More praise

RALPH BUN

"A sensitive, informative, comprehensive, and often heartbreaking biography of Bunche: a great book about a great man. . . . [A] remarkable biography . . . full of restrained passion and narrative skill."
—Stanley Hoffman, *Foreign Affairs*

"A superb biography of one of the great international civil servants—and one of the best-known African Americans—of our time. . . . [Urquhart's] book succeeds by showing, rather than merely telling, what those tumultuous early years of the U.N. were really like, and how Bunche operated as a negotiator and a peacekeeper in Palestine, the Congo, Cyprus, and Kashmir."
—*The New Yorker*

"It was Bunche . . . who in effect invented United Nations peacekeeping. . . . Sir Brian's admirable history shows that what it did in those early years was done with spirit, improvisation, and good sense. Much of the credit goes to that quiet American, Ralph Bunche."
—*The Economist*

"[A] powerful biography . . . reclaiming Ralph Bunche for a generation of readers.
—*London Times*

"Establishes Bunche's place among the most important Americans of the century."
—James O. Freedman, *Boston Globe*

"Provides a wealth of insight into the United Nations and its relationship with member nations, especially the United States."
—*Seattle Times*

"Bunche emerges here as one of the major American diplomatic figures of this century and one of the towering leaders in African American history. Urquhart brings to his work an insider's knowledge of the United Nations, where Bunche scored his most remarkable triumphs, as well as an intimate familiarity with and affection for this highly intelligent, dedicated citizen of the world. . . . A highly credible, exciting portrait of a black American who believed passionately in the principle of international harmony and dedicated himself to the service of honor and truth."
—Arnold Rampersad,
Princeton University, author of *The Life of Langston Hughes*

"Brian Urquhart has performed a great service in giving us a full portrait of this remarkable man, a true activist who was as committed to securing equal rights for African-Americans as he was to achieving peace in the Middle East. This is a book for everyone." —John Hope Franklin, James B. Duke Professor Emeritus, Duke University, and author of *From Slavery to Freedom*

"Ralph Bunche was a citizen of the world whose peace-creating skills the State Department and the United Nations would do well to contemplate in the heat of today's flash fire wars. . . . A welcome addition to African-American, no, to American letters." —William S. McFeely, author of *Grant* and *Frederick Douglass*

"An absorbing, knowledgeable, and highly readable account. . . . This is must reading for those interested in the past and post-cold war future of the United Nations, in the art of multilateral diplomacy, and in the American civil rights movement." —Donald F. McHenry, former United States Ambassador to the United Nations

RALPH BUNCHE

RALPH BUNCHE

An American Life

Brian Urquhart

W · W · NORTON & COMPANY · NEW YORK · LONDON

Copyright © 1993 by Brian Urquhart. *All rights reserved.* Frontispiece photograph courtesy United Nations. Printed in the United States of America.

First published as a Norton paperback 1998

The text of this book is composed in Avanta with the display set in Craw Modern with Bold. Composition and manufacturing are by the Haddon Craftsmen. Book design by Marjorie J. Flock. Maps by Ben Gamit.

Library of Congress Cataloging-in-Publication Data

Urquhart, Brian.
  Ralph Bunche—an American life — Brian Urquhart.
    p.   cm.
  Includes bibliographical references and index.
  1. Bunche, Ralph J. (Ralph Johnson), 1904–1971. 2. Statesmen
—United States—Biography. 3. United Nations—Biography.
I. Title.
E748.B885U76 1993
341.23′3′092—dc20
[B]   92-46564

ISBN 0-393-03527-1
ISBN 0-393-31859-1 pbk

W.W. Norton & Company, Inc., 500 Fifth Avenue, New York, N.Y. 10110
W.W. Norton & Company Ltd., 10 Coptic Street, London WC1A 1PU

1 2 3 4 5 6 7 8 9 0

To Sidney

CENTRAL ARKANSAS LIBRARY SYSTEM
LITTLE ROCK PUBLIC LIBRARY
100 ROCK STREET
LITTLE ROCK, ARKANSAS 72201

Contents

Family Genealogy, page 18

Photographs follow pages 36, 110, 290, and 456

Maps
United Nations Partition Plan, 1947, page 141
The Middle East, page 152
The Congo, 1961, page 301

Preface

For most of the years that I knew him, Ralph Bunche showed little or no interest in writing about his own life and achievements. When urged to do so, he usually said that it would bore him and would be egotistical. He did intend to write the story of his family and had asked his cousin Jane Taylor to help him. By that time, however, his eyesight was failing, his health had gravely deteriorated, and his workload at the UN was still heavy.

Bunche's personal notes have left some record of his thoughts and actions. Although he never said as much to me, several people have told me that he had thought that I might write his biography, as in 1970 I was doing for Dag Hammarskjöld. In this book I have tried, whenever possible, to let him speak in his own words and to describe events from his own point of view.

Bunche, from his college days on, was a prodigious worker, and it would be possible to expand almost any chapter into a full-length book. More and more governmental and other papers relating to the main events of Bunche's life are now becoming available and will enrich future accounts of the various stages of his life. My objective here has been to describe a very full life in a form that will, I hope, be concise enough to hold the interest of the general reader.

My own relationship with Ralph Bunche has naturally been a major factor in writing the book. I first met him in London in late 1945 at the meetings of the Preparatory Commission of the United Nations, and from 1954 until his death in 1971 I worked closely with him at the United Nations as his chief assistant. As will be clear from this book, I had the greatest respect and affection for him, and my feelings are, of course, reflected in what I have written. Bunche was one of those unusual people, rare in public life, whose personality and behavior were unaffected by success or fame. As I said at his funeral, "The grander he got, the nicer and more relaxed he became."*

When Dag Hammarskjöld appointed me to work with Bunche in 1954, Bunche himself was friendly enough but not particularly enthusiastic. He liked to do his own work and disliked delegating authority or having a personal entourage. I thus went through an apprenticeship of being second-guessed, argued with, and generally tested out. This period, lasting two or three years, was the most valuable education I ever had, and at the end of it I entered into a working relationship and a friendship that became a central part of my life. Working with Bunche, especially during crisis periods—Suez and the first UN peacekeeping force, or in the Congo in 1960—was a thrilling experience, and my regard for him steadily increased as the years went by.

When, in 1971, Bunche was obviously dying, I asked him to include in his will an instruction for the disposition of his papers.† I knew that the directors of several great libraries in the United States had visited him, and that each had left his office looking equally satisfied and confident. Bunche resolutely evaded my efforts to make him decide where his papers should be deposited, and instead made me his executor. He did, however, make it very clear that he wanted access to his UN papers and his private notes to be rigorously controlled. After his death, Ruth Bunche and I decided that his alma mater, UCLA, and the UN Archives should be the main depositories for his papers. After Ruth Bunche's death, some personal papers were also placed in the Schomburg Center for Research in Black Culture in New York City.

I wish to clarify one important question of terminology. Ralph Bunche always used the word "Negro." It was, he said, "an ethnic term with no objectionable connotation at all. It describes my ethnic roots, and I have always had a deep pride in those roots." The term "African American" was not current in Bunche's lifetime, and I do not know how he would have viewed it. In this book, therefore, except in direct quotations, I have used the term "Black American," which Bunche often used himself.

---

*A friend said of the great jazz musician Dizzy Gillespie: "He never took advantage of who he was, and he never acted like a star. I don't know how stars get from here to there, but Dizzy walked down the street."[1] This is a good description also of Ralph Bunche.

†This request revealed that Bunche, who had always said he didn't like lawyers, had failed to make a proper will, an omission that was quickly remedied with the help of Sidney Rosoff, who became his lawyer and a devoted friend of the whole Bunche family.

It would be impossible to mention by name all of the people who have helped me and with whom I have discussed this book over the years, and I thank them all. I must especially thank Ralph Bunche's cousin, the late Jane Taylor, the historian of the Johnson/Bunche family, for all her help and for her invaluable comments on and additions to the manuscript. I am also deeply grateful to Joan Bunche and Ralph Bunche, Jr., for all their support.

In 1982, when I was still working at the United Nations, I began to feel that the years were going by very rapidly and that I must start collecting and organizing the material for this book—something that my own working hours and travel program made impossible. The Rockefeller Foundation, in the person of John Stremlau, responded by providing for a research assistant for two years to work on the project. I wish to express my thanks to the Rockefeller Foundation for this providential help.

When I left the UN in 1986, I was fortunate enough to be invited by Franklin A. Thomas, the President of the Ford Foundation, to become Scholar-in-Residence in the International Affairs Program at the Foundation. This has allowed me to pursue a number of projects, including this book. It would be difficult to express the degree of my gratitude to Franklin Thomas and the Ford Foundation for an arrangement that has made writing this book a pleasure and has also made what would otherwise have been my retirement years more lively and interesting than I could ever have imagined.

My wife, Sidney, as always, has been an invaluable commentator, editor, and supporter. I am also very grateful to Arthur Schlesinger, Jr., for reading over the wartime chapters, and to Professor Edwin M. Smith of the University of Southern California for looking over the manuscript as a whole. I thank Professor Lawrence Finkelstein for his comments on the pages on trusteeship, decolonization, and the San Francisco Conference, and Sir Anthony Parsons for reading the chapter on Bahrein. Milton Grant has given important advice on the photographs.

I have been extremely fortunate in all the help I have received from W. W. Norton. In particular I thank Donald Lamm and Hilary Hinzmann for their suggestions, editing, and unfailing encouragement.

Marcia Bikales, my assistant at the Ford Foundation, has been a tower of strength and enthusiasm in the preparation of this book. Her positive critical faculties are second only to her extraordinary skill with the word processor, and I am deeply grateful to her.

When I went to the Ford Foundation in 1986, I took with me Barbara Nelson, who had been collecting material for this book since 1983. She continued to work on this and other projects until her death in April 1992, acquiring a unique knowledge and understanding of Ralph Bunche and his achievements. Without her perceptive and devoted work, carried on dauntlessly during a five-year battle with cancer and completed only a few days before her death, I could not have written this book. Barbara's radiant personality, her vibrant imagination, and the integrity of her character will be long remembered by all of us who worked with her.

BRIAN URQUHART

Tyringham, Massachusetts
March 1993

In affectionate memory of
Barbara Helena Wilson Nelson
1940–1992
who did so much to make this book possible

RALPH BUNCHE

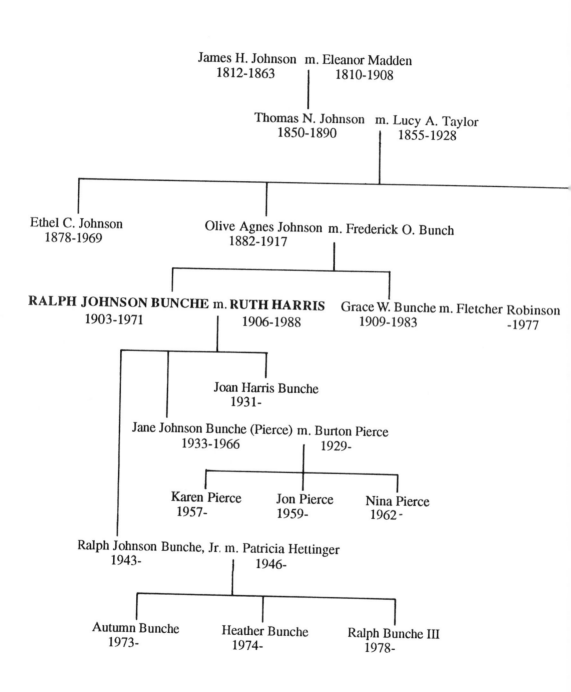

Ralph Johnson Bunche
Family Genealogy

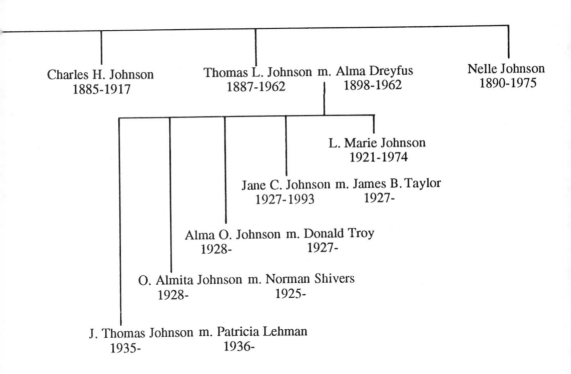

Charles H. Johnson
1885-1917

Thomas L. Johnson m. Alma Dreyfus
1887-1962   1898-1962

Nelle Johnson
1890-1975

L. Marie Johnson
1921-1974

Jane C. Johnson m. James B. Taylor
1927-1993   1927-

Alma O. Johnson m. Donald Troy
1928-   1927-

O. Almita Johnson m. Norman Shivers
1928-   1925-

J. Thomas Johnson m. Patricia Lehman
1935-   1936-

Prologue

On a damp Mediterranean winter day in early January 1949, the white aircraft of the United Nations mediator in Palestine brought Ralph Bunche to the island of Rhodes. He had come to undertake what was widely regarded as an impossible task, the negotiation of armistice agreements between the new state of Israel and her four Arab neighbors. On his success rested the hope of an end to the war that had plagued the Middle East since the proclamation of the state of Israel eight months before.

When Bunche had left Rhodes more than three months earlier, he was in shock from the assassination, by the Stern Gang in Jerusalem, of his friend the UN mediator Count Folke Bernadotte. Now, as Bernadotte's successor, he faced a task as urgent as it was daunting. In the next few months, in a virtuoso display of personality, stamina, and skill, he successfully negotiated the four armistice agreements and gave the Middle East seven years' respite from war, as well as the vital first step toward a peaceful settlement—a settlement that, tragically, has not yet come about. Some called Bunche the new Colossus of Rhodes, and he was universally recognized as a major international resource for a world in turmoil and transition.

Bunche brought to his vocation in the United Nations the vitality and spirit of a remarkable family, the intellect of a scholar, the analytical skill and experience of a field anthropologist, and the passion for justice of a member of an oppressed minority. Before coming to the United Nations he was already known as a strong and radical voice in the fight for racial equality and civil rights in the United States, as the leading American expert on Africa and on colonial affairs, as one of the authors of the Charter of the United Nations, and as a determined advocate of decolonization.

Bunche's achievement as mediator in Palestine, for which he was awarded the Nobel Peace Prize, made his name known all over the world. He continued, until his death more than twenty years later, to work at the United Nations as its principal negotiator of international conflicts and disputes, and as the founder, main architect, and director of UN peace-keeping operations. He gave an example of international service which has never been matched either in its effectiveness or in its integrity. "I rely only on reason, candor and truth," he wrote just before his death. "They stand firm enough without support from emotion."

Throughout his years of success and public acclaim, Ralph Bunche remained as he had always been—down-to-earth, humorous, kindly, and unpretentious. He continued to be more concerned with achieving results than with getting the credit for them, more interested in people than in celebrities, more moved by the struggles of the young and the disadvantaged than by the caprices and favors of the great and famous. He forgot neither where he had come from nor the very real and unresolved human problems which the UN had been set up to tackle. He was intensely proud to be both American and black, but was strongly critical of America's failures, especially as regards his own people. He never wavered in his conviction that the United Nations must, and could, be made to work. As the third secretary-general of the UN, U Thant, said of him at his death, he was "an international institution in his own right."

1

Beginnings

A Proud Clan

"We were a proud family—the Johnson clan," Ralph Johnson Bunche wrote in 1967. "We bowed to no one, we worked hard and never felt any shame about having little money."[1]

Ralph Bunche's great-grandfather James H. Johnson, a Baptist preacher and freedman from Virginia, married Eleanor Madden in the mid-1830s in Missouri,[2] then a border state between North and South, with a black population half slave and half free. Eleanor's mother was a house slave and her father a plantation owner of Irish Catholic descent who had decreed that no child of his should be a slave. On June 29, 1842, James Johnson purchased two hundred acres of farming land in southern Illinois at public auction for $3.34 an acre. This farm, near Alton, Illinois, has remained in the family. The Johnsons had six sons and five daughters, all of whom survived to adulthood.

Ralph Bunche's grandfather Thomas Nelson Johnson, like the rest of his siblings, attended school and read and wrote well. Although Thomas did his stint on the farm, he had a passion for learning and went to Shurtleff College in Alton, where, in 1875, he was one of very few nonwhite graduates. He was trained as a teacher, organized literacy classes for former slaves, and taught night school at churches in the area. One of his students was a pretty, shy young girl, Lucy A. Taylor. Lucy Taylor was born in Sedalia, Missouri, on March 10, 1855, to a house slave, Emmaline, and an Irish landowner. At the end of the Civil War, Emmaline had taken her children, Lucy and Frank, to Alton. After a year of school Lucy got a job as a maid with the Root family, who took an interest in her, treated her as part of the family, and sent her to night school at the Salem Baptist Church, where she and Thomas Nelson Johnson, her teacher, fell in love.

After a long wait so that Thomas could finish college, they were married on September 8, 1875.

Thomas Johnson's passion was education and in particular the education of former slaves. He took a position as teacher in a small school for black children in Indian territory near Fort Scott, Kansas, where his first child died in the primitive conditions of the place. Lucy and Thomas had ten children in fifteen years, of whom only five lived to adulthood. Their second child, Ralph Bunche's mother, Olive, was born in Kansas on April 3, 1882. In 1885 they moved to Waco, Texas, where Thomas Johnson became the principal of a school for Black American children. He gave any unused money from his salary to buy books and supplies for the school, and he edited a weekly paper, the *Texas Baptist Star*. His hobby was astronomy. Thomas and Lucy Johnson's life was happy and fulfilling, but in November 1890 Thomas, at the age of forty, succumbed to malaria. On his deathbed he charged his eldest daughter, Ethel, to take care of her mother, which she did, to the exclusion of virtually all other interests, for the rest of her mother's life.

At thirty-five years of age, Lucy Johnson found herself a widow with five children and no money. She sold her husband's books and telescope, and a concert was organized to raise money for the family's trainfare back to Alton, Illinois. Back at the Johnson farm in Alton, the bereaved family settled in for two years, until unwanted attention from an old suitor* and inadequate schools prompted Lucy Johnson to move her family to the sandy little town of Michigan City, Indiana, on the shores of Lake Michigan. Her husband's share in the Alton farm allowed her to buy a house. To support her children Lucy worked as a chambermaid in the Vreeland Hotel, or in the knitting mills or the chair factory. They lived on Fourth Street, a long curving road leading out of town along the lake, and her daughters have recorded idyllic accounts of their small white cottage and of life on the lakeshore, especially of the Pine Hollow, where they played, winter and summer, and where their German and Dutch neighbors held parties and dances. The Johnson children were only allowed to watch these parties from a distance because their mother distrusted the effects of the large barrel of beer that was always present for the occasion.

Olive usually stayed at home as housekeeper while the others worked, and she ruled the children of the neighborhood with a gentle tyrant's hand, coming down especially hard on bullies. Local baseball matches

---

*Thomas Johnson had never beaten his children. Lucy was not sure the Alton suitor would follow his example.

were important occasions for the family, and at one of these Ethel and Olive met two itinerant barbers, Fred Bunch and John Taylor. Taylor, the older and less prepossessing, had no success with Ethel, but Fred Bunch,* from Zanesville, Ohio, was young, well dressed, and good-looking, with smooth olive skin and bold black eyes. He was traveling with the circus, working as a barber and a barker outside the tents. Olive fell in love with him and eventually married him in Detroit.

Looking for better work and school opportunities for her children, Lucy sent Ethel to Detroit to report on jobs and accommodations, and she moved her family there in the fall of 1900. She had made a tremendous effort to raise her children as their father would have wanted. Olive was now eighteen, and her brothers, Tom and Charlie, were thirteen and fifteen respectively. With their support, Lucy herself no longer had to go out to work.

In Detroit they finally settled in a one-story frame house, white with green shutters and a long front porch, at 434 Anthon Street, in a semirural area about a mile from the Detroit River, near Fort Wayne. Their neighbors on each side were English gypsies who, according to Aunt Nelle Johnson, "though dirty and thievish were good neighbors," mostly engaged in horse-trading, fortune-telling, and genteel thievery.

Ralph Bunch† was born into this warm and talented family—"something of a clan with my maternal grandmother at its head"—in the frame house on Anthon Street on August 7, 1903.‡ The only known details[4] of

---

*The Springfield, Ohio, *News-Sun* of September 18, 1949, recorded that Mrs. Hattie Roberts Bunch, and her husband, Absalom, a farmer and contractor of Mechanicsburg, Ohio, had taken seven-year-old Fred as a foster child from the Madison County children's home in Mt. Sterling, Ohio, and brought him up. In December 1949, when Ralph Bunche was much in the news as the UN mediator in Palestine, a Mrs. Alex Roberts from Granville, Ohio, wrote to him on behalf of "your grandma Bunche as she can no longer use her right hand." Grandma Bunche was ninety and was disappointed not to have met Dr. Bunche. (Grandma Bunche—and the local newspaper—had added the *e* to the family name by this time.) Mrs. Roberts, her sister-in-law, commented on how much Ralph Bunche looked like his father. Ralph Bunche had intended to visit Grandma Bunche in Mechanicsburg but had to go overseas, and when he returned he received a clipping telling of her death. The clipping, incidentally, omitted the "e" from the name.[3]

†When the family left Albuquerque in 1917, his grandmother decided to give Ralph and his sister, Grace, a start on their new life in Los Angeles by adding an "e" to their family name. At the same time his aunt Nellie dropped the "i" from her name and became Aunt Nelle.

‡After 1940 the official date given for his birth was 1904. He was, in fact, born in 1903 and his school and UCLA records show this date. In the early 1940s, when he asked his aunt Ethel for his birth certificate, it could not be found. She therefore took the family Bible to a notary to get a substitute birth verification. The date given in the bible was 1904. "And

this event are that the birth pangs lasted all night and into the afternoon of the next day, and that in the evening Tom and Charlie, rushing home from an exciting sandlot baseball game, raced, as was their habit, for the Morris chair in the parlor, unaware that the newborn Ralph was lying there. Only a fast tripping action by Aunt Ethel sent the racers sprawling and saved the infant from harm.

Fred Bunch was a good barber, and he worked at a large, well-appointed shop downtown. He was described to his son many years later by the son of a fellow barber, Edgar Roberts, as "a lovable carefree chap who couldn't sit still."[5] Even at this early stage Fred seems to have been something of an outsider in the Johnson family circle, although he lived with the family in the Anthon Street house. He was intensely jealous of his beautiful wife, Olive, with her dark eyes which smiled on everyone. Around 1907, the Bunch family moved successively to Cleveland, Ohio; Knoxville, Tennessee; and then to Toledo, Ohio, where Ralph's sister, Grace, was born in 1909. They were in dire financial straits, and Ethel, on traveling to visit them in Toledo, found Olive sick, coughing, and cold, Fred out of work, and the family living in one room. She took them back to Detroit, where Olive was diagnosed as having tuberculosis. Lucy Johnson cared for the children while Olive spent two years in a sanitarium. There was no room for Fred in the house to which the Johnsons had moved, but he visited his children frequently.

A performance of *Carmen* in September 1968, at the Metropolitan Opera in New York, stirred Bunche's earliest memories. "It was a very pleasant feature of my childhood," he wrote, "that there was so much music in the Johnson clan." Music was a central feature of Johnson family life, and many happy hours were spent around the old square piano on which Olive accompanied the singers. Ralph's earliest musical memory was his mother singing "I Wonder Who's Kissing Her Now." Uncle Tom's rendering of "Toreador" and "The Two Grenadiers" also remained vivid in his memory. Aunts Ethel and Nelle and Uncles Tom and Charlie, with Olive as accompanist, formed the Johnson Quartette, which achieved a modest fame in the Detroit area. Later on, they got good notices when they presented a sketch, "The Heart of a Hero," at the Concordia Hall in 1913. A review in the local paper, *The Leader*, noted

---

how old am I?" Bunche wrote to Ethel and Nelle in February 1941. "Until you folks sent that affidavit when I got my first passport I thought I was born in 1903, but you stated it from the family bible as 1904. What is the correct date? Am I 36 or 37, and why?" Bunche seems not to have pursued the matter and to have accepted 1904 as his birth year. Aunt Ethel also gave Ralph's sister's birthdate as 1910 instead of 1909.

that "Ralph Bunch as the office boy can get a position at the Leader office any old time."

"My childhood days were poor days," Ralph Bunche wrote, "but happy ones and filled with music. Because of my liking for music, I used to trot around behind the itinerant street bands—the 'German bands'—and the organ grinders which were a cultural fixture of Detroit in my boyhood. It made music, even bad music, exciting." In his penultimate year, 1970, when he could hardly see to write, he scrawled another note on music.

When "Toreador" was being sung at last night's performance of Carmen at the Met, my mind was flooded with vivid boyhood memories of our household in Detroit always ringing with music whenever anyone was home. Tom especially stood out in my memory—a rich baritone voice, mellow and, with good volume. I could see him standing beside the old upright piano. (I wonder whatever became of that prized instrument?) . . . My recollections of the family scenes around the old piano bring the family warmly to life. Ethel, always dramatic, lively, laughing and blushing, fast-talking in her distinctly contralto tones. Nelle, the soprano and perfectionist—deadly serious about her singing and very proud of her ability to hit above high C; Charlie, the tenor and a good one, but an even better drummer. Mama was the accompanist, but I'm not sure she could read a note. . . .

Bunche remembered his father's taking him to a sort of Western musical in Detroit and being reprimanded for being in shirtsleeves. The first stage musical he ever saw was *No No Nanette* with Nana Carroll in Los Angeles. Bunche loved it, and "I have been a musical buff ever since. I still thrill to hear *Tea for Two*."[6]

Among other pleasures of his boyhood days in Detroit Bunche recalled

hitching my sled in winter onto the tailgates of horsedrawn beer trucks; swimming on Belle Isle in the summer and in the river down by the ice-house; . . . the thrill of the circus parade, and particularly the calliope at the end of it, when Barnum and Bailey came to town—and the still bigger thrill of slipping into the big tent under the canvas sides;* rooting for the Tigers and especially Ty Cobb; hawking newspapers on the streets—and how we yelled!—and the excitement when "Extras" came out as they frequently did then and never do now.[7]

There was "shinny"—street hockey with tin cans and shaped branches for sticks—and baseball with stuffed Bull Durham tobacco sacks as balls, and

---

*In May 1968, when he took his three grandchildren to the circus at Madison Square Garden, Bunche lamented the absence of "dust and animal smells, sideshows and the Wild West act at the end with cowboys and Indians and also a chariot race. The high trapeze artists . . . look much more daring when they perform at the top of a tent."

games of "Run, Sheep, Run" and "Tippy." There were skates and sleds and a skate-wheel scooter.

The Johnson family were swept into the fervor of religious revival at the Second Baptist Church, where the Johnson Quartette were the Glee Club's core, and the family moved to 542 Monroe Avenue to be nearer the church. They occupied a second-floor flat above their Jewish landlady, "old lady Rheinstein," who was occasionally driven to distraction by Charlie's indefatigable practicing in the attic on the snare drum. "Mrs. Johnshon, Mrs. Johnshon," she would call up the stairs, "tell your son to stop de drummin'! He is knockin' de very paper off de walls!"[8] Monroe Avenue, a mixed-race neighborhood, had shops and a streetcar line, but the family's social life centered on the church. Later still they moved a few blocks to 366 Macomb Street. Charlie and Tom, the chief providers of the family, worked at the Diamond Match Co., and later on at the Tullar Hotel downtown. Charlie also earned good money by playing the drums in orchestras, including the Mills dance orchestra, the best black band in Detroit.

Like his sister Olive, Charlie developed tuberculosis, and his sister Ethel sent him to Albuquerque, New Mexico, in May 1914. Olive followed him in September of that year. Ralph's grandmother Lucy Johnson brought Ralph to Albuquerque in October 1915 by the Santa Fe Railroad. Fred, broke, later joined them there by "riding the rails." After the two had given concerts throughout the Midwest for a year, Tom went to Kansas City, and Nelle, to Corsicana, Texas, as a teacher. The family days in Detroit were over.

Albuquerque in 1915 had little or no industry and was primarily a place where people, especially asthmatic or tubercular patients, went for their health. The Johnsons first lived in a little adobe house on Fifth Street. A neighbor, Yola Brinson, recalled,

It was easy to be kind to Olive, because she was so gentle and good. I used to think she was about as near an angel as anyone I would ever see. Ralph used to come and sit in my kitchen and talk as I worked. He was a great talker, but a dreamer too. He used to look at the range of blue mountains through the window, gaze at the white line of rock trail along their top, and then say decisively, "Some day I'm going to walk those mountains." I like to think of that remark as prophetic.[9]

The Johnsons picked up their musical pursuits in Albuquerque. Ralph's mother, Olive, liked to go to Sunday-afternoon band concerts in Old Town. Ralph would put his mother on the trolley and then run to meet her at the other end. This both developed his athletic stamina and saved money.

Ralph's most vivid recollections of Albuquerque were of hunting expeditions on the mesa with Uncle Charlie. They would bring back cottontails, jackrabbits, and quail. In his later years he recalled the delicious flavor of quail broiled in butter and also his grandmother's stewed chicken and dumplings, baked apple dumplings, and homemade biscuits, bread, and ice cream. Among his school friends in Albuquerque were many Indians and Mexicans. He did well in school, but liked to talk in class. His teacher, Miss Emma Belle Sweet,* sometimes stood him in a corner with his face to the wall or gave him a rap over the knuckles to discourage this habit, but Bunche remembered with affection her class, in which he was one of two black students in a group of thirty-six, an integrated group in which "there was no differentiation, no outsiders."[10]

For most of the time in Albuquerque the family lived in an adobe house at 621 North Street. Anxiety over the health of Charlie and Olive overshadowed an otherwise happy time. Olive's tuberculosis was complicated by a rheumatic condition which caused her to hobble. In October 1916 her husband, Fred, who had not been living in the Johnson house, left Albuquerque to look for regular work. Although he was supposedly going to send for Olive and the children when he was in a position to support them, his departure probably further drained Olive's will to live. For a time it seemed that Charlie's health was improving, but, after taking a job as a brakeman on the railroad, he got soaked by a cold rain one night and suffered a severe setback. Olive slowly declined, and she died in February 1917. During the burial service, Grace cried inconsolably at the graveside and refused to leave. Finally, Ralph put his arm around his sister and gently walked her away from the grave.† Charlie, despondent about his health and his inability to settle his mother in a house of her own, blew his brains out with a shotgun three months later. Tom and Nelle came immediately to Albuquerque.

His mother's death when she was thirty-five and he was thirteen years old, and the suicide of his much-loved and admired uncle Charlie, put a tragic end to the first chapter of Ralph's life. In 1967, after attending the funeral of a friend's mother, he wrote:

Now, more than ever, I seem to regret that I lost my mother when both she and I were so young. I feel cheated to have been deprived of her. I have retained

---

*In 1962, in Atlanta, Bunche presented his old teacher with the "Golden Key Award" and $1,000 "for lifetime dedication to children."

†Grace told this to Jane Taylor.

an image of her as a pretty, very sweet and romantic lady, a dreamer, accomplished in music and poetry, and always an invalid. I can never get it out of my mind that on that night of her death in Albuquerque she had asked for milk and there was none in the house because I had drunk it up.

Ralph treasured a letter, the only letter of his mother's he had, which Olive had written to her brother and sister Tom and Nelle a year before she died. It is a long letter, starting with evocations of their childhood, and saying that she is trying to be less frivolous and superficial, and more like Nelle.

I'm still largely superficial Nell, but I'm learning a little bit everyday; how to be happy, contented, how to supersede hate with love and best of all, how to live more in the Reality of things, nearer to God. I'm still grumbling a little, still complaining of my health at times, but I have high hopes and strong conviction that health and happiness are for me. I'm even beginning to get back snatches of my long forgotten ambitions Nell, such as I had when I went to school, wrote crude verses, and dreamed of being a poetess. . . . Ralph has done fine in school this year, in study and application, and I know you will be glad to know that his temper is improved. . . . We have relapses into old ways, but they are less frequent. Fred is working steadily as usual, and we're continuing to make ends meet, and combining contentment with it, which has been a revelation to me as a remover of worry. The roses were beautiful in our yard Nell, they are almost gone, but the fragrance was lovely while it lasted. We're all glad Tom sent the piano. . . . It's just as calm and beautiful, this eve, here, as you can imagine, you know Nell, one of our typical New Mexico sunsets. . . .[11]

She ends by thanking all her brothers and sisters for their help and kindness. It is easy to imagine how such a letter would compound Ralph's sense of loss.

Lucy Johnson's indomitable spirit at first seemed broken by the double tragedy. After Charlie's suicide, shock and grief enveloped her and Ethel, and for a while her children despaired of her surviving. Then a Christian Science counselor revived the spark of life in her, and she realized that with Ralph and Grace to care for her duty was not done. There was no reason to stay in Albuquerque any more, and Tom went to Los Angeles to look for lodgings. Fred Bunch had lost his main reason for coming back to the Johnson family. His difficulties in holding a job for long did not sit well with the industrious Johnsons, some of whom, particularly Aunt Ethel, were certainly not well disposed toward him.* From

*Fred Bunch married again after Olive's death. He made contact once, in 1928, with Aunt Ethel in Los Angeles, in an effort to talk to Ralph's sister, Grace. Ralph Bunche never saw

now on Lucy Johnson, Ethel, Nelle, and Tom were in sole charge of Ralph and his sister.

Los Angeles, with a population of half a million people in 1918, was, even in its less wealthy sections, a city of space, trees, grass, and flowers, with a celestial climate. In 1919 the house on 37th Street (now 40th Place) and Central Avenue where the Johnson family settled, and where Aunt Nelle lived until her death in 1975, was in a white middle-class neighborhood which began to change rapidly in the 1920s. Jefferson High School was a half-block away. Twenty-five blocks up Central Avenue there was an area of honky-tonk cafés and the Hummingbird Dance Hall— rough territory, especially at night. There were no "ghetto" areas in the sense of large and poverty-stricken concentrations of a particular ethnic group. As late as 1940 Watts had a mixed population—black, white, Mexican American, and a smattering of Indians—in which Black Americans numbered just 50 percent. The city had few, if any, of the massive problems and frictions which have, in later years, brought it much unwanted attention.

Asked in 1968 what made him "tick," Ralph Bunche replied that, though he hadn't given the matter much thought, certain motivations and guidelines had much to do with his career.

Most of this guidance came to me from my maternal grandmother who reared my sister and me after we lost our parents in childhood. She instilled in me a desire to do my best in anything I tried to do so that I could have a sense of achievement and experience pride. She taught me the value of self-respect and dignity. She told me to be proud of my origin, of my family and of the society in which I live. I learned from her that hard work can be enjoyed and can be highly rewarding. Although having little education herself, she appreciated the value of education and insisted that I should get as much of it as possible, and the best possible.[12]

Lucy Johnson—Nana, as Ralph and the family had always called her—was often described by her grandson, and perhaps most vividly in an article entitled "My Most Unforgettable Character."[13]

Nana could be regarded as an optional Negro. She was entirely Caucasian in appearance. Her twin brother, Frank, in fact, "passed over" into the white sector as a youth. "White" as Nana was outside, she was all black pride and fervor

---

him again, but he kept, in a box that contained his most valued treasures, the tiepin his father had given him when he left Albuquerque. Bunche contacted Fred's second wife, Helen, in an effort to find his father, but she didn't know where he was.

inside. . . . Nana was fiercely proud of her origin and her race, and everyone in our "clan" got the race-pride message very early in life. It has stuck with me.

Nana's authority was such that, although she almost never imposed or asserted it, it was accepted as a matter of course.

She was small—almost tiny—soft-spoken and shy. But she was strong, very strong, in character, will and spirit. She was outspoken and a tartar when aroused. And so very wise and far sighted.

Nana was deeply religious—a straitlaced Baptist—and morally strict, especially about Sunday observance. Once, in Los Angeles, Ralph slipped out to a movie theatre on a Sunday, but an earthquake caused the audience to leave in a hurry in the middle of the show. To his surprise he encountered his aunt Ethel on the way out, and they had to admit to Nana where they had been. Nana simply pointed out that God had given them a warning to refrain from such errors in future, and the next time would not be so easy.

Ralph was the only family member who had not been baptized as a child. In the summer of 1927, on his way from UCLA to Harvard, he stopped in Detroit to visit the Reverend Bob Bradby of the Second Baptist Church. Bradby told Bunche that nothing would convey his gratitude to Nana better than a telegram telling her that he had at last been baptized as a Second Baptist. When Bunche protested that he had not heard the "call," Bradby assured him that a good deed for Nana was in itself a religious act and would constitute both the "call" and a valid response. Ralph was baptized on a Sunday morning before an overflow congregation, which made a generous offering to help him at Harvard. Nana was greatly pleased.

Nana thought her brother's "passing over" to white society had been a grave mistake, but she explained to Ralph that he had done it not because he thought white people were better, but only to try to escape from the hardships of white prejudice against Negroes. Nana was intensely proud of her black ancestry and told Ralph and his sister to be proud of their race and their family.

Always protect your self-respect and your dignity. Never pick a fight, but never run away from one either if your dignity or an important principle is involved. Let no one ever "lowerate" you.

These precepts had a vast influence on Bunche in later life.

In and out of school, I have always been motivated by a spirit of competition, particularly when pitted against white people.—I suppose this was an inevitable response to Nana's constant admonition to "let them, especially white folks, know that you can do anything they can do."

Another of Nana's characteristics, her swiftness to react to any hint of a racial slur or insult, also had a profound effect on Ralph. An unfortunate Los Angeles traveling salesman for cemetery plots, deceived by her appearance, told her, "We only sell plots to white people—no niggers or greasers in this cemetery." After asking him to repeat this remark, she excused herself to fetch a broom from the kitchen and chased him out of the house.

Nana tirelessly monitored Ralph's education. At the Thirtieth Street Intermediate School (now John Adams Junior High School), a predominantly white school where Ralph was enrolled when the family arrived in Los Angeles in 1917 and where he stayed until 1919, she found out, after noting Ralph's lack of interest in schoolwork, that he had been enrolled, as black students almost invariably were, in vocational classes (shorthand, commercial arithmetic, etc.), on the assumption that he would not be going to college. Nana told the principal, "This boy is going to college and he must be ready for it," and insisted that he be placed in classes that would fit him for college.

A portrait of Bunche at the predominantly white Jefferson High School was provided by one of his teachers, Dr. Cecilia Irvine, to whom Bunche had written in 1959 on the occasion of her retirement. In reply Dr. Irvine wrote:

I would like to picture to you the boy you were. You were distinctly a thorough-bred who walked with a springy step, always you seemed completely at ease with the world and always looked up. I think, more than anything, I remember you with your head held high. I remember your grandmother. I met her just once. She was dressed in black with a Queen Mary black hat, and I have never forgotten the emanation of power from that tiny figure.

At Ralph's graduation ceremony in 1922, Mr. Fulton, the Jefferson High School principal, a well-meaning but insensitive man, made the mistake of saying to Nana: "Mrs. Johnson, we are very sorry to see Ralph leave Jefferson. We like him here. He has been a good student and a good athlete. In fact, Mrs. Johnson, we have never thought of Ralph as a Negro." Nana retorted, "You are very wrong to say that. It is an insult to Ralph, to me, to his parents and his whole race. Why haven't you thought of him as a Negro? He is a Negro and he is proud of it. So am I. What makes you think that only white is good?" And with a few more well-chosen words, she said a tart "Good day" and left with Ralph.

Before coming to Los Angeles the Johnson family had always lived in mixed neighborhoods. In Detroit there were only a few blacks in the whole city, and the district they had lived in was mostly inhabited by recently arrived Austrian and German immigrants.[14] There was thus relatively little prejudice against Black Americans, community prejudice at that time being mainly directed against new immigrants, particularly Italians pouring in from southern Europe and threatening to undercut wages and living standards. Consequently, in his early years Ralph knew very little about the "Negro problem" and racial prejudice, although he heard all sorts of hostile racial epithets applied to Italians, and later, in Albuquerque, to Mexicans and Indians. Nana was suspicious of foreigners, but, as recorded by Ralph, laid down a firm family line on the matter. "Negroes have no business running down anybody. Anyhow, people who can sing and like tomatoes and bananas as much as those Italy folks do can't be all bad."

It was only in Los Angeles that Ralph first began to develop real racial consciousness, having even "some inner feeling of resentment about not being 'Negro' enough, compared to my negro chums.* . . . By contrast, I felt something like the interlocutor in a minstrel show and somehow racially short-changed."[15]

Hints of prejudice, as well as acts of discrimination, had, however, occurred periodically from Ralph's earliest days. He could recall a train journey to Knoxville, Tennessee, when he was about six years old. The conductor informed his mother that they must move back to the coach for "colored" passengers. His mother indignantly refused, and after an argument the conductor gave up.

My mother later explained to me what had happened and why, and particularly why she could not move and maintain any dignity and self-respect. She told me we were lucky not to have been arrested. I was shaken by the experience because I feared for my mother's safety and for my own, since the conductor got red in the face with anger and shouted at us.[16]

Ralph was chased out of the municipal park in Knoxville because blacks were not allowed there. In Albuquerque, when he was with his mother in the nickelodeon at the Busy Bee Theatre, an usher insisted they move to the area reserved for blacks. Once again his mother refused, saying their money was as good as anyone else's.

Their arrival in Los Angeles in 1917 was marked by a racial incident.

*Bunche's group on Central Avenue consisted of George Duncan, Charles (Sandy) Saunders, Wilalyn Stovall, Melvin Thistle, and Erskin and Charlie Ragland. Their theme song was, "There'll be some changes made."

Tom, who was pale-skinned like Nana, had gone on ahead and rented a frame bungalow on Griffith Avenue, on the east side. Just before they moved in, the white owner saw Ralph and Aunt Nelle, who were darker, realized that his new tenants were black, and, before they arrived with the moving van, changed the locks. He had not reckoned with the Johnson spirit, however; on moving day they never hesitated. "We have paid our rent," Tom said, "and we are going in." He put his strong shoulder to the door and pushed it open. The family stayed for the full period for which the rent had been paid and then moved to their permanent home, which Nana called "our little Garden of Eden," on East 37th Street. There was some muttering from the neighbors, but, as Nana pointed out, the neighbors were mostly renting, whereas the Johnsons had *paid* for their house.

Although he did extremely well and led his class at high school, Ralph, despite the protests of some of his teachers, was excluded from the Ephebian Society, the citywide student honor society. "On angry impulse," Bunche wrote in 1969, "I decided to leave school, abandon graduation. Then I thought of my mother's words, 'Ralph, don't let anything take away your hope and faith and dreams.' I decided that I could get along without the honor society." This racial insult was only corrected thirty years later when Ralph M. Lloyd, the president of the Ephebian Society, conferred honorary membership on Bunche after Pheneus Singer, who had been chosen in Bunche's place, had written to say that Bunche should have been chosen instead of him.[17]

Ralph enjoyed Jefferson High. He had some good teachers and everyone liked him. He particularly remembered his basketball coach, Si Tipton, with affection and admiration. Tipton constantly urged Ralph to relax and taught him how to do it, an invaluable asset in the pressures of his later life. He was already thrilled by learning and enjoyed a wide range of reading, from *Lorna Doone* to Dickens, Shakespeare, and the New Testament. He was the valedictorian of his high school class and its graduation speaker, choosing as his topic "Our New Responsibilities." He had trouble memorizing his lines, and when he came to a dead halt in the middle he was rescued by a prompt from a black classmate, Leonidas Simmons, who had heard Ralph rehearsing his speech and had memorized it. After Ralph's address Leonidas Simmons sang a song called "The Wren" by Benedict.

While at high school Ralph worked as a delivery boy for the *Los Angeles Times* and later on got a job in the paper's printing plant, working from 5:30 P.M. to 1:00 A.M. as a "pig boy," whose function was to carry lead bricks to the linotype machines. On Saturday nights the pig boys staged wrestling matches on the concrete floor of the print shop. The printers chipped in for a pot for the winner. On an outing with the pig boys, Bunche and his friend Charlie Matthews were refused access to the "Venice plunge," a public swimming pool. Nana eventually made him leave this job because she had heard that printers tended to die of consumption.

Bunche always claimed that he would never have gone to college but for Nana's foresight and insistence. For a young black man in east-side Los Angeles there was little incentive to go on to higher education, and college seemed very remote from the day-to-day, immediate concerns of his boon companions. While at high school Bunche had learned carpet laying at the City Dye Works and was making good money. He ran around with a spirited group of young black friends, most of whom, like himself, were athletes. They were proud of their athletic prowess, but were otherwise aimless and without ambition. Of Ralph and his friends only three went to college, "two because their parents could afford to send them, and I because Nana wouldn't hear of anything else." Nana lived long enough to see her grandson graduate "with the highest honors" from UCLA in 1927. Her last letter to him, on November 24, 1928, ended with the words "Will you finish at Harvard this year?" She died seven days later.

Above, left: Emmaline Banyon, born in slavery. Ralph Bunche's great-grandmother and mother of Lucy Taylor Johnson. *Above, right:* Ralph Bunche's great-grandmother, Eleanor Madden Johnson, born in slavery. Mother of Thomas Nelson Johnson. *Below:* Ralph's grandmother Lucy Taylor Johnson, in her wedding dress. Alton, Illinois, September 1875.

Ralph's grandparents Lucy and Thomas Johnson, with Ethel, Charlie, and his mother, Olive *(sitting in front)*. Waco, Texas, 1885.

Thomas Johnson with his students. His daughter Ethel is on the left of the second row from the top. Waco, Texas, 1888.

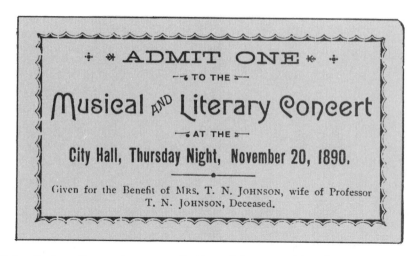

✣ * ADMIT ONE * ✣

─ᴥ TO THE ᴥ─

Musical ᴬⁿᴰ Literary Concert

─ᴥ AT THE ᴥ─

City Hall, Thursday Night, November 20, 1890.

Given for the Benefit of MRS. T. N. JOHNSON, wife of Professor
T. N. JOHNSON, Deceased.

Ticket for benefit to raise money for Lucy Johnson and her family to return to
Illinois after the death of her husband, Thomas Johnson. Waco, Texas, 1890.

Ralph's mother, Olive Johnson Bunch, and father, Fred Bunch. Detroit, 1902.

Ralph Bunche's birthplace—434 Anthon Street, Detroit, 1903.

July 4, 1907—A picnic at Belle Isle, Detroit, "where hundreds of canoes filled the lagoons" (Aunt Ethel's words). *Top row, left to right:* Fred Bunch, Ralph, Lucy Taylor (Nana), Olive Bunch, Ethel Johnson.

Ralph, at about age ten.

Ralph and his sister, Grace. Detroit, about 1911.

Ralph's first recorded public appearance was in this production with the Johnson Quartette. *Left to right:* Ethel, Charlie, Nelle, and Tom. Detroit, 1913.

LOOK! LOOK! LOOK!
SEE WHAT'S HERE

JOHNSON QUARTETTE

With Talented Cast in the Domestic Drama

"THE HEART OF A HERO"
AT TOWN HALL, SANDWICH
Monday, April 21st, 1913

SYNOPSIS

ACT I---Morning at the Westover mansion. Cyrus in search of a wife. The runaway pony. A confession of love.

ACT II---Em gives Cyrus a little advise. Salina and her father. A secret of the past. Discharged.

ACT III---Salina plays detective. Denton still scheming. The forgery. Accused. And I can prove it."

ACT IV---Evening. Denton's last card. The uprising of the men. Cyrus takes a hand. The tables turned. The crowning of love.

CAST OF CHARACTERS

In the Order in Which They Appear

Cyrus Bodkkin (A Lone Widower) -	Mr. Chas. Johnson
Caroline Westover (The Squire's Sister)	Miss Ethel Johnson
Seth Marlow (To Self and Honor True) -	Mr. Horace Page
Gilbert Westover Esq. (Owner of the Mills)	Mr. Tom Johnson
Tillie Sloan, a village belle,	Miss Mary Lawton
Arnold Payne (Gentleman from the City)	Mr. Chauncey Page
Em, not much of anybody,	Mrs. Madeline Foster
Salina, the Squire's daughter,	Miss Nellie Johnson
Clarence Denton (An Enemy in Disguise) -	Mr. Adolph Osby
Robert, office boy, -	Master Ralph Bunch

MISS ETHEL HARRIS, Accompanist.

LOCAL TALENT WILL ASSIST DURING CHANGE OF SCENES.   CURTAIN 8 O'CLOCK
GENERAL ADMISSION 25 CENTS.   RESERVED SEATS 35 CENTS.

Given for First Baptist Church, Sandwich, Ont.

THE RECORD PRINTING CO., Ltd.

Ralph with his mother and his Uncle Charlie. Albuquerque, New Mexico, 1916.

Nana at 1219 Griffith Avenue, her first home in Los Angeles, 1918.

Above, left: On the three-time winning team of the Southern Conference basket-ball championship, UCLA (then University of California, Southern Branch), 1926. *Above, right:* UCLA senior, 1927. *Below:* 1927 beach picnic at UCLA. Ralph is in the center in a wool cap.

2

UCLA, Harvard, and Howard

Genesis and Catalyst

"UCLA was where it all began for me; where, in a sense, I began; college for me was the genesis and the catalyst."[1] Thus, at the dedication, in 1969, of Ralph Bunche Hall on the UCLA campus, Ralph Bunche eulogized his old school. With his pay as a carpet layer Bunche had, in the summer before going to college, acquired a jalopy and had spent a wild summer with his friends, careening up and down Central Avenue, fired by bathtub gin and apple brandy. Only Nana's insistence had kept him to his enrollment at UCLA, but about halfway through his freshman year he realized that he could hold his own and began to see that Nana had been right.

In Bunche's time UCLA (then called University of California, Southern Branch) was still on the old Vermont Avenue campus (now Los Angeles City College), and he earned much-needed cash trimming the ivy on the old buildings. The student body was relatively small—some thirty-six hundred in all—and in the rather cramped quarters of the old campus it was possible to know a large number of its members. Bunche was extremely gregarious. He had many friends and plenty of girlfriends, and he loved parties and excursions. He remained in touch with many of his UCLA friends throughout his life and, on later visits to Los Angeles, he would try to see as many of them as possible or gather them together for a party. His UCLA photograph album shows a popular and handsome young man having a wonderful time.

Bunche knew many of the professors, and they seem to have been remarkably accessible. He remembered in particular the dean of the College of Liberal Arts, C. H. Rieber, a philosopher from Berkeley. Rieber's incisive mind, rich store of knowledge, dry, pointed humor, and rapierlike use of words made a lasting impression on Bunche. Rieber's door was always open, and Bunche could drop in whenever he liked. Rieber kept a box of cards on which he wrote down aphorisms and sayings that had impressed him. One of these defined cooperation as "doing what I tell you to do." Bunche wrote that with Rieber he was "unfailingly cooperative."[2]

Bunche's career at UCLA was an all-round success. He became a respected scholar. He practiced the arts of oratory and debate and became president of the Southern Branch Debating Society. He wrote articles for the UCLA newspaper, the *Daily Bruin,* and was a star of the basketball team. As his basketball coach put it, he was "a versatile young man of limitless energy. . . ."[3]

While at UCLA Bunche suffered two serious physical setbacks, both of which affected him for the rest of his life. Toward the end of his first year, he began to suffer severe headaches, which were at first attributed to long extracurricular hours as janitor in the women's gymnasium. The trouble was later traced to a piece of barley straw in his left ear which had festered. The first mastoid operation was botched and necessitated a second operation, which left Bunche deaf in his left ear for life. During his hospital stay, he managed to escape for an afternoon, catch the Red Car (the fast streetcar), attend a UCLA football game, and return to his hospital bed undetected. He returned to school at Nana's urging in the fall of 1923.

Bunche's athletic achievements in high school had earned him an athletic scholarship at UCLA, and his next injury, on the football field, resulted in a blood clot in his left calf which had to be permanently and tightly bandaged with cotton gauze. In later years stress and fatigue could make this condition extremely hazardous. At UCLA, however, it merely caused Bunche to switch from football to basketball. He was on the varsity team which won the Southern Conference basketball championship three years running. His three miniature golden basketballs were particularly treasured possessions, and many years later, when he was told that his house in Queens, New York, had been burgled, they were the first things he asked about. (They were safe.)

A variety of jobs supported Bunche in his time at UCLA, although he continued to live with his family on 37th Street. He worked as a houseboy for the silent-screen actor Charles Ray, and for a time he and Charlie Matthews pooled their resources to buy an old Model T Ford for $25 and organized a cleaning service for stores and lunchrooms. The ROTC was barred to him because of his punctured eardrum, but Colonel Palmer, the head of ROTC at UCLA, allowed him to attend the summer session at Camp Lewis in the Pacific Northwest anyway, and he hitchhiked up there to save money. A friend in Seattle who was a waiter on the Admiral Line coastal liner *H. F. Alexander* persuaded him to embark as a stowaway for the return journey to Los Angeles. He was soon discovered and put to work in the galley shelling peas. He did so well that he stayed aboard working in the galley for the rest of the summer. The next summer he worked on the boat again as busboy and petty officers' messman, thus putting aside a decent sum of spending money for school. All his life Bunche remembered the call-boy's song which roused the crew of the *H. F. Alexander* each day at 5:00 A.M.

> *Sleepin' good,*
> *Sleepin' good.*
> *Gimme dem covers,*
> *I wish you would.*
> *I know you're tired*
> *and sleepy too,*
> *I hates to do it*
> *But I'se got to do,*
> *For you must rise and shine*
> *For dis Admiral Line.*[4]

Bunche's time at UCLA seems to have been extraordinarily free of racial incidents, and one of the few he recorded is a strong tribute to UCLA. At the opening practice of the freshman basketball team a student from Louisiana went to the coach, Caddy Works, in great distress to say that by some mistake there was a colored fellow on the team and that his parents in New Orleans would never tolerate his playing with a black teammate. Works replied that he sympathized with his problem, but there was an easy solution. "Just go over and turn in your suit," he said. Faced with this alternative the boy decided to stay, and Works paired him at guard with Bunche. The two soon became friends.[5]

Bunche was active in interracial discussions both at UCLA and at other nearby colleges,* and he took an enthusiastic part in oratorical contests at UCLA. His contribution to one of these in 1926, on the proposition "That man may dwell in Peace," survives. It opens with Bunche's favorite quotation, the words of Isaiah,

They shall beat their swords into plough-shares; and their spears into pruning hooks; nation shall not lift up sword against nation, neither shall they learn war anymore.

---

*As the official debating society did not accept him, Bunche and some friends set up their own debating group, the Southern Branch Debating Society.

Beneath the surface of its rhetoric, more critical themes emerge—opposition to imperialism, colonialism, and racism—including one or two extraordinarily perceptive remarks. For example,

There is not the slightest doubt that by vicious use of propaganda, preying upon the racial and nationalistic hatreds of the peoples of the world, this universe could very shortly again be transformed into a seething cauldron of infuriated nations.

Bunche saw two essentials for a peaceful future—"international organization, involving *every* nation of the world; and the full development of the International Mind or Will." He described the League of Nations and the World Court as "inspiring harbingers of future world harmony," and deplored the United States' lack of participation in them. He asserted that "social education" could gradually generate the necessary international will to achieve genuine peace. He deplored "ethnocentric chauvinism" and urged that it be overcome by education and through the media. In his later career Bunche turned such themes into practical action.

He made a much more hard-hitting speech, "Across the Generation Gap," at about the time of his graduation to a predominantly black adult audience.[6] The most outspoken part of this speech relates to the setting up of a "For Colored Only" swimming pool in Los Angeles. Bunche was certainly also recalling his own exclusion from the "Venice plunge." He saw the segregated swimming pool as the thin end of the wedge of discrimination in Los Angeles and called for total resistance to it as a sign of racial pride.

Whatever may be the attitude of you older people toward this dastardly practice of insolently slapping the Race in the face, I can tell you, in all sincerity, that there is a violently smouldering fire of indignation among those of us who are younger in years and who have not yet become inured to such insults. . . . I want to tell you that when I think of such outrageous atrocities as this latest swimming pool incident, which has been perpetrated on Los Angeles Negroes, my blood boils. And when I see my people so foolhardy as to patronize such a place, and thus give it their sanction, my disgust is trebled. Any Los Angeles Negro who would go bathing in that dirty hole with that sign "For Colored Only" gawking down at him in insolent mockery of his Race is either a fool or a traitor to his kind.

The only way to break down "this infernal inferiority complex which besets so many of our kind," Bunche told his seniors, was ever-increasing education, which was the only means by which the Negro could compete with other peoples.

We must meet their standards or be left in the rut. And heaven knows we've been in the rut long enough already. . . . You know it's often said of our Race that we are "kings of the alibi." We can have more good intentions and do less than any other people on earth.

In urging his audience to support the young Negro, he concluded,

We have *youth*—we have *racial pride* and we have *indomitable will* and boundless optimism for the future—So we can't help but come out on top of the heap! . . . We'll make you all *proud* of the young Negro.

With the support of his teachers Bunche had insisted on majoring in political science, although at that time black students usually studied law, medicine, or for a career in the church. He was already beginning to see international affairs as the field that interested him most. He graduated from UCLA in 1927 with highest honors in political science and, having the highest grades in his class, was the valedictorian at the commencement ceremonies.

He consulted Dean Rieber as to a suitable topic for his speech. Rieber suggested it would be good to read something that "would mellow my soul." He took down a volume of the poems of Edna St. Vincent Millay and told Bunche to take it to the beach, lie on the sand, read the poems, and reflect, assuring him that in this way he would soon think of a suitable topic. Bunche followed his advice and came up with "The Fourth Dimension of Personality." His theme was the need to develop philosophical and spiritual qualities to give meaning to the pragmatic side of life. One member of the Board of Directors of the university was so impressed that a student would emphasize the philosophical and spiritual side of life that he gave Bunche a $100 check to help him with his graduate-school expenses.

Bunche's commencement speech was the utterance of a highly intelligent and idealistic young man. Stating that "Humanity's problem today is how to be saved from itself," he argued the importance of developing the "socially valuable man." Attacking excessive materialism, he extolled the qualities of vision, international-mindedness, and that "Olympian sympathy which overleaps the boundaries of craft or class or country, and creates new worlds from old." He ended with a rousing peroration on human fellowship and some lines of Edna St. Vincent Millay.

The world stands out on either side,
No wider than the heart is wide;
Above the world is stretched the sky
No higher than the soul is high. . . .

This high-flown speech contains hints of most of the elements which formed Bunche's approach to the great challenges of his career. There is no mention, however, of the views on race and racial discrimination which he had already partly formulated and publicly expressed. All his life Bunche had a rigid sense of decorum, and he evidently felt that the commencement exercise at an institution which had been good to him was not the place to vent his strongest personal preoccupations.

The grant of a fellowship at Harvard to do graduate work in political science was providential. However, it only covered tuition. As usual, the Johnson family rallied round, and Tom, who had been a mixture of father and brother to Ralph during his growing up, teamed up with Nelle to give concerts at various churches to raise money for his trip east and his living expenses. Led by Mrs. Alice Patton, who had been impressed by his commencement speech, the ladies of the Iroquois Friday Morning Civic and Social Club of Los Angeles, "believing that every true and loyal citizen of the Race will be glad to help this worthy young man financially, that he may be unhampered in his first year at Harvard," set out to raise a Ralph Bunche Scholarship Fund of $1,000. They exceeded the target. In 1969, when Tom Johnson's grandson Ronald Taylor was going to Yale, Bunche sent him a check "in recollection . . . of the good will and generosity of the black women of the Friday Morning Club of Los Angeles who in 1927 helped me to Harvard."[7]

On May 11, 1927, while he was still at UCLA, Bunche had written to William E. B. Du Bois, the foremost Black American intellectual activist of the time, telling him that he had been granted a scholarship at Harvard.

Since I have been sufficiently old to think rationally and to appreciate that there was a "race problem" in America, in which I was necessarily involved, I have set as the goal of my ambition service to my group.

He told Du Bois he had already been active in interracial discussion groups at UCLA and other colleges.

But I have long felt the need of coming in closer contact with the leaders of our Race, so that I may better learn their methods of approach, their psychology and benefit my own development by their influence.

He asked how he "can be of service to any group this coming summer, either in the east or in the south."[8]*

"I have definitely decided," Bunche wrote to Dean Rieber at UCLA after five weeks at Harvard,

*Du Bois replied, on June 7, "I do not know of any opening for you just now, but I shall keep your case in mind."

to cast my lot in the realm of the scholarly rather than the purely legal, and from now on will bend every effort toward the attainment of the Ph.D. The conversations which I was fortunate enough to have during my trip this summer with some of the leaders of my race, influenced me considerably in making the decision. That trip was an education in itself to me and it has revealed to me the tremendous amount of work there is for each of us to do during our stay on earth.[9]

For the rest he told Dean Rieber of the novelty of the changing seasons and of how Harvard "seems to grow on one day by day." "The football team," he added, "is pathetic."

There were not more than thirty or forty black students at Harvard when Bunche arrived there. He became a lifelong friend of two of them who roomed in the same house, Ma Clark's. William Hastie became the first black federal judge, and Robert Weaver, an economist, was active in the New Deal and later served as head of the Housing and Home Finance Corporation in the Kennedy administration and as Secretary of the Department of Housing and Urban Development under President Lyndon Johnson. He also saw a lot of John P. Davis, who was studying English literature and later became the national secretary of the National Negro Congress and founder and publisher of *Our World*, a leading black magazine. Their late-night discussions, especially on race relations in the United States, were an important part of Bunche's higher education.

Robert Weaver has described Bunche in their Harvard days.

His advance notices were rave, and he lived up to them. We lived in close proximity and had almost daily contact, both in playing cards with a strict time schedule, discussing what university students talk about, and reserving the weekends for serious bull sessions, where race relations and strategies for attacking the color line were the dominant themes. . . . Bunche was extremely attractive, quite vocal, articulate and approachable. He made male and female friends with ease and charm, and he had a well developed sense of humor, which embraced the capacity to laugh at himself. What impressed me most about Ralph in those days was his optimism. I soon realized that it was not rooted in wishful thinking, as is often the case, but rather based on a long history of overcoming obstacles and an uncanny ability to produce stupendous amounts of work over long sustained periods of application. I watched his capacity grow in proportion to the critical nature of the issues. It maximized the impact of his knowledge, the brilliance of his personality, and was in my opinion the chief factor in his spectacular career.[10]

Bunche's main spending money at Harvard came from working in the secondhand bookstore of John Phillips in Harvard Square. He got a job there more or less by mistake in his first week, having been given a letter of introduction to Phillips from a UCLA professor with a view to securing Bunche a discount on books. Phillips, who had just advertised for help, assumed that Bunche was an applicant and, before Bunche could explain, took him on for $10 a week to work after school hours. Phillips was so myopic he did not notice that Bunche was black, and only became aware of this much later, by which time Bunche had already proved himself invaluable. He told Bunche that he might not have taken him on if he had realized at their first meeting that Bunche was black, and he was honest enough to add that he would have been very wrong to reject him.[11] In 1956 Bunche wrote to Phillips, who was ill, recalling his happy days in the bookstore and the wonderful surprise when, later on, Phillips had come to hear him speak in Los Angeles, where Phillips lived after his retirement. When Phillips died Bunche wrote to his son, "Whenever I am back in Cambridge I inevitably walk by the bookshop and think back to those days when your father did me the good turn of employing me in the shop."[12]

Bunche impressed his teachers, and with his master-of-arts degree he received, in June 1928, the Thayer Fellowship. He declined the fellowship because he had just received an invitation to become an instructor and to organize the political-science department at Howard University in Washington, D.C.* This appointment to set up and direct a political-science department in the foremost black university of the United States provided Bunche not only with a major academic challenge but with a base for a wide variety of outside activities. According to Sterling Brown, a professor of English at Howard, Bunche "developed the Department of Government into one of the most appealing and cogent departments at Howard. He was a first-rate teacher, solidly grounded, able to communicate, exacting but understanding; able to inform, to liberalize, to inspire his students."[13]

Bunche also stood up for his students when necessary. Kenneth Clark led a group of students picketing the segregated restaurant in the Capitol building and was arrested. Mordecai Johnson, the president of Howard, fearing that Clark had jeopardized the college's congressional appropriation, demanded that he be brought before the faculty disciplinary committee. Bunche, as a member of the committee, argued forcefully that Clark and his group should be rewarded, not punished, for their demonstration, and won over the majority of the committee.[14]

Howard seems to have stimulated Bunche's radicalism, which had

---

*Professor Percy Julian of Howard had learned of Bunche's prowess at Harvard and got Howard University to offer him the post.

not been much in evidence at Harvard. Charles P. Henry describes the University as

a unique black institution in the thirties. Under the leadership of President Mordecai Johnson, a remarkable group of black scholars was assembled, and intellectual stimulation was supreme. Johnson was unlike many black college administrators of the day. His faculty members often had different lifestyles or serious personal problems. And he was criticized by government officials for permitting communists to speak on campus. The result was a "black Athens" that attracted such intellectual lights as Abram Harris, Sterling Brown, E. Franklin Frazier, Charles Thompson, Alain Locke, Charles Wesley, Ernest Just and, of course, Ralph Bunche. Harris, Brown, Frazier, Locke, Bunche and Emmett Dorsey were particularly close and often met at Bunche's house, which was on campus. Other friends at Howard were William Leo Hansberry, Hyland Lewis, and John A. Davis. While Harris was seen as the intellectual leader of the group, Bunche was viewed as the most accessible to students. . . . His leftist views seemed far from orthodox. He and his colleagues at Howard distrusted the "black bourgeoisie," but they had no illusions about the masses or unions. Race and class were inseparable components of their approach.[15]

Bunche soon began to find Howard a confining environment from which he often sought escape. Mordecai Johnson was not an easy person to work for. Others have described him as an autocratic man of God, with no milk of human kindness, and as a better preacher than manager.[16] "Mordecai Johnson, the president of the college," Bunche told Lillian Ross of *The New Yorker*, "once openly criticized me in a faculty meeting. 'Bunche is going all the way to Africa to find a problem,' he said. Negro colleges are petty places. The horizon is very limited, very narrow. They can be a graveyard. . . . They know they exist as expedients. They're not in the free, competitive market. I had to get out."[17] There can be little doubt that the pervasive segregation of life in Washington, D.C.—a shock after Los Angeles and Cambridge, Massachusetts—greatly contributed to Bunche's feelings of claustrophobia at Howard. It was also a major factor in his later choice of a career. "Living in the nation's capital," he remarked later, "is like serving out a sentence. It's extremely difficult for a Negro to maintain even a semblance of human dignity in Washington."[18]

Howard University proved to be an understanding patron for Bunche. He was active on the faculty from 1928 to 1933 and remained professor of political science there until 1950, when he finally came to terms with the fact that he would never return to academic life.

In Bunche's first year at Howard he met his future wife. Ruth Ethel Harris was born in Montgomery, Alabama. Her father, Charles Oscar

Harris, was educated at Oberlin and Howard and was for thirty-five years chief mailing clerk in the Montgomery post office, where he was affectionately known as "Colonel Harris." He was highly respected by both whites and blacks. Ruth was one of ten children, on whose education most of the family money was spent. After Ruth graduated from Alabama State Normal, the family moved to Washington, D.C., where Ruth got a job teaching and took night classes at Howard until she could satisfy the requirements for a bachelor's degree.

One day in October 1928 Ruth was sitting at home with some girl-friends, all young teachers, gossiping about school and about eligible young men, when Mortimer Weaver, Robert Weaver's brother, who was a professor at Howard, called to say he would like to drop in and bring a new young colleague who had just arrived to teach political science. Soon after the guests arrived the talk turned to a forthcoming dance. Ruth was to be partnered by Mortimer Weaver, but one of the girls, Thelma, had no escort. When it was suggested that Bunche should take her, he announced firmly but politely that he was going to take "that quiet little girl sitting back there on the piano bench." (Ruth was an extremely pretty young woman.) The brashness of this announcement silenced everyone into acquiescence, and neither Ralph nor Ruth looked for, or at, another partner ever again. After they met, Ruth enrolled as a student in one of Bunche's political-science classes and was able to confirm for herself that he was an exacting teacher. They were married in Ruth's brother's house in Washington on June 23, 1930.[19]

Before they could be married, Bunche had to return to Harvard, on leave from Howard, in the fall of 1929 to complete his preliminary coursework for a doctorate, and nearly a year of passionate correspondence ensued. This was a grueling year for Bunche. Commenting on the suicide of the most brilliant graduate student of the Harvard Medical School, Liddell Davis, he wrote to Ruth, "They pile it on and pile it on to see how much we can stand." In addition, he was wrestling with German, a language that exasperated him. His competitive spirit stood him in good stead. "I have been competing so long in this academic grind," he wrote on January 17, "that I just can't stand to see any of these fellows do better work or get better marks than I do. . . . I'd rather pass out than let one or two of them in particular beat me." These and other preoccupations were such that the economic disasters of 1929 and the onset of the Great Depression are not mentioned in the correspondence.

In the demanding conditions of graduate work at Harvard Ruth's letters were a lifeline, and when a day or two passed without one the mail

was filled with recriminations and dark surmises. Bunche's somewhat di-
dactic epistolary style and his exigent nature often ruffled the romantic
surface of their correspondence. In a bad mood—"one of my spells"—he
tended to write nagging, critical, pompous, and ungracious letters he later
regretted. He also tended to make general statements on the nature of
their future married life—on matters of "doubt," "trust," "confidence,"
and "faith"—and even suggested a form of mutual psychoanalysis
through exchanging lists of things each of them particularly disliked so
that they could avoid them when they were married. Ruth was remarkably
loving, patient, and understanding, although she occasionally protested, as
when she deplored Ralph's "condescension" toward her. It is possible that
Bunche's persistent use of the word "little," as in "my little girl," had
begun to grate.

Of the two, Bunche was the more self-absorbed. He worried about
the effect of school on his temperament. On February 2, 1930, he wrote:

I sometimes wonder if I am too broad for my age, or in advance of it, or whether I
have misinterpreted what I have thought to be the moral standards of my fellow-
men, as I have seen them portrayed by my fellow class-men. It may be that my
experiences and contacts at white schools have injured my moral fibers.

And, on April 13,

I have ever had a rather sensitive temperament—easily wounded, extremely im-
pressionable. I wonder what effect the testing and buffetting my sensitiveness has
received up here this year as a result of a very unsatisfactory existence here will
have upon my disposition.

But in better moments, which certainly predominated, it is clear that he
was getting remarkable support from his supervisors and that his self-
confidence was steadily growing.

Bunche's health, and to a lesser extent Ruth's, occupy a great deal of
space in the letters. Bunche was always concerned about his health, and
indeed he had much to worry about.* While at Harvard he was beset by
headaches, indigestion, and respiratory and dental problems, and ended
up in May in the Stillman Infirmary to have a tonsillectomy, an operation
on his sinuses, and a serum injection for the blood clot in his left leg. He
told Ruth that the pressure of work had addicted him to cigarettes, an
addiction he only shook off twenty years later.

*His aunts, evidently recalling the family history of tuberculosis, had earlier been so wor-
ried about his health at Harvard that they persuaded him not to take the long journey west
for Nana's funeral.

Financial worries were always on his mind. He was living on a very tight margin with no time to earn spending money. Until two months before their wedding he and Ruth did not know what they would live on during the summer, although Bunche, always a stickler for independence, was adamant that they would not live in Ruth's mother's house in Washington. They worked it out that for three months in Cambridge they would need $700, which included $40 a month for board at Ma Clark's and the down payment on a much-longed-for Ford. Miraculously, the General Education Board gave Bunche a $400 scholarship to work on his thesis during the summer, and Howard University confirmed his assistant professorship for the coming academic year. Bunche triumphantly passed his general examinations in June and made a down payment on the $619 price of a blue Ford coupé with a rumble seat.

Their daily correspondence in the year before their marriage both attests to their mutual devotion and presages the tensions which later sometimes troubled their life together. Bunche felt strongly both the need for the stability of married life and the yearning for knowledge and experience, not to mention a decent livelihood. These requirements were not always compatible. Although he told Ruth repeatedly that once they were married they would never again be apart, soon after their first child was born he was on his way to Africa to research his doctoral dissertation, and wrote from Paris on June 23, 1932, to apologize for missing their second anniversary. On their third anniversary he wrote from Harvard, "I'm going to finish up this blooming thesis this summer so there'll be no more cause for any future separations." But the future almost always turned out to be another series of separations.

3

Howard and Beyond

Too Broad for My Age?

The economic collapse of 1929 and the ensuing decade was a traumatic period both in American and in black experience. Bunche was maturing at a time—for Black Americans, at any rate—of tantalizing steps forward in the face of forbidding fundamental obstacles, of flickering hopes and waves of despair. Oscar De Priest, elected as a Republican member of Congress in 1928, was the first black congressman from a Northern state. In 1929, De Priest told a rally in Harlem that Negroes would never make substantial progress until they elected political leaders whose fortunes depended on their ability to fight for black interests in Congress. In 1930, the Temple of Islam, forerunner of the Black Muslims, was founded. In 1931, the Scottsboro Nine trial of black youths charged, in highly questionable circumstances, with the rape of a white woman became a worldwide *cause célèbre* and triggered off a battle between the NAACP and the communist-oriented International Labor Defense for the right to represent the defendants.

When Franklin Roosevelt won the presidency in 1932, black voters were only beginning to turn to the Democratic Party. Roosevelt soon began to appoint some Black Americans to responsible posts in his administration, and his wife, Eleanor, was obviously sensitive to race problems. By 1933 more than one-fourth of urban Black Americans were unemployed, and by 1934, in Northern and border states, 52 percent of Black Americans, compared with about 12 percent of whites, were on relief. In 1935, the National Council of Negro Women was founded by Mary McLeod Bethune. In the same year the NAACP bitterly criticized Roosevelt for failing to present or support civil-rights legislation. Nonetheless, in the 1936 election Roosevelt gained increasing support from black voters.

The hero of the 1936 Berlin Olympics was the black athlete Jesse

Owens, who won four gold medals—and was publicly ignored by Adolf Hitler. In the same year the Supreme Court required the University of Maryland to admit a black student, Donald Murray, to its graduate law school. In 1937, Bunche's Harvard friend William H. Hastie was made judge of the Federal District Court in the Virgin Islands, the first black federal judge in United States history.

Small gains were made in eliminating discriminatory employment practices in a number of places, but in general discrimination in employment persisted. In New York and Chicago, the "black renaissance" of which Bunche's Howard friend and mentor, Alain Locke, had been a prophet, made black musicians, performers, and athletes national figures. In 1939, Marian Anderson, denied the use of Constitution Hall in Washington by the Daughters of the American Revolution, sang to an Easter Sunday crowd of seventy-five thousand at the Lincoln Memorial. In 1940, Benjamin O. Davis, Sr., became the first black general in the history of the U.S. Armed Forces, and Roosevelt announced that black strength in the armed forces would be proportionate to black population totals, although troop integration was still ruled out. In 1941, Robert Weaver, another of Bunche's Harvard friends, was put in charge of the government's effort to integrate Black Americans into the national defense program.

Bunche never felt any urge to go into politics as such, but he waded into this tumultuous decade with the weapons he knew best, a passionate sense of responsibility, a remarkable capacity for detailed research, a keen and trained analytical mind, and the polemical and debating skills he had begun to develop at UCLA and Harvard. Throughout his life Bunche displayed a prodigious capacity for concentration and work. His output for the period from 1930 to 1940 was continuous and weighty, including speeches and articles in scholarly periodicals, a lively correspondence, full-scale studies such as his Harvard dissertation on "French Administration in Togoland and Dahomey," a related short book, *A World View of Race,* and some three thousand pages of monographs for the Gunnar Myrdal study which became *An American Dilemma.* Some projects—his study on non-European groups in South Africa, for example—remained uncompleted. In this period the competitive and brilliant student and academic developed into a major authority in his own right, an acknowledged expert who completed one task only to be immediately involved in another.

Unlike most of his black contemporaries Bunche had had, from the beginning, the elements of a strong world view, which is presumably what he meant when at Harvard he wondered "whether I am too broad for my age." Certainly he was deeply concerned with the problems and future of his own race, and he remained so throughout his life. But he saw these problems in the wider and deeper perspective of the national disaster of the Depression and of worldwide oppression, exploitation, racial prejudice, injustice, poverty, and lack of opportunity. These were the broad challenges which fired his sense of responsibility and his vocation. His discontent with Howard University, apart from President Mordecai Johnson's autocratic leadership style, was largely due to what he regarded as its too narrow and parochial concerns and interests, as well as the inescapable fact that it symbolized the exclusion of black academics from the faculties of all major American universities. Bunche was interested in improving the lot of the oppressed peoples of the world, not just the oppressed minorities of the United States. Indeed he saw them as indivisible parts of the same great problem.

The decade of the 1930s was a free-for-all of ideologies and ideas from both left and right. Although Bunche was undeniably on the Marxist left ideologically, he had a sure instinct for the basic interests of the people he wanted to help. His stringent commentary, criticism, and advice played an important part in keeping the causes he championed on a steady and pragmatic course. In a crucial period for the black population of the United States he played both an intellectual and a practical role.[1]

In 1931 his doctoral thesis was still Bunche's main preoccupation. He had accepted a $2,000 Rosenwald Fellowship and had agreed to work on a comparison of French colonial administration in the French colony of Dahomey and in the French-administered League of Nations mandate of Togoland.*

Bunche had intended to spend the academic year 1931–32 in Africa and Europe, but he was offered the job of assistant to President Mordecai Johnson of Howard, which gave him both administrative experience and increased pay. He also wanted to wait for the birth of his first child, Joan, who was born in December 1931. He finally sailed for Europe on June 15, 1932, tourist class on the *Europa*. † He spent over four months in France,

---

*In an edited version of Bunche's journals in South Africa, *An African-American in South Africa,* edited by Robert R. Edgar (Ohio, 1992), p. 5, Edgar writes that Bunche had originally intended to work on a comparison of the experience and assimilation of mixed-race people in Brazil and that of Black Americans, but had been steered toward Africa by Edwin Embree, the head of the Rosenwald Fund, because he "thought that US Negroes might get 'dangerous' ideas in Brazil." In a memorandum of May 21, 1941, to W. C. Haywood of the Rosenwald Fund, Embree hotly denied this allegation.

†He had been told that there was less racial prejudice on the German Line than on the British Elder Dempster Line.

collecting data and reports from the French Colonial and Mandates Office, and in Geneva, doing background research and meeting with officials of the League of Nations. He then went to French Togoland and Dahomey to study colonial administration at first hand, returning to Paris in mid-January 1933.

On his first transatlantic trip Bunche was impressed by the vast quantities of food, but less so by some of the American passengers: "a crude group of Georgetown fellows who are continually drunk."[2] A plane catapulted from the ship took his first letter to Ruth. A number of distinguished black passengers, including the poet Langston Hughes, were on board, headed for the Soviet Union, which was then ardently wooing black intellectuals.

There were also Black American intellectuals and artists in Paris, many of whom frequented a nightclub run by a singer known as Bricktop, who became Bunche's lifelong friend. At her establishment the specialty was corned-beef hash with a poached egg on top. In the Latin Quarter Bunche happened upon a communist rally protesting the Scottsboro case.

Mrs. Wright, the mother of two of the Scottsboro boys, was on exhibition and gave what appeared to be a memorized and well-rehearsed version of the affair. I met her afterwards and found her to be exceedingly ignorant. She doesn't seem to know what it's all about.* . . . The French are excitable, wild, woolly.

Bunche went to the races at Longchamps and visited the main sights of Paris. He wrote to Ruth:

Paris is truly a beautiful city, but I don't care much for it or for the French. . . . French food is *terrible*—I've had indigestion and mild dysentery ever since I've been here. . . . The French are very ordinary looking people. You will be particularly disappointed with the appearance of French women, even in the fashionable districts. . . . They do, however, dress themselves and their children superbly.

He was also struck by the extraordinary degree and contrasts of racial intermingling to be seen everywhere in Paris.

Bunche had not been in Paris a week before he became acutely homesick. Although he was on a tight budget—the Rosenwald Fellowship and expense money from Howard† —he began to beg Ruth to join him,

---

*In February 1936, in a rousing speech to the Scottsboro Boys Defense Committee, Bunche said, "The Scottsboro boys are martyrs to Southern injustice and intolerance. Justice, not those boys, is on trial in Decatur."

†In a letter of April 22, 1932, to Dean Davis at Howard, Bunche set out his own expenses as follows:

bringing the six-month-old Joan. After a series of yearning letters from Bunche, including some lectures on the necessity of molding the character of his baby daughter and preventing her from sucking her thumb, Ruth and Joan arrived on July 22.

Bunche departed alone for West Africa on November 5 on the French ship *Foucauld*. Many of his fellow passengers were Martiniquian and Guadeloupian French colonial-service workers returning to their posts with their families. Most of Bunche's time in Africa was spent in the offices and installations of the colonial regime. The overwhelming poverty of the people dismayed him, but he greatly enjoyed this first African visit—the colorful markets of Dakar, a trip to the north in Togo in a van in which people were "packed like sardines," but in which he, being "classified as European," was allowed to ride in front with the driver. He visited Abomey in the interior, and saw the ruins of the old Dahomean kings' palaces and the tomb of Behanzin, the great Dahomean monarch who was conquered by the French. He was also impressed by the alcoholic intake of most French colonial civil servants.

Bunche's feelings about colonial Africa and his first direct experience of colonialism were expressed in a letter on December 1 to Robert Weaver from Lomé.

Sitting out here on the veranda of the Hotel de France under a brilliant tropical sky and with the lazy rumble of the tropical Atlantic in my ear. . . . There is, of course, the inevitable colonial gramophone grating away and this being French jurisdiction, the music is terribly French. . . . This is a marvelous country and after seeing a bit of it and its people, one is apt to become more puzzled than ever as to what is to become of it, or even what *should* become of it. . . . One may suggest, but easier than all is to criticize—the problem being so grand and the men fiddling about with it so small. . . .

Returning from Dahomey via Accra, Monrovia, Freetown, and Dakar, he rejoined Ruth in Paris in mid-January 1933, and then returned

---

Roundtrip fare to Europe and return	$250
15-day trip from Hamburg to Lomé (1 way)	$245
Return trip	$245
Allowance for inland travel expenses	$200
Tropical equipment	$200

This will leave a balance of only $860 to cover all the other expenses such as passports, visas, living expenses, etc. on the continent and in Africa for from 10 months to one year. Nothing at all is left for emergency.

to his post at Howard University. Their second daughter, Jane, was born in May 1933.

Bunche spent the summer vacation in Cambridge working on his dissertation. Although his adviser, Arthur N. Holcombe, as well as others who followed its development, believed it had great promise and should be made into a book, Bunche had extreme difficulty in concentrating on his work. "This thesis is a terrible grind—every word has to be carefully weighed, every statement doubly checked." He was dissatisfied with the quality of the background materials he had collected in Paris—"these old French reports" which are "inadequate and inaccurate." He was moody and was smoking excessively. He attributed his distraction to profound loneliness and longing for Ruth, and sometimes also to her failure (with two small children at home) to write him letters that were long or expressive enough.

For her part, Ruth, already feeling the burden of looking after the little girls, resented her husband's being away so often, in spite of his repeated assurances that after the thesis was written there would be no more separations. For all these assurances, when the prospect of a project in Puerto Rico came up in August, he wrote to Ruth,

If I could do something big on assignment like that, I might work up to something better than Howard offers—you see, I don't intend to spend my life down there if I can help it. I hate the thought of going back into that atmosphere again. . . .

Bunche's dissertation, which gained him his doctorate of philosophy in February 1934 and also won the Toppan Prize for the year's best dissertation in the field of government, set the stage for his subsequent work in the United Nations on trusteeship and decolonization matters.* "The study herein recorded," he wrote in the preface, "is stimulated by a deep interest in the development of subject peoples and the hopes which the future holds for them." Quoting John Stuart Mill's warning that the government of one people by another merely means that the people so governed are kept as a "warren or preserve—a place to make money in, a human cattle-farm," Bunche commented,

It is doubtful that the territories of Togo and Dahomey are little more than this today. Moreover, there seems to be but slight disposition to make them more.

*In spite of the urgings of his dissertation committee at Harvard, Professors A. N. Holcombe, Rupert Emerson, and George Benson, Bunche's dissertation, 450 pages long, was never published.

Bunche believed, however, that the very process of exploitation gave Africans the knowledge and techniques which they could use to their own advantage, as well as making them unwilling

to continue to accept the virtual tyranny of French administrative bureaucracy. Sooner or later, as the educated class of natives increases in numbers, the French will be confronted with the difficult problem of the colonial administration of backward peoples, viz., that there is no apparent peaceful means of transition to full self control. This condition is already looming larger on the horizon in neighboring British Gold Coast. The French will be able to postpone this day of reckoning longer than will the British perhaps, because France finds it possible to mollify the élite by giving them racial and social equality.

Bunche's ambition to provide "a peaceful means of transition to full self-control," which was at the heart of his later efforts in the United Nations, probably took root at this time.

Bunche foresaw that the awareness of the colonial peoples of West Africa of the abuses of the French colonial administration and of their inability to do anything about it under the colonial regime would stimulate national consciousness and unified action. He was shocked by the economic and social backwardness of the African population and their primitive living conditions. He noted, however, that the peasants had been left unmolested in their lands and were thus "reasonably secure against the extreme abuses incident to the plantation and location systems." Although Togo (formerly a German colony) was a League of Nations mandate and Dahomey was a colony, there was little actual difference in the treatment and status of the natives in the two places, and the natives themselves appeared to be totally oblivious of the distinction.* Bunche was critical of the annual French reports to the League of Nations Mandates Commission, reports that had a tendency "to paint pictures of roseate hue which do not represent the actual conditions." He felt that this should be remedied through visits of inspection and through giving the natives the right of petition and appeal to the League. This idea took practical shape in Bunche's later work on the UN Charter and in the Trusteeship Division of the United Nations Secretariat. He felt strongly that the treatment of a mandated territory as an ordinary colony "seems to defeat the intent of the spirit of international trusteeship which inspired the mandates system." That system, Bunche concluded,

*In a speech to the UN Trusteeship Council in 1950, Bunche cited this ignorance as an argument for sending UN visiting missions to, and for receiving petitions from, UN Trust territories.

has only begun a great work which still remains to be performed—it is important that the mandate principle assure to these territories an unselfish, helpful administration, which will offer them an opportunity to properly prepare themselves for the eventual day when they will stand alone in the world. The African is no longer to be considered a Barbarian, nor even a child, but only an adult retarded in terms of Western civilization. This Western civilization now surrounds him in his daily life, and he consumes it greedily. Assured of strong and helpful government under a sound mandate system and a liberal colonial policy, he will be assured a balanced diet and be spared the pains of social indigestion.

For the year 1933 these were perceptive—and prophetic—words.

Bunche's analysis of colonialism, as well as of the problems of Black Americans, was informed by a strong Marxist strain of economic determinism. Although race was certainly a factor in imperialism, in the 1930s he was convinced that the predominant motive for imperialism was greed, and that economics were the basis of racial oppression. Imperialism, he believed, was an international expression of capitalism.[3] There could be no doubt that the general pattern of domination was white over nonwhite, and Bunche strongly resented the fact that throughout the world so many nonwhites were exploited by so few whites. He was determined to work for, and lived to see, a world which, as he put it in 1959, "is not by any means a 'white man's world.' "[4] Bunche hoped and believed that coalitions among oppressed peoples would eventually create a radical change in the world, just as an alliance of black and white American workers could create change in the United States. In the world at large the catalyst would be the revolt of oppressed peoples and their alliance against colonialism and imperialism.

The radical agenda of the 1930s included the Depression and the New Deal; the struggle against racial discrimination; the relevance of Marxist ideas; the aspirations and incursions of the American Communist Party; the rise of fascism; and, ultimately, the Second World War, America's role in it, and the place of Black Americans within that role. The titles of a few major items of Bunche's large written output for the decade give some indication of the development of his own interests in this agenda.

1928   "The American City as a Negro Political Laboratory"
1928   "The Negro in Chicago Politics"
1934   "French Administration in Togo and Dahomey"
1935   "A Critical Analysis of the Tactics and Programs of Minority Groups"

1936   "Triumph? or Fiasco?" (a critique of the First National Negro Congress)
1936   "Education in Black and White"
1936   *A World View of Race*
1936   "Fascism and Minority Groups"
1937   "African Survival in the New World"
1937   "Culture Conflict in South Africa"
1939   "Programs of Organizations Devoted to Improvement of the Status of the American Negro"
1940   "The Role of the University in the Political Orientation of Negro Youth"
1940   "The Negro's Stake in the World Crisis"

Bunche's opening theme in *A World View of Race*[5] anticipated the basic premise of Gunnar Myrdal's *An American Dilemma*. "No other subject can so well illustrate the insincerity of our doctrines of human equality and the great disparity between our political theory and our social practices as that of race."

A World View of Race starts with a lengthy sociological discussion of racial theories and situations worldwide, drawing on Bunche's extensive reading and studies as well as on his experience in Africa. An important section devoted to race and imperialism is followed by a long disquisition on race in the United States.

Race is the great American shibboleth. . . . It is one of the great factors in confusing the American populace in its effort to understand the fundamental conflicts and issues confronting society. It has been one of the most serious obstructions in the alignment of the population along lines of natural class interests.

Bunche asserted that economic competition is the basic cause of racial persecution and that, therefore,

The Negro must develop . . . a consciousness of class interest and purpose, and must strive for an alliance with the white working classes in a common struggle for economic and political equality and justice.

Pseudo-scientific racial theories, in Bunche's view, lent themselves conveniently to the exigencies of political and economic control. By causing group divisions and conflicts they assisted the process of domination and exploitation of the many by the "self-chosen few." With the Nazi racist ideology in mind, Bunche asserted that "racial crises threaten not only the future of the United States but the peace of the world." However, beneath such overt manipulation of racial issues, "the lines are forming in a different manner. Race issues appear but tend to merge into class issues. Throughout the world the issue between working and owning classes is sharpening." The great struggles of the future, Bunche wrote, would be between the haves and the have-nots, and numerical strength would be on the side of the have-nots. "And so class will some day supplant race in world affairs. Race war then will be merely a sideshow to the gigantic class war which will be waged in the big tent we call the world."

This run-of-the-mill Marxist ending* does scant justice to the solidity of much of the analysis in *A World View of Race*. In later years Bunche himself said that *A World View of Race* was not a very good job and had soon become outdated. He complained that it had had to be written too hastily, "within a week, in fact."[6] But fifty years later, in a world of fewer "haves," more "have-nots," and "North-South" tensions, his prophecy of a world class war, shorn of its Marxist overtones, still strikes an ominous chord.

Liberal thinkers in the 1930s, including people in the Roosevelt administration, tended to emphasize class and economic considerations, not least because they were easier to handle politically than questions of civil rights. In a period of acute economic crisis they apparently believed, as Bunche came to believe later on, that racial change could, and would, come through economic and political change in the context of what Roosevelt's secretary of the interior, Harold Ickes, called the "new democracy" of the Roosevelt welfare state.[7]

Bunche found himself in disagreement with most of the current approaches to the problems of Black Americans. He accepted neither W. E. B. Du Bois' formula of a "Negro Nation within the Nation" nor the ideas of black liberal reformers like Charles S. Johnson who believed that the combined forces of technology and liberal reform within the New Deal were actually changing the existing structure in favor of Black Americans. Nor did he find himself in sympathy with established black organizations such as the NAACP—of which, much later, he became a National Board member—or the National Urban League. He regarded them as incorrigibly middle-class and elitist in their thinking and out of touch with

---

*"My writings and speeches are getting me labelled 'Red,' " Bunche wrote to Ethel and Nelle in September 1936, "but I only write and speak what I consider to be the truth—the logical deductions from the given situations—and I intend to continue to do so. When I can no longer do that I'm ready to give up my job."

problems of the large majority of Black Americans. He was also leery of grass-roots groups which supported economic boycotts—"Don't Buy Where You Can't Work"—as both racially parochial and likely to worsen black employment opportunities. He was concerned that that they would widen the gap between white and black workers "by boldly placing the competition for jobs on a strictly racial basis." It was, he wrote,

absurd to assume that the Negro, deprived of the advantages of full participation in American life today, will be able to gain . . . advantages or acceptable substitutes for them by setting himself up in a black political and economic outhouse.[8]

Although race and racism were an essential element of the problems of Black Americans, Bunche believed at this time that it was a mistake to assume that their problems were basically racial in nature. Most of these problems, he felt, stemmed from the wider failure to improve the standard of living of the working classes. He believed that much black racial ideology was simply a reaction to white racist assumptions and practices and to the biases of the dominant white culture, and did not therefore address the primary needs of Black Americans.

Bunche was always skeptical of overoptimistic or facile formulations, and popular ideas had to undergo the test of his rigorously analytical mind before he accepted them. As a radical scholar-activist, his first ambition, as he had told W. E. B. Du Bois in 1927, was to serve the cause of Black Americans by promoting constructive political and social thinking on their problems, and he helped to organize two conferences for this purpose. At Howard University in 1935 he worked with his Harvard friend John P. Davis, who had served for three years as executive secretary of the Joint Committee on National Recovery but was critical of the New Deal,* to organize an ideologically diverse, black assessment of the New Deal. The conference, on "The Status of the Negro Under the New Deal," provided the platform for Bunche's most wide-ranging attack on Roosevelt's policies. "For the Negro population," he told the conference, "the New Deal means the same thing but more of it."[9] He argued that the New Deal, far from aiming at fundamental social and economic changes, was designed to create an unstable balance between big business and the laboring masses, with a strong tilt in favor of the former, and with only a halfhearted attempt to curb the abuses of capitalism. The New Deal planners, caught between the opposing concepts of government control of the means of production and full freedom for private industry, had ended

*Davis was later to join the Communist Party.

up doing very little to achieve an equilibrium between the two. In the end they had weakened the independence of the working masses and increased the power of the capitalists. Even worse, New Deal planning and welfare policies had tended to legitimize economic oppression of Black Americans. The National Recovery Administration had perpetuated the inferior economic status of Black Americans by legalizing occupational and geographical wage differentials, while the Agricultural Adjustment Administration had left black sharecroppers and tenant farmers at the mercy of the big white farmers. Such policies ensured that Black Americans would be economically and racially isolated in future. Bunche referred to the New Deal scathingly as a "great relief program" which produced at best a precarious livelihood for millions of distressed workers and farmers, but which failed to change any of the traditional racial stereotypes held by white people. It thus served only to "crystalize those abuses and oppressions which the exploited Negro citizenry of America have long suffered under laissez-faire capitalism, and for the same reasons as in the past."

After the Howard conference, Bunche joined with John P. Davis and A. Philip Randolph, the legendary leader of the Brotherhood of Sleeping Car Porters who had fought the Pullman Company for twelve years to win recognition of the first major black trade union, to create the National Negro Congress. Bunche was increasingly concerned with what he saw as the failure of black leaders to create the strategy and organization necessary to challenge the political status quo. The objective of the National Negro Congress was to provide the basis for a broad coalition of black and white progressive interests, trade unions, and religious, civic, and fraternal bodies. It was to formulate a comprehensive program for social, political, and economic change and to "unite the masses of Negroes behind a definite program."[10] Its underlying assumption was "that the salvation of the American Negro and the solution of all his vital problems is to be found in working class unity and mass pressure."[11]

The first organizing conference of the NNC was held in Chicago on February 14–15, 1936. There were 817 delegates from 585 black organizations. Randolph was elected president, and Davis national secretary. Several communists and communist sympathizers took part. Randolph's keynote speech bore strong resemblances to Bunche's speech at the Howard conference the year before. "The New Deal is no remedy," he said. "It does not seek to change the profit system. It does not place human rights above property rights, but gives the business interests the support of the State."[12]

The press reports of the NNC meeting had tended to be sensational, and Bunche set out to give a more sober appraisal in "Triumph? or Fiasco?"[13] As the title implies he was already experiencing some doubts about how the NNC would turn out. There were far too many Negro groups and organizations, he wrote, advancing every conceivable program "from licking the boots of wealthy white philanthropists to revolutionary communism." The need was for a definite program behind which all could unite "in order that the mass numbers of the Negro population may be effectively employed. . . ."

The most significant achievement of the congress had been to bring together black leaders and professionals with black manual workers, which was, "to say the least, an educational experience for the Negro leaders and the professional and white-collar groups." The predominant theme had been the necessity for black participation in a militant American labor movement through which working-class unity and mass pressure could be channeled. Although some of the resolutions contradicted others, they had covered an immense range of subject matter. The business resolutions were, in Bunche's view, particularly weak, and he especially deplored the congress's failure to adopt Randolph's keynote theme of industrial union-ism. But, for all these shortcomings,

for earnestness and purpose and hard work its equal has never been seen in the history of the American Negro. . . . The difficult problem is how to reach the Negro masses with the cogent, realistic message of labor organization.

After inveighing against "false Negro prophets," Bunche sounded a note of doubt about the comprehensive composition of the congress.

Perhaps a Congress composed only of representatives of organizations actively engaged in the labor struggle could achieve more—but could it effectively reach the greater masses of the Negro people? To do so it would still have to contend with the black demagogues, the professional Uncle Toms, and the socially igno-rant ministers of the gospel. . . . Its [the NNC's] fundamental purpose should be to make Negroes socially conscious, to give them a realistic understanding of their mass position as workers in society, to promote labor orientation and to stimulate the enrollment of the Negro masses in the ranks of organized labor.

At the 27th Annual Conference of the NAACP in July 1936, in a speech on "Fascism and Minority Groups," Bunche began to develop a theme which was soon to become central to his thinking, the place of Black Americans in the forthcoming fight against fascism.

Fascism is the last desperate effort of capitalism to preserve itself at all costs, and to do so, therefore, it must destroy labor groups, labor organizations, all the rights that labor has won for itself over a long period of years of struggle—that alone gives sufficient reason for the Negro . . . to bend all his energies to fight against this monster.[14]

At this point Bunche's knowledge of European fascism was limited, but he certainly believed that the seeds of fascism existed in the United States. In this speech, for example, he referred to William Randolph Hearst as "our leading fascist," and he derided the idea that fascism could not happen in the United States. The answer to fascism could only be "the establishment of a solid front of all working class peoples throughout the country."

Bunche maintained his interest in Africa, and in May 1936 organized a conference at Howard on "The Crisis of Modern Imperialism in Africa and the Far East," a subject he was to pursue during the following year's journey to Europe and Africa. Bunche had consulted Donald Young, a race-relations specialist at the Social Science Research Council, about funding for a project on the impact of colonial rule and Western culture on Africans as seen by Africans themselves.[15] Young told him that the SSRC would require that he undergo research training in cultural anthropology before he could be funded to embark on such a project. This training would include study with three leaders in the field, Melville Herskovits* at Northwestern University, Bronislaw Malinowski at the London School of Economics, and Isaac Schapera at the University of Cape Town. Bunche agreed and was agreeably surprised when the SSRC gave him a two-year grant, rather than the one year he had asked for.

After a summer stint at Swarthmore running a race-relations institute, he spent the last months of 1936 and January of 1937 at Northwestern and the University of Chicago, working under the supervision of Herskovits, to whom Bunche had been introduced by his Howard colleague Abram Harris before his first trip to Africa in 1932. Although Bunche and his friends seem to have spent a lot of time at Northwestern complaining about him, Herskovits became a respected mentor and a lifelong friend. Herskovits certainly had a high regard for Bunche and his academic associates at Howard. They were "the only group known to me among the negroes able to approach the tragedy of the racial situation in this country with the objectivity that comes from seeing it as the result of the play of historic forces rather than as an expression of personal spite and a desire to hold down a minority people."[16] In introducing Bunche to Isaac Schapera he wrote, "one thing you can count on, and that is that he will meet these

*Herskovits, a pioneer in African studies, is now chiefly remembered for his much-debated thesis , expressed in his 1941 "Myth of the Negro Past," that American black culture owes much to African culture.

situations [racial discrimination in South Africa] as they arise, with a very clear head and a detachment that is as admirable as it is unusual."[17]

Bunche's constant absences from home and the prospect of another long separation in the coming year were already a source of deep anxiety for Ruth. On July 9, 1936, she wrote,

Ralph, the next two years seem like a nightmare to me. I hate to think of it. It keeps me awake at night. I want you to have everything good and all the success in the world, but I do hate to see our family break up. It seems like a death to me. . . .

Ruth was distraught by the girls' constant squabbling, and she lamented, as she was often to do in the future, the fact that her husband was not there to help. She was still teaching first grade during the day, and found the dual responsibility exhausting and exasperating. She had disagreements with her mother about dealing with the children and was more and more housebound in the evenings. Although Bunche himself was unquestionably tormented by his separations from his family, he did not always choose the most felicitous way to express his feelings. "I love you and the children more dearly each day, Ruth—" he wrote on October 12, "nothing impresses that on me so much as being away from you."

For some months they had been discussing whether Ruth and the two girls should accompany Bunche to Europe. Finally, on January 10, 1937, Bunche recorded in his diary, "Special delivery from Ruth announcing she has decided to make the round-the-world trip with me. That pepped me up plenty. She's a sweet girl."

4

England 1937

This Staid Little Isle

The family sailed for England on the *Berengaria* on February 5, 1937. During a stopover in New York Bunche went to a night-club to hear Leonidas Simmons, who had prompted him in his high school commencement address. On the boat he made the acquaintance of Ellen Wilkinson, a fiery socialist member of the British Parliament, who opened up many socialist and international doors for him in England and was immensely hospitable throughout their stay.

The family's first impression of England was of "dirty and disappointing" lodgings in Golder's Green, and they soon moved to better digs in Earl's Court. Bunche, though greatly enjoying his stay, had ambivalent feelings about "this staid, glum and curt, though always 'courteous' little isle."[1] In his international, socialist mood he was naturally suspicious of the world's major imperial power. He found the English racially prejudiced in a far more subtle way than Americans, but prejudiced nonetheless. As a champion of the workers he was appalled at the state of the English lower classes. "The masses really are in bad shape physically, scrawny, rotten teeth, etc."[2] As a dedicated tourist, he took a lot of trouble to get seats outside Buckingham Palace for the coronation of George VI in May 1937, but he commented, "The whole thing was very colorful but what a cheeky flaunting of excess wealth before these poor millions. . . ." As an anticolonialist he was naturally influenced by the views and feelings of the young African radicals with whom he spent much of his time, and he was surprised to see "no anti-imperialist section or slogans" in the May Day parade.

England in 1937 was a frustrating place for a young, left-wing idealist. The economic and social conditions of the poor were appalling. The Conservative government, hopelessly unprepared for war, was picking an undignified and expedient path through the fires that were about to engulf Europe. Britain was noninterventionist in Mussolini's invasion of Abyssinia as well as in the Spanish Civil War, the two causes that most engaged the British left. It was still appeasing Hitler, who had just embarked on a program of forceful European expansionism. Britain was defensive but arrogant about the empire, proclaiming the virtues of indirect rule but strongly resistant to independence movements and their leaders. Bunche's natural friends were people who were engaged in various forms of protest against such attitudes—the Labour Party, the left-wing intelligentsia, and the early proponents, both British and African, of decolonization.

Bunche's academic base in London was the London School of Economics, and, in particular, Bronislaw Malinowski's Thursday-afternoon seminar on "The Comparative Study of Culture." Malinowski had a worldwide reputation as the founder of the "functionalist" school of anthropological fieldwork, and Bunche faithfully attended his seminar, as well as two or three others. He variously described Malinowski as "very whimsical," "vain and dogmatic, but extremely able,"[3] and even something of a charlatan. He found the seminar immensely stimulating, while questioning much that was said and remaining aloof from the cult surrounding Malinowski and the doctrine of "functionalism." "There's never been a primitive religion so demanding as 'Malinowskism' is here. But I ain't converted. The Baptists dipped me in a tank and couldn't convert me, and I know damn well I can't get no kind of religion in a classroom."[4]

Malinowski's seminar was the gathering point of a remarkable group of young Africans, some of whom were to play an important role in the independence struggle of the postwar period. Jomo Kenyatta, a Kikuyu from Kenya, was perhaps its most impressive member ("goatee à la Edgar Brown," Bunche noted on their first meeting[5]) and Bunche saw him frequently. He took weekly Swahili lessons with Kenyatta and met him constantly at LSE, at home, and at social gatherings. Kenyatta cut a flamboyant figure in the gray, bowler-hatted London of 1937. He wore a red fez in class and, when lame, used a spear instead of a walking stick. "He claims to hate the British and to trust few, if *any*, white men."[6] Use them but don't trust them was Kenyatta's motto. "Kenyatta loves Russia and the Scandinavian countries and their peoples," Bunche noted. "But he seems to be an intense racial chauvinist rather than a Marxist, though he spent a year and four months at school in Russia. Said he was treated royally."[7] One of Kenyatta's deepest grievances against the British was that, in the government's report on the 1922 revolt in Kenya, the British had reduced the number of dead from two hundred to twenty-five. Toward the end of his stay in London, Bunche was asked by Malinowski to mediate in a furious row between Kenyatta and an English graduate student called Goodfellow, ostensibly over the use of research material. It was Bunche's first success in the field of mediation.

A typical meeting of this African group was a gathering in Bunche's lodgings on the evening of March 31. It included Kenyatta and Peter Koinange, then at Cambridge, both from Kenya; Addo, Kessie, Afurata, and deGraaf Johnson from the Gold Coast; and Myanza and Akiki Nyabongo from Uganda. The Gold Coasters claimed that they were far more independent and aggressive than the Nigerians. Everyone agreed that educated Africans tended to be individualistic and self-centered and that there was little hope for pan-africanism or African unity. The lawyers in the group were "very verbal and rhetorical but not too sound."[8] Some of the party got rather drunk, causing Kenyatta to denounce them for lack of self-discipline and courtesy. If a white man had been present, he said, and had asked him whether Africans were ready for self-government, he would have had to say no.

The most important Black Americans in Bunche's London life were George Padmore and Paul Robeson. Padmore, whom Bunche had taught at Howard, had become a "perfervid pan-africanist and a racial chauvinist,"[9] and had just written *Africa and World Peace*, with an introduction by Sir Stafford Cripps. His home was a center for radical Africans and Black Americans in London, and he was organizing a bureau and a journal of African peoples, later called the International Africa Bureau, in which Bunche agreed to help. He was also a popular speaker at rallies about the war in Abyssinia and for relief for the Republican victims of the Civil War in Spain. Bunche opposed pan-africanism, which he perceived as a distraction from the right road to African liberation, the hope of which, in his view at the time, lay in a fundamental change in the political and economic structure of the imperialist nations themselves. Padmore was sponsoring Max Yergan, another Black American ("seems to be very C.P." [Communist Party], noted Bunche), who asked Bunche to serve as a board member of his newly formed African Affairs Committee.* Yergan, who had a South African girlfriend, Frieda Neugebauer, for whom he had left his wife and children, offered to arrange for Bunche to go to Spain. Ruth strongly opposed this, "but it would be a wonderful opportunity for me as

---

*Bunche never attended a meeting of this committee and finally concluded that it was merely a self-promoting device for Yergan. On April 29, 1940, he told Yergan to remove his name from the committee's letterhead.[10]

a political scientist."[11] Nothing came of it, however, or of Bunche's attempt to get an Italian visa to go to Abyssinia.

Paul Robeson, at the height of his fame as a singer and an actor, lived in London and was working at the Pinewood Studios at Denham, outside London, on a film called *Jericho.* Eslanda (Essie) Robeson invited the Bunches over to meet Max Yergan. Robeson was "anti-white and all out for USSR,"[12] but he seemed to be having a wonderful time in London, with a beautiful house, a chauffeured Daimler, and splendid dressing rooms at Denham. His wife, Essie, was warm and immensely friendly and gave Bunche her Ciné Kodak movie camera to take to Africa. Robeson enchanted Bunche during a family dinner by cuddling Joan and Jane, who had initially been shy, and singing to them. Bunche, perhaps influenced by Robeson's paeans of praise, visited the Intourist office in London to set up a trip to the Soviet Union, but nothing came of that either.

For all his mixed feelings about the place, Bunche had a wide range of contacts in England. At the Dominions Office, Malcolm Macdonald, son of former Prime Minister Ramsay MacDonald, was immensely helpful in planning Bunche's forthcoming African trip and smoothing the way with the South African authorities. Lord de La Warr at the Colonial Office was equally friendly, and Bunche was given a free run of the Colonial Office library for his research work. De La Warr also undertook to write in his behalf to the governors of the African colonies Bunche was going to visit. Ellen Wilkinson took the Bunches to parties and entertained them in the House of Commons, where Bunche enjoyed seeing Lloyd George, Stanley Baldwin, Clement Attlee, Sir John Simon, and others debating. He went to fervent socialist rallies addressed by Attlee, Cripps, Norman Thomas of the American Socialist Party, and others, on fighting fascism and on the liquidation of imperialism, where clenched fists were raised and the "Internationale" was sung. C. R. Buxton, a Labour M.P.; Ethel Mannin, a social activist; Lady Rhondda, the owner-editor of the left-wing periodical *Time & Tide,* and Julius Lewin, a South African who was also studying at LSE,* entertained him. Lewin introduced him to Harold Laski, the well-known socialist guru and head of the London School of Economics, whom Bunche found "active and full of talk."[13] Professor Hugh Jones, who became another lifelong friend, had Bunche to stay for a weekend at Oxford, where he met, among others, Professor J. L. Myres, the great historian of ancient Greece; Margery

---

*After the war Julius Lewin came to New York for a year to work for Bunche in the UN Trusteeship Department.

Perham, England's ranking academic authority on colonialism; the historian Sir Alfred Zimmern; Sir Arthur Salter, who was credited with inventing the convoy system in World War I; A. L. Rowse, later an eminent historian; and the then well-known left-wing historian and publicist, G. D. H. Cole.

The Bunche family's social life in London was astonishingly active. Apart from African and British occasions there were many family outings and expeditions. Although British conditions—the cold and damp, and the difficulty of keeping the house warm—were a source of complaint, this was a uniquely happy period of family life,* with Bunche taking a very full part in the domestic chores. Joan and Jane went to school at the Froebel Institute and flourished. The family did a lot of shopping together, and since a neighbor, Mrs. Crichton, was a willing babysitter, Ralph and Ruth could go out together in the evening to the theatre or the movies or to see friends. Bunche went to Wimbledon several times and saw Donald Budge beat Baron Gottfried Von Cramm in the finals for the Davis Cup.

Their happiness was only very occasionally marred by Bunche's temper or Ruth's nagging. A persistent grievance was the amusement arcade, or sports palace, in the Haymarket. When one or the other of the girls was sick, which was often, Bunche used to take the Underground to the all-night pharmacy in Piccadilly Circus for the necessary medicaments and then go on to the Haymarket amusement parlor, where he was surprisingly successful, winning cigarettes and, at various times, a clock, a desk lamp, a chest of kitchen silver, a casserole dish, a watch, and a combination cigarette case and lighter. His addiction to this place seems to have infuriated Ruth, who was already "grumpy" at the prospect of his long absence in Africa.

In all this round of intellectual stimulation and social activity, Bunche worked less hard than usual and wrote relatively little. It was a welcome pause for reflection at a time when he was receiving a great number of new impressions. In London he contemplated writing various books—"The Negro and the Federal Government," "The Constitutional Status of the American Negro," and "What the Educated African Thinks." The latter idea got as far as a detailed questionnaire and long sessions with Kenyatta and other Africans. His London stay also forced him to think about the looming catastrophe of war and its consequences.

---

*"We have been extremely happy," Bunche wrote to Ethel and Nelle in September 1937 from the boat train to catch the boat to South Africa, "since we left America last February. Living over here drew all of us closer together than we had been before."

One note in his diary reads, "Greater bargaining power for Africans as result of war."[14]

Racial discrimination—as a general problem, as a matter of principle, and as a feature of his own life—was always with Bunche. As a highly intelligent and successful man he could not escape it and had no wish to ignore it. On the boat from New York he noted "enquiries about my nationality," and, in his search for new lodgings in London, "one clearly prejudice rebuff." He observed his daughters' reactions and noted, "The kids have no recognition of color differences in people. They seem simply to take it for granted that there are black, brown and white people and have no curiosity about the differences."[15] On June 22, when Joe Louis beat Jim Braddock for the world heavyweight title, the British press printed many snide racial comments, and at a film showing of the fight a man sitting behind Bunche, for whom the Louis victory was a historic moment, kept talking about "that darkie." Bunche glared at him to no avail, and on the way out said to him, "Well that darkie certainly gave Braddock a hell of a beating, didn't he?"[16]

Such irritations came to a climax in Bunche's anxiety about getting into South Africa. His English friends were worried that he would have difficulties with accommodations there and would be harassed,* but he was set on going and was determined to do nothing to jeopardize his chances. Thus he was concerned when George Padmore read his name out at a protest rally on the Abyssinian war, "since govt's. detectives were assuredly on hand,"[18] and he avoided getting too close to people he knew to be communists. He was right about the British government's interest, as the following letter in the Colonial Office archives indicates:[19]

Downing Street
29th June, 1937

SECRET

Dear Merrick,

With reference to my letter of the 6th of May about Professor R. J. Bunche, I think it well to tell you that while he has been in England he has apparently been pushed into touch with some of our black undesirables. We do not know what his relations with them are, or whether he is in any degree sympathetic with them. It is quite on the cards that he has simply been led astray by names and did not realise the sort of people that he was going to meet, but I pass this on to you. It has reached us from a very confidential source and, of course, should not be

---

*Paul Robeson asked him if he would have to "walk in the gutter" in South Africa. "I told him that I never walked in the gutter, at any time or anywhere, and that goes for So. Afr."[17]

disclosed. I ought to add that there can be no doubt about Bunche's credentials, so it is to be hoped that his connexion with the scaly lot is purely accidental.

                                                    Yours sincerely,
                                                    (signed) J. M. W. Flood

J. E. S. MERRICK, ESQ., C.M.G., O.B.E.

As a result of Malcolm MacDonald's efforts Bunche finally got an interview with a Mr. Scallon at South Africa House. Scallon looked over his credentials, was suspicious that his doctoral thesis had been on French colonial policy, and said that the South African government would be very annoyed if Bunche made any speeches. Bunche assured him that he was engaged in scientific study rather than missionary work. Scallon remained hostile and obstructive, but Malinowski and Schapera intervened with the South African minister of the interior, Jan Hofmeyer. When Bunche learned from Schapera in Cape Town that his entry into South Africa had been approved by Pretoria, he again visited Scallon. Scallon denied any knowledge of the matter but was finally persuaded to look in Bunche's file, where the telegram was found. Even then, Scallon delivered a long lecture on his distrust of American missionaries and his contempt for the natives before giving Bunche his landing permit. Bunche managed to contain himself during this humiliating interview, and described Scallon in his diary as "a real S.O.B."

Racial discrimination also complicated his travel arrangements. At the outset, the Holland-Africa Line, in the absence of an approved landing card, demanded a deposit for the return trip in case Bunche was refused admission to South Africa. Their suspicions had been aroused by the fact that on the South African immigration form, under "Race," Bunche had written "American." When his landing permit finally came through in June a new complication arose. Bunche had a berth in a double cabin and was worried that he would lose it if a white cabinmate objected to his presence. Julius Lewin volunteered to handle this delicate matter for him and found out that the races *were* kept separate on Holland-Africa boats and that the boat was fully booked. Representations to the shipping-line headquarters in Amsterdam resulted in Cook's calling Bunche in most courteously to change his ticket, "in accordance with certain last minute shifts that were necessary." Bunche got a better cabin, which he shared with a charming young Dutchman called Rees, who was an employee of the Holland-Africa Line. Bunche was right. European racial discrimination was more subtle but just as deep-rooted as American.

Padmore and Kenyatta were at the station on July 27 to see the

Bunche family off to Holland. They stayed in The Hague, which they loved, while Bunche talked to various colonial officials. The Dutch were lyrical about indirect rule, of which Bunche was highly skeptical, but he found the Dutch had a much broader attitude to race than the British. He was much amused at repeated and glowing references to the mulatto wife of a colonial official called Muhlenfeld. "She's certainly their exhibit A," he wrote.[20]

The family spent Bunche's thirty-fourth birthday in Brussels and then had three weeks in Paris before Ruth and the girls were to sail for New York on the *Queen Mary*. They visited the World Exhibition and saw all the sights, including Josephine Baker at the Folies-Bergère. (Josephine Baker became a family friend.) Bunche saw the family off at Cherbourg with a heavy heart. He stayed on the dock until the liner pulled out, the little girls shouting "Goodbye, Daddy," for nearly an hour. He returned to London alone.

5

Africa and Asia

Ping-Pong and No Jim Crow at the Capitol Theater

Jomo Kenyatta, Peter Koinange, and Julius Lewin were at Victoria Station to see Bunche off on the boat train on September 12, 1937. "The world," he wrote to Ethel and Nelle from the train, "has never felt so immense to me before, nor have I ever been so lonely in it." The sea voyage on the *Boschfontein* was long but uneventful. At Ping-Pong he could beat everyone on the ship except the table-tennis champion of Kenya, but when the Ping-Pong tournament was organized he noticed that the purser did not ask him to sign up until some of his Ping-Pong partners protested. He stayed out of it anyway. He spent many of his evenings with the steerage passengers, who seemed to have a far more enjoyable time than those in superior accommodations. At meals he listened politely to much South African talk about the inferiority of the natives, Boer bigotry, and the gold industry's dependence on cheap native labor. "No J.C. [Jim Crow] in dining room tonite at dinner," he noted with surprise on the first night. "I would have a tougher time on a boat headed for Florida or Texas." Although his fellow passengers soon became friendly, he had to sit through a lot of talk about the hopeless mental backwardness of black South Africans, and Mr. Ruben, a Jew from Johannesburg, apologized to him for using the word "nigger." "I just keep mum and listen," Bunche wrote. "A nigger is a nigger even in the middle of the ocean."[1] He had no problem with the immigration authorities in Cape Town, but was required to pay a £5 deposit "for good behavior."

In Cape Town, he stayed in a "colored" household at a house called Arabesque above the city below Table Mountain.* His hosts were Dr.

---

*The house was in "District Six." In 1960, this area was declared "white" under the Group Areas Act, and its vibrant community of 55,000 "colored" people was forcibly evicted. In 1979 its dwellings were demolished, and the site remains derelict to this day—a monument to the criminal folly of apartheid.

A. H. Gool and his wife, Zairunnissa (Cissie), daughter of a Malayan father and a Scottish mother. They lived in a new and comfortable stucco bungalow. Cissie Gool—whose father, Dr. Abdullah Abdurahman, had been a leader in the fight for the rights of the Indian and "colored" population—was a keen city politician, the first president of the National Liberation League, and a good if absent-minded parent. In 1938 she was elected to the Cape Town City Council, of which she remained a member even when she was listed as a member of the Communist Party in 1950. Bunche became much attached to the Gool children, Marcina and Shaheen, and later helped to bring Marcina to school in the United States. Colored life in Cape Town centered in the busiest part of District Six, Hanover Street, "Cape Town's Lenox Avenue," where"Negroes [are] so mixed up . . . the place looks like Harlem."[2] Another of Bunche's guides in Cape Town was Harry Snitcher, a socialist campaigning for complete colored-white equality, who was active in the Liberation League and took Bunche to all sorts of meetings and offices. Bunche noted that Snitcher's household seemed to be "divided between Bolshevism and Zionism."[3]

Bunche's basic interest was the political, economic, and social status of the non-European groups of South Africa. His mentor in this project was Professor Isaac Schapera at the University of Cape Town, whose academic seminar he attended and who advised him on his program and itinerary. He spent October in and around Cape Town, meticulously recording his meetings and experiences. His travels eventually took him to Lesotho, Alice, Thaba'Nchu, Bloemfontein, Mafeking, Johannesburg, Benoni, Pretoria, and Durban.

As always, racial discrimination was a constant companion, but once again in a different key. Bunche noted the "Europeans Only" signs and the separation of the races, although "Schapera [is] still surprised that I don't get thrown out of the 1st class train."[4] On long-distance trains things were more complicated. As a colored person who was also a distinguished visitor, Bunche had a reserved first-class compartment all to himself on most trains. In his isolation he was waited on obsequiously by both white and black railway staff. On his departure from Cape Town for Maseru, seeing the reservation sticker bearing the inscription "Col. Male," he at first assumed he had the company of a military man, until he realized it was a description of himself.[5] His compartment was guarded with scrupulous care to prevent any racial mixing, although sometimes "I . . . don't know whether I'm 'passing' or not . . . brown and kinky-headed as I am."[6]

On his travels in South Africa, Bunche stayed, as far as possible, in black or "colored" homes and relied on friends—white liberal, as well as

black and colored—to escort him around. He kept up a relentless schedule
of meetings and visits which usually went on well into the night, after
which he spent the small hours writing up his notes. He went down a mine
outside Johannesburg and visited union halls and jails as well as schools
and hospitals. From Durban he spent a week on a native location where he
found the sense of isolation and the discomfort oppressive.

As a Black American Bunche was looked on by black South Africans
with curiosity and admiration as a member of a group which had made
progress in a predominantly white society. He found that black personalities like Joe Louis, Jesse Owens, Duke Ellington, Fats Waller, and Paul
Robeson were heroes to black South Africans. "Paul you surely are an idol
to the Bantu," he wrote to Robeson ". . . when one mentions American
Negroes they all chorus 'Paul Robeson and Joe Louis'—the more sophis-
ticated may add Jesse Owens and Duke. . . ."7 Although he had undertaken to avoid public speaking, he felt obliged to make encouraging statements when pressed to do so, in an effort to counter the negative image of
themselves under which black South Africans seemed generally to labor.
He sought to encourage them by highlighting the achievements of Black
Americans as judges, civil servants, scholars, and performers. He found
black South Africans, especially the younger ones, often ashamed of their
own culture, and wanting only to adopt white standards and customs. "I
insisted to Scallon at South Africa House in London that I am not a
missionary. But any American Negro visiting South Africa *is* a missionary
whether or not he wills it. But he doesn't have to be a *religious* missionary."8

Bunche's general objective, as agreed with Schapera, was to study the
impact of South African official policies on non-European South Africans,
or, as he put it in his notes, "How can this handful of whites keep these
millions of blacks down?"9 Bunche's journal provides a rich and astonishingly detailed account of people, conversations, crowds, events, happen-
ings, atmosphere, and institutions. A stream of anecdotes vividly illus-
trates the pervasive separation of the races within South Africa and the
subtle shifts of tone and emphasis within that basic separation. He was
impressed by the lack of solidarity among non-European South Africans,
the antagonism between "coloreds" and black Africans, and the lack of
energetic leadership. There seemed to be little real challenge from black
political organizations to white rule. Bunche was also concerned about the
dependence of black organizations on white liberals, whose role he believed to be to discourage any sign of black militancy.

During his South African stay, Bunche attended three important political meetings—the first session of the newly created Native Representative Council in Pretoria, the third meeting of the All African Convention, and the Silver Jubilee meeting of the African National Congress, both the latter in Bloemfontein. The meeting of the Native Representative Council gave a painful impression of black impotence. It was run by a schoolmasterish and autocratic European, D. L. Smit, the secretary for native affairs, who dominated the agenda, limited debate, and treated the native councillors like schoolchildren. Bunche found the councillors timid, badly prepared, and frivolous. The other two meetings were no less dispiriting, and at the ANC meeting Bunche was so outraged at the servility of some of the speeches that he felt compelled to point out that black South Africans could not hope to take their country back unless they could effectively harness their own labor power and build their own organizations.

Somewhat to his surprise, Bunche himself had no really disagreeable racial experiences in a land clearly riddled with race prejudice. He even found his racial background to be something of an asset in his research work. "I am reasonably convinced," he wrote in his report to the SSRC, "that an American Negro, endowed with a reasonable amount of common sense, tact and a fair sense of humor, can do effective fieldwork even in South Africa, once he gains admission to the country, of course."[10]

Bunche was particularly homesick over Christmas, and by January 1, 1938, when he boarded the SS *Tasman* from Durban, headed, via Laurenço Marques, Beira, and Zanzibar, for Mombasa, he was exhausted and lonely. He managed to write his quarterly report to his sponsor, the SSRC, while on the boat. The passengers were friendly but boring, and he had a much-needed rest. From Mombasa he took the night train to Nairobi, dining en route with a Captain Neil-Stewart of the Criminal Investigation Department. His African friends believed he was being followed, and Neil-Stewart told him that he himself would be receiving reports on Bunche's activities from some of his African contacts. Bunche replied, "What good will a lot of blank reports do you?"[11]

In Nairobi he was met, at Kenyatta's instigation, by a large delegation of the Kikuyu Central Association, who arranged much of his program. He stayed with an Indian, R. P. Dass, and ate and played tennis at the Indian Gymkhana Club. Once again his days and nights were filled with visits and discussions with Indian and African informants, varied occasionally by an interview with the governor or a member of the colonial administration. Bunche took an encyclopedic interest in everything he saw and heard. He made notes on everything, including road accidents, native markets, and, of course, the racial situation. He also took twelve thousand still photographs and fourteen thousand feet of film with Essie Robeson's cine-camera. He noticed that there was no "J.C." [Jim Crow] in the Capitol Theater or in the crowd watching the Kenyan mixed European-Indian hockey team beat the South African–Rhodesian team. He disliked most of the missionaries he met—"narrow, prejudiced against any radical native and self-righteous."[12]

From Nairobi he visited Chief Koinange, the father of his London friend Peter Koinange, ten miles outside Nairobi at Kiambu. The chief and his wife loaded his car with flowers and bananas and urged him to come to stay. The Kikuyu Association took him to Tigoni to get evidence on the government's unjust land policy. They slaughtered and cooked a lamb for him so that he could eat meat with them, and conferred on him the name Karioki, "he who has returned from the dead," referring to one whose ancestors had left Africa in slavery and had come back to his native land. They also offered to provide him with a personal servant and cook, an offer he accepted when he went on safari.

When he went back to stay with Chief Koinange at Kiambu, Bunche brought gramophone records by Robeson, Josephine Baker, Fats Waller, and Benny Goodman. "It's incongruous listening to Fats and his 'yas, yas' way out there in the native reserve."[13] He was disconcerted to find the ewe that was to be killed for his welcome feast waiting meekly outside his tent at breakfast time. He found Chief Koinange both fascinating and wise, but was apprehensive of the attentions of his youngest wife. Koinange arranged a luncheon with five chiefs, and during Bunche's stay the governor also came to meet the Kiambu people.

Bunche had seen a film of Kikuyu circumcision rites taken by a Dr. Guy Johnson, and the Kikuyu Central Association arranged for him to witness such a ceremony at Githiga. The rites, which lasted from 1:30 to 6:00 P.M., were "the most gruesome, bloody spectacle I've ever seen."[14] They were a combination of butchery and fortitude. Bunche filmed the male and female ceremonies "with close-ups of the dancing and the surgery."*[15] He noted that the Kikuyu practiced the rites "as an emblem of their national self-assertion, and a recompense for lost power."[16]

By mid-February he was ready to start on a longer safari. He had acquired, for £40, a Ford station wagon which gave constant trouble, and he set out in this uncertain vehicle accompanied by Obidiah, a clever and

*Bunche showed these films to the older Johnsons in Los Angeles in the summer of 1938. Jane Johnson Taylor, who was ten at the time, recalled her fury that she and her twin sisters were not allowed to see them.

resourceful driver, and a cook called William, who was better at complaining than at cooking. The clay roads were rough and extremely skiddy when wet, and Bunche had little experience of life in the wilds. He was understandably apprehensive about the trip, and his mood was not lightened by letters from home.

Ruth, living in her mother's house in Washington, was back at her double duty of teaching and looking after the children. She was lonely and often resentful. She had arrived back from Europe to find their house and belongings trashed by a tenant. The children got whooping cough, she was worried about polio, and things had gone steadily downhill for her. "I carry a blue feeling with me all the time," she wrote Bunche, and she had worked it out that he had been away from home for more than half of the five years of their marriage. After pointing out that he at least was having a fascinating time, she wrote, "I believe I come out on the worst end. . . . Training children without a father and especially in a house with other people is a hard task."

Her often gloomy letters, which also reminded Bunche of the "University mess I have to return to next year," compounded his anxieties about setting out on safari. He wrote from Kisumu on February 15:

I was already pretty much in the dumps about starting on this tough safari, and your letter indicating that everything is all wrong made me feel even worse . . . not to have decent food or sleeping accommodations week in and week out, and to be forever slapping at insects, feeling dubious about every bite of food eaten and drink of water taken, dosing with quinine, being parched with heat in the day and shivering with cold at nite, packing and unpacking bags continually, writing notes, notes, notes, day and nite etc., etc.

Nonetheless, with "excitement in my heart, much conjecture as to whether our little old Ford would hold up on bad roads in my mind, a few pounds in my wallet and Jo Baker's record of 'I've got a message from the man in the Moon' ringing in my ears," he set out through the Rift Valley. He stopped in Nakuru and visited Dr. Louis Leakey's excavation camp. Leakey told him that the hotels in Nakuru would not accommodate him and gave him a shelter to sleep in. They had a long discussion of Kikuyu customs.

From Kisumu, on Lake Victoria, he drove into Uganda to Kampala. He observed the Kabaka, the king of the Baganda, arrive for a ceremony in a custom-built Buick, and endured the usual fourteen-hour days of interviews, visits, and note writing, before driving through Uganda to the Belgian Congo. He found the Congo inhospitable and spent several nights

in the car amid the roar of lions and the whine of mosquitoes. He saw the
Ruwenzori range and the pygmies of the Ituri Forest before regaining
British territory at Bukoba on Lake Victoria. After a rest in a large bungalow provided by the district commissioner, with whom he discussed native
administration, he went back to Kampala, where Margery Perham had
arranged for him to lunch with the rather unimpressive British governor.

By March 28 he was back in Nairobi and spent the next week with
Koinange, assembling his life story in marathon conversations with the old
chief. "His philosophical answers, with Kikuyan proverbs as illustrations,
to my opinionate questions were superb. He's a grand and wise old
man."[17] At a "farewell tea" Koinange presented him with a spear and
shield.

Bunche attended a big Kikuyu Central Association meeting at
Kabuko at which "I was received like the Governor."[18] On April 14 his
friends gave him a great send-off at the Nairobi station, and then, as was
the Nairobi custom, drove seventeen miles to the Athi station to give him
another send-off. In Mombasa he interviewed, among others, the wily Sir
Abu Ben Salim and Major Cavendish-Bentwick, "the great defender of
settler interests."[19]

Bunche's time in Africa was of immense importance to his future
work. It also made him look at the race problem in the United States as "a
part of a universal pattern which applies to minority groups and to non-
European peoples throughout the entire world."[20]

By April 19, when he embarked on the *Boutekoe,* "a terribly dinky
and dirty little freighter" headed for Singapore, he was "more fatigued
than I can ever remember being."[21] It was "a great relief to have the
African safari behind me and I was lucky not to have contracted any
serious illness there. . . . I'm heading home now and I'm happy."[22] He was
able to relax on the boat with good food, many back numbers of *Time*
which Ruth had sent him, and a great deal of Ping-Pong and deck tennis.
"The passengers on board are very snooty," he wrote to Ruth, "and so am
I. They stuck me at a table alone with the only other non-white on board,
a half-caste from Java."

As always happened, Bunche's personality and intelligence quickly
overcame racially motivated hesitations. Although the passengers "made
the inevitable reference to the natives as 'niggers,' which I ignored but
noted,"[23] he was soon sought out as the fascinating person he was. He
discussed the Dutch colonial system in Java into the small hours with a
Dutch judge, and enjoyed similar discussions with British and other pas-

sengers. He also managed to finish his notes on East Africa.

The twelve-day voyage also gave him a chance to reflect on more personal matters. He had tried to persuade Ruth to meet him in Hawaii on his voyage home, but she demurred because of the children and also because of the cost. "The separation has helped me to take stock of my own shortcomings as a husband, too," he wrote to Ruth from the ship.

And while these are admittedly many—my stubborness, selfishness, harsh temper and irritability, to mention only a few—none is so serious that it can't be overcome, and I have definitely and systematically conditioned myself this year so as to overcome them. If I'm not a better husband hereafter than I've been in the past then I will know I am absolutely without self-control and self-will, Ruth. For I have analyzed myself carefully this year, and I think I know what are good and what bad traits in me. . . .

He reached Singapore on May 1 and explored the town and Johore with the friends he had made on the boat. On May 8 they reached Batavia, where he visited schools and other colonial institutions. He was impressed by the racial liberality of Dutch colonialism. "Interesting sight to see all the races mixed in one class-room after East Africa."[24] He went on to Soerabaja, Bali, and Djokjakarta, where he witnessed the governor's Garebeg Moeloed ceremony at the sultan's palace with vibrant gamelan music. On May 28 he embarked on the *Tjisadane* bound for Hong Kong via Macassar, Balikpapan, and Manila. He was "travelling in a semi-daze now, tired and homesick,"[25] but at least a year of work was behind him and he was heading for home.

In Hong Kong the realities of mainland Asia crowded in on Bunche. "I can never forget the thousands of Chinese I saw sleeping on the sidewalks of Hong Kong, nor the hundreds of beggars, mainly women and children, who accosted me."[26] The clouds of impending war were looming. Bunche had wanted to go to Canton from Hong Kong to get some idea of conditions in China under the Japanese occupation, but

I got to thinking that I had no right to take such a risk because of my family responsibility, so I stayed in Hong Kong. And, for the first time, the Japanese bombed [the train] that Thursday night, scoring direct hits on 3 coaches and killing and injuring many passengers. . . .[27]

The letter ends with an already familiar refrain, "No more separations for me."

Bunche had intended to return to the United States from Hong Kong on the P&O liner *Empress of Asia,* but it was full, so he took passage on the Norddeutcher Lloyd *Scharnhorst.* They sailed up the Yangtze River to Shanghai, where there were many warships. From Shanghai Bunche made an excursion to Chapei, "lousy with stupid-looking Jap soldiers." On the *Scharnhorst,* overhearing a dialogue between a close-cropped Nazi and a "blonde, tousle-headed English boy who had offended the Nazi by making derogatory remarks about Hitler,"[28] he was reminded of the other partner in the future Axis. The boy had accused Hitler of chasing people out of Germany. The Nazi answered, "You don't like Jews either, do you?," to which the boy responded with the classic reply, "Some of my best friends are Jews." All further blandishments from the Nazi were rebuffed, and the boy turned away. He was later warmly congratulated by an American passenger, Mr. Mandelbaum.

The *Scharnhorst* docked in San Francisco on July 7. "Not much excited about getting back to the States," Bunche wrote. "First thing I saw on front page of S. F. Chronicle was a report of lynching of a negro in Miss."[29] His spirits picked up when Ruth and the girls met him three days later in Los Angeles, where they visited the family and friends for several weeks. They stayed with Aunts Ethel and Nelle in the old house, and the younger members of the Johnson family got to know the relative about whom their elders had spoken with such reverence and pride. For once there was no early prospect of another separation. Bunche was home to stay for the next six years.

6

An American Dilemma

A Slave for the Swedish Simon Legree

During his absence in Europe and Africa Bunche had become a full professor at Howard, which added considerably both to his status and to his income. After his adventurous year and a half abroad, it was an effort to get back into the routine of academic life and teaching. He wrote to Mel Herskovitz:

My most serious task right now is to digest enough information concerning what has happened on this side of the water during the twenty months I have been away, so that I can teach my classes in American Government and Constitutional Law without the necessity of discussing East Africa and the Dutch East Indies.[1]

He had managed to escape the position of dean at Howard, and so "I am free to go about my job teaching and writing with nothing to worry me but committee assignments."[2]

Bunche had intended to start work at once on his study of the status of non-European groups in South Africa, leaving East Africa and the Dutch East Indies until later. He wrote to Cissie Gool in Cape Town on December 27:

I am amazed at the number of close parallels there are between your situation and ours here. The pattern of racial (within the broader class pattern, of course) persecution and exploitation is universal. . . . I do think it is important for us to establish some close connecting links with you down there. Both the International committee on African Affairs and the N.A.A.C.P. would very much like to keep abreast of the activities of the Liberation League and other organizations working on behalf of the non-European peoples of South Africa.

In this letter he also commented on "the ever present trend of fascism," but on the other hand, "the vigorous reaction of the American public against recent German activities and policies is encouraging." In February 1939 he was still hopeful of completing his South African study and accepted the $500 Anisfield Award for this purpose.

By that time, however, he, along with a number of other black intellectuals and academics, was already working part-time with Gunnar Myrdal, a Swedish social economist whom the Carnegie Corporation of New York had taken on as director of "a comprehensive study of the Negro in the United States, to be undertaken in a wholly objective and dispassionate way as a social phenomenon."*[4] This study was to become, in 1944, the monumental *An American Dilemma: The Negro Problem and Modern Democracy.* "Between my university work, the South African study, and fooling around with the Carnegie survey," Bunche wrote Herskovits on May 23, 1939, "I have been run ragged lately."

Bunche did not get down to working on his South African notes until October 1940, and then other pressing responsibilities soon stopped him again. Thus much of his vast collection of notes and photographs from the 1937–38 trip stayed unsorted in their boxes, and the immediate purpose of the African trip remained unfulfilled. It had, however, provided Bunche with an invaluable, firsthand preparation for his work in the OSS and the State Department, and later on in the newly established United Nations.

Bunche was ambivalent about becoming involved in the Myrdal study, although the authorities at Howard urged him to do so and to postpone his South African work, and Donald Young concurred. Young had introduced Myrdal to Bunche and Herskovits and had taken them on a tour of Harlem nightclubs, which, to Bunche's amusement, had failed completely to distract the two older professors from their intensive discussion of racial problems. Bunche was worried about letting the South African notes grow cold and again abandoning his department at Howard, which had suffered greatly during his absence. He was also uneasy about Myrdal's survey. He had had for some years a rather similar project of his own in mind but had been unable to get started on it for lack of either funds or time. After working with Myrdal since late 1938, he was doubtful "about the possibility of doing all that Myrdal wishes done by September 1940, which he has fixed as the deadline. I am afraid that more has been bitten off than can possibly be digested in this time."[5]

For all his doubts, the challenge of the Myrdal study was irresistible,

*The Carnegie Corporation had decided that no American social scientist could approach the subject objectively. After considering several former British colonial administrators, they chose Myrdal.[3]

and by June 1939 he was fully engaged in this large and ambitious enterprise. Myrdal's group consisted of six top staff, thirty-one independent
workers, thirty-six assistants, and fifty experts.[6] The basic material submitted to Myrdal consisted of forty-four monographs, some fifteen thousand
pages in all. The monographs were based on the field notes from hundreds
of interviews. Bunche was one of the six top staff and the staff member
closest to Myrdal. He wrote four of the monographs, the most important
of which, and the last to be finished, was "The Political Status of the
Negro," 1,660 pages, nineteen chapters and three annexes, dictated at a
gallop in August 1940.* His other three monographs for the study were
"Conceptions and Ideologies of the Negro Problem," "The Programs,
Ideologies, Tactics and Achievements of Negro Betterment and Interracial Organizations," and "A Brief and Tentative Analysis of Negro
Leadership."

The Myrdal study was by far the largest and most comprehensive
investigation of race relations in the United States that had ever been
attempted. Previous research had tended to avoid suggestions as to public
policy or social reform, and the New Deal itself had preferred economic
initiatives to efforts in the politically explosive field of civil rights. Myrdal,
however, saw his task as to provide not only information but also a guide to
policymakers. As Bunche put it,

We feel that a frank appraisal of the position of the Negro minority in the United
States at this time will constitute a striking document and one that should be
extremely helpful to the Negro in his struggle for equality.[7]

Although Myrdal had assembled a heterodox team of experts representing widely different views, he himself was the final arbiter of the
finished work. His team included a number of outstanding black intellectuals—Sterling Brown, Doxey Wilkerson, Franklin Frazier, Alain Locke,
and Kenneth Clark among others—but Bunche established a uniquely
close relationship, both professional and personal, with Myrdal, and the
four monographs he wrote were among the most articulate and the most
influential as far as the final work was concerned.

Kenneth Clark "had the opportunity to listen to [Bunche], Myrdal
and other senior associates discuss their findings and interpretations. . . . I
was constantly impressed by Bunche's clarity of mind, his courage, his
intensity and his humanity. . . . He seemed incapable of pretense. . . . He

*It was published in 1973, after Bunche's death, as *The Political Status of the Negro in the
Age of FDR* by the University of Chicago Press.

would listen to the ideas of research assistants with as much interest as he would listen to the opinions of Myrdal. And he would evaluate these ideas with objectivity, and without condescension."[8]

Myrdal and Bunche soon developed a strong mutual respect and conducted a running debate across the whole subject. They differed on many important matters. Myrdal considered Marxism to be a fatalistic dogma and disagreed with Bunche's view that working-class solidarity was the best basis for ending racial division and that the future of Black Americans would largely depend on fundamental political and economic change. Myrdal was skeptical of an interracial working-class alliance as the basis for the struggle for civil rights and believed that the white working class itself was a bastion of racism. He saw the hope for change, rather, in the American creed of liberty, equality, and fraternity inspiring the Supreme Court and the U.S. administration to give new voting power to Black Americans.

Myrdal certainly cherished his relationship with Bunche, who himself afforded a striking example both of the limitations imposed on outstanding Black Americans and of their great potential. He was strongly influenced by Bunche's work on the effects of racial oppression on black character and culture, as well as by his views on black leadership and the self-defeating nature of some trends in black political thought. In the final book their views often diverged, Bunche's belief in a socialist transformation of society as the best hope for Black Americans giving way, in *An American Dilemma*, to Myrdal's social-engineering approach and his view that Black Americans should try to adjust as far as possible to the values and behavior of white middle-class society.

The writing phase was preceded by a prolonged period of fieldwork, which Bunche had insisted on, and during which he was at Myrdal's headquarters in New York. Bunche had three field assistants, Wilhelmina Jackson, a Howard student, James Jackson from the labor movement, and a white man, George C. Stoney, from the Henry Street Settlement in New York. Stoney, who did about half the interviews, had a particular talent for drawing out his interlocutors and vividly recording their language and reactions. The interviews were conducted almost entirely in the South, with particular emphasis on Alabama, Georgia, North Carolina, and South Carolina.

In October 1939 Bunche took to the road himself for his first visit to the South, to be joined later by Myrdal, who was anxious to have direct experience of the fieldwork. He left Washington for Richmond in his Ford on October 17, "loaded down with bags, dictaphone, camera, typewriter, questionnaires, etc."[9] In those days a Black American from the North embarking on a trip to the South aroused considerable interest. Some friends expressed the hope that Bunche would come back alive; others inquired whether he was taking a gun. Miss Houston,* the Bunches' housekeeper, "assured me that I would encounter no trouble with 'crackers' just so I said 'sir' to them."[10]

After he left Washington, the South quickly made itself felt, with "White Only" signs and discriminatory episodes at every turn. Of the chairman of the Inter-race Committee in Richmond, Bunche wrote,

> He was smooth and complacent as silk—a professional inter-racialist. Rode down in the elevator with him and he talked with me before his white fellow citizens, but was his face red and how he did duck away when we hit the street.[11]

Bunche was already into his usual fieldwork pattern—days and evenings packed with interviews and visits, followed by note transcribing into the small hours, this time into a Dictaphone.

In Portsmouth, Virginia, he stayed in the home of his researcher Wilhelmina Jackson, and they went to Norfolk for interviews before moving on to Hampton and Raleigh, where Bunche typed up a long letter of instructions to Myrdal, who was joining him in Charleston. So far, despite the obvious signs of racial segregation, he had found the whites he had interviewed civil and even cordial, though he was irritated by an insurance-company lawyer dealing with damage to his car inflicted by a white female driver.

> When I had to to describe the accident he told me to describe it to him and he would dictate it to the stenog. I informed him that I was used to dictating and would dictate to her directly—I put on dog and went too fast for her, tho Daisy could have taken it.[12]

Myrdal's arrival broke the controlled calm of Bunche's journey. In the South Myrdal "thought he was on a lark," Bunche wrote later, "and I was always on the verge of being lynched because of his playful pranks. We actually had to run for it a couple of times. . . ."[13] Myrdal showed all the arrogance, naïveté, and sense of mischief of some European intellectuals and seemed to have very little idea of the risks which Bunche, and to a lesser extent he himself, were running.† At each stop they would part

---

*Ruth Houston Mackenzie stayed with the Bunche family until after Ralph Bunche's death.

†His daughter, Sissela Bok, refers to Myrdal's "habits of free-wheeling debate and mercilessly irreverent joking."[14]

company, Myrdal to the best hotel and Bunche to whatever accommodation his friends and contacts could find for him.

The trouble started mildly enough on their first night in Charleston when Myrdal decided he wanted to go out for a beer. In spite of the assurances of the hotel elevator boy to Bunche that "they won't know what you are," they ended up in a "negro hole-in-the-wall where we got beer while creating a sensation." Bunche was perpetually trying to calm the ebullient Myrdal down, not always with success. At Faber's Fair in Charleston, "Gunnar slipped in to see the Fat White Lady and then came out feigning shock at this terrible display before Negroes. Faber became scared. . . ."

November 1 in Savannah was a typical day. Bunche had been writing up his notes until 3:00 A.M. He picked up Myrdal at his hotel at 10:30 A.M. and visited the collector of taxes. Bunche interviewed the head of the YMCA, and then they met the editors of the morning and evening papers. A long sidewalk conference with Judge Emmanuel Lewis was followed by a talk with McKelvey, a self-made Negro contractor. They had dinner with the assistant manager of the North Carolina Mutual Insurance Company, and went on to interview the owners of a Negro funeral home, after which Bunche was taken to a PTA meeting. They got to bed at 11:30.

They moved on to Macon, where Bunche stayed with another funeral-parlor operator, who took him to the Jim Crow room of a white restaurant. "Hartley, a big Negro businessman, sat up on a stool in that rough backroom café, without any consciousness of its significance."[15]

Bunche often had to persist with the desk clerk when calling on Myrdal in his hotel, the clerk usually calling Myrdal to say offhandedly that "some fellow" was waiting to see him. In Atlanta they were joined by Arthur Raper, a white Southern sociologist,* who also failed to quiet Myrdal down. While sitting in a black café, Myrdal started quoting from an interview with a planter including his use of the word "nigger." "I had to tell Gunnar he'd ruin all of us doing that. Just as when we were 'passing' in Charleston he sat down and loudly began to discuss the negro problem."†[16]

Trouble started in earnest with Myrdal's interview in Atlanta with a Mrs. J. E. Andrews, editor of the *Georgia Women's World*, whom

*Raper's memorandum, "Race and Class Pressures," concerning extralegal violence in the South, particularly impressed Myrdal.

†Bunche normally despised "passing" as beneath his dignity, but because he was working with Myrdal on a tight schedule it made sense to stay together as much as possible.

Bunche later described as "psychopathic." Bunche was absent from this event doing other interviews, and the next day they moved on to Greenesboro, visiting an old plantation house and a rural, one-room, one-teacher school on the way. Once again they separated, Myrdal to the Colonial Terrace Hotel, and Bunche to the house of a Dr. Baker, reputed to be the only black home in town with an inside bathroom. In the evening they visited a convict camp outside town, where Bunche had an excellent opportunity to talk with the prisoners because he was not invited, with Myrdal and Raper, to eat with the commandant. They returned to town and parted as usual, and Bunche drove eight miles out into the country to interview an old black farmer. When he returned to Dr. Baker's house the children told him that his friends had been by four times to see him. Bunche called the hotel only to learn that Myrdal's party had checked out. He was already worried at the possibility that Myrdal's indiscretions had caused him to be run out of town. Myrdal and Raper arrived again at Baker's house at 11:00 P.M. and told Bunche the party was leaving right away for Alabama.

In the car Bunche learned that Arthur Raper's wife had called to say that Mrs. Andrews had sworn out a warrant for Myrdal's arrest on a personal-insult-and-defamation charge. Apparently Mrs. Andrews' tirade about miscegenation and the alleged sexual appetite of black men had provoked Myrdal to ask "mercilessly irreverent" questions—whether she had had a subconscious desire to have sexual intercourse with blacks; whether she had black blood, etc. Mrs. Raper reported that the Atlanta police were watching the trains for Myrdal and were searching for him everywhere. The lawyers whom Raper had consulted said that nothing could keep Myrdal from arrest if the police found him, and they had advised him to skip out of the state.

Bunche drove the party steadily through the night, through Macon and Columbus, reaching Tuskegee, Alabama, at 4:30 A.M. Myrdal, unrepentant, was already looking for more trouble by suggesting they all three book into a white hotel. "Myrdal kept marveling at what a perfect instrument of repression the upper classes have in our legal system, and how effectively it can be used vs. the Negro." He asked Raper plaintively, "What did Magna Carta say—doesn't it protect me?" Raper announced that he was leaving the party on the grounds of illness, and Bunche wrote, "I am aching too. This trip is too taxing."[17] He was already experiencing serious difficulty with an undiagnosed and crippling pain in his right leg.

In Montgomery Bunche photographed Ruth's old home and saw some of her childhood friends. Myrdal was attacked as a "damn Yankee" by some drunks in a café but finally convinced them that he was a Swede. The party went via Mobile to New Orleans, where Bunche had to get treatment for his leg. Myrdal told the manager of his hotel that there was a prominent Negro educator with whom he wished to talk and drink cocktails in his room. The manager said that was all right but his Negro friend would have to enter by the service entrance and come up by the service elevator. "I told Myrdal I didn't subject myself to J.C. for social purposes and that he would have to come to me. He did."[18]

The schedule in New Orleans was, if possible, even more hectic and comprehensive than before. It included an effort to talk to black prostitutes about race relations, payoffs, police brutality, etc. This proved to be something of a farce. A young taxi driver called Whitey drove them vainly around the town until at last they spotted a black woman called Hilda who recruited Helen, "another ugly, crippled gal," to answer their questions in an "ugly, dingy, dilapidated room." The women's customers, it transpired, were only white men, for no black man would take them even for free. The higher-class bordellos were closed because of an imminent election, but they did at last find a male homosexual and a girl who insisted on staging a "show" for the party before answering any questions—"professional pride apparently. Anyway it was a complete flop as the faggot could not do anything with a woman and kept saying he needed a man." They got home at 2:00 A.M.

Another hazard arose on the road to Meridian. Myrdal had insisted on giving a ride to a white girl, to whom he then took a strong dislike.

All of his hate of the South rained down on her in his bitterly sarcastic questions and statements. . . . I feared she might get so angry that she would ask to get out and then tell some Mississippi cracker that the "nigger" driver and communist foreigner had insulted her. Then we would be in for it.[19]

Fortunately, the girl elected to get out at Hattiesburg to visit some relatives, and they drove on safely to Tuscaloosa. On the road to Birmingham they stopped for Myrdal to interview the white guards of a Negro chain gang and to take some movie shots, and later on to visit poor white families while Bunche interviewed their black counterparts. Myrdal seemed to grow more and more indiscreet in his conversations. He was often insulting to the officials he interviewed, and Bunche felt they were extraordinarily lucky to get away with it.

Myrdal left by air for New York on November 18, "leaving me with this damned car and close to a thousand miles between here and home."[20] On November 19, "With nothing but home on my mind," he set out from Birmingham, reaching Washington exhausted at 2:30 P.M. on the following day.

His preoccupations with the volatile Myrdal had not prevented Bunche from constantly pining for home. Ruth had written to him, "This is the fifth week you've been away and you said you'd be gone three. Oh well, I suppose I'm a perpetual widow." After teaching a class of fifty all day, she found her own children increasingly exhausting and hard to manage. It worried both parents that they were, in Bunche's words, "too severe on Joan and Jane. Am going to make an earnest effort to ease up when I return home."[21] There was now, for once, a good prospect of a long period at home uninterrupted by long absences. They were also planning a new house of their own. "We wish emphasis to be placed on warmth and utility rather than show," Bunche wrote to the architect, Hilyard Robinson, in May 1940. ". . . our tastes in design seem to lean toward the conventional and conservative." They finally moved into this house, 1510 Jackson Street, N.E., in June 1941.

The early months of 1940 offered a brief respite from the Myrdal study while the fieldwork went on, but in April Bunche wrote to Herskovits, "I am back on my slave routine for the Swedish Simon Legree. . . ." He had embarked, mostly in Washington, on the four monographs which had to be completed by September 1 and would total more than three thousand pages. He was happy neither with the results nor with the limitations imposed by Myrdal's deadline. In the rush to get the materials together, there had been little time for reflection or analysis, and the result was, he wrote in a characteristically frank preface, "A terribly hurried, poorly integrated, and roughly written job."[22] However, "The Negro in politics has remained a virgin field for research, and thus assembled data of all kinds are at a premium."[23]

Bunche mentioned ten subjects which had been left undone or superficially treated. These included the shift in black preference from the Republican to the Democratic Party, and an analysis of Southern liberalism and its effect on black political status in the South. To compensate for the lack of attention to northern Black Americans, he had added to the monograph on "The Political Status of the Negro" a subtitle, "With Emphasis on the South and Comparative Treatment of the Poor White."

As an analysis of the problem this monograph does not now appear very original. As in previous works, Bunche tended to overemphasize economic factors and class conflict as the basic problems of the Black American. Nonetheless, the text has a sense of immediacy and reality which is still arresting. The quoted remarks of the interviewees, both black and white, jump out from the page and are often astonishing in their frankness and brutality. A devastating picture emerges of the corruption of politics and electoral practices, of the disenfranchisement and the complete freeze-out of blacks in local politics*—an account of which Myrdal made full use in *An American Dilemma*. Social mores and prejudices created a climate of intimidation, a "harsh, hostile and rigid application of the law and often something more than the law,"[24] as far as the registering of Negroes was concerned. The almost paranoid white fear of black equality is matched by the terrible apathy and hopelessness of blacks themselves. Myrdal's main theme in *An American Dilemma* was the contrast, especially in the South, between the American creed of liberty and equality, and the actual treatment of Black Americans. Whatever its shortcomings "The Political Status of the Negro" gives an unforgettable and detailed picture of black life in the American South at the beginning of the Second World War.

Bunche's writings for Myrdal reflect one significant change in his own thinking, his attitude to Roosevelt and the New Deal. Four years after criticizing the New Deal as "the same thing and more of it" for Black Americans, and "a great relief program," he now saw parts of it at least as positive. The inclusion of Black Americans in voting on cotton referendums in the South or the participation of black farmers in the Tenant Purchase program, Social Security, and wage-and-hour legislation were important steps toward a recognition, by white and black producers, of parallel economic interests. He was also encouraged by decisions of the Supreme Court upholding the Wagner Labor Relations Act, the principle of social security, and the Fair Labor Standards law, as important steps toward bettering the condition of Black Americans. He regarded the activities of black New Deal advisers, some of whom were his friends, as "first feeble steps in a desirable direction—the full participation of the Negro in administrative government."[25] He felt that the Roosevelt administration had "for the first time . . . given broad recognition to the existence of the Negro as a national problem . . . though the basic evils remain untouched."[26]

There is already an extensive literature on *An American Dilemma*, its importance, its influence, and its current relevance.[27] The book was un-

---

*A paper on "An Analysis of the Dynamics and Mechanisms of Disfranchisement," which Bunche presented to the Annual Conference of the American Political Science Association in December 1940, nearly four years before *An American Dilemma* was published, was widely regarded as a pioneering work in this field.

questionably a monumental landmark in the literature on black America and had a vast influence.* Most Black Americans initially regarded it as a great and positive contribution to their cause. Coming out in 1944, when World War II had sparked a new determination among Black Americans to achieve their full rights, *An American Dilemma* was certainly timely. As long as black activists were seeking to join the American mainstream through integration, it also provided a useful guide for action. Predictably, it was attacked from the outset by Marxists and the radical left, later joined by the far right and Southern segregationists.

Myrdal's book provided a new understanding of the racial problems of the United States as well as a new sense of the urgent need to resolve those problems. Walter Jackson writes:

An American Dilemma . . . helped to create a new racial liberalism that influenced political leaders, judges, civil rights activists, and thousands of educated white Americans. Myrdal's study was the key text in shaping a liberal orthodoxy in support of civil rights, desegregation, equal opportunity, and the assimilation of blacks into mainstream American culture. These ideas proved to be remarkably durable for twenty years after the publication of *An American Dilemma*—an extraordinarily long life in the turbulent world of racial politics. . . .[28]

In the 1960s, after the 1965 Voting Rights Act and the Watts riots, as black activists turned more radical, violence mounted, and the civil-rights movement fell into disarray, the basic tenets of the book's racial liberalism were increasingly questioned, and its relatively optimistic outlook began to be seen as outmoded. In a period of confusion and acrimony Myrdal's ideas seemed to lose much of their relevance. The dilemma he had defined had developed into a complex of different but equally dismaying dilemmas. The basic problem, however, remained, and with it the historical place of *An American Dilemma*.

*When Gunnar Myrdal died in May 1987, the *New York Times* obituary recalled footnote 11 to the U.S. Supreme Court's 1954 ruling that segregation in public schools was unconstitutional. In listing sources to prove that schools could not be "separate but equal" because separation implied and enforced inferiority, the footnote to the Court's ruling read, "See generally Myrdal, *An American Dilemma*, 5/8/1944."

7

Prelude to War

Black America's Stake in World Crisis

While Bunche was completing the four monographs for the Myrdal study,* the war in Europe, and in particular its significance for Black Americans, began to dominate his thinking. The spring and early summer of 1940 had seen Hitler's tanks roll triumphantly into Denmark, Norway, Holland, Belgium, and France, and, viewed from the United States at least, the fall of Britain might well follow at any time. On May 1, Bunche bade an emotional farewell to Gunnar and Alva Myrdal, who were returning to Sweden to play their part if Germany invaded their country.

Bunche saw the rise of fascism and the triumphs of Nazism in Europe as a direct and mortal threat to Black Americans. He believed that a Nazi victory would increase the likelihood of fascism in the United States, and that American fascism would relegate Black Americans permanently to the status of an inferior racial caste. The defense of Western democracy, whatever its shortcomings, was therefore of paramount importance to Black Americans, and Bunche was determined to alert them to their imminent danger. He had for long been skeptical of the quality of black leadership in the United States. "Because of the extreme provincialism of its organizations and leadership," he wrote in July 1939, "the Negro population suffers from stagnation in its social thought. . . ." If they did not develop better organization and leadership, "the black citizens of America may soon face the dismal prospect of reflecting upon the tactical errors of the past from the gutters of the black ghettoes and concentration camps of the future."[1]

---

*He formally finished this work on September 21, 1940, although he kept in touch with Myrdal throughout the latter's work on *An American Dilemma*.

The Third National Negro Congress was held in Washington in April 1940. It was a disillusioning experience, redeemed only by the courageous conduct of A. Philip Randolph, and after it Bunche formally broke with the congress, saying that the "NNC had dug its own grave" and that it "would now be reduced to a communist cell."[2] By 1940 the NNC had lost its original diversity and no longer represented Bunche's hopes of establishing an alternative to the more traditional black organizations. The meeting was dominated by the Communist Party and the party-line unions of the Congress of Industrial Organizations (CIO). "The Negro rank and file did not know what it was all about."[3] Its resolutions condemned Roosevelt and the "imperialist" war of Britain and France and praised only the Soviet Union, which was, at that time, Hitler's ally. Nazi and Soviet totalitarianism were equally ignored. Randolph, standing against this overwhelming tide, denounced the Soviet Union along with the other totalitarian nations and urged the Congress to remain independent, nonpartisan, and "built up by Negro effort alone. . . . He ridiculed the assumption that the Communist Party, aligned with the political course of the Soviet Union, could pursue a constructive policy with regard to Negro interests here."[4] Most of the audience walked out during his speech, and, unable to agree with the resolutions passed, Randolph resigned his presidency.

"It took both courage and honesty to do what he [Randolph] did," Bunche wrote.

Randolph was stating the obvious truth; namely, that the Negro problem cannot be worked out through an escape based on easy formulae, whether the formula be in terms of affiliation with the Communist Party, the C.I.O., the Republican Party, the New Deal, or whatever organization. In the Negro problem there is no substitute for intelligent, independent thinking and courageous action.[5]

Randolph's place was taken by Max Yergan, Bunche's London acquaintance, "a rank neophyte, a former YMCA secretary . . . who can only parrot slogans laid down in the party tracts."[6] Bunche was particularly disgusted with the performance of John P. Davis,* with whom he and Randolph had started the congress in 1936. Davis, who had just visited the Soviet Union, was re-elected as national secretary.

*Bunche told a civil-service investigation in March 1943 that already in 1936 "Triumph? or Fiasco?" finished him with the congress, "because John P. Davis doesn't relish criticism or objection." He had attended the 1940 meeting of the congress "over the objections of John Davis" as a representative of the Carnegie Corporation working on the Myrdal study.[7]

He knew . . . that when he openly pledged the Congress to a pro-Soviet policy, and when he stated that American Negroes would not fight against the Soviet Union, that the Congress would be publicly branded as a communist front. Davis also knows that it is not possible to build up a mass movement among either Negroes or whites in this country under the banner of the Communist Party. . . . The result is certain to be an intensification of Negro red-baiting. I think that the responsibility for this rests with John Davis, and my own belief is that he did it on orders. In my mind it amounts to deliberate sabotage of the organization. . . . He coolly allied the interests of the American Negro with the foreign policy of the Soviet Union as reflected in the line of the American Communist Party.

The National Negro Congress would, Bunche prophesied, be reduced to "devout party members, close fellow travellers, and representatives of the C.I.O. unions.[8]

The self-immolation of the National Negro Congress caused Bunche to search for other approaches to the problems of Black Americans at this critical time, and it certainly influenced his changing assessment of the New Deal. In June 1940, with the news from Europe more disastrous every day, he wrote to Charles Dollard at the Carnegie Corporation suggesting that the Myrdal study should have a special additional section about the effects of a totalitarian triumph in Europe on the Western Hemisphere, on the United States, and on the Negro in the United States. "Perhaps," he wrote, "the greatest weakness of all of us to-day is not being easily enough alarmed about what transpires in the outer world." The aim of the study would be twofold: to define the black stake in the present world conflict, and to examine the role of Black Americans in current plans for mobilization for national defense,

lest the Negro be frozen out of things completely. . . . The utterances we now hear daily from the lips of Negro intellectuals indicate a confusion and bewilderment that are indeed alarming. . . . There is an abysmal ignorance, among Negroes, of those forces which are destined to shape their ultimate position in society.[9]

Bunche went on to give a detailed outline of the issues that should be studied.

Bunche also wrote an impassioned letter to William Allen White's newly formed Committee to Defend America by Aiding the Allies. "I wonder if it has occurred to your Committee that American Negroes have more at stake in this moment of supreme world crisis than any other group of Americans?" In spite of abuse, exploitation and vilification in the United States,

every thinking Negro knows that our hopes, our aspirations, the future of our children, are inseparably bound to the future of this great country. . . . The Negro citizens ask only that they too be fully mobilized, that they be given full opportunity to strike vigorous blows on behalf of democracy.[10]

In his search for new approaches Bunche had requested, on May 3, an interview with Mrs. Roosevelt. To his surprise, he immediately received an invitation to lunch at the White House on May 13. Noticing some uneasiness on the faces of the functionaries who greeted him at the White House, he asked Mrs. Roosevelt if she had known in advance that he was black, for he had assumed that no invitations to the White House were extended unless it was known exactly to whom the invitations were going. Mrs. Roosevelt replied that she had *not* known Bunche was black, although as she looked at his questions on her way down to meet him she had thought he might be. In any case, with her it was a matter of no importance. She had often invited Black Americans to meals, and she never asked in advance about the racial composition of delegations.

It was a sunny spring day, and they lunched on the White House portico on jellied soup, chicken salad, and blancmange with cherries in it. Mrs. Roosevelt was cordial and completely informal, and Bunche felt very much at home.

She has very clear blue eyes and is a very intelligent woman. I don't believe I have interviewed anyone about whose sincerity I am more impressed. On many things she is perhaps not profound nor too well informed as to details, but she thinks clearly and consistently.[11]

Bunche had prepared ten questions, which Mrs. Roosevelt answered with enthusiasm. She was convinced that if the economic situation in the United States got worse the plight of Black Americans would get worse, and that if Nazism triumphed there would be severe racial repercussions in the United States. Many Americans admired things that "worked" and would therefore favor a triumphant Nazism and its American counterpart. Obviously, Black Americans must have equal citizenship rights, but the issue of social equality was always confused by Southerners with the question of intermarriage. This was the point, she told Bunche, on which her discussions of racial equality with the vice-president, John Nance Garner of Texas, invariably foundered.

Mrs. Roosevelt was extremely gloomy about international developments and regarded the situation of the European Allies as virtually hopeless, while America itself was totally unprepared for war. If Nazism triumphed there was a grave danger that the United States, in which there were many Nazi spies and agents, would be engulfed. She felt that the real battle for democracy had been in Spain, but both Britain and France had abstained from it. As a result Nazi political and racial creeds were threatening civilization itself.

In September Mrs. Roosevelt asked Bunche for a memorandum on the black worker and his struggle for justice. Bunche responded with a forcefully argued paper based on the premise that Black Americans had three basic problems: the right to work, the right to remuneration on the basis of merit and performance, and the right to advance in salary and rank, also on the basis of performance. He made a devastating analysis both of white stereotyped conceptions of blacks and of current black approaches to the problem. He asserted that economic justice was important not only to Black Americans but for the preservation of respect for the democratic institutions for which America might soon have to fight. The right to work and to proper compensation for work were one side of the democratic coin; political and civil liberties were the other side. Either side was meaningless without the other. At a time when employment of Black Americans in defense industries was about to become a burning issue, such a cogent and forthright articulation of the problem, delivered to the heart of the White House, may well have had some impact.

His exchanges with Mrs. Roosevelt certainly stimulated Bunche's own thinking. Speaking of the position of Black Americans in the current crisis, he wrote, "The Negro must make his immediate choice from imperfect, buffeted democracy on the one hand, and totalitarianism on the other." He blasted the indifference to the war then fashionable among Black Americans of all classes and the soapbox logic "of the communists and traditional anti-imperialists," and provided a devastating analysis of Hitler's *Mein Kampf* and its real meaning. For Black Americans the vital question about the war was, Who will win it? "The Negro faces grave dangers from the repercussions of a Nazi victory in Europe—less from the possibility of direct invasion than from the penetration of Nazi ideology. . . ." The United States had many of the raw ingredients of a native fascism—racial intolerance, mass poverty, admiration for practical success and things that ostensibly "work," a naïve mass public easily impressed by demagogues, many wandering, discontented, and futureless young people, political, economic, and social chaos in the South, and a profit-loving class which would do anything to salvage its vested interests.

The Negro is no longer indispensable in this country. He is entirely dispensable everywhere. He is increasingly a relief burden. . . . Fascism is a highly rational system. Its ends justify its means. And its ends are to organize the resources of the state for the benefit of the master race. White supremacy under fascism or "100% Americanism" could seal our doom.

He ended by listing the likely practical measures—very similar to those applied to the Jews in Nazi Germany—which such a regime would apply to Black Americans.[12]

In October 1940 Bunche wrote to Julius Lewin, who was now at Witwatersrand University in Johannesburg, that he was in favor of the United States' going to war, "and rather selfishly so; conditions here are such that a Hitler victory would inevitably result in an American brand of fascism that would, of course, mean the end of me and my people."[13] To Harold Laski, soliciting an article for the *Journal of Negro Education*, Bunche wrote:

There are many Negroes here . . . who are inclined . . . to jump to the dangerous conclusion that there is little to choose between an imperfect American or English democracy, often abusive to non-white populations, and a Nazi "new order" . . . This is a racially suicidal view.[14]

Bunche's study of non-European groups in South Africa had been put aside for the Myrdal study, and he only got back to it in October 1940. "I am trying to drag myself back to the African field notes," he wrote to Willard Park, "but I have developed such a revulsion toward work since my sentence on the Carnegie Project expired that it is very difficult."[15] Africa had also to be seen in the context of world war. "They [the Africans]," Bunche wrote in October, "are the innocent pawns in the disgusting spectacle of the so-called civilized nations and their rulers fighting each other to death. . . ." In peace, Africans suffered brutal economic exploitation; in war, Africa was "a bloody battlefield in which the great 'civilized' nations of Europe fight each other like mad dogs over a bone." Though Africa had no voice in the war, it was not permitted to stay out of it. However, since the First World War the democratic European colonial powers had been obliged to allow some progress in their colonies, if only in response to liberal voices at home, and Africans were beginning to develop effective organizations of their own, just as Black Americans were doing. The future of Africa was "inseparably tied to the outcome of the present war," to the crucial choice between totalitarian, racist, fascist imperialism, and democratic imperialism. Hitler's Nazism "embraces boldly and fundamentally a racial theory more severe and more brazen than any the modern world has known—more formal, more deliberate even than that to be found in our own deep South." In the context of an Aryan master-race, Nazi statements habitually referred to blacks as "animal-like," whereas in England, sorely beset though it now was, colonial Africans could still make their voices heard and present their grievances. "If Hitler and Mussolini win this war," Bunche concluded, "the future of the African will be one of abject, hopeless slavery."[16]

Bunche was very conscious of the threat to other minorities, especially the Jews, and was deeply apprehensive of mounting anti-Semitism. "For the Negro," he wrote in 1941, "certainly anti-Semitism is a dangerous luxury." Jewish and Negro organizations should cooperate because "In large measure their problems—their grievances and their fears—are cut to a common pattern."[17]

Bunche wrote, lectured, and organized tirelessly in the period before the United States came into the war, with his sights still firmly fixed on the basic requirement for black Americans. "The Negro in America has but one fundamental objective," he wrote in July 1941:

to attain the full stature of American citizenship. . . . In a world where democracy is gravely besieged, the United States must consider seriously the implications of its own failure to extend the democratic process in full to some thirteen million of its citizens whose present status tends to make a mockery of the Constitution.[18]

A very practical application of this objective arose with the enormous expansion of the defense industry. In the early stages of this process Black Americans had found it virtually impossible to secure jobs in defense industries, except, perhaps, as janitors. On April 28, 1941, Bunche, together with A. Philip Randolph, was one of seventeen signatories of a letter to President Roosevelt pressing him to dispense justice in the distribution of jobs in national defense. When no immediate response was forthcoming, the NAACP approved Randolph's plan for a march of a hundred thousand Black Americans on Washington. The plan was very much in the spirit of Bunche's memorandum to Mrs. Roosevelt of the year before, and he supported it warmly. On June 25 President Roosevelt issued Executive Order 8802, forbidding employment discrimination in government and defense industries and establishing the Fair Employment Practices Commission. The march was called off.* When Pearl Harbor was bombed five months later, the NAACP called on Black Americans to give wholehearted support to the war effort.

Bunche was now an established figure—a full professor, an articulate and outspoken protagonist of practical policies to improve the lot of Black Americans, and a respected authority both on racial and African prob-

*In his *Free at Last: The Civil Rights Movement and the People Who Made It* (New York, 1991), Fred Powledge states that the modern civil-rights movement began in 1941, when Randolph threatened President Roosevelt with a march on Washington.

lems. In Washington he had constant cause to reflect on the ironies of racial discrimination as it still constantly impinged on his own life, albeit in a more muted and subtle way. As he noted in 1941:

There's a lot of irony in this American racial situation. I'm sitting in a Pullman out of Raleigh, NC, en route for Washington, DC . . . writing notes in defense of the Amer. democracy. I could get the Pullman reservation only through deception. . . .*[19]

His friend Todd Duncan, a baritone in the original cast of *Porgy and Bess*, wrote to him of his embarrassment at the fact that at the National Theater in Washington, his Black American friends would not be able to see the show. Bunche and some of his Howard colleagues got the backing of the Central Labor Union for picketing the theater and then went to the manager. After a long wrangle the manager opened the theater to Black Americans for the whole of the run of *Porgy and Bess* in Washington.[20]

Bunche carefully monitored the effects of racial snubs on his children. On a Sunday outing, the Bunches, accompanied by his Howard colleague, Abe Harris, a respected black economist, and his wife, were refused entry by an extremely embarrassed white attendant to a Great Falls park owned by the Virginia Power Company. Bunche noted that Joan clearly understood the situation but wasn't either disturbed or puzzled by it, merely accepting it as just another racial incident. He later recorded the following exchange with Joan.

Joan: Is George Washington a white man?
Bunche: Yes.
Joan: Then why was he *our* president?
Bunche: Franklin Roosevelt is white, and he's our president.
Joan: Oh, is *he* white?

A nine-year-old friend, Louise Sherefsky, gave Joan an unsolicited introduction to the intricacies of the race question, saying that colored schools were inferior and that she and Jane should come to *her* school. "Jane," she said, "is white, and they wouldn't know what you are." She also told Joan that the Bunche family was mixed, only Miss Houston being really black. She added, for good measure, that Woodward and Lothrop, the Washington department store, wouldn't serve Jews.

Although there was a school within easy walking distance of their new house, at 1510 Jackson St, NE, Joan and Jane had to be transported

*Bunche had had one of his former students who could "pass" pick up the ticket.

three miles across town to a black school. Bunche was in a car pool with two white colleagues at the time, and they often dropped Jane off on their way to work. Jane always insisted, even in the pouring rain, on being dropped off at the corner, and Bunche eventually found out that her black classmates, seeing two white men in the car, would give her a hard time. This mirror-image racism upset Bunche almost as much as the original article.

Bunche once described the effects of discrimination to James Green, a colleague in the State Department.

You white folks just don't understand what we black folks go through. A black man like me, who has a sense of humor, can survive; a black man like Paul Robeson, who doesn't have a sense of humor, takes to wine, women, song, and communism.*[21]

It never occurred to Bunche to move out of Washington during the war, or to work there ever again after it. With the entry of the United States into the war, he was about to enter public service and an entirely new phase of his career.

*Asked in 1949 to comment on a statement by Robeson that American Negroes would never fight the Soviet Union, Bunche replied, "Paul should stick to singing. . . . He's had some very unpleasant experiences here, as all of us have had. He's resentful of the injustices as all of us are. I know that when he went to Russia he was very well received, and that may have influenced him to follow the party line. . . . I think he's radically wrong."[22]

8

World War II Washington and the OSS

Irreplaceable at Any Price

In June 1941, after nearly two years of war, Hitler, triumphantly in control of Western Europe, invaded the Soviet Union with stunning initial success. On the other side of the globe, Japanese expansionism and war-readiness loomed ominously over a United States still at peace. As it became less and less likely that the United States could stay out of the war, the American defense effort went into high gear.

An essential element of this effort was information and intelligence, and on July 11, 1941, President Roosevelt announced the creation of the Office of the Coordinator of Information (COI), out of which there later sprang the Office of Strategic Services (OSS).* Colonel William J. Donovan, a Republican Wall Street lawyer, was in charge of COI, while the poet Archibald MacLeish ran a parallel organization, the Office of Facts and Figures. Both operations were housed in an annex of the Library of Congress. Donovan considered "an intellectual base essential for a job of channelling public information,"[1] and immediately began to assemble a team of scholars, journalists, intellectuals, and writers for the combined task of public information, defense information on any country where U.S. forces might be involved, propaganda, and psychological warfare.

In June 1941, in response to a request from the fledgling COI for an African specialist, the Harvard history department had mentioned Bunche as a possibility, quoting the Harvard constitutional historian, Benjamin Fielding Wright, who "characterized him as one of the few—perhaps the only—Negro graduate student he has known at Harvard who

---

*Later still, after World War II, the OSS evolved into the Central Intelligence Agency.

[was] able to compete for fellowships on equal terms with the better white students."[2]

In August, Conyers Read, an eminent Elizabethan historian at the University of Pennsylvania with a lively interest in public affairs, who was to be Bunche's boss at OSS, cabled Professor C. H. McIlwain, "Shall I take him?," to which McIlwain replied that Bunche was "the best graduate student of his race at Harvard in my time." Even Harvard seems to have been unable to judge Bunche on his ability without reference to his race. On September 10, two months before Pearl Harbor and the United States' entry into the war, Bunche was appointed as senior social-science analyst in the Library of Congress at a salary of $4,600 a year.

Bunche had strong feelings about the obligations of public service and the behavior dictated by those obligations. Although he continued to express his opinions forcefully to his colleagues, he was acutely conscious, in his new job, of the necessity for discretion and restraint in his public statements. Thus, from 1941, although his convictions remained as strong as ever, his public voice was to some extent muted. In public service Bunche experienced at first hand the complexity of the decisions that governments—especially democratic ones—have to face, and the narrowness of the options that are usually open to them in critical times. During his years of public service, while remaining as outspoken as ever in the confidential circle of his colleagues, he scrupulously avoided public activities or statements which might be damaging or embarrassing to the government or organization he was serving.

His entry into public service did not in any way change Bunche's personal demeanor. Throughout his life he remained remarkably free of pretension and of the desire to claim credit or win public acclaim. He never boasted of his achievements, and it was difficult to get him even to talk about them. His friend Kenneth Clark put it well. "I never did see any difference between Ralph Bunche, the person, the human being, and Ralph Bunche, the public figure, the statesman. . . . He was incapable of flamboyance, even temporary egoism and posturing. He was concerned with the task at hand and his possible contribution to the attainment of the desired objectives."[3]

In the Office of the Coordinator of Information Bunche was responsible for work on the British Empire in Africa, which included Kenya, Uganda, Tanganyika, Nyasaland, Zanzibar, the Rhodesias, South Africa, the South African protectorates, and South-West Africa. He set about the task with his usual mixture of scholarly thoroughness and practical common sense. He told Conyers Read that he intended to build up information on all possible aspects of these areas and to keep fully abreast of current events, including the attitudes and day-to-day problems of native populations.[4] He was not encouraged by his first look at the resources of the Library of Congress on Africa. "Much reliance seems to be put on encyclopedias," he commented.[5]

Bunche threw himself into the work at OSS with all his usual commitment, fired also by the conviction that there was very little time to lose. Commenting, in February 1942, on Africa's strategic importance in the war, he wrote that in view of "revelations of Nazi foresight and efficiency in their 'blueprint' for Africa, it is more important than ever to anticipate all possible needs there."[6] With American military operations in the offing, Bunche suggested sending army doctors to Africa to study health problems and to prepare a manual on conditions and on the precautions to be taken. There should also be military manuals on native peoples if the "native legend of America as a liberalizing force in the world" was to be preserved. "The elite African especially is even more sensitive on racial matters than is the American Negro."[7] The war also had to be explained to the native African population with, if necessary, abundant and imaginative illustrations. Native nationalism was "a force to be reckoned with" and must be studied and understood. Bunche suggested sending Black Americans to Africa as unofficial representatives to enlist popular support for the allied cause.

Bunche wrote the manual on North Africa for the U.S. troops who were to fight there. His efforts did not pass unnoticed. "The men who finished the mission course," Undersecretary of State Edward R. Stettinius wrote to him in March 1943, ". . . have expressed their great appreciation of your work in grooming them for their job, particularly for giving them the economic, geographic and sociological background of the country to which they are going."[8]

Bunche lost no opportunity to seek out firsthand sources of information. He interviewed Free French officers, Belgian colonial administrators, or British civil servants with a view to getting as accurate a picture as possible of conditions and attitudes. One preoccupation that seemed to be shared by the representatives of all the European colonial powers was the probable impact of the high pay-scale of Black American troops on native African soldiers. The fact that black American soldiers still served in segregated units made less of an impression on them.

If victory was to be assured, it was also important for the United States to understand the point of view of the European Allies, especially the colonial powers. The two most sensitive areas were conditions in

Africa, where the European colonial powers were already apprehensive of United States enthusiasm for decolonization, and European reactions to the American race problem as manifested in the behavior of the United States Army overseas. Even before large numbers of American troops had crossed the Atlantic, Bunche pointed out that a large-scale demonstration of American racial discrimination in the United Kingdom through the presence of black and white U.S. troops "threatens to prejudice British civilian opinion against the United States."[9] A typical problem would arise in pubs or restaurants in London, where white American soldiers would expect black soldiers to be barred.* Such an affront to the code of racial tolerance prevailing in Britain would not only cause serious resentment, but would create strong reactions among British colonial populations. Bunche had learned that Africans in London were already apprehensive about the situation, and he suggested an urgent effort to explain the American race problem to the British, either through British experts like Margery Perham or by sending suitable Americans for that specific purpose. "The British have rarely seen a Negro intellectual," he noted.[10]

Bunche was particularly concerned with the place of Black Americans in the U.S. war effort. The American Communist Party, which had been driven to a contemptible volte-face by Hitler's invasion of Russia in June 1941, was still trying to make the black cause its own, with steadily decreasing success. Bunche was anxious to maximize the black role in all parts of the war effort. He personally wrote to the Capitol Transit Company of Washington, D.C., suggesting that it employ black drivers to compensate for the shortage of white drivers, in a reversal of its "racial employment policy."[11] He suggested that the Office of War Information produce documentary films on Negroes in war industry and on Negroes in wartime affairs,[12] but urged that emphasis be placed on the indispensability of black manpower to the war effort rather than on "romantic principles of 'justice,' 'fair-play,' 'democracy,' etc." It was essential, for example, to avoid any suggestion of coercion by the Fair Employment Practices Commission, which should be seen as a war-production agency harnessing all available manpower to the war effort, rather than as a coercive social-reform unit.[13]† The development of a corps of trained black workers was

---

*The British writer Philip Toynbee had all his front teeth knocked out in London in precisely such a situation, when he protested the demand of a young United States officer that two black soldiers leave the pub where he was having a drink.

†Bunche's preoccupations on this score were justified by events in Detroit and Mobile, Alabama, the following year, when white workers violently protested the employment and promotion of black workers.

also important to the economic future of the South after the war.

Aided by a small staff, Bunche was coping with a vast workload of strategic surveys, psychological-warfare roundups, and other routine work. As Conyers Read described it, he

maintains contacts with pertinent US and foreign agencies, arranges and conducts interviews, pursues independent research at the State Department and the War and Navy Departments. He is called into conference constantly in connection with present operations in Africa and is one of four members of OSS to represent the United States in the forthcoming conference at Quebec under the auspices of the Institute of Pacific Relations.[14]

The Institute of Pacific Relations Conference at Mont Tremblant, Quebec, in December 1942 was, Bunche later wrote,

the best international conference I've ever attended—Lord Hailey, Sir Frederick Whyte, Creech Jones; Ramaswami Mudaliar, Sir Zafrullah Khan; Lester Pearson, Paul Martin, Brooke Claxton, Hugh Keenleyside; Leo Pasvolsky; Paul Hasluck— laid basis for United Nations Chapters 11, 12, 13 [of the Charter].[15]*

The two main questions before the conference were:

1. What steps can be taken by the United Nations to aid in the better prosecution of the war and in the establishment of conditions of racial, political and economic justice and welfare?

2. How can this discussion be made the basis of the practical program of the United Nations during and after the war?

Apart from its intrinsic importance in formulating objectives and policies for the postwar world, the meeting offered a unique opportunity to discuss both wartime and postwar problems with highly placed Allied representatives.

At Mont Tremblant, Bunche was the rapporteur of the round table on social and demographic matters, and his report both reflected his previous experience and foreshadowed his future responsibilities. The discussion took place in the framework of the Atlantic Charter, which Roosevelt and Churchill had signed in August 1941 on the battleship *Augusta* off

---

*Hailey and Whyte were distinguished colonial administrators. Mudaliar (India) and Zafrullah Khan (Pakistan) represented their countries at the UN after the war. Creech-Jones became minister for colonial affairs in the British postwar Labour government. Pearson and Martin both served as foreign minister of Canada. Brooke Claxton was Canadian defense minister in 1946–54. Pasvolsky was the moving spirit in drafting the UN charter. Keenleyside pioneered the economic development role of the UN. Hasluck became governor-general of Australia.

Newfoundland. The aims of paragraphs 4 and 5 of the Charter were improved labor standards and security, and freedom from fear and want. Whether these and other provisions of the Charter were meant to apply primarily to the victim nations of Europe, or to the world at large and especially to colonial territories, was to be a matter of some controversy throughout the war years. Bunche never had any doubt that the Atlantic Charter must be made to apply to all peoples, *especially* those in colonial territories. The Mont Tremblant Conference provided the springboard which was to launch him on this mission and on his own career as a leader in decolonization and trusteeship matters.

The underlying premise of Bunche's report to the conference was that the criterion for the sincerity of the colonial powers in preparing their colonial areas for self-government must be a "unanimous and humane recognition of the basic right of these people to a decent and dignified existence—a right they have never realized." His peroration got an ovation from the conference. Schemes of future international organization, he concluded, must be

the realization of the hopes, if not the clamorous demands, of the vast millions who struggle tragically to eke out a meagre existence. The real objective must always be the good life for all of the people. International machinery will mean something to the common man in the Orient, as indeed to the common man throughout the world, only when it is translated into terms that he can understand: peace, bread, housing, clothing, education, good health, and, above all, the right to walk with dignity on the world's great boulevards.[16]

The Mont Tremblant Conference, snowbound in a beautiful resort, opened up a new world for Bunche, and many of the people he met there were to play an important part in his life at the United Nations. As he wrote to Ruth:

A real cross section of the world's population, and most of them both intelligent and sociable. I am right in my element as you can imagine. . . . My tongue is wagging all day long and most of the night. . . .[17]

At Mont Tremblant Bunche also got a foretaste of the very real problems which would become pressing as soon as the war was over. Foremost among them in his mind was how to make the process of decolonization as voluntary and nonviolent as possible. The cooperation of the colonial powers would be indispensable to the success of this process. Bunche was impressed by the expertise and seriousness of colonial officials such as Lord Hailey, Lord Lugard, Malcolm MacDonald, and Sir George Gater, and also by the sincerity of politicians like Arthur Creech-Jones, who was to become the minister for colonial affairs in the British postwar Labour government. He tended, therefore, to react sharply to what he regarded as ill-informed, unrealistic, and woolly thinking on this vitally important matter. A case in point was the American "Committee on Africa, the War, and Peace Aims," which had published its views at about this time. Bunche wrote:

Self-appointed Committees who pine for political control by Africans and tell the European governments how to control their colonies cause extremely bad feeling among the Allies. . . . Does the Committee realize that colonial matters are debated freely in the British Parliament, who, to date, are their own best critics? If the Americans want to set up in Africa an ideal colony, why don't they make Liberia a decent place in which to live, thereby setting an example and something to show our allies. . . . Criticism detached from all responsibility is meaningless, and causes considerable trouble not only in Africa, but elsewhere.[18]

By 1943 Bunche was beginning to feel the limitations of his work at OSS. Because all of Africa would soon be in the hands of the Allies, the continent had a "role of diminishing consequence for the OSS," he wrote to his OSS supervisor.

I have a very vital stake in the outcome of the war. I have, in fact, for some time hankered after something a bit closer to the front line. Had I not been rejected by Walter Reed [Hospital] with a recommendation of no waiver in my physical exam for a commission last fall, I would now be in uniform for Special Services.[19]

The Mont Tremblant Conference had whetted Bunche's interest in postwar planning, especially for the colonial areas of the world, and he had begun to feel that his work at OSS had too narrow a focus.

For its part, the OSS, having recognized and profited from Bunche's unique qualities and qualifications, was extremely reluctant to lose him. "Bunche is perhaps the foremost authority in America on African problems," Conyers Read wrote in November 1942.[20] And again,

he ought to number among the highest paid men in R & A. His knowledge of Africa is unique, his diligence in research very remarkable, and his tact in personal contacts outstanding. . . . Many attempts have been made by other agencies to secure his services which he has resisted because he feels he can make a greater contribution to the war effort where he is. . . . He would be absolutely irreplaceable at any price. . . .[21]

As the tide of war turned and victory in the foreseeable future began to seem possible, Bunche's interest in, and concern for, planning for postwar decolonization steadily increased. The United States engagement in African affairs at that time was largely for war-time military purposes. "It seems scarcely tenable that . . . we will pull out when the shooting stops with no continuing sense of responsibility for the future of the continent."[22] At Mont Tremblant, Bunche had felt that the American delegation had made "a rather pitiful showing with respect to the factual data on the colonial problems of the Pacific" by comparison with the professionalism and expertise of the representatives of colonial powers. Nor were there in the United States competent private groups which systematically studied postwar African and colonial problems, as there were in England. "At this late stage in the game the US is ill-prepared to cross swords with Britain and the colonial nations of Europe on colonial problems or planning."[23]

Bunche also felt that an opportunity was being missed. "The present disposition of the British Government . . . is to recognize an international responsibility for the future of colonial areas and peoples." Bunche had had twelve years of unusually wide international contacts on colonial questions. In that time, "I have had but one unpleasant experience that could be attributable to my race, and that was at the hands of a minor official of the Government of the Union of South Africa." He had found that his race was never a handicap, and often an advantage, in dealing with European colonial officials. Bunche urged that someone, preferably himself, should talk to the British and also gain access to the wealth of material on colonial matters which was available in London.[24]

The OSS did not take up this proposal, and Bunche's desire to move on increased. At a conference organized by the Canadian Institute of Public Affairs at Lake Couchiching, north of Toronto, in August 1943, he had noted a significant change of mood among the European participants. Though the British were "as usual . . . impressively represented,"[25] all the American representatives were unofficial. At Mont Tremblant, the year before, there had been great interest in American policy. At Lake Couchiching, there was much criticism from Allied representatives that the United States had not defined its postwar foreign policy or objectives. The American intervention in North Africa was now viewed as an obstacle to French unity, and some Europeans were evidently becoming suspicious of what the United States might do in Europe itself. Bunche concluded that there would be little or no European postwar gratitude to the United States, and that European provincialism would reassert itself, "once Europe is freed of the Axis military heel of course."[26] There was thus an urgent need to formulate policy on colonial affairs and to increase contacts and discussion with the Allies.

In Washington the only work being done on postwar Africa was in the State Department in Leo Pasvolsky's Division of Political and Economic Studies. Leo Pasvolsky, a brilliant Russian émigré, had been borrowed from the Brookings Institution by the State Department to be the mastermind of the postwar planning effort which culminated in the United Nations Charter. Bunche had been called in early in 1943 by Pasvolsky's staff to sound him out on working on a "colonial charter" for the postwar world. Only Benjamin Gerig, a former member of the League of Nations Mandates Section, was working on this project at the time, but, Bunche observed, "he has little knowledge of the actual problems and conditions of Africa."[27] The OSS doggedly resisted Bunche's move to the State Department.

Paradoxically, the war years in Washington were, for the Bunche family, the most domestic period of their entire married life. They saw friends, went out in the evenings, and had regular weekends during which Bunche tended his garden and enjoyed their new house. Their third child, Ralph Jr., was born at 5:12 A.M. on September 18, 1943, and Bunche took two weeks' leave "nurse-maiding, sterilizing bottles, making formulae, seeding lawn, etc. . . ."[28] That he could, and would, do this shows not only his enthusiasm for the event itself, but also the relatively undemanding nature of his schedule at OSS.

Racial segregation in Washington did not succumb to wartime pressures. "Couldn't make Schorske's* cocktail party," Bunche noted in January 1943, "for lack of gas and unwillingness to ride Va. J.C. bus with Ruth."[29] An episode which especially enraged Bunche occurred when the family dog died and the children wanted it buried in the local pet cemetery. Bunche drove there to make arrangements and found that there was one section for white people's pets and another for black people's. This made such an impression on him that, when President Truman offered him the post of assistant secretary of state in 1948 and sent Dean Rusk to New York to persuade him, Bunche cited the incident as an example of his reasons for refusing to live in Washington in peacetime.[30]

There was at least some progress in official circles. In the office, "I get along fine," he wrote to Ethel and Nelle, "and though I have a white woman assistant and three other white men on my staff, I've encountered no difficulties." Outside the office things were less certain. "Had lunch with Willard Park . . . in Commerce Department cafeteria," he noted in

*The historian Carl Schorske was working in OSS. Another OSS friend was the historian Arthur Schlesinger, Jr.

May 1943. "Despite Willard's doubts there was no trouble." A considerable breakthrough occurred when Dean Rusk took Bunche to lunch in the Officers' Dining Room at the War Department. This was the first time a Black American had lunched there, and "our innocent stroll into the dining room was quite an incident for its day." However, Dean Rusk's commanding officer fully supported him and there were "no lasting repercussions."[31] "The funny thing," Rusk wrote in 1991, "is that neither Bunche nor I realized it was off limits to blacks. We were just hungry."[32]

"As I think you know," Anson Phelps Stokes* wrote to Bunche early in 1944, "we have long advocated having a few colored men of the highest character and ability given posts of importance in the Department, and have felt that the plan could not be started out better than by your selection."[33] The competition for Bunche's services actually came to a head at the end of 1943. Dr. William Langer, the director of research and analysis at OSS, tried to persuade Pasvolsky to let Bunche stay at OSS and work part-time for the State Department, but Pasvolsky insisted that Bunche had to work for State, although he could remain the "spiritual adviser" of the Africa section of OSS. The State Department formally requested Bunche's transfer on December 8, 1943, and on January 4, 1944, he was sworn in as an officer of the Department of State.

*Anson Phelps Stokes, founder of the Phelps Stokes Fund, was a pioneer in race relations and had written to Undersecretary of State Edward R. Stettinius about Bunche.

Howard University Social Science Conference, 1935. W. E. B. Du Bois is in the center with Professor Emmett Dorsey and Bunche on his right. George O. Butler, professor of economics, is at extreme left of front row. Fred Minnis is second from right in the front row. John Syphax, Charles Lofton, J. B. Browning, and Hylan Lewis are among those in back rows.

Above, left: With Ruth, Jane, and Joan after returning from Africa and Asia. Los Angeles, August 1938. *Above, right:* With Gunnar Myrdal at Jackson Street, Washington, D.C., summer 1943. *Below:* The Bunche family house, 1510 Jackson Avenue, N.E., Washington, D.C., summer 1943.

With Count Folke Bernadotte and Prime Minister Nokrashi Pasha of Egypt. Cairo, June 1948. UN PHOTO

Keeping track of a press conference given by Count Folke Bernadotte. Tel Aviv, June 1948. UN PHOTO

A last farewell to Bernadotte. Bunche, Carey Seward, and General William Riley (saluting). Haifa, Israel, September 19, 1948. UN PHOTO

The acting mediator addresses the Security Council on the fighting in the Negev. *Seated at table, left to right:* Faris al Khouri of Syria, Vassily Tarassenko of Ukraine SSR, Jacob Malik of USSR, Sir Alexander Cadogan of Britain, Bunche, Trygve Lie, Warren Austin of the United States and president of the Council, and Arkady Sobolev, UN assistant secretary general. Paris, October 19, 1948. UN PHOTO

Reading the text of the armistice agreement to the Egyptian and Israeli delegations—Colonel Sherine and the Egyptian delegation *on the left; at center table,* Constantin Stavropoulos, General William Riley, Bunche, Henri Vigier, UN observers Colonel Millert and Colonel Langlois, and Bill Mashler; *on the right,* the Israeli delegation: Reuven Shiloah, Yigael Yadin, and Walter Eytan. Hôtel des Roses, Rhodes, February 24, 1949. UN PHOTO

Relaxing during the armistice negotiations with a game of billiards, Yigael Yadin looking on. Hôtel des Roses, Rhodes, February 1949. *Below:* A lighter moment on Bunche's last flight—to Stockholm. *Far right:* Doreen Daughton, Bunche's chief secretary, and William Stoneman *(two seats behind her).* April 11, 1949.

With Eleanor Roosevelt at dinner in Bunche's honor. Waldorf-Astoria Hotel, New York City, May 9, 1949. *Below:* King Haakon of Norway receives Bunche and Ruth after the Nobel Peace Prize presentation ceremony. Oslo, December 10, 1950.

Ruth and the children at home. Parkway Village, New York, 1949. *Left to right:* Joan, Ruth, Ralph Jr., and Jane.

9

The Road to San Francisco

The Hardest Working Conference

As assistant secretary of the navy in the First World War, Franklin Roosevelt had been painfully aware of the lack of preparation for the Paris Peace Conference and the serious mistakes that had resulted. Postwar planning had therefore been a function of the State Department since December 1939. Immediately after Pearl Harbor in 1941, in a move that displayed remarkable confidence in the outcome of the war, Roosevelt instructed Secretary of State Cordell Hull to establish in the State Department a special staff to plan for the peace. This staff, led by Leo Pasvolsky, set out to deal with every problem that might come up at the peace conference. One section dealt with postwar boundaries in Europe, another with reparations, and a third with the disarmament of enemy powers.

Later on, another section was set up under Harley Notter to work on a new league of nations and a new international court of justice. Benjamin Gerig headed the group that dealt with the old League of Nations mandates system which had been set up to deal with the colonial possessions of the defeated nations after the First World War. Gerig's function was to consider what to do about colonies after the war and to develop out of the old mandates system a new and more dynamic "trusteeship" system. Bunche had only been in the Near Eastern and African Section of the State Department for a fortnight when Gerig asked for his transfer to Gerig's International Security Organization section to assist in the work on trusteeship. Bunche's chief, Philip E. Mosely, the head of the Territorial Research Staff, resisted this move, and it did not actually take place until July 1944.

By the time Bunche arrived at the State Department in early 1944, the main postwar policy objectives of the United States as regards colonies—or "dependent territories," as they were officially called—had been drafted but were still under intensive discussion. The concept of a trustee-ship system to replace the League of Nations mandates system was already well established, but the original idea that *all* colonial territories should undergo a period of trusteeship under the new international organization as a preparation for full independence had been successfully sidetracked by the British. All that was left was a trusteeship system that would apply to the former mandated territories of the League of Nations, to the colo-nial territories of defeated enemy states, and to territories voluntarily placed under trusteeship by their administering powers, should any wish to do so. The British had also succeeded in persuading Hull that the goal for dependent territories should be self-government, but not necessarily independence.

The outline of U.S. postwar policy also included the idea of a general declaration of principles governing the administration of *all* colonies. In May 1944 Bunche played a key role, as an adviser to the American govern-ment delegation to the International Labor Conference in Philadelphia, in securing the adoption of a recommendation on Minimum Standards of Social Policy in Dependent Territories. Since the representatives of the colonial powers at Philadelphia never even suggested that labor and living standards in dependent territories were not a proper matter for interna-tional concern, this was something of a breakthrough for the view that the Atlantic Charter applied to the whole world rather than just the parts of it that bordered on the North Atlantic. Bunche certainly saw it as a useful precedent for a broader declaration on dependent territories at the up-coming San Francisco Conference on International Organization.

The immediate preoccupation of Harley Notter and his staff was the preparation for the Dumbarton Oaks Conversations in Washington, D.C., scheduled for late August, 1944. The purpose of the conversa-tions—between the United States, Britain, and France on one side, and the Soviet Union in a first phase and China in a second—was to get agreement on the main outlines of the charter of the new world organiza-tion. The members of Pasvolsky's team were not only to serve the Ameri-can delegation but also to "function as the international secretariat of the conference."[1] Gerig's group had worked hard on a proposal for the con-version of the League of Nations mandates system into a new trusteeship system, but in the end the subject of trusteeship was not to be discussed at Dumbarton Oaks at all.

The absence of trusteeship from the agenda at Dumbarton Oaks was the result of a domestic political row in the United States—a titanic struggle between the War and Navy Departments on one side and the State Department and the Department of the Interior on the other. The problem was the former German islands in the North Pacific—the Mariana, Caroline, and Marshall Islands—which Japan had controlled under a League of Nations mandate since the First World War. Under the trusteeship system as originally conceived, these islands would have become United Nations Trust Territories, a notion totally unacceptable, for strategic and national-security reasons, to James Forrestal, the secretary of the navy, and Henry Stimson, the secretary of war, who originally wanted simply to annex the islands. The struggle nearly destroyed the concept of trusteeship altogether, and in the effort to save trusteeship, the declaration on dependent territories was jettisoned. The problem of trusteeship was finally resolved at the last moment before the San Francisco Conference by the invention of a new category of United States administered "Strategic Trust Territories," which would be under the supervision of the Security Council, where the United States had the veto. The last official decision taken by President Roosevelt, two days before his death and two weeks before the opening of the San Francisco Conference in April 1945, was to approve a United States proposal on the principles and machinery of the trusteeship system, including Strategic Trust Territories.

Although much of the force and ingenuity of U.S. postwar planning for colonial and dependent territories was consumed in this domestic battle, the development of the postwar system remained an important part of the Pasvolsky team's task. It is difficult to determine Bunche's precise contribution to this work in the pre–San Francisco period. His colleague James F. Green called him "a very energetic and imaginative officer and an excellent team member,"[2] but, as another colleague, Lawrence Finkelstein, has written, "Dr. Bunche himself was too busy making history to record it."[3] Certainly Bunche was an increasingly active and influential member of the team that prepared the road to San Francisco.

At Dumbarton Oaks, in late August 1944, since the trusteeship system could not be discussed, Bunche and his colleagues on Gerig's staff inevitably played a peripheral role, confined largely to taking the record of meetings. For Bunche, it was a valuable education for the ultimate test, the San Francisco Conference. The key to success at Dumbarton Oaks was the drafting of proposals in the "formulation groups" of each main committee, and he had the opportunity to watch some world-class experts—Alexander Cadogan and Gladwyn Jebb of Britain, Arkady Sobolev of the Soviet Union, and Leo Pasvolsky—engaged in the art of drafting of which he himself was shortly to become an international master. In the daily meetings of the U.S. delegation and at the various social events, he also got to know many of the people he would deal with in San Francisco, including Victor Hoo of China, who was to be his first boss at the United Nations.

The Dumbarton Oaks meetings coincided with dramatic developments in the war. Paris and Marseilles were liberated between August 15 and 20, and Brussels on September 15. By August 15 Bucharest and Warsaw had fallen to the Red Army, and India had been cleared of the Japanese. The end of World War II was at last in sight.

The Dumbarton Oaks meeting agreed on most of the outline of the charter of the new world organization, including its name, the United Nations. There were three main sticking points. The Soviet Union insisted that permanent members of the Security Council must be allowed to vote on, and exercise the veto in, disputes to which they were a party. They also "left Stettinius and Cadogan breathless"[4] by insisting that the sixteen Soviet republics must all be founder members of the United Nations.* Both these issues were finally settled at the summit meeting at Yalta in early 1945. The third sticking point was the total absence, due to the interdepartmental struggle in Washington, of any discussion on trusteeship and dependent territories.

In late October, two weeks after the Dumbarton Oaks Conversations ended, Pasvolsky set up a group of officers in the State Department to prepare for the San Francisco Conference, where it would no longer be possible to postpone the issue of dependent territories and trusteeship. Bunche was a member of this team.[5] He was also occupied in numerous other tasks, such as preparing statements on dependent territories, including one for President Roosevelt for a speech to the Foreign Policy Association, and advising the Pentagon on army policies concerning black troops. In December he was promoted to associate chief of the Division of Dependent Areas Affairs under Ben Gerig.

An understanding of the attitudes of the main colonial powers, Britain and France, was a vital part of the preparation for San Francisco. In January 1945, for the 9th Conference of the Institute of Pacific Relations, on Security in the Pacific, Bunche traveled down to Hot Springs, Virginia, with an acquaintance from Mont Tremblant, Arthur Creech-Jones, the British Labour Party's expert on colonial affairs. Creech-Jones, who, as

*In 1991, on the collapse of the Soviet Union, these republics, in addition to Ukraine and Byelorussia, became independent members of the UN.

colonial secretary in the postwar socialist government, was to remain both a reformer and a dogged defender of British colonialism, displayed a mischievous interest in the newly formed Dependent Areas Division of the State Department and asked half-seriously if it would deal with American dependent areas, not to mention the fifteen million dependent black people of the United States. Creech-Jones' facetiousness indicated his skepticism about postwar plans for colonial territories, and he asserted that the native peoples of the British Empire would greatly prefer making slower progress under British control to entrusting their fate to international arrangements. He also maintained that mandated territories like Cameroon or Tanganyika would do much better economically as colonies than as independent states. He admitted that the principle of accountability for colonies was gradually becoming acceptable in Britain, although not yet to the government, but on no account could accountability include sanctions or international inspection.

Bunche dealt with some of Creech-Jones' points in a speech in February in Cleveland, Ohio.[6] He cited the Anglo-American Caribbean Commission as an encouraging development for the peoples of an area which was entirely dependent.* He also dealt with Creech-Jones' taunt about the American Negro problem and the colonial question.

There is utterly no connection between the two problems. . . . The Negro is an American, and his struggle is directed exclusively toward one objective: the full attainment of his constitutional rights as an American citizen. Unlike the colonial peoples, the American Negro, who is culturally American, has no nationalist and no separatist ambitions.

As to colonialism and the coming San Francisco Conference,

The modern world has come to the realization that there is a great moral issue involved in the perpetuation of colonial systems. That issue, stated boldly, is whether any people are morally good enough to rule permanently over another.

Because the answer to that question was self-evident, the colonial system was—and had to be—self-liquidating.

It cannot be questioned that the colonial regimes of the United Kingdom, France and the Netherlands have brought much progress to the dependent peoples of the Far East. . . . The issue, then, resolves itself into questions of timing, acceleration of progress toward self-rule, and the mechanisms that may be devised to speed up the process of colonial liquidation and to discharge the obligation of accountability.

*Bunche was appointed American commissioner on this commission in September 1945.

These were the basic aims which Bunche would be pursuing at San Francisco and at the United Nations.

French attitudes on the future of colonialism were very different from the British and had been enunciated in a conference of French colonial governors and administrators in Brazzaville in early February 1944. In analyzing this conference Bunche set out to distinguish the rhetoric of the conference from the reality of French colonialism. The phrase "self-government" had been rendered in English at the Brazzaville Conference, to show that it had no equivalent in the French language or in the French concept of the proper relationship between the colonies and the metropole.

The implication is very strong that Brazzaville clung tenaciously to conventional French policy of integration and assimilation of colonial territories and their peoples. . . . The results of the Conference on the whole should be interpreted as the rejection of the idea of international trusteeship. . . . It would seem that the French dream of a united France, with one hundred million Frenchmen, has not been dissipated.[7]

On February 26, 1945, Mrs. Roosevelt had written to Secretary of State Edward R. Stettinius* that "it might be extremely useful in our relationship with South and Central America as well as the Near East" to have some black advisers in the U.S. delegation at San Francisco. She suggested Channing H. Tobias and Dr. Ira D. Reid. In a draft reply that was never sent, Acting Secretary of State Joseph Grew wrote,

You may be interested to know that Dr. Ralph Bunche took an active and important part in the Dumbarton Oaks talks and has served with distinction in the office . . . which has primary responsibility for the preparations for the San Francisco conference. He is an able and outstanding young Negro leader and has made a favorable impression on all those with whom he has come in contact.

On April 12 Bunche "was in conference . . . when shocking news of President's death was received at 5:40. MacLeish: 'a black day for the things we stand for.' " Six days later, on April 18, as technical expert to the delegation of the United States, he left on the Pre-Con Special for San Francisco for the Conference on International Organization which was to produce the United Nations Charter.

The whole Pasvolsky group were on the train, and they worked throughout the journey on the final United States plan for trusteeship, which had yet to be approved. The Johnson family and Bunche's sister

*Cordell Hull had retired due to ill health in October 1944.

Grace came to visit the train during its stopover in Los Angeles. The party arrived in San Francisco in the late afternoon of April 22, and were taken in navy buses with a police escort to their hotels. Bunche shared an apartment in the Alexander Hamilton Hotel with Walter Kotschnig of the State Department. On April 25 he attended the opening meeting in the Opera House, where the foreign ministers and dignitaries of the fifty founding members of the United Nations were assembled. He observed Secretary of State Stettinius ostentatiously looking at his watch during the minute of silent tribute to President Roosevelt. "I did feel a bit proud this afternoon," he wrote to Ruth, "at being the only Negro who sat on the first floor. . . ."

On April 26 there was a night meeting of the full United States delegation to approve the draft proposal on the trusteeship system. Among those present were Senators Tom Connally of Texas and Arthur Vandenberg of Michigan, Governor Harold Stassen of Minnesota, Representative Sol Bloom of New York, and Dean Virginia Gildersleeve of Barnard College. The head of the delegation, Secretary of State Stettinius, arrived late, and Bunche, who was keeping the record, noted "Mr. Stettinius arrived at this point accompanied by a photographer. After pictures were taken, the meeting was resumed."[8] The meeting went into executive session to consider three amendments put forward by the army and navy. Stassen said that the technical experts and advisers had "done a fine job on an extremely difficult subject." At 11:40 P.M., the United States position on trusteeship was at last finalized.

For Bunche this was the beginning of "the hardest working conference I have ever attended."[9] The conference was divided into four commissions—on General Provisions, the General Assembly, the Security Council, and International Judicial Organizations. Trusteeship was dealt with in the Fourth Committee of the Second, General Assembly, Commission.[10] Harold Stassen led the U.S. delegation on this committee. Stassen had resigned the governorship of Minnesota to join the U.S. Navy and was a commander on Admiral Halsey's staff in the Pacific when he was recalled by President Roosevelt* to join the U.S. delegation to the San Francisco Conference. When he flew into San Francisco Stassen had no staff and gratefully accepted the State Department's suggestion of Gerig and Bunche, both of whom he interviewed. He also asked Harvard and

*Roosevelt had apparently remembered a speech at a Gridiron dinner in which Stassen, a Republican, had said that isolationism was dead, that there was only one president of the United States, and that Republicans must cooperate in getting the United Nations off to a good start.

Yale for the names of promising students of international relations who had been wounded in the war, and took on Cord Meyer and John Thompson. Stassen felt that he had "the sharpest staff in all San Francisco."[11]

Because there had been no discussion of trusteeship at Dumbarton Oaks, all the groundwork of getting international agreement on a coherent trusteeship proposal had to be done at San Francisco. The five-power consultative group on trusteeship met for the first time on April 30. The United States team were Harold Stassen, John McCloy, Artemus Gates for the navy, Abe Fortas, a stalwart supporter of the concept of trusteeship, from Interior; and Ben Gerig. Bunche was the secretary of the group. The work started with separate basic drafts from the United States and Britain and some four hundred pages of amendments from other countries. It was Stassen's job, with Bunche's help, to merge all this material into a consolidated single working document. This immense labor was achieved by May 17, when the Conference's Fourth Committee accepted Stassen's consolidated paper as the basis for its discussions.

Bunche enjoyed working with Stassen who, at thirty-eight—two years younger than himself—was then a likely presidential candidate.

He is an easy person to work with, provided you don't mind working. He goes at a terrific pace and demands plenty of materials prepared for him—but he reads and uses it, and that is gratifying. . . .[12]

Stassen was equally appreciative of Bunche's dedication and brilliant mind.[13] Bunche was not impressed with the rest of the delegation, who seemed to him to compare unfavorably with the outstanding ability and professionalism of leaders like Vyacheslav Molotov and Anthony Eden.

Stettinius is a complete dud, whatever the press may say about him. He is simply in a job for which he has utterly no qualifications and about which he knows nothing. He can't make a move w/o asking someone what to do. Except for Stassen, and to a lesser extent Vandenberg (both Republicans) the US Delegation is equally weak. . . .[14]

Trusteeship was, in Bunche's words, the "hottest subject" at the Conference and attracted a great deal of attention. The pace was frenetic. "I scarcely know where one day ends and the next begins," he wrote to Ruth. "We live in a very nonreal world of our own making. We are in San Francisco but not of it." There was no time to see friends like Essie Robeson, who was a visitor at the Conference. "Even VE [Victory in Europe] Day didn't stir up a ripple out here,"[15] although Stettinius, as president of the Conference, called on the Conference to stop its work for a minute of silence on May 8 at 11:00 A.M. to honor the victims of the war in Europe.

Bunche's life was an endless round of attending meetings, writing papers for Stassen, and keeping records of discussions. There were moments when exhaustion bred disillusionment with the abrasive reality of high-level international dealings. "There is practically no inspiration out here—every nation is dead set on looking out for its own national self interest,"[16] he wrote in the middle of the Conference. On May 21, he reported,

Trusteeship, which is about the most important job unfinished, is moving along slowly. It is a tough fight at every step, but we keep on battling and I think we may get something half-way decent out of it. Stassen made one bad blunder on the independence issue but we have been working hard to make up for that one, and the chances are good that we'll write independence into the document after all.*[17]

The British were insisting, successfully, that independence could only come as part of a process of natural evolution. The final text of the "Declaration Regarding Non-Self-Governing Territories" (Chapter XI) reads

to develop self-government . . . and to assist them in the progressive development of their free political institutions, according to the particular circumstances of each territory and its peoples and their varying stages of advancement . . .

In the trusteeship chapters, however, in Article 76(b) there is a reference to "Self-government or independence as may be appropriate to the particular circumstances of each territory. . . ."

According to Lawrence Finkelstein, who was in the U.S. Delegation staff, Bunche played a major role behind the scenes in getting the declaration included in the Charter.[18] Because of the internal battle over the Japanese islands, no decision had been taken in Washington to introduce a declaration of principles governing all dependent territories, so the U.S. delegation in San Francisco could not take an official initiative on the subject. Fortunately, the British, apparently unaware of the paralysis of the U.S. delegation, introduced a flimsy draft designed to counter what they believed would be a much stronger American proposal. This British proposal, unwittingly, became the basis for the declaration in Chapter XI. The Australians, under the dynamic leadership of Foreign Minister Her-

---

*Bunche felt that Stassen should not have opposed the inclusion of the word "independence" in the declaration, since the British representative, Lord Cranborne, was going to oppose it anyway and should have been left to do it on his own.

bert Evatt, had worked on colonial issues during the war, and their views were much nearer those of liberal Americans than of the conservative British. Bunche quickly identified the opportunity and informally passed a copy of the U.S. draft of the declaration (which the U.S. delegation had no authority to use) to the Australians, who used it in their proposal to amend and strengthen the British draft. Much of the original U.S. draft of the declaration thus appeared in the final version of Chapter XI of the Charter ("Declaration Regarding Non-Self-Governing Territories").

Another fruit of Bunche's informal contacts may be found in Article 80 of the Charter, the "conservatory clause," designed to preserve existing arrangements in the period after the League mandates system lapsed and before new trusteeship arrangements were negotiated. Bunche had been contacted at San Francisco by the Jewish Agency for Palestine, who were anxious that the protection for the Balfour Declaration afforded by the League of Nations Palestine mandate should not be allowed to lapse. Some believe that the wording of Article 80 reflects this concern.[19] Arab representatives, for their part, supported the conservatory clause because they believed it protected Arab rights in Palestine under the League of Nations mandate. This caused a prolonged controversy at the conference. In the end the clause had little effect on the Palestine issue, because Palestine never came under the trusteeship system.

The culmination of the work on trusteeship came in the meeting of Second Commission at 8:30 P.M. on June 20, six days before President Truman was to arrive for the formal adoption of the Charter and the final session of the Conference. Field Marshal Jan Christiaan Smuts of South Africa, the father of the League mandates system, presided, and, in paying a tribute to Stassen, welcomed the articles on trusteeship as "one of the most important pieces of work that has been done at this Conference."*[20] By its two parts, the first putting all colonial powers under certain obligations, and the second providing for the trusteeship system,

the principle of Trusteeship is now applied generally. . . . All dependent peoples will have the benefits of the new administration. They will also have the United Nations Organization seeing that they do get these benefits.[22]

In responding to the tributes to him, Stassen, with characteristic grace, said,

*A *Newsweek* poll of foreign correspondents at the end of the conference rated Stassen and Herbert Evatt as having had the greatest impact on the formulating of the final text of the Charter.[21]

It fell to my lot simply to have the honor of standing up in the Committee and making the motions. The work was done by Mr. Gerig and Mr. Bunche of our delegation.*[23]

Bunche wrote:

Stassen, Gerig and I received full credit for winning the toughest fight of the Conference. We have a Trusteeship Chapter in this Charter, tho many thought it could never be pulled off. It is not as good as I would like it to be, but better than any of us expected it could get—there were long periods here when it seemed that we would lose and would have no Chapter at all. A good part of the phraseology, inc. some of the most difficult provisions was drafted exclusively by me. It is a thrill even for your blasé old hubby to see his own writing in it†—writing over which he struggled for long, long hours in a desperate effort to break what often seemed to be impossible impasses. . . .[24]

Assessments of the work at San Francisco that resulted in Chapters XI, XII, and XIII of the Charter vary. Mr. Forde of the Australian delegation called Chapter XI ("The Declaration Regarding Non-Self-Governing Territories") "the most far-reaching declaration on colonial policy in history." Lawrence Finkelstein, who was a junior colleague of Bunche's at the conference, commenting forty years later on Chapter XII ("The International Trusteeship System"), wrote that the U.S. delegation had been shackled by the military demand for control over the Japanese islands and had therefore been unable to perform at its full potential at San Francisco. Thus a "denatured Trusteeship system" limited to a handful of territories had emerged, instead of a system embracing all colonies. "The trusteeship they preserved," he wrote, "was a shell."[25]

Bunche himself evaluated the result at the end of 1945 in an article in the *Department of State Bulletin.* [26] "The San Francisco Conference recognized that the problem of the dependent peoples has come to be widely accepted as a matter of proper international concern. . . ." Thus three out of nineteen chapters of the Charter were devoted to it. He described the trusteeship system not as a substitute for, but as an improve-

*Stassen gave a copy of the proposed charter to Bunche with this inscription: "To Ralph Bunche, able participant in our interesting negotiations. Best Regards, Harold E. Stassen." After the war, when Stassen was president of the University of Pennsylvania, the university gave Bunche an honorary degree.

†Much later, in a letter of January 31, 1952, to his daughter Joan, who had asked for help on a college assignment, Bunche mentions "the phrase of Chapter XI 'whose people have not yet attained a full measure of self-government' (which, incidentally, I drafted at San Francisco)."

ment on, the League mandates system, being far more dynamic, precise, and authoritative, with the Trusteeship Council as a principal organ of the United Nations. As for the problem of dependent territories, the declaration, although unique, did not specifically mention independence, but "by official Conference interpretation" it recognized independence as one of possible alternative goals. The paramountcy of the interests of the inhabitants of dependent territories had been recognized for the first time in an international agreement. The international community was now committed to the advancement of dependent peoples, because "the best guarantee of world security is a world of free, self-respecting, and prosperous peoples."

The original idea of trusteeship as a preparation for self-government for *all* dependent peoples had already been sidetracked during the war years by the opposition of the colonial powers, and after the war it was overtaken by the force and urgency of the movement for colonial independence. Nor did all mandated territories become Trust Territories. Neither Palestine nor South-West Africa became a Trust Territory, and both became long-lasting problems for the United Nations. Nonetheless, the three chapters of the Charter on dependent peoples and trusteeship gave a momentum and a legitimacy to decolonization which allowed the process to be completed within thirty years of the San Francisco Conference, putting an end to the long era of colonial empires, and radically changing both the geopolitical map of the world and the membership of the United Nations. Bunche was to continue to play a central role in this historic process.

The signing of the Charter at San Francisco was a landmark in international relations. The conference, taking place while the war was still going on and with its horrors fresh in the minds of statesmen, was able to agree on a blueprint for international organization which was in many ways radical, and remarkably prescient. After this promising start, the East-West struggle—the Cold War—stunted the development of the world organization for nearly forty years. Decolonization was one of the comparatively rare success stories of the United Nations in the Cold War period.

In Bunche's own career, San Francisco was certainly a landmark. He was now a respected international figure of proven stature and ability. Public service had called him, and he had responded with all of his ability and strength. Already in March 1945 he had said, "I have the feeling that these years in Government service have been the most useful years of my life."[27] In San Francisco his thoughts began to turn to the possibility of a career in international service. He wrote to Ruth:

Many of my colleagues here are convinced that they will be working in the new intl. org. within a year. That's a decision we will have to make before long . . . if things go right. . . . In many ways it would be great for all of us and especially the children—a new life, new surroundings, good schools, no ghettoes and no jim crow."*[28]

For all the grind and the preoccupations of the conference, in his letters home Bunche's thoughts turned again and again to family matters, and especially to his children.

As for the girls . . . we have both been at fault in being too severe with them. . . . We ought to try to see if more love and less censure and nagging won't do the trick. We really never have taken them close to us. We have never really shared our own great love with them. I doubt that either of them have any deep feeling of love for us. We have been their masters rather than their loving parents. I know that in this regard I am criminally culpable. . . . We *must* change. . . .[29]

In a letter to his daughter Jane he says that he has been

too harsh to you and Joan . . . but that is just to make you work harder and to keep you from thinking you are too good. . . . I'm going to make a special effort to be a kinder and a better Daddy. . . . I know you will make a special effort to be helpful and kind to Mommy. You and Joan may be too young to fully appreciate her now, but I assure you that the day will come when you will. You see, I know, because I too had a kind and lovely mother, and I lost her when I was just one year older than Joan. . . .[30]

The contrast between Bunche's behavior in the office and at home was a theme that was to become perennial in their correspondence. He wrote:

Everyone out here with whom I work says I am the most liked person in the Dept. because of my disposition, courteousness and reputation for fairness. My office conduct seems to be excellent. Yet I don't seem to carry the same traits to my home. I know that at home I have too often been fractious, ill-tempered and even crude. I can't for the life of me figure out why, for I love my wife as life itself, and I love my children. I'm surely going to try to do better when I return. . . .[31]

*No decision had yet been taken about the location of the United Nations, but Geneva, Switzerland, seemed a strong possibility at this time.

International service, on which Bunche was about to embark for life, was to put even greater strains on himself, on Ruth, and on their marriage than any they had so far experienced. It was, however, to prove an irresistible call.

10

Building the United Nations

Opting for International Service

Building an international organization on the foundation of the United Nations Charter was the function of the Preparatory Commission of the United Nations, which was to meet in London in the autumn of 1945. On September 11 Bunche was designated as an adviser to Edward R. Stettinius, the United States representative on this commission. Adlai Stevenson was Stettinius' deputy, and many friends from San Francisco were on the delegation. In a very serious-minded team of advisers, Bunche's down-to-earth humor and quiet self-confidence stood out. He treated everyone, from foreign ministers to secretaries and doormen, with the same kindly interest. In fact, he seemed more interested in young and unknown people than in celebrities. He himself was treated with respect, and a hint of trepidation, by the officials of the European colonial powers.

The main work of the Preparatory Commission was carried out by an Executive Committee which consisted, among others, of Philip Noel-Baker and, occasionally, Ernest Bevin for Britain, Andrei Gromyko for the Soviet Union, Lester Pearson for Canada, Jan Masaryk for Czechoslovakia, Wellington Koo for China, and Herbert Evatt for Australia. It was an impressive and unusually effective group, intent on the business at hand and not yet paralyzed by postwar disagreements or the East-West struggle that was to become the Cold War.

Postwar London, where Bunche arrived on September 20, was quite a shock after Washington. He wrote to Joan and Jane:

London isn't the same as when all of us saw it last in 1937. It is a badly battered city, living conditions are bad, food and fuel are scarce, prices are high, but the English people remain the same—proud, brave and reserved. . . . It is grey and somber, like the weather. There is no gaiety. The great hordes of people look grim and weary. . . .[1]

Although the American delegation had PX privileges and free movies, Bunche was always hungry. London was still full of American soldiers. Of Piccadilly, he commented, "What a sight! Too many Yanks and too many loose gals."[2]

The work in the Executive Committee, where Bunche's concern was trusteeship and the setting up of the Secretariat, was nothing like as taxing as at San Francisco: "Plenty of talking and conferring, but not so much writing."[3] The first clouds of the Cold War were already beginning to dim the bright vision of San Francisco. The Soviets were claiming the trusteeship of Libya, and the Council of Foreign Ministers (U.S., U.S.S.R., Britain, and France) was already bogged down on postwar arrangements in Europe.

In the subcommittees of the Executive Committee Bunche found many old friends from previous meetings, and for the first time he was actually representing his own country.

This Conference gives me the very best opportunity I have ever had, since I am the sole US representative in my committee and must rely entirely on my own judgement. I know that I have the respect of every member of the Committee.[4]

The effort to set up the strongest possible Secretariat organization and to establish conditions and rules for an effective Trusteeship Council still provided plenty to fight about. Bunche championed the liberal approach to dependent territories against the rearguard actions of the colonial powers, who were determined to minimize the Trusteeship Council's impact in such matters as the examination of reports, supervisory visits to territories, and the right of the inhabitants to submit petitions. Bunche was equally determined that the new system would be a significant advance over what he had seen of the League of Nations mandates system in French Togo in 1933. It was, he wrote of one meeting,

a one-man fight against the British, French and Dutch. . . . The struggle, which was a battle of wits, knowledge of the Charter and original procedures and ability to do quick and expert drafting, continued until this afternoon. In the end the Committee sustained every important position I had taken. . . .[5]

His performance did not go unnoticed. Bunche told Ruth:

Gerig said that some of the foreign delegates had told him that I was the most able negotiator the Americans had here, and Stettinius asked that that statement be entered into the record.[6]

The Council of Foreign Ministers was considering, among other things, the future of Italy's prewar territories in Africa: Libya, Somaliland, and Eritrea. In Washington on Labor Day, before he left for England, Bunche had received an urgent demand from Secretary of State James F. Byrnes, who had succeeded Stettinius in July 1945 and was on his way to London, for drafts of trusteeship agreements for these territories. Over the holiday weekend Bunche, Larry Finkelstein, and Tom Power each produced the draft of one agreement, Bunche taking Libya. Bunche was surprised to learn that the foreign ministers were considering naming Italy, a wartime enemy, as the administering power, and instructed his colleagues to make the agreements as strong as possible in protecting the rights of the inhabitants and maximizing the supervisory powers of the United Nations. He hoped thus to create the model for an ideal trusteeship agreement.[7] After he reached London he worked on these agreements with the American delegation to the Council of Foreign Ministers. "These agreements are extremely tough drafting and I have worn myself out on them tonight," he told Ruth.[8]

In mid-October Bunche was sent to Paris as a member of the United States delegation to the Conference of the International Labor Organization. The delegation was headed by Frances Perkins, the former secretary of labor under Roosevelt. After the Conference, Perkins paid a warm tribute to Bunche for his work in the committee on dependent territories. This was a difficult committee since the majority of its members represented the colonial powers, for whom better working and social conditions in the colonies would be very expensive.

Mr. Bunche was notable for his helpfulness and his skill in drafting wording which avoided clashes; for his ingenuity in finding proper compromises, and for wasting no words, making few speeches, and industriously keeping the committee at work on its principal objectives. . . .[9]

As Bunche himself put it,

Playing a leading role, speaking plenty, but it's short crisp statements. . . . Haven't lost an amendment since the first one.[10]

"Paris and Parisians very depressed and depressing," he wrote. Like London, Paris was swarming with American soldiers. There were acute shortages of practically everything, and the people were "dispirited, defeated, insecure, hungry and shabby."[11] Once again the food—especially at the Café de La Paix, where the delegations entertained—constantly made Bunche sick, and he longed to leave. He was thus delighted when

Alger Hiss, from Washington, instructed him to return to the United States immediately. After a nightmare three-day journey by air, via Prestwick (twice), Iceland, Labrador, and New York, complicated by weather and constant mechanical breakdowns, he arrived back in Washington on November 10.

Bunche's departure for London in September had provoked unusually strong resentment on Ruth's part. She had felt he had been cold and inattentive when she and Ralph Jr. had seen him off at the station, and a telephone call from La Guardia Airport the next day had made matters worse. "As we were both excited—she from an attempted housebreak the night before—the conversation was neither coherent nor pleasant," Bunche noted.[12] There followed a series of recriminatory letters, and the situation was exacerbated by the fact that Bunche's letters from London were always seriously delayed.

Bunche's success in San Francisco had convinced Ruth that he had fundamentally changed, and she became increasingly suspicious and resentful of his absences from home. For the first time racial resentment began to surface in her letters. "Are your white friends supplanting us?" she wrote on the night Bunche left Washington.[13] She noted again and again the contrast between his behavior at the office and at home.

I know you think you are the Miracle Negro with the whites, but I am sure you are just a novelty and whom they can get two men's work out of one from you, though it may be killing you and hurting your family. . . . Achievement is a grand thing and I am very proud of yours but we shouldn't let it blind us to the values of life. . . .[14]

In Bunche's absence, Ruth ruminated endlessly on both past and future absences.

I must realize that as you grow more important you will be away from us the best part of our lives and I'll always have the responsibility of rearing the three children alone.[15]

Each time you write: "I'll never go again unless I can take you all." How many times have you said this and how many times has it happened? . . . I often wonder if some things you tell me are only pretty words on paper. . . .[16]

Ruth soon apologized for these tirades, saying that everything had piled up—a new baby at the age of thirty-seven, two adolescent girls, a big home that was hard to manage, the difficulty of ever getting out of the house, and, of course, Bunche's absence. Unfortunately, Bunche had not received this conciliatory letter when he responded to its predecessors on September 29, expressing incredulity at Ruth's expressions of distrust.

Ruth, you well know that I am obsessed with a burning desire to excel in everything I undertake. This is why I work so hard in my jobs and missions. I am also always conscious of the handicap of race, and much of my conduct in the presence of whites is not at all the result of any special feeling about them, but a calculated and deliberate intent to prove to them that I am, despite my race, their equal if not their superior in intellect, ability, knowledge and general savoir-faire. As you know, I have no bosom friends in either race and seek none, since I am entirely satisfied to go along with my family alone. . . .

He was also worried about the future and how to pay for college for the girls, and had to make money by making a success of his job.

I have put everything I have into that and have also got no little thrill out of the fact that I have been pioneering and doing the impossible for one of our group. . . .[17]

Ruth's mood alternated, as on future occasions when he was away, between resentment and expressions of love and admiration. She was in a by no means uncommon situation—a loving, extraordinarily supportive wife caught in the domestic drudgery of family life while her husband traveled the world on fascinating assignments. Bunche was always on the lookout for her letters anyway. "Ruth's letters were very cheering," he noted on November 6. "If she would only *trust* me!"[18]

Bunche's life consisted of two principal elements only—his work and his family. He had few hobbies or distractions. He was certainly an old-fashioned husband and expected to be agreed with and obeyed at home. When tired, he could be short-tempered, demanding, and sometimes dismissive and impatient. By the standards of a later generation, he was something of a male chauvinist. He was also an old-fashioned father, fully prepared, when he thought necessary, to apply the strap. Believing that education was the only reliable route to success, he was always insistent on his children's excelling at school, and at times this severely strained his relationship with them.

Being an old-fashioned husband and parent, Bunche had a rigid view of the sanctity of marriage. Although he was an extremely attractive man often surrounded by admiring women, there was never, in all the years, the smallest hint of infidelity. For all the ups and downs and absences, his marriage and his family were sacred, and extramarital affairs, let alone separation or divorce, were inconceivable to him.

Bunche had few close friends outside his family circle. In spite of his periodic statements to the effect that he never took a vacation, the family made a number of expeditions together later on—to Europe, to Hawaii, to Los Angeles, and elsewhere—and as soon as Bunche had relaxed, they almost always had a good time. He loved watching sports on TV or going to games with Ralph Jr. Although he was so often away from it, his family was the center of his life.[19]

Only six weeks elapsed before Bunche was on the road again. He had been appointed as a member of the U.S. delegation to the first session of the United Nations General Assembly, which was to meet in London in January 1946. This time he went by sea, on the *Queen Mary*, with the other members of the delegation, Stettinius, Eleanor Roosevelt, Senators Tom Connally of Texas and Arthur Vandenberg of Michigan, John Foster Dulles, Abe Fortas, and the usual team of advisers. The *Queen Mary* was still a troopship with no amenities, and the voyage was extremely dull. A highlight was "Mrs. FDR promenading in long strides and widow's weeds including a black beret."[20] In delegation meetings it was agreed that one of the main U.S. objectives in London would be to recapture the initiative and leadership on the dependent-territories issue. They were greeted at Southampton by Adlai Stevenson and by the mayor of Southampton in full regalia carrying a huge gold mace. London was bitterly cold, and Bunche immediately fell sick.

Bunche was uneasy about the United States delegation. He felt that Mrs. Roosevelt was the only really conscientious member, with a sense of responsibility and a readiness to listen to expert advisers. James F. Byrnes, the secretary of state, decided everything on a political basis and was despised by the staff. "Byrnes makes his own decisions in his own way and is no team man. . . . The US position is weak, vacillating and stumbling."[21]

Bunche worked most closely with Dulles, who had been assigned the trusteeship and dependent-peoples items. Dulles was "a far cry from Stassen," Bunche wrote.

He doesn't know the subject, doesn't apply himself as Stassen did, and seems to devote most of his time to playing party politics along with Vandenberg. He doesn't follow advice very well, but doesn't know enough to get along without it. . . . He just doesn't have Stassen's ability, astuteness or graciousness. . . . He is a ponderous, dull person without any sparkle.[22]

Vandenberg was "profane, blustering, wisecracking and very unsuccess-fully trying to bludgeon his way through his committee."[23] Abe Fortas was, as usual, a tower of strength, but he resigned on January 14, "a great loss to my cause, as Fortas is the only Trusteeship adviser who thinks as I do."[24]

Bunche's main preoccupation at this first session of the General As-sembly was to protect and strengthen the as yet unformed Trusteeship Council, and to encourage the submission of trusteeship agreements so that the council could be set up. In his speech to the Assembly on January 17, Ernest Bevin announced that Britain would put under trusteeship all the African mandated territories it administered, and that Transjordan would become independent. The question of the mandated territory of Palestine, however, would have to await the findings of the Anglo-Ameri-can mission of inquiry. Soon thereafter, Australia made similar undertak-ings for Nauru and New Guinea, New Zealand for Western Samoa, and Belgium for Ruanda-Urundi. South Africa, which was already suspected of planning to annex the mandated territory of South-West Africa, was nega-tive, along with France, which only came forward some time later on the French mandated territories. There would, however, be a solid basis for the work of the Trusteeship Council once the promised agreements had entered into force.

Working with them in London did not decrease Bunche's doubts about his seniors in the delegation. When Dulles was grounded by weather during a junket to Germany, Bunche spent some exasperating hours coaching Congressman Sol Bloom to make a speech in Dulles' place. Bloom was mainly interested in talking about himself, telling wise-cracks, and boasting of his parliamentary prowess in the House of Repre-sentatives. On the day of the speech, Bloom called to say that his doctor had forbidden him to go out in such weather, so the task fell to Benjamin V. Cohen, Stettinius' legal adviser. Bunche lamented:

Cohen was horribly unimpressive in his halting speech and creaky, quavering voice. He sounded like he was eighty. . . . This diplomacy by amateurs is appalling even to a neophyte like me."[25]

Stettinius replaced Byrnes as the head of delegation on January 26, and the advisers began to be listened to again.

Trygve Lie of Norway was appointed secretary general of the United Nations on January 29, "a big hurdle over." Bunche got his first sight of his future boss at a meeting of the Security Council. "He is a huge, flabby-looking man," who was said by the British foreign office to be "a

politician first, last, and all the time."[26] Bunche was soon approached by a
young Chinese, Ping Chia Kuo, the secretary of the Assembly trusteeship
committee, about becoming assistant director of the Trusteeship Department in the future UN Secretariat. Bunche gave no answer, reflecting that
a nice Chinese boy like Kuo, who knew nothing about the subject, should
be working for *him*, rather than the other way round.[27]

At the first session of the General Assembly of the world organization
it had pioneered, the voice of the United States, unquestionably the
world's most powerful nation, was strangely muted. Ernest Bevin was
already delivering tough anticommunist speeches while the United States
was still nervous about opposing the Soviet Union. "Bevin expressed what
they all feel but are afraid to say," Bunche observed.[28] The Security
Council met for the first time on January 17 and immediately, in the first
of a forty-year series of East-West brawls, became embroiled over Soviet
troops in Azerbaijan, and Western forces in Greece and Indonesia.

For Bunche the most testing task at the Assembly was the framing of
the Assembly's resolution on non-self-governing peoples. Article 73(e) of
the Charter required the colonial powers to transmit to the secretary
general, "for information purposes," reports on economic, social, and educational conditions in their colonies. Bunche knew that if the General
Assembly took no action on, or notice of, such reports, they would simply
be filed, and the procedure would become a meaningless bureaucratic
exercise. It was therefore important to give attention and meaning to the
reports on colonial territories. The United States was not prepared to take
any official action to build on the very limited obligation contained in
Article 73(e). However, according to Lawrence Finkelstein,

Bunche found a way to work informally with the Chinese delegation, which
introduced the proposal that led to the creation, at first, of the Ad Hoc Committee on Information from Non-Self-Governing Territories and, later, of its more
lasting replacement. He thus had a significant part in laying the basis for what
proved to be an important United Nations function affecting all dependent territories in subsequent years.[29]

In its final form the resolution which the Assembly adopted on non-self-
governing territories also required the secretary general to summarize all
the information received from the colonial powers in his annual report.
"Chapter XI [of the UN Charter] thus may be said to constitute something approaching an international charter of colonial administration,"[30]
Bunche told a Canadian audience six months later.

Bunche had also been instrumental in getting included in the non-self-governing-territories resolution a sentence recognizing "the problems of the non-self-governing peoples as of vital concern to the peace and general welfare of the world community."[31] This statement made the future of colonies a political matter as well as a question of economic, social, and educational advancement. Only three days after the Assembly had adopted the resolution, Bunche was gratified to hear the Egyptian delegate, arguing the Indonesian case against the Netherlands in the Security Council, refute Ernest Bevin's argument that the case fell under the domestic-jurisdiction clause of the Charter (Article 2.7) by quoting that very phrase of the Assembly resolution.

It was good to hear my words being used in this important international affair and also to see Chapter XI, which I had drafted to so large an extent, being effectively invoked.[32]

His influence on Dulles had also sufficiently increased that Dulles made a strong speech, drafted by Bunche, in the General Assembly, endorsing the general responsibility of the UN for dependent peoples and "the goals of self-government or independence to be sought under Chapter XI."[33] In a letter to Wilfred Benson of the International Labor Organization, who was soon to become his opposite number for non-self-governing territories in the United Nations Secretariat, Bunche wrote that the trusteeship committee of the Assembly had "adopted a resolution very much broader than that recommended by the Preparatory Commission. . . . Chapter XI ["The Declaration Regarding Non-Self-Governing Territories"] gradually comes into its own."[34]

When Bunche got back to Washington in mid-February he was uncertain about his future. It was generally assumed that he would become a member of Stettinius' team in the U.S. delegation to the United Nations in New York, but he was also being urged to serve in the newly established UN Secretariat, at least during its formative stage. Ben Gerig, in discussing the matter with Alger Hiss, pointed out that the most immediate task was to complete the negotiation of enough trusteeship agreements to ensure that the Trusteeship Council could be set up at the next General Assembly session in September 1946.[35] Getting general agreement on the draft agreements submitted by the British and Belgian governments would be a formidable task, and the Secretariat of the Trusteeship Department also had to be organized. To make matters more complicated, Victor Hoo, the Chinese UN assistant secretary general for trusteeship, was going to be in hospital for most of the summer. Gerig therefore recommended that, although Bunche would formally be assigned to the Stettinius mission, he should be loaned to the Secretariat for some weeks during the summer.

On April 22 Bunche joined the UN Secretariat on temporary loan for six weeks as acting director of the Trusteeship Division. He stipulated only that he bring with him his State Department secretary, Mary Carey, because she was "accustomed to the pace at which I work." At the same time his friend Wilfred Benson was appointed director of the Division of Non-Self-Governing Territories. Benson, who was British, was a tireless crusader for dependent peoples and took much of the heat generated by the resentment of the colonial powers at what they saw as unwarranted UN interference in colonial questions. Both he and Bunche were motivated by the conviction that the colonial age was inevitably coming to an end, and that it must be concluded in the best possible conditions for the dependent peoples themselves. Bunche wrote:

The needs and expectations of all of us in the strenuous days of modern times are great enough, to be sure, but the needs and the expectations of the non-self-governing peoples are greater. The reason is simple. They start with less, and therefore they both need and aspire to more.[36]

Each time Bunche's temporary term of service in the Secretariat expired, Victor Hoo begged for a prolongation, until, in December 1946, Secretary General Trygve Lie finally asked the United States to release Bunche for a permanent post in the Secretariat as Director of the Trusteeship Division. This was a considerable blow to the State Department, and especially to Ben Gerig, Bunche's immediate boss, who told Bunche:

I shall always consider your stay in New York as only temporary. . . . Personally I feel about your going a little as if about two motors had suddenly dropped off our C-54 while crossing the Atlantic. . . . I have never worked with anyone who was more congenial and helpful and, as I look back on our pleasant association together, I recall that we never once had the slightest difference arise between us.[37]

Bunche wrote a heartfelt reply.

As you have often told me, we have certain unique qualities which made it possible for us to work together day in and day out without friction and with perfect understanding. I look upon my new post as a purely temporary assignment and hope that some day, not too distant, I may return to the Department and resume my pleasant associations there.*[38]

For all his affection and respect for Gerig, this letter was disingenuous. Bunche knew very well that working in the State Department would

*Bunche remained in the UN Secretariat until his death in 1971.

not afford him anything like the scope and the possibilities of a senior post in the United Nations. Trusteeship and decolonization were, after all, the ideas to which he had given all his energy and thought in the past two years, and there was now a possibility of turning them into a historic reality. Nor did Bunche relish the prospect of life in segregated Washington in peacetime, especially as a respected public official for whom embarrassing allowances would have to be made, while his family and other Black Americans would still be subject to Jim Crow conditions. "Ruth and I both felt strongly," he wrote to Bill Hastie, "that the children would have much better educational and cultural opportunities in New York than in Washington."*[39]

At this time Bunche still intended to return eventually to academia. He was a full professor on leave from Howard, and offers from other universities were pending. He certainly wanted to believe that, when the work of setting up the UN was done, he would become a professor again. Meanwhile he settled into his work at the United Nations, then temporarily located at Hunter College in the Bronx,† with his customary energy and thoroughness. He had already shown, at San Francisco and in London, how much one motivated and skillful middle-level official could do to advance the cause of dependent peoples, an issue which he regarded as "a searching test of the ability of the post-war world to give effect to the ideals and principles for which World War II was fought to its victorious conclusion."[41] In the United Nations he was, at last, a senior official in charge of his own division and, in the absence of Victor Hoo, an influential adviser to the secretary general.

When Bunche took over the Trusteeship Division there was still no sign of the trusteeship agreements that had been promised at the Assembly session in London earlier in the year, and without them the Trusteeship Council could not be set up. There was nothing in the Charter to authorize the secretary general to take an initiative in such a matter, but in early June Bunche proposed that Trygve Lie should formally ask the mandatory powers to transmit trusteeship agreements to him by September 3.

*"In Washington, the Nation's capital, Lincoln the Great Emancipator sits majestically in his great armchair behind the marble pillars, and overlooks a city which does not yet admit his moral dictum that the Negro is a man; a city in which no Negro can live and work with dignity; a city which, administered by Congress itself, subjects one-fourth of its citizens to segregation, discrimination and daily humiliation. Washington is this nation's greatest shame precisely because it is governed by Congress and is the capital of a great democracy. Washington, of all American cities, should symbolize and vitalize that democracy."[40]

†Now Lehman College. The UN moved to the Sperry Gyroscope Factory at Lake Success, Long Island, in July 1947, and to its permanent headquarters in Manhattan in 1951.

Trygve Lie enthusiastically agreed to this idea, and the letter went out at the end of June. Bunche's staff also took the initiative in preparing questionnaires and rules for the handling of petitions, and in making preparations for the council's visits to Trust Territories. Bunche and Benson followed up the Assembly's resolution on non-self-governing territories by getting Lie to ask all member states for their views on what were the non-self-governing territories referred to in Chapter XI, to enumerate those under their jurisdiction, and to indicate the form in which they wished to supply the UN with information on the territories. Thus, at the outset, Bunche set a tradition of activism by the Secretariat in trusteeship and decolonization matters.[42]

The General Assembly met in the converted skating rink at Flushing Meadows, New York, on October 23, 1946, and was formally welcomed to the United States, in a stirring address, by President Truman. Bunche was the secretary of the subcommittee which examined each trusteeship agreement before it was passed on to the Assembly for approval. The atmosphere had greatly deteriorated since the London meeting in January. Field Marshal Smuts, in an attempt to have the territory incorporated into South Africa, was now refusing to convert the mandate of South-West Africa to a trusteeship arrangement, a move that enraged Jawaharlal Nehru's sister, Mrs. V. L. Pandit, who was representing India. The Soviets, trying to appear as the champion of dependent peoples, had become abusive and uncooperative. Nonetheless, by November there were eight trusteeship agreements before Bunche's committee, six in Africa—Tanganyika, Togoland, British Cameroons, French Cameroons, French Togoland, and Ruanda-Urundi—and two in the Pacific—New Guinea and Western Samoa. The General Assembly finally approved the agreements on December 13, allowing for the formal setting up of the Trusteeship Council on December 14. The negotiation and processing of these agreements had been a backbreaking task for Bunche, and Lie's executive assistant, Andrew Cordier, wrote to him, "if it had not been for your superlative services it is really doubtful whether we should have a Trusteeship Council at this moment."[43]

In the following year, much of Bunche's time was spent in running the Trusteeship Council, which met for the first time on March 26, 1947. The people of the eight Trust Territories totaled at that time some fourteen million, so the council's responsibility was considerable. Its work in setting living conditions, hearing petitions, and sending visiting missions was also—as Trygve Lie, in a speech written by Bunche, told the Council's first meeting—"of great significance to hundreds of millions of people in other non-self-governing territories which today lie outside the trusteeship system."[44] Not for the first or the last time, Bunche was critical of his own compatriots. As secretary of the Trusteeship Council, Bunche found Francis Sayre, its first president,

obstinate and not a little thick. . . . He's ponderous, voluble and pompous: acts like a nervous old lady in the Chair. . . . Doesn't *savez* French and though he has me taking notes on French discourses, he nods understandingly while they speak—for the benefit of the gallery.[45]

Ruth was still living in Washington, and Bunche commuted there for weekends. This was unsatisfactory for everyone, and in November 1947, after Bunche's return from his first stint in Palestine, the beloved house at 1510 Jackson Street in Washington was sold, and the family moved to New York. They settled into an apartment in a new development, Parkway Village, on the Grand Central Parkway, relatively near Lake Success. Parkway Village was at that time almost entirely occupied by members of the Secretariat and delegations to the UN.

Racial pressures in New York were far less open than in Washington but by no means nonexistent. One of Bunche's first acts when he joined the Secretariat was to protest about the space for the designation of race on the UN's personnel forms, which had been copied from United States models. He noted how conscious of color and race New Yorkers were as they watched the UN's limousines, and how, in contrast, the non-Americans on his UN staff seemed to be oblivious of racial differences. When he decided to send the girls away to school, the vice-principal of the George School, a Quaker school in Bucks County, Pennsylvania, informed him that "as a matter of procedure we have never enrolled a child of Negro background."[46]

Trygve Lie consulted Bunche about the difficulty of finding housing, especially for nonwhite members of the staff. One reason the Bunches were in Parkway Village was that New York Life and Metropolitan Life Insurance, which owned Fresh Meadows and Peter Cooper Village in New York City, the other two UN housing projects, could deny occupancy to nonwhites. Bunche recorded with sardonic amusement the occasions when well-meaning colleagues who wanted to work for him assured him that they would "work like a nigger." He continued to have problems in trains and restaurants south of Washington, and urged that the UN, as far as possible, not do business with companies or firms which violated the fundamental Charter principles of equality of race, sex, language, or religion on which the United Nations was founded.

Although he still had some reservations, Bunche had thrown in his lot with the United Nations, at least for the period during which the trusteeship system was being set up. He was soon to be diverted from this task by the problems of a League of Nations mandate which never became a United Nations Trust Territory—Palestine.

11

Palestine

A Ghostwriting Harlot

Of all the problems that have faced the international community since World War II few have proved as resistant to a peaceful solution as the question of Palestine. After the Balfour Declaration of 1917 established a Jewish homeland in Palestine, the relationship of Jews and Arabs in Palestine had grown increasingly tense. The persecution and attempted extermination of the Jews of Europe by Hitler during the Second World War vastly increased the number of Jews desiring to settle in Palestine, and also the hostility of the Palestinian Arabs. The mandatory power for Palestine, Great Britain, desperately struggling to recover from the strains and losses of World War II, found itself universally pressured and squeezed by the conflicting demands of Jews and Arabs in Palestine and by their respective allies and sympathizers in the outside world.

In the House of Commons on January 31, 1947, Winston Churchill dramatically voiced Britain's dilemma in a devastating attack on the Labour government's record in Palestine and on its alleged cowardice in dealing with Jewish terrorists who had taken British soldiers hostage.

How long are you going to stay there, and stay there for what? Is it in order that, on a threat of killing hostages, we show ourselves unable to execute a sentence duly pronounced by the competent tribunal? Let us stay in the Canal Zone and have no further interest in the strategic position of Palestine. I never thought we had a strategic interest there. We have broken our pledges to the Jews. . . . It is said that we must stay, because if we go there will be a civil war. I think it very likely, but is that a reason why we should stay? We do not propose to stay in India. The responsibility for stopping civil war in Palestine ought to be borne by the United Nations and not by this overburdened country. . . . We should definitely give notice that unless the United States of America comes in with us on a fifty-fifty basis in all the bloodshed, odium, trouble and worry, we will lay our mandate at the feet of the United Nations.[1]

On April 2, the British government, as a first step toward dumping the Palestine question on the United Nations, asked for a special session of the General Assembly to consider the question of "constituting and instructing a special committee to prepare for consideration of the question of Palestine." The Assembly decided, on May 15, to set up an eleven-member Special Committee on Palestine (UNSCOP) with "the fullest powers to ascertain and record facts and to investigate all questions and issues relevant to the problem of Palestine." Trygve Lie appointed Victor Hoo, the assistant secretary general for trusteeship, as his representative for this Committee. Although Hoo had a Mexican deputy, Alfonso García Robles, who later shared the Nobel Peace Prize for work on disarmament, Lie obviously realized that some heavyweight assistance was going to be needed. He therefore appointed Bunche as "special assistant to the representative of the Secretary-General." For Bunche and Ruth, who had planned a summer vacation in Colorado and with the Johnson family in Los Angeles, this was an unwelcome surprise and a personal disappointment.

The caliber of the committee, the first official body in the seemingly endless involvement of the UN in the Palestine question, left much to be desired. With its membership of six diplomats, four jurists (which Bunche felt was too many), and one professor, Bunche characterized it as "just about the worst group I have ever had to work with. If they do a good job it will be a real miracle."[2] The committee was quite obviously incapable of writing its own report, or even of making its own arrangements. It recognized this itself at the outset by making Bunche, even though he was a member of the Secretariat, the chairman of its subcommittee on arrangements, and in the end he did virtually all the report-writing as well. Some of the top Secretariat members were not much better than the committee members.

I'm disgusted with the people I have to work with—both Committee members and Secretariat—they are all so petty, so vain, so striving and not infrequently either vicious or stupid.[3]

Victor Hoo was a vain, pleasure-loving lightweight. The chairman of the committee, Judge Emil Sandström of Sweden, was a charming and cultured man, but a weak and indecisive chairman. The Indian delegate, Sir Abdur Rahman, had "more bark than bite; a likable old fellow" but

MEDITERRANEAN

Sidon

LEBANON

Damascus

Tyre

SYRIA

El Quneitra

Acre
GALILEE
Safad

Haifa

Lake Tiberias

SEA

Nazareth

Es Suweida

Der'a

Irbid

Jenin

Tulkarm

Mafraq

Nablus

Jordan River

Tel Aviv–Jaffa

Es Salt

Ramallah

Amman

Jerusalem
Jericho

El Azraq

Bethlehem

DEAD SEA

Gaza

Hebron

Khan Yunis

JORDAN

Rafah

Beersheba

El Karak

El 'Arish

NEGEV

El Jafr

Ma'an

THE UNITED NATIONS
PARTITION PLAN (1947)

EGYPT

Jewish State

Umreshresh

Arab State

Aqaba

International Zone

SINAI

Gulf of
Aqaba

was strongly and outspokenly anti-Jewish. Mr. Justice Ivan Rand, the
Canadian delegate, was "grumbling, neurotic, egocentric and garrulous
. . . a one-man sabotage team. He relates every problem to Canada and
talks incessantly."[4] Enrique Fabregat of Uruguay, already noted in the
UN for the length and fatuousness of his speeches, was a "Latin buffoon,
without trying or knowing."[5] Jorge García Granados of Guatemala was,
Bunche felt, unscrupulous and unprincipled as well as "petty, vain and
garrulous."[6] Karel Lisicky, the Polish member, was "alternatively bellicose
and wise-cracking; completely negative: self conscious."[7] Nicolaas Blom,
the Dutch representative, Bunche characterized as a "tight-fisted, not
very bright Dutchman; rather a lightweight,"[8] and he noted with some
glee that, on a visit to the Church of the Holy Sepulchre in Jerusalem,
Blom had managed to fall into the tomb of Nicodemus.

On the other hand, Alberto Ulloa, the Peruvian member, was "quiet,
self-effacing, highly intelligent and knows what he stands for."[9] Nasrollah
Entezam, the Iranian, was "polished, not deep but has know-how; as a
Muslim he is fair but very much on the spot."[10] Valedo Simic, the Yugoslav, was "quiet, dignified, good-humored, no temperament, very intelligent and earnest."[11] John Hood, the Australian, was "intelligent but has
no force,"[12] and tended to drink too much, while his eccentric assistant,
Sam Atyeo, was a bull in a china shop who had invented nicknames for all
the members (Pre-Fabregat, Shifting Sandström, Hoo Stole My Brains
Away, Hoo Leans on Bunche all Day, etc.) which inevitably became generally known and caused much distress.

This very mixed crew were embarking on an immensely important
and difficult, if not impossible, task. The Arab Higher Committee, which
was supposed to represent the interests of the Palestinians, had already
announced that it would not meet with the committee, because the
United Nations, by refusing to adopt the "natural course" of terminating
the mandate and declaring independence for Palestine, had ignored
Palestinian rights. The Arab Committee called for a general boycott of
UNSCOP among the Arabs of Palestine. On the Jewish side, the committee's arrival in Palestine coincided with a strong reaction by Jewish underground fighters to British measures against Jewish terrorism. This often
assumed the form of taking British soldiers as hostages for Jewish terrorists
under death sentence. Apart from terrorism, the greatest problem for the
British authorities was illegal Jewish immigration. The immigrant ship
Exodus (formerly *President Garfield*) arrived in Haifa and was sent away
by the British during UNSCOP's sojourn in Palestine. There was also a
major split between the Jewish Agency, which officially represented the

Jews of Palestine and favored partition, and the more extreme under-ground elements, the Irgun Zvai Leumi and the Stern Gang, which were violently opposed to it.

The British authorities, in their own reserved way, also caused great problems for UNSCOP. They insisted, against the wishes of the committee, on giving testimony only in private. They wished to be informed in advance of whom the committee was interviewing, a manifest impossibility in relation to groups like the Irgun, which had been outlawed and was being hunted by the British.

At the heart of the Palestine problem was Jerusalem. The ancient city contained layer upon layer of history—Jewish, Roman, Muslim, Arab, Christian, Turkish, British. It was a place of unique significance for three great religions. Exiles pined for its golden stones and its walled mysteries, its pellucid light, its sparkling air. It was a paradise held hostage by the passions of conquerors and prophets and by the caprices of history, a magical city, doomed to strife and hatred.

When the committee arrived in Palestine by air on June 14 Jerusalem was an armed camp.

British are everywhere and they all carry guns. As you go thru the streets you're constantly stopped by sentries and control centers and required to show your pass. Buildings are surrounded by barbed wire, pillboxes and road-blocks are abundant. Armed guards patrol the building in which we live.[13]

On the committee's first day of work, June 16, 1947, the British heightened the tension by sentencing five Jewish Irgun terrorists to death, and two to fifteen years in prison. The locals, however, told Bunche that things had become a great deal quieter since UNSCOP's arrival. In the next six weeks the committee traveled two thousand miles within Palestine, visited Lebanon, Syria, and Transjordan, and investigated displaced-persons camps in Germany and Austria. Bunche's first task was to organize this intensive itinerary.

After being received by the British high commissioner, Sir Alan Cunningham, at Government House, and touring the holy places, the committee set about its program of field trips and interviews. Bunche was particularly impressed by Chaim Weizmann, the "great old man" of Israel, then seventy-four years old. After he and Sandström had lunched with Weizmann in Weizmann's charming house in Rehovoth, Weizmann asked Bunche to return alone for lunch on Sunday, July 13. Gershon Agronsky, the editor of the *Palestine Post,* and Isaiah Berlin, the celebrated Oxford philosopher whom Bunche had met in Washington during the war, were also there. Weizmann was evidently anxious to get his moderate views firmly across to UNSCOP. "The Jewish Agency boys," Bunche noted, "obviously have it figured out that I will prepare the first draft of the report and are cultivating me steadily."[14]

Some of the interviews were more exciting than others, because they had to be undertaken clandestinely and even with some element of risk. Such efforts included visits to the headquarters of the Haganah, the mainstream Jewish military organization, where Bunche met Moshe Dayan and Yigael Yadin for the first time. Far more complicated was a call on Menachem Begin, the leader of the Irgun Zvai Leumi, which Bunche described as "my most exciting adventure in Palestine."[15] Since Begin, as the leading terrorist, was underground and had a price on his head, this was no ordinary interview. It was arranged through Carter Davidson, the Associated Press correspondent, who communicated the plan to Sandström in the men's room of the British Sporting Club in Jaffa, where the Committee was having lunch.[16] Bunche, Sandström, and Hoo pulled out of the UNSCOP convoy visiting the docks and booked into the Park Hotel in Tel Aviv, ostensibly to have a swim in the Mediterranean. Davidson contacted them there and, after dinner, drove them to the apartment of the poet Yaacov Cahan in Bialik Street, where Begin was awaiting them.

Bunche took the record of this three-hour meeting and asked most of the questions or prompted Sandström to ask them. The Irgun position was uncompromising and diametrically opposed to the views of Weizmann and the Jewish Agency. Eretz Israel, the homeland of the Jewish people, comprised, Begin told them, Palestine on both sides of the Jordan, including Transjordan itself, because the forefathers of the Jews, three thousand years before, had conquered Palestine from what was now Transjordan, crossing the Jordan from east to west. Irgun aimed to create a Hebrew republic under a democratic government in this entire territory. The millions of Jews who wished to come to Palestine should be repatriated immediately, a move that was only being prevented by illegal British rule and the British armed forces. There was enough room in Palestine for everyone, both Jews and Arabs. Since Britain was controlling Palestine by force, Irgun could only achieve its aims by force. Begin was strongly critical of the Jewish Agency's complicity with the British. The Irgun rejected partition, which would merely put the Jews in a ghetto behind an artificial boundary, and would fight against it, since all Palestine was Jewish territory by right. Begin dismissed as mere British propaganda the notion that the Arabs would oppose Jewish immigration or that the Arabs would go to war. Sounding a note often heard from subsequent leaders of liberation movements, he concluded, "We are not just a handful of fanatics. We exist and gain strength, even though our struggle brings troubles to the Jewish people. We fight for freedom."[17] Begin agreed that there should be no publicity about the meeting: "Irgun always keeps its word," he said. "Ask the British; they will tell you so."[18]

Bunche arranged for the Irgun to approve his record of the meeting, and when they returned the script they also arranged for a contact with Bunche when he got to Geneva, the password being "Regards from Mr. F."

The meetings with the Jewish Agency were more down-to-earth and less conspiratorial. Both Ben-Gurion and Weizmann made highly persuasive presentations. After they had presented the Agency's position publicly, Aubrey (later Abba) Eban, Moshe Shertok (later Sharett), and David Horowitz sought out Bunche to elaborate the proposals for partition that the Jewish Agency would find acceptable.

Bunche was bothered at the imbalance between Jewish and Arab presentations in Jerusalem, and he managed to talk privately to Hussein al-Khalidi of the Arab Higher Committee. The imbalance was to some extent rectified by the committee's visits to Beirut, where it had agreed to meet Arab leaders, as well as to Damascus and Amman. King Abdullah of Transjordan had insisted on UNSCOP's coming to Amman, and the committee flew there from Beirut on July 24 in three flimsy-looking DeHavilland aircraft flown by British pilots. "Crafty Abdullah," Bunche noted, "seeing the possibility of enlarging his domain by partition of Palestine, wants to present his case at Amman rather than in Beirut."[19] Like Weizmann, Abdullah stressed the urgency of solving the Palestine problem. He was good-humored, moderate, and impressively intelligent in his informal talks with the members of UNSCOP, saying that there were many possible solutions but what was necessary was to adopt one and enforce it. He parried with great skill all efforts to pin him down, saying that if the Jews had been treated justly elsewhere, there would be no Jewish, and therefore no Palestine, problem.

After the meeting Abdullah called Bunche back to look at a picture of his father, who, he said, was buried in Jerusalem and had told him to look after Palestine. The king asked Bunche where he was from and expressed surprise on learning that he was American, saying "that I might be taken for an Arab. I assured him that there were all complexions in my country, and he laughed."[20]

On July 25 they left at last for Geneva to write the committee's report. After trying to digest all the conflicting statements he had heard and the contrasts he had seen, Bunche was not sanguine about UNSCOP's task.

One thing seems sure, this problem can't be solved on the basis of abstract justice, historical or otherwise. Reality is that both Arabs and Jews are here and intend to stay. Therefore, in any "solution" some group, or at least its claim, is bound to get hurt. Danger in any arrangement is that a caste system will develop with backward Arabs as the lower caste.[21]

Like everyone else who has tried to tackle the Palestine problem, Bunche felt increasingly frustrated. He wrote to Ben Gerig:

The longer we stay, the more confused all of us get. The only thing that seems clear to me after five weeks in Palestine is that the British have made a terrible mess of things here. About the only subject on which both Arabs and Jews seem to be in agreement is that the British must go.[22]

He told Jim Green, "I am now a Near East expert, completely befuddled."[23]

Bunche was by now convinced that any "solution" would inevitably involve bloodshed, and the responsibility was already weighing heavily on him. He wrote to Ruth:

. . . the mental strain is the heaviest I have ever experienced. This Palestine problem is so complicated and serious that many of us walk about in a continuous state of frustration.[24]

It was hot in Geneva, and Bunche sometimes crossed the street from his hotel to a park bench on the edge of the lake to work.

A couple of weeks in Geneva is as long as anyone ought to remain here, beautiful vacuum that it is. You remember how I used to hope that UN hdqs. would be in Geneva? . . . I've revised my opinion on that now. . . . It is like being out of the world altogether and terribly boring—the climate is bad too. . . .[25]

Bunche was tired and was, for the first time, having serious trouble with his eyes, which were inflamed from the heat and dust of the Near East. He was even reduced to listening to the band in the park for several evenings because he could not work. His cousin Jane Johnson, who was on a student tour of Europe, visited him in Geneva, and Bunche greatly enjoyed taking her out to dinner.

As the time for decision neared, the mediocrity of the UNSCOP membership became a serious problem. It was a problem which worried other people besides Bunche, including the Jewish Agency representatives, David Horowitz and Aubrey Eban, who were clearly desperate for a decision on partition as soon as possible. The Irgun contacted Bunche through a mysterious woman's voice on the telephone saying, "I have regards from Fred." After an elaborately arranged rendezvous at the main Geneva railroad station, he was driven to see "Fred," who, it turned out, only wanted to denounce the Jewish Agency for cowardice and to say that the Irgun would never accept partition.

UNSCOP's lack of leadership or strong personalities made it impossible for the committee itself to make progress on its report. "The Secretariat obviously must show more initiative," Bunche wrote, "or this will be a fiasco." Sandström had taken to submitting long incoherent papers of his own, which Bunche found impossible to revise. He therefore got Hoo and García Robles to agree that the Secretariat should produce a draft of the committee's report.

The committee itself was agreed on independence and the termination of the British mandate, but on virtually nothing else. Bunche therefore began writing into the early hours of each morning. By August 10 he had finished a paper on partition and written the outline of a proposal for a federal state, "but it is not very convincing. No 'solution' is."[26] The more he worked with UNSCOP, the more he came to distrust, perhaps excessively, the motives of its members.

The obvious trouble is that a number of the committee members and alternatives are anti-Semitic and will support Jewish Agency claims for a Jewish State as a means of dumping world Jewry on the Arabs. This goes for Rand, the Canadian delegate, Mohn, the Norwegian, the Australians, the Dutch and the Guatemalans.[27]

Bunche was beginning seriously to doubt that UNSCOP could ever agree on a report on Palestine. The committee's dithering was also having bad effects farther afield, because the journalists who were in Geneva to cover UNSCOP had nothing to do but speculate. Bunche, for example, found himself being written up as anti-Semitic in the Hebrew press in Palestine on the fantastic grounds that he didn't want a Jewish independent state because Black Americans would then ask for their own state too. Fortunately, in Constantin Stavropoulos, the legal counsel, and John Reedman, the economic adviser, he had two excellent colleagues. It was Reedman who informed the committee that if partition was to mean two viable independent states they would have to be linked by an economic-

and-customs union. In other words, there was, realistically, no such thing as pure partition.

On August 15, in desperation, Sandström asked Bunche for a draft of a confederation (partition) scheme for the committee to discuss the following day. Bunche completed this task at 2:30 A.M. This was the first time the committee had ever been able to get down to a concrete discussion, and they welcomed the draft enthusiastically.

The improvement was short-lived. The chairman "lets the Committee wander in circles and never ties anything up,"[28] so that meetings were a total waste of time, leaving all the individual members to ride their personal hobbyhorses and disrupt the proceedings still further. On August 18, Bunche, totally exasperated, informed Victor Hoo that he was leaving in a week no matter what happened. He proposed that UNSCOP should divide itself into three subcommittees—on boundaries, on the structure of a confederation (partition), and on a federal structure. Bunche worked with the group on confederation until the federal-structure group asked him to draft their report, which he did overnight. The federal-structure subcommittee accepted it. Unfortunately, in Bunche's absence Judge Rand more or less destroyed the subcommittee on confederation. "He's the most irascible, voluble, argumentative old cuss I've ever seen," Bunche noted, "and knows nothing to boot. . . . Canada could not possibly have done worse."[29]

Bunche then had to draft a trusteeship agreement for Jerusalem for the group that was considering the holy places. He was exhausted, his eyes were failing, and he was acutely homesick. Nevertheless, on August 25, besides alternatively assisting the federal, the partition, and the holy-places groups, he wrote the arguments for the partition report. "They were about as good as those I wrote for the federal state. A ghostwriting harlot!"[30] He then spent the whole afternoon revising the federal report, which was to become the formal minority report. The next day, August 26, was also devoted to writing and drafting, with an occasional visit to the committee room to observe the disgraceful antics of the partition (confederation) group, some members of which were walking out or threatening to switch to the federalist minority, who had already approved their report.

Bunche, by now totally disgusted, told Hoo he was leaving the next day. Hoo, realizing that any hope of a report would be dashed by Bunche's departure, protested strongly, and it was finally agreed that Bunche would leave on August 29. Perhaps because of this exchange, on the afternoon of

August 27 the committee suddenly agreed to put everything to a vote. This done, the main chapters of the report could be written. Bunche wrote all three of them, working without a break from 6:00 P.M. until 6:00 A.M. on the morning of August 28. He then packed, on the off-chance that he could catch a plane later in the day.

What UNSCOP had voted on was a partition plan with an economic union, but without prescribing specific boundaries. The Arab and Jewish States were to become independent after a two-year transitional period. Seven members voted for it (Canada, Czechoslovakia, Guatemala, Netherlands, Peru, Sweden, and Uruguay). Three members (India, Iran, and Yugoslavia) voted for the plan for a federal state, of which the Arab and Jewish states would be provinces with a common capital in Jerusalem. The Australian member abstained on both votes. Since the partitionists couldn't agree either on precise boundaries or on the status of Jerusalem, they were not very elated. Bunche commented, "Their artificial union—partition—won't have a shoo-in in the General Assembly. Federation won't either."[31]

Bunche continued to draft the rest of the committee's report, its recommendations, a report on Arab and Jewish claims, and, with Reedman, a note on the viability of two states in Palestine. Having finished his work at last, he found, to his exasperation, that his flight to New York had been canceled. He finally left on August 30, the day before UNSCOP formally adopted the report he had written. He reached Washington via Prestwick, Shannon, Gander, Detroit, and New York on September 1. "And now to rejoin my family! The Palestine episode is over," he noted with an unusual lack of realism.

On August 31 UNSCOP published its report, which consisted of the majority report on partition, the minority report on a federal state, and eleven unanimous recommendations. These included the termination of the British mandate; the responsibility of the United Nations for administering Palestine in the transitional period and preparing it for independence; the preservation of the sacred character of the holy places; urgent international arrangements for some 250,000 distressed European Jews in assembly centers; and the economic unity of Palestine.

Bunche was by no means happy with this outcome, although it was largely his own handiwork. He wrote to Ruth:

I have written two solutions this week . . . and they are the only solutions which are being considered. So in any case, whatever the solution decided upon . . . the basic paper will have been mine. . . . I'm not at all satisfied with my scheme [the partition plan], but this is the sort of problem for which no really satisfactory solution is possible. The best that can be done is a reasonable and workable compromise, and I worked out my proposal on that basis.[32]

Both the majority and the minority reports were rejected by Arab leaders and all sectors of Arab opinion. Any idea of a Jewish state was denounced. "Any attempt," the Arab Higher Committee proclaimed, "to impose a solution contrary to the Arabs' birthright will lead to trouble, bloodshed, and probably a third world war."[33] The Zionist General Council, on the other hand, approved the majority report by a vote of sixty-one to six at its meeting in Zurich on September 3.

British and American officials alike considered the partition plan both unworkable and unfair to the Arabs of Palestine.* Loy Henderson, director of the Office of Near East and African Affairs in the U.S. State Department, warned the U.S. delegation to the General Assembly that the plan would have to be implemented by force, resulting in much bloodshed and suffering and in all probability making the Palestine problem "permanent and still more complicated in the future."[35] There was, however, increasing pressure from public opinion in the United States to support the majority plan, which provided for a Jewish state, and the United States embraced the partition plan on October 11.

Bunche played little part in the follow-up of the Palestine report in the General Assembly. He was only too glad to be done with UNSCOP, to return home, and to resume his work in the Trusteeship Department. His absence had aroused Ruth's strong resentment. He had missed their seventeenth wedding anniversary, and she had once again been left alone with two teenage girls and with no plans for the summer. The mails from Palestine were slow and unreliable, but Bunche's letters, full of interest and activity, may well have made matters worse. Ruth's constant catalogue of complaints about the girls caused Bunche to write:

It seems we have really failed in rearing those two. Maybe it has been because I have been away so much but I doubt it. My presence only puts more fear in them. . . . I hate to admit failure and if you didn't have to suffer the pangs of childbearing I'd like to start all over and see if we couldn't do a better job with Ralph and whatever the next one would be.[36]

Ruth's letters were bitter and often acrimonious.

*Secretary of State (since January 1947) George Marshall had carefully read both the majority and the minority reports and was surprised at the quality of the analysis—"an unwitting tribute to Ralph Bunche, who had drafted both. . . ."[34]

I've an excellent article on the arteries that I'm saving for you. . . . The description somehow fits you: "hypertensive man almost invariably fits into a pattern—restless, ambitious, energetic go-getter, works ceaselessly and with tremendous purpose and almost never takes a vacation . . . body build—short, stocky and broad-chested . . ." How's your blood pressure, Ralph?[37]

She again catalogued old grievances and contrasted the glamour of Ralph's life with the labor and tedium of her own. Meanwhile, Bunche, under severe pressure in Jerusalem, blew up.

I received your letter written July 2. I am returning it enclosed. . . . I was not angry at the things you said in it—just disgusted and amazed that you could be so vicious. . . .[38]

This letter crossed with an abject apology from Ruth for her previous letters, urging him to ignore what she had said. The storm passed, but the resentment at Bunche's repeated absences remained and increased, along with a nagging worry that in some way they had both failed Joan and Jane. At least Bunche was at home from September until the New Year.

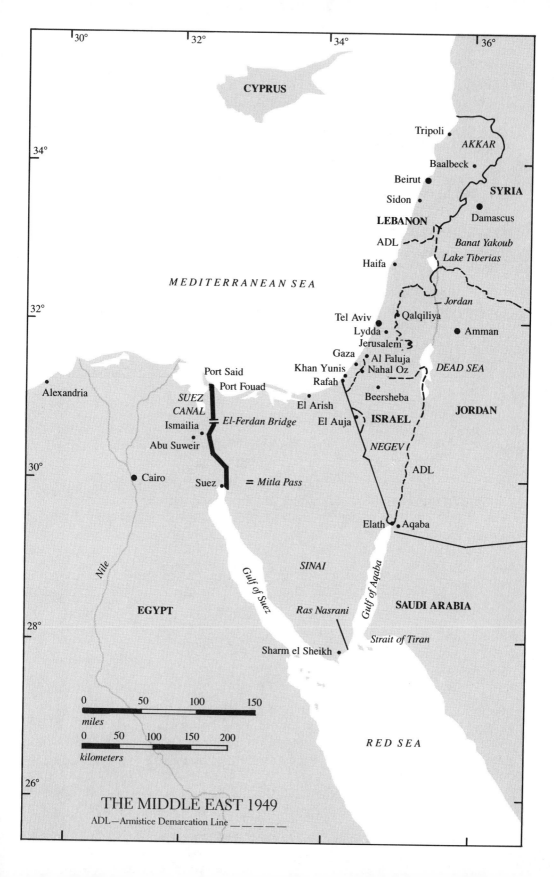

30°   32°   34°   36°

CYPRUS

34°

Tripoli ●
AKKAR

Baalbeck ●

Beirut ●

Sidon ●
SYRIA

LEBANON
Damascus ●

ADL ‒ ‒ ‒
Banat Yakoub
Lake Tiberias

Haifa ●

MEDITERRANEAN SEA

32°
Jordan

Tel Aviv ● ● Qalqiliya

Lydda ●
Jerusalem
● Amman

Gaza ● ● Al Faluja

Khan Yunis ● Nahal Oz
DEAD SEA

Port Said   Rafah ●
Port Fouad   Beersheba ●   JORDAN

Alexandria ●   El Arish ●

SUEZ   El Auja ●
CANAL   *El-Ferdan Bridge*   ISRAEL

Ismailia ●   *NEGEV*
Abu Suweir ●

30°   ADL

Cairo ●

Suez ●   = *Mitla Pass*

Elath ● ● Aqaba

SINAI

Nile   *Gulf of Suez*   *Gulf of Aqaba*   SAUDI ARABIA

EGYPT   *Ras Nasrani*   *Strait of Tiran*

28°

Sharm el Sheikh ●

0   50   100   150
miles

0   50   100   150   200   *RED SEA*
kilometers

26°

THE MIDDLE EAST 1949

ADL—Armistice Demarcation Line ‒ ‒ ‒ ‒ ‒ ‒

12

With the Mediator in Palestine

A Friendship and a Tragedy

On September 23, 1947, the United Nations General Assembly set up a committee to consider UNSCOP's report and the Palestine situation in general. The committee became the focus of intensive lobbying both by the advocates of partition and by the Arabs who opposed it. Representing the two opposites were Chaim Weizmann of the Jewish Agency and Jamal el-Husseini of the Arab Higher Committee, and it was they who summed up the two cases at the conclusion of the committee's debate on October 13. On November 25, the committee approved the partition plan by a vote of twenty-five to thirteen with seventeen abstentions. This was just short of the required two-thirds majority, and the lack of only one vote prevented the committee from approving an Arab proposal to request an advisory opinion from the International Court of Justice as to whether the General Assembly had the right to partition Palestine against the wishes of the majority of its inhabitants.

An immense lobbying effort was deployed to secure the necessary extra votes for the partition plan when it came to a vote in the plenary session of the General Assembly. Haiti and Liberia, which had abstained in the *ad hoc* committee, and the Philippines, which had not participated, were main targets of the lobbying, and all three voted for partition in the Assembly vote on November 29. In all, seven of the seventeen countries which had abstained on November 25 voted for partition on November 29. The historic decision on Palestine was a very close-run thing, and, as Bunche had predicted, partition was no "shoo-in."

On November 29, with thousands of spectators from the largest Jewish city in the world trying to get into the temporary Assembly hall, the converted ice-skating rink at Flushing Meadows, the majority plan for partition was approved by thirty-three votes to thirteen with ten abstentions. All Arab and Muslim states voted against it and then walked out. The United Kingdom abstained on the grounds that, as the mandatory power, it would only give effect to a plan that was agreed upon by both Arabs and Jews and which did not have to be imposed by force. In Palestine the Arabs declared a three-day general strike, while the Jewish population rejoiced.

The November 29 decision of the General Assembly set out the boundaries of the Arab and Jewish states and the city of Jerusalem, as well as a plan for economic union.[1] It also set up a timetable for the transition from mandate to partition. The British would leave not later than August 1, 1948, and the Arab and Jewish states would come into existence within two months of the British withdrawal. To supervise the transitional period a five-member UN Palestine Commission would be set up, to which the British would progressively turn over the administration. The commission would establish the frontiers of the Arab and Jewish states and the city of Jerusalem and set up councils of government in each state, which would in turn progressively take over from the commission, which would also prepare the machinery for economic union. The fact that the Arabs had already violently denounced this splendidly logical program and the British had said they would not give effect to it made the whole exercise somewhat academic.

Nonetheless, the commission (Bolivia, Czechoslovakia, Denmark, Panama, and the Philippines) was duly constituted, and Trygve Lie appointed Bunche as its Principal Secretary, "the single bright element in the picture," as Lie later put it.[2] The commission held its first meeting in New York on January 6, 1948. Until its demise in May it was, even by United Nations standards, an unusually forlorn exercise. The next few months witnessed a display of American inconsistency, British evasiveness, Arab intransigence, Jewish determination, and violence in Palestine itself, which steadily undermined both the capacity of the mandatory power to govern, and any possibility of realizing the partition plan.

Bunche knew better than anyone the possible pitfalls and disasters of this situation, and he devoted his energies to advising Lie and the commission on how at least to avoid the worst. He was also aware of the very poor quality of the commission itself. His deputy, the perceptive Spaniard Pablo de Azcarate, wrote:

If the plan was defective, and if its adoption by the General Assembly took place in conditions which were far from ideal, what barred the last hope of seeing it executed was the Palestine Commission. . . .[3]

Azcarate believed that

the presence of the Commission as actually composed, with the peculiar characteristics of its members, its internal quarrels and its arbitrary and unjustifiable
hostility to anything of British origin or initiative, would have been catastrophic
for UN prestige in the Middle East.[4]

The British were almost totally uncooperative, and Bunche was determined that the commission should not go to Palestine unless and until
minimum conditions for its work were established. The chief preoccupation of the British authorities, Azcarate wrote,

lay in impeding by every possible method the presence in Palestine of anybody or
anything remotely connected with the UN, and in particular with the Palestine
Commission.[5]

The British believed that the commission's arrival in Palestine would en-
rage the Arabs and delight the Jews, thus greatly increasing their already
almost insuperable problems of maintaining law and order. The British
ambassador at the UN, Sir Alexander Cadogan, initially informed the
commission that it could arrive only two weeks before the British departure. Bunche asked him how a completely new civil administration could
be set up in two weeks and noted Cadogan's "sheepishness" in trying to
dodge the question. Bunche was determined that a showdown on this
matter should take place in New York before the commission departed,
rather than in Palestine itself,[6] and he prepared a tough questionnaire for
Cadogan, designed to smoke the British out of their total noncooperative-
ness. He also used the commission's reports to the Security Council,
which he wrote, for this, among other purposes.

Meanwhile, the tide of violence rose steadily in Palestine. A series of
killings and counterkillings between Arabs and Jews largely replaced the
previous pattern of attacks on the British, who were rapidly losing control
of the situation. On February 22 an explosion in Jerusalem's Yehuda
Street killed fifty-two people, mainly Jews. On April 9 the Irgun killed 250
Arab civilians in an attack on the Arab village of Deir Yassin, causing the
first major flight of Palestinian Arabs and marking the beginning of the
Palestinian refugee problem. A spreading guerilla war began to engulf
the territory.

Lie and Bunche searched earnestly for a means of controlling violence and bloodshed after the mandate ended. Lie was convinced that a
basic issue of international order was involved and that, if the threat of
force to abort the General Assembly decision on partition were to succeed,

a disastrous international precedent would be set. This view was also reflected in the reports to the Security Council which Bunche wrote for the
commission. Lie instructed Bunche to draft a proposal to the Security
Council for the establishment of a United Nations force and a ruling that
violence could not be used against UN bodies or decisions. Lie did not, in
the end, transmit this proposal to the Security Council because the
United States insisted that the Council did not have the right, under the
Charter, to enforce a General Assembly decision such as the partition
resolution. The commission reports, however, continued to mention the
necessity of some unspecified international force in Palestine.

In February the British began to urge that a small advance party of
the Palestine Commission be sent to Palestine. Bunche was derisive of this
maneuver, believing that the British only wanted to show some token of
cooperation with the Security Council. Four people were not likely to
have any effect on the chaotic situation in Palestine, and he therefore
pressed for a much larger party and guarantees of the necessary freedom
for it to act effectively. On February 22, Bunche saw off the advance
party, led by Azcarate and Constantin Stavropoulos, at La Guardia Airport. "My conscience hurt," he noted. "The biggest explosion yet [the
Yehuda Street explosion] occurred in Jerusalem today."[7] On its arrival in
Jerusalem the advance group was restricted and discouraged by the British, cordially received by the Jews, and boycotted by the Arabs. Azcarate
constantly urged the necessity of a truce and suggested that it should be
monitored by neutral military observers.

The United States now added to the confusion. There was already
speculation that the United States might abandon the partition scheme,
and Jewish organizations in the United States mounted an intensive lobbying campaign to avert such a move. In spite of this, on March 19, the
United States ambassador at the UN, Warren Austin, informed the Security Council that, in the belief that partition could not be achieved unless
it was imposed by force, the United States was proposing the suspension
of the Palestine Commission and the holding of a special session of the
Assembly to consider placing Palestine under UN trusteeship.

Lie, facing a development which he regarded as a betrayal of the
United Nations by the United States, seriously considered resigning. The
Jews also regarded the U.S. move as a betrayal, and Weizmann stated
that, after Austin's proposal, Zionists "had no choice but to 'create
facts,' " a phrase and an activity that were to become distressingly familiar
in succeeding years. Most Arab leaders were delighted. Bunche wrote to
Ben Gerig:

As you can well imagine, we in the Trusteeship Department received the surprise US proposal on temporary trusteeship for Palestine with mixed emotions and not a little shock. I thought you liked us. The prospect of having Jerusalem on our hands was staggering enough. We are looking forward to details of the trusteeship proposal with great interest.[8]

In Palestine the violence increased, and on April 23, following Azcarate's suggestion, the Security Council appointed a Truce Commission[9] composed of the representatives of members of the Security Council that had consular representatives in Jerusalem (the United States, France, and Belgium), to supervise the implementation of its previous cease-fire resolution.[10] The Palestine Commission reported to the April special session of the General Assembly that Arab hostility, British noncooperation, mounting violence, and the failure of the Security Council to provide the "necessary armed assistance" had prevented it from carrying out its task, and prophesied chaos, bloodshed, and starvation in Palestine. In the Trusteeship Council Bunche got Shertok and al-Khalidi to agree to a truce in the Old City of Jerusalem. The month-long Assembly session produced little but talk. It did not rescind the partition resolution, and the idea of trusteeship was abandoned. Arthur Creech-Jones, the British delegate, did, however, mention the need for a neutral authority to fill the gap that would result from British withdrawal and to work for a permanent solution. Thus the idea of the mediator in Palestine was born.

Such was the prelude to the mediation effort in Palestine. As the end of the mandate approached and the British progressively relinquished responsibility, the situation in Palestine deteriorated rapidly. While the Jewish Agency was actively preparing for a provisional government in the Jewish sector, there was total disorganization and lack of leadership on the Arab side. Incidents like Deir Yassin and the flight of Arab Palestinians also tended to increase the area controlled by the Jews, who, by the end of the mandate, controlled Tiberias, Haifa, Jaffa, Acre, and most of the new city of Jerusalem.

On May 14, the British high commissioner, Sir Alan Cunningham, accompanied by the last British officials and soldiers, left Haifa on a cruiser of the Royal Navy. The state of Israel was proclaimed on the same day. The General Assembly's partition resolution was cited as the legal basis of the new state, although its boundaries were not specified as those laid down in the partition resolution. In New York, Francis Sayre, representing the United States, was addressing the Assembly on the question of

Jerusalem when word began to circulate that President Truman had recognized the new state of Israel. It transpired that the only person who had been told of this move in advance was the chief U.S. delegate, Warren Austin, and he had been so upset that he had gone home without telling anyone else. After checking the Associated Press news ticker, another member of the U.S. delegation, Philip Jessup, mounted the rostrum in some embarrassment and read the recognition announcement to the Assembly.

The following day Egypt informed the Security Council that Egyptian forces were entering Palestine "to establish security and order instead of chaos and disorder,"[11] and they were soon joined by forces from Jordan, Lebanon, Syria, Iraq, and Saudi Arabia. The guerrilla chaos of the previous months had given way to full-scale war.

On May 14 the Assembly established a "United Nations Mediator in Palestine" for a number of purposes, of which the most important was to "promote a peaceful adjustment of the future situation in Palestine."[12] The mediator was to be chosen by the permanent members of the Security Council, who announced, on May 21, the appointment of Count Folke Bernadotte of Sweden.

On the evening of Thursday, May 20, Bunche had been to a party at the Park Avenue apartment of Marshall Field, the publisher of *PM*, a New York afternoon newspaper, in honor of Henry Lee Moon's new book, *The Balance of Power: The Negro Vote.* When he got home he found that Lie had been trying to reach him. Lie wanted Bunche to go to Paris within a couple of days to meet Bernadotte and to proceed with him to Palestine "for a short period."[13] Bunche's title was to be "Chief Representative of the Secretary-General in Palestine." This request, virtually impossible to refuse, came as a considerable shock both to Bunche and to Ruth. Although he was to leave for Paris on Sunday, on Saturday he drove Ruth and Ralph Jr. to the Westtown School in Pennsylvania to see the girls. On returning at midnight, he went to his office at Lake Success. He finished packing at 4:00 A.M. and left for Paris at 2:00 P.M. on Sunday, May 23. Many old friends, including his colleagues from the Trusteeship Department, Larry Finkelstein, Wilfred Benson, and Heinz Wieschhoff, came to see him off.

Bunche met Bernadotte at Le Bourget on May 25, having "hired a nice looking Hispano-Suiza for the Count."[14] The count, as head of the Swedish Red Cross, wore a white Red Cross uniform with many medal ribbons and was accompanied by his American wife, Estelle, a secretary, and a valet. His personal physician was expected on the following day. Bunche wrote:

The Count is affable, speaks good English, fairly tall and slender, deep-lined face but nice-looking. . . . He is eager to get to work. Emphasized frankness and punctuality. Says if he advances an idea he relishes criticism provided it is accompanied by an alternative plan.[15]

He wrote to Ruth:

I think we will get on well, for he seems to be a man who will listen seriously to advice.[16]

Bunche soon found out that Bernadotte had a low opinion of the partition resolution.

The UN had chartered a DC-3 from KLM for the mediator's personal use. The plane was to carry both UN and Red Cross insignia. Bernadotte directed that the plane should also be painted white, setting the style for all UN planes ever since. They left Le Bourget on May 27 for Cairo via Athens. Approaching Cairo they had their first taste of the Near East war zone when the control tower refused to radio the number of the landing runway because "this would give the enemy the direction of the wind and Egypt is at war. Musical comedy stuff," Bunche noted.[17]

In Cairo, which was in the grip of a heat wave, they began the relentless round of interviews with ministers and representatives of different factions which was to occupy most of the summer. Two days later they were escorted into Haifa by four British Tempest fighters, and drove, under a heavy Haganah escort, to Tel Aviv, from which they shortly departed for Amman.

Bernadotte's first task was to stop the fighting, which, as long as it continued, made any mediation effort impossible. On May 29 the Security Council had called on all the fighting parties to order a cease-fire and observe a truce for four weeks, during which no new fighting personnel would be brought into the area. The mediator was instructed to get agreement to this appeal and to monitor the truce, for which purpose military observers would be provided. Prime Minister David Ben-Gurion and his foreign minister, Moshe Shertok, were suspicious of this resolution, which had been drafted by the British, and believed it would cost the Jews their current military advantage. Nonetheless, Tel Aviv accepted the cease-fire in principle on June 1, provided others did the same. The Arabs, although faced with an imminent ammunition shortage and a hopelessly divided command, also believed that they were making military headway and were less forthcoming.

The Security Council had authorized Bernadotte to set the date of the cease-fire, and, after a further whirlwind round of the Arab capitals, he decided, on June 7, to set the day and hour—6:00 P.M. (GMT) on Friday, June 11—when the truce would come into effect. He also stated that if his cease-fire proposals, which had been written by Bunche on the plane between meetings, were not accepted unconditionally, he would go straight to the Security Council.* For Bunche and Bernadotte, who were waiting in Cairo, June 9, the deadline which Bernadotte had set for acceptance of the truce, was, in Bunche's words, "a day of watchful waiting." The Arab acceptances came in before the deadline, but Israel's acceptance, relayed through John Reedman in Haifa, was forty minutes late. "Count hugged me," Bunche noted.[19]

Overcoming this first hurdle had given Bunche a better idea of Bernadotte. He wrote to Ruth:

There has really never been anything like this. The Count has much of Myrdal's dynamic quality, and we keep hopping from one place to another like mad in our plane and often on just a few moments' notice. As soon as we land anywhere we begin to confer and leave for some place else immediately the conference is over. I get practically no sleep and miss many meals.[20]

Azcarate, who had a ringside seat but was not part of Bernadotte's entourage, saw the mediator in a rather different light.

I got the impression of a man wholly preoccupied with the idea of speed and activity, anxious to appear as someone who came to the point at once and knew his own mind. . . . There was rather too much activity, rather too much coming and going, counting the minutes, taking rapid decisions and carrying them out without the time for proper reflection and all in a somewhat confused and chaotic manner.

Later on, he wrote:

The Count gives me the impression of a man who is lost in a labyrinth who yet continues walking with great speed and decision as if he knew exactly where he was going.

Bernadotte liked publicity and had a "marked predilection for the spectacular and the ostentatious."[21]

The way was now clear to begin the actual mediation process, but the arrival in Jerusalem on June 11 of the first truce observers added a new and completely novel responsibility for Bunche, who had not only to direct them but to elaborate the principles and establish the practical basis on

*In Amman, Glubb Pasha had told Bunche, "both sides love to haggle and bargain. They should be told to take it or leave it."[18]

which they would work. This was the first UN military-observer group—
indeed, the first UN peacekeeping operation—and there were no precedents for it. The first and most basic principle was strict impartiality and
objectivity. Bunche also insisted that the observers should be unarmed,
something alien to the traditional military mind. He believed that this was
vital for the observers' own safety and would put them above the conflict
they were monitoring, whereas carrying individual weapons would only
endanger them. Bunche's rule became the accepted practice in all UN
observer missions.

The truce had to be supervised in such a way as to give no military
advantage to either side. Before the full team of military observers arrived
and could be deployed, Bunche had to use whatever members of his own
small staff he could spare to check the shipment of war materials and the
influx of immigrants at airfields and ports. The mediator's plane was
pressed into service for observation over Jerusalem, Amman, and Haifa.
One UN official found himself monitoring the huge British supply dump
at Suez. The cease-fire lines also had to be defined. In Haifa, John Reedman, hearing shooting outside the city, took a taxi to the spot, picked up
the local Israeli commander, and took him to the local Arab commander
to arrange for the shooting to stop. The observers wore UN armbands and
carried UN flags, but the UN flag was exactly the same blue and white as
the Israeli flag. For this reason, the observers' vehicles were painted white
with "UN" in huge black letters on the sides and top. This also became
the standard practice for all UN observer missions.

Until reinforcements could arrive, the monitoring of the truce imposed a heavy additional burden on Bunche and his staff—one for which
they used the night hours, after the count had retired. Everything had to
be improvised. Communications were slow, and sometimes nonexistent,
until Major General Frank Stoner, later of RCA, came out to install the
UN's first field-radio network. Bunche also asked for coastal-patrol vessels
and small aircraft of the Beechcraft type. Three United States destroyers
and a French corvette were made available, as well as three U.S. C-47s.

The initial target was for twenty-one observers each from the three
countries of the Truce Commission, but the buildup was agonizingly slow.
Trygve Lie was anxious to supplement the military observers with a
United Nations Guard Force,* especially for use in Jerusalem. Although
Bernadotte had asked for a thousand UN guards to monitor the demilitari-

---

*Forty-three years later, a UN Guard Force was deployed in northern Iraq to monitor and
protect humanitarian relief operations for the Iraqi Kurds.

zation of Jerusalem, Bunche had strong reservations about this idea, and his doubts were fully justified when some forty guards were recruited in New York and sent to the area without indoctrination, training, or discipline. The conduct of these "soldiers of peace" on their first night on the town in Beirut was such that they were immediately and permanently repatriated to New York.

His by now open-ended working hours prompted Bunche to remind Andrew Cordier, Lie's executive assistant, of Lie's promise that he would be in the field for only two or three weeks. Cordier told him that the high quality of his work would make his replacement difficult. Bunche replied that he could easily take care of that.

The first four-week truce held surprisingly well, although it was marred by three serious incidents. The arrival of an illegal immigrant ship, the LST *Altalena,* which beached itself off Tel Aviv, was a direct challenge to the new Israeli government and its observance of the terms of the truce. Ben-Gurion ordered the Haganah to open fire on the ship and on the Irgun forces defending it. The second major breach was the blocking of agreed-upon food convoys to Jewish settlements in the Negev by Egyptian forces, which also fired on a UN plane. The third was the refusal of the Arab Legion and Iraqi troops to permit the flow of water to Jerusalem. Two local arrangements made in Jerusalem during the first truce lasted until the 1967 war. A no-man's-land was established between the belligerents and greatly reduced friction between them; and Mount Scopus, a mainly Jewish enclave containing the Hadassah Hospital and the Hebrew University, was demilitarized and put under the supervision of UN observers.

To facilitate the mediation effort, Bernadotte's headquarters was moved to the Hôtel des Roses on the island of Rhodes on June 13, while a truce-supervision headquarters was established in Haifa. Bunche wrote to Ruth:

Rhodes is a beautiful island, but the weather has been extremely humid—everything is damp, even the paper I'm writing on. The sea breezes keep the temperature down, however. . . . The hotel is very close to the sea and I can look out my window and see the Turkish coast not far away.[22]

He had no time to enjoy the place, however, or even to take a quick swim.

The truce brought no softening of the position of either side on basic issues. The Arabs rejected partition and a Jewish state, while the Jews were adamant on a Jewish state with unrestricted immigration. On June 19 Bernadotte told Lie that he saw no chance of getting agreement on a future settlement in Palestine by July 9, when the four-week truce would expire. He therefore proposed to prolong the negotiations and the truce by making rather vague preliminary suggestions to the parties rather than formal proposals on basic questions. He also intended to work for the demilitarization of Jerusalem. Both Bernadotte and Bunche tried to get Lie himself to visit the Near East to show support for their efforts, but Lie always found a pretext to avoid such a visit.

Since the middle of June Bernadotte, in accordance with a procedure suggested by Bunche, had been conducting exploratory talks with the parties with a view to determining the main areas of disagreement, and the issues on which agreement might reasonably be hoped for. Bunche had worked out a list of leading questions as a basis for their talks with the parties. What, for example, was the Jewish attitude to the return of Palestinian refugees to the areas occupied by Israel that did *not* belong to the Jewish state under the partition resolution? What restrictions on Jewish immigration would the Arabs insist on? And so on.

Up to this point the mediator had made no proposals of his own regarding a settlement. On the evening of Midsummer Day, June 22, Bernadotte asked his senior advisers on Rhodes to develop suggestions based on common sense, justice, and the realities of the situation after six weeks of war. Bunche presided over this brainstorming process and gave free rein to Constantin Stavropoulos, John Reedman, Henri Vigier, and Paul Mohn, his senior staff. In the course of the discussion they all developed and changed their own ideas significantly, and Bunche put the results together at the end.

After three days of intensive drafting, Bernadotte, on June 28, sent envoys with written suggestions to the various parties in an effort to establish whether there was any common ground on which to continue the mediation effort. He hoped—vainly, as it turned out—that the parties would send representatives to Rhodes for further discussion of his suggestions.

Bernadotte suggested that the boundaries of the two states would be negotiated with his help and on the basis of suggestions made by him. Palestine, as defined in the original mandate—i.e., including Transjordan—might form the basis of a union of the Arab and Jewish states. Bernadotte's territorial suggestions were bound, in any case, to be highly controversial. All, or part of, the Negev, which had been awarded to the Jews in the partition plan, was to be included in the Arab state. All, or part of, Western Galilee, which had been awarded to the Arabs, was to be included in the Jewish state. The city of Jerusalem was to be included in

Arab territory, with municipal autonomy for the Jewish community and special arrangements for the protection of the holy places.

This last suggestion was a particularly explosive issue with the Jewish side. Bernadotte's and Bunche's thinking was certainly influenced by the fact that the dominant international crisis of the summer of 1948 was the blockade by the Soviet Union of the Western Sectors of Berlin—a vivid example of the problems of a divided city set in a hostile environment.* Bunche and Reedman both felt strongly that an international regime for Jerusalem wouldn't work. Unlike Berlin, there were no sectors, nor were there forces to guarantee the arrangement, and the Jews were only in a small part of Jerusalem, and in a very tenuous position.[24]

Bernadotte's suggestions were intended to provide a purely exploratory and informal basis for further discussion and mediation, but leaks in Cairo and in Tel Aviv made it necessary to publish them as a document of the Security Council.[25] This gave the suggestions a formal standing they were never intended to have and almost certainly sent a misleading and fatal message to Bernadotte's future assassins. Bunche, who wrote most of the suggestions,† felt the truce had come too early for the parties to accept them. He told Ruth,

I feel almost certain they will be rejected by both sides. When that happens we will come straight to Lake Success and report to the Security Council.[26]

A visit of Arab and Jewish "consultants" to Rhodes in the previous week had not given any grounds for optimism. Bunch wrote:

My patience with Arabs wearing thin. They refuse to face realities and peddle myths; they speak of "justice" as though it were a robe specially tailored for Arabs. Even though intelligent they often speak like children—e.g., Shukairy telling us the Arabs treat Jewish POWs so well Jews all want to be taken prisoners. Jews (Shiloah and Kohn) much more intelligent and sensible.[27]

Nor was it an easy time to be with Bernadotte: "C[ount] B[ernadotte] can't stand waiting—difficult period waiting for reactions to our suggestions."[28] This pause in their activities was "a terrifying period for us."[29]

As Bunche had foreseen, both parties rejected the mediator's sugges-

*Bernadotte wrote: "Jerusalem would be surrounded by territory completely controlled by the Arabs. It is undesirable—or so I felt at that time—to set up an international zone . . . inside any given state or zone." Bernadotte goes on to mention Berlin as an example of such an arrangement.[23]

†In his personal notes for June 27 Bunche wrote, "Drafting of the introductory statement, most of the ideas and suggestions and territorial annex were mine."

tions. The Israelis said that the proposals ignored both the General Assembly's partition resolution and the fact that a sovereign state of Israel had already been established within the area assigned to it by that resolution. The inclusion of the Arab state in the kingdom of Transjordan radically changed the problem. The Israelis violently objected to what they termed the "disastrous" suggestion that Jerusalem would be included in Arab territory, and urged that Bernadotte reconsider his whole approach to the problem. The popular and press reaction in Israel was violent and included allegations that Bernadotte had Nazi sympathies and was a British agent. In some circles, he had become, after Ernest Bevin, the most hated man in Israel. The Arabs, no less forcefully, rejected the suggestions *in toto* as promoting "realization of all Zionist ambitions: and aggravating an already grave situation."[30] They offered counterproposals for a unitary state in the whole of Palestine.*

In the Security Council, echoing the Israelis, the Soviet Union denounced Bernadotte's suggestions as a violation of the General Assembly decision and asserted that the mediator was contributing to the prolongation of the fighting and interfering in the establishment of two independent states in Palestine. The Soviet Union especially objected to the suggested enlargement of Transjordan and accused Bernadotte of collusion with the British to safeguard Britain's strategic, political, and economic interests in the region.

Meanwhile the four-week truce was running out, and Bernadotte requested the Security Council to prolong it. Arab political leaders had always tended to ignore the realities of their military situation and, regardless of the facts, to declare great victories, thus building up the public belief that the Arab armies were invincible, which in turn forced the Arab governments to be increasingly intransigent. They now objected to prolonging the truce on the grounds that the truce gave the Jews the advantage, allowing them to consolidate their new state and to continue immigration. On July 8, when the negative Arab reply on prolonging the truce was received, Bunche noted, "Arabs must either be mad or assured of British supplies."[31] Transjordan's Arab Legion, bearing the brunt of the fighting in and around Jerusalem, was short of ammunition. The legion's British commander, Glubb Pasha (John Bagot Glubb), far more realistic than the Arab leaders, knew that the British would not provide the needed ammunition, a fact confirmed to Bunche by Sir Alec Kirkbride, the British

*Bunche drafted, within hours of their receipt, measured and detailed replies to both the Israeli and the Arab rejections of Bernadotte's suggestions.

ambassador in Amman. It was thus literally vital for Transjordan that the truce to remain in force. Nonetheless, in Cairo on July 4, the Transjordanian prime minister refused to agree to a prolongation of the truce on the grounds of Arab solidarity.

By July 8 the breakdown of the truce seemed so inevitable that Bunche, while in Haifa to pay his respects at the coffin of a French observer who had been killed the day before, gave orders for the evacuation of UN observers and personnel. On his return to Rhodes that evening an urgent message arrived from King Abdullah asking Bernadotte to come to Amman at once, and they decided to leave at 5:00 A.M. the next day. Bunche's hope of a good night's sleep before the trip was dashed by a call from New York. A transatlantic telephone call in Rhodes entailed a perilous dash by jeep ("the most dangerous part of this mission") to "Radio City," the Marine Signal Corps truck on top of the highest nearby hill. Bunche was usually summoned in the small hours. On this occasion he got to bed at 1:15 A.M. and had to be woken early next morning by Bernadotte, delaying their 5:00 A.M. takeoff by twenty-five minutes, The truce officially ended at 6:00 A.M.

In Amman, King Abdullah greeted them at the palace door and asked Bernadotte, "Why did you let the cease-fire end?" Bernadotte, taken aback, answered that in Cairo the Transjordanian prime minister had been the most outspoken of all in rejecting the truce. The king replied, "You must force us." Abdullah, facing a serious military crisis, was evidently appalled at the Cairo decision.* He urged that the Security Council demand a cessation of the fighting, if necessary under the threat of force, as a face-saving measure for the Arabs. He was also concerned about getting the Egyptians out of Palestine as soon as possible, and was even willing to accept Bernadotte's suggestions as a basis for future discussion. Abdullah said that if Bernadotte could succeed in getting the Security Council to exert the necessary pressure to maintain the truce, he would use all his influence to induce the Arab states to accept continued negotiations.

After leaving Abdullah, Bernadotte and Bunche, at Bunche's urging, decided to go at once to New York. Through the American chargé d'affaires in Amman Bunche sent a message to the State Department urging that the Security Council take immediate and strong action to bring the

---

*Glubb later described his own feelings on hearing of the Cairo decision not to renew the truce: "My heart sank. 'Why?,' I exclaimed, 'what madness! What resources have they got? What do they think they can do?' . . . I can recollect no precedent in history for such irresponsible action on the part of those in power."[32]

Arab states to their senses and to permit them to change the Cairo decision without loss of face.

Bernadotte believes that if Security Council should adopt resolution threatening use of all provisions of Charter including armed intervention, Arab States would back down.[33]

Bunche and Bernadotte flew back from Amman to Rhodes via Haifa, where Bunche countermanded the order for the evacuation of the UN observers. They left for New York on the following day. Before taking off Bernadotte appealed to all parties to observe a ten-day unconditional cease-fire during his absence from the area. The Israelis immediately accepted. There was no reply from the Arabs.

Bunche spent much of the flight to New York writing Bernadotte's report to the Security Council and formulating the unique request it contained. On July 13 Bernadotte asked the Council to *order* a cease-fire and the demilitarization of Jerusalem, threatening the use of coercive measures under Articles 41 and 42 of the Charter* in case of noncompliance. Bernadotte urged the Council to make it absolutely clear that the United Nations would not permit the Palestine issue to be settled by force. He warned the Council that to supervise the new truce he would need about three hundred more military observers with adequate transport and communications.

On July 15, after an acrimonious debate in which the Soviets denounced Bernadotte, the British, and King Abdullah, the Council adopted a resolution ordering the parties to desist from military action and to agree to an immediate and unconditional cease-fire in Jerusalem.[34] The truce was to remain in force until there was a peaceful adjustment of the situation in Palestine, a stipulation that turned out to mean indefinitely. Theoretically at least, the July 15, 1948, resolution is still in force today. Bernadotte set the time for the cease-fire as 3:00 P.M. (GMT) on July 18. He and Bunche left New York for Rhodes on July 17.

This unusually forceful action by the Council owed much to the persuasive powers of both Bernadotte and Bunche. The five tumultuous days in New York had afforded Bunche little time for his family, and he left again with a heavy heart. His stay in the Middle East with Bernadotte had followed a by now disconcertingly familiar pattern. The short absence he had been promised had been progressively prolonged. Ruth had again

---

*Article 41 provides for the use of sanctions by the Security Council. Article 42 provides for the use of armed force if sanctions prove to be inadequate.

felt slighted by his lack of attention on his departure from La Guardia Airport in early June, and his cables of apology from Gander and Paris had little effect. Several acrimonious letters had followed, taking up the usual themes and harping especially on a new one. "But *you* weren't sorry to go. Now, honestly, were you, Ralph? A little more fame and publicity. And that's what really counts, isn't it?"[35] Again complaints about the drudgery and loneliness of her life, his preoccupation with his work, his conduct at home, and his continual absences had filled diatribe after diatribe, crossing with Bunche's descriptions of a fascinating and sometimes hair-raising mission.

I would, Ralph, like to be treated with just as much dignity and respect as other wives of men in your kind of position are treated by their husbands (especially in your white circle).[36]

When the letters finally arrived, Bunche answered with cold anger.

We risk our lives out here almost everyday. We land our airplane on fields too small for it, on deserted and war-gutted fields; we stroll through sniper's territory—I stood last Saturday in Jerusalem on the spot where my friend Tom Wasson was killed.* So I really don't know whether I will ever get back from this assignment. And when I get letters like the ones yesterday I really don't give a damn. I am so tired and so harried that it would really be a relief. . . . Even Arabs and Jews have more faith in each other's word than you have in mine. Well, I'm catching enough hell on this assignment without getting more of it in my mail. I think it better that if people can't write pleasant letters they had best write none at all. . . . I'm sorry for this unpleasant letter, but I'll not bother you with any more, of any kind.[37]

On their eighteenth anniversary, June 23, Bunche relented with a cable and a loving anniversary letter, to which Ruth responded with full apologies. Equilibrium was once again restored, but on July 17, after only five days at home, another prolonged absence loomed.

By the time Bernadotte and Bunche got back to Rhodes on July 19, all the Arab states had announced their compliance with the Security Council resolution. Bunche noted that "if Arabs accept, this means virtual surrender on question of Jewish State."[38] His most immediate task was to set up the expanded machinery for monitoring the truce. It was a slow and frustrating business.

---

*Thomas Wasson, U.S. consul in Jerusalem and a member of the Truce Commission, had been shot by a sniper on May 22 and died on May 24.

On July 19, Bunche had drafted cables to the foreign ministers of the U.S., France, and Belgium asking for the immediate dispatch of more observers. The response, though small, was enough to set up the expanded truce supervision organization. On July 20, five C-47s arrived in Rhodes carrying sixty-six officers—forty Americans and twenty-six Belgians. Bunche spent the following day briefing them. He was impressed by their quality. "Many of the US officers," he noted, "are southerners. They apparently felt nothing about my presence alongside the Count."[39] By July 22 the first observers were in the field, and Bunche was working on the overall plan for truce supervision. He noted:

Arab position now is pitiful. They cannot continue to fight and know it. Yet their public opinions are so hot the government officials are frightened stiff. Heads will fall. Syria and Iraq especially dangerous.[40]

By July 26 they had only 105 of the projected 300 observers and no guards for Jerusalem, causing Bernadotte to cable to New York, "You notice without doubt that I am mad, and I believe I have the right to be. . . ."[41] Bernadotte told the U.S. consul general in Jerusalem, John J. MacDonald, that he would resign if no help was forthcoming.

Bunche was intensely loyal to people he worked closely with, and Bernadotte was no exception. He liked, and got on well with, Bernadotte, which was natural since Bernadotte, although he unquestionably took responsibility for the final decisions, was dependent upon Bunche for the work which led up to them. Bunche was mildly skeptical of the extent and expense of Bernadotte's entourage—a doctor, a secretary, a valet, and a considerable Swedish military staff. "Count's personal staff jumps when called by him," he noted, "rest of us don't."[42] Bunche maintained a respectful informality with Bernadotte, and in Rhodes they met regularly early each morning in their dressing gowns on a balcony overlooking the sea.

By July 27 Bunche was able to send to New York, for circulation to the Security Council, his plan for the supervision of the truce and the instructions to the observers. This document, the foundation stone of the technique that later became known as "peacekeeping," contained the following key passage.

The Observer must be completely objective in his attitudes and judgments and must maintain a thorough neutrality as regards political issues in the Palestine situation. The fundamental objective of the terms of the truce is to ensure to the fullest extent possible that no military advantage will accrue to either side as a result of the application of the truce.[43]

Bunche again insisted that the observers should be unarmed, both for their own safety and as a symbol of their being above the conflict.

Bernadotte and Bunche were becoming increasingly concerned with a largely unanticipated result of the violence in Palestine, the swelling tide of Palestinian refugees. The Israeli government was totally unresponsive to approaches on this matter, arguing that the return of refugees under truce conditions would seriously prejudice the security of the Jewish state, especially in Jaffa and Haifa. The Israelis were not prepared to readmit any substantial number of Arab refugees as long as a state of war existed. In any case, Shertok told Bernadotte, the space vacated was needed for Jewish immigrants from Arab countries. When the Arabs were ready to conclude peace treaties with Israel, the refugee problem would be part of the general settlement.

Bernadotte felt the Israelis were showing "signs of a swelled head" in categorically refusing to consider the refugee problem,[44] and he was sufficiently exasperated by their response to send a message on August 1 to the president of the Security Council asking that the Council insist on the return of the three hundred thousand or more refugees before their situation became desperate, if necessary differentiating between those of military age and others. At the very least, Bernadotte felt, the right of the refugees to return to their homes at the earliest practical date should be reaffirmed. He was even thinking of asking for a special session of the General Assembly to consider the matter, but none of his efforts succeeded in stemming, or reversing, the tide of refugees. More than forty years later the Palestinian diaspora and a vast refugee problem remains at the tragic and explosive core of the Arab-Israeli problem.

The position of the mediator was becoming dangerously eroded in the Middle East itself. On August 6 Philip Jessup, the acting U.S. representative at the UN, in warning of the dangers of abandoning the idea of an international regime for Jerusalem, cabled the secretary of state,

It is our hope that it will be possible to avoid a situation wherein the Mediator again makes proposals which are considered unrealistic by both sides and rejected by them.

Jessup believed that the best way of avoiding this would be by developing a concerted British-American position which would be communicated to the mediator and strongly supported by the two governments with the principal parties in the Middle East.[45] A far less restrained view came from the newly arrived U.S. ambassador to Israel, James G. MacDonald,* in a cable to the State Department.

*Not to be confused with the U.S. consul general in Jerusalem, John J. MacDonald.

I do not think that the United States should be overly influenced by the views of either the Mediator or the British. The former, so far as I can judge, is almost complete discredited not only among the Arabs but among the Jews. His inability to enforce his "decisions" and his loquacious pronouncements have left him neither substantial moral authority nor dignity.[46]

Bernadotte himself had certainly become increasingly disillusioned with both sides, as well as impatient with the members of the United Nations for the delay in providing adequate numbers of observers. In a talk with the U.S. chargé in Cairo on August 7, "He commented that the role of peacemaker for Palestine was decidedly no easy one."[47] After returning from New York on July 19, he continued his round of meetings with all concerned, trying to inject a sense of realism into the Arabs and some restraint into the now ebullient Israelis. Shertok assured him that there was no question of a lack of confidence in the mediator, but was opposed to the demilitarization of Jerusalem, to which the Israeli forces had now established a land bridge.* He was also adamantly opposed to the return of Palestinian refugees. He was, however, prepared to discuss converting the truce into an armistice as a step toward a settlement.

Bunche told Ruth, who was reaching the end of her tether with the children and was desperate for him to come home, that they had one more tour of the capitals to make before he left for New York.

This may be the most hazardous trip of all because public opinion in some of these countries is very much inflamed just now, and for the first time feeling is running against the Mediator and his staff. We are all being attacked in both the Arab and the Jewish press. The Arabs are especially angry about the Mediator persuading the S[ecurity] C[ouncil] to *order* the Arab states to cease fire [Bunche describes antiforeign riots in Cairo, Amman, and Baghdad]. . . . It is really a marvel that neither the Count nor anyone of his party has ever been sniped at out here. Just in case, I'm enclosing the will I told you about.[48]

Judging from this letter, Bunche still regarded the Arabs as more potentially homicidal than the Israelis.

On August 4 Bunche arrived back in the United States. Bernadotte had asked him to try to get more support in Washington both for the observer operation and for the effort to demilitarize Jerusalem. After talks at Lake Success he went to Washington on August 8 for talks with Assistant Secretary of State Dean Rusk and Secretary of State George Marshall.

*The Israeli press, encouraged by leaks from the government, had had a field day with the alleged details of Bernadotte's plan for the demilitarization of Jerusalem. One rumor was that Bernadotte was requiring every male member of the Haganah to leave Jerusalem, thus destroying the economic life of Jewish Jerusalem.

Bunche described to Marshall the Near East situation as it appeared to himself and Bernadotte. Most Arab governments had come tacitly to accept the realization that the Jewish state was there to stay, but no Arab government could admit this publicly for fear of arousing public opinion. The cease-fire order might eventually allow the Arabs to come to an open admission of the fact of the state of Israel. The Jews had made considerable military gains and were conscious of their superior strength. Jewish public opinion was at the height of nationalistic fervor, and the Jewish state was not afraid of the future.* On the other hand, the Israeli government knew that Israel could not exist without the support of the international community.

The boundaries prescribed in the partition plan of November 1947, Bunche told Marshall, were no longer pertinent since the Israelis had occupied nearly all of Galilee, and the conditions no longer existed for a separate Arab state linked to the Jewish state in an economic union. Bernadotte wanted to know the views of the United States and the United Kingdom on the future territorial settlement in Palestine, believing that if the U.S. and U.K. were in agreement, there was a chance that both Jews and Arabs, while strongly protesting, would go along. Jewish demands would be very large at the beginning, and the Arabs would need a formula to placate an aroused public opinion, but Bunche believed there was still scope for a settlement, provided that it had the firm support of the U.S. and Britain.

Bunche told Marshall that Bernadotte's preliminary thinking on the matter was that the valuable land in most of Western Galilee, already conquered by the Israelis, should go to them, while in return the Arabs should get most of the Negev desert. Bernadotte felt that a UN administration of Jerusalem would be unworkable and that Jerusalem should therefore nominally be under Jordanian sovereignty with local autonomy for the Jewish population, the whole arrangement being supervised by a UN commission.[49]

Although the Arabs would not deal directly with the Israelis, they were prepared to deal with the United Nations, and this had already made possible a series of local agreements for withdrawal of soldiers from critical points such as Mount Scopus and the Latrun pumping station. The mediator urgently needed impartial military observers to fill the vacuum at such points. He had concluded that observers in national uniform would be

---

*On July 30, after a meeting in Tel Aviv, Bunche had noted, "Israelis now swashbuckling and Shertok pompous. Jewish imperialism rampant already."

more respected than UN guards, and was now hoping to get 250 observers—one hundred each from the U.S. and France, and fifty from Belgium—to observe the truce in Jerusalem.

Marshall saw no difficulty about the observers but, as a military man, was concerned at the enormous administrative problem of running small teams of officers who were not self-supporting. As regards the eventual boundaries of Israel, the U.S. was consulting with the British, but had as yet reached no final conclusions.

In this extraordinarily noncommittal conversation, no one appears to have given Bunche any indication that the United States was critical of Bernadotte's ideas about Jerusalem, although in a subsequent cable to the U.S. ambassador in London Marshall told him that Bernadotte's views, *except on Jerusalem*, were similar to Washington's.[50] Thus, Marshall wrote, if Bernadotte stated what, on the basis of the facts and justice, seemed to him the most equitable frontier for Israel, the United Kingdom and the United States would then publicly support him. Later in August, however, Marshall instructed the U.S. ambassador in Stockholm to call on Bernadotte to discourage him from putting forward to the General Assembly any suggested territorial solution until the U.S. and the United Kingdom had agreed on a common policy on the matter.[51]

On August 12 Bernadotte left Rhodes for Stockholm to attend a Red Cross conference and to catch up with his personal affairs. Bunche, in New York, kept in touch with him in a series of confidential reports. While making progress on getting more observers and planes, he was also pondering Bernadotte's next step. He told Bernadotte that, when Washington and London had agreed with each other as regards his ideas about Jerusalem and boundaries, the result would be informally communicated to him by them. He also suggested that Bernadotte should submit his report not to the Security Council but to the secretary general, for transmission to all the members of the UN. Bernadotte's thinking was also developing. He told A. Katznelson of the Israeli mission in Stockholm that he had withdrawn his suggestion that Jerusalem should come under Arab rule, although he did not believe internationalization of the city to be a practical solution.[52]

Bunche spent the rest of August in New York with his family. He was due to leave on August 31 for Stockholm to pick up Bernadotte and return to Rhodes. On the day of his departure, Trygve Lie called him into a meeting with Arthur Lourie, a senior Israeli diplomat. Lourie was protesting Bernadotte's proposal to limit further entry into Israel of men of military age. Lie, who had many reservations about Bernadotte, was clearly unhappy with this proposal too. Lourie reminded Bunche that it was the critical question of immigration that had brought the Jews to the breaking point with the mandatory power, Britain, and that Bernadotte's proposal could only lead to a head-on clash. Bunche, though defending Bernadotte, said he would discuss the matter with him in Stockholm. He left for Stockholm with an uneasy feeling that, quite apart from the Arabs and Israelis, his own secretary general was not very solidly behind Bernadotte and himself either.

Bunche's two days in Stockholm were his first experience of Sweden. He found that Swedes, especially the rich ones, believed that a Soviet invasion was imminent. Even Countess Bernadotte was sending family valuables to the United States. In Bernadotte's circle "everyone seemed to have a title."[53] Many people in Stockholm were violently critical of Bunche's old colleague, Gunnar Myrdal, now the Swedish minister of trade, whose policies they blamed for Sweden's economic difficulties and dollar shortage.

They left Stockholm on September 1 for Rhodes, stopping briefly in Paris to see Trygve Lie, who asked Bernadotte to submit his report not later than September 13. In Geneva they picked up a small staff to deal with the growing Palestinian refugee problem. They reached Rhodes on the afternoon of September 3.

Bunche was "not enthusiastic about seeing Rhodes again, . . . same place, same weather, same faces,"[54] and devoted himself to tightening up the staff arrangements and the truce observer mission and getting the refugee relief operation under way. On September 6 he and Bernadotte set out on a round of visits. In Alexandria they found the Egyptians and the Arab representatives more realistic and restrained than on previous occasions. Azzam Pasha, the secretary general of the Arab Higher Committee, told Bunche that the Arab leaders had had doubts about him at first because of his role in the UN Special Committee on Palestine (UNSCOP), but now accepted him without question as a fair and honest man. In Amman they lunched with King Abdullah, who was "his usual dreamy-eyed, nodding, polite self."[55] In Tel Aviv they found the Israelis also in a more restrained mood. Shertok seemed less assertive than usual and less adamant against the demilitarization of Jerusalem. Bunche noted:

Change in atmosphere here. Shertok and all his advisers no longer in shirtsleeves. They are all dressed up with ties and jackets. Shertok has a secretary taking verbatim notes of everything he says. The military officers now all have epaulettes and rank insignia and wear proper uniforms.[56]

The British consul in Jerusalem informed Bernadotte that Britain and the United States had worked out a common line on Palestine which would be communicated to him shortly. Bunche was confident that this would be based on his talks with Secretary of State Marshall in Washington and would give vital support to Bernadotte's own report. "My New York mission paying off;" Bunche noted, "if this comes off, it's my greatest success."[57]

After three days and nights of intensive work on Bernadotte's report, they learned that emissaries from the two powers, Ambassador Robert McClintock for the United States and Sir John Troutbeck for Britain, would be arriving in Rhodes on September 13. "They are really taking it seriously," Bunche noted. "Count elated." When the two representatives arrived, ostensibly to discuss the Arab refugee problem, Bunche found, as he had hoped, that their position was extremely close to the views expressed in his draft of Bernadotte's report on virtually all points.* Working each night into the small hours, Bernadotte and Bunche put the finishing touches to the report by September 15. Its substance was basically in line with the policy outlined by the two emissaries, except that McClintock mentioned the possible necessity of giving a part of the Negev to Israel, to which Bernadotte was opposed.

Both at the time and later it was claimed by the Israelis and some others that the Bernadotte plan simply reflected British policy and the British strategic interest in maintaining control, through Transjordan, of the Negev. The British had developed this policy even before the mandate ended, and Bernadotte and Bunche must have been aware of it. The United States was certainly aware of British views on the Negev and was at this time apparently beginning to disagree with them. In early August Bunche had told Secretary of State Marshall that, since the Israelis had already taken the valuable land in most of Western Galilee, which had been allotted to the Arabs in the partition plan, Bernadotte felt that the Arabs should, in return and as a matter of justice, get most of the Negev desert, which had been allotted to the Israelis. This idea was incorporated in the Bernadotte plan because it seemed to Bernadotte and Bunche to provide an approximately just arrangement which might make it possible

---

*Sidney Bailey writes: "When they [the emissaries] arrived in Rhodes on September 13, Bernadotte's report had already been completed and no changes were made as a result of the visit. Bernadotte's ideas for the future were, as it appears, almost identical with those of the Foreign Office and the State Department: the Partition Plan should be amended so that the Jews should be given valuable lands in Western Galilee . . . but in return for this acquisition should permit the Arabs to take over most of the Negev."[58]

for the Arabs, however reluctantly, to accept the plan. There are those, however, who are still convinced that Bernadotte and Bunche were simply manipulated by the British.[59] In any case, the Bernadotte plan, if there was to be any hope of its succeeding, needed the general support of the United States and Britain.

When the discussion with the emissaries turned to tactics and timing Bernadotte insisted, against the arguments of McClintock and Troutbeck, that it was imperative to bring the Palestine situation before the General Assembly at the earliest possible time. Otherwise, he believed, the situation would deteriorate greatly, and possibly irretrievably. Only rapid UN action could allow Arab leaders to channel public opinion at home into accepting a solution that they, in spite of much bluster, now admitted to be inevitable. Israel, for its part, might well take the situation into its own hands if the General Assembly appeared not to consider the Palestine situation as urgent. The Americans would have preferred to rely solely on Bernadotte's proposals, supported by the U.S. and Britain, rather than risk a bitter and perhaps inconclusive debate in the Assembly. They agreed, however, that if the matter was to go to the Assembly, it should be rushed through, preferably by acclamation. It was agreed that Bunche should draft a resolution setting forth the essence of the mediator's recommendations, for the use of possible sponsors. McClintock reported to Secretary of State Marshall:

My overall impression . . . is that Bernadotte, who has taken an immense amount of first-hand testimony, has come from last-minute talks with leaders on both sides, and who is sternly determined to advocate only a solution based on equal justice to both sides, feels that now is the optimum moment: that if not "now" it is "never," and that the General Assembly must seize the opportunity.[60]

Bernadotte signed his report at the Hôtel des Roses early on September 16,* and it was transmitted to Lie in Paris on the same day. In his transmittal letter he wrote:

I would emphasize that an extremely crucial stage has been reached on the Palestine question, and it is this conviction which alone prompts me to be so bold as to suggest that steps should immediately be taken to bring the urgency of the matter to the attention of the General Assembly.

The most significant and controversial part of the report,[61] which Bernadotte hoped might serve as a "reasonable, equitable and workable basis for settlement," was the suggestion as to frontiers between the Arab

---

*Bunche and his staff had worked day and night for six days on the 130-page report. Bunche wrote the introduction, the basic factors, and the conclusions and proposals—in fact, the meat of the report.

and Jewish territories, which, "in the absence of agreement between
Arabs and Jews, should be established by the United Nations."[62] Ber-
nadotte believed that if such a formula was firmly backed by the General
Assembly neither side would forcibly resist it. The Negev would go to the
Arabs, Galilee to the Jews, and central Palestine would be divided accord-
ing to the boundaries laid down in the partition resolution.[63] The Arab
territory would probably be merged with the territory of Transjordan.
Jerusalem and the holy places would be placed under effective United
Nations control, with maximum feasible local autonomy for its Arab and
Jewish communities, free access to the holy places, and religious freedom.
(This was a radical departure from the suggestions Bernadotte had circulated in June.) Arab refugees would be given the right to return home at
the earliest possible date.

In his conclusion Bernadotte stated:

A first essential in Palestine today is an immediate cessation of hostilities. But that
is only a first step, for the question must be answered, at some stage, whether the
international community is willing to tolerate resort to armed force as the means
for settlement of the Palestine issue. . . . Ending the use of force in Palestine will,
in fact, make possible an eventual peaceful settlement.[64]

The report thus pointed the way to the armistice agreements which were,
in the end, its only lasting result.

Bernadotte's report differed from his earlier suggestions in several
important ways. Among other things it recognized the existence of a
totally independent state of Israel without restrictions on its foreign, defense, or immigration policies. Jerusalem was now to be placed under UN
control, as foreseen in the November 29, 1947, resolution. The fate of
Arab Palestine was to be decided by the Arab governments in consultation
with its inhabitants, although still with a recommendation that it should
be merged with Transjordan. Haifa and Lydda (Lod) Airport were to
become free ports.

While the report was being written, Bunche was also dealing with
serious incidents on the ground. On September 4, Arab irregulars blew up
the Latrun pumping station. On September 6, as a result of a communications failure, two French UN observers, deplaning at the Gaza airstrip,
were killed by Saudi irregulars under Egyptian command. On September
12 three Arab villages south of Haifa were attacked and destroyed by the
Israelis. In all of these cases Bunche denounced the perpetrators, demanded punishment and, where possible, restitution, and reported to the
Security Council.

Bernadotte left Rhodes for Jerusalem on September 16, leaving

Bunche behind to clear up and check all the details of the report. Bunche said goodbye to him at 6:00 A.M., when the count came in, before taking off, to see how the staff were doing with the report and to sign it. Bunche himself was to rejoin Bernadotte the following day in Jerusalem, and they would then go on to Paris, where the General Assembly was convening.

Bunche left Rhodes at 8:00 A.M. on Friday, September 17, for Beirut, where Bernadotte's plane was to pick him up. The plane was late, and then another forty-five minutes was lost in repairs of a minor mechanical failure. In Haifa, the entry point for Israel, there was a further half-hour delay while the Israelis queried the British passport of Bunche's secretary, Doreen Daughton.

Bunche's party finally landed at Jerusalem's Kalandia Airport in the late afternoon. Driving into the city, they were stopped at the Israeli checkpoint at the Mandelbaum Gate, where there was more trouble over Doreen Daughton's passport. The Israeli officer in charge had already left for the Sabbath, leaving in charge an Israeli corporal who spoke no English. Bunche, who had never been late for a rendezvous with Bernadotte, was furious. General William Riley, the chief UN observer, was finally permitted to go ahead in a jeep to inform Bernadotte that Bunche was delayed and to get help from the Israelis. After another twenty minutes, a UN observer accompanied by an Israeli liaison officer sped up to the checkpoint. The liaison officer shouted to Bunche to get into the car at once, and then told him that Bernadotte had been assassinated. They drove to the YMCA building and found the bodies of Bernadotte and a French observer, Colonel André Sérot, being laid out in the same room where UNSCOP had held its first meeting the year before.

Bernadotte, although he was a stickler for punctuality, had waited more than half an hour for Bunche, with whom he was going to look at Government House in Jerusalem as a possible headquarters. During this waiting period, a French observer, Colonel André Sérot, had come over to talk to him. Sérot's wife had been saved from a Nazi concentration camp in 1945 by the Swedish Red Cross expedition led by Bernadotte. When it became clear that Bunche was not going to show up, Bernadotte asked Sérot to join him, and they set out for Government House in an open car, with Frank Begley, the UN chief of security, in front next to the driver. Bernadotte was on the right rear seat, Sérot in the middle, and the Swedish chief of staff, General Lundström, on the left. On the return journey from Government House the party was stopped in the Katamon quarter by a jeep pulled across the road. The UN people and Captain Moshe Hillman, the Israeli liaison officer with the party, assumed it was a regular

Israeli checkpoint and were therefore not worried when three armed
men—apparently soldiers, in khaki shorts and shirts and carrying machine
pistols—proceeded to check the cars in the count's caravan, walking on
each side of the road. When the man on the left reached Bernadotte's car,
he immediately opened fire, killing Bernadotte and Sérot instantly.[65]

A Jewish underground organization, Hazit Ha-Moledeth (The Fa-
therland Front) claimed responsibility for the assassination, but there was
no doubt that it was a cover organization for the Lohamee Herut Israel
(Lehi), better known as the Stern Gang. The decision to kill Bernadotte
was taken by three men of the Lehi central committee, Nathan Friedman-
Yellin (later Nathan Yellin-Mor), Dr. Israel Sheib (later Israel Eldad) and
Yitzhak Yezernitsky (later Yitzhak Shamir, and a prime minister of Israel). The man who shot Bernadotte was probably Yehoshua Cohen, later
a friend of David Ben-Gurion.

Lehi, like the Irgun Zvai Leumi, had been violently opposed to the
partition plan, to the UN truces, and to the demilitarization of Jerusalem.
Lehi saw Bernadotte as the main obstacle both to Israeli annexation of
Jerusalem and to Jewish control of the whole of Palestine. Its daily bulle-
tins had violently denounced the mediator and the UN truce supervision
since June, and had repeatedly alleged that Bernadotte had been a Nazi
agent and was currently an agent of the Nazi's successors—presumably
meaning the British.[66] In an interview in 1971, Baruch Nadel of the Stern
Gang* said,

We knew that if Bernadotte with his magnetic personality and all his influence
came and talked with his plan in Paris, the General Assembly would decide for
this plan and endorse it. So we had to kill him on this day."[67]

Arkady Sobolev, the Soviet assistant secretary general for Security
Council Affairs, who was in charge in New York during Lie's absence in
Europe, immediately cabled to Bunche, designating him as the head of
the Palestine mission, a decision endorsed by the Security Council on
September 20, when it appointed Bunche acting mediator.† After cabling

*At the time of the assassination, Nadel was a journalist with the Stern Gang newspaper,
Ha-Mivrak.

†A dissenting voice in this appointment was Sir John Troutbeck of the British Middle East
Office in Cairo, who had seen Bunche in Rhodes the previous week. Bunche, he cabled to
the Foreign Office, "would be an unfortunate choice. As an American he would be suspect
to the Arabs. He has the reputation whether justified or not of being a convinced pro-
Zionist. From my own short acquaintance with him I should say he is a competent official
rather than a statesman. I believe Señor Azcarate would be a far better choice." Troutbeck
was overruled.[68]

Ruth, "Sad but safe. Love Ralph," Bunche had little time or disposition to worry about the undoubted fact that, as Bernadotte's deputy and chief adviser, he was certainly intended to have been one of the victims. He wrote to Ruth:

Just think. That was only the second or third time since we've been out here that I wasn't riding next to him in the back seat of the car. It just wasn't my time to go, I guess.[69]

Bernadotte's assassination had a traumatic effect on the UN staff and observers, and Bunche's first task was to rally them. General Lundström, who had been in the car with Bernadotte, had to be restrained from pulling all the military observers out and asking for an Israeli police guard at the YMCA.

In a telegram to Shertok, Bunche told the Israelis that Bernadotte's murder had done the Jews more harm than the Arabs could ever do, especially as regards international opinion and support. After denouncing the murder as an "outrage against the international community and an unspeakable violation of elementary morality," he pointed out that Bernadotte, at the time of his assassination, had been in the presence of an Israeli liaison officer, Captain Hillman, and was within the Israeli lines. His safety was therefore an Israeli responsibility. Bunche also referred to the campaign against the mediator which had been building up since June.

I feel obliged to record the view that the prejudicial and unfounded statements concerning the truce supervision attributed to you and Colonel Yadin as having been made at your press conference in Tel Aviv on Thursday, September 16 . . . are not the kind of statements which would be calculated to discourage reprehensible acts of this kind.

He also had to make a detailed report to the secretary general on the tragedy.

Bunche got to bed at 5:00 A.M. on September 18 and got up again at 8:00 A.M. to supervise the loading of the bodies on a Red Cross ambulance for the journey to Haifa. He stayed behind to confer with the chairman of the Truce Commission, American Consul General John J. MacDonald, and left by air for Haifa from Kalandia at 11:30 A.M.

Arabs very sympathetic as we passed through, with little trace of elation that the Jews had made such a terrific mistake. Arab Legion paid impressive honors to the ambulance convoy as it passed their lines.[70]

In Haifa Bunche went to the Zion Hotel and talked to Shertok on the telephone. He then went to the truce-supervision headquarters for a staff meeting called by Lundström—"a monstrous performance. What an old fool."[71] Lundström had apparently misread Sobolev's cable and believed he himself had been designated to take Bernadotte's place. He thought he would be playing Bernadotte's role in Paris and even told the staff meeting so. Bunche noted:

Then I moved in—I had been quiet until then and had let him run the meeting in his crude way. I quietly told him that no one of us would go to Paris unless specifically invited, that his going was by no means definite, that the cable made me head of the mission, that the Mediator's plane was a UN plane and would return directly to Palestine from Stockholm, and I took over the meeting from that point on.[72]

Once again Bunche worked through the night, which was probably the best way to cope with the tragedy. "I am completely exhausted but not shattered," he wrote on September 19.[73]

In a long reply to Bunche's cable on September 19, Shertok wrote that there was evidence that the assassination had been carefully planned and that the preparations for it were completed before Thursday, September 16, so that his and Yadin's statements could have had no relation to the crime. Bunche returned to the subject of the Israeli government's attitude in his reply to Shertok the following day. Commenting on an article in the *Palestine Post,* he wrote that some of the attributed statements impugned the motives of the truce supervision organization and could only lead to the conclusion

that our operation was deliberately partial and unfair. I refer, of course, to the statement that the Mediator's staff appeared to be laboring under a "political theory" that firmness must be shown towards your government, while a policy of patience and leniency was to be shown towards Arab governments.

Bunche categorically rejected this thesis, saying that there had not been, and would not be, any willful policy of discrimination against either side.

In Haifa, at 5:00 A.M. on Sunday, September 19, Bunche went to the hospital to escort the two coffins to the airport. They were loaded onto an American C-47 transport. The mediator's plane carried the count's staff and an escort of UN observers. Bunche found it very hard to watch the mediator's plane take off without him on this sad mission. He had had to choose between escorting Bernadotte's body to Stockholm and staying on the job at a critical time, and he had no difficulty in deciding which Bernadotte would have wanted him to do. He sent General Stoner, his communications expert, to represent him in Stockholm. While he was in Haifa he arranged that the bullet that had been extracted from Bernadotte's body* should be sent to Countess Bernadotte.

After seeing the mediator's plane off, he drove to Tel Aviv to see Shertok. He now had an armed Israeli escort, and three Haganah soldiers followed him everywhere. He found Shertok sad and contrite. Shertok expressed horror at the outrage and described the elaborate steps that were being taken to apprehend the murderers and to wipe out the terrorist bands. In the end these words proved much stronger than any action taken. No one was ever tried for the murder of Bernadotte.†

Bunche's own safety had now become a matter of general concern. In Paris Lie told Eban that Israel was responsible and should provide him with complete protection.‡ When he landed at Kalandia, the Jerusalem airport, with General William Riley, now chief of staff, they found themselves leaving the airport alone except for two Arab Legion armored cars. Riley, a U.S. Marine, remarked that after Bernadotte's murder none of the observers cared to risk riding with them. Their reception at the Mandelbaum Gate, however, was very different from that on September 17. Israeli guards were lined up to salute Bunche, and an Israeli liaison officer escorted him to the YMCA with two jeeploads of soldiers, one in front and one in back.[75]

Bunche was anxious to pin down the truce, which was still shaky, as well as the demilitarization of Jerusalem. Even in the days immediately after Bernadotte's murder, he frequently had to deal with violations of the truce, including an Arab attack on a UN-supervised food convoy from Tel Aviv to Jerusalem on September 22, in which an Israeli liaison officer and three civilians were killed. On September 20 he met with the Truce Com-

*Five other bullets had passed straight through the count's body.

†The Swedish Foreign Ministry report on Bernadotte's murder, published on March 9, 1950, states that the Israeli investigation had been conducted with "astonishing negligence," and that virtually none of the ordinary measures for such an investigation had been taken. Of the 266 members of the Stern Gang rounded up in the week after the murder, only two had been imprisoned, and they were released under an amnesty twelve days later.[74]

‡Two years later Robert Lovett, who in 1948 was undersecretary of state, told Bunche that the U.S. government had been so worried about him that U.S. security agents had been sent to the Near East. These agents had uncovered an extremist assassination plot aimed at Secretary of State Marshall and Bunche in Paris, to be led by a Bella Jacobs. Neither the U.S. nor the French government had been able to find these would-be assassins.

mission in the same room where Bernadotte's and Sérot's bodies had been laid out, and urged them to take up again the demilitarization of Jerusalem. He found the commission members highly skeptical of the efforts being made to apprehend Bernadotte's assassins and spoke to the head of the Israeli Criminal Investigation Department on the matter. He also took pains to disabuse the Israeli Foreign Office of the story they were putting about that Bernadotte had refused an escort.[76]

The shock of Bernadotte's assassination soon wore off, and on September 22 the Israeli government issued a statement strongly objecting to Bernadotte's proposals on the Negev and on Jerusalem.* On the same day the United States announced its acceptance of Bernadotte's report "in its entirety." Abba Eban, in Paris, expressed his astonishment to the Americans and was told that

these three words not inadvertent. Americans anxious to avoid long delay and reach swift conclusion at psychological moment now favoring decisive action. . . . Themselves willing listen arguments in committee, but undisposed far-reaching changes in report.[77]

Bunche spent from September 23 to 25 writing a full report to the Security Council on the assassination of Bernadotte and Sérot.[78] The report was a heavy indictment not only of the terrorists but also of the ambivalence of the Israeli authorities. Bunche first described the continuing threats of the Stern Gang, which culminated in the concluding words of their September 6 bulletin, "the task of the movement is to oust Bernadotte and his observers. Blessed be the hand that does it." He also described the steadily intensified attacks in the local Jewish press on both the mediator and the Truce Supervision Organization, accusing both of bias and discrimination. The government, in spite of warnings by the mediator's staff, had done nothing to counteract these unfounded attacks. On the contrary, statements by responsible officials had tended to support them. Bunche explained that Bernadotte had always taken the position that the provision of an armed escort in the places he visited was at the discretion of the local authorities, who presumably would know best the extent of the protection necessary. In these circumstances the conclusion seemed inescapable that the Jewish authorities in Jerusalem had been negligent about the mediator's safety.

*After Bernadotte's assassination Bunche had suggested that the publication of the report should be deferred until September 27, but it was already being distributed by the time his message reached Paris.

These assassinations constitute a critical challenge from an unbridled band of Jewish terrorists to the very effort of the United Nations to achieve, by means of mediation, a peaceful adjustment of the dispute in Palestine.

Bunche asked that "urgent measures be taken to insure that the aims of the United Nations in Palestine should not be frustrated by criminal bands or by any individuals or groups who might hope to profit from the acts of such bands." To Lie, in transmitting his report, he wrote:

In its preparation we took into account our obligations to an innocent man who was killed, and the morale of our observers, as well as the broad political implications. We could have said much more, but not much less. All that has been said can be thoroughly documented.

In a broadcast on September 27 Bunche emphasized the irony of Bernadotte's assassination only twenty-four hours after he had signed a report that "accepted without question the existence of the State of Israel, and which had strongly urged that the truce in Palestine must be promptly superseded by a permanent settlement." In this broadcast he strongly endorsed Bernadotte's conclusions as "the most sound and practical means of achieving this end" and expressed the hope that the General Assembly would,

at an early stage in its deliberations, take that decisive action which alone can ensure that Count Bernadotte's life, and the lives of the five other gallant men who have fallen in Palestine in the service of the United Nations will not have been wasted.

Before Bernadotte's assassination Bunche had hoped and believed that his time in Palestine was at an end and that, after a few days with Bernadotte in Paris, he would be able to go home. "Now I am trapped," he wrote to Ruth, "and my future plans for the moment at least, are much less definite."[79] For Ruth, Bernadotte's assassination precipitated a torment of worry and anxiety. "I was never so stunned and shocked in my life," she wrote on September 17. "I turned cold all over and it seemed as if my whole world had collapsed." She was deeply concerned for Bunche's health and safety, and desperately anxious for him to leave Palestine. "Please get out of Palestine as soon as you can," she wrote, "and stay out."[80] But she was also very conscious of the obligation imposed on Bunche by his appointment as acting mediator, and her letters were supportive and understanding. Her feelings were matched by her husband's. He wrote:

The crucial work to be done here would not permit me to accompany Bernadotte's body to Stockholm. I'm trying to keep the lid on the truce. . . . This is a grim business I'm in. My knowledge of your love for me is all that keeps me going.[81]

Joan and Jane, deeply anxious for their father's safety, constantly called home from school for news of him.

Bunche got back to Rhodes on September 26 totally exhausted. He wrote:

It is a great relief to be back on peaceful Rhodes. . . . I've been completely knocked out since arriving here—all the strain I've been under since 17 September came down on me. This has been the worst ten days I will ever experience in my life.[82]

On September 28 Lie asked Bunche to come to Paris immediately. Before leaving he sent another report to the Security Council, deploring the worsening situation in Palestine and the threat it constituted to the authority, prestige, and even the safety of the truce supervisors.[83] To date, six men, including the mediator, had been killed and seven wounded, and the observers, their vehicles, and their aircraft were frequently under fire. Bunche asked the Security Council to use its authority to remedy this situation, and especially to bring home to the parties their obligation to ensure the safety and safe conduct of the observers and the representatives of the mediator.

Bunche himself was now guarded around the clock. Although the Jewish press was still attacking him as they had attacked Bernadotte, and Bunche's main task in Paris was to defend the Bernadotte report, "which I wrote anyway,"[84] the Israelis certainly wanted to avoid responsibility for a second assassination. When he learned that he was to leave for Paris at once, he cabled to Ruth to come over quickly. She and Ralph Jr. sailed from New York on the *Queen Mary* on October 15.

13

The Acting Mediator in Paris

Walking Just as Straight a Line as I Know How

Bunche arrived in Paris on October 8. For the first and last time in his UN career, he was his own boss, responsible only to the Security Council, and with considerable freedom to act independently. In the next two months he took the lead both in the General Assembly, over the Bernadotte report and the Arab refugees, and in the Security Council, over the truce and the Israeli campaign in the Negev. He also proposed the form and nature of future approaches to the Palestine problem.

The 1948 session of the UN General Assembly in Paris was a dramatic international gathering in a city that was still struggling to throw off the trauma and misery of war and occupation. George Marshall, Ernest Bevin, Vyacheslav Molotov, and Andrei Vishinsky were among its many stars. Under the leadership of Eleanor Roosevelt, the session produced a landmark in the history of human civility, the Universal Declaration of Human Rights. At the same time the Security Council was grappling with the first great crisis of the Cold War, the Berlin blockade. The UN was housed in the buildings of the Musée de l'Homme, which had been the center of the Paris World Exhibition which Bunche had visited with Ruth in 1937—a central pavilion and two curving wings looking across the Seine to the Eiffel Tower.

Before he left for Paris Bunche knew that discussion of Bernadotte's report would be delayed. Although the United States and Britain were prepared in principle to submit, with other members, a joint proposal embodying Bernadotte's proposals in broad terms, the Berlin crisis was the dominant issue in Paris. The Arabs hoped to delay the debate on Palestine until after the American presidential election in November, and seemed to prefer the freezing of the current situation in some kind of armistice arrangement to making a final settlement. Abba Eban noted on September 30 that whereas the Americans and British were anxious to use the shock of Bernadotte's assassination to get the Bernadotte plan endorsed quickly, the Arabs, as usual, had come to Israel's aid by insisting on a postponement of any decision in the hope of preventing the General Assembly from coming to grips with the problem at all.[1]

Bunche had lively discussions with Eban and Michael Comay on the Bernadotte plan. Eban told him that Israel would reject any attempt to detach the Negev from Israel and would, if necessary, react by putting up additional settlements in the Negev. Bunche explained that Bernadotte had hoped to use the desert areas of the Negev as an inducement to the Arabs to make concessions elsewhere. He was particularly irritated by the persistent Israeli allegation that the British had dictated Bernadotte's proposals on the Negev for their own strategic reasons. As he informed the Israelis, Bernadotte himself had originally put forward the idea after a sleepless night, and it had been written into his report days before the British and American representatives had arrived on Rhodes.

Bunche's first preoccupation in Paris was to insist that the Israelis provide better security for UN representatives in Israel.* When, on October 14, the Security Council considered his report on the matter, Bunche payed a tribute to the courage of his people in Palestine as "a real inspiration" and described the hazards which they faced. "They are unarmed; their only protection is the United Nations armband and the United Nations flag, often augmented by a white flag."[2] Many of the Council members congratulated Bunche on his own courage and on his clear and outspoken statements.

On October 14, before the Assembly could take up the Bernadotte report, serious fighting between Israeli and Egyptian forces broke out in the Negev. As Bernadotte had anticipated, the Israelis were evidently anxious to "create facts" on the ground before the matter was discussed in the Assembly and had launched a preemptive strike to avert the possibility that, under American and British pressure, the Assembly would adopt the Bernadotte plan, which allotted the Negev to the Arabs. An Egyptian attack on a convoy supplying an Israeli settlement in the Negev served as the pretext for a well-prepared and massive offensive, originally called Operation Ten Plagues. The Israelis captured Beersheba on October 17. During the final stages of the presidential election campaign in the United

---

*In Paris, Bunche himself had a permanent escort of three French detectives, and his efforts to dispense with them were unavailing. His concern that they should be properly fed in restaurants provided the overture to many meals.

States, Israel was exerting maximum pressure on President Truman to reverse Secretary of State Marshall's approval of the Bernadotte proposals.

Dan Kurzman's biography of David Ben-Gurion gives some idea of the Israeli game-plan.

On October 22, after stalling the UN for a few days, Ben-Gurion had to give the cease-fire order to his commanders. . . . The Arabs were on the run, and he had to keep them running. But not for the moment in the Negev. If he defied the United Nations now, Truman himself might give up on Israel, and the new State could not risk losing American support.

Instead, six days later, Ben-Gurion ordered an offensive in Galilee and into Lebanon.[3] The truce broke down in Jerusalem on October 15 and, a week later, on the Lebanese border.

At Bunche's urging, which provoked "a tiff with Eban,"[4] the Security Council, on October 19, called for an immediate cease-fire, withdrawal of all forces to their previous positions, and freedom of movement and access for the UN observers.[5] By the time a cease-fire, ordered by Bunche as mediator, had come into force on October 22, an Egyptian division, in which Egypt's future president, Gamal Abdel Nasser, was a major, had been cut off at Al-Faluja, northeast of Gaza. Eban, representing Israel on the Council, was at loggerheads with Bunche throughout this episode. Israel resented Bunche's demands for withdrawal in the Negev, and Eban's indignation reached its peak on October 31 in a cable to Sharett in which he accused Bunche of lack of impartiality, high-handed conduct, and "irresponsible self-assertedness" in embroiling the United States in open conflict with Israel just before the election.[6] At the same time the Egyptian side regarded Bunche's attitude as unduly soft on the Israelis.

The Negev action, unlike previous violations of the truce, had been a major military offensive. Bunche, on whose reports the Council based its debate, told the Council on October 28 that, despite the cease-fire, the position of the opposing forces made an early resumption of hostilities almost certain, and also threatened the whole future of the truce itself. What was needed was no longer a mere interruption of hostilities, but a transition to a permanent condition of peace—the indispensable condition for an eventual settlement of the Palestine problem. It was time, Bunche told the Council, for bolder and broader action, such as a

clear and forceful declaration by the Council that the parties be required to negotiate . . . a settlement of all outstanding truce problems in all sectors of

Palestine with a view to achieving a permanent condition of peace in place of the existing truce. Such a negotiation would necessarily aim at a formal peace, or at the minimum, an armistice which would involve either complete withdrawal and demobilization of armed forces or their wide separation by creation of broad demilitarized zones under United Nations supervision.[7]

On November 4, the Council called on all parties to withdraw to their October 14 positions and to negotiate permanent truce lines and such neutral and demilitarized zones as seemed necessary.[8] It also appointed a committee of the Council, consisting of the five permanent, and two nonpermanent, members, to advise the mediator with regard to his responsibilities under the resolution. This resolution was a considerable retreat from the Council's October 19 decision because it opened up the possibility of negotiating new truce lines, thus accepting to some extent the Israeli *fait accompli* in the Negev and putting the final responsibility on the mediator. Bunche, however, noted, "Negev resolution adopted and vindicated my actions,"[9] and Eban urged Sharett to stall on any response and to be sure that the White House was informed that the U.S. delegation were aligned "with most extreme British position."[10] The Egyptians resented what they regarded as the Council's pusillanimity, but, because their own military situation was so weak, were eventually forced to accept the resolution.

On November 9 Bunche submitted proposals, in the form of a draft resolution, to the Council, which, at his insistence, met in private session. These proposals recognized that "the transition from truce to a definitive end of hostilities is an indispensable condition of an ultimate peaceful settlement of the basic political issues" and called upon both sides to "undertake immediately through the good offices of the Acting Mediator, the settlement of all outstanding problems of the truce in all sectors of Palestine." The resolution called for the establishment of an armistice involving the separation of armed forces by the creation of demilitarized zones under UN observation, and "such ultimate withdrawal and reduction of their forces as will ensure the restoration of Palestine to peacetime conditions."[11] He also proposed a provisional demarcation line in the Negev, and on November 13 he called on Israel and Egypt to withdraw their forces to this line by November 19. On November 19 Bunche stated that he was satisfied that both Israel and Egypt had complied with his instructions to establish provisional truce lines in the Negev.

On November 16 the Council, following up Bunche's proposals, recommended the conclusion of armistice agreements in all sectors of Palestine.[12] There ensued one of those chicken-and-egg arguments for which the Middle East has become famous. Bunche, who was unhappy that the Council had merely called for, rather than *ordered,* an armistice, had immediately asked the governments in the Middle East to give him their views on the procedure for negotiating the armistice agreements as soon as possible. Egypt refused to talk about an armistice before the November 4 withdrawal order in the Negev had been acted on by Israel, whereupon Israel, which regarded the November 16 resolution as toning down the harshness of the November 4 resolution,[13] refused to withdraw its troops because of Egyptian noncompliance with the November 16 armistice resolution.

The stalemate continued for three weeks until, in early December, Bunche made a brief visit to Tel Aviv and Cairo. In a two-and-one-half-hour talk with Ben-Gurion, he got very little except a tribute to Bernadotte and himself for their devoted efforts. The Israelis knew very well that Egypt desperately needed to extricate itself from its military and political impasse but was inhibited from doing so by the humiliating situation of the Egyptian division trapped at Al-Faluja.

On his return to Paris Bunche suggested bridging the gap between the November 4 and November 16 resolutions by reassuring each side of the other's intentions. Specifically, he proposed that Israel would agree in principle to permit the withdrawal of the Egyptian forces at Al-Faluja; that the UN chief of staff, General Riley, would negotiate the procedure for the withdrawal in stages under UN supervision; that, simultaneously, permanent truce lines would be negotiated; and that Egypt would guarantee that the troops released from Al-Faluja would not be employed against the Israelis.[14] The Egyptian government finally announced that it would take part in the armistice negotiations as soon as the Israelis withdrew to the truce lines fixed by the mediator.

The shift from maintaining the truce to negotiating an armistice, as signified by the Council's November 16 resolution, made it easy for Israel to consolidate its conquest of the Negev, an early example of the successful technique of "creating facts." By skillful manipulation of the Al-Faluja situation, the Israelis also forced the Egyptians into the negotiation of an armistice at a time when the Egyptian military situation was catastrophically weak.

Just before Christmas Egypt complained of a new, large-scale Israeli attack into the Southern Triangle of the Negev. Bunche, from New York, submitted detailed reports on the fighting for the Council's December 28 meeting, strongly criticizing Israel's expulsion of the UN observers from its area of operations.

In view of all the above circumstances I must report to the Security Council my inability to supervise effectively the truce in the Negev, since UN Observers are being refused access to the area on the Israeli side, and since, as indicated in Mr. Eytan's message of 22 December, the Government of Israel feels bound to reserve its freedom of action. I must also report my view that the intransigent attitude assumed by the Israeli authorities on the situation at Al-Faluja is a major factor in preventing progress towards implementation of the Resolution of the Security Council of 16 November.[15]

The Council, on December 29, once again called for an immediate cease-fire and cooperation with the mediator and the truce supervisors.[16] A forceful message to Israel from President Truman was delivered on December 30.[17] Fighting flared up again, followed by yet another Security Council resolution, and a cease-fire was finally arranged for January 7.

The effort to maintain the truce was more than enough of a task for one person in Paris, but Bunche was simultaneously following up on Bernadotte's report, in the fading hope that the historic moment that Bernadotte had perceived would not be missed. Other international preoccupations, particularly the Berlin crisis, as well as the maneuvers, both diplomatic and military, of the Israelis and the self-defeating intransigence of the Arabs, had already eroded the American-British resolve briefly evoked by Bernadotte's murder. In September Secretary of State Marshall and the British had seemed willing to try to put through a settlement of the Palestine question which, though neither side agreed with all of it, neither could refuse. The General Assembly's First Committee—the main political committee—finally began its debate on Bernadotte's report nearly five weeks later, on October 15.

Bunche opened the debate with a tribute to Bernadotte, who "but for that crime in Jerusalem committed by a band of despicable gangsters . . . would be speaking to you now."[18] He characterized Bernadotte as

not only my chief but a treasured friend. . . . He was an utterly honest and fearless man, completely independent in his thinking, and thoroughly devoted to the effort to bring peace to Palestine. He had no axe to grind, no vested interest to serve.[19]

Bunche went on to a forceful analysis of the "inescapable logic of the situation in Palestine with which this Assembly is now confronted," and its three main features—the proclamation and vital reality of the Jewish state, the resort to forceful measures by the Arab states, and the intervention of the Security Council. Although the imposed truce of July 18 was a permanent cease-fire order, it was regarded by both parties as more a temporary than a permanent arrangement. The armies still confronted each other in full battle array. Such a situation could not last indefinitely and must be superseded by something more durable and secure—either a formal peace or an armistice.

The intensity of feelings on both sides had made it impossible for the mediator to bring the two parties together to achieve a settlement, not least because the Arabs had steadfastly refused to meet with Jewish representatives, even in the presence of the mediator, for fear that such a step might be taken as a tacit admission of the right of the Jewish state to exist. This did not mean that Bernadotte had concluded that the Palestine problem could not be solved by peaceful means.

There was an alternative which derived precisely from the very rigidity of the parties who were at the same time in the predicament of having to defy the Security Council in order to resort to the simple expedient of trial by force of arms.

Bernadotte had been convinced that the combination of the injunction against military action by the Security Council and firm political decisions by the General Assembly could bring both sides to acquiesce, however reluctantly, in any reasonable settlement which had the stamp of approval of the United Nations. In the words of Bernadotte's report:

What is indispensable is that the General Assembly take a firm position on the political aspects of the problem in the light of all the circumstances since its last session, and that its resolution be so reasonable as to discourage any attempt to thwart it and to defy the Security Council order by the employment of armed force.[20]

Bunche saw two imperative needs for resolving the Palestine question. The first was a reasonable basis for the assumption that neither side would again resort to force to achieve its ends. The second was for the Assembly, representing the international community, to set forth its position on the fundamental political issues. These issues were: permanent peace in Palestine; the existence of the Jewish state; the boundaries of such a state; international guarantees for these boundaries; the future status of Jerusalem; the disposition of the Arab-controlled area of Palestine; guarantees of the rights of all inhabitants of Palestine; repatriation and resettlement of Arab refugees; and the nature of continuing United Nations involvement. Bunche urged that Bernadotte's conclusions be used as a basis for the Assembly's decisions on these matters. Bernadotte had not believed that either Arabs or Jews would embrace his conclusions in their entirety, but he did think that the United Nations "speaks with considerable authority in Palestine."[21]

Bunche's statement was both balanced and pragmatic. The following day Dean Rusk cabled from Paris to Robert Lovett in the State Department that the statement

should relieve tension of those who've been afraid of rigidity in precise detail. . . . Bunche's statement as a whole gives full credit to Jewish side and should steady the nerves of those who are being bombarded by partisan propaganda.[22]

Bunche himself was under few illusions as to the willingness of the Assembly to act firmly. Eban, reporting on October 20 on a luncheon with Bunche,

found him chastened, doubtful whether any outcome Assembly likely, in any case only very general resolution feasible. Expressed his dissatisfaction Council weakness, especially American complacency at Israel's advance [in Negev]. . . . Reticent on Negev, adding significantly Israel interest lies allowing Egyptians some foothold in part of Negev.[23]

According to Bunche, Michael Comay, who also attended this lunch, was not quite as bland as Eban and told him that "others may be assassinated by fanatics if the Negev is denied to the Jews."[24]

In an interview with Larry Lesueur of CBS on October 17 Bunche was skeptical of the prospect of formal peace in Palestine, but thought a *condition* of peace might be preserved if the Assembly was prepared to take

the necessary unequivocal decisions concerning fundamental political issues. . . . New international machinery is necessary in my view. The mediation function has run its course. There is really not much more to be expected from one-man mediation.

Bernadotte had suggested a UN conciliation commission, which Bunche wholeheartedly endorsed.

The campaign against the Bernadotte proposals continued. On October 25 the Israeli mission in Washington told Sharett that Marshall had informed President Truman that the U.S. delegation in Paris was ready to present a joint Anglo-American resolution proposing the adoption of the Bernadotte plan in its entirety.

Our friend in White House* explained [to] Truman detrimental effect such action both on settlement and his own interest. Consequently instructions sent

*Probably Judge Samuel I. Rosenman, who was advising Truman on Palestine and on its impact on the impending presidential election.

Marshall abstain from presentation such resolution and avoid any statements on Palestine without previous clearing White House. . . .[25]

Bunche continued to steer the debate in the First Committee of the General Assembly. In a statement to the committee on November 25, seeking to clarify Bernadotte's intentions, Bunche leveled a counterblast at allegations, frequently made in private by the Israelis and recently publicly aired in an American periodical, *The Nation,* that representatives of the U.K. and U.S. had written significant parts of Bernadotte's report, especially on the Negev. Categorically denying this allegation, Bunche described it as

a contemptible slander of a dead man, and a slur on the honesty and integrity of a thoroughly honest person who sacrificed his life in unselfish service to the United Nations.

Bunche noted that similar boundary proposals had been put forward in Bernadotte's first suggestions to the parties in the previous June.

Pointing out that both sides had condemned Bernadotte's conclusions, Bunche acknowledged the Arabs' right to refuse to recognize the Jewish state, but challenged their claim to have the right to resort to force.

By the Arabs the [Bernadotte] report has been denounced for alleged crass and pragmatic acceptance of the *fait accompli* without regard to right and equity. By the Jews, on the contrary, it is condemned for not perceiving and accepting, to use Mr. Shertok's words, the "inexorable logic of events" which are asserted to entitle the State of Israel not only to territory envisaged in the 29 November resolution but also to a number of other "territorial improvements" beyond those limits.

Bunche felt that, for all the complications, the area of the Palestine dispute had been vastly narrowed in one year.

Today, despite the familiar torrents of protest, the issue of the Jewish state, and with it the issue of immigration, have been settled for all practical purposes. Even as regards boundaries, the points remaining at issue relate almost exclusively to the Negev and Western Galilee. The future status of Jerusalem remains to be determined, and a new and urgent issue, that of the future of Arab refugees has arisen as a result of the fighting.

In conclusion Bunche listed seven points to guide the Assembly in its attempt to find a solution: affirmation of the state of Israel and its membership in the UN; a strong call to the parties to resolve their differences through direct or indirect negotiation; the establishment of a conciliation commission; clear guidance to this commission; the strongest possible international guarantees for the boundaries, which could be changed only by mutual consent; affirmation of the right of Arab refugees either to return or to compensation; the determination of the future of Jerusalem with a special international status under UN supervision, with local Arab and Jewish autonomy. Bunche also urged that the office of the mediator be terminated as soon as the Palestine Conciliation Commission was organized, and that the functions of truce and armistice supervision be transferred to the Conciliation Commission at the same time. These points were to become the main substance of the Assembly's final decision on December 11.

On November 30, in a supplemental report to the Assembly, Bunche again urged the Assembly to exert its influence on the Palestine question.

I am thoroughly convinced that the action which the General Assembly may now take will be decisive in determining whether the Palestine problem will be quickly settled or will drag on with increasing ill-will between the parties and a continuing threat to the peace of the world. In this regard the critical issue is whether the General Assembly will assist a settlement by an unequivocal expression of its conclusions as to the desirable basis of a settlement, or whether it will shift the entire burden of the settlement to the parties themselves.

On December 11, the Assembly, rejecting British proposals to approve the territorial provisions of the Bernadotte report, passed a resolution which, among other things, established the Palestine Conciliation Commission, which was "to assume in so far as it considers necessary in existing circumstances, the functions given the United Nations Mediator. . . ."[26] Bunche certainly believed that with the establishment of the Palestine Conciliation Commission, his term as mediator was coming to an end and that he would soon hand over to the commission. On the following day he left for New York to see his family (Ruth had left Paris in mid-November) and have a long-delayed medical checkup.

The weeks in Paris had been, even by Bunche's standards, astonishingly intensive. Quite apart from a rigorous round of appointments and meetings, the volume of statements, letters, instructions, and reports to the Security Council on the truce, to the General Assembly on the mediation effort and on the refugees, and to his representatives in the Middle East—clear, forceful, and unambiguous, and all written originally in long-hand—constitute an extraordinary achievement of intellectual analysis, stamina, and constructive judgment. Bunche's qualities of courage, responsibility, clear thinking, comprehensive drafting, and sheer endurance offered a refreshing contrast to the diplomatic and political shifting and turning of the governments in the General Assembly. It was a lonely effort, throughout which Bunche remained exactly as he had always been—friendly, unpretentious, humorous, and incredibly hardworking. Working round the clock with his close associates in an improvised office looking over the roofs of Paris, he discouraged, as far as possible, all personal publicity and did his best to evade the attentions of journalists.

The hostility of the Israelis to the Bernadotte proposals and to Bunche's opposition to their campaign in the Negev and other *faits accomplis* was not only expressed in private conversations and diplomatic cables. Partisan journals in the United States were also useful mouthpieces. A classic example was the campaign against Bunche by Freda Kirchwey of *The Nation,* which coincided with the Israeli offensive in the Negev. Kirchwey even importuned Trygve Lie, to whom she wrote,

It is my hope that upon reading the article[27] you will agree that the situation is one urgently calling for an investigation by you of the fashion in which an honorable decision of the United Nations [the partition plan] is being contravened with the help of representatives of the United Nations.

To his credit, Lie responded to this letter with a blistering rebuttal, but the canard that the Bernadotte plan had been written by the Arabists of the U.S. State Department and the British Foreign Office was still trotted out, and Bunche was even attacked for criticizing the Israeli authorities at the time of Bernadotte's assassination.

Nor was Bunche confident of the quality of the support he was getting from his own organization. Trygve Lie was strongly biased in favor of Israel, and he certainly was not happy that a member of the Secretariat was in such a prominent and independent position as the Palestine mediator. Bunche had come to view Lie as a lazy, vain, and self-centered man, who nursed petty prejudices and was anything but objective on major issues such as Palestine. The secretary general's refusal to visit Palestine when he and Bernadotte had suggested it had not impressed Bunche with either Lie's courage or his sense of responsibility. When Bunche arrived in Paris from Rhodes after Bernadotte's assassination the first words Lie spoke to him were, "Have you had your picture taken with that SOB Evatt yet?" (Herbert Evatt, the Australian foreign minister, was the current president of the General Assembly. He and Lie were deeply jealous and suspicious of each other.) Later on, when Bunche had charged the Israelis with violating the truce in the Negev, Lie, at a lunch for top

Secretariat officials, yelled down the table to Bunche, "Ralph, you are a good number 2 man, but not a number 1"[28]—a remark in which it was hard not to detect a racial overtone.

Hostility to Bunche sometimes took even pettier forms. An attempt was made to deny him the mediator's salary, to which he was clearly entitled—Lie claiming that Byron Price, the American assistant secretary general for administration, was blocking it, while Price claimed that Lie was responsible. Bunche regarded this petty insult as indicative of Lie's and Price's jealousy of his position. Only in June 1949 did he finally receive the remuneration that was due to him,[29] by which time Bunche had successfully negotiated the armistice agreements, and Lie had radically changed his attitude.

Herbert Evatt made no secret of his own unqualified support for Israel, and Bunche was aware that Evatt was jealous of him and lost no opportunity to subvert his authority as mediator. Michael Comay, for example, reported, after a meeting with Evatt on December 14, that Evatt had said Bunche "was essentially a weak person, and very much controlled by the Foreign Office and the State Department. . . ."[30] Evatt's jealousy had reduced him to playing back Israeli propaganda to the Israelis themselves.

"I need hardly tell you," Bunche wrote to Karel Lisicky, who had been chairman of the defunct Palestine Commission,

that I am not at all happy to find myself on this very hot seat. . . . I am doing the best I can, but I fear that is not enough. There are so many complications, interferences, pressures, maneuvers and intrigues that at times I quite despair of finding a way out at all. I am just a fill-in, however, and that is consoling.[31]

His friends, thinking of Bernadotte's fate, were worried about Bunche's safety. Walter White, the secretary of the NAACP, wrote to say that in New York he had found "one of the damnedest campaigns I have ever run into—of an apparently organized Jewish attack on you regarding the Negev." White had been pointing out to his Jewish friends that the whole cause of the Jews "was being damaged by their prompt assertion that anyone who does not do precisely as they wish is therefore guilty of having sold out to the British, the Arabs, or somebody else."[32] Bunche replied:

Most of my fan mail (chiefly from New York) is not pleasant reading these days. I am neither surprised nor hurt by it. In the sort of work on which I am now engaged this kind of attack must be rated as an occupational hazard. The purpose, of course, is to discredit me and also the Bernadotte report. It is not inconceivable that it may have a substantial measure of success. As long as I am on the job I shall continue to call each play just as I see it. When the Arabs are wrong I put the finger on them, and I'll do precisely the same with the Jews come hell or high water, and despite the fact that I have had a purely personal sympathy for their cause. That's the only way I know how to play the game.[33]

A violent outburst from an unexpected source particularly pained Bunche. W. E. B. Du Bois, whom he had so greatly admired in his youth, attacked him in a speech to the American Jewish Congress at Madison Square Garden for betraying the interests of the Jewish people. Du Bois apologized to his audience "in the name of the American Negro for the apparent apostasy of Ralph Bunche . . . to the clear ideals of freedom and fair play, which should have guided the descendant of an American slave." Du Bois implied that Bunche had sold out for money and power. He also linked Bunche to a "disgraceful betrayal" of the Jews by the Department of State as the heirs to British imperialism. Bunche never forgot, or forgave, this multiple insult, although Du Bois later praised his performance as mediator. In 1951, he refused to serve as a sponsor for a testimonial dinner for Du Bois on his eighty-third birthday because of Du Bois' attack on his integrity and objectivity. "It would be sheer hypocrisy for me now to pretend that I had forgotten this insult from a man who, up to that time, I had always considered to be a truly great personality, to be admired and deeply respected, and with whom I had always had the most cordial relations."[34]

The Arabs, who resented the Bernadotte report as much as or more than the Israelis, were more restrained and less personal in their criticisms. They had not yet learned the art of turning their disagreements with the mediator into an aggressive and derogatory public campaign.

To his old Howard colleague, Alain Locke, Bunche wrote:

I don't like misrepresentation, of course, and I am aware that in some quarters I am labelled as anti-Semitic. But all that is an occupational hazard in this controversial job. Trouble is the public gets political settlement mixed up with the truce supervision, and unfortunately I have been handling both, and walking just as straight a line as I know how.[35]

14

Armistice Talks in Rhodes— Egypt and Israel

Holding a Bear by the Tail

Bunche had tried very hard to get Bernadotte's proposals for a Palestine settlement endorsed by the General Assembly. He knew better than anyone that neither Arabs nor Israelis liked the proposals, but that in itself created a certain balance, and with full support from the outside world it was just possible that the Bernadotte plan could have been made to work. Now the opportunity—slim though it had been—had been lost. The alternative was to negotiate an armistice regime which would at least give the Near East a more stable situation than the often violated truce, as well as a firmer basis for the work of the Palestine Conciliation Commission.

On January 6, 1949, Bunche, who was still in New York, informed the president of the Security Council that the Egyptian and Israeli governments had unconditionally accepted his proposals for a cease-fire to be followed immediately by direct negotiations on an armistice between the two governments under United Nations chairmanship. The cease-fire in the Negev came into force on January 7. Realizing that this agreement might soon evaporate under the pressures of the military situation, Bunche decided to go ahead with the negotiations without waiting for the Palestine Conciliation Commission to get organized.* The armistice

---

*The Palestine Conciliation Commission, the members of which were France, Turkey, and the United States, had its first meeting in Geneva on January 17. The commission's morale and its estimate of the feasibility and importance of its task were indicated by the behavior of the United States representative, Joseph B. Keenan, who failed to attend the commission's first meeting. Bunche had seen Keenan, evidently in the throes of a severe hangover, in New York, and described his appointment as a "scandal." Keenan was replaced by Mark Ethridge, later the publisher of the Louisville *Courier Journal.*

negotiations between Israel and Egypt opened on Rhodes on January 12 under Bunche's chairmanship.

Even before Bunche left New York he had a foretaste of the complications to come. The Egyptians were sore about last-minute Israeli military gains in the Negev. The British were "hopping mad" about five RAF reconnaissance planes which the Israelis had shot down in the desert. The Israelis were worked up about British forces that had landed at Aqaba. For a time it looked as if the Rhodes negotiations might blow up before they started, and Bunche sent "all kinds of strong cables"[1] to calm things down. Nor was he encouraged, during a last-minute shopping expedition, to be told by a Fifth Avenue salesman, "I see you're leaving tomorrow. I suppose you are still trying to take the Negev from us."[2]

Arriving on January 11, Bunche found Rhodes depressingly familiar, except that it was now *cold* and damp. There was no heating in the Hôtel des Roses, and the food was worse than ever.

There was no model and no precedent for the negotiation on which Bunche was about to embark. The reality of the military situation was relatively simple. Egyptian weakness and incompetence had made possible the *fait accompli* of Israel's conquest of the Negev, in open breach of the truce. No available pressure, either political or military, was strong enough to persuade Israel to withdraw from the Negev. The objective of the armistice negotiations, therefore, was to produce a more stable situation by getting Egypt to accept the Israeli conquest of the Negev in exchange for the evacuation of the beleaguered Al-Faluja garrison and the undisputed occupation by the Egyptian army of the coastal strip between Gaza and the frontier.

The political situation was more complex. The Israelis, from President Weizmann on down, felt passionately about the Negev and saw no reason why Egypt, which had never accepted the General Assembly's partition decision, had tried to crush Israel by force and had been decisively defeated, should be compensated with a part of the Negev. The Israelis were also determined to extract the last ounce of advantage from the humiliating situation of the trapped Egyptian division—Egypt's best—at Al-Faluja.

The Egyptian government was in a very difficult position. The Egyptian public had never been told the dismal truth about the much-touted triumphs of the army. The politicians were therefore far more bellicose and unrealistic than the soldiers. Moreover, other Arab countries were watching Egypt's performance, and their own conduct vis-à-vis Israel would be greatly influenced by it.

The physical arrangements in Rhodes—even the appalling food—were, on the whole, advantageous to the mediation effort. For the first and only time Arab and Israeli negotiators were living in the same hotel and eating in the same dining room on a remote island where there were no alternatives and no distractions. "Israel occupied the larger part of one floor," Walter Eytan wrote, "and Egypt the floor immediately above. It was an excellent arrangement. All the parties concerned were under the same roof, yet each enjoyed almost perfect privacy."[3] The main recreation in the Hôtel des Roses was Ping-Pong and billiards, at which Bunche excelled. Rhodes presented no incentives for dallying or staying a moment longer than was necessary. A determined mediator could use these conditions as an additional element of pressure.

The talks opened in a relatively congenial atmosphere. The delegations arrived in Rhodes on the afternoon of January 12. The Israelis were represented by Walter Eytan, Reuven Shiloah, and Elias Sasson on the civilian side, and, on the military side, by Colonel Yigael Yadin, the chief of staff of the Israeli army, with a staff that included Yitzhak Rabin. The Egyptians had a predominantly military delegation, including Colonel Seif El Dine, Colonel El Rahmany, and a young honorary colonel, Ismail Sherine, who was a cousin of King Farouk. After meeting both groups informally, Bunche assembled them for an opening meeting on the afternoon of January 13. It was a surprisingly cordial occasion, with handshaking all around and none of the usual problems about agenda or procedure. Bunche felt they were off to a good start.

In his opening statement Bunche laid down his own broad interpretation of their task on Rhodes, which was to give effect to the Security Council's resolutions of November 4 (withdrawal of forces) and November 16 (armistice). The Rhodes meeting was very specifically *not* a peace conference to settle all the complicated political issues, which was the function of the Conciliation Commission. "I can readily think," Bunche told the opening meeting,

of a million ways to stall, delay, obstruct and stalemate these discussions should anyone care to do so. I trust there will be no tendency to be rigidly legalistic, picayunish about detail, or recriminatory. There are many eyes here, and motes can readily be found in them. . . . You cannot afford to fail. You must succeed. I have faith that you will succeed.[4]

Later on that night Bunche drafted a declaration of basic principles to guide the discussions, and these were accepted on the following day. This declaration was also designed to serve as a preamble to the eventual armistice agreement and stipulated: scrupulous respect for the injunction of the Security Council against the use of military force; no aggressive actions to be planned or executed by either party; respect for the right of each party to its security and to freedom from fear of attack; and the acceptance of the armistice as an indispensable step toward peace in Palestine.[5] The agenda was equally simple: Al-Faluja; delineation of armistice lines; withdrawal of forces; reduction of forces.

Bunche was fully sensitive to the impact of outside events on the armistice negotiations, but he was also anxious to minimize that impact. The British, whose influence on Middle Eastern events tended to be baneful, had landed a considerable force at Aqaba to reinforce Transjordan just before the Rhodes talks, alarming the Israelis and providing a pretext for them to drag their feet concerning the Negev. Although Bunche was furious at what he regarded as an act of wanton sabotage, he was anxious to avoid debates in the Security Council that would inevitably lead to public recriminations between Egypt and Israel. He therefore did not submit a report to the Council on the British adventure. Bunche was also anxious to have the support of the other Arab states for the armistice negotiations and sent Stavropoulos to Amman, Beirut, and Damascus on January 14 to line up similar negotiations to follow immediately on the Egypt-Israel talks.

When Bunche decided to go on the offensive about getting the trapped Egyptian division out of Al-Faluja, the cordial façade of the opening meetings began to crack. During the night of Sunday, January 16, he drafted a plan which he gave to the Israelis and Egyptians on the following day. It provided for the Egyptian division's withdrawal under exclusive United Nations supervision, after which the division's heavy equipment would be held in UN custody until the armistice became effective. This plan was ostensibly approved with surprising ease at a formal meeting the same evening. Thus, in an atmosphere of false optimism, the discussion of the next item, the armistice lines, began on January 18. "Good progress here," Bunche, who had had no time to write letters, cabled to Ruth.[6]

Unfortunately, the Israelis, in agreeing to January 24 as the date for the Al-Faluja evacuation, had assumed that there would be an armistice agreement by that time, but in his separate meetings with the two sides on the armistice lines Bunche soon encountered serious disagreements. On January 23, when it became clear that agreement on the armistice was a long way off, the Israelis informed Bunche that they would not, after all, allow the Egyptians to withdraw from Al-Faluja on January 24. Facing the first major crisis of the talks, Bunche called in Eytan to give him a personal appraisal of the Israeli position. He told Eytan that the Israelis seemed unwilling to make any significant concessions and "wished the Egyptians to sign a blank cheque."[7] Eytan protested and blamed the confusion on Bunche's optimism that the armistice would be signed before January 24. Bunche denied having made any such forecast. ("Humbug," he commented in his notes.[8]) Eytan reported to Tel Aviv that "we have more or less succeeded in antagonizing Bunche by what he considers our rigid and ungenerous attitude," and expressed the fear that it would be very bad for Israel if the Al-Faluja business were to come up in the Security Council.[9]

After sending a description of the situation to Washington, which had just granted Israel a $100-million loan, Bunche called in the Egyptians, who were dumbfounded when he told them that the Al-Faluja evacuation was to be postponed. He told them to sleep on the news overnight; he would advise them in the morning about future action.

On the following day, in order to "save the Conference (although personally I thought the Egyptians should leave)," Bunche presented a three-point program to the Egyptians and then to the Israelis. He proposed: a strong, and signed, cease-fire agreement of indefinite duration; Israeli permission for food and medical convoys under UN supervision to go to Al-Faluja; and a three-day adjournment of the talks so that the delegates could consult their governments. This was accepted by both sides, and the talks were saved.

Eytan felt that they had all learned a lesson about overoptimism and not relying on purely oral understandings. He paid a backhanded tribute to Bunche, "a most remarkable man. . . . Incidentally . . . at times under Bunche's pressure I felt almost as Hacha* must have done before Hitler." Eytan also recorded Bunche's rebuke to his colleague John Reedman. When Reedman had said that if he were an Egyptian he would walk out of the conference, Bunche rounded on him, saying, "Well, you're not an Egyptian and never will be." Eytan also told Sharett that he felt the Israeli line was too rigid.[10] Eytan, for all the acrimony of the recent exchanges, was evidently developing a considerable respect for Bunche.

Bunche was glad of the three-day respite. He slowed down on work, played billiards, and took the opportunity to become better acquainted with Eytan and Yadin as well as with Seif El Dine. He also dealt with a smuggling ring that had developed among the temporary UN radio operators in Haifa by ordering the immediate dismissal of anyone suspected of

---

*Emil Hacha was president of Czechoslovakia in 1938 at the time of the Nazi takeover of his country.

smuggling. To Ruth, in his first letter since leaving New York, he complained that with the endless days and nights he was "virtually paralyzed with fatigue—a new experience for me." He did not see any way out "unless a miracle happens," and told Ruth that he had asked the Security Council to be relieved of his thankless and unpleasant task, which could be taken over by the Conciliation Commission.*[11]

The negotiations resumed on January 27, but there was no change in the position of either side on the armistice lines. The wrangling went on day and night, with interludes during which Bunche drafted compromise proposals. "Neither side anxious to meet the other," Bunche noted, "but both want me to persuade the other. What a life!"[13] Bunche tried persuasion in separate meetings, in a joint night meeting with coffee and drinks and sandwiches, and night after night of drafting and map-marking, but all to no avail. "Neither side," Bunche noted, "will wish to take responsibility for terminating the negotiations and so [both] will try to shift that responsibility to me."[14] He informed Trygve Lie that prospects for an agreement were virtually nil unless effective intervention occurred from outside, possibly from the Security Council. Lie urged Bunche to "keep going and smiling."[15] Bunche's pessimism caused enough alarm in Washington for U.S. Assistant Secretary of State Dean Rusk also to send a message to him.

We have been much encouraged by your masterly direction of the Rhodes talks, and even though auspices [sic] may not now seem bright, we do hope you will stick by the job until it is finished. While fully conversant with your desire to return, we feel that no one but yourself should shepherd these delicate negotiations at this time. Conciliation Commission can then build on the foundations you have established.[16]

Bunche already had good reason not to take the Conciliation Commission seriously. When he had invited the Commission to come to Rhodes to lend support in the talks, they had merely offered to send an observer. Later on, the commission tried to insist on Bunche's coming to Beirut at the climactic point of the Israeli-Egyptian negotiations. He eventually learned that the commission, though anxious not to get involved because the armistice talks might fail, were jealous of all the atten-

*On January 17, Bunche had reminded the Security Council that the Conciliation Commission had held its first meeting that day in Geneva. He suggested that at the appropriate time the Security Council "would invite Conciliation Commission to undertake those functions deriving from Security Council resolutions now exercised by me."[12] The Conciliation Commission responded that it hoped Bunche would be able to preside over the Rhodes negotiations up to their conclusion.

tion focused on him in Rhodes and, in particular, of the mediator's personal aircraft.

Bunche's discouragement did not last long, and on January 30 he called in both delegations to tell them he was stepping up the pace. He promised them three substantial papers first thing on the following day. He also sent out invitations to Jordan, Lebanon, and Syria to engage in armistice negotiations. The first of the three papers was a draft armistice agreement, the object of which was to put both parties on the spot by devising a reasonable and fair compromise that was below their minimum demands on crucial points but which would be embarrassing for them to refuse. Neither would like it, but both would find it equally difficult to reject. The other papers were on the armistice lines and on the withdrawal and reduction of forces. Bunche finished these drafts at 5:00 A.M. on January 31 and got up again at 9:30 A.M. to give them to the two delegations.

The Egyptians reacted by sending Colonel Sherine to Cairo for instructions. The Israelis told Bunche that the draft would "cause trouble," to which he replied that "we already had plenty of trouble and a little more wouldn't hurt."[17] They followed up with numerous amendments to the parts of Bunche's draft which protected Egyptian claims or tried to give effect to the Security Council November 4 call for withdrawal. The Israelis claimed the need for offensive forces in Beersheba for protection against the Arab Legion and the British forces at Aqaba. As Bunche had foreseen, they claimed that his draft was "unfair" because, if the Egyptians accepted it and Israel rejected it, Israel would be blamed. "With this agreement both parties are trapped," Bunche noted.[18] Yadin even went so far as to intimate that the draft was loaded in favor of the Egyptians. "I stopped him pronto and indignantly demanded a retraction, which Yadin very humbly and apologetically gave."[19] Yadin's complaint was that Bunche's proposal gave Egypt the Al-Faluja garrison, Gaza, Rafah, El Auja, and all her prisoners, which was out of proportion to what Israel was getting and would give other Arab states the false impression that Israel desperately needed the armistice.[20] Bunche gathered that the Israelis' real objection to his proposals was they set a floor below which the Egyptians would not go, whereas if there had been no such proposals the Egyptians might in the end have been forced to swallow the Israeli position in its entirety.

Bunche's initiative was immensely ambitious in scope. It dealt not only with the outline of the armistice agreement, but with the Al-Faluja problem and El Auja, a strategic point on the Egypt-Israel frontier recently captured by the Israelis. It also made practical suggestions on the many disputed points of the armistice demarcation lines, as well as on the reduction and balance of forces on both sides. Finally, it set up a mixed armistice commission under UN chairmanship to supervise the armistice. Many of these proposals were important not only for the negotiations between Egypt and Israel, but as a model for the other armistice agreements.

While awaiting Colonel Sherine's return from Cairo, Bunche sent his plane to fetch Mark Ethridge, the new U.S. member of the Conciliation Commission, from Athens. He learned from Ethridge that President Truman, recently re-elected, was disturbed at the unsettled conditions in the Middle East and was willing to apply pressure when and where needed.* Bunche was to tell Ethridge when and where. During the wait, Bunche beat everyone at billiards and wrote to Ruth.

There is a cat and mouse game going on here between each of them [Egyptians and Israelis] and me—they would be happy if I would terminate the negotiations and thus relieve them of any responsibility. But I am not going to take that rap. . . . It's like having a bear by the tail and being afraid to let go. God knows I want to let go, as I am dying to come home and be with you and Ralph† and get some rest.[23]

Early on the morning of February 3, the Egyptian response arrived. "For once the Egyptians showed clever tactics—they accepted the compromise draft with only minor, non-substantive modifications. In doing so they put the Jews on the spot."[24] Sherine had had a difficult time in Cairo because the military wanted to get out of the mess while the politicians wanted to act tough. Eytan's reaction to the Egyptian response was subdued, and he told Bunche that "Egyptian thinking was a puzzle to him. He was getting 'bored,' he added."[25]

Bunche worked through the night to put the Egyptian and Israeli comments into a single composite draft, which was considered at an informal joint meeting the following afternoon. Eytan did most of the talking

---

*The joint Anglo-American position on Palestine was becoming somewhat strained. Dean Acheson, who had just become secretary of state in the second Truman administration, on being approached by Ernest Bevin, wrote of his "all-too-vivid memories of the pains attendant upon efforts to co-ordinate Palestine problems with Bevin."[21] Bevin, for his part, scrawled on the text of a telegram communicating a request from Washington to support U.S. approaches to Egypt, "I must be very careful. We have not been approached direct and I do not want to be involved any more in these talks with USA. . . . I shall be let down when it suits the President [Truman]."[22]

†Joan and Jane were away at school.

in his donnish way, which infuriated the Egyptians. Sherine was "way out of his depth and frightened as a rabbit," and he irritated Eytan and embarrassed his own people by constantly blurting "4th and 16th" over and over, referring to the key Security Council resolutions.[26] Although his social contacts were impressive and he was about to marry King Farouk's divorced sister, "as a negotiator he's nil."[27]

Bunche had sent Reedman home because his daughter was seriously ill, and he was surprised to learn from him that the prevailing view at UN Headquarters in New York was that the Egyptians alone were responsible for holding up the talks, another triumph for Israeli propaganda. Nonetheless, in the joint meeting on February 4 Bunche had a feeling that the prospects for an agreement were improving, a trend which Eytan had already sensed a week earlier.[28]

On February 5 a constructive discussion of the armistice lines between the military representatives supported Bunche's more optimistic view, and for the first time he believed that, if some compromise could be reached on El Auja, an agreement would definitely be in sight. The British force in Aqaba was frequently mentioned as a reason for the Israelis to hold on to El Auja and Beersheba, and Bunche asked Lie to sound out the British about removing it. He wrote a long personal appeal to Eytan and followed it up with a two-hour talk with him and Yadin. Bunche felt that Yadin was holding up the agreement because he really wanted a total Egyptian surrender.[29] Bunche sent Stavropoulos to Damascus again to deal with Syrian hesitations about armistice talks, since the imminence of the other armistice negotiations was an important element of pressure on both the Egyptians and the Israelis.

On February 5, U.S. Secretary of State Dean Acheson, acting on behalf of Truman, sent a message to Prime Minister Ben-Gurion urging Israel to accept Bunche's compromise proposals.[30] This elicited a strong response from Sharett,[31] who was particularly critical of Bunche's proposals on El Auja, which, he said, was a vital strong point against a future Egyptian attack. Bunche dealt with this same point in a reply to a letter from Sharett, pointing out that the truce applied in the Negev, and Israel had taken El Auja long after the truce came into effect.

Bunche was usually sympathetic with the underdog in any situation, and he was concerned at the arrogance and impatience of the Israelis on Rhodes. He told Yadin that the real test of political greatness, both in a nation and in a military leader, was the ability to accept victory gracefully. Yadin's impatience was shortly—and accidentally—to be responsible for a setback. The military talks on the armistice lines, which had begun on

February 5, had shown unexpected promise. In the military meeting on the afternoon of February 8, Yadin became so irritated at Colonel She-rine's remarks about Beersheba that he threw his pencil down on the table. Unfortunately, the pencil bounced and hit Colonel Seif El Dine's rows of medals. Although Yadin apologized profusely, the Egyptians were deeply insulted and, according to Yitzhak Rabin, who was representing the Negev command in the Israeli delegation, discussions in the military group were badly affected for some days.[32] Bunche scolded Yadin about this behavior and also about his complaint that the Egyptians were build-ing fortifications at Al-Faluja. The Israelis, Bunche told him, had been violating the truce for months by refusing to obey the Security Council order to release the Egyptian division, and they were in no position to complain about anything the Egyptians did there. Yadin admitted to Bunche that much of the Israeli intransigence on the Negev was for bargaining purposes with King Abdullah of Transjordan, who had now agreed to start negotiations as soon as the Egyptian armistice was con-cluded. The Egyptians were evidently also thinking of Abdullah and mak-ing sure they did nothing that could possibly help him.

Bunche spent several days doggedly drafting compromise formula-tions. He was dead tired, nauseated by the hotel food, and exasperated by the intransigence of his interlocutors. He wrote to Ruth:

I talk, argue, coax and threaten these stubborn people day and night, in the effort to reach agreement. I make a bit of progress here and another bit there, but it is *so* slow and so arduous. Sometimes I feel that I should just tell them to go home and forget about an armistice. . . . This is killing work. I haven't been out of the hotel for two weeks now. . . .[33]

One day we are all certain that there is no possibility of agreement and that the conference will break up in failure, and the next day one side or the other will make a concession, and we lift our hopes again and get back to work.[34]

To Lie on February 10, Bunche reported,

Negotiations proceeding with tortuous but steady progress toward agreement. Daily discussions and compromise drafts producing results, but continuing pres-sure from all sources remains indispensable. Have informed Conciliation Com-mission I would welcome them taking over armistice negotiations at any time they consider appropriate and I mean it. This is a killing assignment.[35]

The Egyptians had been insisting that the Israelis must evacuate Beersheba, and the Israelis had been refusing to accept a UN neutral zone at El Auja, which the Egyptians would accept. "Both say they are willing to sit for months."[36] The news that Transjordan had agreed to armistice negotiations only stiffened the Egyptian position, because they feared that the Israelis were trying to improve their bargaining position with Transjordan at the expense of Egypt.[37] However, on February 13 Eytan told Bunche that Israel would withdraw from El Auja provided, as Bunche had suggested, the place became the seat of the mixed armistice commission. He was also conciliatory on a number of other points. Bunche's own mood improved because he had abandoned the hotel food for a diet of American military K rations.

There was now movement on almost all points and a general feeling of optimism. Beersheba was now the stumbling block, but after consulting Eytan, Bunche asked Transjordan to send its delegation to Rhodes on February 23 to commence negotiations on an armistice agreement on February 25. Eytan reported that on the morning of February 13, "thanks to the friendly atmosphere and the smallness of the room,"[38] they had made rapid progress with the Egyptians, and that he had no doubt they would reach agreement on Bunche's new draft on El Auja. Bunche cabled to Lie, "Consideration tomorrow of formulations modified in light of today's discussions may reveal green light. . . ."[39] He also began to prepare a party for both delegations after agreement had been reached.

Yadin and Shiloh came back from Tel Aviv on February 16. Bunche had already warned the Egyptians that Israel would refuse to evacuate Beersheba because of its importance as a defense against the Arab Legion in the eastern Negev, and Yadin confirmed this. All other issues, Bunche told Lie on February 16, were either settled or well on the way to solution. Bunche felt that, although they were technically correct about Beersheba in the light of the November 4 resolution, the Egyptians would be very foolish to hold up the agreement on this basis, since their right to press their claims on Beersheba in the eventual peace negotiations would be safeguarded by the terms of the armistice agreement. He asked for Lie's help in persuading them of this.[40] According to Eytan, Bunche asked the Egyptians point-blank whether they would allow the negotiations to fail on Beersheba. To an Israeli representative who complained of all the benefits the Egyptians were getting and asked what *Israel* was getting, "Bunche replied without hesitation, 'The Negev.' I hope he is right."[41]

By February 18 the Israelis were growing impatient. Bunche "put the heat on both delegations,"[42] and the Egyptians agreed to take the draft agreement to Cairo to discuss it with their government. On Saturday, February 19, in a marathon series of meetings which ended at 3:00 A.M. on

Sunday, Bunche got agreement from both delegations on everything except Beersheba. Bunche told Lie that this was the one issue on which he desperately needed help. If, in spite of Beersheba, the Egyptian response to the whole agreement was favorable, it could be signed by February 23. "If unfavorable, negotiations will be adjourned. Our fingers are severely crossed."[43] Bunche suggested that Lie should tell the Egyptian foreign minister, Mahmoud Fawzi, that in his opinion the Israelis were not bluffing over Beersheba and would walk out if Egypt attempted to renew negotiations on the matter. He should also point out to Fawzi that the armistice agreement would accomplish for the Egyptians what the Security Council had been unable to do since November 4, 1948. In view of the disastrous Egyptian military position, this was a unique opportunity and a thoroughly honorable agreement.[44] Lie saw Fawzi three times in three days in an effort to get Egypt's acceptance.

Bunche worked through the night on the final draft of the armistice agreement until 8:00 A.M. on Sunday, February 20, ate ham and eggs, and went to bed at 8:30 A.M. He arose at 1:00 P.M., and, in a joint meeting at 4:00 P.M., read the final draft agreement to both delegations. They agreed on everything except the question of Beersheba. Monday, February 21, the day on which the Egyptians left for Cairo to discuss the draft agreement with their government, was a day of enforced idleness and letdown. Bunche bought materials for a suit and other clothes and went to a tailor to have them made up. It was a lovely day and the first time he had been out of the Hôtel des Roses for more than two weeks. Tuesday was another almost unbearable day of waiting, and Bunche went on board the U.S. destroyer *Hanson* to celebrate Washington's birthday. He played more billiards, recorded a message for Israeli radio for release if the agreement was signed, and ignored a message from the Conciliation Commission to the effect that the Commission expected to see him in Beirut that night.

On Wednesday, February 23, the Egyptians returned from Cairo at 1:00 P.M. with the full agreement of their government. Bunche scheduled a simple signing ceremony for 10:30 A.M. on the following day. He also got the Egyptians to agree to a joint supper party that night, the first time they had met socially with the Israelis. The Egyptians insisted that a supply of food and drink they had brought back from Groppi's in Cairo be used for this purpose. They even agreed to the press's being invited to the supper.

The party was a great success. Colonel Yadin beat Colonel Sherine at billiards. A mixed doubles at Ping-Pong pitted Bunche's British secretary, Doreen Daughton, and Sam Souki, an Egyptian reporter, against Yadin and Hassan Moher, an Egyptian. "Some combination for the Near East!"

Bunche noted.[45] As they retired to bed at 4:30 A.M., Yadin thanked Bunche profusely for his work, saying, "Patience pays."[46]

The signing ceremony the next day was short and dignified. After it was over, Bunche held the delegations back in order to present them with Rhodes pottery plates with the inscription "Rhodes Armistice Talks— 1949."* "We then went to the airfield to see the Egyptians off. They are a nice bunch, and in a way I was sorry to see them go."[48] Bunche saw the Israeli delegation off early the following morning. At the airport, Yadin's staff gave him a long package to open. It contained a pencil.[49]

Congratulatory messages flooded into Rhodes from all over the world, but the first and the most welcome was a long cable from Ruth. Her recent letters had tended to be morose, but the cable more than made up for them.

I am very proud and happy for you. It's been a hard job and you've done a fine piece of work. . . . It's wonderful that it is ending this way, for all the time and work you and the others have put into this. . . .[50]

Bunche wrote her:

Yours was the very *first* I received and the most precious. Since yours came I have received many others, from Ben-Gurion, Shertok [Sharett], the Egyptian Commanding General, Lie, Lester Pearson, Dean Rusk and the folks in Trusteeship.[51]

On February 24, President Truman, in expressing his gratification over the news from Rhodes, added:

I wish also to congratulate the United Nations Mediator, Dr. Ralph Bunche, whose untiring efforts have so greatly contributed to the success of these negotiations.

The world press was also enthusiastic. According to *Time* magazine:

The armistice agreement was in large part due to the immense ability, patience, tact and unflagging good humor of Ralph Bunche, Negro social scientist—who had taken over the role of martyred Count Folke Bernadotte. Several times during the seven weeks of negotiations, agreement had seemed hopeless. Each time Dr. Bunche had thought of something to keep the talks alive. By the last week, the negotiators on both sides had come to regard him as the new Colossus of Rhodes. His labors, said Walter Eytan, had been "superhuman." Said Seif El

*Walter Eytan recalled: "At one point we floundered in what seemed insuperable difficulties. Dr. Bunche called us into his room, opened a chest of drawers and showed us the plates. . . . 'Have a look at these lovely plates!' he said. 'If you reach agreement, each of you will get one to take home. If you don't, I'll break them over your heads.' "[47]

Dine: "one of the world's greatest men." A somewhat back-handed tribute also came from a young US army officer, a southerner, who was a member of Bunche's staff: "I always swore I'd never work for a Negro. Well, Dr. Bunche is a real man. His color just happens to be a little different."[52]

In Egypt, there were no hostile demonstrations, as had been feared. The press concentrated on the valor of the Egyptian army and Egypt's respect and support for international organizations working for peace.[53] The official communiqué, while paying tribute to Bunche, stated that "the agreement has no political character . . . and does not affect in any way the political destiny of Palestine."[54]

Israelis, though unanimously positive, tended to look at the achievement in a different light. The armistice agreements were the first phase in a permanent peace which never came, but they established legality in a previously anarchical situation.[55] Abba Eban later wrote:

For eighteen years the armistice agreements were the only recognized framework of relations between Israel and its neighbors. . . . The 1949 agreements remain, to this day, the only successful example of an Arab-Israeli compromise leading to a contractual obligation.

Eban contrasted the later "fiasco" of the Palestine Conciliation Commission with the "zest and drive with which Bunche had responded to his opportunities," and went on to make a point made by many other Israeli leaders, that Bunche's success was due to his arranging for Israel to negotiate separately with each Arab state, whereas the Conciliation Commission made the mistake of convening all the Arab states together.[56]

15

Armistice Talks—
Jordan and Israel

Such Trickery, Deceit, and Downright Dishonesty

Bunche did not have much time to savor his spectacular success. He was nursing a heavy cold and preparing for the Israel-Transjordan talks which were to start in one week's time, on March 1.* The Israel-Transjordan talks were very different from the struggle of the previous seven weeks. There was now the model of an armistice agreement to build on. In addition, many of the problems had been, or were being, worked out directly between King Abdullah and the Israelis in the king's winter palace at Shuneh in the Jordan Valley in secret meetings which had started after Moshe Dayan and Colonel Abdullah el-Tell had agreed on a cease-fire in the Jerusalem area on November 30, 1948.[1] The Israeli-Lebanese negotiations, which were less complex than the others, were also due to start—at Naqoura, on the Lebanon-Israel border—and Bunche sent his deputy, Henri Vigier, to represent him.

The Transjordanian delegation arrived in the mediator's plane on the afternoon of February 28. There were five Arab Legion officers and two civilians—"unimpressive, timid, and not very bright."[2] Bunche could get little out of them, and they were obviously "on a string with rigid written instructions." They had to use the United Nations uncoded radio for communication with Amman, which meant that the Israelis could monitor all their instructions. A highly experienced Israeli delegation, headed by Reuven Shiloah and including Colonel Moshe Dayan, arrived on March 1.

---

*The Transjordan government had originally suggested that the talks be held in Jerusalem rather than Rhodes, but Bunche had insisted on Rhodes.

"Transjordan delegation," Bunche cabled to Lie, "reluctant to meet with Israelis and timid about meeting with me. Negotiations under these conditions extremely tedious if not maddening."[3] On March 4 Bunche finally induced the Transjordanians to attend a joint formal opening meeting, at which, ignoring Bunche's request that they shake hands with the Israelis, they sat stolidly in their seats. Bunche, furious at this lack of courtesy, immediately called the meeting to order, raced through the agenda, and adjourned it. He rebuked the Transjordanians for their rudeness and told Shiloah, who was incensed, not to take any hasty action, for the incident was not yet closed. He then called Colonel Jundi, the Transjordanian chief delegate, to his room to meet Shiloah and Dayan. They shook hands and were soon happily talking away in Arabic, with Shiloah translating for Bunche's benefit. Jundi apologized, saying that he had understood that the introductions were to take place at the end of the meeting rather than at the beginning, and the first crisis of the talks was resolved. Paradoxically, the incident had made possible what Bunche had so far been unable to arrange, an informal joint meeting of the delegation heads.

Simultaneously with the Transjordanian negotiations, Bunche was directing the Lebanese armistice negotiations on the Israel-Lebanon border and trying to put some fight into his representative, Henri Vigier, a former League of Nations official who tended to adjourn the talks at the slightest difficulty. Bunche sent off a strong message to Sharett insisting that the Israelis get all their troops out of Lebanon as soon as the armistice was signed, and drafted a compromise formula to put the talks back on track. On March 17 he told Lie that he felt so strongly about the Israeli efforts to change the frontier and keep troops in Lebanon after the armistice* that if the Israeli position did not change, he would seriously consider withdrawing from all the armistice negotiations and returning to New York. The Israel-Lebanon armistice agreement was signed on March 23.

Bunche got on well with Shiloah and Dayan, but found the Transjordanians stiff, scared,† and reluctant to do anything until their emissary returned from Amman. Only on March 8 was Bunche able to get the military representatives to work on the armistice lines, by which time the

---

*After their invasions of Lebanon in 1978 and 1982, the Israelis finally managed to establish an Israeli-controlled "security zone" in southern Lebanon.

†One very good reason for this was certainly that the real negotiations were going on between King Abdullah and the Israelis at Shuneh, and the Rhodes delegation had to await their outcome.

talks were threatened by Israeli military moves in the southern Negev toward Aqaba.* Israeli forces reached Um Reshresh (now Eilat) on March 10. Bunche called in Shiloah and insisted on the urgent need to sign a cease-fire agreement. He called on Israel and Transjordan to halt all military moves in the Negev. He also sent Paul Mohn to Aqaba to see what was really happening.

This is political jockeying by Transjordan to establish a fictitious fighting line to cut Jews off from the Gulf of Aqaba, and by Jews to justify their access and claim.[5]

On March 11 both sides signed the cease-fire agreement, which Bunche reported to the Security Council—the third agreement at governmental level he had negotiated between Arabs and Jews—"and these are the only three in history."[6]

Bunche was indignant at this new Israeli military venture "smack in the middle of the armistice negotiations with Transjordan. Good Faith!"[7] He had been particularly disturbed at questions in the British House of Commons as to why he had been so slow to report on the Israeli advance in the Negev. He discussed with Stavropoulos and Reedman until five one morning whether he should resign over this breach of faith and of the truce. He told Dayan that if the matter came up in the Security Council the Arabs would claim that he had agreed to the Israeli advance. He would then have to demand an Israeli withdrawal, and when Israel refused he would have to resign. Dayan told Bunche there had been no Israeli advance but, rather, a deployment of forces which replaced the previous Israeli control of the territory by reconnaissance, and that there had been no military clash with the Arab Legion. Bunche said the movement was still a violation of the truce.[8] To add to his exasperation, he received word from Damascus that the Syrians would not agree to armistice negotiations—"the fools are just inviting Jewish attack."†[9]

In spite of these alarms and excursions, on March 13 both delegations asked Bunche to submit a compromise proposal on Jerusalem. He felt too tired to embark on it that night and found it such a tough assign-

*David Ben-Gurion described the operation as follows: "After the [Egypt-Israel] agreement had been signed the Defence Minister ordered the army to liberate the southern Negev, part of which was controlled by the Arab Legion."[4] Israel claimed that this area had been allocated to Israel in the November 29, 1947, partition resolution, and she therefore had a right to take it over. This was a violation of the truce.

†Syria finally agreed to armistice negotiations on March 17 after receiving a further message from Bunche through Vigier.

ment that he called off all meetings for the following day and worked on it until four the following morning. He was mystified that there was still no complaint from the Transjordanians about the new Israeli military presence at Um Reshresh, near Aqaba. The explanation was later provided by Glubb Pasha, the commander of the Arab Legion. As a result of the Israeli numerical superiority of ten to one over the Arab Legion, the relentless Israeli encroachments in the Negev and the Hebron area, and the Israeli threat to attack the Arab Legion if it took over the positions of the Iraqi troops stationed north of the Dead Sea, "King Abdullah's anxiety became too deep to resist. . . . He contacted the Israelis direct. . . ."[10]

Bunche knew that the inconsequential discussions on Rhodes were to some extent a cover for the talks at Shuneh, where Dayan was to go on March 18. He presented his Jerusalem proposals on March 15. The Jordanians accepted most of them but the Israelis

rejected them on the grounds of "too much internationalization, which is premature." Humbug, but the debate resulted in both sides agreeing on existing lines, thus resolving the Jerusalem bugaboo in the agreement.[11]

On March 18 Bunche adjourned the talks for three days so that the delegates could consult their governments and ascertain the results of the talks at Shuneh.*

With the Syrian negotiations in sight, the Lebanese agreement almost concluded, and a probable agreement at Shuneh, Bunche felt that the end of his work was at last in sight. In anticipation, he sent to Lie the draft of a Security Council resolution terminating the office of mediator and setting out the transition from the mediator to the Conciliation Commission. He also received an urgent message from Dean Rusk asking when he would be back and cautioning him "not to mortgage your future" in the meantime—a warning that the Truman administration was interested in securing his services.

Bunche was now feeling acutely the strain of juggling continuous crises on different fronts. He told Ruth that he wanted to go to Stockholm on his way home.

I have been thinking a lot about poor Folke Bernadotte lately†. . . . When my work is ended here in a week or two I would like to fly to Stockholm in his former plane—for one day—just to place some flowers on his grave. . . .

*Shiloah was instructed not to tell Bunche about the Shuneh talks, because King Abdullah wanted no one, including his own government, to know of them. Shiloah said Bunche knew about them already.[12]

†Bunche had insisted on keeping the title "acting mediator" out of respect for Bernadotte.

You can't imagine what it takes to hold these monkeys together long enough to squeeze agreement out of them. And such trickery, deceit and downright dishonesty you have never seen. I swear by all that's Holy, I will never come anywhere near the Palestine problem once I liberate myself from this trap. . . .[13]

After being delayed by weather, the Israeli and Transjordanian envoys finally returned to Rhodes on March 23. A breakthrough came the next day when the Transjordanians accepted the Israeli proposal that the armistice line south of the Dead Sea should follow the international frontier, and the Israelis accepted the existing lines to the north, where Iraqi troops were stationed. The meetings at Shuneh had evidently worked. There were, however, maddening delays as instructions from Amman failed to arrive,* and on Sunday, March 27, a day when food poisoning hit most of the inhabitants of the Hôtel des Roses, Bunche set a deadline of one week to conclude the work. Another session was to be held at Shuneh, and both delegations had been instructed to go home again on March 29 to clear up remaining questions. Bunche worked all night to have a draft armistice agreement ready for them to take home with them.†

Another period of waiting ensued, enlivened only by a military coup in Syria, the arrival of Rusk's message about Bunche's future, a threat to assassinate King Abdullah, Israeli advances in the Hebron area, and fittings with the tailor. Also:

While I was eating lunch I was slapped on the back of the head and who should be there but Percival L. Prattis, as loud, wrong and crude as ever. He came in unannounced from Menton on the Riviera via Rome and Athens. Took some pictures, asked some dumb questions, drank too much before dinner and got raucous and then sleepy after dinner.[14]

On April 1 Shiloah and Dayan returned to Rhodes with the news that agreement had been reached at Shuneh on all outstanding points. The modifications to the line in the North favored the Israelis, and around Hebron the Arabs, but the Israelis had achieved a significant enlargement of their coastal strip. Bunche commented:

Another deal, and as usual the Palestine Arabs lose. Abdullah, of course, is mainly interested in extending his rule over Arab Palestine and getting the Jews to accept it.‡[15]

*Possibly because King Abdullah was encountering opposition in Amman to the concessions he had made at Shuneh.

†In his notes Bunche recorded, "Even Rosenne said my draft agreement is good." Shabtai Rosenne was the highly critical Israeli legal adviser.

‡Similar thoughts may have occurred, two years later, to Abdullah's assassins. Among the

Both delegations were now supposed to have similar instructions, and Bunche revised the draft armistice agreement to conform to the instructions Shiloah had shown him. The Transjordanian representatives who had remained in Rhodes were furious at the deal and took it out on Colonel Jundi when he returned on April 2. For the first time, the instructions brought by both delegations referred to the "Hashemite Jordan Kingdom," signifying a deal whereby Abdullah got Israeli acceptance of his hegemony over Arab Palestine while the Israelis got the rest of the Negev and an expansion of their coastal strip.

Once again Bunche and his staff worked all night to have the agreement ready for the next day, and after many last-minute delays the signing was set for 7:30 P.M. on April 3. Bunche had lost his glasses and had great difficulty in reading out the agreement at the meeting. In his own statement, while congratulating the delegations on concluding "a virtual non-aggression pact," he added, in expressing the hope that peace would be restored in Palestine, "I think particularly of the Palestinian Arabs, who by and large have been the innocent victims of the dispute."[17] Bunche presented the Rhodes pottery mementos to the delegations and again presided over a celebratory buffet supper. It was altogether a less joyous occasion than the Egyptian-Israeli affair, and was overclouded by the bitter differences among the Transjordanian representatives.

After supper Bunche and Reedman played billiards and then wandered out to the Café Pindos for a glass of beer, to listen to the music and to watch the dancing. "It feels good not to be drafting," Bunche noted.[18] In spite of the discontent of some of the Jordanians, the writing of the agreement—twelve long articles and two detailed annexes—was an achievement for which both sides expressed their warm admiration. The mood brightened on the following night, when the Jordanians gave a party at which everyone fraternized and had a good time. The band of the USS *Winston* played and "it developed into the best party Rhodes had ever had."[19] The evening ended with the guests' singing "Auld Lang Syne."

The Syrian armistice talks were to open the following day, April 5, in tents in the no-man's-land between Mishmar Ha Yarden and Rosh Pinna. Bunche had no intention of presiding over them and delegated the responsibility to Vigier and General William Riley, the United States ma-

---

accused was Colonel Abdullah el-Tell. The U.S. consul general reported that Jerusalem Arabs were extremely bitter over the agreement, which turned over sixteen villages and thirty-five thousand Arabs to Israeli control.[16]

rine who had become chief of staff of the Truce Supervision Organization. Bunche told Ruth:

I can be of more use to those talks in New York than out here, since it will be primarily a matter of applying UN pressure (and US) to one or both parties. . . .[20]

To Lie's cable telling him of the Israelis' desire that he personally conduct the Syrian negotiations, he replied that if the Syrians had been willing to come to Rhodes he could have done it. As it was, he would supervise the negotiations from New York.

It is doubtful that at this time I could serve effectively in another round of negotiations. I am completely worn out physically and mentally after three months of uninterrupted negotiations. . . .[21]

Bunche flew to Beirut on April 5 to talk to the Conciliation Commission and to the Lebanese and Syrians. His program was soon interrupted by news that the Israelis, on the first day of the negotiations with the Syrians, had taken up a new military position across the Syrian border, apparently for bargaining purposes and to try out the Syrians. Bunche, faced with frantic Syrian threats to counterattack, sent strong messages to Tel Aviv, Lake Success, and Washington and stayed up all night monitoring the situation. The Israelis finally withdrew on April 7.

Bunche returned to Rhodes on April 8 to pack up, play a final game of billiards with Reedman, and say goodbye to the locals and to the USS *Winston*, whose captain gave a party for him. He finally took off at 9:10 A.M. on April 9. His plane buzzed the Hôtel des Roses and the USS destroyers *Winston* and *Larsson* before flying to Venice for the night, and then to Geneva, where he spent the next evening with Gunnar Myrdal.*

The flight to Stockholm on April 11 was Bunche's last journey in the mediator's plane. He was met by Estelle Bernadotte and stayed at the Bernadotte home, Dragongården. After laying a wreath on Bernadotte's grave, he spent the rest of the time with Countess Bernadotte. They discussed at length the proposed publication of Bernadotte's diary and agreed that it should be held up until it could be translated for Bunche to check it. Bunche was already anxious that breaches of confidence might undo the work of the previous months.

After a stop in Paris to deal with a large shopping list from Ruth,† he

*Myrdal was executive secretary of the UN Economic Commission for Europe at this time.

†Shopping was one of Bunche's favorite forms of recreation, and both he and Ruth were tireless shoppers—he for hats, clothes, and mementos of all kinds; she for perfume, gloves, and household furnishings.

embarked on the *Queen Mary* and arrived in New York on April 18. Ralph Jr. and Ruth were on the pier, along with Trygve Lie and batteries of reporters and photographers. New York City provided a police motorcycle escort all the way to Parkway Village. Later in the day Lie sent roses to Ruth and gave a lunch at his house in Bunche's honor.

16

The End of the Mediation
and the Nobel Prize

Peacemaking Not for Prizes

Bunche came home to a hero's welcome. His negotiation of the armistice agreements was almost universally regarded as a formidable achievement. A young U.S. Marine officer, F. P. Henderson, who was on General William Riley's staff, has given a vivid picture of Bunche on Rhodes.

Dr. Bunche's conduct of the six weeks of negotiations was superb in every way. Bunche was not an impressive man at first sight, physically of medium height and build. He was a chain smoker, his clothes usually rumpled with cigarette ashes on his coat and vest, his manner quite relaxed and informal. Anyone who had any official or social contact with him soon realized he possessed an outstanding intellect and a broad range of knowledge. He had a quick grasp of subjects presented in briefings or reports and always asked the right questions or suggested sound alternatives. . . . Whenever he raised a question or alternative our reaction usually was, "Of course. Why didn't we think of that?" He had a very warm and attractive personality, magnetic in a low-key, soft-spoken way. . . . He requested, not ordered, people to do things. He was quick to praise good work, and I do not recall him ever chewing out anyone. Socially, he was an asset to any party or affair, large or small, friendly and approachable to "all sorts and conditions of men" (and women), and a lively conversationalist with a sense of humor. . . . He had the sharpest and most agile mind, the most complete knowledge of matters being considered, the most accomplished negotiating techniques, and the ability to avoid acrimony or hard feelings on anyone's part. . . . Throughout the negotiations Bunche held no press conferences and made no public statements or announcements, and the delegations also observed his wishes on this.[1]

Henderson thought that Bunche's race helped him in dealing with his interlocutors on Rhodes, and that it dissociated him in their minds from bitter memories of colonial rule.

The actual nature of the Rhodes achievement was deliberately concealed by Bunche himself on the grounds that any detailed disclosure would be unfair to the people he had been dealing with. His own notes on the negotiations remained locked in his safe until his death and were never shown to anyone.* For the same reason he was uneasy about the publication of Bernadotte's diary, *To Jerusalem,* and made a number of modifications to it before it was published in 1953.

In later years, accounts by the different parties created conflicting mythologies about the Rhodes talks, although all agreed that they had been brilliantly conducted. On the whole, Israeli participants claimed that there *had* been direct negotiations, whereas Arab participants asserted that the exchanges had taken place through the mediator. In fact there was some truth in both these assertions, and, as Bunche had intended, each side was free to give its own interpretation of what had happened. For his part he would give none, and steadfastly refused to do so whenever the matter came up. "I wish it to be known," he stated in February 1968, when there was a rumor that the Arabs would soon be ready for direct negotiations and Rhodes was cited as a precedent,

that I have never made any comment for publication about any aspect of those talks and do not intend to make any at this time even to correct mistakes. . . . Therefore, although I have extensive personal notes on what actually transpired at Rhodes, I have nothing to add at present to what was said in my reports to the Security Council. . . .[2]

During the mission of Gunnar Jarring, the United Nations special representative in the Middle East appointed in 1967, the so-called "Rhodes formula" was constantly mentioned. On October 9, 1969, the Israeli Foreign Ministry spokesman said that "the Rhodes formula is the equivalent of a 'face-to-face' meeting with the Arabs," a statement which the Egyptian government spokesman promptly rejected, adding that "no direct negotiations had taken place at Rhodes." Bunche told Jarring that he had deliberately refrained from describing to the Security Council the performance and interactions of some of the personalities who had played

---

*The one known, but unintentional, exception was a chambermaid in the Hôtel des Roses in Rhodes who fortunately spoke no English. One day, in a hurry to get to a meeting, Bunche inadvertently left the notes he had written the night before on his bedside table. When he realized this, he dashed back to his room, only to find the notes gone. The chambermaid was summoned, and the hotel manager interpreted. Had she found the notes? "Oh yes." Then where had she put them? "In the usual place, of course, under Dr. Bunche's shirts."

an important part at Rhodes because he was sure the press would treat such reports sensationally. After Rhodes he had also deliberately played down his own third-party role and played up the cooperative attitude of the parties,

not for any reasons of false modesty, but because I and my colleagues at Rhodes at that time earnestly believed that the armistice agreements were only a first step towards a full and enduring peace. . . . In any case, by now the Rhodes waters have been so muddied by self-serving interpretations that one can't see the formula for the mud.[3]

Bunche's most specific description of the Rhodes proceedings occurs in a 1967 letter to Theodore Draper, who was writing about the Middle East negotiating process in the *New York Review of Books.*

Negotiations were carried on with the delegations separately by the Acting Mediator, and the two delegations in each case were brought together by the Acting Mediator only to formalize agreements already worked out. Most of the proposals and drafts were prepared by the Acting Mediator and his staff. The sole exception to this procedure came towards the end of the two negotiations when small groups of military officers from the two sides met under the leadership of the UN Chief of Staff to prepare the maps showing the armistice lines on the basis of the agreed positions arrived at in the negotiations.[4]

In 1970, in trying to avoid making Jarring's task more difficult, Bunche stated, "This is the sort of thing where each side makes its own interpretation and sometimes, when it suits its convenience, history gets invented."[5]

There were few doubts about Bunche's own performance. The Israelis, with whom he had more arguments than with anyone else, were particularly generous in their praise.*Ben-Gurion wrote, "Dr. Bunche handled the negotiations with great skill and gradually brought the two sides closer to agreement, initially on minor questions and then on major ones as well."[7] Yitzhak Rabin recalled Bunche's unfailing patience and good humor and his sense of timing, which allowed him to work out agreements before submitting difficult issues to joint meetings. The Israeli military representatives were astonished at Bunche's detailed understanding of the military situation.[8] Dayan commented:

It was difficult not to be impressed by Dr. Ralph Bunche's handling of the sessions. . . . He spoke little and listened to others with intense concentration. It

*Walter Eytan wrote, "He was gifted, some thought almost a genius, at drafting; sooner or later he was able to contrive a formula to defeat almost any problem."[6]

seemed as though he was trying not only to hear what was being said but also to penetrate the mind of the speaker to discover what lay behind his words. He displayed a great deal of charm. Within minutes of meeting someone for the first time he could establish a rapport and created a mood of amiability and trust.

On Bunche's drafting ability, Dayan wrote:

When the parties failed to agree he could draft a formula so that each could interpret it in his own way. When I questioned him on this approach, he said the basic aim at the time was to bring an end to the fighting. Later, when the parties would discover that on certain items they did not get what they expected, they would not renew the war on that account, but the realities of life would shape the appropriate arrangements.

Dayan noted that in the case of Article VIII of the Israel-Jordan armistice agreement, the "appropriate arrangements" turned out to mean that Jordan denied Israel access to the Jewish holy places in Jerusalem for the next nineteen years.[9]

Another Israeli negotiator who was both admiring and critical was Shabtai Rosenne. "The physical demands he [Bunche] made on himself and on his staff, and on each delegation, were staggering," Rosenne wrote. Rosenne was critical of a number of aspects of Bunche's mediation, including the fact that there was no time limit on the armistice agreements and therefore less incentive to work for a permanent peace. But, he concluded,

he was fair and open to argument and persuasion and to me was the incarnation of belief in the UN—not the United Nations as viewed through the rose-tinted spectacles of a wishy-washy ideology but the UN as a necessity for the preservation of mankind in the nuclear age.[10]

The ever-skeptical Pablo de Azcarate also had some reservations about the end result of Bunche's virtuosity. After acknowledging Bunche's "great intelligence and exceptional energy," Azcarate wrote,

His unlimited capacity for work, enabling him to ignore the difference between night and day that the normal person has to take note of, must have tried the stamina of his own staff and that of the two delegations to the utmost. And I have a shrewd suspicion that on more than one occasion, agreement was reached as a result not so much of concessions freely and voluntarily obtained as of the physical and mental exhaustion of the delegates. . . .[11]

In August, when the mediator's post was finally abolished, the Security Council expressed "its deep appreciation of the qualities of tact, understanding, perseverance and devotion to duty of Dr. Ralph J. Bunche."[12]

Bunche received many offers from universities, including Harvard, Stanford, Berkeley, and the University of Pennsylvania, and he was still tempted to return to academic life. He was also showered with testimonial dinners, awards, and honors. On April 21 Dean Rusk informed him that the State Department wished to offer him the position of assistant secretary of state for Near Eastern, South Asian, and African Affairs. While in Rhodes Bunche had already told Ruth, "I do not intend to go back into the service of the US government. I don't want to live in Washington again and I simply *won't* take any assignment which would take me away from my family again."[13] Secretary of State Dean Acheson and Rusk had been pressing him on the matter and were discouraged by Bunche's negative attitude.* They had even offered to make up any discrepancy in salary between the UN and State Department jobs, but that was not the point, and Bunche dismissed the suggestion as a special arrangement that he could not possibly accept anyway. On May 25 he went to Washington to meet President Truman. Bunche explained to the president that he wanted to stay with the United Nations, and he very frankly gave his reasons for not wishing to return to Jim Crow Washington. Truman was understanding,[15] and Bunche remained on excellent terms with him. Bunche gave a press conference in the White House explaining and confirming his decision before returning to New York.

At the seemingly endless round of events honoring his achievement in Rhodes Bunche developed a newly self-confident speaking style. A typical event was the award dinner in his honor given by the American Association for the United Nations in the Grand Ballroom at the Waldorf-Astoria on May 9. On the platform were, among others, Mrs. Roosevelt, Trygve Lie, the principal UN ambassadors, Mrs. Herbert Evatt representing her husband, Abba Eban, and Bunche's old friends William Hastie and Walter White. There was a letter from Truman, a long and enthusiastic speech from Eban (who in the preceding months had not always been so wholehearted an admirer), and a warm tribute from Lie. Bunche, typically, paid a heartfelt tribute to his colleagues on Rhodes before proceeding with his speech. He was optimistic about the prospects of the United Nations' bringing peace to Palestine, although the most

---

*Acheson, wrongly, ascribed Bunche's refusal to his wish no longer to be "taken up with these seemingly insoluble problems. His most heartfelt wish was for relief from them, not deeper involvement. How often I was to remember and echo his wish!"[14]

far-reaching problems remained to be solved. In his conclusion he introduced a paragraph which became a sort of trademark and credo.

I have a deep-seated bias against hate and intolerance. I have a bias against racial
and religious bigotry. I have a bias *against* war; a bias *for* peace. I have a bias that
leads me to believe in the essential goodness of my fellow man; which leads me to
believe that no problem of human relations is ever insoluble. I have a bias in favor
of both Arabs and Jews in the sense that I believe that both are good, honorable
and essentially peace-loving peoples, and are therefore as capable of making peace
as of waging war. I have a strong bias in favor of the United Nations and its ability
to maintain a peaceful world.

In the hour of his international triumph Bunche never forgot the
problems of his own people. In recalling that the Charter stood not only
for peace, but for peace with justice and equality for all peoples, he reminded his fellow Americans

that all of us who have a sense of justice and fair play must contribute to the
solution of a problem on our doorstep which is perhaps more complex and baffling
even than the Palestine problem, if our own great country is to be enabled fully to
live up to the principles of the Charter. . . . This our country clearly cannot do as
long as fourteen million Negroes are deprived of many of their fundamental rights
and are denied political, economic and social equality. I believe that you will agree
with me that racial bigotry makes mockery of both the Constitution and the
Charter.

These comments were met with loud applause, and Bunche ended with a
moving plea for the hundreds of millions of colonial peoples yet to be
"afforded a full opportunity to determine their own destinies."[16]
These themes reappear in many of Bunche's speeches at this time. A
fuller denunciation of the racial situation in the United States appeared in
his acceptance of the NAACP's Spingarn Medal* at the 40th Annual
Convention of the NAACP in the Hollywood Bowl on July 17, 1949.
After expressing his joy at this award, Bunche said that it would be as
nothing to his elation if he had been able to say, "There need be no more
Spingarn Medals nor any other awards to Negro Americans. For there is
no longer any distinction among Americans because of race or color. . . ."
The speech both registered the progress made and called upon Black
Americans to join in the struggle to become "American in full." Bunche
juxtaposed this struggle with that of the colonial peoples in the world

*Joel E. Spingarn, chairman of the board of directors of the NAACP, had initiated the
award in 1914. It was a gold medal given annually for the "highest or noblest achievement
by an American Negro."

outside and expressed the belief that both would triumph through the democratic process, a system in which nothing is impossible. Denouncing racial prejudices and stereotypes in the United States, he said that he liked American democracy and the American way of life "so well that I wish to see its practice fully squared with its profession."[17]

Bunche had been firm in his resolve to stay on as mediator only until the Syrian-Israeli armistice agreement was concluded, and he initially believed that this would be a matter of days. The mediator's position gave him a certain distance from the daily routine of the UN, and also provided a welcome limitation on his availability for other tasks. On May 4 Lie called, "very upset," to ask him to make a statement supporting Israel's admission to UN membership, which was then pending in the General Assembly.* Bunche refused on the ground that his position as mediator, as well as the current difficulties in the Israeli-Syrian negotiations, would make such a statement by him inappropriate. To U.S. Ambassador Warren Austin he added that he felt Israel needed to "come clean" on a number of matters—a full report on Bernadotte's assassination, the Arab refugees, the internationalization of Jerusalem, and the final boundaries—matters which he hoped would be taken up at the forthcoming meetings of the Palestine Conciliation Commission in Lausanne.[18]

The Israeli-Syrian negotiations had started badly with an Israeli incursion into Syrian territory, but they were also complicated because they had to deal with the sole instance in which Arab forces were occupying territory beyond the international boundary—territory which had been allocated to Israel in the partition resolution. Bunche had anticipated this problem in discussions with the Israelis on Rhodes and had asked specifically whether the Israelis would agree not to advance when the Syrians withdrew. He had received a negative reply. He continued, however, to advocate this basic objective from Lake Success through Eban.[19] Bunche's idea was that, pending a full peace settlement, the area up to the Syrian border evacuated by the Syrians—the Hula Valley, below the Golan Heights—could become a demilitarized zone under UN control, with zones on each side limited to purely defensive forces.† The armistice agreement would specifically provide that the armistice line would in no

*Israel was admitted to membership on May 11, 1949.

†Bunche always maintained that this idea had come to him on Rhodes when he was unable to sleep after an infuriating conversation with his friend and legal adviser Constantin Stavropoulos. Stavropoulos, who was devoted to Bunche but was in some ways extraordinarily insensitive, had stoutly maintained, as a scientific fact, that whites were intellectually superior to blacks.

way prejudice the ultimate defining of the boundary.

Although the Israelis accepted the outlines of this compromise on May 11, for bargaining purposes they insisted on a demilitarized zone on the Syrian side of the frontier as well. Bunche told Vigier, who was conducting the negotiations, to tell the Syrians that realistically they could not expect a better basic arrangement unless they were prepared to face further fighting.

Practical situation is that Syria is left all alone and Israelis know it. In my talks with other Arab representatives here I find no great concern about Syria's plight. It will be advisable for Syrians to make the best of a bad situation.[20]

By this time the Israelis and others were comparing Vigier's performance unfavorably with Bunche's and publicly regretting that Bunche was not on the spot to conduct the negotiations himself. Both Vigier and Bunche deplored this effort to drive a wedge between Bunche and his representatives. When the Israelis in New York suggested that Bunche should fly to Syria, he told them that apart from his full confidence in Vigier and Riley he was "undergoing a cure long overdue."[21]

The negotiations were suspended on May 17, with each side accusing the other of intransigence. To break the deadlock Bunche proposed a meeting at the frontier between the Israeli prime minister, David Ben-Gurion, and the head of the Syrian military government, Colonel Zaim. When the United States suggested on May 23 that Bunche should return to the Middle East, he replied that such a move would short-circuit his immediate aim of forcing a meeting between Ben-Gurion and Zaim. He felt that the Israelis could not expect Syrian withdrawal unless they too were prepared to make some concessions. The Israelis, for their part, again suggested that Bunche's absence was a factor in the faltering of the negotiations because "his skill as a mediator is matched by the confidence and esteem with which he is regarded by all parties concerned."[22]

Bunche's new formula for a compromise concentrated on the necessity of completely separating the armed forces of the two sides by establishing a demilitarized zone in the area between the armistice line and the international frontier. The idea was both to minimize friction and to safeguard the territorial claims and interests of both sides pending the final settlement, which was to be negotiated by the Conciliation Commission. If this formula was rejected, he told Vigier, he would renew his appeal to Zaim and Ben-Gurion to meet, and if *that* failed he would go to the Security Council. Before he could send this proposal, the Israelis agreed to Foreign Minister Sharett's meeting with Zaim. Bunche tried to persuade Zaim to agree to this, on the grounds that Sharett was solely responsible for Israeli foreign policy. Zaim, however, preferred that Sharett meet with the Syrian foreign minister first. The Israelis rejected this and urged Bunche to go ahead with his new formula. Eban threatened, unless Bunche could get the Syrians to withdraw, to go to the Security Council and tell the "unedifying story of the mediating effort." He reported that Bunche appeared "shaken, confused."[23] Bunche was certainly exasperated, both by Eban's long and self-righteous homilies and by the fact that Zaim, who was willing to meet Ben-Gurion, had refused to meet Sharett, who in turn was unwilling to meet the Syrian foreign minister.

Bunche told Vigier to give his compromise proposal, which had the strong backing of the United States, to both sides on June 8. The Syrians authorized their delegation to discuss this proposal on June 13, but a new complication now arose in the form of an Israeli incursion into the Government House demilitarized zone in Jerusalem, in violation of the Israeli-Jordanian armistice agreement. Although Bunche rebuked the Syrians for trying to use this extraneous event as a stick to beat the Israelis with in the armistice talks, he also told Eban that if the Israeli troops did not withdraw he would resign as mediator, giving the Israeli violation and the discrediting of the Jordanian-Israeli armistice agreement as the reason. The Israeli troops withdrew, and the talks reconvened on June 16.

A further delay ensued because Zaim did not want to agree to evacuating Syrian troops from the future demilitarized zone before the plebiscite in Syria which was scheduled for June 25. Bunche explained this to Eban and urged the Israelis to be patient, and on June 24 he was able to announce that both sides had accepted his compromise proposals as a basis for negotiation. He urged both sides not to get bogged down in details about civil administration of the demilitarized zone, pointing out that similar arrangements under UN supervision had worked well previously and could be more easily worked out as a practical matter on the ground after an agreement in principle had been reached.

With Bunche and the United States leaning alternatively on both sides, the end was at last in sight. The agreement was signed on July 20 on the top of Hill 272, near Mishmar Ha Yarden. The following day Bunche told Vigier that he would now make his final report to the Security Council and would have no further responsibilities in the Palestine question. His offices in the area, including Rhodes, could therefore be closed.

In his report[24] Bunche recommended the termination of the mediator's office, which, now that the Conciliation Commission was in existence, no longer had any useful function. He suggested that the Council should declare unnecessary the prolongation of the truce, but reaffirm the order of July 17, 1948, to desist from all military action. He presented his suggestions to the Council on August 7, urging, among other things, that the parties get rid of "the entire heritage of restrictions which developed out of the undeclared war."* In its resolution of August 11 the Council adopted these suggestions and paid a generous tribute to the work of both Bernadotte and Bunche.

Bunche was at last, for the time being at least, free of the Palestine problem. He had a very measured estimate of his achievement, which he knew to be flawed. "The way I always saw the Palestine affair (and still do)," he wrote to Sam Souki, the United Press Cairo correspondent who had been in Rhodes,

was that we had to try to make the best out of a bad situation. That sort of approach rarely leads to a *good* result, but only something *less bad.* That, apparently, is where things now rest. At least, I hope so. But the hapless refugees are still on the hook. They are the *real* victims of the affair.[25]

Bunche had always assumed that the armistice agreements would be a short-lived stage before a full settlement. In later years he frequently expressed his astonishment that they themselves had become a sort of status quo.

On disembarking from the *Queen Mary* in April, Bunche had declared that his top priority was an "extended leave of absence for the sole purpose of rest"[26] and added that he had had no leave since the summer of 1941. The unfinished business of the mediator, the Israel-Syria armistice agreement, had taken longer than any of the other agreements, and, even though he was five thousand miles away, it had occupied much of his time and energy during the early summer. Although he was taking things comparatively easy, Bunche only got away on holiday in late July. He took the family to Los Angeles and stayed in the home of Will Rogers, Jr. At his cousin Jane Johnson's marriage to James Taylor on August 21, Ralph Jr. was the ring-bearer and Joan and Jane were hostesses at the reception.

On September 22, 1950 Bunche was having lunch in the UN Delegates Dining Room when his secretary, Doreen Mashler (she had married his assistant in Rhodes, William Mashler, the previous year), came to

*The most obvious of these was the Egyptian ban on Israeli shipping in the Suez Canal.

inform him that he had been awarded the Nobel Peace Prize. He was doubtful whether, as a member of the Secretariat, he should accept such an award and wrote a letter declining it on the grounds that "peace-making at the UN was not done for prizes." Lie, however, insisted that the letter should not be sent, since the award was also a tribute to the Secretariat and would be good for the UN.* That evening, while he was dining at home with Ruth and the children, the telephone rang and a voice said, "Ralph, this is the President." It was Truman calling to congratulate him.

After an audience with the Pope, two days' shopping in Paris, and a visit to the Berlin Olympic Stadium, where Hitler had tried to ignore Jesse Owens in 1936, Ruth and Bunche arrived in Oslo for the Nobel ceremony on Sunday, December 10.

On the following day Bunche gave the Nobel Lecture in the Aula (the great hall) of Oslo University, "in a dark and perilous hour of human history, when the future of all mankind hangs in the balance. . . ." The Korean War was raging, and the United Nations forces had suddenly had to confront vast hordes of Chinese troops. The Cold War had never been so hot. In his lecture, Bunche forcefully championed the UN struggle in Korea as an essential fight against aggression, and stressed the absolute necessity of the United Nations' having sufficient means to deal with acts of aggression. He spoke of Europe and the necessity of liquidating both the legacy of World War II and the impasse between East and West if the United Nations was to play its full role. He looked beyond the boundaries of the Western world. There was an "urgent necessity of a new orientation—a global orientation," and it must take account of the peoples of Africa and Asia, who constituted the majority of the world's population and who could no longer be ignored. The liquidation of colonialism must be accelerated, and "a friendly hand must be extended to the peoples who are laboring under the heavy burden of newly-won independence, as well as to those who aspire to it."[28]

Bunche believed that the United Nations, used properly, provided the only sure way of applying "reason's voice" to the affairs of nations and of developing a "wholesome international morality." He emphasized that

the United Nations exists not merely to preserve the peace but also to make change—even radical change—possible without violent upheaval. The United

---

*When Bunche told Dag Hammarskjöld this story, Hammarskjöld said, "Good for you. But if *I* had been Secretary-General, you would have *sent* that letter."[27]

Nations has no vested interests in the status quo. It seeks a more secure world, a better world, a world of progress for all peoples. In the dynamic world society which is the objective of the United Nations, all peoples must have equality and equal rights.[29]

His Nobel Lecture brought together all the themes Bunche had worked on separately at different stages in his past career, as well as most of the goals which he was to pursue in the United Nations for the next twenty years. Some—comprehensive decolonization, for example— seemed radical in 1950 but in 1992 are already a part of history. Others— like the development of an "international morality," or collective resist- ance to aggression—are only now beginning to be discussed as practical possibilities.

One of the most important sources of Bunche's strength was his unswerving commitment to general principles and basic objectives, a vi- sion that encompassed events without becoming hostage to them. How- ever murky the political climate, however steep or treacherous the path, he knew where he was going and how he should conduct himself.

17

Anticlimax

Not Much Statesmanship

The Nobel Peace Prize was by no means the last of the honors heaped on Bunche, and in the early fifties he did a prodigious amount of public speaking. His main themes were the United Nations and its potential; freedom and democracy, and especially American democracy; and civil rights, racial prejudice, and bigotry, with particular reference to race relations in the United States. He addressed conferences, organizations, colleges, and commencement ceremonies at a rate of four or five major speeches a month. He even took part in the Hollywood Academy Awards in 1951, taking Jane Taylor with him and presenting Oscars to Darryl Zanuck and Joseph Mankiewicz. He received twelve honorary degrees in the first six months of 1951. He wrote all his speeches himself, and they have a distinctive tone—tough but moderate, idealistic but pragmatic, optimistic but with a profound sense of human weakness and of the immense obstacles to be faced in the pursuit of peace and justice. Bunche cherished the opportunity to make contact with a wide variety of audiences outside the United Nations and to take his message abroad, especially to young people. He concentrated particularly on the American South, always insisting that the audiences be integrated. After a triumphal reception at the University of Arkansas in May 1952 he wrote to Ruth:

I can't understand why it is that I seem to go over so well in the South (except with Negroes of course) for I always talk very straight to them about the race problem. I thought the audience would never stop applauding last night. Everyone white and Negro alike, insists that these visits of mine do a lot of good. I hope they are right.

In the three frustrating years after his return from Palestine, he evidently felt that public speaking was one of the most useful things he could do.

For all the honors and public recognition, Bunche's return to New York and to his job in the Trusteeship Department was something of an anticlimax. Instead of being the leader and inspiration of a life-and-death enterprise of urgent international importance, he was once more a senior official in an international secretariat under the uncertain leadership of Trygve Lie.

On June 27, 1950, Bunche had attended an unusual lunch in the Stockholm Restaurant, on Jericho Turnpike, near Lake Success on Long Island. Among those present were Trygve Lie, Ambassadors Malik and Soldatov of the Soviet Union, Ambassador Ernest Gross of the United States, and Mahmoud Fawzi, the foreign minister of Egypt. President Truman had just announced that the United States would give military assistance to South Korea through the United Nations. The luncheon was the last diplomatic social event of the pre–Korean War period. With the exception of Malik and Soldatov, who were boycotting the Security Council in protest against Taiwan instead of the mainland People's Republic representing China at the UN, the guests left the lunch in a hurry and repaired to the Security Council, which in the evening voted for the United Nations to intervene with force against the North Korean invasion of South Korea. The Council designated the United States as the "Unified Command" of the UN forces. Bunche wrote:

This was the crucial day for the UN. It was either decisive action or the certainty of starting a new chain of Manchukuo, Ethiopia and Munich episodes. The UN is saved, and so is the world."[1]

From the outset, Bunche viewed the Korean action as a turning point both in the Cold War and for the United Nations. Later in the year, when the very existence of the UN forces in Korea seemed to be threatened by the appearance of vast numbers of Chinese troops, he declared that Korea provided the vital lesson that the UN

must have readily at its disposal, as a result of firm commitments undertaken by all of its members, military strength of sufficient dimensions to make certain that it can meet aggressive military force with international military force, speedily and conclusively.[2]

Unfortunately the Cold War itself made such preparedness, which depended on the work of the UN Military Staff Committee,* impossible.

*The Military Staff Committee consists of the chiefs of staff of the five permanent members of the Security Council. China, France, the then Soviet Union, the United Kingdom, and the United States.

The early 1950s were a low point in the history of the United Nations Secretariat. The Security Council action on Korea, and Trygve Lie's strong public support of it, caused the Soviet Union to boycott the secretary general; even Soviet written communications were no longer addressed to the secretary general but to "The Secretariat." Other senior United Nations officials also ceased to deal directly with the countries of the Soviet bloc, and Lie requested his senior colleagues to refuse even social invitations from those countries. The intrusion of the Cold War into the work and official relationships of the Secretariat, combined with the desperate and uncertain fortunes of the United Nations forces in Korea in the first year of the war, spread a chilling cloud over the early enthusiasm and dedication of the UN staff.

Lie's troubles over Korea were compounded by a parallel development on the American side, the anticommunist witch-hunt which reached its grotesque apogee with the activities of Senator Joseph McCarthy of Wisconsin. The witch-hunters found a happy hunting ground among the American members of the Secretariat. In articles in the press, in Senator Pat McCarran's Internal Security Subcommittee of the Senate Judiciary Committee, and later in McCarthy's own committee, the public impression was created that, in the unsubstantiated words of the U.S. federal grand jury on December 2, 1952, there was infiltration into the UN "of an overwhelmingly large group of disloyal US citizens, many of whom are closely associated with the international communist movement."[3]

Trygve Lie's attempts to deal with the so-called "loyalty question" played havoc with the morale of the Secretariat as well as with his own relations with his staff. This miserable period at the United Nations was dramatized, on November 13, 1952, by the suicide of the UN's brilliant American legal counsel, Abraham Feller. In commenting on this tragedy, Bunche denounced the pressures which the witch-hunt had imposed on Feller as Lie's chief legal adviser and mourned the loss of a gifted and idealistic colleague and friend.

Bunche spent virtually the whole of 1950 in New York with no significant periods away from home, although various attempts were made to get him on the road again. Lie wanted him to go to Kashmir, in partnership with Admiral Chester Nimitz, who had been appointed as UN plebiscite administrator, to resolve the threat which India's claim to Kashmir, and Pakistan's reaction to it, posed to peace on the subcontinent. Bunche reacted strongly and negatively to this idea. The director general of UNESCO asked him to become his deputy. He was consulted from time to time on the Palestine question, but had nothing to do with the day-to-day running of the armistice regime he had created.

On a trip with Ruth and Ralph Jr. in August 1950 to Cambridge, Massachusetts, where Harvard had offered Bunche a professorship,* Ralph Jr. developed a high temperature. His temperature went down and then up again while the family was on vacation in Twin Lakes, Connecticut, and a week later, detecting stiffness and soreness in his neck, the doctor took a spinal tap and diagnosed polio. Bunche and Ruth were distraught at this news, and Bunche called Eleanor Roosevelt in New York. She put him in touch with the National Foundation for Infantile Paralysis, which arranged for the boy's treatment in New York Hospital. Watched over day and night by his anxious family, Ralph Jr. eventually recovered completely. Bunche received word that his son's recovery was complete just a few hours before he learned of the award of the Nobel Peace Prize.

The Middle East did not remain quiet. On July 20, 1951, King Abdullah of Jordan was assassinated in the Al Aqsa Mosque in Jerusalem. He was, Bunche wrote,

a unique personality in the modern world. He was a philosopher and a poet, but he was also realistic and politically very astute. He was one of the most charming men I have ever known. In all my dealings with him in connection with the Palestine dispute, I found him always friendly, reasonable and one whose word could be fully trusted.[4]

Bunche was increasingly dismayed with the failure to press forward to a settlement of the Palestine question. In November 1951, after talks in Paris with Arabs and Israelis, he urged the disbandment of the Palestine Conciliation Commission, which had just informed the General Assembly that in its nearly two years of existence it had been unable to make any progress. Bunche felt that, far from advancing matters, the commission's very existence had retarded progress by allowing the Arab states to give a semblance of cooperation while maintaining a totally intransigent attitude.

If the states concerned are willing to compose their differences, they are always free to do so by direct negotiation. If they choose to resort to the good offices of the United Nations, they can always apply to the Secretary-General. If there is a will there is a way, but unless there is a will—a mutual will in this case—no amount of institutional ingenuity will be of any avail.[5]

*Bunche's appointment as professor of government at Harvard was announced on October 27, 1950. Bunche never took up this appointment, and in the end the chair was given to McGeorge Bundy.

Bunche pointed out that the armistice agreements provided for their own revision and could be extended to provide a solution for interstate problems up to and including a complete peace settlement. Such an approach would avoid the Conciliation Commission's fatal blunder of putting all the Arab states together in the peace negotiations. If the commission was abolished, the Truce Supervision Organization and the UN Relief and Works Agency for Palestine Refugees (UNRWA) could continue to deal with the security situation and the refugees, while

the removal of the fig-leaf now covering the nakedness of the Arab refusal to advance towards peace—a fig-leaf represented so far, quite unintentionally, by the Palestine Conciliation Commission—would either force the intransigent party to come out into the open with its real attitude and face the consequences, or resort to the expedient of revising the armistice agreements in order to advance towards a settlement in a less obtrusive manner than by formal peace negotiations.[6]

Because the UN Headquarters in Manhattan was still under construction, the General Assembly again met in Paris in the fall of 1951. Ruth's health prevented her and Ralph Jr. from accompanying Bunche, and he went to Paris without enthusiasm on November 4. It was an uninspiring session. The Cold War, starring U.S. Secretary of State Dean Acheson and Soviet Deputy Foreign Minister Andrei Vishinsky, was at its coldest, and the battle between Trygve Lie and the UN's Staff Association was at its height. Bunche found the charms of Paris much diminished, and his aversion to French food increased. In the evening he usually retired to his hotel room to eat biscuits and fruit or dined in small restaurants with his staff, Doreen and William Mashler, Heinz Wieschhoff, and Bozidar Alexander. He was no longer the center of attention, as he had been in 1948.

The Assembly session itself was a lackluster affair. Bunche wrote:

I'm very much afraid that this Assembly will be a total failure. It is very depressing and if no progress is made here the UN will be greatly weakened. There isn't much statesmanship in evidence, and very little good will or sincerity. It looks bad for the world.[7]

Bunche's work in Paris was almost entirely with the Fourth Committee of the Assembly, which dealt with trusteeship and non-self-governing territories. The tide of decolonization was gathering momentum and creating many unwanted pressures on the colonial powers. The French were under pressure concerning their territories in North Africa, while South Africa was successfully fighting off attempts to remove South-West Africa from its control. Bunche spent much time either dissuading the

French and South Africans from walking out of the committee, or coaxing them back after they had done so. He was also concerned with protecting the petitioners from Africa—Sylvanus Olympio of Togo or the Herrero Chiefs from South-West Africa—from French or South African pressure. Bunche noted:

Some poetic justice, that I, who had such difficulty getting admitted to South Africa in 1937, should be playing a very influential role in the General Assembly resolutions of the past few years which finally resulted in [South African] Union being virtually isolated on South West Africa question.[8]

Bunche was longing to go home, and he became increasingly exasperated with the committee and with the delaying tactics of those, including some of his own staff, whom he suspected of wanting to stay in Paris over Christmas. He finally got home on December 23.

As Bunche grew older he found the prolonged absences from home increasingly hard to bear. Although Ruth's letters had been a great support, in Paris he had missed her and the family acutely. He had not even much enjoyed seeing all the old friends—from Africa or the Middle East, or expatriate Americans in Paris—as much as he would have in earlier years.

Ruth and Bunche had been meaning to find a house of their own ever since they had arrived in New York in 1946. In Parkway Village they were, in Ruth's words,

Still living where the girls don't even have a place to keep their things and their clothes, where everything is so packed up and put away that one can't even use his things or cook properly, little Ralph can't even enjoy his toys and with no place to study, no place for you and me to keep our clothes, and we can't even invite friends here. . . .[9]

Bunche addressed himself to the housing problem on his return from Paris, and on April 12, 1952, he put down a deposit on a house in Grosvenor Road, Kew Gardens, Queens. The owner, a Mr. Sturm, was an admirer who brought the price down from $60,000 to $51,500 for the Bunches, as well as offering to sell them anything in the house that they wanted. They both loved the house, with its space and its garden, and it remained the Bunche home until Ruth's death in 1988.

Bunche had been irritated to hear from Clark Eichelberger of the United States UN Association that the new president, Dwight Eisenhower, though praising him highly, had also told Eichelberger that he doubted that I should talk about the Negro problem so much in my speeches, since I am a "citizen of the world" now and can leave the race struggle to others. Nonsense—I have an obligation to carry on that struggle.[10]

Even in Bunche's own life there were plenty of reminders, ranging from the ridiculous to the serious, that the struggle was by no means won. Typical of the former was his experience at a dinner in 1950 which Lie gave in honor of Crown Princess Martha of Norway. Bunche was seated next to the wife of the head of Swedish-American Lines, a bibulous American-born Mrs. Lundbeck, who, when Lie proposed a toast to President Truman, whispered to Bunche, "I hope he chokes." "Who? Mr. Lie?" Bunche inquired. "No, the President," she replied, and proceeded to denounce Truman's modest origins. When Bunche rebuked her, Mrs. Lundbeck said, "You talk like one of those people who believe colored people ought to be equal." This led to a heated discussion of the alleged mental inferiority of blacks, after which Mrs. Lundbeck said, "Tell me, would you let your daughters marry colored men?" Bunche drew a deep breath and replied, "Why, my dear lady, I don't think I would object. My daughters happen to be colored. They are necessarily colored because I am colored. In fact, I not only am colored but I am an American Negro." Mrs. Lundbeck panicked and said Bunche was different, and, in trying desperately to defuse the situation, asked him if he had been to Norway. He said he was about to go. "What for?" she asked. "The Nobel Peace Prize," he answered. "Who's getting it?" "Well, as a matter of fact, I am." Mrs. Lundbeck later complained she had not been properly briefed.[11]

In all the publicity attendant on the Nobel Prize, Bunche was constantly referred to as "the grandson of a slave," even when receiving an honorary degree at Columbia University. This tendency infuriated Ruth and was bitterly resented by his family, especially Aunt Ethel, who regarded it as an insult to the memory of her father, who was never a slave, and had been a college graduate and a school principal.* Aunt Ethel was even more incensed later on when a book on Bunche repeated the canard.[13] Bunche also disliked the constant references to himself as the "first American Negro" to do this or that,[14] which he found a demeaning and irrelevant qualification and an implied slur on all Black Americans.

In his closing speech at the NAACP convention in Atlanta in July 1951, Bunche castigated the United States Senate for failing to pass civil-

---

*Bunche's grandmother, Nana, as the daughter of a house slave, spent her early childhood years in slavery. She did not suffer abuse. She recalled having to scrub the back of the mistress of the house when she bathed.[12]

rights legislation. "I can never be fully relaxed in Atlanta, fine city that it is . . . ," he said, "since I abhor racial prejudice and its evil end products, discrimination and segregation." He pointed out that a black soldier then fighting in Korea, even if he had the Congressional Medal of Honor, could not rent a hotel room in Atlanta, whereas a white deserter, or a traitor, or a communist conspirator could easily do so. The Atlanta police provided a motorcade to take him from and to the airport.

When traveling in the South Bunche was on the alert for discrimination in hesitations about hotel bookings or tables in restaurants, and he took up each case in the conviction that only thus could people be eventually shamed out of discriminatory practices.* Every now and then he received confirmation of this belief. The Quaker George School in Pennsylvania had turned away his children on racial grounds in 1947. In 1951, the school's senior class asked Bunche to be its commencement speaker, and he politely but firmly refused, giving his reasons. The next year he received a letter of thanks from the sponsor of the invitation "for the kind service you did us by sticking to your principles." His courteous refusal had caused the school to change its admission policies.[15]

The United Nations was not immune to discriminatory practices either. In July 1952 Bunche discovered that a black member of the Secretariat, Edith Jones, was being fired on the orders of Trygve Lie because she had been going out with a boy from Norway whose parents had complained to Lie. Bunche confronted Lie and had the dismissal rescinded.

Bunche was no negative complainer or protester for the sake of protesting. He returned again and again, in his public speeches, to the glory of American democracy, "the greatest experiment in the history of human society,"[16] and its complete incompatibility with the realities of racial discrimination in the United States. He never ceased to proclaim his own pride both in being American and in being black. His ideas, and the positive cast of his thinking at this time, were most eloquently expressed in an address to the 45th Annual Convention of the NAACP in Dallas on July 4, 1954, just after the Supreme Court decision in *Brown* v. *Board of Education,* which ruled that school segregation was unconstitutional since "separate education facilities are inherently unequal."

---

*In Charleston, West Virginia, in 1950, for example, while traveling with the Indian diplomat Mrs. Pandit, Bunche was informed by the manager of the Daniel Boone Hotel that no room had been reserved for him and that he was to be the guest of Dr. Spaulding, a black resident of Charleston. Bunche told the manager that he was there at the governor's invitation and needed to get the facts straight before the press conference at noon. A room was quickly made available.

I am here not only because I am a Negro and proud of it. I have come because I am an American and proud of it; because I have a fervent belief in democracy as the only way of life worthy of free men; because I believe that winning full equality and full integration for the Negro citizen is indispensable not only to him but to the nation; because I believe that proving the ability of democracy to have unqualified application to all people irrespective of race and religion is imperative to the cause of freedom throughout the world . . . ; because I believe that proving the virility of our democracy is one of the strongest blows we can strike at aggressive communism; and finally because I have children and am determined to do all that I can to ensure that they will be complete Americans . . . and without the handicaps of race which you and I have had to suffer. . . .[17]

Of the Supreme Court decision Bunche declared,

I had never imagined that legal phraseology could be so beautiful, that a court's decision could read like poetry. But that is because the decision of the Court . . . marked encouraging progress in democracy, advance in the removal of the racial stigma from the innocent children of a very large segment of the nation's population, and confidence in our ideals, our constitution and the good sense and decency of the American people.[18]

As to whether the decision would be effectively implemented, Bunche noted that the communist press was already scoffing at the Court decision as an empty gesture in the Cold War. "How could any good Americans support and join the Communists in that stand?"[19]

Bunche went on to analyze the realities of the changing racial situation, particularly in the light of the Cold War and the urgent necessity of validating American democracy. "The Negro asks only that American democracy march on its black as well as its white feet."[20] He urged that reason should now supplant emotion and blind prejudice in giving blacks the equality they were entitled to.

I do not contend that prejudice is a myth. I do say that it is not as vigorous, deep-rooted and omnipresent as it once was, and that with many it is today worn as a loose garment.[21]

The nature of the problem itself was changing.

This problem of race is now less than it used to be a problem of economics and politics and more a problem of our minds, our thinking and concepts. It is the mental images, the stereotypes, that we have to combat . . . the almost universal concept of an American as an Anglo-Saxon Protestant. . . . I am a Negro and can speak only for myself, and I say to this audience that I do prefer to be with "my own kind," but my "own kind" are Americans, all Americans, and I do not give a hang what their color or religion may be so long as they believe in our way of life and our democratic destiny. I suspect that most Negroes feel the same way.

Bunche ended this ringing declaration of faith in progress and in American democracy by declaring,

I think it is no idle dream to expect that by the date of the centennial anniversary of the Emancipation Proclamation in 1963 the back of the entire system of segregation and discrimination will be permanently broken.[22]

Bunche was, strictly speaking, accurate in this forecast, just as he proved to be accurate in his predictions of the speed of the decolonization process. What he did not as yet foresee were the disappointments and the vast economic and social obstacles that were, in the next two decades, to blight the promise both of civil rights in the United States, and of decolonization in the world at large.

Bunche was evidently happier out on the speaking circuit than in the claustrophobic atmosphere of Lie's Secretariat. In April 1952 he was surprised to be asked by Lie, at the request of the British and French, to "go easy" on colonial questions and to instruct his staff to press less hard on such matters as visiting missions to trust and colonial territories.[23] He was unable to respond positively to this suggestion.

Because his work at the United Nations had become more and more routine, for once Bunche had time for his family and for the theatrical and show-business evenings in New York which he greatly enjoyed. He loved plays and musicals and the parties after them, and delighted in the opera. He and Ruth became friends with Leonard Lyons, the *New York Post* show-business columnist, and Bunche's doings and sayings often appeared in Lyons' column.

Bunche was an avid baseball fan, and had gloried in Jackie Robinson's historic breaking of the color barrier in major-league baseball in 1947. Robinson became a family friend, and Bunche had a pass for Ebbets Field. At a Dodgers–Giants game in August 1952, he had a chance encounter with General Douglas MacArthur, who, in the previous year, had been dismissed by President Truman from his command in Korea. To Bunche's surprise, MacArthur said that the trouble with the United Nations was that it was too much a captive of the United States, which exerted far too much influence in the world organization. MacArthur believed that modern weapons had caused war to become outmoded, and that political leaders who still thought in terms of power and war were behind the times. The Dodgers won, 9–1.

18

The "Loyalty" Question

An Unseemly Farce

On November 10, 1952, Trygve Lie surprised both the General Assembly and his Secretariat colleagues by announcing his resignation. The Soviet boycott of his office over Korea and the McCarthy witch-hunt in the Secretariat had made Lie's position increasingly difficult. He wanted, he said, to hand over to someone who had the united support of the membership. Lie had delayed his resignation until the Korean War had taken a better turn for the United Nations forces and there was talk of an armistice. He had waited to announce his decision until the foreign ministers of the five great powers had arrived in the Assembly, in the hope that they would be able to agree speedily on a successor.

Lie's hope of a quick succession was not realized, and only on March 31, 1953, after the fruitless consideration of a long list of candidates,* was the Security Council able to recommend Dag Hammarskjöld of Sweden to the General Assembly as Lie's successor. Hammarskjöld was not well known outside his own country, and the members of the Security Council were under the impression that he was a nonpolitical technocrat. Certainly none of them had any inkling of the driving sense of mission, the intellectual virtuosity, or the moral commitment that were to make Hammarskjöld's eight years at the United Nations a landmark in the history of the organization.

*The list included Carlos P. Romulo of the Philippines, Lester Pearson of Canada, Mrs. V. L. Pandit of India, Prince Wan Waithayakon of Thailand, Nasrollah Entezam of Iran, Charles Malik of Lebanon, Padilla Nervo of Mexico, and Ahmed Bokhari of Pakistan. The unwritten agreement that no national of a state which was a permanent member of the Security Council could be Secretary General ruled Bunche out as a candidate.

Bunche had never met Hammarskjöld, knew nothing about him, and was as curious as all his Secretariat colleagues about the new boss. He certainly had no idea that he would soon be embarking on a working partnership with a man whom he came to regard as "the most remarkable man I have ever seen or worked with. . . . I learned more from him than from any other man."[1]

At the time of his arrival in New York to take up what Trygve Lie had told him was "the most impossible job on this earth," Hammarskjöld was, even by Swedish standards, an enigmatic figure. He was improbably young-looking for his forty-eight years and seemed modest and diffident almost to a fault. It was only on closer acquaintance that diplomats, and his colleagues in the Secretariat, began to glimpse the quality of his mind, the firmness of his purpose, and the strength of his integrity and character.

Hammarskjöld, a shy man, was seldom easy in his initial encounters with the people he worked with. Bunche was no exception, and their early relationship was marked by considerable misunderstanding on both sides. Hammarskjöld's most immediate concern, apart from the impending armistice in Korea, was to resolve the so-called "loyalty" question involving American members of the UN staff, and to reorganize the Secretariat. He had also to establish relationships of trust with member governments and especially with Washington, where the Eisenhower administration had just taken office. One of Eisenhower's first moves after his election had been to offer Bunche the job of deputy to Henry Cabot Lodge, the new U.S. ambassador to the UN, a post Bunche had politely declined, saying that he liked his job at the UN too much to leave it.[2]

During the summer Bunche continued with his usual work and his program of public speaking. He had little contact with the new secretary general. At a time when the UN was under continuous attack, not only by Senator McCarthy but in much of the Western press, Bunche concentrated his speeches on passionate and forceful expositions of the importance of developing the real nature and potential of the world organization. He spent most of January 1953 on an intensive speaking tour in India and Pakistan, returning via Cairo and Jerusalem, where he renewed contact with many friends from the mediation period.

In June Bunche flew to Washington to invite President Eisenhower to address the American Political Science Association, of which Bunche was president-elect.

He [Eisenhower] keeps talking, rapid fire, but not very deeply or clearly. He told us "You have to get away from this and see it from a distance or you go nuts." Got impression he is not very happy in the job.[3]

In August Bunche took the whole family with him to Switzerland while he attended a Quaker conference on international affairs at Clarens. Unfortunately Ruth's mother became seriously ill, and Ruth had to return early to the United States, leaving Bunche with Joan, Jane, and Ralph Jr. He evidently greatly enjoyed this experience, and they all got on very well together.

Hammarskjöld had spent the summer of 1953 getting the "loyalty" question under control and making plans for the reorganization of the Secretariat. In the process he personally visited every department of the Secretariat to determine how the various activities of the Secretariat had originated and whether they were still justified and relevant. This process took more than a year to complete, but already in the fall of 1953 he had made some preliminary decisions. One of these was to create two new posts, undersecretaries without portfolio,* for the top United States and Soviet officials, who would deal with "special high-level problems."

Although Hammarskjöld had Bunche in mind for one of these posts, Bunche himself first heard of it in a roundabout way from Jawaharlal Nehru's sister, Mrs. V. L. Pandit. Mrs. Pandit had asked Hammarskjöld if Bunche could attend a seminar on Gandhi in India in October. Hammarskjöld had not wished him to take part on the grounds that he wanted to protect Bunche from too much public attention.

He went on to say that he understood from a source which had usually been reliable, that they were brewing up trouble for me in Washington on the basis of my past associations, etc. He [Hammarskjöld] told her that he was "frightened" about it, since he had it in mind to make me his number two man in the organization.[4]

Hammarskjöld had told Mrs. Pandit that he had hesitated to say anything to Bunche himself since he was not certain that anything would happen and did not want him to worry.

Bunche, who was always extremely open and direct in his dealings and at this time hardly knew Hammarskjöld, was puzzled at such an indirect approach. Two days later, at a Freedom House dinner in New York, he had a chance to sound Hammarskjöld out himself. Talking with Bunche before the dinner, Hammarskjöld had criticized Eisenhower's attorney general, Herbert Brownell, for his recent attack on Harry Truman for being "soft on communism," saying cryptically that he knew plenty about "police reports" and how unreliable they were. Bunche said that, as an American citizen, he was wondering whether it was not his

*This title gave rise to much hilarity and was soon changed to "undersecretary general for special political affairs."

duty to leave the UN so as to be free to raise his voice against the evil forces at work in American society.

After they had sat down to dinner, Hammarskjöld passed Bunche a note written on the back of his place card saying that after what Bunche had said it was urgent that they "talk about his future plans for two minutes" at the end of dinner. Subsequently, in a quiet corner of the hotel lobby, Hammarskjöld began to expound his plans. "I [Bunche] found him difficult to follow and understand" —a common experience for those talking to Hammarskjöld for the first time. Bunche gathered that he was to be one of the two top officials closest to Hammarskjöld's own office. Bunche, in some surprise, asked Hammarskjöld what would happen to the Trusteeship Department, which he had created and directed from the beginning. Hammarskjöld did not seem to understand Bunche's concern, but informed him that his new post would be political and that he was "my candidate." Bunche asked him if he had mentioned all this to the United States, and Hammarskjöld said he had not.[5]

Bunche seems to have totally misconstrued Hammarskjöld's stilted remarks and believed that, after what he himself had said before dinner, he was being given a hint that he might not have a place in Hammarskjöld's reorganization plan because Washington might veto him.

He [Hammarskjöld] said not one word concerning my service to the organization or of regret that I could not continue in Trusteeship, which he knows is my field of special interest and knowledge. He seemed to me to be cold, if a bit shamefaced, about it all. When I told him I was devoted to the UN and at his disposal, he half laughed and half shrugged it off. I have the feeling that for some reason he is not very happy about my presence here.[6]

Bunche had mistaken Hammarskjöld's shyness and difficulty in establishing personal relations for deviousness and pusillanimity.* It took some time for him to realize his mistake.

The witch-hunt for "disloyal" American officials in the Secretariat had been going on since 1950, creating a growing rift between Lie and his staff and jeopardizing many careers. The press chimed in from time to time. A long article in the *Saturday Evening Post* in November 1951 entitled "The Sinister Doings at the UN," by one Craig Thompson, was fairly typical. It alleged that "communist wreckers" had infiltrated the whole Secretariat, and suggested that "Stalin's purpose" was to make life miserable for Trygve Lie.

*Constantin Stavropoulos believed that Hammarskjöld delayed in establishing close contact with Bunche because he wanted to be sure of his own grasp of UN matters before taking on someone so highly qualified and experienced.[7]

In such a climate, it was inevitable that the witch-hunt would eventually involve Bunche. The Institute of Pacific Relations, with which he had had dealings long ago, was a particular obsession with the witch-hunters, because it was associated in their minds with the so-called "loss of China." The National Negro Congress, of which he was a cofounder, had become dominated in the early 1940s by the communist left. He himself had been decidedly radical in his formative years.

One of the UN staff members called before the Senate Internal Security Subcommittee (the McCarran Subcommittee) was Jack Harris, a senior officer in the Trusteeship Department's research section. Bunche had known Harris in the OSS, where he had been in charge of OSS intelligence in South Africa, and had recruited him to the UN on the strength of his excellent credentials as an Africa expert. Harris, who had informed the subcommittee that he had been recruited by Bunche, had invoked the Fifth Amendment in refusing to tell the subcommittee whether he was a member of the Communist Party at the time of his employment in the UN. He was subsequently dismissed by Lie.*

In October 1952 the McCarran Subcommittee had declared, incredibly, that evidence had established the participation of UN officials in "a full-scale operation of subversive activities directed against the security of this nation."[8] The federal grand jury, appointed in June 1951 to investigate subversive activities and espionage, echoed this charge in its final report on December 2, 1952.

In January 1953 President Truman, as one of his last acts as president, had issued Executive Order 10422, which stipulated that all U.S. nationals in international organizations should be subjected to a loyalty investigation. This order was a serious blow to the Charter principle of Secretariat independence. To deal with its repercussions, Lie had appointed Bunche to an advisory panel to assist him on cases involving charges of subversive activity. By February 1953, two months before the end of Lie's term, American members of the Secretariat were being fingerprinted by the FBI in the UN building, provoking further outrage among their Secretariat colleagues. *Pravda* had a field day with all this and called Lie the "front man and agent of the State Department" who had "rushed to the aid of the Senate inquisition. . . ."[9]

On March 10, 1953, Bunche himself was summoned by the Senate Internal Security Subcommittee counsel, Robert Morris, to a meeting

---

*A group of three international jurists, appointed to advise Lie, had ruled that taking the Fifth Amendment constituted grounds for dismissal. When Bunche had urged Harris not to take the Fifth Amendment, Harris replied that he would not become an informer. This was Bunche's first hint that Harris might have Communist Party connections.

with Senators Jenner and Welker at Foley Square Courthouse in New York. The senators were courteous enough and asked him if he had ever been a Communist Party member and about Jack Harris. They also asked about Max Yergan, who had taken over the National Negro Congress in 1940 when A. Philip Randolph had resigned, and about Paul Robeson.

After the meeting Bunche wrote to Jenner expressing his surprise at being summoned to Foley Square.

I would have taken it for granted that my long record of service to my country, and my public utterances, written and oral, throughout my adult career, were more than adequate testimonial to my unqualified loyalty to my country and to my unwavering devotion to the American way of life. . . . At some point in our discussions, Senator Welker, I believe it was, suggested that perhaps it would have been wiser not to have done some of the things I did in the thirties. Seen from today's perspective that may be true. But in the thirties the common and urgent enemy of peace and freedom was Hitler and his Nazi creed. Today it is communism alone. The lines now are much more sharply drawn, and the perspective of each of us is much simpler and clearer.[10]

Bunche also pointed out to Jenner that Harris was cleared for secret war work in the OSS, had been denounced the previous year in the Indian communist weekly *Blitz* as an American lackey, and had been strongly and publicly in favor of the UN action in Korea. He was therefore at a loss to know why he should have had any suspicions about Harris.

There was a lull until October, when Bunche was asked by A. M. Rosenthal of the *New York Times* if he had any comment on Jack Harris' testimony before the Internal Security Subcommittee. He replied that Harris was a highly qualified man about whom he knew nothing derogatory.

Bunche himself was now becoming the target of defamatory, if veiled, articles in the right-wing press, which were often followed up by letters from congressmen demanding explanations. In October 1953 the columnist and radio commentator Walter Winchell, a dedicated hitman for the extreme right who was regularly fed information by McCarthy's young assistant, Roy Cohn, and by McCarthy's counsel, Robert Morris, printed the following.

The President will be appalled when a real bigname (he personally applauded on the front pages) is charged as a meeting-attending commie. The man perjured himself when he stated (on a federal questionnaire) that he was never a party member. Two witnesses say they saw him at 2 [sic].[11]

This tortuous pronouncement was an eerily accurate hint of the fabricated case that was about to be mounted against Bunche.

The process against Bunche began on Saturday, January 9, 1954, when he received a phone call at home from Maxwell Rabb, Eisenhower's aide for relations with minority groups.* Rabb asked to see Bunche on the following Monday and arrived with Pierce Gerety, the chairman of the International Employees Loyalty Board. They were friendly but evidently embarrassed and explained that there was unevaluated "derogatory information" in Bunche's file which had to be dealt with. Bunche elicited from them only the fact that it concerned the National Negro Congress and the Institute on Pacific Relations, and he asked them to send him written allegations to answer. On January 16 he received the official interrogatory. The most specific charge was that he had attended a "fraction" [sic] meeting of the Communist Party in John P. Davis' office in May 1935. The meeting's purpose was allegedly to ensure Communist Party control of the National Negro Congress. The other allegations were mainly in support of this charge. The conclusion was that Bunche had been and might still be a "concealed" communist.

Thus began a painful and Kafkaesque period in Bunche's life, an immensely time-consuming episode which disgusted him and which he passionately resented. It coincided with his anxiety over both Ruth's health and the first signs of depression in his daughter Jane. To make matters more intolerable, the proceedings at each stage were deliberately leaked from Washington, giving rise to screaming headlines in the tabloid press. Answering the interrogatory forced Bunche to spend two weeks digging through old files, boxes, crates, and trunks, in a hunt for answers to fourteen allegations. The fact that the charges were patently false made them particularly hard to answer. Bunche wrote his detailed replies to the interrogatory mostly late at night. Bill Hastie came to stay for the weekend to edit them, and Donald Young also went over them. "A tough job under the best of circumstances," Bunche noted, "but this one had to be done at a time when I am busier in the UN than I have ever been."[13] (Bunche was at this time a key member of Hammarskjöld's team, reorganizing the Secretariat, as well as running the Trusteeship Council.) "I worked with determination, grim and angry and at times almost desperate."[14]

---

*According to Eisenhower's biographer Stephen E. Ambrose, Eisenhower told Rabb, "Bunche is a superior man, a credit to our country. I just can't stand by and permit a man like that to be chopped to pieces because of McCarthy feeling. This report will kill his career and I am not going to be a party to this." Eisenhower told Rabb to tell Bunche that he would publicly support him. Bunche told Rabb he would face the charges directly.[12]

On February 12—"Lincoln's Birthday—what a day for me to deliver myself of a document like that"[15]—Bunche had his reply to the interrogatory picked up. It was a document of over one hundred pages with two large batches of exhibits. It is superbly written and gives a vivid picture of Bunche's views and personal history. He opened with an overall reaction to the questions. He had never been a member of the Communist Party, concealed or otherwise. "Its tactics and its revolutionary philosophy are, and have always been repugnant to me." He characterized the charges against him as both outrageous and devious. In analyzing the use of the word "concealed," he surmised that "the source of the so-called 'information' knows my record well enough to realize that a simple charge of Communist Party membership or communist activity on my part would be utterly ridiculous." He particularly resented allegation 14, to the effect that "the communists are in a position to control you,"* and wondered why the authorities had not disregarded this obvious lie on the basis of his well-known record and public statements, as well as of frequent communist attacks on him.

Bunche recalled that he had resigned from Max Yergan's International Committee on African Affairs because he disagreed with Yergan's procommunist ideology. He had denounced the Negro National Congress, of which Yergan became president in 1940, in a memorandum for the Myrdal study, as an organization which the communists "had captured and which therefore would quickly die, as it did." He believed this memorandum was the "first extensive account of how communists and pro-communists won control over a negro organization." After a long survey of his public and academic record, Bunche also recalled that he and Count Bernadotte were often denounced by the Soviets as American or British agents and that his right-hand man in Palestine had been General William E. Riley, a United States Marine. "I may be pardoned for asking what manner of communist it could be who would act as I did in Palestine."

*Bunche believed that Max Yergan, whom he had cold-shouldered at San Francisco in 1945 and had denounced as a slicker and a phony, was behind this curious accusation. An FBI report from San Francisco dated May 19, 1945, quoted Max Yergan as indicating "that Ralph Bunche, a Negro official of the US State Department, is also 'slipping.' However, Yergan is reported to have stated, 'Fortunately, we can control him—if he gets too far out of line we can have him undoubtedly removed from his job for which he is dependent on political favors.'" Bunche had a copy of this report, and was aware of Yergan's campaign against him. After World War II, Yergan became violently anticommunist and in the 1950s was even an apologist for apartheid.

Recalling the many attacks on him in communist publications, Bunche wrote:

I have been regarded and portrayed, here and abroad, as a symbol of American democracy at its best and a walking testimonial of the progress made in race relations in this country. . . . It comes as a shock to me that I must now *prove* my loyalty to the country which has given me so much and whose interests I have served throughout my career with devotion and whatever ability has been at my command.

His accusers had raked in a mass of lesser charges—a letter to Alger Hiss in 1948;* an alleged telegram to one Thaddeus Battle in the Lincoln Brigade in the Spanish Civil War, which Bunche could not recall, although he had been "very definitely against Franco, who was being . . . actively aided by Hitler and Mussolini"; and acquaintance with various communists, including John P. Davis, with whom he was alleged to have associated in Communist Party meetings.

Allegation 14, that the communists were in a position to "control" him, especially incensed Bunche.

Allegation 14 taken in conjunction with the initial charge [that he was a secret member of the Communist Party] says in effect that " Ralph Bunche is a communist because he is one." This isn't an allegation—it is a combination of Gertrude Stein and loaded dice. It does seem to me that if someone were to make an allegation, unsupported by evidence, that I am "Stalin's aunt," I should not be called upon to disprove it. My record gives a categorical answer to this allegation. . . . Nor would it be possible for me to be seduced by the dogma of communism or any other totalitarian ideology. I love personal liberty too much. I believe too profoundly in the sanctity and the dignity of the individual being. I am, and have always been, a vigorous individualist and I instinctively rebel against arbitrary discipline and conformity in thought and action. I would go down fighting before I would be pushed around and subdued. I abhor the slave mentality, the "Uncle Tom," the intellectual or physical coward. I am no maverick; but I have come up in a free society, have learned to treasure freedom as life itself, have thrived on it, and could not accommodate my being to any other diet. . . . I would be less than frank if I did not say that the formulation of the foregoing replies . . . has been a most gruelling and unpleasant chore, not alone for reasons of

*In August 1948 he had written a sympathetic letter to his former State Department colleague Alger Hiss, who in 1953 was in jail for perjury: "The gallant fight you are making is on behalf of the integrity and reputation of every decent American. . . . I want you to know that I am in your corner."[16] Bunche had liked and respected Hiss as his superior in the State Department and believed he should be seen as innocent unless proved guilty.

physical strain, but for psychological violence as well. . . . It is . . . disconcerting and disturbing to be required to defend myself against allegations, involving, in effect, a review of most of my adult life, emanating from unknown and unseen sources, whose credibility, in my estimation, leaves much to be desired.[17]

Although Bunche received constant assurances from Maxwell Rabb that the White House regarded the whole process as absurd and had full faith in him, no word came from the Loyalty Board in the ensuing weeks. Finally, on May 14, he was informed that there would have to be a hearing because two witnesses had indicated a desire to testify against him. When Bunche expressed his surprise, he was told that in the current atmosphere the Loyalty Board could not run the risk of being suspected of protecting communists. The board met on May 25.

The proceedings had a strong element of farce. On the evening of the second day of the hearings, Bunche dined with Eisenhower at the White House in honor of Ethiopia's Emperor Haile Selassie. The first person he met there was Attorney General Herbert Brownell, whose paid minions were Bunche's accusers. Brownell "greeted me effusively and put his arms round me."[18] While the hearings were actually going on, Bunche was visited by FBI agents making a routine inquiry about someone being considered for a high government post, who turned out to be John Foster Dulles being checked for the post of secretary of state. Days before the hearing the White House asked Bunche to do a goodwill tour for the United States in Europe and elsewhere, something which, with his UN position, he could not have done anyway. When the CIA tried to seek his advice on one of its undertakings, Bunche said he was not cleared. The CIA man responded, "You are cleared with us or I couldn't speak to you."[19]

Throughout the ordeal Hammarskjöld publicly displayed his complete confidence in Bunche and deputed his own legal adviser, Ernest Gross, to assist him. He frequently discussed his predicament with Bunche and was unfailingly encouraging.

The Loyalty Board's hearings were brief but intensive. In spite of the confidentiality of the board's previous proceedings, someone had leaked the news of Bunche's hearing.* The New York *Daily News* on May 26 declared that of 1,760 UN cases investigated only thirty-two had been considered serious enough to warrant a hearing, and Bunche's was one of them. The *New York Post,* on the other hand, played up Bunche's distinguished record, Hammarskjöld's support, and the Bunches' attendance that night at the White House dinner. "The last time the President talked

*An ex-communist, Howard Rushmore, a Hearst journalist and a convert to the extreme right, had been tipped off, apparently in the hope of discrediting Bunche and the UN.

with Bunche," the *Post* gushed, "he told him he was too good a man for the US to spare to the UN."

The two so-called "witnesses" at the hearing were black ex-communists, Manning Johnson and Leonard Patterson. They were both retained by the Department of Justice as "consultants to the Immigration and naturalization Service" and had been frequently used by the authorities in deportation cases.[20] They alleged that Bunche had been mentioned as a party member who would advance communist objectives, that Bunche's writings reflected communist concepts and the Communist Party line, that Bunche had read a paper at the 1935 Howard University conference that had given birth to the National Negro Congress, and that Bunche had been present in John P. Davis' office in 1935 for the purpose of discussing communist policy.

Bunche himself, assisted by Ernest Gross, responded strongly to these charges, to questions about his writings, and about Jack Harris and other matters. He thought he might have met Manning Johnson at Howard University and remembered the name because Johnson was quite well known at that time as a labor organizer. He did not recall ever having met Leonard Patterson.

Although Bunche made a convincing impression and received much unequivocal heavyweight support from outside—from Eleanor Roosevelt, and Walter White of the NAACP among many others—he soon realized that only John P. Davis, in whose Florida Avenue office in Washington Manning Johnson claimed that Bunche had attended a Communist Party meeting, could convincingly give the lie to the most damaging charge. He had broken with Davis in 1940 over the communist takeover of the National Negro Congress and was extremely reluctant to resume contact with him. However, after thinking the matter over all night he called Davis in Washington, and Davis willingly agreed to appear before the Loyalty Board.

In 1954 Davis was a prosperous businessman, the publisher of a popular black magazine, *Our World,* a respected leader of the black community in Washington, and a family man with a wife and four children. Although Bunche pointed out that the revelation of Davis' membership in the Communist Party in the 1930s might damage him, Davis insisted on taking the stand. Appearing on the last day of the hearings, he testified under oath that Bunche had never attended any such meeting as alleged. He also described his experiences as a member of the Communist Party in a way which deeply impressed the Loyalty Board with his honesty and sincerity. He had taken the risk, he told the board, of testifying and thus revealing his communist past because he believed Bunche was innocent of the charges against him.

On May 28 the board chairman, Pierce Gerety, announced that all six members of the board had "unanimously reached the conclusion that there is no doubt as to the loyalty of Dr. Bunche to the United States government." Hammarskjöld also issued a statement reaffirming his unreserved confidence in Bunche's outstanding integrity. Bunche himself wrote of the experience that he had "absorbed it philosophically, marking it off as an unfortunate expression of the difficult and often bewildering times in which we live."[21]

The accusations against Bunche caused a considerable stir, both at home and abroad. Walter White of the NAACP called the episode "an unseemly farce" and recalled that Bunche had "inspired millions of non-whites all over the world to resist communist propaganda and keep faith in democracy."[22] Noting the conjunction of the White House dinner and the hearings, Sweden's *Dagens Nyheter* commented, "This strange combination shows to what paradoxes the present political climate can lead."[23] Not to be outdone, the London *Times* pontificated,

The proclivity of the United States government for making itself appear mildly ridiculous at times in the eyes of the rest of the world is probably one of the penalties of a weakened constitution. . . .[24]

On May 28 a Mr. Richter called Bunche's office about a film for students on which Bunche had cooperated with TransWorld Airways, saying that TWA would omit Bunche's part of it unless they could be assured that there would be no adverse publicity for TWA. "He can go to hell," Bunche wrote on his secretary's note recording this call.

In July 1954 the Justice Department announced that it would prosecute the two informers, Johnson and Patterson, for perjury. On April 16, 1955, the *New York Times* reported, under the headline "Brownell Drops Informant Plan," that "salaried witnesses will not be used in the handling of anti-communism cases." Ten years later, in December 1965, Pierce Gerety, Jr., the son of the Loyalty Board chairman and a student at Harvard, was sent by his father to visit Bunche. Bunche told the young Gerety, who said he had always associated his father with witch-hunting, that his father had been an extremely fair chairman and was a man of integrity.

The allegations against Bunche continued to resound in the echo chamber of the extreme right for many years. A combination of anti-communist obsession, racial prejudice, and hatred of the United Nations motivated a weird crew of fanatics, including Theodore Roosevelt's son, Archibald Roosevelt, the columnists Westbrook Pegler and George Sokolsky, and Alfred Kohlberg, the anchorman of the "China Lobby," to persist in denouncing Bunche. They were originally grouped in an organization called the Nonsectarian Anti-Nazi League and enjoyed considerable resources. Bunche had an informant in this organization and was well briefed in advance on its activities. When, in July 1954, the Justice Department announced proceedings against the two informers, the league resolved "to get" Bunche. Johnson and Patterson, the two "witnesses," were in touch with the league and were asking for help in their now very precarious situation. They complained that they had been unfairly cross-examined by Bunche in the Loyalty Board hearings. The league's idea was to repeat their charges publicly so that Bunche would sue for libel. Its members also hoped to persuade Senator Welker to attack Bunche in the Senate and intended to publicize the "martyrdom" of Johnson and Patterson.* When the Joint Committee Against Communism, another extreme-right group, gave a dinner in honor of Joseph McCarthy's amanuensis, Roy Cohn, Archibald Roosevelt equated Johnson and Patterson with General MacArthur as patriots being martyred by the left wing and the *Herald-Tribune*.

The league was quiet until October 1954, when Bunche was awarded the Theodore Roosevelt Medal for Distinguished Service by the Theodore Roosevelt Association. In a letter denouncing this award to the Association's president, Oscar Straus II, Archibald Roosevelt gave a classic demonstration of extreme rightist paranoia. In rehashing the charges against Bunche already dismissed by the Loyalty Board, he referred to the Roosevelt Association trustees as "unwitting tools of the sinister influences that are now so powerful in the country" and, for good measure, described the OSS as a communist front. The Roosevelt trustees persisted in giving Bunche the medal, and in his acceptance speech Bunche recalled that Theodore Roosevelt had also been denounced as a radical.

Although basically conservative in outlook, he became the target for shameless detractors who denounced him as a "radical" and for his altruistic views. In this, too, he would find himself in familiar surroundings today.

At the dinner Bunche was seated next to Archibald Roosevelt's sister, Alice Roosevelt Longworth, who spent the evening telling him how foolish her brother was to attack him.

*In March 1957, Ruth mentioned newspaper reports that Johnson and Patterson were "making speeches about Martin Luther King being a communist and inciting the Negroes of the South to communism."[25]

In January 1955 a fifty-page tirade against Bunche under Archibald Roosevelt's signature was widely distributed. Bunche was convinced that the author was Manning Johnson. He was by now no longer amused at Archibald Roosevelt's antics. Although Ernest Gross was considering a possible libel action, "I am not inclined to make a public reply to an irresponsible attack on my honor of this kind."[26]

In 1957 another Archibald Roosevelt organization, Alliance, Inc., distributed three thousand copies of a brochure on Bunche. Alliance, Inc., also accused Jawaharlal Nehru of being a Soviet agent and attacked the Ford Foundation. This brochure surfaced in a speech by Congressman James B. Utt of California as late as January 1962. Utt's aim was to get the United States out of the United Nations. Bunche refused to respond to these "old and shopworn" calumnies.

On August 19, 1954, Hammarskjöld officially announced the reorganization of the Secretariat, with Bunche as one of the undersecretaries for special political affairs, Ilya Tchernychev of the Soviet Union being the other. They were to undertake "floating assignments," like Bunche's current study of development plans for the Jordan River. Hammarskjöld explained that they would take on important questions that overlapped between departments, which he had hitherto had to handle himself, thus creating a bottleneck. Bunche took up his new duties on January 1, 1955.

19

Peaceful Uses of Atomic Energy

Putting Science above Politics

After a slow start, Bunche had become Hammarskjöld's most trusted colleague. The penciled notes they exchanged during meetings indicate a striking change from the earlier encounters, where Bunche had complained of Hammarskjöld's barely intelligible mumbling and of his coldness and lack of interest. Of all his senior UN colleagues Hammarskjöld probably regarded Bunche alone as his intellectual equal and as a person of equivalent stature to himself. For his part, Bunche, while never overstepping the line of respect for the secretary general's position, felt free to be totally frank in his working relations with Hammarskjöld. Hammarskjöld, who was not always a good judge of character on first acquaintance, brought in several new top officials during his time in New York in the mistaken belief that they had the makings of the perfect colleague, but he quickly became disillusioned with most of them. By the time of the Suez crisis in October 1956, he had realized that, in Bunche, he had the best partner he could wish for, and Bunche's responsibilities steadily increased.

The essence of Bunche's new post was that it had no fixed assignments, and his first major task was in the then new field of the peaceful uses of atomic energy. In his address to the General Assembly on December 8, 1953, President Eisenhower had made a number of proposals for promoting the peaceful uses of atomic energy, including the creation of an International Atomic Energy Agency, and an international scientific conference to be held in the summer of 1955. Hammarskjöld regarded this program as an important new venture and personally supervised its development. He felt strongly that the new International Atomic Energy Agency (IAEA) should be closely linked to the United Nations and under the UN flag. He was also determined to keep control over the preparations for the conference, which would provide the opportunity for the first major declassification of nuclear secrets between East and West. He was suspicious of the activities of the General Assembly on these matters and had Bunche follow them closely.

Hammarskjöld was particularly concerned with setting up the Scientific Advisory Committee which was to guide the preparations for the atomic energy conference. The group was to consist of representatives of nations with nuclear programs—the U.S., Britain, France, the U.S.S.R., Canada, Brazil, and India. Hammarskjöld was determined that its members should be top-level scientists rather than political representatives paralyzed by Cold War antagonisms. By the time the General Assembly decided, late in 1954, to convene the conference in the following August, there were only eight months to organize an unprecedented and immensely complex meeting.

Over the Christmas season and into January 1955, Hammarskjöld himself was completely preoccupied with gaining the release of seventeen American airmen whose aircraft had come down on Chinese territory during the Korean War and who were imprisoned as spies in China. In January, when he journeyed to Peking for that purpose, Bunche was left in charge of the preparations for the atomic energy conference and for preliminary consultations with the members of the advisory committee. As a result of Hammarskjöld's insistence, these were leading scientists— I. I. Rabi for the United States, Sir John Cockcroft for Britain, Bertrand Goldschmidt for France, Homi Bhabha for India, and others equally distinguished. They were still, however, to some extent controlled by diplomatic advisers with a strong Cold War orientation. This was precisely the attitude Hammarskjöld wished to avoid.

In Hammarskjöld's absence in Peking Bunche discussed the problems of the conference with Rabi and other members of the advisory committee. It was already clear that time would be too short for the committee to prepare formal written suggestions. Bunche therefore proposed that Hammarskjöld himself should be the chairman of the committee and the committee should give their advice directly to him. The members of the committee accepted this arrangement, and Hammarskjöld, on his return from Peking, was surprised to find himself chairman of an extremely distinguished group of scientists. He was at first uneasy about this position, as well as at the Cold War attitudes which initially animated some of the scientists. He soon found, however, that the intellectual powers of the group easily transcended such mundane difficulties, and the meetings developed into a remarkably harmonious and effective effort to resolve the very considerable problems of the conference. Hammarskjöld was so impressed with this experience that he duplicated it by establishing advisory committees on the Suez crisis, and on the Lebanon and Congo problems, with varying degrees of success.

Apart from the scientific advisory committee, the main work of organizing this immense scientific gathering was carried out by the secretary general of the conference, Walter G. Whitman, a professor of chemical engineering at MIT, and a staff of young scientists. Bunche greatly liked Whitman and kept a close watch on his activities, giving him support and advice when necessary.* A minor crisis arose when Whitman was due to visit Moscow to discuss the Soviet papers for the conference. Whitman had been a member of the president's Atomic Advisory Committee and was therefore privy to a great deal of highly secret information on the American nuclear program. The Washington establishment, and especially Admiral Lewis Strauss, Eisenhower's atomic energy czar, had convinced Whitman that he might be kidnapped and interrogated under torture if he went to Moscow. They also told him that a visit to Moscow might cost him the confidence of Strauss and the president. Whitman brought his troubles to Bunche.

To Bunche the entire story seemed fantastic and incredible. "The Russians are dangerous but not damned fools."[1] He advised Whitman not to tell Hammarskjöld about the problem, since it would seriously compromise his position as secretary general of the conference and as a member of the Secretariat. The people in Washington who had wanted him to run the conference had to understand that he was now an international official and was going to Moscow in that capacity. He suggested that, if Washington was so nervous, Charles ("Chip") Bohlen, the U.S. ambassador in Moscow, should be consulted. Whitman went to Moscow, where he was received with great enthusiasm and a remarkable degree of cooperation.†

Much of Bunche's time was still devoted to the task of reorganizing the Secretariat. In February, to Ruth's indignation, he spent three weeks surveying United Nations offices in Latin America, and repeated the process in Europe in March. These trips were physically taxing, since Bunche

---

*I had become Bunche's chief assistant late in 1954, when he took up his new position. Bunche put me to work with Whitman throughout the period of the Conference on Peaceful Uses of Atomic Energy.

†I went to Moscow with Whitman on this trip and was instructed to protect him as best I could. He was initially extremely nervous until he realized the truth of Chip Bohlen's observation, when we visited him in the U.S. Embassy in Moscow, that the only real risk Whitman was running was being killed by Soviet hospitality.

now suffered almost chronically from a slipped disk and had begun to experience trouble with his kidneys.*

While in Geneva, Bunche witnessed firsthand the mutual antipathy of Hammarskjöld and Gunnar Myrdal, who had certainly entertained hopes of becoming secretary general himself. Myrdal was at this time the executive secretary of the UN Economic Commission for Europe, a trail-blazing organization which was attempting to bridge the Cold War gulf in Europe. Hammarskjöld had strongly criticized an ECE paper on oil, which he regarded as a sloppy piece of work. To Bunche's amusement Myrdal responded by casting himself as a crusading liberal being hounded by an arch-conservative and an American lackey (Hammarskjöld and Bunche).

Although, throughout 1955, Bunche's main concern was with the peaceful uses of atomic energy and the Secretariat reorganization, his personal contacts in the Middle East kept him in touch with develop-ments there. In July he met privately with Mahmoud Fawzi, the Egyptian foreign minister. Fawzi said that, although he would deny it publicly, 1955 was the year to reach a settlement in the Middle East. There were, however, two minimum conditions—full compensation for Arab lands expropriated by Israel, and a land bridge through the Negev between Egypt and the other Arab States. Fawzi felt that Hammarskjöld's pro-jected visit to the area was of the greatest importance, and that Bunche and Hammarskjöld should deal with Fawzi himself privately, preferably when he was on vacation. Fawzi was to become one of Hammarskjöld's closest friends and confidants on Middle East questions.

The atomic energy conference proved to be an immense scientific, political, and organizational success. Fourteen hundred scientists at-tended, and 1,067 scientific papers on a vast range of subjects were pre-sented during the two-week meeting. A new bridge was built between East and West during what had become the most constructive and prom-ising year for international peace since the beginning of World War II. (An armistice in Korea came into force at the end of July 1955.) This conference also showed that the UN Secretariat, properly led, could suc-cessfully execute complex and politically sensitive enterprises of great im-portance.

During his stay in Geneva for the atomic energy conference, Bunche went to Günsbach in Alsace and sat on a bench in the organ loft while Albert Schweitzer played the organ. "We differed, but in most friendly

---

*He had quit smoking the year before, on a trip to Geneva, where, suffering from a severe cough and sore throat, he asked himself what he was doing doggedly smoking two or three packs a day. He gave up cigarettes on the spot and never smoked one again.

ways, on Africa. He clearly fears nationalism and takes a paternalistic view. The politically-minded African is not at all understood by him."[2] Bunche was rather less tolerant of the unsolicited advice which Schweitzer offered five years later during the Congo crisis.

The other important part of Eisenhower's 1953 initiative on the peaceful uses of atomic energy was the setting up of the International Atomic Energy Agency (IAEA). Here again Bunche played the role of midwife and guardian angel. He took immense pains over the agreement to establish the relationship between the new agency and the United Nations, which Hammarskjöld was determined should be closer and more effective than the relationship of the UN to the existing autonomous UN specialized agencies. Scientists and governments were less enthusiastic about this close relationship, and in the end it was agreed that the IAEA should be "under the aegis of the United Nations," whatever that classical allusion might mean, and would retain its autonomy while having a special relationship to the General Assembly. Bunche also presided over the conference that, in September 1956, just before the Suez crisis, finalized the statute of the IAEA. For the emergency period of the Suez crisis, he had to delegate most of his work on atomic energy.

At the opening session of the new agency in Vienna in October 1957 Bunche was able to save the IAEA, at its birth, from a major embarrassment over its first director general. Lewis Strauss was determined that this potentially important post should go to an amiable but undistinguished Republican congressman, Sterling Cole. The Soviets were equally determined that it should *not.* Strauss was in Vienna to push Cole's candidacy and seemed oblivious of the harm to the new agency that a divided vote on its first head would cause. Bunche wrote:

I found Strauss remarkably unaware of certain facts of international life, namely that a majority vote on an issue of this kind may be only a pyrrhic victory, that many who will feel compelled to vote with the United States may be very unhappy about it, and it might well doom both Cole and the Agency to failure.[3]

Bunche was already bothered by the location of the agency in Vienna, a delightful backwater.

Vienna is a charming place but I am no less convinced that there is no sound reason to have the agency located here. If attendance at the meetings is an index, the interest of the local public is not aroused.[4]

He was even more convinced that a divided vote and a major East-West split on the director general would be a disaster for the fledgling agency. During a reception at Schönbrunn he tackled Strauss and Vasily Emelia-

nov, the chief Soviet representative, and found that, though each wanted
to talk to the other, neither wished to take the initiative. Both were thus
delighted when Bunche suggested they should meet the following day in
his office, where they talked for nearly two hours. Other senior agency
appointments were discussed; Strauss relinquished his dictatorial, take-it-
or-leave-it attitude; and Emelianov asked for a twenty-four-hour delay to
consult Moscow.

When Cole was formally nominated the next day, Emelianov merely
said that he regretted having failed to convince the United States that the
director general should be from a neutral country but, in order to continue
the "business-like atmosphere" of the agency, he would abstain on, rather
than oppose, Cole's nomination. After Cole had been sworn in Bunche
noted that only the Russians were getting credit for their statesmanlike
conduct and that there was a lot of resentment for Strauss' steamroller
tactics, which were attributed to Strauss' wish to get Cole appointed while
a Republican congressional delegation was in Vienna.

There is no doubt that the USA, through its determination to force Cole into the
post, missed a golden opportunity for a major diplomatic stroke. . . . I am sure that
no head of an international organization ever took office in an atmosphere so
frigid and so devoid of any gesture of friendliness. I felt rather sorry for Cole, who
is personable and congenial, but who, I fear, is cast in the role of a sacrificial lamb
in this episode. . . .*5

During his stay in Vienna the United States Embassy delivered a
message from Eisenhower offering Bunche an appointment as a member
of the United States Commission on Civil Rights, which was being established under the recently adopted Civil Rights Law. Bunche expressed his
appreciation and his regret at not being able to accept the appointment in
spite of his lifelong interest in civil rights, "since in my view I could render
the best service by continuing with the United Nations." The following
day, in a message from the White House, Eisenhower's chief of staff,
Sherman Adams, told him that his refusal had not been unanticipated,
and "the President fully agrees with your view that you can best serve the
nation† in the United Nations." Bunche wished to continue working with
Hammarskjöld. He was certainly also skeptical about the commitment of
the Eisenhower administration to a dynamic civil-rights policy.

*Homi Bhabha, the great Indian scientist, told Bunche in Vienna that the IAEA would
not enjoy the confidence of its members, who would prefer to turn to the UN. India, for its
part, would seek no help from the agency.

†Not Bunche's conception of his role in the United Nations.

Bunche's preoccupations with other major issues, and the smallness of his staff, caused him gradually to relinquish his responsibilities for the UN's work on the peaceful uses of atomic energy. He oversaw the even larger second conference on the subject, in 1958, and felt that it was—with twenty-six hundred delegates and three thousand observers—much too big.[6] His energies and attention were by that time largely occupied elsewhere.

20

Suez and the First Peacekeeping Force

The Front Line of a Moral Force

On April 20, 1956, Bunche noted, "Burt asking for Jane's hand at the reception for Autherine Lucy."* Although Bunche and Ruth had been deeply worried about Jane's tendency to depression both at school and at home, they hoped that marriage might steady her. Jane and Burton Pierce, a young business administrator trained at the Harvard Business School, were married on September 22.

Although Hammarskjöld had talked to Bunche about many things, including the Middle East and its personalities, he had, prior to the last months of 1956, somewhat to Bunche's surprise, "never said a word about my experience in Palestine or sought any advice."[1] Hammarskjöld had not consulted Bunche at all about his extensive tour of the Middle East in April 1956, during which he tried to shore up the armistice agreements, which Bunche had negotiated and which, over the years, had been steadily eroded. Bunche observed that Hammarskjöld was putting increased emphasis on the "authority" of the secretary general and on taking more initiatives. After nearly three years and some considerable successes, he had gained great self-confidence.

During the summer of 1956 it became clear that the Middle East was moving toward a new conflict. The situation between Israel and Egypt deteriorated, with raids by Israel into the Gaza Strip, Palestinian "fedayeen" raids into Israel from Gaza, and massive Israeli reprisals. Interna-

---

*Autherine Lucy was a black student whose court-ordered admission to the University of Alabama had triggered a riot, after which the university authorities suspended and expelled her before she had even been enrolled.

tional tension over the Suez Canal reached a critical stage in July when President Nasser reacted to the abrupt and unexplained cancellation of Western financing for the Aswan High Dam by nationalizing the Suez Canal Company. In spite of efforts by Hammarskjöld and others to defuse this situation, Israel invaded Egypt through Sinai on October 29 with the avowed intention of eliminating the "fedayeen" bases. Two days later, to the surprise and dismay of their main allies, Britain and France, acting in collusion with Israel, gave an "ultimatum" to Egypt and Israel to withdraw ten miles from the Canal, and began bombing Egyptian airfields and other targets in preparation for their own invasion of the country.

This immensely dangerous international crisis[2] tore apart the Western alliance and the tripartite agreement of Britain, France, and the U.S., which until that time had been assumed to be the best basic guarantee of peace in the Middle East. The possibilities of Soviet intervention, heralded by missile-rattling statements in Moscow and a suggestion that the U.S.S.R. should join the United States and other UN members with powerful air and naval forces in a military action to support Egypt against the invaders, gave another, sinister dimension to the situation. Hammarskjöld, appalled at the Anglo-French adventure, played a central role in getting the crisis under control. He was the leader in the effort to stop the fighting, to secure the withdrawal of the invading forces, and to provide the peacekeeping force which would not only make that withdrawal possible but would also provide the basis for a new and less violent situation on the border between Israel and Egypt.

In the tumultuous early meetings of the Security Council and the emergency session of the General Assembly on the Suez crisis, Bunche played little or no part. On November 1, the Canadian foreign minister, Lester Pearson, speaking in the General Assembly, announced that he would abstain from voting on a cease-fire resolution on the ground that it was "inadequate to achieve the purposes which we have in mind at this session."[3] Before the next meeting Pearson had told a skeptical Hammarskjöld that a United Nations force, a new concept, might become necessary, and in the early hours of November 2 Pearson proposed the creation of "a truly international peace and police force . . . large enough to keep these borders at peace while a political settlement is being worked out."[4] On the evening of November 2 Bunche and Andrew Cordier, Hammarskjöld's executive assistant, visited Pearson in his suite at the Drake Hotel to discuss this idea further. This was Bunche's first involvement in the Suez crisis.

By November 3 Britain and France were faced with massive and vocal opposition both at home and abroad and were embroiled in an increasingly uncertain military adventure in Egypt. Port Said and Port Fuad at the northern end of the Canal did not officially surrender until November 6, and there was unexpectedly strong Egyptian resistance to an advance down the Canal, which the Egyptians had blocked with a variety of obstacles to shipping. Even while their invasion forces were still at sea on the way to Egypt, Britain and France had announced that they would stop their own military campaign if Egypt and Israel would accept a UN force to keep the peace and to ensure a satisfactory arrangement of the Canal problem. The creation of a UN force thus became the key to the resolution of the crisis, and in the small hours of November 4 the General Assembly formally requested Hammarskjöld to explore the idea and report back.

The gravity and urgency of the situation evidently convinced Hammarskjöld that he could no longer do without Bunche's executive ability and experience of the Middle East. He first asked Bunche to draft the cables to Britain, France, and Israel requesting a cease-fire. These were dispatched at 7:00 A.M. on November 4. Israel accepted the cease-fire on November 5, and France and Britain on November 6. The creation of a United Nations force was now crucial, and at 11:00 A.M. on November 4 Hammarskjöld met with Bunche, Cordier, Pearson, and the ambassadors of Colombia, India, and Norway to discuss the urgent provision of troops. The four countries all offered contingents, and were followed in the next two days by Sweden, Denmark, Pakistan, Finland, Ceylon, Czechoslovakia, and Romania.

The setting up of the first UN Emergency Force (UNEF) was a major development in international relations. The employment by the UN of armed troops instead of unarmed individual observers required new principles and rules, as well as command, staff, and logistical arrangements. Bunche, who had set up and directed the pioneering truce-observation operation in the Middle East in 1948 and had written the basic principles, procedures, and rules of conduct for that operation, was the obvious choice to supervise this new type of international military venture.

Hammarskjöld was initially dubious about the feasibility of a "peace and police force." "Our main concern," he cabled on November 4 to General E. L. M. Burns of Canada, the chief of staff of UN Truce Supervision Organization in the Middle East, who had just been appointed as commander of the new force, is of course whether it is at all possible within a reasonable time to establish such a group with the peculiar conditions which must apply in the choice of nations from which recruitment can take place. My personal lack of optimism is of course no excuse for not exploring the field.[5]

This unenthusiastic mood began to evaporate when Hammarskjöld, on November 5, got down to writing his report to the General Assembly. He dictated it in between meetings, going over it with Pearson and Cordier as he went along. When he had completed a draft that night he gave it to Bunche for his comments, and then went over it again with Pearson and the legal counsel, Constantin Stavropoulos. The report was ready by 2:00 A.M. on November 6 and was given to the British ambassador to transmit at once to London, since Hammarskjöld's report was the basis on which the British were to agree publicly to a cease-fire. The need for quick action had been intensified by a Soviet request for a Security Council meeting on the night of November 5. Hammarskjöld believed that Soviet Prime Minister Bulganin intended to press for joint Soviet and American military intervention, and he therefore wished to be able to give the Council a positive report before the Soviet ambassador addressed the Council.

Hammarskjöld's report was a masterpiece in a completely new field, the blueprint for a nonviolent, international military operation. It was accepted at once by the General Assembly. The next challenge was to mobilize the force and deploy it in Egypt as soon as possible.

Hammarskjöld and Bunche had put together a list of troop-supplying countries they believed to be noncontroversial. In later years Bunche recalled that Hammarskjöld had assigned him the task of putting UNEF together with the words "Now, corporal, go and get me a force." Hammarskjöld addressed Bunche as "corporal" on the ground that with so many generals around it was a more distinguished appellation. The "corporal" soon found himself besieged by indignant ambassadors protesting that their governments' offers had not been accepted. Pakistan was especially upset that India had been accepted and Pakistan rejected.* Bunche had to explain to the angry envoys that the force had to be balanced, politically and geographically, and that Burns needed time to study the type of military organization he needed. Ambassador after ambassador filed into Bunche's office, and many emerged disappointed.

*Nasser at first tried to exclude from the UN force any country that had collective security arrangements with Britain, which meant any members of NATO, SEATO, or the Baghdad Pact.

Egypt had been expected to welcome the news that the force was almost ready, but instead it withheld permission for the force to enter its territory and submitted a list of detailed questions which symbolized Egypt's sensitivity to the presence of foreign troops. Where would the force be stationed? How long would it stay? Would it leave if Egypt wished it to do so? Where would the troops come from? What would be their duties? Considerable time and patience were needed to answer these questions satisfactorily.

Bunche was determined that, in spite of Nasser's procrastination, UNEF should be ready to go in as soon as possible. He therefore suggested to Hammarskjöld that the troops that were already standing by should be moved in United States transport aircraft to a staging area as near Egypt as possible, perhaps in Italy. Hammarskjöld, who knew that speed was of the essence in order to forestall possible acceptance by Egypt of Soviet bloc volunteers,[6] welcomed this suggestion. The Italian ambassador quickly offered Capodichino, the airport of Naples, as a staging area, and the advance guard of UNEF was established at Capodichino by November 10. On November 12 Fawzi called Hammarskjöld from Cairo to tell him that UNEF could come to Egypt provided India and Yugoslavia were included in the force and Canada was excluded. Hammarskjöld accepted India and Yugoslavia but said he had to maintain his position on Canada. Lester Pearson's role in the birth of UNEF and Canada's unfailing support during the crisis could not be ignored. Hammarskjöld was sure they could agree on such matters when he came to Cairo in the next few days. The first UN troops arrived in Egypt on November 15.

The process of setting up UNEF took place in Bunche's conference room on the thirty-eighth floor and proceeded more or less round the clock as the situation demanded. The working group consisted of the military attachés of the countries providing troops; military representatives of the United States, which was providing airlift and some logistics; and the various services of the Secretariat, including the excellent UN field-operations service led by David Vaughan. The group dealt with problems of organization, supply, and transportation as they arose, and it was kept in touch with political developments by Hammarskjöld and Bunche, who dropped in whenever necessary.*

There was no precedent and no military establishment on which to

*With six years of service in the British army in World War II, I was the only person on the thirty-eighth floor with firsthand military experience. Bunche put me in charge of coordinating the work of this group and ensuring that its decisions were translated into action.

base UNEF. Innumerable problems, great and small, had to be resolved urgently, mostly by improvisation. Soldiers from national armies were being asked to plunge into a critical situation without using force and under United Nations command. Such a venture touched on the most sensitive issues of military psychology and tradition, national sovereignty, and national and international law. Hammarskjöld and Bunche handled the major political and legal problems. The working group handled the smaller ones.

An international army plunging into an international crisis has many practical problems. The contingents were to take ten days' rations to Egypt with them from their home countries, after which they would be fed by the UN. The UN had no logistical organization, and, as a stopgap, it was decided to buy the food on the seventeen cargo ships stuck in the Suez Canal. The problem of uniforms and identification was quite literally vital, since some of the UN troops wore British-style uniforms. "As you know," Bunche commented, "the British are about to leave and they lack some popularity in that particular area."[7] What was needed was distinctive headgear easy for a distant sniper to recognize. A UN-blue beret seemed to be the answer, but it was impossible to procure enough berets in time. American plastic helmet-liners, however, were available in quantity in Europe, and were ready, spray-painted UN blue, in time for the first UNEF detachments to wear on their entry into Egypt. Identity cards in four languages had to be formulated in terms simple enough for an Egyptian or Israeli soldier, or a bedouin, to understand. Tent stoves were another problem. Most of the first contingents came from Northern countries and had woodburning stoves, but with no wood in the Suez Canal area or in Sinai, these had to be replaced by kerosene stoves. The nights and days passed quickly in dealing with a hundred similar details.

A seven-nation advisory committee—Brazil, Canada, Ceylon, Colombia, India, Norway, and Pakistan (the countries providing troops)*—had been set up to assist and advise the secretary general on UNEF. Hammarskjöld and Bunche met with the advisory committee for the first time on November 14, the day Hammarskjöld was leaving for Cairo to negotiate with Nasser. Hammarskjöld greatly enjoyed expounding his views and plans at enormous length in small and informal meetings. Apart from the secretary general, by far the most talkative member of the committee was Ambassador Arthur Lall of India; the most thoughtful was Lester Pearson of Canada. Hammarskjöld explained that in spite of the

*Later joined by Yugoslavia.

unsatisfactory nature of some of the Egyptian conditions, which he intended to deal with in Cairo, he had thought it best first to concentrate on getting Egypt to accept UNEF's arrival. "In order to gain the necessary time," he told the committee, "I accepted a certain lack of clarity."[8] Pearson, with a keen eye for future problems, was already concerned about Egypt's claim to have the sovereign right to determine the composition of UNEF as well as to demand its withdrawal at any time. Ambassador Lall vocally championed the opposite point of view.

Since Hammarskjöld did most of the talking, Bunche confined himself to reporting on the numbers and state of readiness of UNEF. He told the committee that there were already twenty-one offers of troops for the force, and 650 officers and men were already in Naples. "This is the most popular army in history," he said, "an army which everyone fights to get into."[9] He explained the advance arrangements for UNEF made by the UN Truce Supervision Organization's observers in Egypt, and the complexity of improvising logistical arrangements. He also explained the reasons for the urgency in getting the operation started.

In this haste we wanted to demonstrate that the United Nations resolution was not an empty gesture, to avoid the development of a vacuum in the area, and to make use of the only quickly available transportation [the U.S. and Canadian air forces].[10]

When asked at a press briefing whether the haste was really motivated by the fear of Russian volunteers' arriving in the area, Bunche parried the question:

The basic reason was that there was . . . a great deal of skepticism about this. This was an entirely new thing. We had a resolution, but I think not many people thought that very much could be done quickly about it.[11]

A new task for the UN emerged on November 18, when Nasser asked Hammarskjöld for assistance in clearing the Suez Canal of the obstacles with which Egypt had blocked it at the start of hostilities.* For this purpose, Hammarskjöld appointed an American general, R. A. Wheeler, former chief of the U.S. Corps of Engineers and the presiding genius of several epic salvage operations, including the port of Cherbourg during the Normandy invasion in World War II. Bunche liked Wheeler (affectionately known as "Spec") and strongly supported him in launching what turned out to be an outstandingly quick and successful clearance operation.

*There were some seventeen major obstacles, including the El Firdan railway bridge which had been dropped across the Canal, a large oceangoing tug, and a freighter full of concrete.

Hammarskjöld's first action on returning from Cairo was to summon the advisory committee, to which he gave a long and, even by his standards, complex account of his talks in Egypt. The arrangements, Pearson commented, were "becoming almost metaphysical in their subtlety. I have no complaint about that because if, from the beginning of this operation, we had attempted to be specific, we would not have had an operation at all."[12] It was Bunche's task to transform Hammarskjöld's "metaphysical" subtleties into practical arrangements on the ground. In particular he had to deal with the sensitivities of Mahmoud Fawzi, the Egyptian foreign minister, and of the British secretary of state for foreign affairs, Selwyn Lloyd, whose main preoccupation at this time was to use UNEF to the full as a face-saving device for extricating the government of Anthony Eden from its disastrous Suez adventure.

By early December General Burns had decided on the military organization of UNEF, and Bunche discussed the details with Fawzi. Things did not always go smoothly. Believing that a good military band was important for the morale of the force, Bunche had secured one from Pakistan. Unfortunately, the prime minister of Pakistan chose that moment to make a strong public attack on Egypt, and Nasser refused to accept a Pakistani contingent. "The less said about this the better," Bunche told Burns.[13]

The effective buildup of UNEF was the basic condition for the British and French withdrawal from Egypt, which Hammarskjöld and Bunche were negotiating with Selwyn Lloyd. When it became clear that UNEF was a serious political and military reality, the British and French agreed to withdraw all of their forces from Egypt before the end of the year. Hammarskjöld declared in a statement written by Bunche:

It may be pointed out that given the experience of the force thus far . . . and the reception it has received in the area of operation, the UNEF, in terms of potential effectiveness in performing its mission, must be rated as equivalent to a substantially larger military body.[14]

For all the immediate pressures, Hammarskjöld and Bunche never forgot that the new institution they were building would also be a model for the future. Immense pains were taken to develop the legal basis for the presence and actions of UNEF in the form of a "status-of-forces" agreement with Egypt, which provided among other things that members of UNEF detained by the Egyptians for misconduct while off duty would be tried not by Egyptian courts, but in the courts of their own country, a novel provision, extremely important for the governments providing troops. Even ostensibly minor decisions had an important bearing on the international nature of future peacekeeping forces. The units arriving in Egypt initially flew their national flags, as they had always done at home. The Egyptians, after a long history of foreign occupation, wanted them to fly only the UN flag. Bunche was determined that this should become the rule for peacekeeping forces. He told the Advisory Committee:

I see no reason for the display of national flags by the contingents since they are in Egypt only as part of the United Nations force and on no other basis.[15]

This question gave rise to some controversy in the advisory committee, and Bunche had to defend his position strongly, arguing that "it was UNEF which has been permitted to enter Egypt, not this or that national contingent." Hammarskjöld backed him up strongly. "My feeling," he said, "is that the matter is . . . bigger than we may be inclined to think."[16] In this, as in many ostensibly small matters, Bunche was determined that the essentially international nature of UN peacekeeping operations should not be diluted.

It was important that the soldiers who had suddenly been incorporated into this experiment should understand the nature of their mission and its historic context. Bunche wrote a message for Hammarskjöld to send to the UNEF troops in Egypt.

You are taking part in an experience that is new in history. . . . You are the frontline of a moral force which extends around the world and you have behind you the support of millions everywhere. . . . Your success can have a profound effect for good, not only in the present emergency, but on future prospects for building a world order of which we may all one day be truly proud.[17]

As soon as Burns had established his headquarters and staff, and UNEF had reached its full strength of forty-one hundred, the running of the emergency force became increasingly routine, and other problems took priority. The most important of these was the Israeli withdrawal from Sinai. Hammarskjöld and Bunche first broached this vital question in a two-hour meeting with Abba Eban, the Israeli permanent representative to the United Nations, in early December. Bunche had known Eban since 1947, when Eban was representing the Jewish Agency at the UN before the establishment of the State of Israel. Hammarskjöld's more recent relationship with Eban had not always been easy. Preliminary discussion showed that Israel's agreement to withdraw would be closely linked with Israel's concept of the correct use of UNEF and of how the withdrawal should take place. Israel had no intention of simply agreeing to restore the conditions of belligerency by land and sea which had given rise to the current conflict. Eban also raised other Israeli concerns—whether, when the Canal was cleared, Israel would have free passage through it; how free passage through the Strait of Tiran to the Gulf of Aqaba and the Israeli port of Eilat could be assured when Israeli forces withdrew from Sinai; and who would control and administer the Gaza Strip. Israel was determined to prevent the "restoration of an offensive order of battle" on its southern border.

Egypt's views were the mirror image of Israeli preoccupations. In a talk with Bunche on December 9 Fawzi had told him that Egypt must bring back its administration to the Sinai and would need some Egyptian military backing to provide a sense of security. Bunche patiently argued that, though the UN had no right to restrict the return of the Egyptians, either civilian or military, to their own territory, such a move was extremely undesirable. Even if the Egyptian position was legally correct, Bunche emphasized that provocative actions must be avoided. Instead there should be the closest possible cooperation with the UN and UNEF.[18]

The talks with Eban continued to little effect. Both Eban and Hammarskjöld were world-class talkers who liked to set out the nuances and finer points of their cases at great length. Bunche, who was laconic by comparison, was usually the one to pin down what little progress could be made through this blizzard of words and to coordinate it with General Burns, who was conducting parallel conversations with Moshe Dayan, the Israeli chief of staff.

Eban wanted an assurance that Egyptian forces would be excluded from Sinai, something that Hammarskjöld and Bunche had no right to give. He was worried about Egyptian belligerency, and about the possible resumption of the fedayeen raids, which had been the main cause of the Israeli invasion of Sinai. In reply Bunche pointed out that "Israel itself is in a position of belligerency, a position in which it remains so long as Israeli troops are on Egyptian soil."[19] In an appeal for a definite timetable for Israeli withdrawal, Bunche told Eban:

the real importance of UNEF is that it does buy valuable time. It is not in itself a political instrument, but it does purchase time in which political developments can take place and progress on fundamental issues can be made. Delaying the entry of UNEF [into Sinai] seems to be a most unfortunate wastage of this time.[20]

With the French and British poised to leave Port Said, and the Canal clearance operation starting up, Eban continued to respond to Hammarskjöld's representations with the same unanswerable questions. Bunche and Hammarskjöld had no right to provide assurances concerning Egyptian actions on its own sovereign territory, where Nasser had a perfect legal right to move his own forces. Nor were Hammarskjöld's efforts helped by belligerent statements from Cairo proclaiming Egypt's intention to continue the fight against Israel. Although the Israeli forces made partial withdrawals from time to time, the General Assembly required Israel's unconditional and total withdrawal from Sinai; Israel, before it withdrew, required guarantees on the Strait of Tiran, on the future situation in Gaza, and on the future role of UNEF. Hammarskjöld was not in a position to give such guarantees.

By January 22, 1957, the Israeli forces remained only on the western shore of the Gulf of Aqaba and in the Gaza Strip, but this was not enough to allay the pressure from the General Assembly. The armistice agreement of 1949 had established Egypt's right to administer Gaza. Sharm al-Sheikh and Ras Nasrani, which dominated the Strait of Tiran, were in Egyptian sovereign territory. On February 2 the General Assembly decided that after the Israelis had fully withdrawn from Sinai, UNEF should be stationed on the Egypt-Israel armistice line to ensure the full observance of the armistice agreement. The arrangements that Hammarskjöld and Bunche made for the stationing of UNEF would therefore be the key element in securing the cooperation and consent both of Egypt and of Israel.

In this delicate balance of conflicting pressures, the press was not always helpful. An article by Thomas J. Hamilton in the *New York Times* in mid-January stated that Egyptian troops were advancing into Sinai as UNEF advanced behind the withdrawing Israeli forces. Bunche complained to Arthur Hays Sulzberger, the publisher of the *Times,* that the article "affords quite a painful example of how the legend of Nasser's 'dictation' to the Secretary-General and the UN thrives on the outright misstatement of fact."[21] Hammarskjöld and Bunche were increasingly exasperated by a press campaign implying that UNEF was slipping into Egyptian hands and thus would be unable to control the fedayeen. During an anti-UN demonstration in Israel, the soldier-politician Yigal Allon called Hammarskjöld an Egyptian slave and demanded his resignation. There seemed little doubt that the purpose of this campaign was to justify Israel's remaining in control of Gaza and the west coast of the Gulf of Aqaba.

In an effort to get a better Israeli understanding of their efforts, Bunche solicited the help of Jacob Blaustein, a Baltimore entrepreneur who had extensive contacts in Israel.* Blaustein, who met with Bunche on February 4, was worried about UN sanctions, which would certainly cripple Israel. He felt that Eban was far too optimistic about the probable line that President Eisenhower would take, and he called Ben-Gurion and some members of the Israeli Cabinet to warn them.[22] Bunche and Hammarskjöld found Blaustein an invaluable second channel to Ben-Gurion and later used him to give advance notice to Israel of their intentions.

Meanwhile, the talks with Eban became steadily more acrimonious, as each side put questions it knew the other could not, or would not, answer. Israel wanted assurances on Egyptian nonbelligerency, and the long-term stationing of UNEF along the west coast of the Gulf of Aqaba; Hammarskjöld required an affirmation of Israel's complete withdrawal from Gaza and its acceptance of UNEF on the Israeli side of the line.

On February 11 U.S. Secretary of State John Foster Dulles presented a statement to Israel urging prompt and unconditional withdrawal from the Gaza Strip so that the future of the area could be worked out through the good offices of the United Nations. While upholding the right of free navigation for all nations in the Gulf of Aqaba, Dulles also called on Israel to withdraw from its positions on the Strait of Tiran, so that UNEF could take over.[23]

As Ben-Gurion continued to temporize and the threat of anti-Israel sanctions became more imminent, President Eisenhower's patience ran out. On February 20, by television and radio, he took his case to the people of the United States. After surveying the events which had led to the impasse, Eisenhower asked:

Should a nation which attacks and occupies foreign territory in the face of United Nations disapproval be allowed to impose conditions on its own withdrawal? If we agree that an armed attack can properly achieve the purposes of the assailant, then I fear we will have turned back the clock of international order.[24]

In the General Assembly on February 11 a sanctions resolution sponsored by the Afro-Asian group had been presented by Lebanon. In his own statement to the Assembly on this matter on February 22 Hammarskjöld set out to provide a basis for Israeli withdrawal without alienating Egypt. He declared

with confidence that it is the desire of the Government of Egypt that the takeover of Gaza from the military and civilian control of Israel—which, as has been the

---

*Bunche had further extensive dealings with Blaustein in 1963–64, when Blaustein financed the Barbara Hepworth sculpture *Single Form* as a memorial to Hammarskjöld in the forecourt of the Secretariat building in New York.

case, in the first instance would be exclusively by UNEF—will be orderly and safe, as it has been elsewhere.

In a long further passage he proposed that Egypt would act through the United Nations to deal with the various problems of Gaza, including "putting a definite end to all incursions and raids across the border from either side."[25] As often with Hammarskjöld's verbal gymnastics, his February 22 statement was designed to give a little to both sides, in the hope they would both eventually have enough incentive to agree to the next step. Two weeks later Bunche would find himself in Gaza trying to convert this elegant formula into practical arrangements for the operation of UNEF.

On March 1 Golda Meir, Israel's foreign minister, faced with the possibility that the United States would no longer block UN sanctions against Israel, announced that Israel would withdraw completely from the Gaza Strip and the Gulf of Aqaba. Mrs. Meir stipulated that UNEF would be deployed in Gaza, that it would take over from the Israeli military and civilian authorities there, and that it would remain responsible for the administration of Gaza until there was an agreed-upon peace settlement. Israel, she stated, would withdraw from Sharm al-Sheikh "in the confidence that there will be continued freedom of navigation for international and Israeli shipping in the Gulf and through the Straits of Tiran." Henry Cabot Lodge, for the United States, declared that these Israeli assumptions did not make Israeli withdrawal "conditional" and were, in any case, mostly restatements of General Assembly resolutions or statements by the secretary general.

The Israelis were happy neither with being pressured by the United States nor with Lodge's statement, while the Egyptians were also highly suspicious of much that had been said. It therefore fell to Hammarskjöld and Bunche to interpret the proceedings of the Assembly in an atmosphere of extreme sensitivity on both sides. Hammarskjöld had never concealed from the Israelis his view that Egypt had a legal right to return to Gaza, nor from the Egyptians his conviction that it would be most unfortunate if they exercised that right. General Burns was told to concentrate on the takeover from the Israelis "in the first instance"—i.e., for the period in which UNEF exclusively would run the administration in Gaza while more definite long-term arrangements were negotiated with the Egyptians.[26] Hammarskjöld told Fawzi that the only real agreement was over the initial UNEF takeover, which he hoped would last for a long period of time, until the Egyptians "raised their eyebrows." Fawzi nodded approval but did not say anything. To the UNEF Advisory Committee

Hammarskjöld explained that it was necessary to "gamble by going ahead on a pragmatic basis, hoping for a slow development in a low key."[27] Bunche was to orchestrate this precarious gamble on the ground in Gaza.

En route to the Middle East, Bunche represented Hammarskjöld at the independence ceremonies of the Gold Coast (Ghana), a welcome respite from the toils of the Suez crisis. It was also a poignant personal experience for Bunche—the ceremonial beginning of the decolonization of black Africa, for which he had worked so long. The guests included many people who had joined him at various times in the struggle—George Padmore and Peter Koinange from his London days; A. Philip Randolph from Washington; Mordecai Johnson from Howard and Mel Herskovits from Northwestern; Sylvanus Olympio from Togo, whom Bunche had befriended and protected in the General Assembly in Paris. Martin Luther King and Adam Clayton Powell represented a newer generation. Vice-President Richard Nixon represented the United States, and the Duchess of Kent Great Britain.

The cheerful and well-organized ceremonies culminated in the Polo Grounds at midnight, when the Union Jack was lowered and the Ghana flag raised before a crowd of more than a hundred thousand cheering people. Visiting Prime Minister Kwame Nkrumah before leaving, Bunche advised him to "tell his people to stop using [the term] 'Massa,' and he said they would if he told them to—and he would do so."[28] Bunche greatly enjoyed the four-day interlude. He had been particularly impressed at the high standard of discourse in the Parliament—"British democratic tradition at its very best here"[29]—and at the evident prosperity of the country, although he foresaw economic problems ahead if the price of cocoa dropped. Also, "They will need to be more careful about corruption which seems to be quite widespread in the government."[30]

On March 9 Bunche arrived in Rome, where Hammarskjöld called him to tell him to go to Cairo immediately. His instructions were characteristically Hammarskjöldian. In the Gaza Strip, Hammarskjöld cabled Bunche, he attached the greatest importance "to a correct handling, even of seemingly innocent administrative matters, in terms of the possible interpretation that may be attached to them." The Secretariat had to risk taking responsibility "for solutions and arrangements with undefined background and for that reason open to challenge although, of course, tacitly so developed as to be consistent with our basic stand."[31] Bunche flew to Capodichino, the UN base at Naples, which he inspected before flying on to Cairo early next morning in a Canadian C-119 Flying Boxcar.

He landed at Abu Suweir, on the Suez Canal, at 3:15 P.M. on Sunday, March 10, and flew on to Cairo with General Burns.

Bunche had arrived at a critical moment in the deployment of UNEF. On March 6 and 7 the Israeli forces had finally withdrawn from the Gaza Strip and from Sharm al-Sheikh, on the Strait of Tiran, and UNEF had taken over in both places. Hammarskjöld, while convinced that he had to go ahead, was worried about the contradiction between Mrs. Meir's insistence on the complete exclusion of Egypt from Gaza and the legal position, which was also the majority position in the General Assembly, that Egypt's right to be in Gaza under the 1949 armistice agreement must be respected. He had concluded that he had to live for a while with this contradiction, hoping that no move on the Egyptian side would bring it to light while he was trying to find a formula to resolve the problem. This was the essence of Bunche's task in Egypt.

The day before Bunche arrived, Brigadier Amin Hilmy, the Egyptian liaison officer with UNEF, told Burns that he had orders to set up his Liaison Headquarters in Gaza to act as a go-between between UNEF and the civil authorities in the Strip. Burns told Hilmy that the initial takeover was to be exclusively by UNEF and referred the matter to Hammarskjöld, who discussed it with Fawzi on March 11, urging him to go slow on such arrangements. Fawzi seemed to be agreeing with Hammarskjöld when the news arrived that Egypt had appointed an administrative governor, Mohammed Latif, who would arrive in Gaza on March 14. Hammarskjöld told Bunche to take this up with Nasser when he met him on March 13.

Bunche had flown to Gaza with Burns on March 11 to see the situation for himself. There had been demonstrations the day before, and the demonstrators, clearly under outside direction, had tried to replace the UN flag at the UNEF headquarters with the Egyptian flag. The UNEF soldiers were obliged to use tear gas and, at one point, to fire over the heads of the crowd. A ricocheting bullet had hit a bystander, who died two days later.

Burns hoped that Bunche "would be bringing some clearer indications of the policy which UNEF was to follow than we had up to then."[32] Burns had spent a sleepless night in Cairo worrying about how his four thousand soldiers would deal with a hostile population of three hundred thousand if it was incited to resist UNEF control of the Strip. Burns shared his worries with Bunche on their two-hour flight to Gaza, and they communicated their concerns to Hammarskjöld, urging him to arrive in Cairo earlier than he had planned. Gaza was quiet enough, and after intensive discussions with the UN people, Bunche flew back to Cairo.

After meetings in the Egyptian Foreign Ministry on the situation in Gaza and the question of the Egyptian governor, Bunche met Nasser for nearly two hours on the next day, Nasser was only politely cordial at first but became more friendly as the talk progressed.

Clearly [Nasser] has a feeling of personal insecurity, which accounts for his frequent smile and giggle, which noticeably become less frequent as he becomes better acquainted and more at ease. Basically suspicious, his thinking is all in political terms.[33]

Bunche was able to get Nasser's firm assurances that fedayeen raids would be prevented, and that the "military burden in Gaza would be left to UNEF," not least because the Strip was militarily impossible for Egypt to defend. He also promised to settle the matter of the Canadian reconnaissance squadron for UNEF which had been held up in protest against a rumored statement by Lester Pearson proposing the internationalization of Gaza. Nasser spoke of the suffering of his wife and children because of his round-the-clock working schedule, a subject all too familiar to Bunche. However, on the most immediate matter, the return of the Egyptian governor to Gaza, Nasser could not be moved, and a similar effort by the U.S. ambassador, Raymond Hare, was also rebuffed.

Burns and Bunche flew back to Gaza on March 14 to be on hand for the entry of the governor, who finally arrived amid much hubbub about 6:00 P.M. They dined in the UNEF mess, where a Swedish officer played the piano, his repertoire including "Don't Fence Me In," which became the UNEF theme song. The city was full of Egyptian flags, pictures of Nasser, and warning signs addressed to UNEF—"Welcome as Guests not as Occupiers," etc.—all of this in a freezing rain.

There were organized celebrations the following day, but the new governor made a short and moderate speech and stopped cries of "UNEF must go" with friendly words about the United Nations, a surprising shift from the hostility of the previous days. It seemed probable that, although Egyptian prestige demanded a symbolic reassertion of Egyptian rights in the Strip, Nasser did not want to antagonize UNEF or invite an Israeli re-entry into Gaza.

Bunche remained in Gaza for two more days, conferring with Burns and his staff and visiting the different units on the line. He discussed problems of internal security, the reinstating of the mayor of Gaza, the marketing of the citrus crop, and the re-establishment of the currency. He was concerned at the emotional and volatile temperament of the Gaza inhabitants, who could easily be turned against UNEF at any time, and he was determined to keep developments in a low key until Hammarskjöld arrived to talk to Nasser. Thus, when a trigger-happy UNEF Danish sentry accidentally killed an Arab man virtually in front of the governor's house, Bunche was quick to order an immediate inquiry and to make a formal apology to the governor. On his way back to Cairo on March 17, Bunche stopped off to inspect the Canal clearance operations with General Wheeler. "Wheeler is delightful," he noted, "and a great operator."[34]

The Israelis were furious at the arrival of the Egyptian governor and protested loudly that they had been deceived into believing that such a return of Egyptian officials would not be allowed. Bunche was blamed for "selling out" to the Egyptians the moment he had arrived in the area. The Israeli press attributed to him statements "welcoming" the Egyptians to Gaza, which he strongly and publicly denied.* The Israeli position was also reflected in many stories in the Western media, enthusiastically joining the Israeli press in declaring the uselessness of UNEF on the armistice line. Bunche was thus caught between the Egyptians denouncing UNEF for colonial behavior in Gaza and the Israeli press denouncing him for surrendering to the Egyptians. "The newspapermen here," Bunche told Ruth, "are the wildest and most irresponsible I have ever encountered."[35]

Mrs. Meir flew to Washington on March 15, and the American press took up the charge. Typical was a piece in the *New York Post* on March 20 accusing Bunche of being responsible for Egypt's "resumption of rule in the Gaza Strip" by "exceeding his instructions." Nasser was alleged to have "induced Bunche to agree to stripping the UN police force of all authority in the Gaza [sic] and to allow Egypt to again seize control there."[36]

On March 17 Bunche flew in a single-engined Otter aircraft to St. Catherine's Monastery, in the mountain fastnesses of Sinai, where a Finnish platoon had taken over from the Israelis. He was deeply moved by this remote and ancient outpost of religion, culture, and learning, with its sparkling sixth-century mosaics, icons and ancient library. From St. Catherine's he flew to Sharm al-Sheikh, a desolate and uninhabited outpost on

*On March 14, exasperated at reports attributing to him comments on the appointment of the Egyptian governor "in which such expressions as 'agreed to,' 'in agreement with,' 'cooperate with,' 'welcome,' etc., are used, Dr. Bunche wishes it known, in order that the record may be straight, that he has made or authorized to be made none of the comments attributed to him other than to say that as a member of the United Nations Secretariat he has no authority to comment one way or another on the action of any member state, nor would it be proper for him to do so."

the Strait of Tiran, and then back to Gaza along the armistice line, landing with only a few minutes to spare before dark. At Gaza he found a
message from Hammarskjöld instructing him to see Fawzi urgently about
Hammarskjöld's impending visit to Cairo.

Hammarskjöld's doubts about his visit to Cairo arose from three
questions: whether it was possible to have a constructive discussion of
arrangements for UNEF; whether a useful discussion of freedom of navigation in the Suez Canal was possible; and whether there was scope for a
settlement of internal-security and administrative matters in Gaza. He
had just had a very tough meeting with Golda Meir and was concerned
that UNEF's position might become false and untenable. Recent developments in Gaza had damaged UN prestige, and he needed Fawzi's frank
evaluation before he decided whether to come to Cairo or not.

Bunche got a "characteristically roundabout and indecisive response" from Fawzi, but he advised that, on balance, Hammarskjöld
should come to Cairo, since he would be strongly criticized if he didn't
make the effort. "Your road will not be inviting. But I believe much of the
road still open although most suspiciously and grudgingly so." Fawzi's
oblique replies had been couched in a fog of parables and obscure references, but he was obviously anxious to avoid Hammarskjöld's canceling his
visit, and had ended by wishing Hammarskjöld bon voyage and welcome
to Egypt. "So do I," Bunche added.[37] Bunche felt that, although the
Israelis were breathing fire in New York and Jerusalem, the actual situation in Gaza provided no basis for their fears or for an Israeli military
action on security grounds. UNEF was in full evidence all over the Strip,
there were no demonstrations, no Egyptian troops, no incitements against
Israel, and the Egyptian governor was self-effacing and unprovocative.

Hammarskjöld arrived in Cairo at 1:00 A.M. on March 21. Bunche
and Burns accompanied him to the Semiramis Hotel, where they conferred until 3:30 A.M. in preparation for the meeting with Nasser, stepping
out onto the balcony to discuss confidential matters in case the room was
bugged. They met with Fawzi all of the following morning, and with
Nasser from 6:00 P.M. to midnight, including dinner. Once again in-
trigued by Nasser's mannerisms, Bunche noted:

Nasser has weird eyes—a wild and rather furtive look, half smile, half smirk. He
frequently broke into the nervous laugh or giggle, especially in the early stages of
our discussion. Once or twice it was semi-hysterical. . . . He has a habit of sitting
forward on the edge of his chair, leaning forward in a semi-crouch, with his
massive shoulders and big head giving him a powerful and rather monstrous
appearance. He is suffering from his sinuses but still made no effort to close the

meeting—it might have gone on endlessly had not Dag, who was tired, brought it to an end.[38]

Of the Egyptian foreign secretary he commented:

Fawzi is always calm and collected and he is basically honest. He is not brilliant but he grasps things quickly and cannot be fooled. He seldom shows any emotion.[39]

At dinner Bunche asked Nasser about the siege of Al-Faluja in 1948 and was surprised to discover that Nasser regarded it as an Egyptian victory. He was unable to tell whether Nasser knew that it was he who, as mediator, had negotiated the end of the Israeli siege and the UN-escorted passage for the beleaguered Egyptian garrison through the Israeli lines.

On March 22 they spent virtually the whole day with Fawzi, and in the evening met with Nasser again for seven and a half hours, this time under a large banyan tree at the Barrage, a dam on the Nile, half an hour from Cairo, where Nasser had a rest house. On this occasion Nasser told Bunche about an attempt to assassinate him in Alexandria, when, although the men on each side of him were hit, he had completed his speech. Bunche noticed that while walking in the park at the Barrage Nasser kept checking to ensure that his bodyguard, with tommy gun at the ready, was following him closely.

Bunche spent the whole of March 24, except for one hour with Fawzi, talking to Hammarskjöld and dictating notes. The results of their talks were mixed. It was clear that the Egyptians wanted to maintain UNEF as a politically significant entity. Hammarskjöld had received a commitment from Nasser that no Egyptian troops would return to Gaza, but this could not be published.* On the duration of UNEF's stay in Sharm al-Sheikh a sort of moratorium was promised "with obvious intention to close eyes to what may happen in Straits of Tiran with a view towards advisory opinion [of the International Court]." [40] Both Gaza and Sharm al-Sheikh were covered by Nasser's promise that there would be no surprises, and Bunche felt that this was as good an assurance as they were likely to get. (As things turned out, the assurance lasted ten years.) There was also a satisfactory, practical agreement on the functioning of UNEF in Gaza. Miraculously, Nasser did not insist on UNEF's being stationed on the Israeli side of the line, which the Israelis continued to refuse categorically.

*As Fawzi had put it, "Somehow, but not formally, we might be too busy elsewhere to send military forces into Gaza."

On the Suez Canal, on the other hand, no progress whatsoever was made. Hammarskjöld attributed this setback to the visit to Cairo earlier in the week of the Indian foreign minister, Krishna Menon, a well-known loose cannon on the international scene. The best that Nasser and Fawzi would agree to was to have diplomatic contacts before issuing the declaration on reopening the Canal to shipping. The Israeli press pronounced Hammarskjöld's visit to Cairo a complete failure.

On March 25, Bunche, Hammarskjöld, and Burns flew to the Canal to join Wheeler in watching the raising of the sunken tug *Edgar Bonnet*. As a result of Wheeler's remarkable efforts, the first ship went through the Canal on March 29, and the Canal was officially declared open on April 8, but not to Israeli shipping.

When Hammarskjöld left for New York on March 27 Fawzi asked that Bunche stay on for another ten days, saying that matters just now could not be left exclusively to "technical" men. Bunche agreed only with the greatest reluctance. He was exhausted by the pace and the long meetings of the past week and was suffering from constant bouts of dysentery. Ruth's feelings made the prolongation of his stay even less palatable. She had bombarded him with bitter letters since his departure from Accra. His failure to take her with him to Ghana or to write letters was the main grievance, and she evidently did not realize that mail from Ghana took more than ten days to reach New York, while letters from Cairo—still a war zone—had to be sent through the UN diplomatic pouch. She upbraided him for his irritability and coldness at home during the recent crisis months, for his alleged pursuit of fame and glory, for neglect of his children, and for a host of specific minor grievances. These letters, as usual, arrived belatedly in Cairo, crossing Bunche's letters to New York.

Bunche's main task in Cairo was to finalize the agreement on UNEF's mandate in Gaza and to try again to soften Egypt's policy on barring the Canal to Israeli shipping. The UNEF agreement proved relatively easy, but its value in defusing Israeli suspicions and Israeli-inspired press campaigns was greatly reduced because Fawzi refused, on the grounds of preserving Egypt's prestige, to allow the most important points—such as establishing a UN zone of control 750 yards deep on the line in Gaza—to be published. As Hammarskjöld told the advisory committee, "it is one of those areas where a government can do much more in fact than it can do in form. Also where something can be fully understood but would cease being a fact the moment it was in the papers."[41]

On freedom of navigation in the Canal, Bunche made no progress at all, although he was joined in Cairo by John J. McCloy, then chairman of the Chase Manhattan Bank and a special consultant to Hammarskjöld on the financial arrangements for clearing the Canal.* McCloy had excellent contacts in Egypt, but he had no illusions that Nasser would ever allow Israeli ships to pass through the Canal. Fawzi told Bunche that freedom of passage was just one aspect of the Palestine question, of which there were so many other aspects—Jerusalem, the rights of one million refugees, or the presence of Israeli forces in demilitarized zones—matters on which no one seemed to be pressing for an immediate settlement. No Egyptian statesman could let Israeli ships pass through the Canal without causing a massive public uprising. In the end, Bunche's only achievement on the Canal was to get Egyptian agreement concerning the monument to the Canal's founder, Ferdinand de Lesseps. The statue had been blown off its pedestal in Port Said by the Egyptians during the Anglo-French invasion. The Egyptians agreed to put it into a museum in Port Said as an historical relic.

At a dinner one night in Cairo, Herbert Norman, the Canadian ambassador, evidently tense and depressed, confided to Bunche his worries about the accusations that Senator William Jenner and the Senate Internal Security Subcommittee had been making for six years about Norman's earlier contacts with communists. "I had many thoughts and recollections of my own as Norman talked to me. I could understand his feelings." Three days later, Bunche was aghast to learn that Norman had jumped to his death from the roof of the Swedish Embassy, the only place he could think of, as he explained in a note to the Swedish ambassador, where he would not run the risk of hitting a pedestrian.

Bunche inspected more UNEF positions on the line, a refreshing relief from the impasse on the Canal and the Israeli press campaign. Recognized by an Israeli patrol on the other side, Bunche asked if there was any trouble. The patrol leader replied, "Not now, because your army is here."[42] Grazing bedouin flocks exploded three mines during Bunche's one-hour stay.

Bunche was to leave Cairo for New York on April 6. The previous evening, a number of American correspondents, including Joseph Alsop, came to his room and fired questions at him for thirty minutes. He sparred and evaded, sticking to public statements and published texts. Alsop tried to provoke him by taking an extreme pro-Israeli position, but Bunche replied only by chiding him for asking unnecessarily provocative questions. He arrived in New York on April 7.

*These included imposing a 3-percent surcharge on Canal tolls to pay for the Canal clearance operation.

For Bunche the unique experience of the trip had been reviewing the troops of UNEF, a force he had virtually created. The political part of the trip had been both exhausting and frustrating, and he was not sanguine about a peaceful future in the Middle East. The Canal, Gaza, and Aqaba situations could all very easily go sour. The Israelis were suspicious, and the Egyptians, who blindly refused to recognize that they had been defeated in the field and then bailed out by the UN, had no thoughts of making peace with the Israelis.

There is nothing to change the view I have had, indeed the firm conviction, since 1949; there can be no peace or real progress towards peace in the Near East until the problem of the Arab [Palestine] refugees is solved. The world evades that one.[43]

In New York the press campaign was still going full-blast. On April 12 Joseph Alsop, perhaps nettled by Bunche's replies to him in Cairo, published an article about a "deal" with Egypt in which Hammarskjöld and Bunche were alleged to have "conceded another cardinal point to President Nasser by agreeing that UN patrols in Gaza should be accompanied by armed Palestinian police under the command of the Egyptian civil governor."* Alsop went on to say that UNEF was now Nasser's border guard. Bunche replied that the understanding with Egypt had been approved by the advisory committee and had involved no "concessions" by the UN, and that final arrangements for UNEF "will have to wait for the response of the Government of Israel to the request by the General Assembly that the force be deployed also on the Israeli side of the Armistice demarcation line."[44] Bunche personally communicated this statement to Ogden Reid, the *Herald-Tribune*'s publisher, and it was printed on the front page of the *Herald-Tribune*. "The net conclusion," Bunche told the advisory committee, "is that the Force is functioning exceptionally well."[45]

Hammarskjöld felt strongly that it was time to re-establish personal contact with Ben-Gurion, and he wrote to him on April 19 suggesting he should visit him to discuss, among other things, the full implementation of the armistice agreement and the deployment of UNEF in Israel. Ben-Gurion replied that he would be happy to see Hammarskjöld but *not* to discuss either of the subjects mentioned. On this unpromising note, Ham-

*As Bunche explained to the advisory committee, he and Burns, noticing that UNEF troops had no means of communicating with bedouin crossing the line with their flocks, had suggested attaching a Palestinian policeman to UNEF patrols as an interpreter. This was apparently the origin of Alsop's tendentious story.

marskjöld and Bunche set off for Jerusalem in early May.

The meetings with Ben-Gurion were notable for the contrast between the friendly mood and the tough substance of the talks. Both Hammarskjöld and Ben-Gurion needed, and wanted, to re-establish a personal relationship in which it was possible to discuss controversial matters, even if they could not agree on them. As Hammarskjöld later said of the meeting, "it brought us out of that somewhat sickly atmosphere in which these matters have been discussed for six months."[46]

Ben-Gurion hugged both Hammarskjöld and Bunche in welcome and then launched into a long accusatory diatribe. He denounced Arab rhetoric against Israel and demanded that it be stopped. Bunche said that he didn't see how the UN could stop political statements by national leaders. As to the Suez Canal, Ben-Gurion said, "It is more than six months since the decision on Suez was taken, Mr. Hammarskjöld, and what have you done?"[47] Golda Meir chimed in to say that the Arabs had learned from the UN's impotence in Kashmir and Hungary.* Ben-Gurion, warming to his own rhetoric, claimed that only Israel's Sinai expedition had prevented the whole Middle East from being dominated by the Soviet Union. Along the way he and Hammarskjöld engaged in many of the politico-philosophical exchanges which they both enjoyed. Ben-Gurion asked why the UN had brought the Egyptians back to Gaza. Bunche said the UN had done no such thing, but the armistice agreement gave them a right to be in Gaza. Ben-Gurion demanded to know why a country that had violated the armistice agreement had a right to enjoy its benefits. Bunche asked if Israel had formally denounced the armistice agreements. Ben-Gurion replied that he was not prepared to discuss the question.

Bunche advised Hammarskjöld not to comment on the pros and cons of the Israeli Sinai expedition "beyond saying that I heard, with great interest, your analysis—fully debated in the UN—now for history to appraise. But much more important to look ahead."[48] The alternatives for the future were between Israel as an armed camp, depending exclusively on military force, and Israel and the UN working together toward peace. At a further meeting on May 10, Ben-Gurion was less excitable and, at the end, put his hand on Bunche's shoulder, saying "that he still thought I was a good person even though he couldn't understand or agree with some of

---

*Bunche often said that Golda Meir was the toughest and most stubborn woman he had ever met, but he respected her. The feeling may have been mutual. When Bunche died, Golda Meir came to the funeral home on a Friday evening in order to be among the first to pay her respects.

the things I had done"[49] (a reference to the Egyptian return to Gaza).

Bunche found Ben-Gurion greatly aged since their last meeting, in 1953.

Ben-Gurion rambles, invents his own distorted history, rants in a semi-buffoonish way, laughs childishly at his own humor, and shows distressing signs of acute senility. He likes to read from the Charter. Golda is remarkably friendly and relaxed; pompous of course but not hostile.[50]

To Hammarskjöld Bunche wrote:

The old man has deteriorated to an unbelievable degree. . . . I fear he now *believes* the false version of history he recites. There is probably more self-delusion here than in Cairo. If he is not deliberately *acting* in order to avoid a serious discussion—and I fear he is *not*—then he is *mad* and we are playing in a Greek tragedy.

Hammarskjöld noted in reply:

His mind is more and more playing old records—which become more and more confused.[51]

Bunche found Ben-Gurion's advisers far more realistic than the prime minister. Arthur Lourie, Gideon Rafael, and Chaim Herzog did not deny the validity of the case for UNEF's being stationed in Israel but said that, for domestic political reasons, it could not be done immediately after the Israeli withdrawal from Gaza. They conceded that the deployment of UNEF and the Canal clearance operation had been impressive and that the UN's insistence on French, British, and Israeli withdrawals might well have averted world war. They felt that Hammarskjöld's visit had gone a long way toward restoring confidence, and that, if the present calm on the Egyptian front continued for a few months, Israel's stance on UNEF and all other matters would soften. "They have a mania about Nasser—all of them. They are also no little sheepish about their present alliance with the French."*[52]

The mania about Nasser prevailed also in private. Apropos of his recent visit to Egypt, Ben-Gurion's wife, Paula, asked Bunche laughingly "why I had once been so nice and then changed," and she asked Hammarskjöld why he, such a nice man, had permitted himself to come under the evil influence of Nasser. Hammarskjöld, noticing the embarrassment of Yigael Yadin at Mrs. Ben-Gurion's question, replied, "Mrs. Ben-Gurion, are you sure that it is not a case of Nasser being under *my* evil influence?"[53]

*The French had, since the Suez crisis and the combined invasion of Egypt, been vocal supporters of the Israeli position at the UN.

For all their differences Bunche—and indeed Hammarskjöld—enjoyed a genuinely personal relationship with the Israelis. Their talks in Jerusalem, although lively and blunt, had been extraordinarily friendly.

Hammarskjöld is much relieved and even pleased with the meetings, which he feared would be an ordeal and completely negative. Nothing immediately tangible was achieved of course or even striven for.[54]

In Jerusalem Bunche was beset by old memories. It was ten years since he—and the UN—had become embroiled in the Palestine question, and his mind went back to those stormy early days. At Kalandia, the Jerusalem airport in the Jordanian sector, there was now a new, modern airport building.

I couldn't help but recall my first landing here with Bernadotte, on the day the first truce began in early June 1948. There was no paved strip then, just markers in the meadow, all buildings had been destroyed, a lone Arab lit a fire to give us wind direction, the KLM white-painted Dakota . . . first swooped low over the field to drive the goats off and then bumped down with none of us knowing . . . what kind of reception we would get or whether the truce was really in effect in Jerusalem. . . . What a mess of barbed wire and sandbag emplacements Jerusalem was in 1947 when in June UNSCOP arrived. . . . Before breakfast, early this morning, out on the veranda in the bright sunlight (6:30) overlooking the Old City—the wall, the domes of the Dome of the Rock and El Aqsa, seeing the Mount of Olives, the Garden of Gethsemane, etc.; Dag and I were remarking the inaccurate impression conveyed by the Bible regarding distances between places in Jerusalem and as between Jerusalem, Bethlehem, etc.[55]

During the summer of 1957 the situation quieted down in Gaza and Sinai, and so did the reactions from Israel and Egypt. Both governments had evidently realized at last that UNEF was a valuable common asset. The press campaign also sputtered and died. Bunche continued to monitor and direct UNEF day and night. The UNEF people, now that they were well established, began to feel that they could do more or less as they liked, and often seemed unaware that a mistake or a false move could very easily jeopardize once again the whole enterprise. Bunche waged an indefatigable but kindly campaign to keep UNEF on the right track, scrutinizing each development and each incident and giving directions accordingly.

The killing pace of the Suez crisis slowed during the summer of 1957, and there was more time for family life, although Hammarskjöld's demands on Bunche remained incessant. On July 8, 1957, the Bunches' first grandchild, Karen Pierce, was born.

Hammarskjöld had asked Bunche to direct a group of senior officials who were to compile a comprehensive study of the UNEF experience— or, as Hammarskjöld put it,

an exposition, in essentially manual form, of the conclusions, principles and draft texts of basic documents deriving from the analysis of the experience which, in a master text sense, may provide fundamental guidance for any future plans or efforts relating to a United Nations force.[56]

An immense amount of work went into this study between December 1957 and August 1958. Unfortunately, Hammarskjöld had failed to explain precisely what he had in mind. When he was presented with the voluminous draft of the report, he received it in polite silence and proceeded to write his own exiguous and nuanced political analysis for the General Assembly.[57]

By 1958 UNEF was generally recognized as a remarkable practical success as well as a triumph of innovative improvisation. In June 1959, after another inspection trip, Bunche told the advisory committee, "Since my last visit two years ago UNEF has become an institution."[58] It was the model for all future peacekeeping operations.

This did not mean that the Palestine issue was in any sense nearer to a solution. In November 1957 the problem of Mount Scopus, the Israeli enclave in Jordan-controlled East Jerusalem which the UN had negotiated in 1948, came to a head. Under the 1948 agreement, the UN escorted Israeli supply convoys to Mount Scopus every fortnight. The Jordanians had become increasingly suspicious both of the content of these convoys and of the activities of the Israelis on Mount Scopus, which was supposed to be demilitarized. In November 1957 after the Jordanians had suspended the convoys, Hammarskjöld, in a brief visit to the area, had got them to agree to a resumption. He then appointed Francisco Urrutia, the Colombian ambassador at the UN, as his personal representative to resolve the dispute. Unfortunately, Urrutia had no experience of the Middle East, and got nowhere. In May 1958, Hammarskjöld sent Bunche to the Middle East to deal with Mount Scopus. Bunche thought that he had succeeded in settling the affair in meetings with Ben-Gurion and with Jordanian Foreign Minister Samir Rifai in Amman. However, only two weeks later, in an exchange of fire on Mount Scopus between the Jordanians and an Israeli police patrol, four Israelis and a UN observer, Colonel J. A. Flint of Canada, were killed.

Though literally a flying visit, this trip to the Middle East had been a particular trial for Bunche and a great worry for Ruth. Since their stay in Vienna the previous September Bunche had suffered from fatigue, loss of

weight, and loss of appetite—early-warning signs of diabetes. Ruth's usual
resentment over his absences had now completely given way to her acute
anxiety over his physical condition. Bunche had for several months refused to take insulin, on the grounds that he didn't want to be "enslaved"
by it. Between January and June 1958 he lost thirty-five pounds. His
condition had reached a critical state by midsummer, when he began to be
treated aggressively for diabetes. He then recovered some of his energy,
although his general condition went into a gradual decline. "Toughest
period of my life so far," he noted. "Pick-up began with radical treatment
on 3 June."[59] By November 1 he was back to 180 pounds.

Organizing the first UN peacekeeping force, the UN Emergency Force in Egypt. 38th floor at the UN, November 1956. *Left to right:* Colonels T. A. Johnson and G. C. Leech of Canada; General John B. Coulter of the United States; Brian Urquhart; Lieutenant General E. L. M. Burns, commander of UNEF; Bunche; David Vaughan, UN director of General Services. UN PHOTO

Metaphysics and pragmatism—Hammarskjöld ponders while Bunche commits their thoughts to paper. New York City, 1956.
PHOTO BY KNUT HAMMARSKJÖLD

Clearing the Suez Canal—Hammarskjöld, Lieutenant General Raymond A. Wheeler (U.S. Corps of Engineers), Bunche, and General Burns watch the lifting of the sunken tug *Edgar Bonnet.* Ismailia, Suez Canal, Egypt, March 25, 1957. UN PHOTO. *Below:* With President Nasser of Egypt. Cairo, March 1957.

Bunche tours UNEF observation posts with General Burns on an inspection trip
to UNEF. Gaza, April 1959. UN PHOTO

Hammarskjöld's photograph of
Bunche on their African tour and
Bunche's inscription. January 1960.

Dag,
Thanks — to you, to your photographic
skill and to that solemn little
beast — for my favorite
portrait of all time and a
cherished souvenir of our
unforgettable African safari.
Ralph

Bunche and Patrice Lumumba meet the press at Lumumba's residence in Leopoldville, Congo. July 20, 1960. UPI/BETTMANN

Visiting President Joseph Kasavubu of the Congo with Dag Hammarskjöld. Leopoldville, Congo, August 1960.

During his abortive mission to Katanga Bunche talks to Katanga's "interior minister," Godefroid Munongo. F. T. Liu is behind them. On the right is Sture Linner with Robert de Rothschild of Belgium. Elisabethville airport, August 5, 1960. UN PHOTO

On the flight to the Kitona meeting with Katanga President Moise Tshombe, Bunche talks with Congo Prime Minister Cyrille Adoula and UN official Mahmoud Khiari. Congo, December 19, 1961. UN PHOTO

The Kitona meeting, *left to right:* Rémy Mwamba, Prime Minister Cyrille Adoula, Foreign Minister Justin Bomboko, Interior Minister Christophe Gbenye of the Congo, Mahmoud Khiari of the UN, Bunche, U.S. Ambassador Edmund Gullion, Georges Dumontet of the UN, Messrs. Meli, Kibwe, Tshombe, and Mwenda of Katanga. December 21, 1961. UN PHOTO

Bunche greets Bedouin children on a later visit to UNEF. El Quseima, Sinai, June 1962. UN PHOTO

With Adlai Stevenson, United States ambassador to the United Nations. February 1964. UN PHOTO

Hearing the complaints of the townspeople of Ktima, Cyprus, and discussing the problems of Cyprus with President Makarios. April 1964. UN PHOTO

A show-biz evening
with Marlene Dietrich
and impresario Billy Rose.

With Josephine Baker and
Ruth.

On the facing page
On to the State Capitol—
the last stage of the
march from Selma to
Montgomery. *Right to left:*
Coretta Scott King,
Martin Luther King,
Bunche, the Reverend
Ralph Abernathy, and
A. Philip Randolph.
Montgomery, Alabama,
March 21, 1965.
UPI/BETTMANN

With Jackie Robinson.

U Thant and Bunche discuss Vietnam with President Lyndon Johnson and Arthur Goldberg, U.S. ambassador to the United Nations, April 4, 1968. UN PHOTO

Bunche's last high-level meeting. U.S. Secretary of State William P. Rogers discusses the Middle East with U Thant. *Left to right:* George Bush, U.S. ambassador to the UN, Rogers, Joseph Sisco, Bunche, U Thant, and Gunnar Jarring. UN, New York City, May 17, 1971. UN PHOTO

21

Lebanon 1958 and the Middle East

Preventive Diplomacy

In September 1957, when Hammarskjöld was reappointed as secretary general for another term of five years, a problem developed in his immediate circle. Anatoly Dobrynin, Bunche's able and amiable Soviet opposite number, was unwilling any longer to occupy a post without a specific function and therefore wished the posts of both undersecretaries for special political affairs to be abolished. The truth of the matter was that in the prevailing Cold War climate a permanent UN official,* especially one of Bunche's ability, was inevitably assigned the most important political tasks. Bunche told Hammarskjöld that as long as he had responsible work to do he was happy with any arrangement that best served the interests of the organization. Hammarskjöld said he had mixed emotions since he wished Bunche both to take over the Trusteeship Department and to stay in his own office. "When you take your new job of 'freeing Africa,'" Hammarskjöld told him, "I hope you will still come in for these talks, since I value them so highly."[1] Hammarskjöld, although he had in mind that Bunche should lead an ambitious program to help the newly independent states of Africa, eventually decided not to make any change, and Bunche remained where he was. The UN was soon immersed in another crisis.

In January 1958 Nasser announced that Egypt and Syria would unite, forming a single nation, the United Arab Republic. The new nation came into existence on February 1. In response to this development, on Febru-

---

*Soviet UN officials took UN appointments for a short time only, after which they returned to Soviet service.

ary 14, Jordan and Iraq formed a federation called the Arab Union. Nasser, annoyed by this turn of events, went to Damascus for a series of rallies in which he publicly blasted the new federation, and renewed tension gripped the already explosive region. In April President Camille Chamoun of Lebanon amended the Lebanese constitution to allow for an unprecedented second term for himself. In May an uprising against Chamoun began in the northern city of Tripoli and soon spread to Beirut, Sidon, and the Beka'a Valley, near the Syrian border. The antigovernment disorders were fomented primarily by Muslim opponents of the government and its pro-Western policy. Many were admirers of Nasser.

This situation brought out the worst in virtually all concerned. Chamoun and his people, in an attempt to involve the United States and the United Nations in supporting them in what was essentially a domestic political struggle, played on Western fears of Nasser and of a Soviet takeover. Nasser was obstinate and unhelpful. The United States and Britain were inclined to believe the alarmist tales of the Lebanese government and to denigrate anyone who doubted them. Israel, Iraq, Turkey, and others joined in the anti-Egyptian chorus for reasons of their own. The Soviet Union lost no chance to make mischief.

The crisis provided a grueling test of Hammarskjöld's skill in preventive diplomacy, but he received little recognition for staving off what could have been a major international disaster—a confrontation between the United States and the Soviet Union in the Middle East—or for preventing a civil war in Lebanon from becoming the national and international catastrophe which it became twenty years later.

Bunche was, as usual, Hammarskjöld's lieutenant in the crisis, this time struggling in a haze of fatigue and illness. His lassitude and loss of weight were alarming. He no longer questioned everyone and everything, or engaged in the prolonged dialogues which so often exposed plausible but unsound proposals. His condition was the more alarming because he refused to admit that he was ill.

By mid-May, with the United States being urged by Chamoun to intervene in Lebanon and the Soviet Union emitting ominous warnings, as Eisenhower put it, "the consequences could easily become drastic."[2] On May 22 Chamoun requested an urgent meeting of the Security Council to consider Lebanon's complaint about the intervention of the United Arab Republic in its internal affairs, specifically by infiltrating armed bands across the border from Syria. The United States, Great Britain, France, Israel, and Iraq lined up behind Chamoun, and the Soviet bloc behind the UAR and Nasser.

A three-man United Nations Observation Group (UNOGIL),*
served by a large group of military observers, was sent to Lebanon. That
Nasser fully supported this move was in itself puzzling if the Lebanese
accusations had any validity. Hammarskjöld went to Beirut to install the
observation group, and also to Cairo to urge restraint on Nasser and to
make sure that he was not allowing infiltration from Syria into Lebanon.

During Hammarskjöld's absence Bunche was the anchorman in New
York and was putting together the large group of military observers required in Lebanon. Hammarskjöld reported to Bunche on his activities in
Lebanon and Cairo, so that Bunche could keep the members of the Security Council informed of what the secretary general was doing. Hammarskjöld's accounts of his efforts were not always easy to translate. For
example:

The surgeon technically most satisfied by last night's operation. Now he must
trust Mother Nature hoping strongly that anxious friends will stay out of the sick
room, keep silent and wait until bandages can be taken off.[3]

Henry Cabot Lodge, to whom Bunche passed this cryptic message, said
politely that while he personally agreed with Hammarskjöld, Washington's attitude on Lebanon was unchanged, although Hammarskjöld's efforts had to some extent discouraged the supporters of direct U.S. intervention in Lebanon.

When the United States refused to intervene, Chamoun's government tried to get a UN force to fight on its side against the opposition.
Hammarskjöld was strongly opposed to any such idea. Mohamed Jamali,
the foreign minister of Iraq, was among those who supported the Lebanese demand. When Hammarskjöld and Bunche pointed out that such a
force would have to shoot its way in, killing a great number of Lebanese,
Jamali replied impatiently, "Yes, but so what?"[4]

When they realized that the observer group was not going to authen-
ticate their allegations, the Lebanese government contrived a virulent
press campaign against Hammarskjöld and the UN, a campaign taken up
happily by the British conservative press and government, which were still
smarting from the Suez fiasco. Bunche called in the Lebanese ambassador
from time to time to protest some of the more outrageous press fantasies
emanating from Beirut and was invariably told that the obviously inspired
press statements should be considered as without validity.

On July 14 the government of Iraq was overthrown by Brigadier

*The three were Rajeshwar Dayal, a senior Indian diplomat; General Odd Bull of Norway;
and Galo Plaza Lasso, a former president of Ecuador.

Abdul Karim Kassem in a particularly bloody coup. Washington and London immediately assumed that this was the beginning of the CIA's favorite nightmare, the Moscow-inspired takeover of the whole Middle East by Nasser. John Foster Dulles warned Hammarskjöld that restraints on U.S. intervention in Lebanon were now lifted. Chamoun's appeals for foreign intervention had triumphed at last, and the U.S. Marines came ashore on the beach south of Beirut at 3:00 P.M. on July 15.

This ill-considered action, which Eisenhower began to reverse the moment he realized that it was both irrelevant and dangerous, nearly derailed all of Hammarskjöld's painstaking efforts to bring peace and constitutional order to Lebanon. It also threatened a major international crisis and gave rise to many acrimonious debates in the Security Council. Fortunately, the U.S. Marines stayed in bivouac near the beach and did not clash with Lebanese forces. Hammarskjöld greatly increased the number of UN observers in Lebanon in order to give the U.S. government a pretext for withdrawing the Marines. And, after a special session of the General Assembly on peace in the Middle East, both the U.S. Marines and the British forces in Jordan were withdrawn. General Fuad Chehab was elected president of Lebanon, and a potentially very dangerous crisis was over.

Bunche played a less prominent role in this crisis than in any other, partly because it was largely handled, in a virtuoso diplomatic performance, by Hammarskjöld himself, and partly because he was seriously ill. A note dated July 16, the day after the U.S. Marines landed in Lebanon, throws some light on his state of health and mind.

Because of my illness and irregular working hours I have sat down to meals with the family at home very seldom in the past few months. On this particular night, I got home early enough to have dinner with Ruth and Ralph—Joan was on vacation in Washington. I was very tired and cross and when Ruth said something that rubbed me the wrong way I slammed down my fork and napkin and stalked away from the table. Some days later when Joan came back and asked how I was doing Ralph Jr. piped up "Oh he's much better now; he's throwing his fork across the table again."[5]

By late August, when he went to Geneva for the Second International Conference on the Peaceful Uses of Atomic Energy, Bunche, though still shaky, was definitely on his way to recovery. His listlessness was diminishing, his appetite was returning, and he could stay awake in meetings.

From Geneva Bunche went to Lebanon for a few days to inspect the observer group he had organized. UNOGIL now consisted of two hundred observers from sixteen countries, with twenty-two light planes and six helicopters. The situation was almost completely quiet, and it was possible to withdraw the observers completely in early December.

Hammarskjöld had been sympathetic and supportive of Bunche while he was wrestling with illness, and their friendship was firmer than ever. Bunche was one of Hammarskjöld's few professional associates who frequently dined with him at his maisonette apartment at 73 East 73rd Street in New York. On November 3, after first dining at 73rd Street, Bunche and Ruth took Hammarskjöld; Bernadotte's widow, Estelle; Leif Belfrage, the head of the Swedish Foreign Office; and Per Lind, who had been Hammarskjöld's first Swedish assistant at the UN, to see Eugene O'Neill's *A Touch of the Poet.* *

Bunche and Hammarskjöld liked to lighten the tedium of UN meetings by exchanging notes. A typical exchange during a debate on Cyprus in the General Assembly's political committee read:

H. Slim [Mongi Slim, ambassador of Tunisia] is a good lawyer—But I begin to wish all lawyers to go to hell.

B. What is it in the legal approach that induces men to abandon common sense and even morality in pursuit of a legal point?

H. Sometimes I believe—as a lawyer and a diplomat—that law is even more demoralizing than diplomacy.[6]

After the Lebanese crisis died down, there was a period of relative calm at the United Nations. UNEF was keeping the peace on the border between Israel and Egypt with great success, but constant vigilance and direction were needed to prevent ostensibly trivial incidents from escalating into major threats. In December Bunche complained to the Egyptian ambassador about the constant reinforcement of the Egyptian troops in El Arish in northern Sinai, movements which the Egyptians claimed to be purely defensive and due to persistent Israeli overflights. Occasional incursions by Israeli patrols needed careful handling. The soldiers of UNEF itself could also cause problems. Three Canadian soldiers went to Tel Aviv, got drunk, and brought back two Israeli prostitutes to the border post. Because it was raining and the women couldn't get a taxi, the Canadians took them on into Gaza, where the Egyptians arrested them. A

*Hammarskjöld had become a friend of O'Neill's widow, Carlotta, and he arranged for O'Neill's last, and unpublished, play, *Long Day's Journey into Night,* to be given its first performance, as O'Neill had wished, at the Royal Dramatic Theatre in Stockholm.

lot of time and high-level exchanges were needed before the Canadians were court-martialed and repatriated and the women sent back to Israel.

In April 1959 Hammarskjöld announced that, in order to maintain direct personal contact with developments in the Middle East, he had asked Bunche to visit Gaza, Cairo, Jerusalem, and Amman. Apart from inspecting UNEF, which he had not visited since March 1957, Bunche had a number of delicate issues to discuss. In Cairo, there was the Canal question, the Egyptian military buildup in Sinai, and the presence of a Palestinian "battalion" in Gaza which was militarily insignificant but politically worrying. He also had a list of matters to discuss with the commander of UNEF, including a growing tendency not to report incidents to New York. In Israel, the *Jerusalem Post* announced his agenda as being to assail Cairo on the Suez Canal blockade, and Amman on Mount Scopus. This article infuriated Hammarskjöld, who wrote on the cable transmitting it, "You should disillusion them in *advance*. You are *not* going for their purposes which—if pressed—may wreck what you need to do. Are they not tiresome!"[7]

Bunche's journey to Cairo was his first experience of travel by jet aircraft. "They take an awful long time before getting airborne," he noted.[8] His talk with Fawzi at his retreat near the Pyramids was an exasperating exercise in friendly elusiveness. Bunche was put off once again on the Canal question, and when he brought up the question of threats to King Hussein's safety on his flights in and out of Amman, Fawzi expressed the hope that there would be no "theatricals," a reference to the fact that Hussein had nearly been shot down by UAR aircraft on a recent flight. A discussion of the Egyptian buildup in Sinai inevitably led to the question whether Egypt wanted UNEF to stay or leave. Bunche questioned whether UNEF could stay if the Egyptian build-up continued, causing Fawzi to say that UNEF was useful and there was no question of asking it to leave. The "communist threat" in Gaza, he explained, made it necessary to strengthen Egypt's hand. When Bunche expressed his dissatisfaction, Fawzi promised to speak to Nasser.

The most satisfying part of Bunche's trip was the six days he spent with UNEF. He was deeply gratified by the discipline and soldierly bearing of the force, and by its fleet of small aircraft lined up for his inspection at El Arish. He noticed, however, that immediately on his arrival at the El-Arish airfield an Egyptian MiG-17 did an air-show takeoff, going almost vertically upward and out of sight—a demonstration in response to the UN's reservations about the presence of Egyptian fighter aircraft on the airfield. As usual, the trip brought back a flood of memories. On landing at Gaza he recalled how in 1948 two French observers had been shot in cold blood on the airstrip by Saudi Arabian soldiers and how the Egyptians who had tried to restrain the Saudis had in turn been shot. "That was Saudi Arabia's total contribution to the Palestine war of 1948–49."9

Gaza itself was thriving and far more prosperous than two years before, and the population was peaceful and contented. Bunche particularly enjoyed his visits to the various contingents, noting with pleasure their different habits—the furious driving of the Brazilian colonel, the moats around Scandinavian camps to keep out snakes, the abundant Slivovitz plied by the Yugoslavs, the Indian bagpipers who played him in to lunch, and the almost lunar isolation of the Swedish company at Sharm al-Sheikh. The people on both sides of the line were working peacefully in their fields, only a few feet apart, under the watchful eyes of UNEF observation posts. A bedouin to whom he was introduced as Dr. Bunche asked him to pull out an aching tooth on the spot in the open desert. It was all a far cry from the tensions, improvisation, and confusion of 1957. Bunche noted:

Seeing UNEF in operation out here and its remarkable success, I do feel a sense of quiet pride in the knowledge, known only to a few out here, that I was primarily responsible for the organization of the force, the getting it off the ground, and have been directing it from the beginning. It is, perhaps, my finest achievement, exceeding the armistice negotiations.10

On the drive to Jerusalem he passed through Al-Faluja, where Nasser's division had been besieged in 1948, and reflected,

It was on this agreement [to allow the Egyptians to withdraw] that Walter Eytan agreed orally and then reneged after hearing from Tel Aviv. I'm glad they let me take the rap with the Egyptians on the grounds that I had "misunderstood."11

In Jerusalem Golda Meir was friendly, although Bunche had to mediate a row between her and the Swedish UN chief of staff, General Carl von Horn. Israeli President Yizhak Ben-Zvi told him that Egypt, being underpopulated, should absorb the Palestinian refugees. "After that, I knew it was time to go."12 Golda Meir gave a luncheon for the Israelis who had negotiated with him in Rhodes—Moshe Dayan, Yigael Yadin, Walter Eytan, and Shabtai Rosenne—and Bunche greatly enjoyed reminiscing, especially with Yadin, now Israel's ranking archaeologist.

Bunche also visited Ben-Gurion at his kibbutz, Sde Boker. They discussed all the usual problems, but Bunche was most struck by an exchange on Bernadotte. Ben-Gurion, after expressing regret at Bernadotte's assassination, added in a stern voice, "but remember what Count Bernadotte did to us." Bunche, incredulous at an apparent defense of the assassination, looked questioningly at Ben-Gurion and asked him to repeat what he had said, whereupon Ben-Gurion repeated the remark. Bunche asked him if he was referring to the Bernadotte report. Ben-Gurion answered sharply, yes.[13]

22

The Congo

First Aid to a Wounded Rattlesnake

For Bunche 1960 proved to be the year of Africa. The independence of Ghana, at the celebration of which he had been present in 1957, had marked the beginning of the avalanche of independence in Africa which, in less than twenty years, left only Namibia still seeking its freedom from South Africa. This momentum was just beginning to build up in 1960.

On New Year's Day, after helping Joan and Ralph Jr. take down the Christmas tree, he left for Monrovia, Liberia, to represent Hammarskjöld at the inauguration of President William Tubman. After a twenty-three-hour flight, he was immediately plunged into a continuous series of ceremonial occasions during which the intense heat was rendered more unbearable by the fact that for most of the events, day or night, the dignitaries were required to wear top hat, white tie, and tails.

At the inauguration, in the un-air-conditioned Central Pavilion,

after Tubman's rambling address, in the midst of which he knelt down and read a prayer (he had some difficulty getting up again, loaded down as he was with medals and probably more than one snort), we had to walk in a 20–25 minute procession, under the full glare of the midday sun, down Broad Street and sundry side streets in our already wilted formal attire to the Executive Pavilion. . . .[1]

The organizers had forgotten to invite the visiting delegations to the subsequent military parade, but Tubman caught up with Bunche and they reviewed the troops together, after which they drank rum and ginger ale. At the Inaugural Ball, Tubman stayed until 3:10 A.M., making it impossible for anyone else to leave. In three days of ceremonies, the only moment of relatively normal life was a talk with Golda Meir, who was representing Israel at the ceremonies, about the ban on Israeli ships in the Suez Canal.

Bunche finally escaped via Accra, where he saw Kwame Nkrumah, surrounded by large and vicious dogs, which were said to have been given to him by Nasser. Nkrumah had already embarked on the capricious and autocratic course which ultimately proved disastrous both for him and for his country. He regarded himself as the natural leader of all independent Africa, a claim not always welcomed by other African leaders. Megalomania tinged with paranoia was already clouding the golden dreams of independence which Bunche had shared at the independence ceremonies nearly three years before.

I had the strong impression that Nkrumah is scared—this was later confirmed by Dan Chapman [Ghana's former ambassador to Washington and, at the time, headmaster of Achimota School], who says he fears assassination, has had his fears fed by some of the insiders and has even consulted witch doctors and asked for potions and white pigeons.[2]

They discussed many things, including the bad press Nkrumah was getting because of the detention without trial of many opponents and Ghana's claims on neighboring Togo. Nkrumah rejected all criticism and took it for granted that everyone should come to him. He spoke sadly of George Padmore, his American mentor, who had recently died in Accra, and whom Bunche had taught at Howard in the late 1920s and had known in London in the 1930s.

From Accra, Bunche went on to Cairo, where he was kept at arm's length on all serious matters on the grounds that Hammarskjöld would be arriving in a few weeks' time. He nonetheless conveyed bluntly Hammarskjöld's disappointment over the Canal question. He then flew on to Nairobi to join Hammarskjöld on the last stages of his African tour, stopping en route at Khartoum and Mogadishu. He arrived in Mogadishu with the Italian administrator for Somaliland, one de Stefano, who required all officials, as well as an honor guard and a band, to turn out whenever he arrived in the capital. "De Stefano is a fat, fatuous, unpleasant civilian, who is generally regarded as a tragedy for Somaliland."[3]

Staying with the British governor general in Government House in Nairobi* was a striking contrast to Bunche's previous visit to Kenya twenty-two years before, when he had lodged with an Indian called R. P. Das. He and Hammarskjöld met with Tom Mboya and Julius Kiano in the

---

*The Governor-General spoke throughout dinner about the uniforms and insignia of British governors and the inadvisability of changing them. "He is obviously superficial and lives up to his own often repeated, self-deprecating 'I am a very simple-minded chap' or 'I am stupid, you know.' He is."[4]

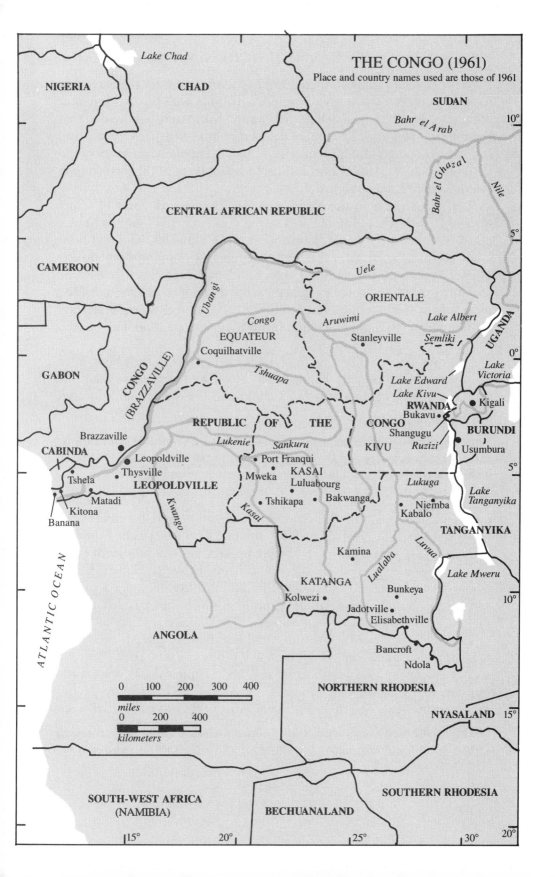

THE CONGO (1961)
Place and country names used are those of 1961

governor general's study. "What a striking development for the Secretary-General to meet alone in the Governor's mansion with the two foremost African leaders!" Bunche noted.[5] Mboya and Kiano were determined that there should be full parliamentary democracy in Kenya that very year and had asked Thurgood Marshall, the NAACP lawyer who was soon to become a U.S. Supreme Court justice, to advise them at the forthcoming London conference on Kenya.

At a reception in the Parliament Building the daughter of Chief Koinange, with whom Bunche had stayed during his 1937 visit to Kenya, asked Bunche to try to get permission for the old chief, who had been banished to the north after the Mau Mau rebellion, to come home to die. He was in his nineties, confused in his mind, and in poor health. Bunche took this up with the governor general, who was sympathetic. Some of the older men at this reception recalled the "baraya" or welcoming ceremony for Bunche in 1937 and called him by his Kikuyu name, Karioki ("he who has returned from the dead").

On January 13 they flew to Entebbe in Uganda, from where, after lunching at Government House, they drove to Kampala to visit the Kabaka (the king of the Baganda), a rather affected young man, educated in England.

He is a rank conservative, seeks by every means to preserve the feudal power he and his chiefs exercise, and is strongly opposed to popular elections which, he complains, the British administration is trying to impose on Buganda.[6]

Bunche felt that, but for the Kabaka's attitude, Uganda could very soon be independent. Once again Bunche met acquaintances from his earlier visit. One, however, the great crocodile Lutembe, who when called used to come ashore to eat rotten meat, had disappeared and was presumed dead.

The tour continued through Somaliland, Ethiopia, Sudan, Cairo, Tunis, and Morocco.* The exhausting schedule was lightened by the comfortable Scandinavian Airlines Convair in which they traveled, and by Hammarskjöld's enthusiasm and curiosity. The impressions that he gained of the problems, diversity, attitudes, and traditions of the African continent provided, as he cabled to Andrew Cordier in New York, "increasingly challenging food for thought at UN." Hammarskjöld was greatly impressed both by the new generation of African leaders and by the immense future problems of independent Africa. He was particularly con-

*Hammarskjöld had already visited Senegal, Liberia, Guinea, Ghana, French Togoland, French Cameroons, British Cameroons, Nigeria, the French Congo, the Belgian Congo, Ruanda-Urundi, Tanganyika, and Zanzibar.

cerned that the crazy quilt of boundaries, imposed on Africa by European colonial powers in the late nineteenth century without regard for economic or ethnic realities, would inevitably impose a crippling legacy on the free nations of Africa. He was determined that the United Nations should assist in this difficult transition.

Hammarskjöld's farsighted and optimistic plans and statements seemed more realistic in the honeymoon atmosphere of the great year of African independence than after more than thirty years of mostly disillusioning experience. Bunche, with a far deeper knowledge of Africa, certainly had a more hardheaded view of the problems ahead. The following years would largely belie Hammarskjöld's vision of a newly free continent marching into the future under able young leaders, helped and advised by the UN.

Bunche's energy was now restored, although he was on a regime for diabetes which he found hard to stick to, particularly when traveling. In early June he was visited by Robert Kennedy on behalf of his brother Jack, who was then campaigning for the presidency of the United States. Robert Kennedy said that his brother recognized that foreign affairs would be the most important challenge facing the new president and needed sound advice by someone who was "practicing" rather than theorizing in the field. Jack Kennedy wanted Bunche to assist him as adviser on international affairs for the rest of the campaign. Bunche demurred, saying that Adlai Stevenson had made a similar request in 1952, and that, as in 1952, he was unwilling to leave the UN.[7]

The story of the Belgian Congo was the darkest chapter in European colonial history. A territory the size of Western Europe had been colonized and systematically looted for over seventy years. It was a fantastically rich country, containing minerals in almost indecent quantity and quality. Gold, cobalt, tin, uranium, and diamonds poured from its mines, and enriched its Belgian masters. It was brutally well organized. From the mountains of Kivu in the East to the Atlantic Ocean at Matadi in the West, from the tropical forests along the Congo River in the North to the scrub-covered uplands of the mining province of Katanga in the South, the colony was run by a bureaucracy of ten thousand Belgian civil servants. It was an economic exploitation machine, involving international corporations, enormous investments and profits, and a complex water, rail, and air transportation system. A network of religious missions tended the souls of the exploited.

The indigenous inhabitants of the Congo had never been permitted to share in the benefits of this remarkable enterprise. In 1960, only seventeen out of thirteen and a half million Congolese had university degrees; there was not one African officer in the Congolese army; and, until 1957, little if any political activity by the Africans had been permitted. The realities of independece had not been discussed.

At the end of May Hammarskjöld told Bunche that he wanted him to go to the Congo to represent him at the independence ceremonies, and to stay a few weeks to advise the new government and explore the requirements for UN assistance. On June 20 he formalized this request in a letter which specified that Bunche was to advise the new Congo government on

questions affecting the application and admission of the Congo to membership in the United Nations and the broad field of United Nations assistance in its technical and other aspects in relation to Congo needs and possible requests.

He was to take with him F. T. Liu,* from his old trusteeship staff; an economist, Henry Bloch; and Sture Linner, a Swede who was to become the UN technical-assistance representative in the Congo.

Bunche left for the Congo on June 23, traveling on the Belgian airline, Sabena. During a stopover in Brussels, at an official luncheon in his honor, he had a dismaying foretaste of the Belgian attitude to the Congolese—an attitude that was to contribute disastrously to the tragedy of Congolese independence. Senior Belgian officials were contemptuously derisive of the new Congolese leaders, especially the prime minister designate, Patrice Lumumba. "The banter back and forth across the table between the Belgian officials in the presence of several Congolese, in the most outmoded paternalistic and condescending tone, was downright embarrassing."[8] He arrived in Leopoldville at 6:00 A.M. on June 25. In another foretaste of the confusion to come, there was no one to meet him and F. T. Liu, and they were rescued by a member of the U.S. Consulate who had been sent to the airport just in case.

Bunche immediately plunged into the Congolese scene. After two hours' sleep, he attended a luncheon given by the Belgian minister for the Congo, Auguste DeSchryver, and the minister for general African affairs, Ganshof van der Meersch, in honor of the newly elected government. It included the future President Joseph Kasavubu, the future Prime Minister Patrice Lumumba, the future Foreign Minister Justin Bomboko, and the UN ambassador designate, Thomas Kanza. They lunched in the residence

*Liu had grown up in Paris and spoke perfect French.

of the former provincial governor, an elegant modern building high on a bluff by the Stanley Monument, looking across the Congo River to Braz-zaville and with a spectacular view of the Stanley Rapids. This was Bunche's first contact with the people with whom he would spend most of his days and nights in the next two months. Mrs. van der Meersch, a devotee of the proselytizing cult Moral Rearmament, introduced Bunche to an MRA representative, a Nigerian in a toga, who told him that his group were there "to bring stability to the country, thus documenting my objection to them."[9]

Bunche summed up his first impressions in a long handwritten letter to Hammarskjöld.* Things seemed to be going reasonably well, and he was impressed by the contrast between the seriousness of DeSchryver and van der Meersch and the attitude of the Belgians he had met in Brussels. The difficulties seemed largely formal, and manageable. For example, the name of the new state was in doubt because the French Congo across the river had already preempted "Republic of the Congo"—one solution being for Leopoldville to adopt the African spelling, "Kongo."† The high Belgian officials had become enthusiastic supporters of the UN, believing that "the Congolese will 'listen' to us and follow our advice, and . . . imply that we alone stand in the way of the Congolese being taken in by Mos-cow."[10] Bunche couldn't help remembering the Belgian boycott of the UN committee on non-self-governing territories and Belgium's unvary-ingly intransigent attitude on colonial problems at the UN.

Bunche had little doubt that the relationship between Kasavubu and Lumumba would soon lead to a showdown, since Lumumba wanted to change the constitution and virtually eliminate Kasavubu's position. Kasavubu, though not an impressive personality, was friendly and a man of integrity. Lumumba was harder to assess. He was obviously young and untried, and had been convicted for embezzlement while working in the post office. "He is tall and sharp-eyed and rather raffish-looking in his mustache and beard and long hair. Whether the latter is an affectation or lack of time for a hair-cut I do not yet know."‡[11] As to the independence ceremonies, it was widely predicted that chaos would reign. President Fulbert Youlou of the neighboring French Congo, for example, had de-manded an important decoration and an escort of ten motorcycles, and

---

*Bunche was living in the Stanley Hotel with no office and virtually no staff. In view of later developments this was a serious weakness.

†It was finally called Congo (Leopoldville), and later Zaire.

‡He got a haircut in time for the independence ceremonies.

there were to be two thousand invited guests for the banquet.

The independence ceremonies on June 30 provided the overture to the subsequent tragedy. King Baudoin of Belgium "led off with a speech which was too paternalistic in tone, overemphasized the Belgian contribution here and made the gross error of praising the early Belgian role here under Leopold."*[12] Lumumba, who was seen to be revising his speech during President Kasavubu's mild response to the king, spoke in words which so profoundly shocked the Belgians that the king nearly left in the middle of his speech. Lumumba's words were harshly anticolonial. "We have known," he said, "ironies, insults, and blows, which we had to undergo morning, noon, and night because we were blacks." Belgian officials had tears in their eyes as they talked to Bunche after the ceremony, but at the ceremonial luncheon Lumumba made a friendly and conciliatory speech ending with a toast to the king. "Lumumba seems to have more than one face. At times he impresses as God's angry young man, but he can also laugh heartily and be excitable or other-worldly."[13] Bunche might have added that Lumumba's aggressive speech was also good Congolese politics, establishing him in the popular mind as *the* independence leader, in contrast to the bland and obsequious Kasavubu, who had, up to that point, been the real father of Congolese independence.

Bunche's next letter to Hammarskjöld, on July 4, was a good deal less sanguine. The takeover of power after independence had been disorderly indeed. The Belgian colonial regime continuing for some time alongside the new one. "There were two governments but little governing."[14] Bunche felt that everyone had started out badly. Lumumba had poisoned the independence ceremonies and grossly exaggerated the heroism of the Congolese struggle for independence, which had in fact come to the Congolese easily and swiftly on the wings of Belgian panic after France had decolonized her African territories. In deciding that the king should come for the ceremonies, Belgian officials had completely misjudged the attitude and temper of the Congolese. Relations between Kasavubu and Lumumba were strained and hostile, and they studiously ignored each other, never speaking to each other unless absolutely necessary. The best hope, although slim, was that the problems of governing the enormous country would prove such a crushing burden that there would be no time for individual power struggles. Like the prevailing weather in Leopoldville, the situation was sultry and overcast, but not yet too hot.

*King Leopold II of Belgium (1865–1909) had established the Congo as virtually a personal fiefdom, in which the brutality and rapacity of his administrators in exploiting the great natural resources of the country had become legendary.

Bunche was appalled at the total lack of preparedness for their new task which characterized all of the new Congolese leaders. They seemed to be mostly concerned about salaries, titles, and cars. There were already daily disorders, and Bunche, while traveling with Thomas Kanza, had had to order his Congolese driver, Pius, to move off quickly to avoid a squad of thugs who were intent on beating Kanza up.

Bunche found his compatriots in Leopoldville obsessed with the possibility of a communist takeover. American officials were perpetually whispering about which Congolese minister was leftist or in touch with Moscow. The wife of an American official had asked Bunche "in most serious perturbation: 'Mr. Bunche, are the *Reds* really coming?' I replied mischievously and not altogether untruthfully, 'My dear lady, they are already here.' "15 Bunche was also irritated with the ubiquitous Moral Rearmament agents campaigning under the arrogant slogan "Moral Rearmament or Communism." "The frightened local industrialists and bureaucrats are just ripe to be plucked under the illusion that MRA can miraculously make the blacks suddenly love the whites."16

Serious trouble began on July 5, when the colonial army, the Belgian-officered Force Publique, rechristened the Armée Nationale Congolaise,* mutinied at its biggest base, at Thysville, between Leopoldville and the sea, and Belgian officers, civilians, and their families fled in panic to the capital. A rumor spread among whites in the capital that a train from Thysville was bringing European evacuees, mainly women and children, some of whom were injured or had been raped. What the train was full of was frightened and bitter people, whose angry denunciations of decolonization, the United States, and the UN added a new element to the already volatile atmosphere. The mutiny soon spread to Leopoldville, the soldiers demanding Africanization of the officer corps, promotions, and better pay. In response to a violent demonstration in front of the Palais de la Nation, Lumumba, on July 5, promised retribution against Belgian officers who had "incited disloyalty" and promoted all members of the army one grade. A brief and uneasy calm ensued.

At 8:00 A.M. on July 8 Bunche was awaiting Kanza at his hotel to discuss the UN program of assistance to the Congo, but it was already clear that something was badly wrong. Military vehicles were tearing about, carrying soldiers shrieking unintelligible slogans. No Belgian officers were to be seen, and were, in fact, at that moment being rounded up by the soldiers. Kanza called to say he was cut off by military cordons. As

---

*The ANC had no Congolese officers at this time.

usual in the Congo, a rich and frightening crop of rumors began to circulate—including one that the troops had arrested Lumumba. A distur-
bance in the street below his hotel room brought Bunche to the balcony to
observe two British journalists and three members of the Israeli Embassy,
including the ambassador, being herded along the street by the soldiers.
Fortunately, one of the Israelis spoke Lingala and persuaded the soldiers
that they were diplomats. A soldier pointed his rifle at Bunche, who
ducked back into his room just before the soldier fired.

Moments later soldiers burst into Bunche's room and ordered
Bunche and Liu to go downstairs—*"Là bas, là bas."* Bunche told them he
wished to get his passport, hid his confidential papers behind the toilet
bowl in the bathroom and, when the soldiers began to shout and to show
signs of becoming trigger-happy, went quietly downstairs with his companions. The lobby was full of soldiers brandishing weapons and some very
frightened guests. After a while, characteristically, the soldiers jumped
into their vehicles and drove off. The hotel help had, meanwhile, taken
fright and left, and self-service became the order of the day. Bunche
noted, "At 2 P.M. it is almost as quiet as a graveyard—is this the calm
before a bigger storm?"[17] Bunche was worried that the situation could
boil up into a "raging anti-white maelstrom, fed by all the grievances of
the past, the stupid conduct of many whites and even now the large
number of arms collected from whites."[18] Even Bunche's car had been
searched for arms by the soldiers, and he had a nightmare vision of a
defenseless city entirely in the hands of a mutinous, officerless army.
When he left the Congo two months later he told the press that he had
never in his life been so frightened as he was at that time. To his son he
wrote,

wouldn't it be ironic though if I should now get knocked around here in the very
heart of Africa because of anti-white feeling—the reason being that I am not dark
enough and might be mistaken for a "blanc."[19]

And to Ruth, "This is the toughest spot I've ever been in—even Palestine
was safe by comparison."[20]

Kanza, worried about Bunche's safety, sent a single Congolese soldier
with a rifle to guard him. Bunche had been convinced since his days in
Palestine that individuals carrying arms invited trouble in times of conflict. For this reason the original UN military observers were unarmed,
and their successors have remained so ever since. The Congolese soldier
was politely requested to leave his rifle behind when traveling with
Bunche.

Bunche's sense of impending disaster was in no way allayed by the new Belgian ambassador to the Congo, Jean Van den Bosch, who told him that by sheer luck he had intercepted and countermanded a request by the Belgian commander of the ANC, General Janssens, to the commander of Belgian troops in the Congo, to put down the mutiny by force. The new Treaty of Friendship between Belgium and the Congo provided that only the prime minister could request the intervention of Belgian troops, and there was no doubt that the whole city would erupt if Belgian forces were to fire on the Congolese. European civilians were already everywhere in flight across the river to the relative stability of Brazzaville.

By July 9 it was clear that the government of Kasavubu and Lumumba was losing whatever control it previously had of the situation, and on July 11 its impotence was underlined by the secession of Katanga, the Congo's richest province. Moise Tshombe, the president of Katanga, had visited Bunche in Leopoldville two days earlier, and Bunche had tried in vain to talk him out of seceding. Tshombe had shown an unhealthy interest in the early history of the United States. "He seemed only encouraged," Bunche wrote later, "when I protested strongly that the US Articles of Confederation had failed woefully to work."[21] Tshombe invited Bunche to visit Katanga as soon as possible.

Bunche reported:

Powder keg here. But full explosion may be averted. Terrific tension among Europeans owing to shock of disillusionment over reliability of Force Publique. Virtual rebellion in the Force due mixture of insistence on Africanization, unrealized expectations of many changes for better after independence. . . .[22]

Active hostility to the Belgians was spreading rapidly. Congolese soldiers were drinking openly and heavily in the streets, and what was left of the European population was terrified. Bunche politely turned down Hammarskjöld's suggestion that he personally might take refuge in Brazzaville with his staff, saying that that would only contribute to the panic.

On July 9 the mutiny spread to Luluabourg, the capital of the Kasai province, and to Elisabethville, the capital of Katanga. For the first time Europeans were actually killed by the mutineers, and on the following day Belgian airborne troops from the Kamina base intervened in both places to protect the white population. More than twenty Congolese civilians were killed by Belgian troops at the Atlantic port of Matadi. The crisis had entered the new and ominous phase which Bunche had anticipated and dreaded.

Bunche got his first intimation that the Congolese might seek military assistance from the UN on July 10 from the United States ambassador, Clare Timberlake, who had been talking to Kasavubu and Lumumba. That afternoon he was invited to a meeting of the Congolese Cabinet, where it became clear that the Congolese government wanted help from the UN but had no clear idea of either what was needed or what might reasonably be expected. The meeting was an emotional one. Lumumba and Kasavubu left in the middle "to make public statements on the situation," and toward the end a telegram arrived announcing that Belgian troops were in action at Luluabourg.

Lumumba and Kasavubu had both insisted on Africanization of the army officer corps but recognized that they would need outside assistance if the military establishment was not to fall apart. After Bunche explained in some detail the possibilities and the limitations of UN military assistance, the government decided to ask for military assistance in strengthening the army for national defense and for the maintenance of law and order. Bunche had in mind getting UN advisers and instructors on the spot as soon as possible. Police experts in the technique of nonviolent handling of riotous crowds would be especially useful in the volatile atmosphere of Leopoldville. It would also be necessary to bring in technicians to keep the vital public services running. Bunche reported all this to Hammarskjöld, who was anxiously waiting in Geneva. He had no doubt, Bunche wrote, that the situation demanded urgent, and possibly unprecedented action. Hammarskjöld decided to return at once to New York to orchestrate an adequate UN response.

In spite of Bunche's warnings, delivered to the Belgians both in Leopoldville and through Hammarskjöld, the deployment of Belgian troops in the main towns of the Congo continued, intensifying the violence as well as the panic among both the white and the black populations. The resulting mass exodus of Belgians included virtually all the administrators and technicians who were to have served the new Congolese government under the Treaty of Friendship. The collapse of law and order was thus compounded by the breakdown of essential services and all economic activity. This added a vast new dimension to Bunche's task, since the UN would now have to take over, temporarily at any rate, the public administration of the country. On July 12 he alerted Hammarskjöld to the need for an emergency airlift of food and for various categories of technicians and administrators.

By July 12 the widespread intervention of Belgian troops had convinced Kasavubu and Lumumba that their primary need was for UN military assistance to deal with Belgian aggression. After their request for United States troops had been politely rebuffed by Washington, they asked Hammarskjöld—by commercial cable, since they were at the time stranded in Luluabourg in an abortive attempt to go to Katanga—for military assistance to fight Belgian aggression. This radical request, made direct to New York from a provincial capital, came as a complete surprise to Bunche in Leopoldville, but he quickly put his mind to the problem of deploying actual UN forces to calm the situation.

While Hammarskjöld was marshaling the Security Council and the African group in New York to respond to the Congo's request, things went from bad to worse in the Congo itself. On the morning of July 13 Belgian paratroops forcibly took over the Leopoldville airport and the European area of the city, where the government and Parliament buildings were situated. Lumumba responded to this development by informing Bunche that he had asked Ghana for military assistance pending the arrival of a UN force. Bunche warned him that an intervention by Ghana would greatly complicate the effort to provide United Nations assistance. At the same time, fearing the reactions of the four thousand Congolese soldiers in Leopoldville, Ambassador Timberlake urged the French ambassador to have the French troops in Brazzaville ready to intervene. Bunche was happy to find that the French ambassador in Leopoldville supported him in strongly opposing this idea.

Only a rapid intervention by the United Nations could now prevent all of the these elements from coming together in a disastrous explosion, and Bunche stressed the urgency of the situation to Hammarskjöld.

I believe UN may be able to save this situation, chaotic as it is rapidly becoming, if some action is taken quickly enough. The two appeals [from the Congo government] together enable UN to do just about anything it may find feasible. Only some manifestation of a "third presence" which definitely should be international, military, but not indispensably fighting men, can save the situation.[23]

Hammarskjöld took up the challenge by calling the Security Council on July 13 to an urgent meeting under Article 99 of the Charter.* Hammarskjöld made three main proposals—technical assistance to the Congo in security administration, the introduction of UN forces, and emergency food shipments. The Security Council took its decision in the small hours of July 14, authorizing Hammarskjöld to go ahead with an operation that was christened ONUC (Organisation des Nations Unies au Congo).†

Hammarskjöld rounded up the first elements of the UN force—from

---

*This article, which empowers the secretary general to "bring to the attention of the Security Council any matter which in his opinion may threaten the maintenance of international peace and security," had never been formally used for this purpose before.

†I joined Bunche in Leopoldville two days later.

Ethiopia, Ghana, Guinea, Mali, Morocco, and Tunisia—within twelve hours of the Security Council decision. He arranged for American, British, and (in the case of Ghana) some Soviet aircraft to transport them to the Congo. Bunche had warned that "swiftness in arrival is more important immediately than quantity,"[24] and that the troops should arrive with as much fanfare and as many UN flags and symbols as possible. He also began to negotiate with the Belgians on their withdrawal and to accustom them to the idea that UN troops would shortly be taking over from them. Hammarskjöld appointed Bunche as the commander of the entire operation pending the arrival from Jerusalem of the Swedish chief of staff of the Truce Supervision Organization, General Carl von Horn, who was to command the ONUC military. From working out of his hotel room with two assistants and one secretary and having to rely on the U.S. Embassy for code facilities and urgent communication, Bunche was about to take charge of the largest UN operation ever launched.

Bunche was already widely respected in Leopoldville. Among the diplomats he was a well-known name. To the Congolese he represented the best hope for the future and for a way out of their troubles. They also viewed him, as they viewed virtually everyone, including each other, with some suspicion. Thomas Kanza, who was slated to represent the Congo at the UN, wrote that in Bunche's relations with the new government "the fraternity of race played a part that could not be under-estimated." On the other hand Bunche's French was rudimentary, so he had to rely on F. T. Liu or an interpreter in his dealings with the Congolese. To the Congolese, at any rate, it also seemed that he could never get away "from the watchfulness of American agents, whether official or merely officious," and thus he could never expect the Congolese to be totally frank with him. Kanza felt that the Belgians saw Bunche

as just another colored man. His position was thus extremely delicate, in that he could never take any position or express any view about the relations between the white colonizers and the black colonized without being misinterpreted and suspected by either or both.[25]

Kanza could not know that some of Bunche's major disagreements were, and would be, with the United States ambassador. As Bunche himself was bitterly aware, his reliance on the U.S. Embassy in the early days for communications was likely to cause serious misunderstandings. Nor was it likely that the Belgians, who had been dealing with Bunche as a ranking international official and colonial expert for nearly twenty years, saw him as "just another colored man." But such Congolese perceptions unquestionably colored their relations with Bunche and added to their limitless store of suspicion.*

The first UN troops—Tunisians—arrived on July 15, and were quickly followed by contingents from Ethiopia, Ghana, and Morocco, so that by July 17 there was already a UN force of thirty-five hundred men in the Congo. On July 16 Bunche made a broadcast explaining the UN effort to the Congolese. The UN troops, he said, came as friends of the Congolese people and were mostly from sister African states. "They will do everything they can to help restore calm, harmony, and safety for all, whites as well as blacks, in this troubled land." He urged patience and moderation. "This alone can save your marvelous country from disaster."[26]

Bunche's call for patience was in vain. Although the UN had deployed thirty-five hundred troops within three days of the Security Council's decision, and had already replaced the Belgian forces in most of Leopoldville, the Belgian troops and the humiliations they had inflicted had become an obsession with Lumumba. On July 18, from Stanleyville, he presented Bunche with the first of a series of ultimatums, in which he declared that if all Belgian troops were not withdrawn within forty-eight hours the government would appeal for aid to the Soviet Union. When Bunche took this up with the Council of Ministers, they made it clear that they totally disapproved of any appeal for Soviet troops and wanted the UN to stay. Lumumba's remark that the UN's delay in expelling the Belgian forces was an "imperialist trick"[27] indicated that Soviet influence was already being brought to bear on the prime minister.

Bunche found the Belgian representatives in Leopoldville no less obstructive than the prime minister. They represented both the mounting fears of all Europeans in the Congo and the public indignation that was creating a political crisis at home in Belgium. Bunche was convinced that the complete withdrawal of Belgian troops and their replacement by UN troops would do more than anything else to save Belgian civilians from harm and restore calm throughout the country. Although Hammarskjöld had conceived of ONUC as a purely African operation, as early as July 17 Bunche cabled him, "In view mounting fear Europeans here I regard it as indispensable to announce quickly . . . inclusion of a non-African contingent."[28] The Swedish Battalion from Gaza and an Irish Battalion shortly

*Lumumba, in one of his frequent rages, asked me why Hammarskjöld had sent *"ce nègre américain"* to represent the UN in the Congo. When I told him that Hammarskjöld had simply sent the best man in the world for this impossible job, he immediately retreated and apologized.

arrived in Leopoldville. Nonetheless, the Belgians seemed intent on stalling, thereby compounding the suspicions of Lumumba and others about
the intentions of the United Nations. With the UN troops arriving in
force, it was agreed that the Belgian troops could soon be withdrawn
completely from Leopoldville, but there were always delays, which served
only to feed Congolese suspicions and Soviet accusations. When Bunche
told General Cuémond, the Belgian chief of staff, that the strategic bases
of Kamina and Kitona would also have to be evacuated, the general splut-
tered, "If that happens we shall need a UN force in Belgium to quell the
revolution."[29]

Meanwhile, the officerless ANC remained a threat to virtually everyone in Leopoldville, and Bunche asked urgently for a group of officers
from African countries to begin its retraining. When he visited the main
ANC barracks, Camp Leopold, on July 17 with Justin Bomboko and
Kanza, the soldiers' resentment of the ministers in their new automobiles
boiled up into a near riot, and they were compelled to leave hurriedly. It
was clear that the soldiers had never heard of the UN and its mission in
the Congo.

The question of how to deal with the Congolese army embroiled
Bunche in a standing disagreement with his own military officers and with
the United States ambassador. General Henry Alexander, the British
chief of staff of the Ghanaian army, had arrived in Leopoldville on July 15
and had, on his own initiative, assumed charge of the arriving UN troops,
a move that had caused Hammarskjöld immediately to appoint Bunche as
interim commander. Alexander was a brave and conventional British officer who believed that the Congolese army must be disarmed if Leopoldville was to be saved. As he once—infelicitously and to Bunche's amusement—put it, "the nigger in the woodpile is the ANC." Alexander was
enthusiastically supported in this view both by the U.S. ambassador and,
when he arrived on July 17, by General von Horn, the UN commander.
Bunche agreed that it was highly desirable that the ANC should not carry
arms but insisted that the Congolese government must first consent to
such a move. Lumumba, obsessed with the continued presence of Belgian
forces, refused. Bunche thus found himself in a situation in which he had
to override his military colleagues and the United States, while at the same
time, by putting the question to Lumumba, he had provided Lumumba
and the Soviets with grounds for accusing the UN of trying to disarm the
Congolese and failing to get rid of the Belgians. It was a very typical
Congolese dilemma.

As the troops came off the transport planes and were deployed all over the Congo except for Katanga, it seemed, in the outside world at least, as if the worst might be over. Bunche was under no such illusions. He told Hammarskjöld:

Risks this operation frightening, but we must take them. Europeans scared and bitter and expecting worst. Africans scared, bitter, expecting miracles. Such as instant withdrawal Belgian troops, food immediately in their outstretched hands, and quick tangible boons from independence. Shudder to think of consequences from an incident involving our troops and members of African or European communities, or worst of all, Belgian troops. We must maintain strictest discipline. Bomboko and Kanza giving excellent cooperation. They alone have education and comprehension, but little authority. For first time, they now show deep fear, of emotional Africans as well as [of] Belgians.[30]

Bunche now had a fair idea of what he was up against. The Belgians, whose long-term policies and short-term activities had precipitated the crisis, were the immediate problem, for until the Belgian troops withdrew the possibility of a widespread and uncontrollable disaster remained.

It is infuriating that the Belgian Ambassador, whose reckless action against which I and others warned him [the deployment of Belgian troops] created this crisis, should now seek to justify new Belgian troop actions by UN inability to cover entire country in a few days.[31]

The Belgians finally agreed that all their troops would be out of Leopold-ville by July 23.

Bunche was also beginning to realize the extent of Lumumba's irra-tionality and instability—a condition aggravated both by his accession to power and by his entourage, an international riffraff of hangers-on, includ-ing the Ghanaian ambassador, whom Bunche characterized as "a fool but dangerous." Lumumba veered wildly between requests for assistance and advice, and ultimatums about the Belgian troops. He was distrusted and feared by his Congolese colleagues, who knew that his demagogic powers could easily produce disastrous confrontations on the streets of Leopold-ville. Bunche's problem was to deal with him firmly without precipitating a physical confrontation between the UN and the forces loyal to Lumumba.

Other problems were less obtrusive but equally frustrating. The Sovi-ets were already embarking on their policy of portraying Hammarskjöld, Bunche, and ONUC as American-run neocolonialists, and lost no oppor-tunity to denounce both UN action and UN reluctance to act. The Soviet embassy in Leopoldville was very large, and its hand could be seen in many of Lumumba's statements as well as in the profusion of Soviet "advisers" to be found lurking in vital installations. A Soviet member of the UN Secretariat, Mikhail Potrubach, sent from New York to join Bunche's staff, proved, predictably enough, to be controlled by the Soviet embassy and, after he had been caught trying to copy some of Bunche's code cables, was quickly sent back to New York. The fact that Bunche, already pictured by the Soviets as an American stooge, found himself in constant disagreement with the U.S. ambassador, Clare Timberlake, and the British ambassador, Ian Scott, made this situation particularly irritating.* Lumumba's ultimatums tended to confirm Washington's obsession with the imminence of a Soviet takeover, and Washington was, in secret, already making its own, ruthless plans for Lumumba's removal.[33]

Bunche had to build up ONUC while he was also trying to cope with the twists and turns of the Congo crisis, and Hammarskjöld gave him all possible support. He got virtually everything he asked for, including a force of more than ten thousand soldiers. The military side was, however, poorly led and organized. General von Horn was a vain and inexperienced commander, more inclined to bluster than to build a strong and disciplined military organization. On the civilian side a staff was needed to run communications, hospitals, the central bank, airfields, police, and all the institutions of a large and complex country, and civilian experts poured into Bunche's headquarters from all over the world. "If we pull this situation out of the fire," Bunche wrote to Ruth, "it will be the closest thing to a miracle I'll ever see. But we're making a mighty try against frightening odds."[34]

Bunche was working around the clock with his new military and civilian staff. In the first days, sporting a blue UNEF fatigue cap to denote his position as interim commander, he spent much time at the airport welcoming incoming contingents and giving them orders to deploy in different parts of the Congo. A small office in the control tower was secured for this purpose. The airport, controlled by young Belgian paratroops and swarming with newly arrived UN troops, was a tense and bustling place. Not all the incoming units were a positive asset. The battalion from Guinea was commanded by a four-star general (commissar) who

---

*Later on, rebutting Soviet accusations in the Security Council, Hammarskjöld said, "It was mentioned that for the first two months my personal representative in the Congo was an American, but it was omitted that this was the natural function of the person in question in view of the position he holds in the UN Secretariat and also because of his unmatched personal record of fighting for the interest of the African peoples and for minorities."[32]

stated on arrival that his sole mission was to fight the Belgians and drive the whites into the sea. He demanded to go immediately to Katanga. His unit was so poorly trained, equipped, and disciplined that a quiet and easy sector had to be found for them, where they could do as little damage as possible to themselves and to the Congolese.

On July 25 Bunche and his staff left the Stanley Hotel for makeshift offices in a new apartment block, the Résidence Royale. The salon was turned into an office and operations room, and Bunche and his staff worked together around a large table. Since internal telephones were non-existent, this arrangement, providing direct communication, was surprisingly practical. The room became known as the "snakepit," and to it repaired virtually everyone—Congolese politicians, diplomats, journalists, or nervous Europeans—who had a question or a problem. The staff ate in a primitive Greek restaurant on the ground floor, or lived on K rations provided by the U.S. Military Air Transport Service.

Outside the Résidence Royale the city of Leopoldville no longer had the appearance of a model colonial capital. Although its native townships were still thronged and pulsing with life, in the spacious central white section of the city, the great villas lay empty in their manicured gardens and time seemed to stand still. Stray dogs, left behind by the fleeing Europeans, scavenged for food around the abandoned luxury cars of their departed masters. The township Congolese, long accustomed to an enforced segregation, had not yet dared to penetrate these formerly sacrosanct white preserves. Occasionally, however, a demonstration by one or another of the "jeunesses"—political youth movements—would pass, shouting, down the main boulevard.

Bunche spent much time with Lumumba and Vice–Prime Minister Antoine Gizenga, or attending sessions of the twenty-eight-member Congolese Cabinet.* These visits were almost invariably frustrating. Typical was an evening meeting on July 20 with Lumumba, who had just returned from Stanleyville, where he had delivered his first ultimatum about the withdrawal of Belgian troops. Lumumba began by indignantly holding the local paper, *Le Courier d'Afrique,* in front of Bunche. The headline read "M. Bunche: L'ONU ne Peut Recevoir d'Ultimatum de Quiconque" and "Ultimatum Rejeté par M. Ralph Bunche" ("Mr. Bunche: The UN Cannot Receive Ultimatums from Anyone" and "Ultimatum Rejected by Mr. Ralph Bunche"). Lumumba said this was an intolerable insult. "I denied having made any public statement . . . but since he kept on had to demand

*The large size was in order to provide for tribal representation.

flatly if he was questioning my word. He climbed down quickly and there was no more of that."[35] Lumumba then complained that the Belgian troops had not left when the UN arrived, "and without mincing words I advised him to look for no miracles."[36] After a series of inconsequential matters Lumumba reverted to his ultimatum, saying that it stood but that the Belgians would not be out of the country by midnight. "I agreed that the latter was the case, said 'alors' [well, then], and that ended the subject. It was never mentioned again."[37] Lumumba then asked Bunche to get the Belgians to release the ANC commander, General Victor Lundula, who had been arrested in Elisabethville, and he started to talk about Katanga. Bunche showed him Hammarskjöld's tough exchange of letters with Tshombe on the Katanga secession. "That melted him completely and for the rest of the talk he was in my hands."[38] Lumumba also told Bunche that the Congolese soldiers guarding the Palais de la Nation were involved in a plot to assassinate him and asked Bunche to replace them with UN soldiers. This Bunche did. He told Hammarskjöld:

The request had an ironic touch since he had just been threatening to run us out of the country. Sitting through such sessions without erupting convinced me that Job had nothing on me. Really.[39]

Lumumba and Gizenga had no experience of conducting business in an orderly way, and conversations were constantly interrupted by diversions—telephone calls which there was no one else to answer, furious inter-Congolese arguments, and wild rhetorical outbursts. To get anything agreed it was usually necessary to enlist Justin Bomboko, the foreign minister (Kanza had left for New York), or Colonel Joseph Mobutu, Lumumba's chief of staff. The general preoccupation with the Belgian troops soon began to give way to an obsession with the secessionist province of Katanga. This was the next challenge which Bunche and Hammarskjöld had to face.

Even amidst the natural resources of the Congo the riches of Katanga were extraordinary. The mines of the great consortium, the Union Minière, produced copper, gold, and tin of exceptional quality. Its capital, Elisabethville, with its agreeable highland climate and its frontier brashness, had, in colonial times, seen itself as the rival of the low-lying, sultry national capital, Leopoldville. Katanga was a name that resounded in the exchanges and the banks of the world.

Katanga's secession was a mortal blow to the prestige—and the exchequer—of the new Congo government. This was an issue which could

neither be ignored nor forgotten. The central government would never
settle down until the Katanga secession was terminated, not least because
the province, and its leader, Moise Tshombe, were widely regarded, with
some reason, as puppets and playthings of the white colonial industrial
world.

For the United Nations in the Congo, the government's obsession
was not the only factor. ONUC had been charged, among other things,
with preserving the borders which the Congo had at the time of its independence. In newly independent Africa secession was inadmissible. Thus
the UN was perforce the monitor and guarantor of the territorial integrity
of the Congo as a whole.

In the outside world the UN Congo operation was, in its early stages,
an object of considerable wonder and admiration, even with people who
normally despised the United Nations. The *New York Post* published an
editorial entitled "The Belated Tribute":

Let the record show that on July 23, 1960, the *Daily News*, lifelong enemy of the
UN and all it stands for, publicly acknowledged humanity's debt to "UN trouble-
shooters Dag Hammarskjöld and Ralph Bunche" for the strenuous efforts they
are making to avert disaster in the Congo.[40]

Walter Lippmann wrote:

This UN enterprise is the most advanced and the most sophisticated experiment
in international cooperation ever attempted. Among all that is so sad and so mean
and so sour in world politics, it is heartening to think that something so good and
so pure in its purpose is possible. No one can say that the experiment will succeed.
But there is no doubt that it deserves to succeed.[41]

The success of ONUC was, in fact, already threatened by three basic
issues—the Katanga secession, the latent split between Lumumba and
Kasavubu, and the Cold War, which divided the UN and was beginning
to make the Congo a battleground between East and West, with ONUC
in the middle. It was Bunche's task to keep the operation on an even keel
and away from these treacherous reefs and cross currents, while at the
same time helping all the people who needed help and doing what was
necessary to preserve the country from further chaos and civil war. There
were seldom any simple answers even to the smallest problems. Later on,
some critics decried our efforts as amateurish or disorganized, but neither
rules, nor precedents nor organization existed for a situation like the
Congo in 1960. Under Bunche's leadership ONUC had, for the most

part, to improvise as it went along. Bunche's insistence on personally
controlling and checking all the activities of ONUC was also criticized
later. To those of us on the spot this seemed the only sensible way of
managing a vast emergency enterprise put together in a hurry, where
many of the staff were new and untried, and where a single mistake could,
and often did, have massive repercussions.

On July 21 Lumumba suddenly decided to visit Washington and
New York, and Hammarskjöld was able to get a firsthand idea of what
Bunche was up against in Leopoldville, before he himself came to the
Congo. Before leaving New York he had asked Bunche and von Horn how
soon ONUC would be in a position to put troops into Katanga without
weakening the UN deployment elsewhere. Bunche gave the earliest possible date as the weekend of July 30–31, provided sufficient transport aircraft were made available. Hammarskjöld stopped in Brussels on his way
to Leopoldville in an effort to get Belgian cooperation for the UN's entry
into Katanga. He not only insisted on the legal case for UN action but also
stressed the international and political risks for Belgium, as well as for the
UN, if the Belgians did not quickly withdraw from Katanga. The Belgians,
however, insisted that the UN's arrival in Katanga would cause an exodus
of Belgian civilians, and that any UN move must be preceded by contact
with Tshombe and representatives of the European population.

Hammarskjöld arrived in Brazzaville on July 28 and crossed the river
to Leopoldville. His time in Leopoldville was both an education and a
considerable shock for him. The Congolese way of doing things, and the
hectic and improvised conditions of the UN operation, were a far cry from
New York and the stately procedures of the Security Council. Hammarskjöld's intention was to instill a sense of reality and patience and to enlist
the Congolese government's support for his efforts. In the absence of
Lumumba in the United States, he dealt with Vice–Prime Minister
Gizenga, who was, if anything, cruder, less gracious, and even more unpredictable than Lumumba, who had, when he wished to be agreeable, considerable charm and charisma. At a reception in Hammarskjöld's honor,
Gizenga launched into a long and insulting speech against the UN, of
which copies were handed out to the guests. Hammarskjöld and Bunche
gave a dinner for the government and diplomatic corps in the Leopoldville
Zoo which was, by contrast, a great success. The zoo had, miraculously,
escaped the man-made chaos of the preceding weeks. The animals were
still living well in pleasant, palm-fringed grounds, where the sultry air of
Leopoldville seemed fresher. After the guests had left, Hammarskjöld,
Bunche, and von Horn took turns conducting the band of the Ghanaian
battalion, which had played for the dinner.

During Hammarskjöld's visit Congolese demands that UN forces go immediately to Katanga grew steadily shriller, drowning out any possibility of Hammarskjöld's explaining the harsh realities of the situation or discussing other vital matters such as the international assistance the Congo now desperately needed. The government's demands were publicly parroted by members of the Soviet and Ghanaian embassies.

On July 31 Hammarskjöld wrote to the Belgian foreign minister, Pierre Wigny, "I must confess that I had not fully realized the continuing deep seriousness of the situation. It may still easily trigger a major confrontation." Hope for a peaceful outcome depended on the Belgian government's declaring that it would withdraw its troops from Katanga as soon as the UN forces arrived. In reply Hammarskjöld received a message from King Baudoin saying, after a grotesque reference to the "civilizing" mission of Leopold II in the Congo, that to withdraw the Belgian troops from Katanga would only create insecurity for the Belgian population and risk chaos.

The diplomatic and political complications and risks experienced in previous operations, Hammarskjöld told Cordier in New York, had been nothing compared with this, and he sent Heinz Wieschhoff to Brussels to tell Wigny that, without some progress on Katanga, the moderate members of the Leopoldville government would vanish from the scene, and the government might resort to violent action, with appalling consequences. The UN effort would break down, and the Congolese government would look for military assistance elsewhere in order to attack Katanga, quite probably precipitating a much wider war. The only reply he got to this appeal was that Belgium was not opposed to the Security Council's decisions on Katanga as interpreted by Hammarskjöld but would make no public statement.

By August 2 Hammarskjöld decided that the situation permitted no further delay. He had just learned from Cordier in New York that Lumumba intended to sack Bomboko and Kanza and that he might well resort to an attack on the UN force. Lumumba, disappointed by his visits to Washington and Ottawa, had evidently decided to play the Soviet Union off against the UN and the West. Hammarskjöld therefore announced that he was sending Bunche to Elisabethville to ensure that there would be no resistance to the UN troops when they landed.* (Bunche had already asked Hammarskjöld to be allowed to go in the first plane to Elisabethville, "thus responding to Tshombe's invitation."42) The idea

---

*ONUC being a peacekeeping force, its soldiers were lightly armed, allowed to use their weapons only in self-defense, and carried in unprotected transport aircraft.

was that Bunche's initial talks with Tshombe and the Belgian representatives in Katanga would be followed up within twenty-four hours by the entry of UN troops.

Hammarskjöld's announcement produced a variety of unpromising reactions. Tshombe said Katanga would resist the dispatch of UN troops to Katanga with force. The Belgians said that law and order prevailed in Katanga and suggested reconstituting the Congo as a federation. Gizenga informed Hammarskjöld that he had "decided" that Bunche should be accompanied by three representatives of the Congolese government with an escort of twenty Ghanaian soldiers—a sure way of aborting the whole mission. Ignoring all this as best he could, Hammarskjöld instructed Bunche to discuss with the Belgians in Katanga the withdrawal of the Belgian troops and their replacement by the UN forces, which would maintain security and, among other things, protect the European population. He could talk to Tshombe and anyone else relevant to the problem, and might expect a disorderly welcome. If he concluded that there was a serious risk that the UN troops would be resisted by force and advised against sending them, Hammarskjöld would immediately leave for New York to request further instructions from the Security Council.

Bunche left ONUC Headquarters early on the morning of August 4, accompanied by F. T. Liu and Sture Linner, now chief of ONUC civilian operations. On the way to the airport, it occurred to him that in Elisabethville he would have to use Belgian channels to communicate with Hammarskjöld in Leopoldville. He therefore devised a simple code which he sent to Hammarskjöld in a penciled note. Abandoning his first idea, which was "Please tell Ruth" for going ahead with the entry of UN troops, and "F. T. Liu is fine" for stopping the operation, he decided on more formal phrases. "Will report soonest" would mean go ahead. "Reporting fully" would mean cancel. On the five-hour flight to Elisabethville in the UN Convair he worked on his papers and wrote to Ruth.

What awaits us we do not know. There may be hostility, of course. . . . I'm dreadfully tired and sleepy as I got less than three hours sleep last night and even that was more than the night before. I cannot begin to tell you how complicated and maddeningly frustrating our operation out here is. . . . It is like trying to give first aid to a wounded rattlesnake. How much longer we can hang on here is anybody's guess. How long I can stand this physically is still another question.[43]

At the Elisabethville airport Bunche found a surprisingly friendly reception. He was met by the chief Belgian officials, Robert de Rothschild and Count Harold d'Aspremont-Lynden, with a guard of honor and a military band. There were also, he noticed, fully equipped military units with arms at the ready, and an impressive number of oil drums to block the runways. In a note which the Convair took back to Leopoldville, he described the welcome to Hammarskjöld.

Thank heaven, *no* Tshombe. To our consternation, some Europeans were even applauding us. Rothschild said that he had *never* been so glad to see *anyone:* I think I know why. We go into meeting immediately. I am ready.[44]

In the meeting with the Belgians and with Tshombe and his "interior minister," Godefroid Munongo, all the stock bogeys of Katanga propaganda were trotted out. If the UN took over, all the Europeans would leave; economic and mining enterprises would collapse; there would be tribal warfare; scorched earth, even poisoned arrows. The UN troops should go to other parts of the Congo, where they were really needed. Tshombe and Munongo were friendly enough, but Bunche's efforts to explain the objectives of the UN in the Congo and the wider dangers of the situation were met with studied incomprehension.

Bunche had the feeling that he would eventually get Tshombe's agreement to the entry of UN troops, but after the meeting Tshombe unexpectedly announced to the press that the decision to send UN troops to Katanga had been canceled. This characteristic trick caused Bunche hastily to issue a counterstatement saying that he was reporting fully to the secretary general and had taken no decision on the entry of UN troops. His inadvertent use of the words "reporting fully" caused confusion in Leopoldville, where Hammarskjöld wondered if he was trying to send the prearranged signal for calling off the operation. Hammarskjöld's only means of communication with Bunche was to send a note by aircraft early on the morning of August 5.

As you know, cancelling of operation on your advice, if based on continuous resistance from Tshombe, would cause me to go straight to the Security Council. . . . You know, of course, that if we call off Simba [the entry of UN troops into Katanga] without recognizable and visible reason and without immediate alternative action here, I am in very deep waters.[45]

Meanwhile, early on August 5, Bunche was having another meeting with Tshombe and had still not decided whether he should call for UN troops to arrive the following day. Although he knew that the opposition of Tshombe and the Belgians contained a large element of bluff, he was apprehensive of the kind of violence that could easily be stirred up by the Katanga government's skillful propaganda and by the manipulation of the

undisguised terror and hatred which virtually the entire population of
Katanga felt for Patrice Lumumba. Nonetheless, he seemed to be making
some progress with Tshombe when de Rothschild and d'Aspremont-
Lynden burst in unannounced, and in a high state of agitation. They
demanded that Bunche go at once to the airport, where feverish preparations were being made to oppose the landing of a UN plane which was
coming to pick up Bunche and was due to land within the hour.

Bunche found the airport like an armed camp expecting an attack.
Katangese soldiers were all over the field, their weapons trained on the
runway. Belgian officers were very much in evidence. Munongo had instructed the airport commandant to block the runway and soon appeared,
wild with excitement and rage, saying that he had ordered the soldiers to
fire on the plane if it landed. Bunche refused to have the plane, which on
his instructions contained no soldiers, diverted, and managed at last to
calm Munongo down by taking him to the control tower and talking with
the pilot of the incoming plane. The plane was allowed to land, provided it
took off again immediately with Bunche on board. Munongo insisted on
going aboard to inspect it.

Fortunately he did not look closely enough, because after we took off I discovered
to my horror that, despite my explicit instructions, some fool in Leopoldville had
permitted arms to be stored on the plane and had also permitted a Ghanaian to
come aboard. Had Munongo, who was a wild man at best, known of this he would
no doubt have fired on us immediately.[46]

The experience at the airfield convinced Bunche that it was too risky
for the time being to bring in unprotected planeloads of UN troops in
uniform. He therefore sent Hammarskjöld, through Belgian channels, a
message, "Reporting fully. Rejoining Leo for purpose," and took off immediately. On receiving the message Hammarskjöld immediately left for
New York to report to the Security Council.

Bunche's decision was a gift to all critics of the UN operation, and
both the Soviet Union and the Congolese government asserted that he
had been taken in by Tshombe. The Soviets, in a memorandum to the
president of the Security Council, demanded that, if such failings continued, the present UN command in the Congo should be replaced, and
that troops should be sent who were prepared to deal with Katanga in the
right way. De Rothschild on the other hand, in a letter to Hammarskjöld,
claimed that he had calmed Munongo down before Bunche got to the
airport, that Bunche's time at the airport had been spent mostly drinking
beer and lemonade, and that the whole incident had been greatly exag-

gerated. Bunche, strongly supported by his companions, Liu and Linner, ridiculed this story, pointing out that it was de Rothschild himself, in a highly excited state, who had insisted that Bunche leave the meeting with Tshombe to deal with the situation at the airport, to calm Munongo down, and to get permission for the UN aircraft to land.[47] Gizenga also broadcast an insulting misrepresentation of Bunche's trip on August 6, to which Bunche issued a firm but civil riposte.[48]

In New York Hammarskjöld managed to get the Security Council, for the first time, to demand the immediate withdrawal of the Belgian forces from Katanga and to declare that the entry of the UN forces was "necessary," although they would not "in any way intervene in or be used to influence the outcome of any internal conflict, constitutional or otherwise."[49] To the Soviet representative, Vasily Kuznetsov, who urged that the UN troops use force, Hammarskjöld replied, "I do not believe, personally, that we help the Congolese people by actions in which Africans kill Africans, or Congolese kill Congolese."[50] In the end Kuznetsov voted for the resolution. It was the last time that the Soviets voted with the United States and the majority in the Security Council on the Congo problem, which was about to become an active issue in the Cold War.

The reaction in Leopoldville to the Security Council resolution was in no way helpful to a solution of the Katanga secession. Lumumba had returned on August 8, and he declared a state of emergency the next day. He assumed that the Council decision would give him the means to end the secession by force and announced that he would soon enter Katanga with his government.

Congolese impatience was now degenerating into a widening mistrust of the UN. There were signs of hostility to the UN force, and some of its African units were becoming restive. If the Belgians did not quickly withdraw from Katanga, Bunche told Hammarskjöld,

I foresee disintegration of [UN] force through development of hostility in populace and desertion by some units through decision of their governments to afford direct military assistance to Lumumba government.[51]

It was increasingly clear that only urgent and renewed action on Katanga would avert a shambles in the capital, and Bunche made plans for the airlifting of three battalions to Elisabethville as soon as Hammarskjöld returned. Tshombe, who was becoming increasingly uneasy, said that he wanted to discuss the entry of UN troops into Katanga with a UN representative. Hammarskjöld replied from New York that he would be coming to Elisabethville himself, although he would accept no conditions. He would arrive on August 12 with military and civilian advisers and two companies of Swedish troops. He informed Lumumba that he would go straight through Leopoldville, and there would be no question of Lumumba or any other member of the Congolese government accompanying him.

Hammarskjöld landed in Leopoldville late in the evening of August 11, intending to take off for Elisabethville early on the following day. Rightly anticipating Lumumba's anger at not being consulted or contacted, Hammarskjöld had spent much of the flight from New York composing a highly sophisticated interpretation of the Security Council's decision on Katanga. Bunche was to present this to Lumumba after Hammarskjöld had taken off for Elisabethville. Unfortunately, Hammarskjöld had written this complex and nuanced document in English, and Lumumba spoke only French. There were no professional translators in the ONUC Headquarters, and, to Hammarskjöld's vast and pungently expressed dissatisfaction, those members of the staff who spoke French all had a shot at translating the memorandum. It took until 4:00 A.M. for Hammarskjöld to be satisfied, and then other important matters relating to ONUC had to be discussed until the moment he left for the airport, so that no one, including Hammarskjöld, had any sleep.

Hammarskjöld took off at 8:00 A.M. followed by four aircraft carrying two companies of Swedish troops. He succeeded, from the cockpit of his aircraft, in arguing Tshombe out of preventing the troops from landing, and thereby opened up Katanga to the deployment of UN troops and the withdrawal of the Belgian forces. His visit was surprisingly peaceful and friendly.

Bunche, meanwhile, had to deal with Lumumba and to present Hammarskjöld's memorandum. The gist of this elaborate text was that the UN force would not be a party to, or in any way intervene in or be used to influence, the outcome of any internal conflict, constitutional or other, in the Congo. Once the Belgian troops were withdrawn from Katanga, the political and constitutional question would be a matter for negotiation between the provincial government and the central government. The UN force could not be used to coerce Tshombe. Lumumba was already furious that Hammarskjöld had gone through Leopoldville without seeing him, and the memorandum added fuel to the flames.

The two-and-one-half-hour meeting started with Lumumba's complaining bitterly that he had not been informed of either Hammarskjöld's arrival or his departure time and had therefore been unable even to meet him at the airport. This had caused many misunderstandings with the press. He then denounced the memorandum, saying that he would deal with the Katanga problem with the help of countries—presumably Ghana and Guinea—which had directly offered him assistance. Lumumba then demanded a UN plane to take his army commander, General Lundula, and some ministers to Katanga. Bunche politely but firmly told him that this would not be done, because the UN would not assist any party to gain advantage in an internal dispute, a principle which could only be changed by the Security Council. The truth, he told Lumumba, was that Hammarskjöld was achieving what the Congolese government wanted, the evacuation of Belgian troops from Katanga and the ending of external interference. Hammarskjöld was shortly returning to Leopoldville for discussions with the government, and Lumumba should study the memorandum so that that he could discuss his differences with the secretary general and, if necessary, appeal to the Security Council for a further interpretation.

Lumumba asked when the UN would get the Belgians out and why the UN was disarming the ANC. Bunche firmly denied the latter charge, and they began to discuss control of Leopoldville's Ndjili Airport, ONUC's lifeline, which Lumumba wanted to take over. After the Belgians left, Lumumba said, there was no need for UN troops to remain in Leopoldville. Bunche told Lumumba that the UN was in the Congo to give all possible help, military and civil, but it could not do this if the government persisted in misunderstandings and recriminations. The UN had already spent more on this operation than any previous effort and had got the Belgian forces out everywhere except Katanga.

Various telephones had been jangling intermittently throughout the meeting, causing Lumumba to jump from one instrument to another in an effort to find which was ringing. At this point he finally made a connection and received a call from Coquilhatville, and after ringing off he seemed calmer. Bunche urged him to talk with Hammarskjöld, and Lumumba said he too was a man of peace and wished to avoid violence or difficulties. He was afraid that the presence of the UN force would in the long run be bad for the prestige of his government, and asked Bunche to consider how the ANC could cooperate with the UN forces. Bunche agreed to consider this carefully and work something out. A meeting that had begun in rage ended with friendly reassurances all around.[52]

The mellow mood did not last. The following day Lumumba once again broadcast all of his criticisms of Hammarskjöld and demanded the withdrawal of all white UN troops from the Congo, apparently because the troops accompanying Hammarskjöld to Katanga had been Swedish.

"Les suédois," he said, *"ne sont que des belges en déguise"* ("The Swedes are only Belgians in disguise"). He also demanded that Ndjili Airport be controlled by the ANC and nonwhite UN troops. When Hammarskjöld returned to Leopoldville on August 14, Lumumba first canceled a scheduled meeting with him and then bombarded him with a series of violently critical letters, the gist of which was that the UN had failed to put its forces at his disposal for the purpose of subduing the rebel regime of Katanga.

Lumumba's rage permanently changed his relationship with Bunche. It also had practical consequences for the UN staff in the Congo. On August 17 two of Bunche's security men, delivering a letter to Lumumba, were arrested and threatened with death before being rescued. In a strong protest to Lumumba about this incident, Bunche pointed out that ONUC was in the Congo in response to Lumumba's own urgent appeal.

We therefore have the right to expect that your government protects us when we conduct affairs with it from insults such as those which have just been committed in the premises of your own residence.[53]

UN employees were assiduously detained at checkpoints and generally harassed. The situation at the airport, where Bunche had arranged a joint ANC/UN guard, was extremely tense. Sixteen Norwegian soldiers arriving on Sabena to report to ONUC were detained as "Belgians," and it took some hours to get them released.

Worst of all, Bunche himself found it increasingly hard to contact Lumumba or Bomboko. "Spirit and morale of staff are high," he cabled Hammarskjöld. "If idea behind morning 16th molestations was to intimidate us it was a dismal failure. But our respect for our 'hosts' is at an all-time low."[54] Bunche, for all his patience, had by now written off the possibility of a constructive relationship with Lumumba, whose irresponsibility and capriciousness seemed to know no bounds. He wrote to Ruth:

That madman Lumumba is recklessly on the attack now—and most viciously—against Dag and the UN—and we will probably be in for a rough time since the public will be stirred up by the radio broadcasts. It is a tragedy, but it looks as though this greatest of international efforts will be destroyed by the insane fulminations of one reckless man. We may well be washed up here in a few days. . . .[55]

Bunche was convinced that Lumumba was deliberately trying to provoke an incident over the airport and that only direct contact with him could settle the problem. UN troops had behaved with great restraint, but, in spite of all Bunche's urgings that they remain cool, tension was rising dangerously, and there was a noticeable tendency among the officers, from General von Horn down, to "rattle sabers." On August 18 Congolese soldiers forced their way aboard a UN transport plane and arrested fourteen Canadian soldiers, beating one of them unconscious. This new provocation created strong reactions among the UN troops, and Bunche issued an Order of the Day paying tribute to the forbearance of the soldiers involved.

They might so easily, and effectively, have dealt with the situation in their own way. Instead, in the interest of the United Nations, they exercised patience and restraint of the most commendable nature.[56]

This episode also caused Bunche to tell Hammarskjöld:

situation developing in such manner that we will quickly be faced with alternative of abandoning Ndjili airport altogether, thus closing it for all practical purposes, or employing force with liberal interpretation of self-defense principle, to hold it.[57]

He asked Hammarskjöld's advice and said he was trying to see Lumumba immediately about the airport crisis. A meeting was fixed for 3:00 P.M. on August 19, but ten minutes before the appointed time Bunche was informed that Lumumba was away and his deputy *chef de cabinet,* a Belgian called Grottaert, would receive him. Bunche declined this crudely insulting invitation, and in the meantime the UN military managed to persuade General Lundula to remove the ANC troops from the airport.

The tensions at the airport also precipitated a wider discussion of the nature of peacekeeping and the objectives of the UN in the Congo. Bunche had been deeply worried about both the divided loyalty and the military capacity of the Ghanaian and Sudanese UN troops at the airport. Hammarskjöld, concerned about the failure of the Ghanaian troops at Ndjili to protect incoming UN soldiers, had written to Nkrumah asking for assurances that he and the Ghanaian contingent in the Congo would give their unreserved support to ONUC. Nkrumah had replied by publishing a memorandum by his British chief of staff, General Henry Alexander, strongly criticizing the orders given to UN troops about restraining the ANC and the failure to disarm the Congolese soldiers. Alexander laid the blame squarely on the UN command, which, he said, had put Ghanaian and other UN troops in an impossible situation.

This attack went to the heart of the technique of peacekeeping of which Bunche was the main architect, and he somehow found time to write a worthy answer.* He took complete responsibility for the orders that had been given and rejected Alexander's criticisms as neither valid nor fair. ONUC was a peace force, not a fighting force, and his aim had always been to avoid UN soldiers having to shoot at the Congolese. Alexander appeared to regard the policy of shooting only in self-defense as a weakness, and he evidently didn't understand the nature of an international peace force. The UN had to have the cooperation of the Congolese government, however difficult that was to obtain, which was why Bunche had overruled Alexander on the disarming of the ANC. ONUC was not an army of occupation. If the UN force began to kill Congolese, its fate would be very quickly sealed. The lapses and mistakes of the Ghanaian troops at Ndjili Airport had nothing to do with unclear instructions. Obviously, the reorganization and disciplining of the ANC was a vital aim, and the UN was at that moment arranging for a team of Moroccan officers to undertake the task.

On August 24 Lumumba once again announced that the ANC would take over control of the airport. After consulting with von Horn, Bunche decided to protest immediately to Lumumba, whom he would inform that if the threat was carried out ONUC would suspend all its operations, military and civilian. Bunche described the ANC at the airport to Hammarskjöld.

The ANC fellows swarm; they're undisciplined and without officers; they whirl about in jeeps with machine guns mounted and cartridge belts inserted; they are drunk and excitable.[59]

Bunche told Hammarskjöld that ONUC troops would not fight to hold the airport without specific instructions from him, but, if necessary, they would fight to regain it for the evacuation of ONUC, and he was confident they could do so. Although Bunche sent him a message urging him to talk before taking military action, Lumumba again made himself unavailable.

In the event, the ANC once again took no action. "Lumumba is

---

*As he was working on this reply on August 20, Bunche received a message from Alexander, volunteering to become executive deputy to von Horn "to help restore confidence in effectiveness of UN command." In referring this message to Hammarskjöld, Bunche pronounced himself "both amazed and insulted at this approach."[58] Bunche was particularly irritated that this message had been transmitted through U.S. Ambassador Timberlake, who was a strong supporter of Alexander's ideas.

more reckless than his 'Generals.' How like Hitler!"[60] Lumumba instead
turned his attention to a "Conference of the African Countries" which
was starting the next day, and the heat was off the airport for the time
being.

   When Bunche gave the good news to the Ambassador Timberlake,
the following dialogue, which Bunche reported to Hammarskjöld, ensued:

Bunche: The heat is off Ndjili, at least for the moment.
Timberlake: Ugh. Why don't you do something to end the G-D blockade
            of the ferry? No pouches, etc.
Bunche: Perhaps the embassies might protest.
Timberlake: What good would it do? You will just *have* to take over the
            force publique [ANC].
Bunche: On what authority?
Timberlake: Just *take* it because you have to.
Bunche: I haven't heard [Henry Cabot] Lodge say anything like that
        in the Security Council.
Timberlake: No, of course not.
Bunche: I hear Czech Airlines have an agreement to run in here.
Timberlake: Yes, right under the UN guns.[61]

   Bunche was now within a few days of leaving Leopoldville. Hammarskjöld had announced on August 21 that Rajeshwar Dayal of India
would take Bunche's place at the end of the month, and for Bunche it was
not a moment too soon. He had come out for a few weeks and had stayed
more than two months. He was exhausted by the unending crisis, which
he described well in a letter to Andrew Cordier, Hammarskjöld's executive assistant, whom he reminded that he had to be home by the end
of August to take Ralph Jr. to visit colleges, which he was determined to
do.

There is never a morning that does not begin without some new excitement—
bayonetted Congolese at the door, trouble at the airport, UN staff arrested, a
complaint also coupled with a new threat from the Prime—or Vice–Prime Minister, the military boys wanting to start shooting etc., etc. The morning starts
always this way and the day continues the same way, virtually, until the next
morning. . . . Yesterday was about the quietest day in some time—we had only
about three tough letters from Lumumba to answer, the commentaries on the Sec
Gen's speech and the Alexander report to do, the mob to disperse in front of the
French Embassy and the case of M. Dieu [a Sabena official who had to be rescued
from prison], and the assault upon and attempted rape of Bob West's wife. We
got to bed early—about 3A.M. . . .

Under this relentless regime Bunche's health had deteriorated. He had lost his appetite, and the varicose ulcer on his leg had become dangerously aggravated. But the factor that weighed most heavily on him was the collapse of his relationship with Lumumba, which, especially in times of crisis, constituted a grave weakness for ONUC. He wrote to Ruth:

The weather begins to get hotter now. Soon it will be steaming. Lumumba gets worse and worse. He is the *lowest* man I have ever encountered. I despise Gizenga, but I hate Lumumba.[62]

With the arrival of the African conference representatives, virtually all of whom urged Lumumba to cooperate with the UN,* the situation in Leopoldville quieted down. Bunche was concerned with finalizing plans for the evacuation of Belgian troops from Katanga in the face of endless prevarications and delays. There was also a new and terrible development, the massacre of the Kasai province's most prosperous tribe, the Baluba, by ANC troops that Lumumba had flown to Kasai in Soviet planes for a future assault on Katanga.

Lumumba visited Stanleyville, his political and tribal base, on August 27, and trouble followed him. By an unfortunate coincidence, an American Globemaster transport carrying Canadian UN soldiers landed at the Stanleyville airport just before Lumumba was expected. There was a large crowd awaiting the prime minister, and, apparently because of a rumor that the Canadians were Belgian parachutists, Congolese police and soldiers attacked and beat the Canadians and the American crew as they deplaned. They were eventually rescued by Ethiopian UN soldiers. The ANC also went on a rampage in the town, invading the UN headquarters. Bunche protested strongly to Bomboko about this outrage, and both General Lundula and Colonel Mobutu apologized and visited the injured in hospital.

Bunche was especially concerned that this incident—the result of the prevailing fear, rumor, and hysteria—would cause a strong reaction among the UN soldiers. The wounded, including six stretcher cases, were flown to Leopoldville on August 28, and the scene was grim.

Military fingers are itching for triggers and civilians would like to have guns. Carl [von Horn] went to airport tonight wearing a sidearm, ready to be "first to shoot." We are moving inexorably toward a clash of arms for simple reason that patience wears thin in face of repeated provocations and of arrogant savagery.[63]

*The only way these delegates could reach Leopoldville was in UN planes, which shuttled them in from Brazzaville.

Nor were some civilians less militant.

Timberlake wild, with loose talk about "closing" US Embassy, "pulling out," no more dollars, and "I told you that you should take over the Force Publique whether or not the government agrees."[64]

Hammarskjöld commented,

Tell everyone to take it easy. Justice will be established in due time.[65]

Andy Cordier arrived from New York on August 28 to hold the fort for a few days until Dayal's arrival. He had arrived at a turning point at which both internal Congolese rivalries and the external East-West struggle over the Congo were reaching a new pitch. When Bunche took Cordier to meet President Kasavubu on August 29, the president and Bomboko were openly critical of Lumumba and the anti-UN campaign, saying the country and its people desperately needed, and wanted, ONUC. Lumumba had recently received a highly visible token of Soviet support in the form of ten Ilyushin-24 transports to carry the pro-Lumumba elements of the ANC. In the outside world also, the Soviet campaign against Hammarskjöld and his representatives in the Congo intensified, soon to reach its peak in Khrushchev's shoe-banging assault on the UN Congo operation in the General Assembly and his strident demand that Hammarskjöld resign. As Bunche left Leopoldville the Congo crisis was moving toward an open and violent confrontation between the factions—a struggle which was mirrored in the Cold War confrontation outside.

In talking to the press on the day of his departure from Leopoldville, Bunche did not speculate on the imminent change in the situation. The operation had put unprecedented demands on patience, understanding, and restraint, "and nowhere have international people responded so well as here." The UN force in the Congo had reached the figure of sixteen thousand, and the last Belgian combat troops were expected to leave that very day. Bunche spoke of the suspicions and misunderstandings which ran deep in the Congo, "a heritage of the past as a colonial state." Nothing like enough had yet been done, and there were many diversions and distractions which must cease before the full dividend could be realized "on the almost miraculous investment that is being made by the world community for the benefit of the people and government of this country."[66] On his return to New York Bunche called the Congo operation "the most challenging and inspiring mission I have ever had."[67]

Within days of Bunche's departure it became clear that the UN effort might not be enough to save the Congo from disaster. On September 6 the Kasavubu-Lumumba government finally broke up, each leader denouncing the other and claiming power. A week later Colonel Joseph Mobutu took over the government with a "Council of Technicians." Mobutu was backed by the West, and Lumumba by the East, while Hammarskjöld and his representatives in the Congo were doubtful of the legality of either. The Congo scene was about to go very quickly from knockabout *opéra bouffe* to violent tragedy.

At the end of August it had still seemed possible that ONUC, with the Belgian forces out at last, might be able to proceed with its task of building up sound government and administration, training the ANC, and resolving peacefully the problem of the secessionist movements in Kasai and Katanga. The formal breakdown of the Kasavubu-Lumumba government, and Cold War partisanship in the UN, effectively put an end to this dream.*

When Bunche briefed Rajeshwar Dayal in New York on his future duties, Dayal was shocked at his physical appearance. "He was obviously very tired and he looked much older."[68] In setting up and running ONUC, the largest and most complex UN peacekeeping and civilian operation, Bunche had discharged an almost impossible task with extraordinary determination and compassion, under a barrage of criticism and second-guessing from many quarters. He had been working in a chaotic situation with an improvised organization and a completely inexperienced government. Those of us who worked closely with him in the Congo came away with greater respect and affection for him than ever.

In the Congo Bunche had also had to defend, and to maintain in action, the basic principle of UN peacekeeping—maintaining peace without using force or taking sides. He had done this in the face of opposition from his own military and from Western representatives, including the United States, knowing very well that any other course would certainly have landed the UN in a bloody debacle which would have quickly put an end to the whole operation.

The Congo crisis also touched directly on an older and deeper part of Bunche's experience, decolonization. Bunche's early career in the State Department and the United Nations had been centered on decolonization and trusteeship. He had done as much as anyone to make these concepts a reality. Decolonization, which in 1945 had been comfortably assumed to be a process that might take seventy or a hundred years, was,

---

*Already on July 23 Hammarskjöld had cabled to Bunche, "If Cold War settles in Congo our whole effort is lost."

by 1960, well on the way to fulfillment.

The Congo provided, in the acutest possible form, a lesson in the practical problems of decolonization in the Cold War context of the 1960s. Bunche had always worked for the earliest possible achievement of independence from colonial rule, believing that only after independence could a country and its people mature and develop. "No nation is ever ready for independence . . ." he wrote in 1961. "How many Western states, including the USA, really were ready at the time of independence? It took the struggle for independence to begin our national unity. . . ."[69] In the Congo, lack of preparation for self-government and the Cold War competition for the fealty and control of new African states combined, as they did later in Angola and Mozambique, to turn independence into a nightmare. Had the Security Council been united, much could have been done to mitigate the crisis of Congolese independence and to lead the Congolese toward a peaceful future. As it was, the unanticipated embroilment in the Congo split the United Nations itself down the middle.

23

The Loss of Hammarskjöld

Great Wisdom, Rare Courage

Bunche returned to New York in time for one of the greatest circuses in UN history. The General Assembly's 1960 session reflected a radically changing world, led by a cast of powerful and charismatic leaders—among them, Eisenhower, Khrushchev, Macmillan, Nehru, Tito, Sukarno, King Hussein of Jordan, Nasser, Nkrumah, Castro, and Sékou Touré of Guinea. The Congo crisis, dramatizing as it did the antagonisms of the different groups, was a central theme of the debate. It symbolized the vast difficulties of recently liberated colonies, the Cold War competition for their loyalty, and the irresistible temptation for small and weak countries to try to manipulate the Cold War to their own advantage. The Congo problem was also a major test of the authority and independence of the secretary general and the UN Secretariat.

The years of the Cold War had hardened Bunche and Hammarskjöld to Soviet rhetoric and intransigence as well as to Western reactions to it. The machinations of some of the newly independent leaders, whose cause they had so ardently championed, were a new tribulation. The activities of the Ghanaian leader, Kwame Nkrumah, who saw himself as the arbiter of all African affairs, particularly distressed Hammarskjöld. "Nkrumah's performance was nauseating and the Ghana-led Soviet ovation even more so," Hammarskjöld noted to Bunche during an Assembly meeting. And again,

Where is the limit between misinformation, bad faith, stupidity and power hunger? All these gibes at the West and no hint of a Soviet problem! Dag.

Bunche wrote back,

He is, after all, an out and out racialist and an unprincipled demagogue with an insatiable lust for prestige and power in Africa—his dream. To realize this dream he will stop at nothing. Ralph.[1]

It was a bitter season all around. The Belgian government delivered a strong official protest at public remarks by Bunche ascribing the Congo tragedy to Belgium's total failure to prepare the Congolese for independence. Hammarskjöld replied that responsible officials had a perfect right to state their opinions, particularly when those opinions were grounded in fact.[2] The strongest attacks came from the Soviet Union. Soviet opposition to Hammarskjöld's policies and actions had now developed into a full-scale attack on Hammarskjöld himself and on the office of the secretary general. Valerian Zorin, a notorious Soviet hatchet man, had replaced the moderate Vasily Kuznetsov as ambassador to the UN, and the attacks plumbed new depths of insult and abuse, to which Hammarskjöld replied in measured but increasingly tough terms. Bunche was in no doubt of the reasons for Soviet rage:

The ferocity of the attacks on the UN may be traced to the fact that the United Nations moved too fast and too well in the Congo and got in someone's way. Something was thwarted there.[3]

The arrival of Khrushchev himself in New York took the dispute to a new level of banality. Although the African countries, by and large, still supported the Congo operation, Khrushchev violently attacked the actions of "colonialists" in the Congo. "It is deplorable," he told the Assembly, "that they have been doing their dirty work in the Congo through the Secretary-General and his staff. . . ."[4] Khrushchev proposed that the office of secretary general be replaced by a "troika" representing the Western powers, the socialist states, and the neutralist countries.

In early October Khrushchev went to new lengths by demanding, in a highly insulting speech, that Hammarskjöld resign. Hammarskjöld dictated his reply before meeting Bunche and Cordier for lunch to discuss it. He asked them to comment only on the style, and the speech remained as he had originally dictated it. It provided a memorable and dramatic occasion, which brought the Assembly, except for the socialist bloc, to its feet in a long, standing ovation. Hammarskjöld concluded:

The representative of the Soviet Union spoke of courage. It is very easy to resign; it is not so easy to stay on. It is very easy to bow to the wish of a big power. It is another matter to resist. As is well known to all Members of this Assembly, I have done so before on many occasions and in many directions. If it is the wish of those nations who see in the Organization their best protection in the present world, I shall now do so again.[5]

Hammarskjöld, who was no orator, was acutely embarrassed by applause. In his postspeech discomfort, he sent a note to Bunche, who was sitting in the Assembly Hall, "Did I read it all right?," to which Bunche replied:

Perfectly. The voice was the most resonant I have ever heard from you; the pace was measured and the enunciation crystal clear—all of which did full justice to the superb text. Thus the greatest—and most spontaneous—demonstration in UN annals. Congratulations. R.[6]

The public fireworks were only a distraction from the unrelenting labor of backing up the crisis-ridden operation in the Congo. Bunche's successor, Rajeshwar Dayal, had arrived in the country at the point where Kasavubu and Lumumba had split, Mobutu had taken over, and there was no strictly legitimate government in the Congo. In maintaining, with Hammarskjöld's full approval, a correct constitutional position by refusing formally to recognize Mobutu's government, Dayal fell out with Mobutu and Kasavubu and infuriated the Americans and British as well.[7] In November, after an acrimonious debate, the Assembly recognized, by a slim majority and under strong American pressure, Kasavubu's and Mobutu's right to the Congolese seat in the Assembly. This development caused Lumumba to leave his ONUC-protected residence in Leopoldville to drum up support elsewhere in the Congo. Mobutu's troops caught and arrested him at Mweka in Kasai province on December 2. Lumumba's arrest opened a new and tragic chapter in the Congo story.

After Lumumba's arrest and reports of his brutal treatment by Mobutu's soldiers, Hammarskjöld tried vainly, through his representatives in the Congo and by appeals to Kasavubu, to save him. In January 1961, it was reported that Lumumba had been taken to Katanga. Hammarskjöld again appealed to Kasavubu to have Lumumba brought back to Leopoldville in decent conditions to answer the charges against him in an equitable legal process. He also demanded, through his representative in Elisabethville, that Lumumba should be treated humanely. Hammarskjöld's appeals were ignored, and the Soviet Union even accused him of complicity in Lumumba's transfer to Katanga. The matter became a *cause célèbre,* and Indonesia, Morocco, and Egypt withdrew their contingents from ONUC in protest, while Nehru criticized Hammarskjöld for his "passivity."

Much worse was soon to follow. Fears over Lumumba's fate came to a head in mid-February, when Munongo, the Katangese "minister of the interior," after a series of sickeningly mendacious descriptions of Lumumba's "escape," announced on February 13 that Lumumba and his companions had been massacred by the inhabitants of an unnamed village. The worldwide uproar which greeted this news was echoed in a violent riot in the Security Council public gallery, where demonstrators battled with the UN guards and hurled abuse at Hammarskjöld and Adlai Stevenson, the United States representative.

Many of the rioters were Black Americans, which evoked a statement from the executive secretary of the NAACP, Bunche's friend Roy Wilkins, that Black Americans were both shocked and horrified at Lumumba's murder and confused by the fantastic complications of the Congo situation. Rejecting the impression given by the press that "American Negroes" had been responsible for the Security Council riot, he said that "obviously this raucous handful cannot be said to represent either the sentiment or the tactics of American Negroes." Bunche, who was reported to have said that the demonstrators were dupes misled by propaganda and by demagogues, endorsed Wilkins' statement. This led to a flurry of angry letters from across the country accusing Bunche of betraying his fellow Black Americans and of helping the white man to keep his hold on the Congo. Bunche encountered, in a demonstration outside the the UN building, a black man carrying a sign reading "Kill Bunche." He asked the man who this Bunche was and received the reply, "I guess he's some joker in the UN." Bunche was saddened and disgusted by the squalid tragedy of Lumumba's death. He had come to distrust and dislike Lumumba, but his murder in Katanga was an unforgivable crime, as well as being a major setback for the United Nations.

The situation gradually cooled down, but events in the Congo kept Bunche and Hammarskjöld fully occupied. In March the Congolese army drove UN Sudanese troops out of the port of Matadi. In April Moise Tshombe, attending a meeting of Congolese leaders in Coquilhatville on the Congo River, was arrested by Mobutu's government, giving rise to another crisis which lasted until June, when he was released. In May Rajeshwar Dayal, with whom Mobutu and Kasavubu refused to deal, resigned. In June there was, at last, a positive development when President Kasavubu asked for UN assistance in reconvening the Congolese Parliament so that a constitutionally legitimate government could be chosen.

The business of directing the Congo operation in a round-the-clock

exchange of cables and directives on political, military, and civil administration questions was managed by Hammarskjöld with a group of senior
officials known as the "Congo Club." Bunche was the ranking member of
this group, which met each evening after the regular business of the day
was done and frequently sat into the early hours of the next morning.
Because three of its principal members—Bunche, Cordier, and Harry
Labouisse—were American, the "Congo Club" became a favorite target
of Soviet abuse.

In December 1960, after Kennedy's election, Bunche had been approached by a member of the new president's staff about a post in the
administration. "I told him that I have a job and am seeking no other
since I am happy in what I am now doing."[8] The only concrete result of
Kennedy's approach was a new FBI investigation of Bunche's record.
Bunche later also discouraged efforts to adopt him as a candidate for the
Democratic nomination for senator from New York. "I have no political
ambitions and in my sixteen years of service in the Secretariat I have
scrupulously avoided all partisan political activity."[9]

Nonetheless, on June 27 Bunche submitted a formal letter of resignation. He told Hammarskjöld that he had always intended to leave before
reaching the retirement age of sixty (Bunche was then fifty-eight).

Considering it advisable at this time, for reasons both official and personal, to
make that intention a matter of formal record, I submit to you herewith my
resignation from the United Nations Secretariat. . . . I take this step for reasons
which are largely private and which merit no recital here, although lately, as you
know, I have become increasingly unhappy about some developments in the
United Nations—particularly the reckless assaults upon you, your office and your
staff, here and in the Congo.

He ended the letter with a tribute to Hammarskjöld's "totally dedicated
leadership" and "impeccable integrity. It is very good, indeed, to be
among your trusted lieutenants, and better still to be your friend."[10] Hammarskjöld immediately appealed to Bunche "not to do this to me now,"[11]
and Bunche dropped the matter, though not before the White House
again inquired, on behalf of President Kennedy, about his availability for a
post in Washington if he left the UN.

It is not entirely clear what caused Bunche to submit his resignation
at this time, although the phrase "to make that intention a matter of
formal record" indicated that he did not intend to push it or expect it to
be accepted. He was certainly bothered, in the light of the violent Soviet
campaign against Hammarskjöld, that the three top officials dealing with

the Congo—himself, Andrew Cordier, and Harry Labouisse—were all American and that this laid Hammarskjöld open to Soviet attacks. In March, in an attempt to correct this imbalance, Hammarskjöld had added three Africans to the Congo team—Robert Gardiner of Ghana, Francis Nwokedi of Nigeria, and Taieb Sahbani of Tunisia. At exactly this time Hammarskjöld was also moving Cordier out of his executive office, and Bunche may well have felt that Hammarskjöld should be free to move him out as well, not least out of fairness to Cordier, his friend and colleague since 1945.

Another reason for wanting to leave the UN was certainly Bunche's longing to take a much fuller part in the growing civil-rights movement in the United States. His health, which had still not fully recovered from his stint in Leopoldville the year before, was also a major preoccupation. In the end, however, his loyalty to, and friendship for Hammarskjöld were overriding, and after Hammarskjöld's appeal there was no question of persisting in his resignation.

The summer of 1961 was a time of severe tribulation for Hammarskjöld and his staff. Apart from the constant strain of the Congo involvement, both the Soviet boycott of the secretary general and the persistent public campaign in the West against his policy in Katanga—especially from the far right in the United States and Europe—were vastly debilitating. There was also a new tendency to question Hammarskjöld's activities in all kinds of other matters, including the administration of the United Nations. In July, by championing Tunisia's cause when French troops, in a brief but bloody action, reoccupied the port of Bizerte, Hammarskjöld also broke with another important UN member, the France of Charles de Gaulle. Hammarskjöld certainly needed all the help and support he could get.

In August the Congolese Parliament, meeting under UN protection on the premises of the University of Lovanium, outside Leopoldville, unanimously approved a government of national unity headed by the moderate Cyrille Adoula, with Antoine Gizenga as vice–prime minister.* With a legitimate and sensible government in Leopoldville at long last, it seemed possible that the UN's troubles in the Congo might soon be over. On August 24 the new government issued an ordinance expelling foreign mercenaries,† the backbone of Tshombe's secessionist army, and asked for

---

*Gizenga remained in Stanleyville and played little part in the Adoula government.

†The mercenaries in Katanga, mostly white ex-soldiers in search of trouble for profit, came from South Africa, Rhodesia, Britain, France, and Belgium.

ONUC's assistance for this purpose. The Security Council had already ruled on the illegality of the mercenaries, and on August 28 ONUC successfully and peacefully rounded up many of them in Elisabethville. A first, and positive, step seemed to have been taken toward resolving the problem of the Katanga secession.

Hammarskjöld was determined that the Congo, and especially the Katanga problem, should not blight the forthcoming session of the General Assembly as it had almost destroyed the previous session. He therefore decided to accept Adoula's invitation to visit Leopoldville. He intended to use the visit to bring Adoula and Tshombe together to resolve their differences.

Bunche and Ruth were taking Ralph Jr. back to Colby College in Maine for the fall semester and were intending to drive on to Quebec for a short vacation, when a call came from Hammarskjöld telling Bunche that he had decided to go to the Congo and wished Bunche to go with him. Bunche returned immediately to New York, where he learned that Hammarskjöld, on reflection, had decided that Bunche should hold the fort in New York and that Heinz Wieschhoff would go to the Congo in his place. When Bunche arrived at the airport to see the secretary general's party off on the night of September 12, Wieschhoff's wife, Virginia, told him of her concern for her husband, who was sick and had a high fever. Bunche immediately volunteered to take his place, but before he could speak to Hammarskjöld, Wieschhoff, who had guessed his intention, assured him that he was recovering and begged him to desist. Bunche reluctantly agreed and stayed in New York.

Departing for the Congo, Hammarskjöld was in a more cheerful frame of mind than he had been for some time. He believed that by getting Adoula and Tshombe together he could make substantial progress on the Katanga problem and so take the first steps to phase out the military component of ONUC. Unfortunately, while Hammarskjöld was in the air on his way to Africa, the UN command in Elisabethville initiated a new move to round up the European mercenaries who had slipped through the net on August 28. The action went disastrously wrong and degenerated into a squalid battle in and around Elisabethville. Thus, when Hammarskjöld, whose first inkling of this development came from a press report during a fueling stop in Accra, arrived in Leopoldville, his first task was no longer to bring Tshombe and Adoula together, but to put a stop to a losing battle in Katanga which was about to cost the UN Congo operation the support of its most important backers.

Washington, where there was a considerable pro-Tshombe faction led by Senator Thomas Dodd of Connecticut, was especially incensed that there had been no warning and no consultation about the new Elisabethville military operation in which the peacekeeping troops were actually using their weapons. On September 14 Bunche talked with Dean Rusk, who was now secretary of state. Rusk had just discussed the Katanga situation with President Kennedy. "His upset tone," Bunche cabled Hammarskjöld, "was clearly reflecting White House alarm."[12] Rusk had asked Bunche to convey his reactions urgently to Hammarskjöld, "which are the following five points, each of which I tried rather vainly, I fear, to counter with facts and reason." Kennedy and Rusk were "extremely upset" that the UN had taken action in Katanga without consulting Washington, which was a major supporter of the UN in the Congo, and the British were "equally upset." The main cause of the U.S. concern was that Adoula's government had nominated Egide Bocheley-Davidson, a pro-Gizenga leftist, as its *commissaire d'etat extraordinaire,* ostensibly to take over from Tshombe in Katanga. Rusk told Bunche that, "if the UN operation in the Congo led to communist control, the Congressional reaction would send Dean back to 'cotton-picking in Georgia.' " Rusk urged that Hammarskjöld should do everything possible to bring Adoula and Tshombe together to agree on some kind of federation or confederation and warned sternly that he would lose U.S. support if the Gizenga line dominated in the Congo. "I anticipate your reaction," Bunche told Hammarskjöld, "and I share it. But they *are* excited in Washington and badly informed."

"What a page in UN history," Hammarskjöld replied.[13] He was particularly incensed that Rusk seemed to be defending the foreign mercenaries, who had been rounded up under a Security Council resolution for which the United States had voted. He asked rhetorically, "what have our critics done in order to bring Mr. Tshombe to his senses?," and added:

it is better for the UN to lose the support of the US because it is faithful to law and principles than to survive as an agent whose activities are geared to political purposes never avowed or laid down by the major organs of the UN.

A UN failure in Katanga would be a major success for Gizenga, whereas a UN success there would end his possibility to gain power. Hammarskjöld urged that the major powers should not react until they knew the facts, and should stick to principles rather than expecting others to break them on their behalf or on behalf of the Welenskys.* Translating into proper language, you may bring these reactions to the notice of Dean Rusk.

Hammarskjöld's message, as interpreted to Rusk by Bunche, had the desired effect. Rusk, Bunche reported the next day, was "much calmer and accepted admonitions in good spirit. He only reiterated hope that UN could bring Adoula and Tshombe together." This had been Hammarskjöld's primary objective in going to the Congo, but before he could attempt it he had to put an end to the fighting in Katanga and to extricate the ONUC forces in Katanga from an impossible situation which was due, at least in part, to their own misjudgment and incompetence.[14]

Bunche's problems with his own compatriots were not yet over. On September 16 he sent a top-secret cable to Hammarskjöld with the opening words "I used this classification primarily because I am ashamed for many eyes to see the substance of this message. I need make no other comment."[15] Bunche was reporting on a talk with Harlan Cleveland, assistant secretary of state for international-organization affairs in Washington, concerning a UN request for U.S. Globemaster troop-transport aircraft, which, according to Cleveland, had run into "a great deal of static." Bunche had particularly objected to Rusk's reported remark that the "real purpose should now be to get fighting stopped and not increase it." Here Bunche added an exclamation mark in brackets. Bunche's objection had provoked a tirade from Cleveland about "gross miscalculation" by UN people in Katanga. To Cleveland's suggestion that Hammarskjöld stay on in the Congo despite the opening session of the General Assembly, Bunche had "expressed confidence that SecGen's independent judgment on this matter would be sound."

Hammarskjöld's reaction to all this was, "waste of time to make comments."[16] He felt that Washington was motivated partly by ignorance of the real situation and partly by a deliberate ignoring of the principles of UN action. Adoula was under strong pressure to send the Congolese army into Katanga and had to be helped to resist that pressure. Tshombe had to be freed from the foreign supporters of Katangese secession, and his army from foreign control, so that he could get together with Adoula. Hammarskjöld was determined to "bring the problem closer to local realities."

To achieve this goal, to silence the increasing chorus of criticism in Western countries which were paying for the Congo operation, and to

*Sir Roy Welensky was prime minister of Northern Rhodesia and a strong supporter of Tshombe.

bring an end to the fighting in Katanga, Hammarskjöld decided, on what was to be the last day of his life, that he himself would meet with Tshombe at Ndola, Northern Rhodesia, on September 18, and, if possible, bring him back to Leopoldville to talk to Adoula. Ignoring efforts by Adoula and others to dissuade him, he and his party took off for Ndola in a UN DC-6 from Leopoldville's Ndjili Airport at 4:30 P.M. on Sunday, September 17.

In the small hours of Monday morning, September 18, Bunche received a telex from Sture Linner, the officer-in-charge in Leopoldville, informing him that Hammarskjöld's plane was missing. He called his staff into the office, and an agonizing period of waiting ensued, until, just before noon, Linner confirmed that the wreckage of Hammarskjöld's plane had been sighted from the air by Colonel Ben Matlick of the U.S. Air Force less than ten miles from the Ndola airport. There was no sign of survivors.

For everyone who had worked with Hammarskjöld, and for the UN itself, his death was a shattering blow. For Bunche it was also the loss of a close friend whom he had admired and respected above all others. As he had done after the murder of Folke Bernadotte in Jerusalem exactly thirteen years before, Bunche took refuge from grief in his work, in carrying on with the task that Hammarskjöld had set, and in maintaining the morale of his colleagues. Although Hammarskjöld's death shocked many of the critics of ONUC into sudden and far more active support of the operation, there was still a great deal to be done. In addition, the gap left by the loss of Hammarskjöld's dynamic leadership had to be temporarily filled until a successor was appointed.*

The crash of Hammarskjöld's aircraft, which was almost certainly due to human error, gave rise to a storm of rumors and recriminations, many centering on the Fouga Magister jet trainer which Tshombe's forces had used to harass the UN forces in Katanga.† In his shock and grief on the day of the crash, Bunche suggested to Linner that the United States might be asked to provide a squadron of jet fighters to dispose of the Fouga and to protect the U.S. transport aircraft that were belatedly being

---

*We also began to discuss the question of suitable memorials for Hammarskjöld. A memorial concert in the General Assembly Hall was quickly organized. Bunche and I also decided to ask the British sculptor Barbara Hepworth, whom Hammarskjöld greatly admired, to create a sculpture in his memory. This in due course took shape in the great *Single Form* which dominates the forecourt of the Secretariat building in New York.

†The Fouga had neither the range, the night-flying capability, nor the ground control to intercept Hammarskjöld's plane at night over Northern Rhodesia.

made available to reinforce the UN troops in Katanga. Linner suggested that, to preserve the political balance, a similar request might be made to Egypt. President Kennedy privately agreed to make eight fighter planes available, but on September 21 Sweden put four Saab jet fighters at the service of ONUC, and four Ethiopian fighters and six Indian Canberra bombers were also sent to Elisabethville, so the request for U.S. fighters was not pursued.[17]

Bunche was worried about the safety of Conor Cruise O'Brien, the UN representative in Katanga. O'Brien, a brilliant writer and Irish diplomat, had been carrying out the impossible job of UN representative in Katanga for the past three months. The fighting in Katanga in September had put him in a very difficult position, and Hammarskjöld had questioned the wisdom of some of his statements to the press, as well as some of the actions which had led to the fighting.[18] On September 22 the *New York Times* speculated that O'Brien would be replaced because of alleged dissatisfaction with his recent performance. Bunche told Linner that "this will slow up execution of any plans, as O'Brien is not to be offered as a sacrifice whether to Tshombe or to the false gods of the press." He urged Linner, however, to get O'Brien out of Elisabethville as soon as possible, "as we greatly fear that his life is actually in danger there."[19]

On September 22 Bunche exercised, for the first time, his prerogative as a Nobel Laureate to nominate someone for the Nobel Peace Prize.* In a letter to Gunnar Jahn, chairman of the Nobel committee of the Norwegian Storting (parliament), he wrote,

No nomination, I am certain, has ever been more natural or clear, for Mr. Hammarskjöld has given new meaning and dimension to dedication and effective contribution to the cause of peace through brilliant statesmanship, great wisdom and rare courage.[21]

On October 23 the award of the Nobel Peace Prize to Hammarskjöld was announced in Oslo. Bunche noted that he was not surprised and commented,

it is saddening that it is only in death the late Secretary-General received this high honor, but he would never have permitted his name to be considered for the prize while serving the United Nations.[22]

*Bunche had resisted pressure to nominate Trygve Lie for the Nobel Peace Prize on the grounds that Lie was his boss and it would therefore be inappropriate. In March 1955 he had been urged to nominate President Vincent Auriol of France. "Most embarrassing," he noted, "for I know not what the hell Auriol has done to deserve it."[20] He later nominated U Thant, and also Galo Plaza Lasso for his work as mediator in Cyprus.

Bunche was no doubt recalling his own hesitation about accepting the prize, Trygve Lie's insistence that he do so, and Hammarskjöld's later comments on the story.

The identification of the remains of the crash victims had been a long and complex process, and the coffins were only flown home to their various destinations on September 28. Bunche went to Sweden, a country in full mourning, to attend Hammarskjöld's funeral at Uppsala on September 29. Before returning to New York, and accompanied by Estelle Bernadotte, he payed his respects also at Folke Bernadotte's grave. Both his Swedish friends had died on September 17, and, but for last-minute developments, Bunche would have accompanied each of them on their final journey. He returned to New York in time to attend, on October 1, the funeral of Heinz Wieschhoff, with whom he had worked since the wartime years in the OSS, and whose place on Hammarskjöld's plane he had offered to take three weeks before.

The death of Hammarskjöld and his companions was a wrenching personal tragedy for Bunche, but his own feelings were never allowed to interfere with his duty as he saw it. He was already wary of the possible repercussions of Hammarskjöld's death on the volatile and violent situation in Katanga. On September 20 he asked General Sean McKeown, the new UN commander in the Congo, for his views on the likelihood that Tshombe would use the uneasy cease-fire that had followed Hammarskjöld's death to build up his military strength with a view to attacking the UN troops. McKeown acknowledged that this was all too possible and asked for armored personnel carriers, armored cars, and light tanks to strengthen the UN forces in Katanga. Within two months Bunche's apprehensions were amply justified.

24

U Thant and the End of the Katanga Secession

I've Done Something for Dag Now

On November 3, 1961, the General Assembly appointed, to serve out Hammarskjöld's term of office, the man with whom Bunche would work closely for the rest of his life. U Thant, the permanent representative of Burma to the United Nations, was one of two people—the other being Mongi Slim of Tunisia—whom Hammarskjöld himself had thought of as possible successors.

U Thant was in almost every way the opposite of Hammarskjöld. He was simple and direct where Hammarskjöld was complicated and nuanced; a man of few words where Hammarskjöld was immensely articulate; a devout conventional Buddhist where Hammarskjöld was inclined to a personal brand of mysticism; a man of imperturbable calm where Hammarskjöld could be highly emotional about his work; a modest and unpretentious middlebrow where Hammarskjöld was unapologetically intellectual; a taker of advice where Hammarskjöld almost invariably had—and stuck to—his own opinion. However, U Thant and Hammarskjöld shared two most essential qualities—courage and integrity.

During the choosing of Hammarskjöld's successor, the Soviet Union, realizing that Khrushchev's "troika"—a three-person secretary general—would never be accepted, had tried to impose on the incoming secretary general a modified troika—a group of undersecretaries representing the three main political divisions of the world to serve as his principal advisers. U Thant persistently refused to accept any such control or restraint, and since, in the meantime, two Americans, Bunche and Andrew Cordier, would have continued to run the Secretariat, the Soviets finally accepted U Thant's nomination to serve out the remaining year and a half of

Hammarskjöld's term. It soon became clear that U Thant would rely on Bunche to continue as his right-hand man. U Thant wrote in his memoirs:

Bunche was an international civil servant in the true sense of the word, and I cannot think of anyone in the operational arm of the Secretariat dealing with political matters who was less nationalistic in his concept and in his approach to problems.[1]

During October it had been agreed that O'Brien should leave Katanga to join the Secretariat in New York, and I, who had been Bunche's chief assistant since 1954, was sent to the Congo to take his place in Elisabethville. After Hammarskjöld's death and the debacle in Elisabethville, the UN's situation in the Congo was not encouraging. The UN military command, in both Leopoldville and Elisabethville, was weak and confused, and the morale and discipline of the peacekeeping troops was uneven and in many cases poor.

In Katanga, Tshombe, his ministers, his mercenaries, and his soldiers believed that they had scored both a military and a moral victory in September, and were encouraged in this belief by their vocal and well-financed lobby in the United States and Europe. They apparently felt that with one more effort they could push the UN out of Katanga altogether. They were spoiling for trouble.

On November 24 1961 the Security Council, exasperated at the lack of progress over the Katanga problem, adopted a resolution denouncing Tshombe's secession and authorizing ONUC to use force to eliminate the foreign mercenaries.[2] This decision, amplified through Tshombe's propaganda apparatus with its habitual calls for scorched earth and poisoned arrows, had a galvanizing effect on the situation in Katanga. Tshombe's soldiers began to harass UN troops, and on the evening of November 28, during a visit to Elisabethville of Tshombe's American patron, Senator Thomas Dodd, they kidnapped, from a dinner party in the senator's honor, the two top UN officials in Katanga, George Ivan Smith and myself. Although George was rescued before the kidnappers could get him away, and I was eventually released after being badly beaten up,* this episode created a considerable stir in the outside world and damaged Tshombe's reputation, even with his Western supporters. Tshombe grudgingly apologized, saying that "enemies of Katanga" had provoked

---

*When Bunche learned that I had been kidnapped, he refused to leave his office until he heard I had been released more or less unharmed. He then called my wife in England and my children at their various schools to prevent their being alarmed by the somewhat sensational press reports of the incident.

the incident in order to disgrace him in the eyes of Senator Dodd.

Tshombe then left for a Moral Rearmament conference in Brazil, and, with more extreme elements in charge, the situation went steadily out of control. After more attacks on UN personnel and ominous moves by Tshombe's forces, U Thant, who in his first press conference, on December 1, had called Tshombe "a very unstable man," ordered his representatives in Katanga to "act vigorously to reestablish law and order."[3] The ensuing battle between the UN and Tshombe's mercenary-led forces lasted from December 5 to 19. Twenty-one UN soldiers were killed and eighty-four wounded, and the casualties on the other side, though never properly tabulated, were certainly considerable.

During this dark period Bunche and the new secretary general unfailingly backed up the embattled forces in the field. They rallied support, including vital logistical help from Washington, dealt effectively with Tshombe's propaganda and the slanted reporting of a segment of the Western press, and kept the General Assembly and Security Council in full and firm support of the UN operation in the field. For once even the Soviets were silent.

Tshombe's people, basing themselves on the September fiasco, had made a serious underestimate of ONUC's capacity to deal with them, and after a week of fighting the end result of the battle was no longer in doubt. Elsewhere, other pressures were coming into play. President Kennedy had strongly supported U Thant and Bunche in their directives to ONUC to establish law and order in Katanga, but the UN's forceful action soon raised questions in the press and in Washington, especially from the Dodd, pro-Tshombe faction. In London, Conservative Prime Minister Harold Macmillan was caught between the Labour opposition, which demanded full support for the UN in the Congo, and his own right wing, which demanded a halt to all British support of ONUC. Meanwhile, the UN forces were about to launch a move to secure key points in Elisabethville. Although Britain was demanding an immediate cease-fire, the United States had agreed with U Thant that there could be no cease-fire until the United Nations reached its "minimum objectives."[4]

Bunche had left New York on December 7 to represent U Thant at the Tanganyika [now Tanzania] independence celebrations in Dar es Salaam. Bunche arrived in Leopoldville via Nairobi on December 12 and was greeted at the airport by Prime Minister Adoula, Foreign Mini-Minister Bomboko, and, in witness to the improvement in Congo-UN relations, a combined guard of honor of UN and Congolese soldiers. Bunche's main concern was the continuing fighting in Katanga. President Kennedy was by now feeling the heat from the right wing in the U.S. Congress and the Dodd faction, and was anxious that the fighting should give way to reconciliation as soon as possible.[5] On the evening of December 13 Kennedy himself called his ambassador in Leopoldville, Edmund Gullion. He wanted to make sure that Adoula understood the importance of early discussions with Tshombe, and that Bunche understood that the UN, having achieved its minimum objectives, should conclude its military operations as soon as Tshombe agreed to enter into serious negotiations with Adoula. After late-night meetings with Adoula and Bunche, Gullion reported that he was "relatively satisfied" that the UN would act in accordance with Kennedy's wishes.[6] Bunche was just as anxious as the president to end the fighting in Katanga. He wished, however, to be sure that this was done in such a way as to strengthen the UN position and put the maximum pressure on Tshombe to make his peace with Adoula's central government by ending the Katanga secession.

Washington had asked the French to put pressure on Tshombe, who, on December 13, appealed to Kennedy to designate a suitable intermediary to help in the negotiations with Adoula. The problem was to get both Tshombe and Adoula to agree to meet without each making conditions that were unacceptable to the other. Tshombe wanted a formal cease-fire in Katanga and negotiations under American auspices. Adoula, believing that military pressure was the only way of getting Tshombe to end the secession, was adamantly opposed to a cease-fire and wanted the United Nations to run the negotiations. To make matters more complicated, a disagreement on these matters had developed between George Ball, the U.S. undersecretary of state, and Adlai Stevenson at the United Nations, as to the American approach.[7] Ball was in favor of the United States' taking the lead in the negotiations. Stevenson felt equally strongly that the UN should do so.

In the end Kennedy advised U Thant that he was designating Ambassador Gullion as his representative to facilitate a meeting between Adoula and Tshombe, and he so informed Tshombe. U Thant then designated Bunche as *his* representative, and Bunche and Gullion divided up the tasks, each taking the ones he could most effectively perform. Gullion was to go to Elisabethville to fetch Tshombe, and Bunche would escort Adoula to the Kitona UN base near the Atlantic coast, where the talks were to be held. As regards the cease-fire, it was announced that, since Adoula would refuse to participate in the talks if there was a formal cease-fire before the talks started, the UN, having attained its objectives in

Elisabethville, would unilaterally *hold* its fire during the talks and only fire if fired on.*

Three days of tension followed for Bunche and Gullion, who had to persuade each of the two principals to arrive at Kitona at the same time and meanwhile not to say or do anything which would allow the other to back out of the talks.[8] On Monday, December 18, Gullion flew to Ndola to pick up Tshombe, and Bunche stayed in Leopoldville with Adoula, whom he brought to Kitona in a UN aircraft on December 19.

The arrangements for the meeting, in the hospital building at the Kitona base, were spartan but adequate. UN Nigerian soldiers guarded the meeting place and the participants. At their first informal meeting on the evening of December 19, Adoula and Tshombe were cool but polite, but they became positively friendly during the evening meal, and there was much laughter. At the formal meeting on December 20 they met alone. In the evening, when Bunche and Gullion were invited to join the meeting, they found a very tense atmosphere. Bunche appealed to both leaders to persevere, stressing how much was at stake and how many lives, both Congolese and UN, depended on their agreement. At midnight, however, all proposals and counterproposals seemed to have failed, the meeting broke up, and the delegations went to pack their bags. Adoula called for the UN aircraft to take him back immediately to Leopoldville.

Fortunately, there was an unavoidable delay in getting the UN plane ready. The crew had to be found, the plane prepared, and, since Kitona had no runway lights, flares had to be lit. Bunche and Gullion put this delay to good use, trying several new proposals back and forth between Adoula on the veranda and Tshombe in his room. The most important objective was to have Tshombe state clearly his renunciation of the secession. He had already stated that he accepted the *Loi Fondamentale,* the Congo's provisional constitution, but he and Adoula had been unable to agree on a joint public communiqué. Bunche and Gullion produced an eight-point declaration which Tshombe would make unilaterally, and this was finally accepted by Adoula.

In this declaration Tshombe recognized the indissolubility of the Congo under President Kasavubu as head of state. He agreed to send his representatives to the constitutional commission in Leopoldville and to allow Katangese deputies to take their seats in the Congolese Parliament. He also agreed that his military forces should become part of the Congolese army. The declaration was accompanied by a letter of understand-

*This idea was contributed by me from Elisabethville.

ing from Tshombe to Bunche, and letters from Bunche to both Tshombe and Adoula. In his letter to Bunche Tshombe said that he would have to get the authorization of the "competent authorities in Katanga" before he published the declaration, a convenient loophole of which Tshombe had availed himself on previous occasions. The reason for Tshombe's letter to Bunche was that Adoula would not accept the declaration if it included this stipulation, although Tshombe had made it clear that his declaration was without reservation. In his letters to Adoula and Tshombe Bunche had written to Adoula that "sincere," and to Tshombe that "effective," implementation of the declaration could resolve the Katanga problem at last.[9]

On this basis, and with some lightning drafting by Bunche and his assistants, the matter was soon settled, and the parties were able to leave at 3:00 A.M., after a brief meeting at which Adoula praised Tshombe for his statesmanship, reasonableness, and courage.

There was naturally much curiosity in the outside world about both the substance and the sponsorship of this brief but extraordinarily successful meeting. Bunche, who arrived back in New York on December 22, gave a full account of the episode in a press conference on the day of his return.[10] He stressed that he and Gullion had stayed away from Adoula and Tshombe at the outset to avoid any idea that they were trying to influence the talks and only took part when they were invited, because at that point the talks were collapsing. The test of the agreement would be in acts more than in words, and an early challenge would be the arrival of the Katangese deputies to take their seats in the Parliament in Leopoldville in a few days' time.

Anticipating a question already raised in insulting terms by the Soviets, Bunche referred to the unusual arrangement by which he had cooperated with the ambassador of his own country in this enterprise.

He had his instructions to follow which in no way affected me, and I had instructions to follow which in no way affected him. . . . I wish to say this: that I am more proud of one fact than anything else in my sixteen years of service with the United Nations and that is that my government at no time has ever attempted to give me any instructions or advice on anything I have had to do in the United Nations.* . . . I am a servant of the United Nations.

Referring to the Soviet ambassador's recent statement that the United States had ordered Bunche to follow Gullion's orders, a journalist asked,

*Presumably, in Bunche's mind, people like Timberlake in Leopoldville in 1960 had simply been trying, without instructions, to exert improper pressure on him.

"Have you any idea what might have led the Soviet representative to make that statement?" Bunche replied, "Not the least." As regards his and Gullion's role at Kitona,

we did try to keep them at it . . . but we did not try to sway them one way or another. We gave them such assistance as we could. We tried formulations, but always formulations which were based on positions which were being taken by the parties themselves, and this was the case with regard to the final declaration that was signed by Mr. Tshombe.

Bunche reminded the journalists that Hammarskjöld's fundamental objective had always been "to bring about peaceful reconciliation of the differences in the Congo. . . . Bear in mind that the basic purpose of Mr. Hammarskjöld's fateful trip to Ndola was to try to induce Mr. Tshombe to come to Leopoldville for this purpose." Bunche recalled his own first effort, on July 8, 1960, in Leopoldville, to dissuade Tshombe from declaring the secession of Katanga. He reflected that in the light of subsequent events, "I was pretty prophetic, more prophetic that I could have realized at that time."

The question of U Thant's re-election to a full term of his own as secretary general began to be discussed in the fall of 1962. In October Bunche noted:

Thant today informed Adlai Stevenson and [Charles] Yost [Stevenson's deputy] in my presence that his decision on his availability for reelection as Secretary-General would be much influenced by "Ralph's intentions," that is, whether "he will stay with me."[11]

On a Sunday in November, U Thant told Bunche point-blank that he must know if Bunche would stay on and stand by him, for otherwise he would not consider staying on himself.

He had many nice things to say about me as an international civil servant, the person he trusted best, etc. He explained the divided feelings he had on the subject—his wife's homesickness, his aged mother, etc., and said if he stayed it would only be to fill out a five-year term, not for another five years [i.e., to serve for five years from November 1961, when he had become acting secretary general].[12]

Bunche liked and respected U Thant, and at this time, and with only three and half years in prospect, it seems not to have occurred to him to resubmit his letter of resignation. U Thant was reappointed for a four-year term on November 30, 1962.

The Kitona agreement and the apparent ending of the Katanga secession had stirred the cobwebs in various far-right attics, and the UN, and Bunche as its main negotiator, again became targets. The egregious Congressman James B. Utt of California laboriously regurgitated the discredited story of Bunche's communist leanings and was firmly put down by Senator Jacob Javits of New York, who published in the *Congressional Record* Bunche's dismissal of Utt's "old and shopworn" charges, which had been "disposed of by the processes which our law has established."[13]

In May 1962 Bunche became sufficiently irritated by the campaign against the UN to launch a counterattack of his own on the critics from both the extreme right and the extreme left. In an address to the convention of the United Automobile Workers in Atlantic City he said:

The United Nations is not dismayed by these representations; it understands well the African proverb that corn cannot expect justice in a court whose judge is a chicken. The rightist detractors are the know-nothings, such as the John Birchers, Buckley and his *National Review,* Soldiers of the Cross, those muddled and addlepated ladies of the DAR and other lunatic fringe groups.

These groups, he said, maintained that the UN was a communist plot, whereas the communists charged that the United Nations was captive to the United States and to Western "imperialists."

The DAR ladies see the UN as a Trojan Horse in the United States and declare that the United States should get out of the UN and the UN out of the United States. You know, I am not at all unhappy about my inability to claim any ancestry with those dear ladies.[14]

These remarks, reported in the *New York Times,* evoked a furious riposte in the House of Representatives from Representative Clifford McIntire of Maine.[15]

Not altogether to Bunche's surprise, a year of shilly-shallying followed Tshombe's declaration at Kitona. Referring to the on-again-off-again contacts between Adoula and Tshombe, Bunche told Adlai Stevenson, "I think one must hold to a most cautious optimism about them, however maddening the delays and antics of both sides continue to be."[16] In July Tshombe celebrated Katanga's Independence Day with great fanfare and immediately thereafter adopted tougher tactics with the UN forces, including a new maneuver of mobilizing hundreds of women and children to harass UN roadblocks. This use of civilians created fresh problems for the UN, and even U Thant was exasperated. In a press conference on July 20 in Helsinki, he called Tshombe and his colleagues "a bunch of clowns" who could not be taken seriously in their relations either with the central Congolese government or with the United Nations. On U Thant's return to New York the first question Bunche asked him was whether he had really used that expression. "He was visibly surprised when I told him that I had. Perhaps he thought such undiplomatic language uncharacteristic of me. Perhaps it was."[17]

In August U Thant proposed a comprehensive Plan of National Reconciliation to Adoula and Tshombe, explaining that the plan was not negotiable, and must be accepted as a whole or not at all. Tshombe at first received the plan with enthusiasm, and then, as usual, began to hedge on several of its main provisions, while the relations between the UN forces and Tshombe's troops became steadily more tense.

At the end of October Bunche spent a week in Leopoldville, thereby missing all but the final days of the Cuban missile crisis.* His main purpose was to make a final attempt to get Adoula and Tshombe to focus on the Plan of National Reconciliation. On leaving Leopoldville he wrote a letter to both of them saying that if their responses were not satisfactory the plan would be abandoned and U Thant would report to the Security Council recommending that various pressures should be brought to bear on Tshombe, including economic sanctions.

During his visit Bunche also discussed with the UN command a military contingency plan, in case the Plan of National Reconciliation should fail. The first phase of this plan would be to attain freedom of movement for UN forces in and around Elisabethville and up to Kipushi, on the Rhodesian border. In the second phase the UN would move to the mining centers of Kolwezi and Jadotville and round up foreign mercenaries. A third phase would deal with mercenaries at Kaminaville. Force was to be used only in the last resort and to the minimum extent possible.

Tshombe, fully aware of this contingency plan, blamed the central government for the failure of the Plan of National Reconciliation, and also claimed that the UN was looking for a pretext to justify the use of force. Paradoxically, his own soldiers seemed to be bent on providing just such a pretext, and on December 24 they began to fire regularly at the UN troops and also shot down a UN helicopter. In the vain hope that the firing would cease, Bunche and U Thant waited until December 28 before giving the order to the UN troops to remove the Katangese soldiers and

*U Thant did not rely on Bunche's advice during the Cuban missile crisis in any case, because he refused to involve his colleagues in controversial situations in which their own governments were directly concerned.[18] He seems to have broken this rule over Vietnam.

mercenaries from the Elisabethville area and to establish complete freedom of movement for the UN in the whole of Katanga.

The UN's military situation in Elisabethville had greatly improved since the previous year. The forces in Katanga were now commanded by two formidable professionals, Major General Dewan Prem Chand, a soft-spoken and courageous Indian officer, and his operational deputy, Brigadier Reggie Noronha, a brilliant Indian cavalry officer—bold and decisive. Tshombe's mercenaries and confused gendarmerie were no match for such commanders. George Sherry, from Bunche's office in New York, was the civilian representative in Elizabethville.

Tshombe contrived—on the diplomatic front, at least—to hold things up one last time by persuading the Belgians and the British, who had large mining interests in Katanga, that if the UN moved on Kolwezi and Jadotville the mining installations in those places would be blown up and a scorched-earth policy would be put into effect throughout Katanga. The Belgian and British ambassadors implored Bunche and U Thant to hold back the UN troops, and Bunche was sufficiently impressed with their arguments to send orders to Robert Gardiner, the Ghanaian officer-in-charge in Leopoldville, to stop the UN forces from crossing the Lufira River and advancing on Jadotville until Tshombe's intentions could be clarified.

In giving these orders, Bunche reckoned without both the UN's antiquated communications system and the get-up-and-go spirit of Prem Chand and Noronha, who, finding little opposition to their advance, pressed on across the Lufira River and entered Jadotville, to the cheers of the populace and a warm welcome from the manager and staff of the Union Minière, Katanga's dominant mining enterprise. Tshombe was reported to have fled to Rhodesia. Gardiner, with some trepidation, informed Bunche of these developments on January 3, 1963.

The crossing of the Lufira River was a very considerable embarrassment for U Thant and Bunche. On December 29 Bunche had assured Dean Rusk and Adlai Stevenson that the UN's military plans were limited. The following day, however, when the UN forces had entered Kipushi, on the Rhodesian border, with no resistance, a jubilant Gardiner had told the press in Leopoldville, "we are not going to make the mistake this time of stopping short. This is going to be as decisive as we can make it." When Stevenson asked for an explanation of this statement, Bunche assured him that no further moves were contemplated for the time being, but that if U Thant made no progress with Tshombe in the next two weeks the UN would move into Jadotville and Kolwezi. The UN forces, Bunche told Stevenson, were under orders to make no further moves without U Thant's approval.[19] Bunche therefore demanded from Gardiner a frank explanation as to why U Thant's orders had been either disobeyed or ignored.

Although the UN forces in the Congo had scored a remarkable success, the outcry caused by the discrepancy between U Thant's statements and the actions of his soldiers could not be ignored. U Thant therefore announced on January 3 that Bunche was leaving that day for the Congo,

for the purpose of consultation with the officer-in-charge and the force commander on a number of matters, political, military and administrative affecting the operation in its present and future activities. The visit of Dr. Bunche has no other purpose.[20]

This bland wording, which was designed to avoid putting blame on the soldiers in the field, persuaded no one that Bunche's urgent departure was for any other purpose than to account for the breakdown of communications between the UN in New York and ONUC. Later on in the year U Thant himself admitted that this was Bunche's purpose and then buried the matter in bureaucratic prose.

After looking into the problem very thoroughly, Mr. Bunche suggested that substantial improvements should be made in ONUC's machinery for communication and coordination internally and with United Nations Headquarters, and he made a number of recommendations in that regard.[21]

Bunche knew that his colleagues in the field in Katanga were expecting a strong rebuke. He also knew that, in spite of orders from New York, they had made significant progress toward a united Congo, an objective for which he and others had been striving since the earliest days of the Congo operation, and which had cost Hammarskjöld his life. It was this aspect of the episode that would finally be remembered. There was certainly no use losing the momentum which General Prem Chand had gained for the UN. During a stopover in Rome on the way to Leopoldville, Bunche cabled U Thant, "The UN definitely has the initiative in the Congo question now and we must keep it,"[22] and he suggested that U Thant issue a statement deploring Tshombe's scorched-earth threats and warning that the UN would make every effort to prevent the application of this policy in Katanga.

In Leopoldville Bunche stressed the routine nature of his visit and admitted that there was often a problem of communication and coordination between UN Headquarters and missions in the field. He told the press that on his last visit he had discussed plans for establishing complete freedom of movement for ONUC in Katanga, and that two phases of that plan has just been carried out with great skill and courage. Recent events had fortified his confidence that with persistence and wisdom ONUC could realize its objectives of law, order, and peace in a fully unified Congo, with all mercenaries eliminated.

One person who was not looking forward to Bunche's visit was the UN commander in Katanga. Prem Chand did not know Bunche well and realized that his lightning advance to Jadotville had caused a considerable row in New York. When Bunche arrived in Elisabethville, however, he went out of his way to put Prem Chand at his ease, and asked if he might stay in the general's house instead of in a hotel. Prem Chand was alarmed when Bunche handed him a letter from U Thant. Bunche, sensing his anxiety, reached into his other pocket and handed him a suggested reply to the secretary general's letter. To Prem Chand's astonishment, the draft described with uncanny accuracy the sequence of events and the military considerations which had caused his troops to arrive in Jadotville before he had received the orders to stop on the Lufira River. In effect the lack of opposition and the momentum of the advance had caused the first phase of the agreed-upon military plan to be telescoped into the second phase.

The following day Prem Chand took Bunche over the whole route of the advance so that he could see for himself what had happened and why.[23]

Bunche, who had made no bones about the embarrassment caused to U Thant, made it clear that communications must be improved and such a breakdown must never happen again.

On the other hand, there is unabashed elation, which I share, at the entry, at long last, of the UN into Jadotville and relief that this was accomplished with a minimum of fighting and of damage to the installations.[24]

Bunche concluded that the problem had arisen from the fact that the UN troops had suddenly enjoyed more success than they were prepared for or used to.[25]

The mood in the outside world was at last beginning to swing in favor of the UN's efforts in the Congo, and Belgium and France were strongly urging Tshombe to accept the Plan of National Reconciliation and put an end to the strife in Katanga. On January 8 U Thant told Bunche, who was in Leopoldville, that the United States was pressing him to make contact with Tshombe, who was in Rhodesia, and not to insist on Tshombe's making a public statement as a prior condition for such a contact. Bunche advised strongly against any contact with Tshombe for the time being. Nothing could be gained from such a contact, and much might be lost.

He is maneuvering in every possible way to get some recognition. His position, after all, is only that of a provincial president, and now, for the first time, he is reduced to size. He should be kept there.[26]

All Tshombe had to do was to state his acceptance of the reconciliation plan and implement it. If the United States was so keen to have Tshombe return to Elisabethville, the U.S. ambassador should speak to Prime Minister Adoula, who was bitterly opposed to Tshombe's return.

The following day Bunche explained the reason for his hard line on Tshombe. "If we could convince him that there is no more room for maneuver and bargaining, and no one to bargain with, he would surrender and the gendarmerie would collapse."[27] In Leopoldville, Ambassador Gullion had been instructed, against his own better judgment, to persuade Bunche to change his mind about an approach to Tshombe. Bunche was infuriated by this message and told Gullion to tell the State Department that a UN approach to Tshombe was "wrong, unsound, out of touch with realities here and would do much more harm than it could possibly do good."[28] He would therefore continue to advise U Thant strongly against the U.S. proposal. Bunche also had to keep in line the top civilian and military people in ONUC, who wished actually to *prevent* Tshombe's return to Katanga. "I am more than ever confident," Bunche told U Thant, "that if we keep on our course, we can be out of the military woods on the Congo operation within a very few weeks."[29]

Bunche returned to New York on January 10. On January 14 Tshombe announced that he was renouncing his secession and would accept the reconciliation plan and give ONUC complete freedom of movement. The UN forces peacefully entered Kolwezi, Tshombe's last stronghold, on January 21, and the Katanga secession, which had caused so much trouble and grief, was finally over. In his notes for that day Bunche wrote:

Big day for the Congo operation. Peaceful entry into Kolwezi . . . That about winds up the military phase and takes us over the big hump—after two and a half years! We ought to breathe a bit easier now. I feel that I've done something for Dag now.[30]

25

Yemen

Going Back Two Thousand Years

The Congo crisis, which for two and a half years had embattled the UN and sapped the energies of the secretary general and his immediate staff, was at last abating. In April 1963 Bunche welcomed General Sean McKeown (the ONUC commander), General Prem Chand, Brigadier Reggie Noronha, and the senior civilians of ONUC to New York for a week of consultations, which was in effect a celebration of the winding up of the Katanga problem. In November U Thant told the Security Council that he was aiming for a complete withdrawal of the military component of ONUC by the end of the year. At Prime Minister Adoula's request, however, a force of five thousand stayed on until mid-1964.

The respite came not a moment too soon for Bunche. Other international problems were demanding his attention, and he was also anxious to find the time to become more involved in the civil-rights movement at home. In June 1963 he went to the funeral, in Jackson, Mississippi, of the slain black civil-rights worker Medgar Evers, "to thank a dedicated and courageous man, who died for a cause as righteous as any cause can be, and who was a hero and is a martyr in the truest and noblest sense. . . ."[1] The FBI faithfully reported on Bunche's presence and remarks.

Bunche was still basically optimistic about civil rights and racial equality. "A true social revolution," he told a Danish audience in July, in a speech largely devoted to the struggle of Black Americans,

is in progress in the United States. . . . The Negro struggle for equality has been won and will soon be completely won. Indeed it is not really the struggle of the Negro but of the American people as a whole.[2]

International crises still dominated Bunche's time and energy. In Stockholm in February 1963 for a meeting of the board of the Dag Hammarskjöld Foundation, he was surprised to receive a phone call from U Thant asking him to go at once to Yemen. He immediately flew to Beirut, where the UN Truce Supervision Organization's DC-3 picked him up and flew him to Taiz in Yemen.

The Yemen problem had surfaced in the UN in the previous year, when, out of three sets of credentials for Yemen, the General Assembly chose those of Brigadier Al-Sallal, who had recently overthrown the Imam and pronounced himself president of the Arab Republic of Yemen. Nasser sent a sizable part of the Egyptian army to support Al-Sallal's government, against which the Imam, with Saudi support, was fighting a fierce guerrilla war.

U Thant had been trying for some months to find a peaceful solution to this potentially very dangerous conflict, a regional power struggle with Cold War overtones. The United States was concerned that an escalation of the war in Yemen, involving Saudi Arabia and the UAR, would jeopardize major U.S. economic and security interests in the Arabian Peninsula, Reluctant U.S. recognition of the Al-Sallal regime had infuriated Saudi Arabia and Jordan. The British were concerned that the war would spill over into the adjacent Aden Protectorate, to which Yemen had made a claim. International tension was further heightened by Nasser's warnings to the kings of Jordan and Saudi Arabia that other Al-Sallals would emerge in their own countries. In February 1963, the United States, in a desperate effort to mitigate the destabilizing effects of its own somewhat schizophrenic policy, decided to send a special presidential emissary, Ellsworth Bunker, to the area. It also sent a fighter squadron to Saudi Arabia to deter Nasser's air force from attacking targets in that country.

Bunche's mission, as the *New York Times* put it, was "to head off the new and deepening crisis in the Arab world. . . . The choice of Dr. Bunche was a reflection of Mr. Thant's concern about the matter."[3] He arrived in Taiz late in the afternoon of March 1 and was welcomed by a large crowd, many of whom were armed with rifles and traditional curved Yemeni daggers. In its collective desire to shake hands with Bunche, the crowd burst through the line of soldiers trying to keep them off the airstrip and engulfed the guard of honor. They chanted slogans hailing Al-Sallal and Nasser and execrating Hussein, Saud, and British imperialism. Bunche reached his car with difficulty, and his party moved slowly out of the airport through a dense, wildly gesticulating mob.

It soon became obvious that the demonstration was completely out of control, and the mob became threatening. At one point a path was cleared so that Bunche could witness the stoning and burning in effigy of King Hussein of Jordan. As they slowly approached the outskirts of Taiz, the crowd's mood changed, and the Yemeni ambassador to the UN, Moshin Al-Aini, who was escorting Bunche, explained gloomily that the crowd had been chewing *qat* and was becoming dangerous. The demonstrators began to rock the car violently, and Bunche felt that his last hour might really have finally come. To make matters worse, the car, an ancient Daimler, was overheating and was likely at any moment to spray the crowd with steam and boiling water, with unpredictable consequences. Al-Aini, as a last resort, ordered the driver to turn sharply off the main road through the crowd. They drove at breakneck speed across a field with the mob in pursuit, and escaped down a side street. Two and a half hours after leaving the airport, they arrived at the decrepit palace where Bunche was staying.[4] Next day the same journey to the airport took eleven minutes.

That following day Bunche flew to the capital, Sanaa, where a combination of Egyptian and Yemeni troops kept the welcoming crowd more or less under control. Nonetheless, outside the walls of Sanaa progress was slow, and banners of "Welcome to the Messenger of Peace" mingled with "Down with the British, Dirty Hussein," and, more prosaically, "The Arab Development and Reconstruction Bank Condemns British Aggression in our Country." This time the car's radiator cap did blow off, scattering the crowd and effectively clearing the way. At the palace, Bunche's short speech from an upper window was wildly applauded.

President Al-Sallal, with whom Bunche had dinner, made a good impression. He seemed a serious man, soft-spoken, calm, and earnest, but seldom smiling. Although he had been imprisoned for eight years and tortured by the Imam's government, he displayed no bitterness, but Bunche had the impression that he could become dangerously impatient if desired results did not come quickly. Al-Sallal denounced the Imam's regime as the worst in the world. It had kept the country, which had an ancient and proud civilization, backward and in isolation. Saudi Arabia's support of the Imam was the main problem.[5]

While in Yemen Bunche received many unsolicited courtesies from the Egyptian commander, Field Marshal Hakim Amr—a large cake, a box of chocolates, oranges, two bottles of whiskey, and, at one point, a huge luncheon tray ("I had eaten already"). The field marshal warned darkly that if the UN couldn't stop infiltration from Saudi Arabia, the Egyptian forces would have to destroy the bases in Saudi Arabia from which it came.

Bunche chose to visit Marab, the Queen of Sheba's legendary capital, where the royalists were said to be strong, and there had been heavy fighting. He flew in an Egyptian helicopter of American manufacture with Soviet radio equipment, and was greeted at Marab by sixty tribal sheikhs, heavily armed and in high excitement over an incident with British forces on the border with Aden. Bunche spent some time calming them down and dissuading them from setting off to fight the British. Otherwise, Marab was quiet, "like going back to a world of 2000 years ago." Bunche was appalled by the "pre-biblical" conditions in Yemen—dirt tracks for streets, broken-down palaces and prisons but no schools, and pervasive swarms of flies. Yemen's only serious road ran from the port of Hodeida to Sanaa and Taiz. It was obviously a country that needed every kind of assistance.

Because the altitude at Sanaa did not permit his aircraft to take off with a full fuel load, Bunche stopped to refuel in Aden and stayed overnight with the British governor, Sir Charles Johnston. This allowed him to get the royalist side of the story. The governor believed that the royalist opposition was strong and would overturn the new Yemen government if the Egyptians left. He seemed to have much misinformation and was quite put out when Bunche refuted his assertion that Marab had been destroyed by Egyptian bombing. Bunche was impressed at the extent to which prevailing royalist sympathies in Aden had dictated a wildly erroneous view of the situation in Yemen. He enjoyed two swims from the governor's private, shark-proof beach.

After his talks in Aden, Bunche decided that he should not visit London on his way home, and, since Ellsworth Bunker was in Jedda, that he should not visit Saudi Arabia either. His only other stop, therefore, was in Cairo. Nasser told him that President Al-Sallal had turned to him as the supporter of Arab nationalism and liberation. After his unpleasant experiences in the recent merger with Syria, Nasser had been reluctant to respond to this appeal from a faraway country, but Al-Sallal, threatened by Saudi assistance to the Imam's forces, had asked, "Will you leave me to die?," and he had sent more than twenty-five thousand soldiers. He was anxious to get them home as soon as possible and had accepted the American idea of disengagement, but the Saudis had turned it down. He had given orders to Field Marshal Amr to stop Egyptian cross-border actions to facilitate Bunche's mission. Nasser told Bunche that King Saud had twice tried to have him assassinated, offering 2 million Egyptian pounds in each instance. When he had asked Saud why he had done this, Saud said he had been misinformed about Nasser.

Bunche thought the Yemen situation could easily deteriorate, with wide repercussions. "I do not exclude the possibility that Yemen could become a Cuba in the Near East." He therefore suggested a plan of action to U Thant. The British should assure Yemen that they would allow no interference in Yemeni affairs in return for a similar assurance from Yemen about Aden and the other British protectorates in the Gulf. The British should recognize the new Yemeni government in return for an engagement by Yemen not to press its claim to the Gulf protectorates. The UN should give urgent technical and economic assistance to Yemen. If Bunker failed to restrain the Saudis, the Security Council might call on all states concerned to refrain from interference in the internal affairs of other states in the region. U Thant might also try to bring King Saud, Nasser, and Al-Sallal together. After his brief look at the conditions and terrain in Yemen, Bunche was very doubtful whether a UN peacekeeping operation would serve any useful purpose.

On his return to New York Bunche found that Bunker had developed a plan for Saudi Arabia to suspend its support to the royalists in exchange for a phased withdrawal of the Egyptian troops in Yemen. The plan would require UN observers to monitor its implementation.* U Thant was initially doubtful about committing the UN to an operation that was likely to be a failure. However, on April 29, he confirmed to the Security Council that Yemen, Saudi Arabia, and Egypt had accepted the plan for disengagement in Yemen. The plan was to be supervised by a mission of two hundred UN Yugoslav soldiers and a small Canadian air unit. It would be called the United Nations Yemen Observer Mission (UNYOM). UNYOM began its operations on July 4.

As Bunche had foreseen, both the political and the physical conditions in Yemen were unfavorable to an effective observer operation. In some areas there was not even an agreed-upon, let alone a marked, border. Nor did either side seem to have any real intention of carrying out the disengagement agreement. They engaged, instead, in a continuing exchange of accusations and recriminations. General von Horn, who had been put in charge of the mission, quarreled incessantly with UN Head-

---

*In the previous year Bunker had negotiated the arrangement by which the United Nations Temporary Executive Authority and Security Force (UNTEA), had presided over the takeover by Indonesia of the former Dutch territory of West New Guinea (West Irian).

quarters in New York and with his own staff, and resigned in a huff in August, to be succeeded by General P. S. Gyani of India, then commander of UNEF in Gaza. Bunche felt strongly that the risks the observers were taking were not justified by either the results or the prospects of success of their mission. What was needed was a negotiator, and U Thant appointed Piero Spinelli, the Italian head of the UN European office, as a special representative to talk to the parties concerned and informed the Security Council that he was terminating UNYOM.

Two years later, in October 1966, Bunche was visited by Moshin Al-Aini, "a man of principle and courage," who had escorted him during his tumultuous arrival in Taiz in 1963. Al-Aini was resigning his post as ambassador in protest against Nasser's action in returning Al-Sallal, who had been in Cairo for two years, to power in Yemen. Al-Sallal, he said, once a courageous man, had been brainwashed and had become an Egyptian puppet. The Egyptian army in Yemen was now an army of occupation, but the people of Yemen would not tolerate it for long. "I hope," Bunche noted, "that I may see him again some day, but if he returns to Yemen now I may not."[6] The following year, in the wake of Egypt's stunning defeat by Israel, the Egyptian forces in Yemen were withdrawn.

The Congo situation had lost much of its interest for Bunche after the resolution of the Katanga problem, and the UN's operations there were becoming increasingly routine and mostly concerned with technical and economic assistance.* There was no movement on Yemen, and the Middle East and Kashmir seemed relatively stable. In the summer of 1963 Bunche was able to take a European trip with Ruth and Ralph Jr. He had found that his idea of a real holiday, which was to stay at home and do as he pleased, was impossible, since he was invariably called back to the office. "All of my colleagues were amazed that I actually embarked on June 27. I guess that I was a bit surprised also." For once the international situation was relatively quiet, yet—

even so . . . I had to deliberate rather hard on whether I should go at a time when the American racial situation was in such a critical state. In May, at a dinner at the White House, at the time of the Birmingham crisis, I had an earnest and constructive discussion of the problem with the President. After attending Medgar Evers' funeral on June 15 I had stated my unequivocal support of the Negro struggle for complete and quick equality and my confidence in the successful

*The UN military forces finally withdrew from the Congo in June 1964, the year in which Moise Tshombe became prime minister of a united Congo.

outcome of that struggle. It appeared to me therefore that there would be little more that I could do in the weeks of July and early August prior to the projected March on Washington. I intended to be back in time for that.[7]

Bunche returned to New York on August 22, and on August 28 he participated in the March on Washington, where Martin Luther King made his "I have a dream" speech.

Bunche accompanied U Thant to greet President Kennedy when he arrived to address the General Assembly on September 20. "His speech was magnificent—in my view the best ever given to the General Assembly." Kennedy was obviously in considerable pain.

He showed difficulty in walking on the long walk to the elevator to the 38th floor and was clenching his fists apparently from pain. He lay down after a while and his doctor was called, probably to give him an injection. . . . He asked for a Bloody Mary.[8]

Kennedy and Stevenson discussed Yemen and pressed U Thant to keep the UN force in the Congo. Bunche took Kennedy to talk to the American members of the Secretariat.

On November 22 President Kennedy was assassinated in Dallas, Texas. Three days later Bunche accompanied U Thant to Kennedy's funeral. Bunche had been informed in October, before Kennedy's death, that he had been awarded the U.S. Medal of Freedom, and U Thant gave him permission to accept it. On December 6 he sadly received the medal at the White House. "Felt honored . . . to receive my government's highest civilian award but could not rejoice in view of our nation's tragedy."[9] The loss of Kennedy hit Bunche especially hard. He had felt far closer to Kennedy's Washington, of which he had been asked several times to become a part, than to the Eisenhower administration. Kennedy, at considerable political risk to himself, had been strongly supportive of the UN Congo operation, and without his support it was unlikely that the Katanga problem would have been resolved. Kennedy was also far more responsive on civil-rights issues than the previous administration. For this reason above all others, Bunche felt "our nation's tragedy" acutely and personally.

26

Cyprus and Kashmir

Providing the Pretext for Peace

On Saturday, February 8, 1964, Bunche and Ruth went, as they often did, to the Metropolitan Opera as the guests of the general manager, Rudolf Bing. Appropriately enough, the opera was Verdi's *Otello,* the tragic story of the Moorish Venetian governor of Cyprus.

Cyprus had achieved its independence from Britain in 1960, but in 1963 intercommunal rivalry between the Greek majority and the Turkish minority erupted in violence, which a large British peacekeeping force proved unable to contain. Although Cyprus was a relatively small island with a total population of six hundred thousand, the Cyprus problem enjoyed a disproportionate importance in the politics of the Cold War. It was a matter of harsh dispute between two members of NATO, Greece and Turkey, and was of considerable strategic importance to NATO. The troubles of Cyprus could not be ignored by the outside world.

The troubles of Cyprus simmered and erupted in a grand historical setting. The seat of an ancient civilization, the legendary birthplace of Venus, the island was an anthology of Mediterranean history. Its mountains, plains, pine forests, olive groves, vineyards, and matchless coastline housed Iron Age, Egyptian, Greek and Roman remains, towering Crusader castles, operatic Venetian ports and fortifications, Turkish mosques, and scores of delightful towns and villages. British rule had bequeathed an efficient civil service, legal system, and police force as well as two world-class strategic military bases. It was sometimes hard for outsiders not to contrast this splendid background with the bitterness and violence of intercommunal feeling and the frequent pettiness of contemporary Cyprus politics.

When, in early 1964, the British decided that they could not sustain the burden of peacekeeping in Cyprus indefinitely, an effort was made, under United States leadership, to substitute a NATO-based force for the British peacekeepers.[1] President Makarios of Cyprus rejected this idea, and on February 7 Soviet Premier Khrushchev warned the NATO powers that any move against the island would be "the source of international complications fraught with grave consequences."

In January 1964 U Thant had sent General P. S. Gyani of India, then commanding UNEF, to Cyprus to report on the situation. Bunche told Gyani that his function was solely to observe and not to discuss a possible peacekeeping force, although it would be useful to have his views on the possible nature of such a force as well as on the risks that it might have to face.

On February 15 the governments of Cyprus and Britain brought the problem to the Security Council, and on March 4 the Security Council authorized the setting up of the United Nations Force in Cyprus (UNFICYP).* Bunche's earlier exchanges with Gyani paid off both in resisting impossible demands from the Cypriots and in formulating the basic functions of the force—

in the interest of international peace and security, to use its best efforts to prevent a recurrence of intercommunal fighting and, as necessary, to contribute to the maintenance of law and order and a return to normal conditions.[2]

The effort to put these bland and carefully qualified precepts into action occupied much of Bunche's time and energy for a long period to come. He was under no illusions as to the complexity of what was ostensibly a relatively small problem. "If you go in there, you'll never get out," he told the Canadian ambassador, William Barton, who had come to see him about Canadian participation in the Cyprus force.[3] Bunche's warning was prescient indeed. Twenty-eight years later Canadian soldiers were still serving in Cyprus. U Thant appointed Gyani as the force commander and Sakari Tuomioja of Finland as mediator.

Bunche brought all his accumulated experience of peacekeeping operations to bear on the problems of Cyprus. In briefing Gyani, he emphasized the vital necessity of independence of decision and action. UNFICYP was not there as the agent of the Cyprus government, and it was not subject to the bidding of any government. In the Congo the Security Council had put the UN force in to "assist" the government, which had caused endless problems and misunderstandings with Patrice

*Bunche wrote a long list of possible acronyms for the Cyprus force, including UNFIC, UNCYMED, UNFINC, UNCYMFI, and UNFORIC.

Lumumba. Through Bunche's efforts, the dangerous Congo formula had been avoided in the Council's resolution on Cyprus. Even so, the force would have to maintain reasonably good relations with the government, which could be very difficult.

I would think it wise to avoid the use of "neutral" and "neutrality," which have political connotations, and emphasize the fact that the UN Force intends to carry out its functions with complete impartiality and fairness . . . and with no political position of any kind on any aspect of the situation.[4]

The commander would have to exercise his discretion and try to settle difficulties by negotiation, avoiding any suggestion of the threat of force. He would have a senior political officer to take the heat on political matters and act as a lightning rod on all the highly charged issues which bedeviled the relations of the two communities in Cyprus.

It was also important to distinguish UNFICYP from its British predecessor. "We do not in any sense inherit from the British anything but the problems and the situation in Cyprus." While implying no bias or criticism against the British, "political wisdom clearly dictates that we must avoid any suggestion that UNFICYP is just picking up where the British left off."[5] Finally, Bunche urged the greatest possible caution and restraint on any firing by the force, particularly in situations where civilians, even if armed, were involved.* "Killing of civilians could quickly make the position of the force untenable."[6]

In April Bunche, on his way to Kashmir, stopped in Cyprus to see for himself how UNFICYP was settling in and to talk to President Makarios and to Fazil Kuçuk, the Turkish Cypriot leader. He found that Makarios had an answer for every question, but usually an answer which left his interlocutor more confused than before. Makarios complained that his Turkish Cypriot opposite number, Dr. Kuçuk, who was theoretically the vice-president of Cyprus, was a good man but too weak to control the Turkish Cypriot community, which was actually controlled by Rauf Denktash, who believed that if his people continued fighting Turkey would eventually intervene. Bunche found Makarios easy to talk to, but "there are strong differences of opinion about the degree of reliability that may be accorded to what he says in such a pleasant and straightforward manner."[7]

Dr. Kuçuk got off on the wrong foot with Bunche by complaining that he had not been shown General Gyani's orders. Bunche replied that

---

*Armed civilians constituted the so-called "security forces" on both sides in Cyprus.

that would continue to be the case, since the orders were an internal communication from the secretary general to the commander and were not shown to any government. (The British had already made a fuss about this.) Kuçuk was a far less skillful performer than Makarios and, though constantly complaining about the situation, did not seem able to suggest practical ways of improving it.

Bunche flew by helicopter to critical points on the island and was horrified by the aftermath of intercommunal fighting, the destruction of Turkish dwellings and mosques, the pathetic groups of homeless and displaced people, and, above all, the hate and suspicion which pervaded the relations between the two communities. He drew up a list of things that urgently needed to be done—getting people back to their homes, getting fortifications removed, stopping harassment and arbitrary searches, getting the Turkish police and civil servants back to work, and getting Makarios and Kuçuk together. He saw that Gyani had an impossibly heavy burden and urged U Thant to appoint a senior personal representative to handle the political side. He was tempted, but for his nationality, to take the job temporarily himself. "It would," he told U Thant, "put me under a handicap in the work in Cyprus and this factor would very soon show up in local criticism. Moreover it would certainly expose you to political attack."[8] U Thant finally appointed Galo Plaza Lasso, a former president of Ecuador, as his special representative in Cyprus.

In June the situation in Cyprus went through one of its periodic spasms, and for a few days it seemed likely that the Turks might invade, but after strong warnings from President Lyndon B. Johnson the storm passed. The situation seemed to get worse as the summer wore on, and General K. S. Thimayya, the distinguished Indian soldier who had succeeded Gyani, referred to "the almost impossible situation that faces UNFICYP in this island at this moment."[9] The Greek Cypriots, as the topdog, tended to disregard and disdain the UN, losing few opportunities to humiliate the force, and the Turkish Cypriots increasingly feared that UNFICYP could not protect them from the Greeks. In the last months of 1964, however, the situation began to improve.

Bunche had always maintained a genial, if distant, relationship with his Soviet opposite number. This had been easy with Ilya Tchernychev and Anatoly Dobrynin, but with their successor, V. P. Suslov, a hardline Soviet apparatchik who was evidently inspired by the diatribes of his Soviet superiors during the Congo period, such a relationship was not possible. Nor was Bunche prepared to indulge Suslov. In December Suslov charged that in refusing to let him see reports on Cyprus before they were published Bunche was "trying to prevent me from carrying out my right-ful duties as one of the principal advisors to the Secretary-General."[10] Bunche replied that he regarded this latter comment as "a gratuitous and petty affront." In all his years at the UN he had submitted reports only to the secretary general, and never to another undersecretary general for review. Suslov evidently had a false idea of their relationship; "my work is not subject to review by you nor is yours by me."

Suslov appealed to U Thant, who, not grasping that an important principle was involved, ruled that Suslov *could* see Bunche's draft reports but that his comments would not be taken account of unless Bunche approved them. Bunche told U Thant that this would not do, because it would "compromise the principle for which I was contending and would create a situation which was bound to lead to irritation." In his disillusion-ment with U Thant's failure to grasp what was involved, Bunche told Adlai Stevenson he had decided to activate his resignation, which had been on file since June 1961. When U Thant learned of this, he was so alarmed that he not only reversed his ruling about Suslov reviewing Bunche's draft reports, but asked for Suslov's recall to Moscow. Suslov left the Secretariat on March 17, 1965.

Another worry was with General Thimayya. The general, who had been chief of staff of the Indian army, was extremely touchy about taking directions which contained any hint of criticism, and also about his health, which was a constant cause of anxiety to Bunche. "I can assure you," Thimayya cabled Bunche in March, "I am not in the slightest bit alarmed as I am in quite good fighting fettle . . . and am visited twice a week by my medical officer."[11] Thimayya died in Cyprus of a heart attack in Decem-ber 1965.

Galo Plaza, who had become the mediator in Cyprus, submitted his report in late 1965. He put forward a plan for settling the Cyprus problem that seemed to most people to be as fair and as reasonable as possible in a situation where there was no perfect solution. He was promptly de-nounced by Turkey and the Turkish Cypriots, who vowed never to accept his mediation again. The Greek Cypriots, equally promptly, responded that they would never accept a mediator *other* than Galo Plaza. The function of mediator in Cyprus thus lapsed.

The Cyprus situation settled down to an interminable round of negotiations, mishaps, pettiness, recriminations, and provocations, re-lieved occasionally by small steps forward. At least, thanks to UNFICYP, the Cypriots weren't killing each other any more. Bunche epitomized his feelings about Cyprus on a later visit when he watched the Kyrenia con-voy, an arrangement by which Greek Cypriots could go through Turkish-controlled territory from Nicosia to the northern port of Kyrenia each day under armed UN escort. He was, not for the first time,

impressed graphically by the tragic senselessness of the situation in this land. . . . This is certainly the only place in the world where men, women and children go to the beach under the protection of ferret [armored] cars, soldiers and police.[12]

On this same occasion, on his departure from Nicosia Airport, Bunche was asked the question that official visitors are always asked by Cypriot journalists: "Are you optimistic?" For once Bunche answered at some length.

I am a professional optimist. If I were not a professional optimist through 21 years in the United Nations service, mainly in conflict areas—Palestine, Congo, here, and in Kashmir—I would be crazy. You have to be optimistic in this work or get out of it. . . . That is, optimistic in the sense of assuming that there is no problem—Cyprus or any other—which cannot be solved and that, therefore, you have to keep at it persistently and you have to have confidence that it can be solved. . . . And so, personally, I am always inclined to pessimism, but professionally I am inclined towards optimism. That makes a good balance.[13]

Doreen Mashler, his longtime personal assistant, surprised Bunche by saying that he must be getting a bit bored with all the "stifling" work he was doing. He, in turn, surprised her by replying that

this was not at all the case, in fact the work on peace-keeping operations as I had found it in recent years was more interesting, and in a quiet way more self-satisfying and rewarding, than any I had done since becoming a member of the Secretariat.[14]

Bunche was very much aware that, in his massive daily, and often nightly, exchanges with peacekeeping operations in the field and with the governments concerned in them, he was not only directing those operations but also building up the precedents, models, and case law of a new international institution with a very important future.

In the dust and heat of a visit to Cyprus and the Middle East in July 1966 Bunche began to be acutely aware of his failing eyesight. While he was in Cyprus he received an invitation from Princess Rainier (Grace Kelly), whom he knew, to come with Ruth to Monaco.* He asked me to clear this with U Thant.

*The trip to Monaco, to celebrate Monaco's hundredth anniversary, was not an unqualified success. Bunche umpired a celebrity baseball game, telling each pitcher that, since he could not see, they would use an honor system, the pitcher telling the umpire what to call. Bunche tripped over a step in a nightclub and bruised his toe, which became infected, so that he had to go to hospital on returning to New York. The trip was cut short in any case, because of a Security Council meeting on Israel-Syria problems.

As you know that is just my social style. The idea is that this would give me an excuse to steal a little vacation and have Ruth join me in England [where he was to go from Cyprus to address the International Institute of Strategic Studies] possibly at Monaco's expense. . . . My main hesitation about the idea relates to the condition of my bad eye which continues to be very troublesome and has shown no improvement on this trip. I have not been using it too much as a matter of fact by having other people do my reading for me.[15]

The Cyprus problem went through one more convulsion during Bunche's stewardship. The activities of the former underground anti-British leader General Gheorgios Grivas, who had become the semiofficial, semiunderground representative of Greek ambitions and anti-Turkish terrorism in Cyprus, had been a dangerously destabilizing factor throughout UNFICYP's early years. In March 1967 there had been a serious incident at Kophinou, and in November Grivas managed to precipitate a pitched battle between the Cyprus police, the Greek National Guard, and Turkish Cypriot fighters at a village called Ayios Theodoros. Once again an armed intervention from the Turkish mainland seemed imminent. All the usual charges and countercharges became intensified on such occasions. During an impassioned exposé by Zenon Rossides, the venerable Cyprus ambassador at the UN, Bunche noted:

On the principle he is basically right, but in presenting his case he is the most exasperating and tedious person imaginable. This has been a sickening day for me. In the talks on Cyprus morality and principle have no place. Turkey's threat of force, fear and cynical pragmatism are controlling.[16]

This was a major international crisis.* On November 22 Arthur Goldberg, Adlai Stevenson's successor as United States ambassador at the UN, urged U Thant to send Bunche to the area, but Bunche demurred, pointing out that the secretary general already had a high-level representative in Cyprus. Bunche suggested instead that the secretary general should strongly appeal to the three governments for restraint and announce his intention to send a personal representative to the three capitals, starting with Ankara, to discuss the crisis. Goldberg wanted Bunche to take this assignment, but Bunche insisted that his Guatemalan colleague, Undersecretary José Rolz-Bennett, who was well liked in the three capitals, would be the best person for the job. A main objective would be to get all the parties to reduce their forces to the 1964 level. In another effort to head off the Turks, President Johnson, on November 29, sent Cyrus Vance to Ankara.

*Bunche had even made arrangements for the evacuation of nonessential UN personnel from Cyprus to a "safe haven" in Beirut.

At 7:30 A.M. on December 3 Goldberg called Bunche to say that Makarios had rejected Vance's final proposal and that Vance, although he had stalled the Turkish invasion, had failed to end the crisis. Anticipating such an outcome if Vance attempted to force Makarios' hand ("too much dependence on the big stick . . . no finesse, too much fanfare and poor drafting"), Bunche had got U Thant to agree to issue his own independent appeal as soon as he knew that Vance's efforts had ended. Bunche had already written the appeal, and it was immediately sent to the president of Cyprus and the prime ministers of Greece and Turkey without consulting their representatives in New York, who could be relied on to hold things up with interminable questions and objections. U Thant called on the three leaders to end immediately any threat to each other's security and to withdraw all forces in excess of their legitimate contingents from Cyprus. If necessary UNFICYP would be enlarged to strengthen its capacity for pacifying the island and supervising the disarmament process.

The three governments, by now eager for a way out of a dangerous situation, responded favorably to this appeal, and the crisis was over. Bunche was even able to catch a 5:30 P.M. flight on the same day to a meeting of the Rockefeller Foundation board in Williamsburg. "I feel rather good about something for a welcome change," he wrote on the plane in his by now large and wandering scrawl.[17]

Cyprus was only one of several conflict situations which the United Nations was attempting to contain. When a cease-fire had been agreed upon by India and Pakistan in 1948 in the war over Kashmir, the UN had stationed a military observer group (UNMOGIP) on the cease-fire line, which ran through the lovely valleys of Kashmir up into the Himalayas to the north. Bunche was responsible for directing this operation, and in April 1964 he went to the subcontinent after visiting Cyprus and Gaza. After talks with the governments of Pakistan and India, he went to Srinagar, in the Vale of Kashmir, and from there inspected the UN observer operation.

In both Rawalpindi and Delhi his conversations gave little hope of a solution of the long-standing problem of Kashmir. Pakistani President Ayub Khan, who was in his pajamas recovering from a hernia operation, said that the Indian dream of an Indian empire in Kashmir was the only obstacle between India and Pakistan, which in all other respects needed each other as allies. He denounced Jawaharlal Nehru as a hypocrite, and the Indians for killing civilians. A war between India and Pakistan, he said, would involve the entire world. Pakistan was seeking an alliance with Peking, because it had a long and indefensible border with China. In

Delhi, where Bunche stayed in the enormous former palace of the viceroy, the Rashtrapati Bhavan, Nehru, though gentler in language, was no less forthright.*

In Kashmir Bunche made long and grueling journeys by jeep over primitive tracks and mountain passes to visit the UN observer posts. Flying conditions in the Himalayas, through passes with the peaks of K2 or Annapurna in the distance, and with rapidly changeable weather, were scenically splendid but nerve-racking. From Bunche's talks with the chief military observer, General Robert Nimmo of Australia, there could be little doubt that the Kashmir situation was deteriorating and could well escalate into war between India and Pakistan. Although the border was closed, Pakistani civilians continued to cross the line to graze cattle or cut grass, and to be shot at by the Indian army. There was also an alarming number of armed civilians on the Pakistani side of the line.

Bunche was disturbed by what he had seen and by the inadequacy of the UN observer group for the formidable problems it was faced with. Although UNMOGIP was a small group of unarmed observers rather than a peace force, it was often required to carry out patrols. Supervision of the Kashmir cease-fire line "would seem to be made to order for a UN peace force, with the function of interposition, as in UNEF."[18] Although the cease-fire line was five hundred miles long, he believed that a moderate-sized force would have a much better chance of success even than UNEF in Gaza and Sinai, "if only because of a desire that I believe to be earnest on both sides to avoid serious trouble along the line." Bunche realized that there was no chance of the Security Council, which during the Cold War period was not capable of considering preventive action, agreeing to such a move at the present time. He had no doubt, however, that, if the situation deteriorated sufficiently, a peace force would be suggested at a point when it would already be too late for it to be effective.

UNMOGIP suffered from a syndrome which was to afflict other successful peacekeeping operations. Because its presence reduced the number of border incidents and prevented them from escalating, its activities received very little attention, either from the Security Council or in the press, and the pressures which were building up on both sides of the line were ignored. India took the position that the Kashmir question was settled and that the cease-fire line would inevitably become the international border. Pakistan took exactly the opposite view and supported the UN observer group precisely as an indication that the cease-fire line was not, and could not be, the permanent border.

*Nehru died on May 27, 1964 and was succeeded by Lal Bahadur Shastri.

Since the conversion of UNMOGIP to a peacekeeping force was a political impossibility, Bunche suggested increasing the number of observers and making them more mobile with helicopters and light aircraft and better communications. He also suggested a much stronger reaction to breaches of the cease-fire, with letters to the governments from the secretary general which would also be circulated to the Security Council, so that the situation and the UN operation itself would become better known to governments and to a wider public.

Bunche's forecast of trouble was amply justified by the events of the following year. In the late summer of 1965, armed infiltrators from Pakistan began crossing the cease-fire line and shooting at Indian patrols. In an effort to avert war, U Thant suggested to both governments that Bunche should visit them again, but he found neither at all receptive to the idea. Instead, Bunche wrote a confidential note to all members of the Security Council describing the ominous developments in the area, and U Thant summoned General Nimmo, the chief observer, to New York. On September 1, 1965, U Thant appealed to the two governments to allow a return to normal conditions, to stop infiltrators from both sides, to withdraw from newly occupied positions, and to stop firing across the line.

There was no significant response to this appeal, either from India or Pakistan, nor was there any reaction from the Security Council. The skirmishing quickly degenerated into a full-scale war, both in Kashmir and to the south, along the international border between India and Pakistan. Given the size of the two armies, the alliance of India with the Soviet Union and of Pakistan with China, and the possibility of bloody intercommunal riots between Hindus and Muslims, this was an immensely serious international crisis. At the urgent request of a now thoroughly alarmed Security Council, U Thant himself went to the subcontinent on September 7 in an attempt to halt the fighting, leaving Bunche in charge in New York.*

In spite of U Thant's appeals for a cease-fire and the "universal recognition that war between India and Pakistan can lead only to disaster for the two countries themselves and for the world at large,"[19] each government's response to U Thant's appeals was hedged about with conditions which the other could not possibly accept. U Thant therefore decided to return to New York put the matter before the Security Council. To symbolize the urgency and importance of the situation, Bunche brought the entire membership of the Security Council, headed by its president, Arthur Goldberg, to Kennedy Airport to meet U Thant on his

*Bunche sent me with U Thant to help him on this important and interesting trip.

return from the sub-continent. U Thant urged the Council to *order* a cessation of hostilities and to ask the heads of the two governments to meet to discuss their differences at the earliest possible time. The Council adopted a resolution to this effect on September 20,[20] and India and Pakistan agreed to end the fighting two days later.

An extremely dangerous crisis had passed. For once Bunche had stayed at home as the anchorman. He had anticipated the Security Council's action by arranging to double the size of the Kashmir observer group so that it could better supervise the cease-fire and withdrawal of forces. He also set up a new observer operation to perform the same function on the India-Pakistan border to the south of Kashmir. In doing this he ran into trouble with Nikolai Fedorenko, the notoriously obnoxious Soviet ambassador, who charged that the Security Council had not been sufficiently consulted on U Thant's actions to halt the fighting. Somewhat to Bunche's surprise, U Thant was deeply hurt by Fedorenko's entirely predictable attacks. Bunche wrote:

The Secretary-General is thin-skinned and takes attacks hard. So was and did Dag, but Dag Hammarskjöld was more of a fighter—he got angry and belligerent as well as hurt.[21]

At this time the French were also challenging the secretary general's authority over peacekeeping operations, and, to Bunche's annoyance, U Thant found it even more difficult to stand up properly to the French ambassador, Roger Seydoux. "U Thant," he noted, "at times chooses to give way rather than stand and fight."[22]

Bunche was well aware that the Soviets often accused him, behind his back, of usurping U Thant's authority. Their efforts in this direction were reflected particularly in press reports from Delhi, and in the complaints of the new Soviet undersecretary, another apparatchik, A. E. Nesterenko, about the setting up and conduct of the vital observer operations which Bunche was running in the subcontinent. Before an official dinner, he learned from the United States ambassador, Arthur Goldberg, that in a meeting of the permanent members of the Security Council Fedorenko had said that Bunche was advising U Thant on the basis of instructions from the Pentagon (the United States Defense Department). Goldberg had immediately demanded an apology and denounced this irresponsible attack, which had seemed to embarrass Fedorenko's staff more than anyone else. At the dinner, Bunche found himself seated opposite Fedorenko, who caught his eye and, to Bunche's amusement, lifted his glass in a silent toast. On the way out of the dinner, Secretary of State Dean Rusk put his arm around Bunche's shoulders and said with a laugh:

Ralph, now I know you are a good international civil servant. I heard about Fedorenko's charge today, and I also have had complaints about you, most recently about some comments you made about US policy in Santo Domingo. . . .*23

On January 4, 1966, Indian Prime Minister Lal Bahadur Shastri and President Ayub Khan of Pakistan met at Tashkent and agreed to withdraw their forces to their pre–August 1965 positions by February 25, 1966. The Kashmir problem remained, however, as a long-lasting time bomb on the international scene.

In the summer of 1965 an uprising against the military government of the Dominican Republic involved the United States in an intervention ostensibly to protect American lives, but actually to prevent the Dominican Republic from becoming what Washington believed might be another Cuba. To cover this intervention, an inter-American peace force was sent to the island, but since the core of this force was the U.S. 82nd Airborne Division the action was widely denounced, the Soviets demanding that the Security Council condemn the United States intervention. The Council temporized by calling on U Thant to send representatives to pin down a cease-fire and monitor the inter-American force, which was generally viewed as an embarrassingly transparent fig leaf for American intervention. U Thant's representatives, in their turn, were seen in Washington as anti-American, a point which President Johnson made forcefully to U Thant during the UN's twentieth anniversary celebration in San Francisco in June 1965. Bunche, who was responsible for directing the UN's representatives in the Dominican Republic, found it "just about the messiest situation we have had to get involved with."24

Bunche's time was not solely taken up by problems of conflict control in distant parts of the world. To his delight, he had been appointed in 1964 to the board of the World's Fair at Flushing Meadows, New York. He was an active and devoted board member, taking care, among other things, that the World's Fair respected "equal-opportunity" employment policies. Whenever he could find a spare hour or two, he visited the fair, and he became an expert and enthusiastic guide for visitors and members of his family. He seemed to see the World's Fair as a symbol of what international cooperation could, and should, be.

*Bunche had been highly critical of U.S. policy on, and intervention in, the Dominican Republic in the summer of 1965.

27

Vietnam

A Senseless and Dirty Business

The war in Vietnam, which, despite campaign pledges of "no wider war," escalated dramatically during the presidency of Lyndon Johnson, had a tragic and lasting effect on the peoples of Indochina and of the United States. In the world at large, however, its impact was surprisingly muffled. The problems of Indochina in the 1960s were never formally taken up in any serious way at the United Nations. As an Asian, U Thant, however, felt passionately that the war was a humanitarian and moral disaster, and that the fighting must be stopped. He made this conviction a personal crusade.

Bunche had strongly disapproved of the United States' involvement in Indochina from the very beginning, and as the war escalated and the U.S. became ever more inextricably committed to it, his exasperation and disgust increased. If, however, he was to play any useful role in the effort to persuade President Johnson and Secretary of State Rusk to seek an early end to the war, he could not express his personal feelings. He greatly respected Johnson's stand on other matters, especially civil rights, and was not prepared to join in across-the-board denunciations of him. Thus he was the only United States Nobel Laureate who refused to sign an advertisement against Johnson and the Vietnam War in the *New York Times*. Bunche set out to help U Thant as best he could in his lonely personal mission to end the war in Vietnam, keeping his own feelings about the war to himself.

For U Thant, Vietnam, which was not officially on the agenda of the United Nations, was an issue of overriding importance, and he doggedly persisted in his informal, and ultimately unsuccessful, effort to end the fighting. He wrote later:

The real issue of the war was not whether the political aims of US policy were right or wrong; the issue was the American conduct of the war. Even if the United States were right politically, it was, in my view, immoral to wage a war of this kind. One does not have to be a pacifist to condemn the napalming and dropping of anti-personnel bombs on hamlets from 35,000 feet above.[1]

To persuade the United States to change its policy was, in U Thant's mind, the key to success, but he personally was not well known, or indeed particularly trusted, in Lyndon Johnson's Washington. Bunche, who knew Johnson, Rusk, and Adlai Stevenson well, was an indispensable ally in U Thant's efforts to bring the United States and its enemies in Vietnam from the battlefield to the conference table.

U Thant's insistence that only political and diplomatic means could solve the problems of Vietnam was not, initially at least, welcome in Washington, and he soon found that Adlai Stevenson, the U.S. ambassador at the UN since 1960, had minimal influence with the Johnson administration. On August 6, 1964, U Thant and Bunche visited Johnson in Washington. This was a formal affair with the Marine Corps band, but at a working luncheon with Rusk in the State Department U Thant urged that emissaries from the United States meet with representatives of North Vietnam for private conversations about ending the war. Thus began "an initiative," U Thant noted grimly, "that was to be rejected by the United States without the President's knowledge."[2]

Believing that Rusk was receptive to his idea, U Thant, on his return to New York, contacted Ho Chi Minh on talks about ending the war. Having no direct access to Hanoi, he used his Soviet undersecretary for this contact, since Peking was strongly opposed to any accommodation with Washington. In September a positive response came from Hanoi, which U Thant passed on to Stevenson, but, to his surprise and mounting dismay, no reaction came from Washington in the remaining months of 1964. When, in January 1965, Bunche asked Stevenson's deputy, Charles Yost, what was going on, he was amazed to discover that Yost knew nothing of U Thant's initiative, and he realized that Stevenson, if he had done anything at all, must simply have mentioned it on the telephone to someone in Washington. Bunche's inquiry stirred Stevenson to ask U Thant about a suitable place for the talks, and U Thant recommended Rangoon, where all the parties concerned had embassies. On January 30 Stevenson at last reported that Washington would not agree to a meeting with North Vietnam, because if news of it leaked out this would demoralize the government in Saigon. On February 7 the United States began bombing North Vietnam, and Hanoi declared publicly that it would not consider talking with Washington until the bombing stopped. Thus ended the first round of U Thant's initiative. The delay in the United States response, and its ultimate rejection of the plan, had already cost him much of his credibility with Hanoi.

At a press conference on February 24, 1965, U Thant declared:

I am sure that the great American people, if they only knew the true facts and the background to the developments in South Vietnam, will agree with me that further bloodshed is unnecessary. The political and diplomatic method of discussion and negotiation alone can create conditions which will enable the United States to withdraw gracefully from that part of the world.

As he noted later,

with those words, whatever utility I might have as a prospective go-between came to an end as far as Washington was concerned.[3]

Twenty-five years later, Dean Rusk described this episode very differently. Asserting that U Thant had simply invented the positive response from Hanoi, and quoting several, rather vague sources to the effect that it had never existed, Rusk concluded a far too defensive jeremiad by characterizing U Thant's initiative as a "cock-and-bull story. . . . Frankly, I thought he had lied like a sailor."[4] This account perhaps sheds more light on Rusk's personal feelings about U Thant than on U Thant's attempts to halt the Vietnam War.

Despite such setbacks U Thant persisted with his efforts both with North Vietnam and with Washington, and Bunche respected him for it. Quoting Gladstone, he wrote, "We cannot believe in the infallibility of any man, but it is restful to be sure of one man's integrity."[5] Bunche was more than ever concerned at the disastrous direction in which the Johnson administration seemed to be dragging the United States in Vietnam. He was also distressed by the problems of Adlai Stevenson, who frequently came to Bunche's office to bewail his difficult relationship with Johnson and Rusk.[6] Stevenson's position with the Johnson administration was even more uncertain than it had been with the Kennedys, and U Thant's efforts and public statements on Vietnam certainly made it worse. Stevenson told Bunche that U Thant's public statement on Vietnam in February had "put him in the doghouse" in Washington and that the UN's rating in Washington was the lowest he had ever experienced. He himself was through, he told Bunche, and would probably have to step down. In a few days, however, the situation improved, and Stevenson decided to stay on, even urging Bunche to encourage U Thant to pursue his efforts on Vietnam. In May Bunche drafted a new appeal by U Thant for talks and a cessation of the fighting.

As far as Stevenson personally was concerned, things came to a head at the UN's twentieth-anniversary ceremonies in San Francisco in June 1965. There was much public speculation that Johnson would use this high-level international occasion to make a dramatic statement on Vietnam. Instead, Bunche noted, there was "widespread and deep disappointment with LBJ's speech—empty and he missed such a great opportunity."[7] Bunche and U Thant were to see Johnson at the Opera House after the president's speech. Arriving at the president's temporary quarters in the tenor's dressing room, Bunche "saw Adlai, red-faced, leaving and I asked him why. He said, acidly, 'he does not want me present.' I immediately told U Thant that in that case I also should leave, and left."[8]

U Thant met Johnson alone and learned from him that the president knew nothing of his earlier initiative* and had therefore been extremely upset at his subsequent criticism of American policy. Johnson amazed U Thant by saying that Averell Harriman was ready to go anywhere and had a plane at his disposal. U Thant told Johnson that unfortunately Hanoi's position had changed since the American bombing of North Vietnam had started, and that Hanoi would now insist on the Viet Cong's being involved in any talks, as well as on a cessation of the bombing.

Ten days later Stevenson dropped dead on a London street. Bunche was shocked and saddened at the death of his old friend. Johnson asked him to be a member of the party, led by Vice-President Hubert Humphrey, which was being sent to London to escort Stevenson's body back to the United States. Coming back on the plane, Stevenson's son, Adlai Stevenson III, told Bunche how restless and unhappy his father had been in his UN post. In spite of—or perhaps because of—his recent humiliating and dismissive treatment of his ambassador, President Johnson was waiting at the ramp at Andrews Air Force Base.

There was much speculation as to who would succeed Stevenson, Bunche's name being prominently mentioned. Bunche told U Thant that under no circumstances would he consider such a shift, not least because

*In October 1966, during an unscheduled visit to U Thant in New York, Johnson repeated that he had not been informed of U Thant's initiative, and Dean Rusk added a new twist by saying that Stevenson (who had died in July 1965) had not been authorized to reject U Thant's proposal. Bunche and U Thant were stunned at this unconfirmable piece of information.

he was opposed to U.S. policy on Vietnam, in the Dominican Republic, on the perennial opposition of the U.S. to communist China taking the Chinese seat in the UN,* and on the Article 19 crisis, where the United States was apparently in favor of suspending the Soviet right to vote in the General Assembly for nonpayment of dues for the Congo operation.†

U Thant's relations with Dean Rusk did not improve. Rusk evidently resented his efforts on Vietnam, which he felt complicated the already controversial policy of the U.S., and U Thant felt that Rusk distrusted him and did not take him seriously. When they met they disagreed about almost everything, leaving Bunche to pick up the pieces. A typical meeting took place in New York the day after Adlai Stevenson's memorial service in Washington. "Dean began to doodle furiously and U Thant was shaking his legs," Bunche noted, referring to the only overt sign of tension which U Thant permitted himself.[10] Rusk, having shelved U Thant's suggestion for a meeting the year before, was now saying that the United States was looking to Hanoi for a sign of willingness to sit at the conference table, but the communists only escalated the war and were totally responsible for everything that was happening in South Vietnam. U Thant strongly disagreed. "The exchange produced no glimmer of hope," Bunche wrote.[11] Rusk seemed bitter, rattled, and jumpy at this meeting. He accused the UN observers in the Dominican Republic of passing military intelligence to Fidel Castro. He also said, in relation to the Article 19 crisis, that if the Soviet Union insisted on peacekeeping operations' being paid for on a voluntary basis only, the United States would demand the same right, and all UN budgetary contributions would become voluntary.

When I pointed out to Dean that we all know the US would not pay for an operation to which it was opposed, as, for example, a UN peace force in the Dominican Republic, Dean shocked us by saying "questions of finance would never arise as we [the U.S.] would not let it land."[12]

*In a speech in Texas on July 13, 1965, Bunche had said that keeping mainland China out of the UN had been a disaster and a great weakness for the UN, and that its admission could not be many years off. Tendentiously reported in the New York *Daily News*, this speech caused a considerable uproar.

†In February 1965 Bunche had written a long letter to Hobart Taylor, a former colleague from Howard University who was working in the White House. Bunche urged that in order to save the United Nations from paralysis, the United States should accept the Soviet offer to make a substantial voluntary contribution as a way of ending the deadlock. "It would not avail very much to save the Charter and lose the Organization."[9] Hobart Taylor passed Bunche's letter to President Johnson.

"U Thant," Bunche wrote later, "is strongly negative about Rusk, whom he regards as anti-UN, generally reactionary, and the leading 'hawk' in Washington, even more so than McNamara."[13]

On the very next day Rusk called Bunche, "as a friend and as an American," to say that he hoped Bunche would do all he could to convince UN delegates, and especially the Arabs, that Arthur Goldberg would be a good successor to Stevenson.[14] Goldberg was stepping down from the Supreme Court to take up the UN appointment. Presenting his credentials the following week,

Goldberg was very formal—even a little pompous—at the beginning. He had a pile of typed pages before him from which he was reading while trying to appear not to be. It was as though he was addressing an audience and he spoke quite loudly. . . . He spoke frequently of his service on the Supreme Court and how difficult it was for him to leave it, and he seemed to have certain mannerisms of the bench, moving his head and shoulders with magisterial dignity and deliberateness and sitting very erect.[15]

Goldberg did not

fumble and stumble and say ooh and aah as Adlai so often did in trying to present U Thant with the position of the United States, whether because he was not thoroughly familiar with it or disagreed with it, we could never be sure. Probably a combination of the two, as we often had the impression that Adlai had not done his homework too well.[16]

Although Goldberg could, on occasion, be pompous and humorless, Bunche came to respect him greatly, both for his ability as a negotiator and for his courage. He was rumored to have accepted the UN appointment largely in the hope of finding a peaceful solution in Vietnam. Johnson, who on July 28 announced that an additional fifty thousand men would be sent to Vietnam to join the seventy-five thousand already there, also asked U Thant, in a letter delivered by Goldberg, to do everything he could to help bring an end to the war.

Your efforts in the past to find some way to remove that dispute from the battlefield to the negotiating table are much appreciated, even highly valued, by my government. I trust they will be continued.[17]

Encouraged by this message and by the arrival of Goldberg, Bunche drafted a new appeal from U Thant to all the fighting parties. Stating that the basis of a settlement should be the military neutralization of Vietnam

and the democratic determination of Vietnam's future through interna-
tionally supervised elections, U Thant appealed for a preliminary dialogue
leading to a more formal conference, the cessation of all hostile military
activities, and the inclusion in the talks of all who were actually fighting
(i.e., the Viet Cong and the South Vietnamese as well as the North
Vietnamese and Americans).

Goldberg told Bunche that this appeal had been passed on to Saigon
and that he believed Washington would react positively. The appeal unfortunately coincided with the U.S. bombing of irrigation systems and
hydroelectric plants in North Vietnam. U Thant protested strongly
against these attacks on nonmilitary targets, which were, he said, tan-
tamount to making war on the people of North Vietnam. His stock in
Washington quickly slumped again, and, far from showing progress, the
year 1965 ended with a distinct hardening of Hanoi's position and the
development of a strong alliance between Hanoi and Peking, which was
now sending massive assistance to North Vietnam.

In early January 1966 Bunche received a phone call at home from
Dean Rusk, who seemed unusually forthcoming and wanted to talk about
Vietnam. Rusk said that the U.S. peace offensive* was in dead earnest and

warned there would be some "harsh developments" if there was no helpful response to it. . . . Dean asked me to call him "anytime" and give him the benefit of
any views I might have on what Washington is doing.[18]

Two months later at the annual Gridiron Dinner in Washington,
Rusk asked Bunche, "Can't you keep U Thant quiet?"† Rusk was irritated
at recent statements about Viet Cong participation in the negotiations
and added, " 'Why doesn't he come out for a coalition government in
Burma?' Rather petty and irrelevant," Bunche noted. "They are very
sensitive and snippish in DC these days."[19] At the dinner Bunche was
seated between Dean Acheson and a Marine general. Acheson was "very
palsy and reactionary" and told Bunche, among many other things, that
the UN should not have gone into the Congo or Cyprus, which were

---

*During a thirty-seven-day Christmas bombing halt, Johnson had published a list of four-
teen points to demonstrate the U.S. willingness to end the war through unconditional
negotiations, and sent high-level emissaries to thirty countries to explain his views. On
January 31 the U.S. brought the question of negotiations on Vietnam to the Security
Council. Debate was blocked, however, by the Soviet Union and France, who objected
that the U.S. was the only fighting party in Vietnam which was represented on the
Security Council. There was also strong objection to the fact that the U.S. request coincided with a resumption of the bombing of North Vietnam.

†U Thant had appealed publicly for a bombing halt on March 9.

matters better left to the great powers. The Marine general opined that "even if we killed all the North Vietnamese in South Vietnam we couldn't win unless we 'killed all the Viet Cong' guerrillas."[20]

U Thant continued his contacts, but with little success and to the scarcely concealed resentment of Washington. Goldberg told Bunche and U Thant that Johnson was "disillusioned" with the UN because of adverse reaction to his San Francisco speech and to the U.S. attempt to have the Security Council discuss Vietnam. Goldberg himself was increasingly frustrated. He had written to Johnson suggesting a three-point peace proposal similar to U Thant's—unconditional cease-fire; a new Geneva Conference on Indochina; and withdrawal by the United States. The letter at first met with adverse reactions in the White House, but in the end Johnson told Goldberg, "Get Rusk on board and I'll take it." Unfortunately Rusk was abroad, and the matter lapsed.[21] As the months dragged on it was clear that Goldberg, representing the "dove" wing of the internal dispute on Vietnam that was now immobilizing the Johnson presidency, was getting steadily further removed from White House thinking.

U Thant continued to try, with diminishing success, to provide a channel of communication between Hanoi and Washington. He did most of this entirely by himself, especially when he was in Asia. Although U Thant trusted him completely, Bunche could not always get a very clear idea of what the secretary general was doing, since his reports were often rather simplistic. In early March 1967 U Thant had a meeting in Rangoon with a delegation from Hanoi. Goldberg's request over the telephone for a written text was Bunche's first inkling that U Thant had made any "new proposals" about talks at this meeting. He discovered that U Thant had given the North Vietnamese his "proposals" orally, and the Hanoi people had taken notes and promised to tell their government about it. Bunche told U Thant that it would be a good idea to have a written text of such an important communication. When he saw the handwritten text that U Thant had produced over the weekend, Bunche was astonished to find that the secretary general had abandoned his previous insistence on a bombing halt. He had thus met current United States demands while making no concessions at all to North Vietnam. When queried, U Thant said he had dropped the bombing halt because the United States wouldn't accept it. Bunche pointed out that this omission, apart from making the proposal unacceptable to Hanoi, would also weaken those in the United States—including Senators Robert Kennedy and William Fulbright—who were calling for a halt to the bombing. He therefore insisted that U Thant include in his new proposal a passage reading:

The Secretary-General reasserts his conviction that the cessation of the bombing of North Vietnam is a vital need, for moral and humanitarian reasons and because it can lead the way to talks to end the war.

"What troubled me most," Bunche noted after revising U Thant's draft,

was the fact that U Thant did not seem aware of how far he had gone and with what implications. What I was saying seemed to take him completely by surprise.[22]

The U.S. accepted U Thant's proposal on March 18, 1967. There were three main points—a standstill truce, preliminary talks, and reconvening the Geneva Conference—and Johnson expressed the hope that serious meetings with Hanoi would start soon. Unfortunately, now that he had the attention of Washington, U Thant had lost the cooperation of Hanoi, which rejected his proposals on the grounds that they favored the United States and equated the aggressor with the victim at a time when the United States was escalating its war effort.

Bunche had foreseen that U Thant would get himself into an impasse by making his latest proposal easy for the United States to accept and virtually impossible for Hanoi. On April 1 he was being talked at by the verbose ambassador of Saudi Arabia, Jamil Baroody.

In listening, or trying not to listen, to Jamil's customary boring harangue, a thought occurred to me as to how U Thant might be helped in the sense of restoring some balance to his position.[23]

He cut Baroody short and dictated a statement which he immediately took to U Thant at the other end of the thirty-eighth floor.

He read it, commented that it would be "a major political decision," paced the floor, turned pale and after about twenty minutes of agony decided to release it.[24]

Bunche's brainwave, as U Thant called it, was an appeal to the United States, in its position as by far the strongest combatant in Vietnam, to break the impasse by undertaking unilaterally to put the standstill truce into effect, and thereafter only to fire if fired upon. There was, admittedly, a limited risk in doing this, but the United States, "with a power and wealth unprecedented in human history," was in a position to afford it. The statement got a lot of attention and the blessing of the *New York Times,* but the impasse remained unbroken.

In April 1967 Martin Luther King was reported to have urged both blacks and whites to become conscientious objectors in the Vietnam War.

Bunche publicly criticized King for what he saw as mixing up the civil-rights movement with the Vietnam peace movement, and thereby doing serious harm to the civil-rights struggle.

His anti-US-in-Vietnam crusade is bound to alienate many friends and supporters of the civil rights movement and greatly weaken it, an ironic twist for a civil rights leader. In my view Dr. King should positively and publicly give up one role or the other—the two efforts have too little in common in any case.[25]

King called Bunche from Los Angeles on April 13.

He was much disturbed about my criticism of his position, which he said had been misrepresented by the press. He denied emphatically that he was for a fusion of the civil-rights and anti–Vietnam War efforts. Said he was a clergyman and had been wrestling with his conscience. Said he had wanted to consult me about some of his recent speeches but had never got to do so. I assured him that his denial or disavowal eliminated any issue between us as far as I was concerned.[26]

Three days later, during a huge anti–Vietnam War demonstration outside the UN, Bunche received the representatives of the antiwar movement—King, Benjamin Spock, David Dellinger, and several others—in his office. Bunche told them of the widespread frustration at the United Nations that the organization had not been able to play a useful role in halting the war. He described U Thant's personal efforts and emphasized the necessity of stopping the bombing and the need for a unilateral initiative by the United States to stop the war, both of which King had endorsed in a speech earlier in the day.

Bunche doubted that King had done either the civil-rights movement or himself much good by his participation in the peace demonstration. His speech had been too moderate for many of his listeners, and he had seemed ill-at-ease, so that it had none of the dramatic impact of his historic "I have a dream" speech at the Lincoln Memorial during the March on Washington. Bunche also deplored the extremist acts and statements which had marked the demonstration—the mass burning of draft cards and insults to the American flag. In particular he had been incensed by the Black Power leader, Stokely Carmichael's ultimatum to Johnson to get out of Vietnam in a month or "we'll close up New York City." Bunche noted:

In the thirties, I was in the front ranks of the civil rights militants and was regarded by many as "radical" and by some as "subversive," but I never made wild or reckless statements, never stooped to demagoguery and never indulged in insults against personalities.[27]

In the closing months of 1967 the gap between Lyndon Johnson and his ambassador at the UN steadily widened. Goldberg complained that he had virtually lost touch with Johnson, and Bunche's and U Thant's efforts became correspondingly less relevant. Bunche had for some time been warning U Thant that Goldberg's position as a confirmed dove, and his cool relations with Dean Rusk, would soon make his position untenable. On October 20, at the UN Association's annual ball at the Waldorf, Goldberg told Bunche that he would be leaving at the end of the year. He did not actually resign until the following April.

In early 1968, U Thant became very active again. In February he had two meetings with representatives of Hanoi, who informed him that Hanoi would discuss all relevant matters with Washington after an unconditional cessation of the bombing. Peking's condemnation of U Thant's "nefarious activities" over Vietnam probably also gave him increased credibility in Washington. He and Bunche visited Johnson in the White House in late February to inform the president of Hanoi's new approach, and it may have had some influence on the partial halt to United States bombing which Johnson announced, together with his refusal to seek re-election, on March 31. Commenting on this announcement, U Thant, who was greatly influenced by astrology, told Bunche that he had foreseen this development in the stars, and especially in the movements of Saturn, as early as the previous November. Bunche, who found U Thant's stargazing propensities bizarre, commented that LBJ was more influenced by polls than by planets.

Three days later Johnson paid another surprise visit to U Thant in New York, this time giving only seven minutes' notice, so that Bunche barely made it to the front door to meet him. U Thant congratulated the president on his statesmanlike decision on the bombing. Johnson asked U Thant for his help and told him, "I am a poor communicator, but I can communicate with you because I like and respect you."[28] Also in early April, Hanoi declared its willingness to begin preliminary talks with the United States. The talks finally got under way in Paris on May 10.

Although the talks made little progress and the fighting soon intensified, now that talks had started U Thant's and Bunche's efforts on Vietnam no longer had a focus. Goldberg resigned on April 25, and was replaced by George Ball. Bunche was outraged that Johnson's announcement of Goldberg's resignation lacked even a perfunctory word of praise or appreciation for Goldberg's service at the UN. "I found this inexcusable. I see it as evidence of pique and pettiness because of Arthur's differences with LBJ over Vietnam."[29] Goldberg unburdened himself to

Bunche with obvious emotion as they flew back to New York together from George Ball's swearing in. He was deeply disappointed at not being asked to return to the Supreme Court and at Johnson's studious avoidance of him. He told Bunche that he had tried to get Bunche's Harvard classmate Bill Hastie, whom he regarded as superior to Thurgood Marshall, appointed to the Court. Bunche recalled his own efforts to persuade Kennedy to appoint Hastie, and his outrage when Byron White was appointed instead.

George Ball did not fare well at the UN. Bunche wrote:

Ball has not caught on here at all. He seems tense, unnecessarily belligerent, and the general feeling is that he is anything but enamored with the UN and that he is rather arrogant.[30]

Ball left after five months to become foreign-policy adviser to Hubert Humphrey in his campaign for the presidency.

Bunche's preoccupation with the war in Vietnam took a personal twist in June 1968, when Ralph Jr. reported for military service. Ruth had felt that something could have been done to prevent his call-up, but Bunche said that he could not properly take any such step and that Ralph Jr. didn't want him to anyway. "You know," he wrote to his son before he left for Vietnam,

how much I deplore the fact that you have to be there at all and how much I wish you'd come home at the earliest possible moment. As you know, the war is totally abhorrent to me. I regard it as a senseless and dirty business. I am sorry that you are anywhere near it and I hope with all that is in me that you will keep out of harm's way. I would be happy also if you can avoid any situation requiring you to harm anyone else.[31]

Ralph Jr. left for Vietnam on November 3, 1969. He refused to have his parents go to Kennedy Airport to see him off, and Bunche and Ruth had a hard time concealing their emotions until he left the house. Bunche wrote:

As I began to think about the boy's departure, I became furious and outraged. . . . Our one son . . . was being taken off to an utterly senseless, useless war, a war that could bring no good to anyone, that no one could possibly win. That our country had never intended to get into, but had got into simply by stages and accidents and now lacked the courage to get out of. I would not like my son to have to go to any war, but if he had to go in defense of his country, he would have my blessing. But to go to war and risk his life when there was really no question of the country's defense or even its interest at stake was just too damned much. I felt like going out into the street and denouncing in the strongest terms at my command the war, all of those who got us into it and those who keep us in it and the establishment in general. Then my rage became the greater when I realized that I was really trapped, that to give vent to my feelings would not only be embarrassing to the boy, but could considerably increase the risk for him by making him a marked man, which is not a healthy situation in a military set up. And so I set off for the office seething, but never revealing my feelings to Ruth for that would only disturb her more. . . . This is a day of intense bitterness for me.[32]

Ralph Jr. returned safely from Vietnam in October 1970.

28

A Darkening Glass

The Abandonment of Dreams

On Saturday, October 9, 1966, Bunche and Ruth got home late from a New York Jets game at Shea Stadium. At 2:10 A.M., the phone rang, and the voice of a police officer said, "Something has happened to someone. We think it is your daughter." Jane's husband, Burt Pierce, sobbing hysterically, then told Bunche that something terrible had happened, and Bunche realized with a sinking heart that his daughter "was lying crushed and dead at the base of her 12-story apartment building from the roof of which, as the police put it, she had either jumped or fallen."[1] Bunche roused Ruth, and they set out at once for Riverdale. Bunche's failing eyesight made night driving difficult, and they lost their way. A kindly police officer finally guided them to the apartment building. The night was an indescribable ordeal for both of them.

Jane's death broke Bunche's spirit, and it took two years and Ralph Jr.'s imminent departure for Vietnam for him to bring himself to write about it. He longed to believe that it was anything but suicide, but an extensive police investigation turned up no evidence to the contrary. In succeeding weeks Bunche spent the nights searching among old papers and in his memories of the past for some clue as to what had gone wrong. Although he had always thought that Jane had the best mind of his three children, she had also always been neurotic, and at Radcliffe he had had to put her under psychiatric care as a condition of her remaining at college. She had been infatuated with her future husband, Burt Pierce, and had married him when she was, in Bunche's words, "a sweet and lovable child, never a woman." Her sister, Joan, for one, had felt that she was too immature for marriage and had married largely because she had longed to get away from home. After all his soul-searching Bunche eventually concluded that she had probably killed herself in a rage while her husband was at a football game.

Jane's death made Bunche re-examine, in the most painful possible way, the history of his relations with his family. "I love her and appreciate her," he wrote two years later, "much more now than I ever did when she lived."[2] He had always been a strict and demanding parent, and very often an absentee father. Such recollections haunted him in the terrible weeks following Jane's death. The tragedy made him more protective and appreciative of Joan, and apprehensive of what would happen to her when she too left home, as she was now intending to do. Ruth was shattered by Jane's death, and for a time seemed on the verge of a complete collapse, her grief sometimes turning to rage and resentment against her husband.

Jane's tragedy came at a particularly troubling time in Bunche's life. His health was deteriorating rapidly in a number of debilitating ways, many of them connected with diabetes. On a speaking tour on the West Coast in February 1966, he had experienced, for the first time, great difficulty in reading his notes, although they were printed in block letters on a special large-type typewriter. He suffered sudden onsets of acute fatigue and weakness. "I don't know yet," he wrote, "the full implications for my active life of the combination of being in my sixties and having diabetes. It is already abundantly clear that the adjustment for me will be extremely difficult."[3] When he learned that Sheikh Abdullah of Kashmir had nearly died from acute diabetes, he wrote,

I feel sorry for him. He is a great figure of a man but diabetes can take him down. It is insidious in that it seems to erode one's life away—sapping strength in many ways and keeping one entirely at its mercy. I sometimes feel like a doomed prisoner.[4]

The worst immediate result of Bunche's diabetes was the progressive loss of his eyesight. Three days before Jane's death he wrote:

I have realized for months that my sight is going and is not likely to return. The hemorrhages seem to have dissolved but apparently have left scars that will permanently obscure my vision. Will there be new ones and will I end up completely blind? If so, it will be difficult but I believe I can adjust and take it philosophically. Right now I do more stumbling than I like and I'm in danger whenever I am on stairs.[5]

The next year his incipient blindness had a very practical consequence.

I am desolate about having only four more days to drive—then, no licence.

And on July 1, 1967:

my first day without a driver's licence—the first time since I was fifteen . . . that I have been unable to drive myself. That came as a great blow for it means a considerable loss of my independence, which I greatly cherish. I dislike being dependent on any one or any thing.[6]

U Thant arranged for UN security officers to take it in turns to drive Bunche. Senior Secretariat officials did not have perquisites such as personal drivers, and Bunche himself felt strongly that such privileges would erode the concept of an austere, international civil service. He therefore hated the new arrangement that his failing eyesight had made necessary, even though it certainly contributed to the safety of other road-users. He also feared that it would cause jealousy among his UN colleagues. For once he was wrong, and all applauded the arrangement. He himself came to like being driven, which allowed him to work on the way to and from the UN, and after this time most of his personal notes were written in the car.

Bunche was extraordinarily accident-prone. When his toe had become infected on his return from Monaco, he did not notice it for some time because he had lost all feeling in his toes.* The infection was therefore well advanced by the time he saw a doctor, who told him, "you may lose your toe, your foot, your leg, or your life," and ordered him to hospital for four weeks. During the great New York blackout in November 1965, he had insisted on walking down thirty-eight floors from his office and was hospitalized. He also suffered from a pinched nerve in his neck and bursitis in his right hip. He nonetheless continued a hectic social schedule of diplomatic lunches and dinners, visits to the theatre and opera, and the parties associated with them, as well as many sporting events.

Losing his driver's license caused Bunche to muse on his old age.

It is astonishing to me that elderliness has come upon me so suddenly. I have been going at full speed for many years with no thought of life coming to an end or even having to slow my pace. Now I find myself pondering the imminence of age 63, with the realization that 70 is just ahead and that not very many years—at least active ones—are left to me. And all sorts of ailments, aches and pains begin to assail me. All this disturbs and even shocks me, for there are so many things I wish to do, things I have been putting off under the unrelenting pressure of a life thus far of always demanding work.[7]

In this frame of mind Bunche had to face a career decision which would determine how he spent his final years. U Thant's term as secretary general was to expire in December 1966. Earlier in that year Bunche had discussed their respective futures with U Thant and had told him that he

*After this, Bunche wore Coward's Safety Shoes with steel toe-caps.

would not stay on when his contract expired at the end of 1966. "I told him that I was tired and my health was not good." Bunche also warned U Thant about the problem of choosing his successor.

> I have been proud of my complete independence from my government and its influence and my record as an international civil servant. I felt that I had served the UN and had been most helpful to the Secretary-General because they [the U.S.] were aware of my independence. When I left, my government may well try to put an American in my place who would have a relationship to his government somewhat similar to that between the Soviet Under Secretary and his government.[8]

Bunche liked U Thant personally and respected his courage and his integrity, although he was very much aware of U Thant's limitations as a negotiator and his occasionally surprising political naïveté. In 1965, Bunche had strongly urged the Nobel Peace Prize committee that the Prize be given to U Thant, not least because it might give weight to his efforts for peace in Vietnam, and he was much annoyed when it went to UNICEF instead—"a gross injustice to U Thant."[9] Bunche also realized that U Thant's stoic calm masked the anxiety and stress which underlay his frequent indispositions, sometimes even putting him in hospital.

> U Thant has the outward appearance of being Buddha-like in his composure and calm. But actually he is quite nervous. When sitting he is often swaying his legs and bumping his knees together nervously; he almost chain-smokes cigars and he frequently paces the floor in his office. His eyes, particularly, betray his malaise. But he has a good sense of humor and particularly enjoys ribaldry.[10]

Bunche's relationship with U Thant was vastly different from his partnership with Hammarskjöld. He felt protective of U Thant and was more like an older brother than a subordinate to him.

Throughout 1966 governments sounded U Thant out about staying on, but he was increasingly disinclined to do so. He was frustrated at the ineffectiveness of his efforts over Vietnam, and there were many other discouragements and irritations—the weakness of the Third World majority in supporting the principles of independent peacekeeping, the myopic and self-defeating antics of African delegations over Rhodesia, and Dean Rusk's often evident hostility, to name only three. It was, all in all, a discouraging period at the United Nations. U Thant also wanted to go home for family reasons.

When Bunche told Goldberg of the situation, Goldberg said that the UN might collapse if U Thant and Bunche both left. At a reception in the

White House in June Rusk had told Bunche, "You will just have to stay on whether U Thant does or not."[11] On August 29 Bunche reaffirmed, in a letter to U Thant, his intention of leaving at the end of the year, mentioning that he had already submitted a letter of resignation in June 1961 but had agreed to stay on because of the Congo crisis.

Knowing me as well as you do, you will appreciate my unwillingness to stay on the job once I feel that I cannot give to it the intensity and quality of work that my standards call for and which the job itself requires.[12]

Bunche told U Thant how much he cherished

the always cordial, friendly and understanding working relationship I have had with you during these past five years. . . . One could never hope for a better chief. To serve under your leadership has been both an honor and a pleasure.[13]

On September 1 U Thant sent a letter to the whole UN membership stating that he would not offer himself for a second term in the belief that a secretary general should not normally serve for more than one term.[14] He then went into hiding for a week. Goldberg, unable to reach U Thant, called Bunche for advice as to the best means to persuade U Thant to stay on. When Bunche told U Thant of Goldberg's approach, he was puzzled that U Thant said he thought matters should be allowed to cool off and simmer down for a few weeks. On September 14 Bunche noted that, for the first time in their association, U Thant gave him

the impression of being "oriental" about his availability for a further term. . . . He simply sits looking rather inscrutable and being uncommunicative—What does this mean? I think he must know that only by a miracle could there be any agreement on a successor to him by 3 November. Indeed he knows that primarily because of his own known wishes [that things should "simmer down"] practically no effort in this direction is being made. Thus when 3 November comes there will be nobody in sight, and U Thant knows that he cannot just walk away from his desk then and leave the UN without a head. Thus the draft becomes inevitable and automatic and also irresistible. . . .[15]

The pressure on U Thant to stay on steadily mounted on all sides. On October 7, during another surprise visit to the UN, President Johnson told him that he was in total disagreement with him about one thing, namely his stated intention not to continue in office. On December 1 four of the permanent members of the Security Council presented to him a written appeal which, at U Thant's request, contained a somewhat muted reference to U Thant's September letter urging the members of the

Council to give their closest attention to his recommendations—a reference both to Vietnam and to the negative Soviet and French position on peacekeeping. "U Thant responded (a bit too quickly, I thought) saying that the appeal was acceptable to him,"[16] and was congratulated by the four ambassadors. Bunche wrote:

U Thant has been a real puzzle to me in these recent days, an enigma. Although I have been convinced for months that he was determined not to stay, in the last few days he has given the impression to me that he wants very much to stay and wished to avoid doing or saying anything which might jeopardize the opportunity.[17]

U Thant's change of heart posed a serious problem for Bunche, and on December 3 he reminded U Thant of his own intention to leave at the end of the year. "U Thant reacted immediately and negatively saying, 'Oh no, Ralph, I wish you to stay. In fact my belief that you would stay was an important factor in my own decision to stay.' " When Bunche demurred, U Thant begged him to stay at least for a year, saying that if things didn't improve he himself would only stay for a year.[18] All the pressure was now turned on Bunche. When he told Goldberg that his eyes were failing, Goldberg replied that he wasn't needed for his eyes but for his knowledge and judgment; Dean Rusk called on behalf of President Johnson with the same message; the Canadians, the British, and the French took up the cry. But U Thant was the only one to whom Bunche was actually obliged to respond.

On January 6, 1967, Bunche sent a formal letter saying "to my very great regret I must inform you of my inability to change my prior decision." Overriding reasons, in large measure personal, dictated this decision, but Bunche was also dismayed at the confused and ignorant attitude of the General Assembly toward peacekeeping, which he regarded as his most important achievement. U Thant again begged him not to leave and refused to listen to his ideas about his replacement. (Among others, Bunche had Charles Yost and Harry Labouisse, then the director of UNICEF, in mind.) On January 27, in a receiving line at the White House, Johnson told Bunche, "Don't you leave the UN." U Thant's insistence continued.

In some of my talks with U Thant about my retirement in recent weeks, he asked me to sit beside him as he sat in the big upholstered black leather easy chair. He always resisted any real discussion of the subject from my point of view and at times we would just sit and say nothing. I once reflected that it was rather like sitting beside Buddha.[19]

On February 20 Bunche at last, reluctantly, gave in.

I need say here only that the reversal of my retirement decision now entails the abandonment of plans and dreams which I, and Mrs. Bunche as well, have been cultivating over the past six years. . . . As you will readily appreciate, to do that has traumatic implications.*[20]

To Valerie Betts, his English pen-pal, Bunche wrote:

In the end, what it came down to was that I could not win U Thant's concurrence in my leaving, and since I did not wish to leave after twenty-one years in an unpleasant atmosphere, I was trapped.[22]

Whatever the reason for Bunche's uncharacteristic lack of firmness, the decision was a fateful one. For Ruth it was the last in a series of disappointed hopes for a normal life, a series that had played itself out since their wedding day thirty-seven years before. Bunche himself was condemned, in deteriorating health, to a grueling job which would leave him no time for civil-rights work, or indeed to write about his life. It is possible that Jane's death had left such a gap in his life and in his self-confidence that, in the end, he may subconsciously have welcomed the pressure to remain in a familiar job that would leave him very little time for thought or reflection.

*To George Harrar, the president of the Rockefeller Foundation, Bunche wrote, "I must forego the pleasure and reward of the ideal opportunity for post-retirement freedom which you and the Foundation have so generously made available to me."[21]

29

The Six-Day War

Hard Facts and a Convenient Scapegoat

I n 1967, despite the usual crop of violent incidents in the Middle East, there was no general expectation of a full-scale war. One-third of the Egyptian army was bogged down in Yemen, while in Israel the government of Prime Minister Levi Eshkol did not seem to be particularly bellicose. A new, radical leftist government in Damascus had, it was true, since the spring of 1966, taken to encouraging rather than suppressing sabotage operations across the border against Israel. Israel reacted to this development with a massive attack, on November 13, 1966, against the Jordanian village of As Samu. Bunche was incensed by this action.

The Israeli attack on As Samu was shameful, unjustified and utterly misguided. They blamed Syria and attacked Jordan. The attack has precipitated dangerous demonstrations and riots in Jordan. The Palestinians in Jordan are denouncing Hussein and hailing Shukairy.* It is a supreme irony that Israel should be responsible for giving Ahmed Shukairy his greatest boost.[1]

The Syrians were not deterred by the Israeli attack on Jordan, and cross-border incidents continued. On April 7, 1967, the Israeli air force bombed Damascus and shot down six Syrian aircraft. Even this failed to discourage the Syrian government, and the Israelis began to threaten large-scale military action if the infiltrations from Syria did not stop.

Bunche was particularly concerned at the worsening situation in Jordan and the potential Palestinian threat to order and to King Hussein's authority. He was also fully aware of the deteriorating situation on the Israeli-Syrian border. After the UN chief of staff in Jerusalem, the Norwegian General Odd Bull, reported a military buildup on both sides in January 1967, Bunche had written an appeal for U Thant to the two govern-

---

*A preposterous figure who headed the so-called "Palestine Liberation Army."

ments urging them to accept without delay an emergency meeting of the Israeli-Syrian Mixed Armistice Commission. The commission's talks broke down after the Israeli air attack on Damascus in April.

What Bunche and U Thant were *not* aware of was the series of misunderstandings, provocations, accidents, misconceptions, and intrigues which eventually precipitated the most disastrous episode in the long history of the Arab-Israeli conflict, the so-called Six-Day War.[2] They did not know, for example, that on May 13 the Soviet ambassador in Cairo, Dmitri Pojidaev, had delivered to the Egyptian Foreign Office a totally unfounded warning that the Israelis were massing up to twelve brigades on the Syrian frontier.* On the previous day, United Press International had reported a threat by the Israeli chief of staff, Yitzhak Rabin, to occupy Damascus, which Rabin later denied ever having made. Ostensibly, these were the immediate reasons why, on May 14, Egypt mobilized reinforcements and began to deploy them in Sinai.

UNEF, after a shaky start, had been one of the UN's outstanding successes. It maintained, for nearly ten years, almost complete calm on the once bloody frontier between Egypt and Israel, and had come to be taken for granted as a more or less permanent arrangement. The main interest which governments showed in it was a perennial desire to reduce its size and cost, and by 1967 it had a total of just eighteen hundred soldiers on a line extending nearly three hundred miles. These peacekeepers were armed with personal weapons for self-defense only. Apart from occasional statements—in Jordan and other Arab countries seeking to taunt Nasser—that Egypt was hiding behind UNEF instead of confronting Israel, UNEF had dropped out of the news. Even the Soviet Union and France, who regarded UNEF as illegal under the Charter and refused to pay their share of its cost, almost never mentioned it. The secretary general routinely reported on its activities every year to the members of the General Assembly—who then quickly moved on to other matters.

The first inkling of a major crisis arrived in New York on the evening of May 16 in the form of a cable from Major General Indar Rikhye, the commander of UNEF. Rikhye had just received, at his headquarters in Gaza, a strangely worded request from General Fawzi, the Egyptian chief of staff. "For the sake of complete security of all UN troops which install OPs [observations posts] along our borders . . . that you issue your orders to withdraw all these troops immediately."[4] Rikhye immediately referred

---

*Active Israeli military strength at the time was two brigades. On May 15 General Bull reported to Bunche that he had no reports from his observers of any buildup.[3]

this request to Bunche, who informed U Thant, and they called in the Egyptian ambassador, Muhammad El-Kony, to ask what Fawzi's message meant and to suggest that his request be withdrawn. El-Kony called Cairo and reported that the request could not be withdrawn and that Egypt had the right to demand UNEF's withdrawal at any time, which was legally perfectly correct according to Hammarskjöld's agreement with Nasser.

Nasser himself apparently wanted only a redeployment of UNEF. Because he had no confidence that the Egyptian army could hold Gaza, he wanted UNEF to stay in Gaza and Sharm al-Sheikh in order to give the Egyptian army freedom of maneuver in case of war. Field Marshal Hakim Amr, who was far more confident of the Egyptian army, wanted UNEF's complete withdrawal. Nasser had told Amr to change the word "withdraw" to "redeploy" in the message to Rikhye, but the courier had already left for Gaza.[5] El-Kony was getting his instructions from the Foreign Office in Cairo, which was apparently working on the assumption that the UN had been requested to "redeploy" rather than to "withdraw" UNEF, the word used in the message to Rikhye. When El-Kony suggested a partial withdrawal of UNEF, Bunche argued that UNEF could not stand aside to facilitate an Egyptian confrontation with Israel in one sector while protecting Egypt's flanks in other sectors. As the memorandum given to El-Kony put it,

The purpose of the UN Force in Gaza and Sinai is to prevent a recurrence of fighting, and it cannot be asked to stand aside in order to enable the two sides to resume fighting.

This argument was later denounced as inflexible by many of U Thant's critics. It was also cited by the Egyptians, after their defeat by Israel, as evidence of Bunche's responsibility for precipitating the crisis.*

Egypt's actions on the ground spoke much louder than its UN ambassador's words in New York. On May 16 Rikhye was asked to withdraw UNEF troops immediately from Al Sabha, the main UNEF post on the international border, and from Sharm al-Sheikh on the Strait of Tiran. He was told that Egyptian troops must occupy these places that very night,[7]

---

*According to Nasser's confidant, Mohamed Heikal, Nasser interpreted Bunche's remarks to El-Kony as an attempt to cut off discussion of redeployment and make Egypt choose between all of UNEF or none, thereby furthering an American-Israeli plot to embarrass Egypt.[6] How much of this was an *ex post facto* effort to depict Bunche as a malevolent conspirator trying to entrap Egypt, and how much Nasser actually believed the story at the time, is not clear. The idea of Bunche as part of an American-Israeli plot is bizarre, to say the least, but even before the war he seems to have been built up, in Cairo, as a useful scapegoat if things went wrong.

and Egyptian troops moved up in both places on the following day. Such Egyptian actions do not, and did not, indicate that a reluctant Egypt was dragged into a trap by an inflexible and possibly duplicitous international civil servant.

On May 17, while they were waiting for further clarifications from Cairo, U Thant and Bunche met with the ambassadors of the countries whose troops were serving in UNEF. At this meeting the UN's legal counsel, Constantin Stavropoulos, stated that, from a legal point of view, once a government withdrew its consent to the presence of a UN peace-keeping force on its territory, the secretary general had no choice but to withdraw the force. The Scandinavian, Brazilian, and Canadian ambassadors expressed their concern but were unable to deny the validity of this legal opinion; the Yugoslav and Indian ambassadors favored the immediate withdrawal of UNEF.

On May 18 El-Kony delivered the formal Egyptian request for UNEF's withdrawal. Bunche had suggested that U Thant send a strong appeal to Nasser to reconsider his decision before it was too late, but when El-Kony learned of this he told U Thant that he had instructions to advise him strongly not to send such an appeal, because any such move would inevitably meet with a stern rebuff. The Egyptians seemed determined not to be talked out of their suicidal adventure. U Thant, who had expressed to El-Kony his apprehensions of the disastrous consequences of withdrawing UNEF, responded to this warning by telling El-Kony that he proposed to visit Cairo himself as soon as possible and wished Ralph Bunche to accompany him. The following day El-Kony returned to say that,

although Ralph Bunche was held in very high esteem in his country "from President Nasser down to the man in the street," he suggested that I [U Thant] should go to Cairo without Ralph, because his presence in Cairo at this time, since he was an American, would be resented at least by a section of the Egyptian people.*8

Bunche assumed that this was a reference to United States support for Israel, as well as to Egypt's resentment of the strong public criticism in the United States of Egypt's request for the withdrawal of UNEF. At all events, U Thant went to Cairo alone.

*Richard Parker has found in Mohamed Heikal's *1967-al-Infijar* ("1967–The Explosion"), an account of the proceedings in New York based on Ambassador El-Kony's telegrams, which indicates that El-Kony's prejudice against Bunche was a serious obstacle to a proper understanding by Cairo of the realities of the situation. Bunche was, apparently, unaware of El-Kony's feelings.

As soon as Egypt's formal request for UNEF's withdrawal was received, U Thant and Bunche briefed the UNEF Advisory Committee,
which Hammarskjöld had established in 1956. When UNEF was first
deployed in Sinai in early 1957, Hammarskjöld had told the General Assembly that if Egypt were to request its withdrawal, "an indicated procedure would be for the Secretary-General to inform the Advisory Committee which would determine whether the matter would be brought to the
General Assembly." U Thant was following this "indicated procedure." It
is striking, in view of all the later criticism of U Thant, that no member of
the advisory committee, or any other member state, asked for an emergency session of the General Assembly or a meeting of the Security Council at this point. The entire responsibility, in a very difficult situation, thus
fell on the secretary general.

Although deeply disturbed at the possible consequences of UNEF's
withdrawal, none of the advisory-committee members questioned Egypt's
right to demand it, and the ambassadors of the countries with the two
largest contingents, India and Yugoslavia, repeated that they would withdraw their contingents at once. They also revealed for the first time that
their ambassadors in Cairo had been informed of the demand for UNEF's
withdrawal on the previous day and had assured the Egyptians that their
contingents would be withdrawn immediately. Thus UNEF had already
been effectively dismantled without Bunche's or U Thant's knowledge.
All the ambassadors urged U Thant to try to persuade Nasser to change
course.

Bunche laid out for the advisory committee the realities that had to
be faced. "There are legal aspects but there is the aspect of hard facts
too." The basis for Egypt's consent to UNEF's presence in Egypt was an
agreement between Nasser and Dag Hammarskjöld. When UNEF deployed in Gaza and on the Egyptian-Israeli frontier in March 1957, the
UN and the Egyptian authorities had agreed that Egyptian forces would
stay five hundred meters away from the border in some places and two
thousand meters in others, and it was in this space that UNEF operated,
since Israel had never allowed UNEF to deploy on the Israeli side. No one
had ever suggested that UNEF could prevent Egyptian forces from moving up to the line on their own territory, which they had now done,
making it impossible for UNEF to continue to perform its function as a
buffer between Egypt and Israel. There was absolutely nothing that
UNEF could do about such a situation.

Another hard fact related to the security of UN troops, for which
Bunche and U Thant were responsible. Bunche recalled Lumumba saying
to him in the Congo:

We do not need any governmental action to get rid of the UN force here. Any time we become displeased with it, all I have to do is to go on the radio and make a statement and the people will be turned against the UN force. The force will not be able to remain here.

That would be precisely the situation in Gaza if UNEF tried to remain against the will of the Egyptian authorities. In fact, it would be impossible even to feed the UN force because its base airport at El Arish was also an Egyptian military airport.

Bunche told the advisory committee members that the Egyptian government was already furious at statements in Western capitals which implied that Egypt did not have the right to request UNEF's withdrawal. Cairo was accusing the United States and others of trying to make UNEF into an occupation force. "Finally," Bunche concluded,

may I say this. Since I have been working closely with the Secretary-General since this crisis developed, I am fully aware of what he has been doing and saying, and I can assure you that he is doing everything under the sun, everything humanly possible, to try, first of all, to save the situation, and failing that, to see it through as quietly and in as orderly fashion as possible. There is no question here of precipitate action. The only issue is whether there will be agreement that the force will be withdrawn. The withdrawal should take place in an orderly way, which must involve transport and many other questions. It is understood that these would be worked out and would take time.[9]

This latter remark hinted at Bunche's intention to string out the process of withdrawal for as long as possible in order to give time for tempers to cool and for Nasser to be persuaded to change his mind.

The orders to UNEF which Bunche wrote for U Thant that evening reflected this intention, and also Bunche's determination that what had happened should not be seen as a reflection on UNEF itself.

The withdrawal of UNEF is to be orderly and must be carried out with dignity befitting a force which has contributed greatly to the maintenance of quiet and peace in the area of its deployment and has earned widespread admiration.

The force would not cease to exist until all its elements had departed. The commander should make clear to his men that the reasons for the withdrawal were of an overriding political nature and reflected no discredit or humiliation on the force itself.[10]

Bunche was in no doubt as to the extreme gravity of the crisis. In U Thant's report to the Security Council on May 19 he wrote:

I do not wish to be alarmist, but I cannot avoid warning the Council that in my view the current situation in the Near East is more disturbing, indeed, I may say, more menacing, than at any time since the Fall of 1956.[11]

The prospective withdrawal of UNEF evoked strong reactions in many quarters. The Israelis, in spite of their initial hostility to UNEF, believed its withdrawal might lead to a resumption of war between Israel and Egypt, although they were still unwilling to have UNEF stationed in Israel in order to preserve it.* Arthur Goldberg voiced Washington's anxiety, and Bunche explained to him what steps had been taken, and why, at the moment, there were no practical alternatives. He told Goldberg that, although the situation was immensely dangerous, the story was not ended and there would be more developments. When Goldberg called again to say that Washington hoped U Thant would go to Cairo, Bunche told him that U Thant had already decided to go and that Cairo had welcomed his decision. President Johnson offered U Thant his own aircraft for the journey. "I did not have the heart to say to Arthur that this was not a very good idea and so in 'chicken' fashion I assured him that I would convey the offer to the Secretary-General."[13]

The Canadians, who had served in UNEF from the beginning, were particularly upset. Ambassador George Ignatieff, exemplifying the general ignorance of the unusual legal history of UNEF, asked U Thant if he would also withdraw the force in Cyprus if President Makarios requested it. Bunche replied that the two cases were completely different. Hammarskjöld and Nasser had agreed on UNEF's entry into Egypt, because at that time the Security Council was paralyzed by British and French vetoes, and the Suez crisis was being dealt with by the General Assembly. The Security Council had set up the Cyprus force, and the Council alone could decide on its withdrawal. Unfortunately, since the Security Council had had nothing to do with UNEF's establishment, the sole responsibility for withdrawing it fell on the secretary general.

In spite of Bunche's warning that Cairo would violently resent any implication that Egypt had no right to ask for UNEF's withdrawal, Canadian politicians were particularly outspoken in their denunciation of Nasser. When it was announced that two Canadian destroyers were being sent to the southeastern corner of the Mediterranean, Egypt reacted by stating that the security of the Canadian soldiers in UNEF could no longer be guaranteed. Canada thereupon instantly withdrew the Canadian contingent, leaving UNEF without a logistics unit or aircraft. The Canadians were the first contingent actually to leave UNEF, and the only one to leave before the war started on June 6.

---

*When U Thant, on May 19, asked Gideon Rafael, the Israeli ambassador, about a report that Foreign Minister Paul Martin of Canada had asked Israel to accept UNEF on Israel's side of the line, Rafael exclaimed, "Ridiculous. Israel is not the Salvation Army and would not be willing to accept UN discards from Egypt."[12]

Public reactions in the West were more outspoken than official ones and greatly complicated U Thant's and Bunche's task by simultaneously raising the temperature, increasing the misunderstanding of the "hard facts" of the case in the West, and heightening the indignation and intransigence of the Egyptians. The London *Spectator* headlined its account "U Thant's War." Joseph Alsop denounced U Thant's action as "poltroonery." C. L. Sulzberger, in the *New York Times,* wrote that U Thant had "used his international prestige with the objectivity of a spurned lover and the dynamism of a noodle," whatever that might mean.[14] There seemed to be an almost total absence of any effort, or willingness, to analyze the brutal nature of the dilemma or of the hard facts that U Thant and Bunche were compelled to face. Instead, much print and energy were devoted to identifying and denouncing a scapegoat.

In an effort to inject some degree of realism into the Western uproar about UNEF, Bunche gave an extensive briefing to the press on May 20. "That I consented to give this briefing," he told the journalists, "can be said, I suppose, to be a measure of the seriousness of the situation in the Near East, because I do not have to tell you that I do not enjoy this."[15] In a masterly exposition of the history and nature of UNEF he pointed out that if UNEF had the right to remain on Egyptian territory without Egyptian consent, it would never have been allowed to enter Egypt in the first place. UNEF was still there, although it could not function once Egyptian troops had moved up to the line.

In this very stormy and ominous situation, U Thant and Bunche had few practical options. Of the two inter-governmental bodies that might have helped, the Security Council was hopelessly and acrimoniously divided on East-West lines and played no useful role at all in attempting to stave off the disaster. The General Assembly required a two-thirds majority to hold a special session, and since the majority believed that Egypt had a perfect right to request UNEF's withdrawal, there was no hope of the Assembly's agreeing even to meet to consider the matter. In Sinai itself, the Egyptian forces had moved quickly to establish the *fait accompli* which was to be their undoing. All remaining hope therefore rested on U Thant's visit to Cairo.

U Thant left for Cairo on May 22. Just before his departure, Gideon Rafael came in to tell him that Nasser should be left in no doubt of Israel's reaction if Egypt attempted to block Israeli shipping going through the Strait of Tiran to Eilat. On the day U Thant left New York, Nasser, accompanied by Field Marshal Amr, went to the forward air base of Bir Gifgafa in the Sinai and announced that Egypt would be closing the Strait of Tiran to Israeli shipping and cargo, and if this meant war, so be it.[16]

Nasser's statement, which he knew would certainly mean war with Israel, is hard to reconcile with the later Egyptian claim that Egypt had been deliberately trapped into the war. During a stopover in Paris, U Thant learned of Nasser's declaration. His first reaction was to return immediately to New York, but it was 3:00 A.M. in New York, and U Thant did not want to awaken Bunche, whose health was a matter of increasing anxiety to him.*[17] He therefore decided to go on to Cairo. When he upbraided Nasser for his statement on the blockade, Nasser said that the matter had been decided for some time and that he had made the statement before U Thant's arrival so that it would not be interpreted as a snub to the secretary general. This was scarcely the reasoning of someone who was trying to find a peaceful way out of a dangerous situation.

U Thant's talks in Cairo were inconclusive.[18] Bunche urged him by cable to warn Nasser in the strongest terms of the disastrous consequences of the blockade of the Strait of Tiran. U Thant proposed a moratorium on all action in the Strait, which Nasser accepted for a period of two weeks provided Israel also observed the moratorium. He would not, however, undertake to call off the blockade completely. Nasser seemed to be extraordinarily confident. On U Thant's return to New York on May 26, Israel flatly rejected the moratorium and also the appointment of a UN special representative whose task would have been to try to defuse provocative rumors and generally to de-escalate the crisis.

During U Thant's absence Bunche had been racking his brains for possible ways out of a disastrous situation. Some of his thinking was reflected in the report that U Thant made, on his return, to the Security Council, which had at last decided to meet on the crisis. Since Israel would not accept UNEF on the Israeli side, would not agree to the revival of the armistice machinery, and rejected a special UN representative, Bunche drafted a resolution to provide a "breathing spell" by calling on both sides to "refrain from all actions which could increase tensions and aggravate the conflict situation," and to support and assist the efforts of the Security Council to find a peaceful solution.

U Thant also decided to appeal to Nasser and Eshkol for restraint, asking Nasser specifically to refrain from interfering with Israel-bound shipping through the Strait of Tiran, and messages were sent accordingly to the Egyptian and Israeli ambassadors. Bunche soon got a call from a very excited Ambassador El-Kony saying that the message was not in accord with U Thant's talks in Cairo, where it had been agreed that the

*Bunche, who insisted on being awakened during the night for any important message, would have been appalled if he had known of U Thant's misguided consideration on this occasion.

moratorium would include an appeal to all countries not to send oil or strategic materials to Israel through the Strait. Bunche was astonished at this provision, which U Thant confirmed, and told U Thant that such a ban on oil and strategic materials would put him in the position of effectively endorsing the blockade and fully implementing it without any further effort by Nasser. The secretary general's appeal was then withdrawn. "I am convinced," Bunche wrote, "that U Thant did not realize the enormity of the mistake he was about to make."[19]

After a week of totally ineffective debate in the Security Council, Bunche's worst fears were realized at 2:40 A.M. on Monday, June 5, when he received a cable from Rikhye announcing that the war had started. The Israelis struck at breakfast time by land and air with devastating effect. In Gaza fourteen UNEF soldiers were killed in the first hours of the Israeli action. The Egyptian air force, most of it parked on the ground, was demolished within a few hours, and the Egyptian army in Sinai was decisively defeated by June 8. In the days before the war Jordan had concluded a mutual-assistance pact with Egypt, and, despite all efforts by General Odd Bull, the UN chief of staff in Jerusalem, to dissuade them, the Jordanians began shelling Israeli forces in Jerusalem. A savage Israeli counterattack secured Arab Jerusalem and the West Bank for Israel within three days. The Golan Heights in Syria were in the Israeli army's hands by June 10. The Security Council, stunned at last into some semblance of consensus, could only watch this shattering upheaval from the sidelines.

Much of Bunche's life work was destroyed within a few days. The armistice regime which he had built vanished virtually overnight. UNEF, the pioneering experiment in peacekeeping of which he had been so proud, had ceased to exist except as a logistical problem. His efforts to prevent the disaster had been ignored or swept aside. The Security Council had bickered and dithered until it was much too late. The Soviet Union, which might have restrained Nasser, had, on the contrary, played a considerable role in provoking the disaster. The United States, which might have restrained Israel, seemed more intent on pointing the finger at Bunche and U Thant. As an additional tribulation, throughout the endless days and nights of Security Council meetings, talks with ambassadors, and the donkey work of winding up UNEF, Bunche was in intense discomfort from a massive and intractable neck infection.

Bunche was under no illusions as to the far-reaching consequences of the war for the UN. He wrote on June 7:

A likely result of the current war in the Near East will be a sharp curtailment, if not a complete end, of UN peace-keeping activities in that area. UNEF is finished and it may seriously be doubted that UNTSO will ever regain the status and responsibility that it has had since 1949. Israel's great military success is bound to reinforce the traditional position of that country that the relations between Israel and her Arab neighbors should be left to direct negotiations and arrangements without any third party (i.e., UN) intervention. . . . The decline of UN peacekeeping cannot fail to affect adversely the standing and prestige of the UN itself.[20]

There was plenty to be done, most of it depressing cleanup work. Cease-fires on the Suez Canal, which was now the border between the Egyptian and Israeli armies, on the West Bank, and in the Golan Heights had to be established and monitored. A great new wave of Palestinian refugees, many of them displaced for a second time, had to be cared for. Government House in Jerusalem, the UN's Middle East headquarters, had to be recovered from the Israelis. The status of Jerusalem once again became an urgent international problem. UNEF had to be disbanded and sent home. The search for a permanent settlement had to be started all over again.

An additional and gratuitous irritation was a farcical episode in the Security Council involving Bunche and the ambassador of Saudi Arabia, Jamil Baroody. Baroody, a Maronite Lebanese, was famous for his lengthy, florid, irrelevant, and frequently obnoxious speeches, which, especially in times of crisis, were dreaded by the members of the Security Council.* While addressing the Council at length on the war and other topics, Baroody observed Bunche talking to U Thant at the Council table. "Do not distract the Secretary-General, Mr. Bunche," Baroody bellowed. "I am talking. I want him to hear every word, my dear Mr. Bunche. He is my Secretary-General" . . . and so on. Bunche was perhaps unreasonably irritated by this buffoonish behavior, not least because he could not reply. He therefore wrote Baroody a letter.

The Secretary-General's work has to go on during the long sessions of the Council, and I frequently consult with him at the table, as do some of my colleagues. Occasionally, I assure you, I have work to do and matters to take up with the Secretary-General which are more important than listening to speeches, even to one being made by Ambassador Baroody.

Baroody reacted furiously to this letter and, after a series of insulting calls to Bunche's office, made a long speech of protest in the Council. The Soviet ambassador, Nikolai Fedorenko, predictably joined in, remarking

*Nonmembers of the Security Council are permitted to address the Council on matters in which they have a *bona fide* interest.

that the name of Bunche "is offensively linked with the notorious 'Congo Club.' " Others sprang in to defend Bunche, and a great deal of time was wasted. To put an end to this unseemly farce Bunche wrote a letter to be read out by the president of the Security Council.

Mr. President, I am very sorry that a letter written by me should have diverted the attention of the Council from its consideration of matters of such transcendent importance. As Ambassador Baroody has said, we have long been friends, and I am happy to hear him say we can continue so. I wrote the letter because I thought my personal dignity, which means very much to me, had been violated publicly. Ambassador Baroody has clearly stated that this was not his intention. May I say again only that I express my personal regret that I should have done anything to interrupt the Council's attention to the extremely pressing problem before it which means so much to so many suffering people.

Baroody, extricated from a ridiculous situation by this statement, rushed over and, to Bunche's acute embarrassment, embraced him and kissed him on both cheeks.

Bunche was determined to keep the historical record straight in the face of ill-informed statements and attacks from many quarters, often from people whose judgment he normally respected. He and his staff wrote two major documents in an effort to put the record straight. The first, "Notes on the Withdrawal of the UN Emergency Force,"[21] came out two days before the war and was a very full account of the history of UNEF and the hard facts of the current crisis. The second was the report he wrote for the special emergency session of the General Assembly, which met on June 17[22] and was attended by many heads of state and government, including Alexei Kosygin and King Hussein of Jordan. This latter document was a definitive account of the facts of UNEF's withdrawal as U Thant and Bunche then knew them, and dealt incisively with the critics in a concluding section on "Main Points at Issue." Bunche concluded with an effort to try to put the UNEF withdrawal in a larger perspective.

The presence of UNEF did not touch on the basic problem of the Arab-Israel conflict. It merely isolated, immobilized and covered up certain aspects of that conflict. At any time in the last ten years either of the parties could have re-activated the conflict, and if they had been determined to do so UNEF's effectiveness would have automatically disappeared.

The report was printed in full in the *New York Times* on June 28.

In times of crisis, rational expositions of the facts of a case are usually the last thing that those caught up in it wish to read. In a major disaster, it is both easier and more agreeable to pillory a scapegoat than to confront reality. Even before the war, Egypt's desire to shift responsibility for the crisis was reflected in a report from Cairo to the *New York Times* by James Reston.[23] The Egyptians had told Reston that they had not planned to get rid of the UNEF troops in the Strait of Tiran. "This, they say, was proposed by the Secretary-General of the United Nations on the grounds that if the UN couldn't keep its troops in one part of the crisis area, it wouldn't keep them in another."[24] Unfortunately, Reston failed to ask the Egyptians how they would have squared the continued presence of UN troops on the Strait of Tiran with Nasser's blockade or why they had demanded UNEF's departure from Sharm al-Sheikh.

Bunche was annoyed that Reston, whom he had known for many years, could have been taken in by such a transparent and self-serving falsehood. "There is not a shred of truth in it," he wrote to the *Times* in a letter pointing out, among other things, that already on May 16 the Egyptian chief of staff had demanded UNEF's withdrawal from posts in Sinai, specifically including Sharm al-Sheikh on the Strait of Tiran, which Egyptian troops had arrived to take over on the following day. "In critical times such as these, of course, it is common in official and unofficial circles alike to indulge in what may be called deception, if one wishes to be polite about it."[25]

The Egyptian effort at self-exculpation gained momentum in succeeding years. U Thant was shocked, in February 1970, to read an interview in which Nasser had said:

I did not intend to close off the Gulf of Aqaba to Israeli shipping. I did not ask U Thant to withdraw UN troops from Gaza and Sharm al-Sheikh. . . . Nonetheless, the UN Secretary-General, on the advice of the American diplomat Ralph Bunche . . . decided to withdraw UN forces, thus forcing me to send troops into Sharm el-Sheikh and to impose the blockade. That is the way we fell into the trap that was set for us.[26]

U Thant sent this press clipping to Bunche, noting that the passage was not included in the Arabic text published in Cairo. Bunche commented laconically, in returning the clipping, "Thanks. Important omission."[27]

Even some of those in a position to know the hard facts succumbed to the need for a scapegoat. George Brown, the famously emotional British foreign secretary, was voluble, if abysmally ignorant, in his criticisms, and later published a bizarre account of the crisis in his memoirs. Bunche was surprised to learn, on June 14, that Dean Rusk had told a NATO ministerial meeting in Luxembourg that U Thant's rapid acceptance of the demand for UNEF's withdrawal had undoubtedly surprised Nasser. Bunche reacted with a stiff note to the United States Mission. "The Secretary-General regards this casuistic comment as unfounded and unfriendly." After describing Egypt's immediate military moves, Bunche concluded,

It is distressing to find that the Secretary of State has thus given support to the current tendency in the United States and some other places to seek a scapegoat for the recent eruption in the Near East.[28]

Rusk, who had his own troubles, appeared in New York on June 20 and was so bad-tempered, brusque, and discourteous, both to U Thant and to Bunche, that Goldberg, who had accompanied Rusk to the meeting, called Bunche afterwards to ask him to tell U Thant that Rusk had been upset by an unpleasant luncheon discussion with the French ambassador over a statement by de Gaulle linking the Vietnam War and the Middle East crisis.*

A few Western journalists, like James Wechsler in the *New York Post*, strongly defended U Thant. Addressing "pro-administration journalists whose real quarrel is with his refusal to accept our simplistic version of events in Vietnam," Wechsler wrote, "He [U Thant] is a bigger man than many of those in our government—and others—who select him as whipping boy when their own inadequacies and ineptitude are exposed."[30]

On June 19 Abba Eban, reacting to what he described as an "intemperate" speech by Soviet premier Kosygin, launched an attack on U Thant in the General Assembly. "What is the use," he declaimed,

of a fire brigade which vanishes from the scene as soon as the first smoke and flames appear? Is it surprising that we are firmly resolved never again to allow a vital Israeli interest and our very security to rest on such a fragile foundation?[31]

For the representative of a country that had refused to accommodate the "fire brigade" and had so dramatically initiated the actual fighting, this seemed self-serving indeed. Bunche enjoyed writing an uncharacteristically sharp reply for U Thant, who told the Assembly that he was surprised at Eban's remarks, not least because, in a recent meeting with him, "I heard no such reaction as Mr. Eban projected to the General Assembly yesterday; nothing like it." For ten years, UNEF's effectiveness had been based on the cooperation of Egypt, whereas, in spite of the intention of

*Twenty-three years later, in *As I Saw It*, Rusk relived his old differences with U Thant with a one-paragraph description of the UNEF withdrawal, different from the version he gave to NATO, but containing even more errors and contradictions.[29]

the General Assembly to have UNEF troops on both sides of the line, "Israel always and firmly refused to accept them on Israeli territory on the valid grounds of national sovereignty. There was, of course, national sovereignty on the other side of the line as well." U Thant also mentioned Israel's refusal, at the beginning of the current crisis, to accept elements of UNEF on the Israeli side.

I have noted Mr. Eban's picturesque simile of the "fire brigade which vanishes as soon as the first smoke and flames appear." Mr. Eban would agree, I am sure, that for more than ten years the UN Emergency Force had been remarkably effective in preventing clashes and in extinguishing the flames of the raids across the line, the terror of the fedayeen.[32]

The debates in the special session of the General Assembly had little practical effect, and the situation on the ground remained unsettled. On July 1 there was a major clash in the Suez Canal area. Bunche therefore suggested that UN observers be stationed on both sides of the Canal to help preserve the cease-fire. It took a week to persuade Egypt and Israel to agree to this, and the observer posts were established on July 11—the most dangerous assignment ever given to UN observers because of the frequent heavy exchanges of fire across the Canal. The egregious Fedorenko, who had a habit of abusing Bunche behind his back while being sickeningly amiable to his face, tried to insist that only the Security Council could authorize the exact numbers and nationalities of the observers on the Canal. This was an important matter of principle, involving, as it did, the secretary general's authority over peacekeeping operations, and Bunche mobilized U Thant to fight for a right that the secretary general had exercised from the very beginning.

I was not sure U Thant would stand up before this challenge, especially since there was evident weakness among those who might have been expected to take a strong position against the Soviet attempt, including Canada, Denmark, the UK and even the US. But U Thant was very firm throughout, and at the end it was Fedorenko who had to back down completely.[33]

Fighting flared up along the Canal again in mid-July, and Bunche worked with the Israelis and Egyptians in trying to get a cease-fire.

I suppose it should be regarded as an encouraging feature of man that these people, who are always so ready to fight, are also ready to stop early on in the fighting if we can help them out of it.[34]

The cease-fire came into effect at 6:00 P.M. on July 15.

There was relief—at least for a while. We had done it again for the Nth time. I got the usual expressions of gratitude from the two ambassadors.[35]

The combatants themselves seemed exhausted by the events of the early summer, and the situation on the Canal and in the Golan Heights gradually settled down to an uneasy and often broken truce. In August, Bunche even managed to have some days off to take his grandchildren to Expo 67 in Montreal.

Bunche remained puzzled by the Egyptian moves which had led up to the war, and a year later he asked Mohamed Riad, a friend of many years who was senior assistant to the Egyptian foreign minister, Mahmoud Riad, if he could throw any light on the matter. Riad described the disastrous process as due to "miscalculations on the basis of misinformation." For a number of ill-founded reasons, including his belief in the superiority of the Egyptian army in equipment and numbers, Nasser was convinced that, in spite of the Tiran blockade, Israel would not go to war alone. To Bunche's astonishment, Riad said that many Egyptian officials had brought themselves to believe that U Thant had wanted to get rid of UNEF because it was a financial burden. Bunche told Riad that two main factors had determined U Thant's decision: Ambassador El-Kony's insistent warning that the state of mind in Cairo was so adamant that no change of course was possible; and the revelation, at the advisory-committee meeting on May 18, that Cairo had already passed the demand for UNEF's withdrawal to the ambassadors of the countries with troops in UNEF and had been assured that their governments would comply.[36]

To the end of his life Bunche ruminated on the Six-Day War and the role he and U Thant had played in the crisis. He was not in possession of much of the information that has since come to light, or of many of the often self-serving and dishonest accounts that have emerged. He remained convinced that, in the political circumstances of the time, there was no feasible alternative course of action that might have avoided the disaster. The miscalculations, the internal politics, the pressures, and the misinformation that drove Nasser to his suicidal adventure had made him immune to appeals to reason. If the United States and the Soviet Union had joined forces and exerted their full influence the story might have been different, but instead their acrimonious mutual hostility had simply made a bad situation worse. No help was to be had from the Security Council, which was neutralized by the Cold War, or from the General Assembly, a majority of whose members believed that Nasser was well within his legal rights and that there was therefore nothing to discuss.

Given the harsh realities of the situation, Bunche did not believe that, in the circumstances, anyone could have handled the situation to better effect than U Thant, whatever his shortcomings as a negotiator. "Since I worked very closely with U Thant's predecessor, Dag Hammarskjöld," Bunche wrote to Eugene Rostow, who had criticized U Thant strongly,

on both the creation and supervision of UNEF, I feel I can say with considerable confidence that Mr. Hammarskjöld would have done exactly what U Thant did with regard to the withdrawal of UNEF, and in much the same way. There was in fact no sensible alternative course, although wishful or frustrated thinking might hold otherwise. . . . There have been so many totally, and sometimes I fear willfully, misleading accounts of the withdrawal of UNEF, in which U Thant is made a convenient scapegoat for the 1967 War in the Middle East. Such accounts, apart from fostering bad history, seriously impede a clear understanding of contemporary international relations including the functioning of the United Nations.[37]

In the years before 1967 the governments which paid for UNEF had complained constantly that it cost too much and demanded that it be reduced in size. The Six-Day War and its consequences showed that a small peacekeeping force with no military power was a far more important element of peace in the Middle East than most governments had realized.

Bunche never shied away from unpleasant realities. If he was convinced that he had done everything he personally could about a problem, he was prepared to accept the criticism and the outcome, whatever it was, and move on. His experiences had made him very much aware that there are some problems, especially international ones, to which, in practice, there is no good solution. The Six-Day War had been a massive disaster for the Arab countries of the Middle East, for the long-suffering Palestinians, and for the United Nations itself. It was an immense setback for the experiments and ventures which Bunche himself had pioneered. Until his death Bunche continued his efforts to keep the historical record straight, but since he could think of no realistic way in which, in the existing circumstances, the crisis could have been handled to better effect, he did not repine.

30

Winding Down

Not Much to Celebrate

The traumatic summer of 1967 took a heavy toll on the physical health as well as the peace of mind of both Bunche and U Thant. It was, in any case, a stultifying period at the United Nations. The organization was mired both in the paralysis of the Cold War and in the new confrontation between the old industrialized countries of the West and the radical and angry new countries of the so-called Third World. The 1945 San Francisco vision never seemed so remote as in Bunche's last years.

In fact, he did not attend the celebration of the twenty-fifth anniversary of the UN in San Francisco in June 1970

because I could not bring myself to feel that there was very much to celebrate about at this time. I have particularly in mind, of course, the situations in Indo-China and the Middle East which continue to frustrate us.[1]

To the British sculptor Barbara Hepworth, who had sent him a message on UN Day, October 25, and with whom Bunche had worked closely in 1964, when Hepworth's great memorial to Hammarskjöld, *Single Form*, was unveiled, he wrote:

Thank you so much for your thoughtful cable, which meant a great deal to all of us here. After the interminable speechifying, editorializing and cliché-ridden pronouncements of pessimism and despair which accompanied the 25th anniversary celebrations, it was refreshing to get a short and simple message from a real friend.[2]

The Middle East remained a central concern, in spite of the discouraging reception afforded to most UN efforts to do something about it. On November 22, 1967, after prolonged negotiations, the Security Council adopted Resolution 242. This historic decision—a compromise based on the return of occupied land in exchange for a full peace—which remains to this day the basis of the search for a Middle East settlement, also called for the appointment of a special representative in the Middle East. U Thant appointed Gunnar Jarring, at that time the Swedish ambassador in Moscow. Bunche had great respect for Jarring, who had been Sweden's ambassador to the United Nations in the late 1950s, and worked closely with him in his ultimately abortive search for a settlement. Jarring made a noble and painstaking effort to pursue his mission, but he lacked the solid support and the economic or political weight necessary to move either the Arabs or the Israelis on the major problems of the Arab-Israeli conflict. Bunche noted:

The Council has given no indication of its position on any of these problems. Thus Jarring has been without guidance or support on specific issues. On general occasions, however, the Council has taken action warmly endorsing the Jarring mission and beseeching cooperation with it. That is to say "To Jarring with love."[3]

Jarring himself became increasingly frustrated. Bunche noted in November 1968:

Gunnar Jarring comes in to see me three or four times every day. He is a very taciturn man but obviously has the need to unburden himself to someone. He tells me about every talk he has and every thought. He seems to sense that he can trust me and that I will not speak to anyone but U Thant about what he tells me and will not tell even U Thant everything.[4]

Jarring liked Bunche and greatly respected his wisdom and his keen analytical mind, which, in Jarring's words, "quickly saw through the traps hidden behind elegant formulations."

Jarring still held his Moscow post and came to New York only periodically, when it seemed possible that something useful could be done with regard to the Middle East. Such occasions were relatively rare, and Bunche devoted much time to encouraging him and suggesting new ways in which he might approach his extraordinarily difficult task. Bunche saw Jarring in Stockholm when he went to represent U Thant at Trygve Lie's funeral in Oslo in January 1969, and persuaded him to come back to New York for a prolonged stay.

Bunche's other main objective in the Middle East was to halt the War of Attrition, as the intensive exchange of high explosives across the Suez Canal had come to be called. The War of Attrition waxed and waned throughout the late 1960s, mostly in the form of heavy artillery exchanges.

It was perhaps the best-documented war in history, with the UN observers reporting, round the clock, every artillery shell or burst of small-arms fire to Bunche in New York. Bunche was deeply concerned with the risks that the observers were running and the periodic casualties in their ranks. Irritated by a journalist's suggestion that the UNTSO observers' emblem should be changed to a sitting duck, Bunche responded:

I cannot think of any guys who have been more truly heroic than these fellows out there on the line now. I do not understand it fully myself. Why the devil they should be risking their hides and their lives every day, I do not know. There is no question of national patriotism or national obligation involved. They are getting nothing out of it. They are certainly not highly paid. They are under fire every day for the United Nations. It is amazing that they stick to it. And not only do they stick to it, but we have none who have even hinted that they would want to leave. I just do not know of any more heroic action in history.[5]

In addition to the War of Attrition, a new form of violence, international terrorism, had emerged out of the Arab-Israeli conflict. International aviation was the main target of this new wave, which focused especially on Israeli, or Israel-bound, aircraft. The hijacking of an El Al aircraft to Algiers led to a lengthy process of negotiation at the UN and elsewhere, which finally ended successfully. When Arab gunmen fired on an El Al aircraft in Athens in December 1968, Israel retaliated with a commando raid which destroyed thirteen airliners at the Beirut airport. The most massive hijacking operation took place in September 1970, when, as a prelude to the Black September Palestinian uprising in Jordan, five jet airliners were hijacked by Palestinian terrorists to Roberts Field in Jordan, three of them being blown up there after the passengers and crew had disembarked. Such incidents occasioned Security Council meetings and lengthy negotiations with various governments or their ambassadors.

In important meetings with the secretary general, Bunche still insisted on taking all the notes himself, which would have been a taxing job even for a healthy, younger man. As his eyesight deteriorated, his writing became larger and more rambling, lines often being written on top of previous lines. The records he dictated, however, remained models of clarity and precision. Bunche also insisted, to the considerable annoyance of his staff, on always being woken up personally by the UN cable office during the night for any important communication from the field. Thus it was quite usual to find, on coming to the office in the morning, that Bunche had transacted a long and complex piece of business by telephone in the small hours of the previous night.

Other crises came and went. In August 1968 news came that the

Soviet Union and other Warsaw Pact countries were massing troops on the Czechoslovakian border. U Thant called in the Soviet and Czech ambassadors and, on Bunche's advice, canceled his departure for Europe and remained in New York, in a vain effort to head off the Soviet invasion.

The civil war which raged in Nigeria over the secession of Biafra was a particularly frustrating and poignant demonstration of the limitations of the UN. Because it was a civil war, the United Nations could not intervene except with humanitarian aid, and the organization's critics did not miss the opportunity to lambaste the UN, and especially the secretary general, who had volunteered his good offices to the warring parties, for inaction and callousness. On a Friday afternoon in July 1968 a young African woman in Nigerian costume burst into Bunche's office in a highly excited state, protesting on behalf of the Biafran victims of the civil war. She said she would stage a hunger-and-sitdown strike in Bunche's office until the UN took action. The UN's security officers wanted to eject her, but Bunche refused to let her be taken from his office by force and tried to reason with her. He had sandwiches brought in, which she refused. The woman eventually calmed down and talked about the war, and after three hours Bunche convinced her that, for all his sympathy with her complaints, it was useless for her to go on sitting in his office. When she got up to leave he told her that she was free to return at any time if she wished to do so.

Another problem of national sovereignty and jurisdiction arose during the visit to U Thant, in August 1969, of Patrick J. Hillary, the foreign minister of Ireland. Ireland was interested in a UN peacekeeping force for Northern Ireland, but U Thant told the foreign minister that the British would never accept such an arrangement. He suggested, however, that he might send a special representative to look into civil-rights issues in Northern Ireland. Asked if he would undertake such a mission, Bunche replied without hesitation that he would do so if U Thant wished, on the assumption that in this case his American nationality would not be a disadvantage. He warned, however, that the British might not be too happy. Although the Irish were enthusiastic at the prospect of Bunche's mission, nothing came of the plan. A few days later Bunche had a chance to observe the other side of the Northern Ireland problem. He described the Reverend Ian Paisley, the Northern Irish Protestant leader, as "a burly man, being intense and vociferous and somewhat frightening in his intensity and in the cold glint in his eye and his masklike countenance."[6] Talking to Paisley made Bunche think of the intercommunal strife in Cyprus, which had persisted, with disastrous results, despite all efforts to resolve it.

It was a gloomy time for other reasons. The assassinations of Martin Luther King* and Robert Kennedy were American tragedies which also personally affected Bunche. Bunche had first met Robert Kennedy when Kennedy was a student at the University of Virginia Law School. Kennedy had asked him to speak at the university and had told him that although the law of the state of Virginia required segregation in audiences in public places, there would be no segregation at Bunche's public lecture. Impressed with Kennedy's willingness to flout the law in a good cause, Bunche accepted the invitation. He had greatly enjoyed meeting Kennedy and his young wife, who had met him at the airport and driven him around Charlottesville. More recently, in 1966, Bunche had shared the dais with Kennedy and Senator Jacob Javits at a dinner in New York. As they were leaving, Kennedy said to Bunche, who had received by far the largest ovation at the dinner, "that was one hell of a hand you got there. I'm glad I don't have to run against you."[7] Bunche had had great hopes and expectations that Kennedy would develop, perhaps as president, into a fearless fighter for civil rights and for world peace.

Robert Kennedy's death hung like a shroud over the 1968 presidential election. When asked how he was going to vote Bunche replied that he had never seen so many bad alternatives.

Hubert [Humphrey] has lost irretrievably his own liberal image. He is now a shadow image of LBJ. He made a grave mistake in accepting the role of Vice President. He became something akin to a court jester in King Lyndon's court. Nixon, in my view, is an utter hypocrite, without conviction or principle. He is a small, ambitious and dangerous man. Thus in November I shall close my eyes, hold my nose and vote for Hubert only because to do otherwise would be to help Nixon. Anything but that.[8]

In December, President-elect Nixon visited U Thant. Bunche had a long talk with the new president, telling him, among other things, that UCLA always beat Whittier, Nixon's college, even in football, to which Nixon responded, "Low blow."[9] The fact that Nixon, accompanied by William Rogers, his future secretary of state, and Henry Kissinger, his future national security adviser, chose to visit U Thant before taking office had evidently mellowed Bunche's opinion of him.

Bunche's somber mood was not relieved by a week at a Pugwash Conference at Sochi, in the Crimea, in October 1969. Apart from two nights in the Swedish Embassy in Moscow with Jarring, he felt cold and unwell the whole time. The Russians, concerned at his failing eyesight, insisted on his visiting the famous Filatov Clinic in Odessa for an eye

*See Chapter 32.

examination. The clinic constructed for him a remarkable pair of eye-glasses that looked like opera glasses. Although he could see slightly better with them, they were so heavy and ungainly as to be unwearable. The discussions at the conference, largely on nuclear matters and attended by both scientists and politicians, deeply depressed him, especially a sophis-ticated debate on ballistic missiles which seemed to him a

numbers game of extinction. . . . I was appalled also by the apparent lack of conscience and feeling of guilt by that select group of men from whose ranks had come those who made possible the nuclear monster, and who indeed even now are preparing even more monstrous and diabolical means of extinction.

At a circus performance in Sochi, he reflected that the clowns and the performing brown bear made more sense and knew better what they were doing.[10]

In these years of trouble and frustration there were some pleasant moments. In May 1969, Bunche went to UCLA for the dedication of Ralph Bunche Hall, the tallest building—eleven stories—on the UCLA campus, and the new home of the university's social science depart-ments.* Bunche told the audience that the occasion was more thrilling to him than the Oslo ceremony where he had received the Nobel Peace Prize. He talked of hope and concluded:

This great hall now bears the name of one who firmly believes in peace; who believes that men can bring themselves to live together on this little planet in harmony, understanding and mutual respect; who believes, in short, in people."[11]

By this time Bunche's speech notes had to be painted in huge letters on large sheets of paper. The director of the UCLA archives secured this unusual text for the university's collection.

The UCLA ceremonies gave Bunche the opportunity to see the Los Angeles members of his family, and it was the last time he saw his aunt Ethel. When she died in the following year Bunche recalled her fierce loyalty to the Johnson family.

Ethel saw in the Johnson family an expression and a renewal of the great virtues of life—love, fidelity, industry, achievement. . . . I owe to Ethel more than I can say. . . . After Nana's death she was a mother to me. I often disagreed with her, particularly in what seemed to me to be an excessive zeal and protectiveness about our family. But I came in time to understand that in upholding the family as she did, Ethel was, in fact, serving and enriching all of us.[12]

*The building was originally to be called the Social Sciences Building at UCLA. When it was completed the student body asked that it be called "Ralph Bunche Hall."

Back in New York, other old memories were stirred by a chance meeting in the Waldorf-Astoria lobby with Peter Koinange, Bunche's fellow student in London and now the foreign minister of Kenya. Koinange was on the telephone and signaled to Bunche to come over and take the receiver. On the other end was Jomo Kenyatta, who had taught him Swahili in London and was now the president of Kenya.

In July and August 1969 Bunche took Ruth, Joan, and Ralph Jr. on what was to be their last trip abroad together. He had a program of visits to Rockefeller Foundation* overseas projects and a speech to make in Hawaii, as well as an official visit to Cyprus, but the duties were relatively light. They traveled to Honolulu, Tokyo, Manila, Hong Kong, Bangkok, New Delhi, Tehran, Istanbul, Beirut, and Nicosia. Although Bunche had another severe retinal hemorrhage in Bangkok, he enjoyed the trip. The highlight for him was a night concert in the Roman amphitheatre in front of the Temple of Bacchus at Baalbek in Lebanon, with the Leipzig Orchestra playing Brahms' Second Symphony. He also managed to see on television in Tokyo the Apollo blast-off, in Manila the astronauts' moonwalk, and in Bangkok the splashdown.

Bunche had not lost his taste for controversy, and his outspoken speeches on the civil-rights question often aroused hostile reactions. He also continued his dogged efforts to set the record straight on the 1967 Middle East war. He enjoyed commenting in the British press on George Brown's memoirs, which appeared in serial form in November 1970, and wrote in the London Sunday *Times*:

Mr. Brown writes much of his own various ideas for dealing with the Middle East crisis, all of which were unavailing. . . . He does not mention that of all the world's leaders, U Thant alone, instead of engaging in rhetorical outbursts at home, went immediately to Cairo . . . in an effort to forestall the dangers of war and to persuade President Nasser to reconsider his course of action. . . . It is a pity that Mr. Brown, apparently in an attempt to mask his own ineffectiveness in a serious crisis, should have been driven to such a reckless and irresponsible attack on another public figure who did everything he possibly could, in the most difficult circumstances, to avert disaster.[13]

Bunche also remained outspoken about matters nearer home. On February 9, 1969, a record snowfall marooned him and other inhabitants of Queens in their homes for three days. Outraged, Bunche fired off a telegram to New York's Mayor John Lindsay.

---

*Bunche was then serving on the Rockefeller Foundation board.

The snowstorm came on Sunday. This message is sent on Wednesday. In all that period no snow plow has appeared on our street or in our vicinity. There are no buses, no taxis, no milk, newspapers or other deliveries, and there have been no trash or garbage collections since last Friday. As far as getting to the United Nations is concerned I may as well be in the Alps. This is a shameful performance by the great City of New York, which should certainly condone no second-class boroughs.[14]

Evidently stung by this missive, which Bunche's staff had shown to correspondents to explain his absence from work, Lindsay called U Thant and accused Bunche of being politically motivated in sending his message. This in turn infuriated Bunche, who told Lindsay that U Thant had nothing to do with the matter. He had sent his telegram as an American citizen, taxpayer, voter, and home-owner in the borough of Queens. "I fail to see," he told Lindsay, "how an appeal to the city's Mayor for snow plow service three full days after the snow ceased falling could be considered to be 'political.' "[15]

Secretary of State William Rogers had become very active in the search for a Middle-East settlement, and in support of Gunnar Jarring's mission. In 1969 the four major powers in the Security Council—Britain, France, the United States, and the Soviet Union—began to hold meetings at the UN in an attempt to devise a basis for moving Jarring's mission forward. This development was regarded with ill-concealed suspicion by Israel, and without enthusiasm by the Arabs.

In 1970, the War of Attrition flared up to unprecedented levels of violence. "By June 1970," U Thant wrote, "three years after the Six-Day War, the chances for peace appeared more remote than ever."[16] In August, however, Egypt, Israel, and Jordan agreed to send representatives to New York for discussions under Jarring's auspices. They also agreed to a standstill cease-fire for ninety days from August 7. Bunche, who celebrated his birthday on that day, said that the fact that for the first time since 1967 soldiers on both sides of the Canal could stroll peacefully in the sunshine was the best birthday present he had had for years. Jarring was summoned urgently to New York, but the arrangement soon hit a snag. The Israelis withdrew their representative, Joseph Tekoah, on the grounds that the Arabs were not observing the cease-fire, and they accused Egypt of moving SAM-2 and SAM-3 anti-aircraft missiles into the Canal Sector. It was not until New Year's Eve that the Israeli representative returned to New York.

Jarring's talks still made no progress, and on February 8, 1971, he tried to break the deadlock. After consulting Bunche, he submitted to

Egypt and Israel a memorandum asking Egypt and Israel to make prior and simultaneous commitments to him on the two key questions—Israeli withdrawal from territories occupied in the '67 war, and the acceptance of a peace agreement by Egypt and, ultimately, by Jordan. To almost everyone's surprise Egypt accepted Jarring's proposal within a week, but Israel reacted angrily, asserting that Jarring had exceeded his terms of reference in proposing that Israel should withdraw to the June 1967 boundaries. This was, in effect, the end of the Jarring mission, and Bunche was now too ill to make the effort to revive it.

Throughout this period, Bunche's health had steadily and inexorably declined. In 1968 a bout of pneumonia had put him in hospital. He found it increasingly difficult to stay awake when he was not actively engaged, and sitting for long hours in the Security Council was a particular torment. The British ambassador, Lord Caradon, who greatly liked and admired Bunche, addressed to him a note in verse during a Council meeting on the Middle East:

> *Our master slept*
> *While watch was kept*
> *Upon the Sea of Galilee—*
> *It's after lunch*
> *And Dr. Bunche*
> *Shows equal equanimity.*

Bunche was delighted with this effort and would have liked to reply in kind, but, "Alas, I find that in Bunche there may be rhythm, but no rhyme."[17]

In November 1969 Bunche noted that for three months he had endured constant and sometimes excruciating pain in his left arm and shoulder from arthritis and bursitis, and Darvon made him nauseated.

My ailments have now become cumulative—diabetes, circulation in the left leg, loss of vision and sinusitis, frequent nausea, chronic constipation, discharging ear and punctured eardrum, albumen in the urine, loss of feeling in toes and fingers and occasional high blood pressure.[18]

Nonetheless, he somehow continued his official and social schedule. The problems of civil rights and race in the United States were more critical than ever, and there was still one more international negotiating challenge.

31

Bahrain

So Successful That Hardly Anyone Noticed

As Britain's influence was withdrawn from the Persian Gulf in the late 1960s, a new balance of power and new rivalries were emerging in that strategically and economically vital region. With the imminent departure of the British, the island sheikhdom of Bahrain, a British protectorate, was in a particularly vulnerable position. Bahrain had been under Persia's sovereign jurisdiction until it had been seized by the Arab al Khalifa family in 1783 and subsequently brought under British protection early in the nineteenth century. For over a century Persia had claimed the sovereign rights over Bahrain if the British left. Modern Iran regarded Bahrain as its Fourteenth Province, keeping empty chairs for Bahrain's deputies in the Majlis, the Iranian parliament. Iran's claim was strongly opposed not only by the British and by Sheikh Isa bin Sulman al Khalifa, the ruler of Bahrain, but also by Iraq, Saudi Arabia, and other Gulf states. The situation had all the makings of a serious conflict in a very sensitive part of the world.

U Thant was first approached on the Bahrain question by the British and the Iranians in early 1969 after the Shah had publicly rejected the use of force over Bahrain,* and he agreed to undertake a "good-offices" mission to try to resolve the problem. The objective was to get Iran, Britain, and the ruler of Bahrain to agree on a mechanism by which the views of the people of Bahrain could be ascertained and the result approved by the Security Council. Such an arrangement would allow Iran to give up its claim without loss of face. U Thant turned the problem over to Bunche, and a year of intensive negotiations ensued.

*The Shah apparently had no intention of fighting for Bahrain and said on a number of occasions to Sir Denis Wright, the British ambassador, "the pearls have run out; the oil is running out; what is the good of Bahrain to me?" On the other hand, the Shah needed a respectable pretext for giving up Iran's historic claim to Bahrain.[1]

The matter was extremely delicate so that, in addition to negotiating skill and mutual confidence, total discretion and secrecy were essential. Bunche's discussions, which he kept completely to himself, were mainly conducted with Mehdi Vakil, the Iranian ambassador to the United Nations, and Anthony Parsons, Lord Caradon's brilliant head of chancery at the British Mission to the United Nations. Parsons had previously served as British political agent in Bahrain.

The early discussions were frustrating. The Iranian government wanted a full plebiscite in the island, a course rejected by Britain and the ruler of Bahrain. Both feared the unpredictable consequences of Nasserite propaganda and knew that organizing a plebiscite in a semi-feudal autocracy would be extremely difficult. It was only when the shah of Iran suggested that the choice of a mechanism should be left to the secretary general that Bunche's talks with Parsons and the Iranians began to make headway. Parsons wrote:

It was a long and difficult business. Dr. Bunche was mortally ill and nearly blind, but mentally alert as ever. In spite of his infirmity, his devotion was total. . . . Dr. Bunche was on his last legs and I had to read the documents aloud to him.[2]

Parsons was astonished at Bunche's analytical powers and verbal memory. He could recall old texts with complete accuracy and could suggest drafting changes just as if he were able to see the written words on the page.[3]

Bunche felt strongly that if the secretary general was to be given a free hand in ascertaining the wishes of the Bahrainis, he must choose a method which could not, after the event, lay him open to charges of collusion in a put-up job. Though he recognized that the ruler of Bahrain would not accept a plebiscite, he was suspicious of his insistence that the secretary general's personal representative should consult only a carefully chosen list of "existing organizations." He insisted that the representative should be free to consult individuals. The Bahrain government eventually concurred.

The negotiations on these procedural matters went on for the rest of 1969. By December the British and Iranians reached an agreement, but it was still necessary to get the agreement of the Bahrainis, who, being by far the smallest and weakest party involved, were not unnaturally apprehensive. Bunche was the obvious choice to inspire the necessary confidence, and he reluctantly agreed to meet with the ruler's representatives in Geneva.

Bunche was by this time in such poor health that he could not face the prospect of sleeping away from home. He therefore left New York by the Swissair night flight on December 30. He arrived in Geneva at

8:15 A.M. the next day, met with the Bahrainis, and took the afternoon flight back to New York. The meeting achieved its purpose. The Bahrainis, realizing the effort that Bunche had made, and having the opportunity to meet the secretary general's personal representative, Vittorio Winspeare Guiccardi, were reassured that the UN mission was in good hands. They agreed on the special representative's method of operation. "Geneva trip went well and was worthwhile," Bunche cabled to U Thant, who was in Senegal, ". . . no hitches. Awaiting receipt of formal request. Hope all goes well and happy new year."

In March 1970 Iran and Britain formally requested U Thant to send a personal representative "to ascertain the true wishes of the people of Bahrain with respect to the future status of the Islands of Bahrain."[4] Winspeare arrived in Bahrain in late March.

Bunche, who had kept this fragile vehicle on the road successfully for a whole year, was determined that nothing should go wrong in the final stretch. It was something of a miracle that there had been no leaks, or indeed any press reports at all, during the long months of negotiation, but until it was successfully concluded the operation remained extremely sensitive. Bunche therefore sent Winspeare a comprehensive letter of instructions. It was the last such directive he was to write.

Tact and restraint must be the watchwords, and any unofficial discussion of the work of the mission must be avoided.

There could be disastrous consequences for the mission if there should be the least basis for an allegation that any member of it was seeking to influence the Bahrainian views. Discussions of local politics should likewise be taboo. This is a mission for wise men only, from top to bottom. . . . We approach this exercise with complete impartiality. It will be only the people of Bahrain who will speak conclusively.[5]

Bunche continued to monitor and advise Winspeare's mission until Winspeare left Bahrain for Geneva on April 18 to write his report.

My conclusions have convinced me that the overwhelming majority of the people of Bahrain wish to gain recognition of their identity in a fully independent and sovereign state free to decide for itself its relations with other states.[6]

The Soviet ambassador, predictably, complained that U Thant had exceeded his authority in the Bahrain matter. In the reply he wrote for U Thant, Bunche described the meaning of "good offices." Sometimes states approached the secretary general directly for his help on a delicate matter.

They explain that they do so because they feel that a difference between them may be capable of an amicable solution if dealt with at an early stage quietly and diplomatically, and, therefore, it will be inadvisable to take the particular matter before the Security Council or to consult its members individually on it. . . .[7]

The Security Council welcomed the solution of the Bahrain problem on May 11 with congratulations all around. Lord Caradon made a somewhat fatuous tribute in verse ("Thank God that Bunche is with us still / and his indomitable will."), and summed up the achievement in a comment to the *Christian Science Monitor*.

So the favorable factors have converged and met—British restraint, Iranian magnanimity, United Nations impartiality, Italian fairness and judgement . . . and Arab dignity and self-respect, an irresistible combination.

The Bahrain negotiation was a textbook example of settling a dispute by quiet diplomacy before it degenerated into conflict.[8] U Thant noted that

it was the first time in the history of the UN that the parties to a dispute entrusted it to the Secretary-General's good offices by giving a *prior pledge* to accept without reservation the findings and conclusions of his personal representative,

and he warmly acknowledged Bunche's role.[9] Ironically, the very smoothness of the negotiation ensured that it got little public attention. As U Thant put it, "the perfect good offices operation is one which is not heard of until it is successfully concluded, or even never heard of at all."[10]

In Bunche's mind the Bahrain negotiation had been uniquely important for the UN. It was the first time a secretary general's recommendation had led to action by the Security Council. It had greatly enhanced the concept of the secretary general's good offices. And it had established the principle that it was possible to ascertain the wishes of a people by a method short of a plebiscite, a principle that could have relevance to other intractable problems, such as Kashmir.[11] The British Mission in New York concluded its report to London on the Bahrain case with the words "At this end the main credit goes to Dr. Bunche, whose good will, patience and skill were truly exemplary."[12]

32

Civil Rights and Race in the United States

This Is My Country Too

"One ever feels his two-ness," W. E. B. Du Bois wrote in 1903, the year of Bunche's birth,

an American, a Negro; two souls, two thoughts, two unreconciled strivings; two warring ideals in one dark body. . . . The history of the American Negro is the history of this strife—this longing to attain self-conscious manhood, to merge his double self into a better and truer self. He would not Africanize America, for America has too much to teach the world and Africa. He would not bleach his soul in a flood of white Americanism, for he knows that Negro blood has a message for the world. He simply wishes to make it possible for a man to be both a Negro and an American, without being cursed and spit upon by his fellows, without having the door of opportunity closed roughly in his face.[1]

Bunche himself faced the problem of ethnic dualism in a positive and determined way. He was proud both of his ancestry and of his nationality. "I only ask that the one be as much respected as the other."[2] As regards terminology, "The word 'Negro' for me is an ethnic term with no objectionable connotation at all. It describes my ethnic roots and I have always had a deep pride in those roots."[3]

Honored and respected the world over, the fact remained that, at home, for all his fame, Bunche was a leading member of a still disadvantaged and increasingly resentful minority group. The more famous he became, the more Bunche brooded on this, not least because of the exceptional treatment he himself now invariably received. There had, admittedly, been landmarks of progress and signs of hope, but by the 1960s it was distressingly clear that the "American dilemma" persisted and, in the urban ghetto, was taking larger and more intractable forms. In Bunche's declining years this bitter reality became his dominant preoccupation.

In his own life, reminders of racial discrimination and bigotry were still never far away. Accounts of Bunche's achievements were prefaced, with a monotonous predictability, with phrases like "the first Negro to . . ." or "the grandson of a slave" (not true; he was the great-grandson), which whites apparently believed to be complimentary, but which Bunche and his family found obnoxious and patronizing. There were still annoyances in hotels. When Bunche was on a visit to Birmingham, Alabama, in February 1959, the mayor of Birmingham gave him the Key to the City but he was refused a room in the Dinkler-Tutwiler Hotel. He had the same experience at the Dinkler Hotel in Atlanta in July 1962. Bunche's appointment to the Harvard Board of Overseers in 1959 was attacked, ineffectually, by the extreme-right Veritas Foundation.

A widely publicized incident in 1959 concerned the West Side Tennis Club in Forest Hills, where the U.S. National Championships and Davis Cup matches were then played. The tennis pro at the club had coached Ralph Jr., then at the Choate School in Connecticut, and suggested he become a member. His application was turned down by the club's president, Wilfred Burglund, on the grounds that the club was closed to Negroes and Jews. Bunche, as a matter of principle, publicly protested and received wide support, including that of Senator John F. Kennedy of Massachusetts. The club's Board of Governors then announced its president's resignation and informed Bunche that his application would receive "courteous and prompt attention." Bunche declined the offer ("I'm too old for tennis"[4]) but said he would take the matter up with Ralph Jr. when he came home from school. After hearings with New York City's Commission on Intergroup Relations, the club announced a change in its membership policy.*

Neither Bunche nor his son had any overwhelming desire to belong to the West Side Tennis Club. Bunche had simply felt obliged to protest against bigotry at an important sporting institution.

I question no one's right to dislike, even to hate, me as an individual and to refuse any association with me. But when I am rejected solely because of my race, thus automatically refusing every Negro, this is bigotry. There should be no room for bigotry in the house of democracy.[5]

Bunche had given his sister Grace the money for a down payment on a house of her own in Los Angeles, and in July 1961 she wrote,

*Arthur Ashe was playing for the first time at the West Side Tennis Club in the Eastern junior championships at exactly this time.

I want you to know how happy we are in our new home. This community is an all-white one, and we were not welcomed with open arms. One dear lady told the broker that sold us the house that he had upset the block. This is really my first time running into anything of this sort, so I guess Alabama is not too far way. For Sale signs have been flying ever since we arrived. . . .[6]

Still nearer home, Ruth, when exasperated by Bunche's absences, tended to criticize his white colleagues for what she perceived as their hypocritical attitude toward him. "*None* of them," she wrote in 1959, "no matter how broadminded, would want their children to marry your children—no matter how highly they regard you or like you."[7]

Bunche did not need such relatively trivial episodes to remind him of the rising tide of black resentment at the unfinished business of civil rights and racial integration, or of the growing impatience that was making "progress" a dirty word for the majority of Black Americans.

The word progress has almost become a bad word because progress has now become synonymous in thinking with gradualism and . . . gradualism has run its course. . . . The promise of the Constitution, which is almost 200 years old, has been unfulfilled as to the basic promise of equality and rights for the black American. . . . If you are a resident in the ghetto, and that's where the majority of Negroes now live, then you know that the term progress is meaningless. . . . The conditions in the ghetto in terms of segregation, discrimination, are worse now than they were ten, fifteen years ago when the intensified Civil Rights struggle began. . . .[8]

It was this sense of time and momentum lost, and human suffering and outrage increasing, that drove Bunche's efforts on civil rights in his last years. It also compounded his frustration at the failure of his several attempts to retire from the UN, where his position made it impossible for him to play as active a role on civil rights as he would have wished. As in his earlier and more radical years, he was determined to do whatever he could to keep the civil-rights movement on a sound course, and to discourage what he regarded as false prophets or diversionary and self-defeating ideas. It was not always plain sailing. Bunche's international fame and prominent position made him an easy mark for accusations that he was out of touch with, or not sufficiently caring of, the plight of the mass of Black Americans, especially when he publicly opposed what he considered to be irresponsible or reckless actions.

Not everyone, though, perceived Bunche's international success as detracting from his domestic influence. John Hope Franklin had written, "Negroes were heartened when Ralph Bunche . . . joined the United

Nations to work with the Trusteeship Council. They hoped that this Negro specialist would, somehow, be able to advance substantially the welfare and interests of those people who would be unable to promote their own interests."[9] Nor was Bunche's early work forgotten. A. Philip Randolph was quoted as saying:

Important as Dr. Bunche's work for the United Nations has been, I remember him best for his early commitment to the civil rights campaigns during the 1930s and 1940s. Our movement was young then, and it was totally committed young people like Ralph Bunche whose spirit and resilience, in the face of overwhelming odds, gave strength to the rest of us. His assistance during campaigns for a fair employment practices commission and an end to racial segregation in the military was invaluable. These important campaigns laid the foundation for the progress we were to achieve during the 1950s and 1960s.[10]

While younger and more radical black leaders sometimes criticized him for lack of involvement, Bunche was frequently accused, especially in the U.S. Congress, of improperly using his international position to further civil-rights causes or to criticize the United States, and his strong pronouncements often evoked floods of hate mail and abuse.

Bunche had come a long way from the Marxist radicalism of the 1930s, but his basic convictions remained the same. As Charles P. Henry has put it, "Bunche's views on race and human rights remained consistent, and only the strategies for achieving self-determination changed."[11] He was adamant on the evil of racism, from whatever source. "We do not have to become racists ourselves to win our struggle," he told the NAACP convention's "Youth Night" in 1962. "In my judgment black bigots are no better than the white breed. I both scorn and pity white bigots; I despise those who are black."[12] Though deploring the slow pace of change, he was convinced that protest action within the law and without violence was still the best option for Black Americans fighting their way into the mainstream of American life, and that genuine equality of the races was the only valid ultimate goal.

I want to be a man on the same basis and level as any white citizen. I want to be as free as the whitest citizen. I want to exercise, and in full, the same rights as the white American. I want to be eligible for employment exclusively on the basis of my skills and employability, and for housing solely on my capacity to pay. I want to have the same privileges, the same treatment in public places as every other person. But this should not be read by anyone to mean that I want to be white—I am as proud of my origin, ancestors and race as anyone could be. I want to go and do only where and what all Americans are entitled to go and do.[13]

Bunche's opposition to separatism became, if anything, stronger in the face of its several advocates in the 1960s. In 1965 the NAACP had dissociated itself from "Black Power" doctrine on the grounds that, as Roy Wilkins put it, "it is the ranging of race against race on the irrelevant basis of color. It is the father of hatred and the mother of violence." Bunche did not dismiss the concept of Black Power out of hand and felt that in reaching out to the mass of Black Americans and fostering unity and combined effort it could serve a useful purpose. But he disagreed completely with black nationalists who denounced integration. "They are hard put to it to define the alternative . . . for there is really no other goal than integration that will make any practical sense."[14] "Stokely Carmichael, Rap Brown, Floyd McKissick, Adam Clayton Powell," he said at UCLA on February 21, 1968, "can and do speak with great eloquence and gusto about black power, but they falter when it comes to talking about the end results of the exercise of black power."

Bunche's lifelong conviction that integration was the only acceptable goal for Black Americans had been reinforced by time and experience. The

fantasy of separation . . . is simply a new version of the escapism of the Garveyites of the thirties, with their vain dream of escaping to Africa where there was no place and no welcome for them. I care nothing about a mythical separate black man's country. I want equality here, for this is my country too.[15]

I think the Black Muslims are pitifully wrong and misguided. . . . I have always held, and still hold, that the Negro can and will win his struggle for full equality in this society. Implicit in the doctrine of the Black Muslims is resignation to the Negro's inability ever to win this struggle, and therefore he must accept the doctrine of separation of the races, which ironically, is the core of the philosophy of the white supremacists.[16]

Full equality was the birthright of Black Americans.

I am a Negro, but I am also an American. This is my country. I own a share in it, I have a vested interest in it. My ancestors helped to create it, to build it, to make it strong and great and rich. All of this belongs to me as much as it belongs to any American with a white skin. What is mine I intend to have and to hold, to fight, if necessary, to hold it. I will not give up my legacy in this society willingly. I will not run away from it by pursuing an escapist fantasy of an all-black road to an all-black society—the illusion of a black heaven.[17]

Bunche was equally exasperated with some white attitudes.

Those who oppose integration generally refer to it as "mixing the races." This is a ridiculous conceit, since it assumes that the major preoccupation of Negroes is to "mix" with whites. They should know that we have far more important preoccupations—making a living and bringing up our children properly, for example, not to mention trying to keep our peace in the face of many provocations. We are not the least interested in "mixing."[18]

If Bunche was opposed to the doctrine of separation, he disliked even more the tactics and rhetoric of some of its advocates. In all of his experience of racial discrimination Bunche had never allowed himself to become bitter or to feel racial hatred. He was outraged by Malcolm X's remarks to a rally in Los Angeles on the crash of an Air France charter aircraft at Orly Airport in which many of the cultural leaders of Atlanta were killed. Malcolm X was reported by *Time* to have said that

a very beautiful thing has happened. . . . I got a wire from God today. . . . He dropped an airplane out of the sky with over 120 white people on it. . . . we will continue to pray and we hope that every day another plane falls out of the sky.

Bunche commented,

This utterance could only come from a depraved mind. We do not have to become racists to win our struggle.*[19]

Bunche was generally skeptical of extremist black leaders and their aims, and they in their turn were skeptical of him. Stokely Carmichael, for example, who was more concerned with economic empowerment than with violence, was quoted as saying, "The food Ralph Bunche eats does not fill my stomach"[22]—or, more colloquially, "You can't have Bunche for lunch." Long ago, in 1936, Bunche had written that black leaders who relied on a "racial interpretation" led "negroes up the dark, blind alley of black chauvinism."[23] Although Bunche had worked with him on integrating the staff of the 1964–65 World's Fair at Flushing Meadows, New York, he regarded much of Congressman Adam Clayton Powell's behavior as reprehensible. When Powell proclaimed that Black Americans should boycott the NAACP because it had white people in high positions, Bunche responded:

I think such a statement is absurd and deplorable. It is basically a racist statement and I'm against racism whatever its source. . . . The fact that the Negro wins,

*There is a story that, after his visit to Mecca in 1964, Malcolm X visited Bunche to make his peace with him.[20] I can find no record of such a visit. However, at Kennedy Airport on his return from Mecca, Malcolm proclaimed, "A blanket indictment of all white people is as wrong as when whites make blanket indictments against blacks."[21]

increasingly, white support for his struggle for equality is to me a most encouraging and reassuring social fact, and I would wish to encourage it . . . not reject it.[24]

When Powell was quoted in the New York *Amsterdam News* as saying that Black Americans "had not heard from Ralph Bunche since we helped fight to get his son into the Forest Hills Tennis Club," Bunche replied, "As to Mr. Powell not having heard from me since then, this may be due to the fact that Adam does not speak in the deep South as I do and seems to avoid NAACP meetings." Bunche went on to list fifteen speeches he had given in the South on race relations and integration. In the March on Washington he had not seen Malcolm X at all, and Powell only briefly when a group of congressmen put in a short appearance at the Lincoln Memorial. What Malcolm X and Powell really disliked, Bunche wrote, was his strong stand against any form of racism, white or black.[25]

However, when the House of Representatives, overriding the advice of its party leaders, voted to exclude Powell for misappropriation of funds and other improprieties, Bunche publicly denounced the decision as a punitive strike against Powell and his Harlem constituents, and as an action motivated by racial prejudice which would not have been taken against a white congressman. Bunche was denounced for this statement by Representative Earle Cabell of Texas, who accused him of exploiting his United Nations position to interfere in American politics.

Bunche found a strong ally for moderation and common sense in Jackie Robinson, who had broken through for Black Americans in major league baseball and at this time wrote a column in the *Amsterdam News*. Robinson also was intermittently denounced by black radicals for having sold out to the white establishment. The athlete even went so far as to tell Bunche that they were both targeted for assassination, "because we are too integrated in the white society and were so strong in support of integration."[26]

Although he did not always agree with its leaders, Bunche strongly supported the growing civil-rights movement, and its main groups and their leaders: NAACP (Roy Wilkins), the National Urban League (Whitney Young), the Southern Christian Leadership Conference (Martin Luther King, Jr.), the Congress of Racial Equality (CORE) (James Farmer), and the Student Nonviolent Coordinating Committee (SNCC) (John Lewis). In 1956, when Martin Luther King, Jr., was organizing a bus boycott in Montgomery, Alabama, Bunche cabled to him:

I greatly admire and warmly congratulate you all. I know that you will continue strong in spirit and that you will stand firm and united in the face of threats and resorts to police-state methods of intimidation. Right is on your side and all the world knows it.[27]

Bunche admired King's bold social activism and emphasis on non-violence. He anxiously followed King's 1963 drive against racial discrimination in Birmingham, Alabama, and the confrontation with the dogs and cattle prods of the chief of police, Eugene "Bull" Connor. When King was awarded the Nobel Peace Prize in 1964, Bunche warmly congratulated him, but "at the same time I felt it was a mistake to ignore in the award Roy Wilkins and the NAACP, the true pioneers in the field who actually made King's efforts possible."[28] On his way to Oslo to accept the Nobel Prize, King, accompanied by Andrew Young, had dinner with Bunche in New York.

The murder, in June 1963, of the NAACP's Mississippi field secretary, Medgar Evers, at his home in Jackson seems to have intensified Bunche's desire to participate actively in the civil-rights movement. He attended Evers' funeral and denounced his murder as a "foul and cowardly deed" and "a national disgrace." "The Negro of today," he said, "can be infuriated but no longer intimidated."[29] Bunche warned that the only possible result of such acts would be the intensification of black demonstrations and violent black reactions.

On the first day of the 1960s, Bunche, leaving for an extended trip in Africa, had expressed the belief that the back of segregation had been broken and that achieving integration was now a matter of time.[30] In this optimistic estimate he had not taken full account of the changing nature both of the race problem in the United States and of the civil-rights movement. By 1960 the black population of the United States was predominantly urban and located for the most part in Northern cities, increasingly blighted by problems of housing, unemployment, and education, many of them a by-product of racial discrimination. The black protest movement, originally a middle-class movement to secure black constitutional rights through court action and legislation, was shifting to a broader mass movement giving more emphasis to direct action than to legal solutions, more insistence on overcoming poverty and cultural deprivation than on securing constitutional rights.

Bunche welcomed mass participation in the civil rights movement.

Impatience . . . has been a prime motivation in the heroic actions of Negro youth—and some white youth too—in the sit-down, bus boycott, freedom ride,

campus strikes and demonstrations and other protest activities of recent years—
activities in which I have rejoiced because they mark a new awakening for the
Negro and courage in support of bold action. . . . Such demonstrations were not
only timely, they were long overdue. Actions of this kind have accelerated the
pace of progress in the achievement of social justice by dramatizing the struggle
for all the world to see. . . .[31]

Harry Truman had blasted the student sit-in movement and remarked, "If
anyone came into my store and tried to stop business, I'd throw him out.
The Negro should behave himself." Bunche commented:

I would have been happier if Mr. Truman had said, as I believe would have been
the case, that the problem wouldn't have arisen because he wouldn't have had
segregation in his store.[32]

Two months after Evers' murder, on August 28, 1963, the great
March on Washington provided the context for King's electrifying "I
have a dream" speech. Bunche marched and then spoke at the Lincoln
Memorial, along with Roy Wilkins, Whitney Young, James Farmer, John
Lewis, A. Philip Randolph, Walter Reuther of the United Auto Workers,
and representatives of all the churches. He later described the march as
"almost a religious experience."[33] After the march, its leaders were received by President Kennedy.

In the summer of 1964 there had been riots in black areas of New
York, Philadelphia, and other Northern cities. During the first three
months of 1965, Martin Luther King launched a prolonged campaign in
Selma, Alabama, in support of the right of Black Americans to register as
voters. King himself was arrested in early February along with 766 others.
On March 5, King announced his intention to organize a march from
Selma to Montgomery, the state capital, to present a petition to Governor
George C. Wallace demanding the right to vote and protesting police
brutality. Governor Wallace banned the march, but seven hundred
marchers set out anyway and were driven back by state troopers using
cattle prods and tear gas. King made another attempt two days later and
was stopped again, but on this occasion one of the marchers, a white
Unitarian minister, Dr. James Reeb, was beaten up and died of his inju-
ries, causing widespread indignation and a demand for federal intervention. On March 12 President Johnson announced that he would submit a
voting-rights bill to the Congress and asked for an injunction against
interference in peaceful demonstrations. He later mobilized two thousand
National Guardsmen and one thousand military police to protect the
marchers.

On March 19 Bunche enthusiastically accepted King's invitation to join the new march on March 21, in spite of the fact "that chronic phlebitic condition precludes any lengthy marching, but I managed the March on Washington with no difficulty."[34] When he arrived in Selma King told him, "Ralph, your presence gives a new dimension to our effort."[35] King, Ralph D. Abernathy, and Bunche led the march. Along the way they kept themselves informed, with a small transistor radio, of new developments, including bombings in Birmingham. Bunche walked for over nine miles.* He then had to return to work at the United Nations, but came back to rejoin the march as it entered Montgomery. He commented that the march was "a technique that can be very useful, if judiciously planned and timed to make sure it will not boomerang. It is a fine tactic when used right, and Dr. King knows how to use it right."[37]

"By God, we are here! Little more need be said," Bunche began his speech on March 25 outside the Statehouse in Montgomery, where Governor Wallace was still refusing to receive the voting-rights petition. Bunche paid a heartfelt tribute to King's "superlative leadership." Rejecting Wallace's denunciation of the marchers as "outsiders" and "meddlers," he said:

I am here as an American; an American with a conscience, a sense of justice and a deep concern for all of the people and problems of our country. . . . I say to Governor Wallace that no American can ever be an "outsider" anywhere in this country. . . . And lest the Governor has forgotten it, Alabama lost its attempt to leave this Union more than a century ago. Apparently he has forgotten it, for I see the Confederate flag flying up there over the dome of the Capitol. . . . That flag should have come down over a century ago. . . . In the UN we have known from the beginning that secure foundations for peace in the world can be built only upon the principle and practice of equal rights and status for all peoples, respect and dignity for all men. The world, I can assure you, is overwhelmingly with us.[38]

This speech earned Bunche an even larger harvest of hate mail than usual, a typical offering being a postcard to "Rev. Dr. Ralph Bunche Jr." reading,

> Hey d'ere Niggershit
> Yo' marchin' right to de gas chamber
> Maccabee

---

*The FBI, reporting to the president and secretary of state on Bunche's participation, said that he could not walk for more than one and a half hours and that he needed a private room because "he lives on the needle." The FBI did not see fit to explain that as a diabetic Bunche needed insulin shots, and that he also had phlebitis.[36]

Despite the deaths and the violence that occurred on the fringes of the march, Bunche was finally convinced of the merits of this kind of action. No doubt recalling his research in the South for Gunnar Myrdal's *An American Dilemma* twenty-six years before, he wrote, "The most important single factor, in my view, has been the overcoming of fear by the Negro in the South. When he could no longer be easily intimidated, a great stride forward had been taken."[39]

The problems and the effects of the ghetto had preoccupied Bunche from his earliest studies of the plight of Black Americans. In 1941, when he was trying to alert his black compatriots to the mortal danger of Nazism, he commented on the narrow and self-centered nature of black thinking about world affairs. "This is the inevitable consequence of the physical and intellectual ghetto existence that has been imposed upon us by the white man's hard-bitten prejudices. . . ."[40] In 1947 he wrote that though the ghetto dictated "a decided provincialism . . . a tendency toward the short view and emphasis on the local scene . . . an exaggerated racial chauvinism," there were positive effects as well.

The harsh ghetto life . . . has unquestionably developed in [the Negro] certain traits which have assured his survival and have made possible his development; an essential hardihood; an ability to take suffering in his stride; a certain callousness; an elemental cynicism; an indifference to odds against him; an artificially stimulated group pride; a peculiar form of self confidence . . . a burning resentment. . . .[41]

Bunche came back time and time again to the ghetto as the ultimate symbol of segregation.

The logic of American democracy seems to be self-evident. If we are all Americans—not Negro Americans on the one hand and white Americans on the other, but just Americans, there should be no separate working or living for any of us, no group segregation, and no racial ghettoes.[42]

He feared the capacity of the ghetto for breeding demoralization and defeatism.

We must face it, there will be some Negroes among us who will claim to prefer segregation to integration. . . . Inevitably there will be some who are just too weak, too timid, too lacking in self-confidence, too incompetent, or just too plain lazy to wish to risk competition in the open field beyond the ghetto.[43]

After riots in several Northern cities the previous year, the worst riot of all took place in the Watts section of Los Angeles on August 11–16,

1965. Having grown up in Los Angeles,* Bunche felt this particularly keenly.

Unspeakable tragedy has occurred in Watts—tragedy for the city, for the nation and, most particularly, for the American Negro and his cause. . . . There was no "insurrection" in Los Angeles; the rioting had no politically motivated leadership or organization and no rational purpose. . . . The ominous message of Watts, I fear, for all America, is that it has produced, raw and ugly, the bitterest fruit of the black ghetto. . . . There is but one remedy: city, state and national authorities must quickly show the vision, the determination and the courage to take those bold—and costly—steps necessary to begin the dispersal of every black ghetto in this land.[45]

The summer of 1966 was again a period of racial tension and urban riots—in Chicago, Cleveland, Brooklyn, Omaha, Baltimore, San Francisco, and Jacksonville. A few urban projects, such as the Bedford-Stuyvesant Renewal and Rehabilitation Corporation in Brooklyn, were started, but there was no massive governmental response to the tragedy of Watts and other urban ghettos. Meanwhile, a more radical black approach flourished. Floyd McKissick of CORE, defining "black power," asserted that "it takes shock to wake this nation up," and put forward six basic objectives, including black control of government in areas where the Negro was in the majority, the development of militant leadership, and a black consumer bloc to counter unscrupulous manufacturers and merchants.[46] In October, in Oakland, California, Huey Newton and Bobby Seale founded the Black Panther Party, the aims of which included reparations for the wrongs done to Black Americans, the release of all black prisoners, and the trial of Black Americans by all-black juries. The SNCC leader, H. Rap Brown, speaking from the riots in Cambridge, Maryland, was quoted as telling his followers, "You'd better get yourselves some guns. The only thing honkies respect is guns." Black Power and black nationalism seemed to be a rising force. Such developments inevitably created a strong white backlash.

Again, in 1967, there was a "long hot summer" of rioting, starting in Newark, New Jersey, where 26 people died and fifteen hundred were injured. In July, in Detroit, Michigan, where Bunche's first years had been spent, four thousand soldiers were needed to quell the disorder, and im-

*In December 1969, in an interview with Sam Donaldson on ABC's *Issues and Answers,* Bunche said, "I came up in a ghetto, East Side Los Angeles, the apparent ghetto of Watts." He soon received an irate letter from Aunt Nelle. "Where did you ever get the idea that you grew up in the black ghetto? When you were growing up this street of ours was almost entirely white."[44]

mense damage was done. In a long note written during this summer, which was also the summer of the Six-Day War, Bunche asked himself, "What can be said realistically about a complete separation of the races in this country?" The concept was

born of a despair about the black American ever being accepted equally and treated decently in a predominantly white society in which all aspects of life are controlled by and for whites and which is going to remain that way in the foreseeable future. It is an expression of the complete loss of hope and faith in the American society, in its promise and its dream of equality and integration, motivated also by animus against whites and a virulent black racism.

On the practical level, however, there was no real possibility of a black state coming into existence, and the crucial condition for total separation could not therefore be met. What was left was partial separation. Black Americans, already largely segregated in ghetto communities, would demand increasing local autonomy through insistence on decentralization.

But it is painfully obvious that the black communities can never be economically viable except on an intolerably low standard of living as compared with the white community. Bedford-Stuyvesant can never hope to come close to Manhattan in terms of wealth, employment and other opportunities. Therefore, the black American, under partial separation, will continue to have his economic life in the white sector. The practical result of this in time will be an American version of apartheid."[47]

This somber assessment only strengthened Bunche's conviction that the key to the future must be massive action to disperse the "forced, collective ostracism"[48] of black urban ghettos, with their perennial harvest of frustration, bitterness, despair, hatred, and desperation, which now so frequently erupted in mindless, self-destructive violence. "No racial peace can exist in our country so long as ghetto existence is imposed on one-tenth of our total population."[49]

Bunche developed the themes of this note into a paper on "Upheavals in the Ghettos,"[50] and, in a noteworthy departure from his usual practice, submitted it for publication to Look magazine. Look had already commissioned a series of articles on the subject, but suggested that Bunche's long article should be immediately syndicated in six sections. Bunche did not favor this idea, and in the end the paper had a small private circulation only. Focusing on the crisis of the ghettos, it is a distillation of all his experience and ideas on the race problem.

The paper starts with a harsh premise.

The majority of Negroes are ghetto dwellers, and the ghettos embody all of the worst and most intolerable injustices of racial discrimination. . . . Twenty-one million disillusioned and potentially disaffected citizens could become a mortal cancer in the body of this society.

Bunche felt that urban racial skirmishing could even lead eventually to racial civil war, starting with "ghetto guerrilla fighting in the brick and concrete jungles of a modern metropolis."

Bunche viewed the reaction to the riots of many white officials, in particular Governor Richard Hughes of New Jersey and Mayor Hugh Addonizio of Newark, as showing a total misunderstanding of the phenomenon they were trying to deal with. They seemed to believe that the riots were a conspiracy or an insurrection inspired by "criminal elements" rather than the end result of black grievances.

My shame at Negro conduct in Newark at the time was quickly mixed with dismay and fear at the attitudes revealed in . . . public statements by highly responsible officials in the troubled areas. . . . I may repeat that Newark's ghetto, as Detroit's and all the others, was ready to explode. All the ingredients were there. Any spark, a relatively trivial incident, could set it off. It required no plan by criminals.

Bunche went on to describe the growing impatience of Black Americans with continuing underprivilege:

the people of the ghettos, particularly outside of the south, can see little change in their political and economic status as a result of civil rights activity and the civil rights legislation adopted in Congress, and no gains at all in other spheres. They are still just as black, segregated tightly in their housing, their schools, their hospitals, their churches. After working hours they generally see only black people, except for the white shopowners and the police of the ghetto.

There is serious and dangerous disillusionment among Negroes from the inability of the traditional methods of struggle—appeal to the courts, to the administration, and to public opinion—to achieve new breakthroughs at the racial barricades. There has been enough of a slowdown in progress towards full equality to warrant the conclusion that the old methods, embodying gradualism, have run their course. . . . There is an increasing conviction among Negroes that only militant tactics can henceforth produce results. . . . This can readily lead to the defiance of authority. The line between denunciation and defiance of authority and actual rebellion against it can be instantly erased by the heated emotions generated by a single incident. That is one way riots are born. Every ghetto to-day, therefore can conceive them.

Bunche went on to describe the emotional nature of ghetto riots.

At the moment of participation, the riots are, to the participants and no doubt to the onlookers as well, triumphs of liberation, of throwing off shackles, of getting out from under white domination. . . . The atmosphere characteristic of riots is both macabre and bizarre. The mobsters, particularly the young ones, are often festive, yelling and laughing as they race along, breaking every plate glass window in sight, hurling the fire bombs and stealing anything they can tote. . . . They are exhilarated with even this fleeting moment of "liberation" which they know will soon be ended.

Anarchy reigns,

until police and troops restore order, which they cannot fail to do. Then, the rebellion over, what it was against, the ghetto, stark symbol of oppression, remains, charred, broken, uglier, meaner and more brutish than ever.

It was an "unpleasant fact" that the United States as a whole was racially "prejudice-ridden." "Negroes, possibly increasingly, become anti-white or at least come to regard all whites with suspicion or skepticism." For their part, whites, often without really knowing it, nurture prejudice. "They will *treat* the Negro as equal, but there are precious few who will *accept* him on their own plane as a person."

In recent years the pace of integration had slowed almost to a standstill.

All of the relatively easy steps have been taken—those that cause only a minimum of inconvenience and disruption to the mores of the white community. . . . Any significant new advances require an all-out *acceptance* of the Negro as a person— in residential areas, in the schools, the churches, in organizations, in the power structure, in every aspect of life."

The orgies of breaking and burning

are not only criminal, they are indescribably stupid as well. . . . The breakers and burners are a minority within a bitter minority. . . . But even as they burn and rob they are over-expressing in their recklessness a dissatisfaction that is burning painfully inside every Negro in the country to-day, inside or outside of the ghettos. I am no exception.

"Black Power," Bunche felt, was a symptom, not the cause, of racial violence. He characterized this movement as "a sloganized, grossly over-simplified exploitation of the disillusionment of Negro Americans . . . which would have neither meaning nor impact without the ghettos." Black Power was long on sensational slogans ("burn, baby, burn") but, like the civil-rights organizations the Black Power leaders despised, short on tactics and tacticians. Its leaders owed their fleeting prominence not to anything they have accomplished but to the perverse addiction of the American press to the sensational and to its readiness to publicize extreme, absurd and even inciting statements by persons of no real consequence. . . .

As before, Bunche dismissed Black Power separatism as "racist and escapist." To him the only valid goal was still total integration as an absolute right of all Americans. He recalled previous separatist movements in the 1930s—Marcus Garvey's "Back to Africa" movement, the National Movement for the Establishment of the 49th State, the Peace Movement of Ethiopia, the National Union for People of African Descent, W. E. B. Du Bois' idea of a black economic, political, and social structure within the walls of segregation, and the Communist Party's "misguided and infantile line of self-determination for the Negro in the blackbelt. . . . The promise of an all-black Elysium is, of course, an escapist dream."

Given the ominous situation, especially in the cities, Bunche concluded that

there is only one true measure of racial progress; the extent to which . . . the ghettos are diminishing. . . . By that standard, the American Negro has made and is now making very little progress.

There was no denying that since the Second World War there had been significant advances for Black Americans in many fields,

but what is too little understood is that the fact of this progress itself creates an ever more insistent demand for more progress. It can be said to have the force of a social axiom or law that the more progress there is toward equality by a disadvantaged people, the more insistent they will be in demanding full equality without further delay.

In the riots, the forces of law and order were bound to get the upper hand in the end. Then the responsible officials would turn their attention to measures for a return to so-called "normal" life—rebuilding and rehabilitating the shattered areas. But,

If these disasters are not to be repeated—a much broader, bolder and more imaginative approach will be required. . . . A more shiny ghetto will be no protection against it being again reduced to a ruin.

By comparison with blacks under apartheid in South Africa,

American Negroes are held in their ghettos by a more insidious force than law and one more difficult to attack: racial prejudice among whites, expressed in political, economic and social barriers.

Pouring assistance of all kinds into the ghettos was not the answer, and too much assistance might transform the ghetto into an urban reservation for Black Americans. Assistance programs were only a palliative—albeit an immediate necessity—and offered no cure for the ghetto problem, which stemmed from a state of mind as well as body. Massive assistance would create neither self-respect nor mutual respect.

Bunche's "inescapable conclusion" was that the ghettos must be eliminated—broken up, their black populations dispersed, and white people drawn into the area by deliberate incentives in housing, institutions, businesses, and other features. "A radical social surgery is required to relieve our urban communities of the malignancy of the black ghettos. The prognosis calls for surgery, not for slow treatment." There was one question which only the president, governors, and mayors could answer, and it did not need to await the report of President Johnson's National Advisory Commission on Civil Disorders (the Kerner Commission). That question was, why there was not the vision, courage, and determination at least to set in motion and coordinate a "policy and program, jointly conducted and financed, to eliminate the black ghettos, to disperse their black populations, to resettle them, to achieve physical integration in this society."

Such a goal could be achieved only with tremendous effort and at staggering cost and would require a pooling of resources by city, state, and national governments. Even so, the cost would be less than a few months of war in Vietnam or of placing a man on the moon; and small compared with the cost of future riots. "I would like to hope that no cost will be regarded as too great to save American cities from becoming racial battlegrounds."

Bunche's call to arms was not published, and those who read it—Senator Edward Brooke of Massachusetts, for example—did not pursue it. Bunche did not wish to make a public appeal unless he could be sure in advance that it would be helpful, and in any case his position at the United Nations limited his ability to play a role in American domestic politics. People in Washington were fully preoccupied at this time with the war in Vietnam and the imminent presidential election. Some of Bunche's thesis finally appeared in the conclusions of the report of the Kerner Commission the following year.

Our nation is moving toward two societies, one black, one white—separate and unequal. . . . What white Americans never fully understood—what the Negro can never forget—is that white society is deeply implicated in the ghetto.

White institutions created it, white institutions maintain it, and white society condones it.[51]

The Kerner Commission also recommended pursuing integration by combining ghetto "enrichment" with policies which would encourage Negro movement out of central city areas. It emphasized that the primary goal must be a single society.

Bunche had been a trustee of the Rockefeller Foundation since 1955, and was due to leave at the end of 1968, after he reached sixty-five, the mandatory retirement age. At the trustees' meeting in Williamsburg in December 1967, he made an emotional appeal on the subject of poverty and racism and urged the Foundation to give priority to the fundamental problem of eliminating the black ghettos. His eloquence, and the strength of his feelings, had an electric effect on the board,* and some of its members recalled the occasion as the most memorable of all the board meetings they had attended. The result was a general feeling that the foundation, at this critical national juncture, should change direction, and a joint trustee-staff subcommittee was established then and there to study how this could be done. Its chairman was Thomas J. Watson, Jr., the president of IBM.

The subcommittee had great difficulty in pinning down what Bunche's aim of eliminating the ghetto meant in terms of a program. It therefore decided to meet with outside experts—philosophers, activists, and scholars—to try to clarify its recommendation to the Rockefeller board. Among these experts were Kenneth Clark, the renowned black educator and psychologist; Daniel Patrick Moynihan, then director of the MIT/Harvard Joint Center for Urban Studies; Robert Weaver, Bunche's fellow student at Harvard and currently secretary of housing and urban development; and Roy Wilkins, the director of the NAACP. At one of these meetings, Bunche suggested an intensive study of a particular ghetto to work out a blueprint for changing its character, and the subcommittee members seemed to be sympathetic. General agreement, however, was not the same as specific programs, and the discussion began to move away from eliminating the ghetto to smaller and less formidable objectives. One idea, which predated Bunche's initiative, was to update *An American Dilemma* to cover the ghetto problem.

*The board's members at that time included Douglas Dillon, former secretary of the Treasury, ambassador, and banker; Barry Bingham, publisher of the Louisville *Courier-Journal;* Father Theodore Hesburgh of Notre Dame; and President Robert Goheen of Princeton.

A later subcommittee meeting, in March, heard, among others, the black nationalist Floyd McKissick of CORE; a radical community organizer, Saul Alinsky of the Urban Areas Foundation; and Ted Watkins of the Watts Labor Community Action Committee. The discussion focused on the Negro and the power structure. McKissick urged that Harlem should have its own, locally controlled fire and police departments, schools, and businesses. The subcommittee and the staff finally came up with a list of four possible program areas—leadership and support training, reforming ghetto school systems, research and action, and medical and community-health programs. One of these would be selected for concentrated effort by the Foundation. The research-and-action topic might include a pilot project for ghetto dispersal.

In commenting to Watson on these ideas, Bunche noted the subcommittee's misgivings about the foundation's attempting to formulate a blueprint for eliminating a particular ghetto.

I must say it seems to me to be entirely feasible and within reasonable financial limits. . . . As you say, Tom, the ghetto is still with us despite all the effort and money expended, but the point is that little or none of this effort and money has been directed at the fundamentals of the problem—that is eliminating the ghetto rather than improving life and conditions in it. In this respect, in my view, billions more can be poured into the ghettos in palliative efforts without appreciably changing the present sinister trend in the deterioration of race relations in our country. . . . I am disturbed that what is to me the decisive consideration is not mentioned at all, namely that of integration and whether it is to be any longer regarded as a realistic objective. . . .

Bunche felt strongly that the aim should be stated not in terms of "dispersal" but of what was required to eliminate the ghetto in the sense of changing its character as a ghetto.

This would be a case study not in eliminating a selected ghetto but in what would be required to do so, how it could be done and at what estimated cost, given the community and governmental will to make the effort.

The case study

should be undertaken by the Foundation, not as "one of its many efforts," but as a major and priority project taking precedence over any other projects in the equal opportunity or human rights sphere.[52]

This letter, and his single-minded view of what ought to be done, may well have disturbed the subcommittee, and on May 15, Bunche was astounded when Watson announced, "matter-of-factly and with great satisfaction" over the telephone, that the members of the subcommittee were unanimously agreed, except for Bunche, to drop any consideration of the suggested survey of a selected ghetto.[53] Bunche felt that Watson had been lobbying, and a heated exchange of nearly one hour ensued. Watson threatened to resign as chairman, and Bunche threatened to resign from both the subcommittee and the board of the Foundation and to make public his letter of resignation. Watson was sufficiently disturbed by this exchange to call John D. Rockefeller III and tell him of his dispute with Bunche. Rockefeller then telephoned Bunche and appealed to him to attend the next subcommittee meeting. He assured Bunche that he would call on him at the outset to defend his project.

At the meeting on the following day, although Bunche spoke first, the other members were either indecisive or subtly negative, and after two hours Watson announced that since no one but Bunche supported the ghetto project it could be considered as put aside. Bunche protested sharply. John Rockefeller made a conciliatory statement which Bunche took up and "used for all it was worth," and it was finally agreed that the foundation would go ahead with the project and would select a director for a preliminary investigation of the feasibility of a major study aimed at transforming a ghetto.[54]

The search for a director dragged on through the summer as several distinguished possibilities turned down the foundation's invitation. Bunche sharply disagreed with a proposal that, instead of appointing a director, they should commission various papers. With Bunche's strong endorsement, Dr. Kenneth B. Clark was finally appointed as director of the Metropolitan Applied Research Center in September. Like Bunche, whom he knew from Howard University and from the Myrdal study, Clark was a strong proponent of full integration.

By the time Clark's study got under way Bunche had left the board of the Rockefeller Foundation. The study was constantly delayed and prolonged. It accumulated a large volume of papers and surveys and initiated some useful educational and leadership projects. It did not, however, succeed in articulating a practical overall approach to the dispersal of a ghetto. The Metropolitan Applied Research Center finally went out of business in July 1976. An objective of such magnitude was undoubtedly beyond the scope of a single private foundation, and Bunche's dream of an initiative that would galvanize action on the ghetto remained unfulfilled.

Bunche was at a meeting of the Security Council on April 4, 1968, when he received the news of Martin Luther King's assassination. Although he had had his disagreements with King, he admired and greatly respected King's integrity, his dynamic leadership, his courageous moderation, and his resistance to all forms of racism. Bunche wrote:

The world has lost one of its most earnest, respected and commanding voices in the allied causes of peace, freedom and the dignity of man. . . . The world's leading contemporary exponent of non-violence is now gone, all too ironically by an act of savage violence.[55]

Bunche's attendance at the funeral in Atlanta was "the saddest journey I have ever made," and he was

sick at heart, both because of the assassination and shameful aftermath in the epidemic of eruptions in so many of our cities. . . . Ours is an enigmatic country. Until his death Dr. King was tirelessly and fearlessly leading the black revolution, championing the cause of the poor, the deprived, the oppressed everywhere; upholding peace. . . . Now King, no longer the foremost revolutionary leader, hated by many in a racist society and widely feared, has become a national hero, our foremost martyr, and is nationally mourned with unprecedented scope and intensity—To mourn a man to this degree has to mean some degree of respect and sympathy not only for the man but for what he stood for, his ideas and ideals, his goals, his work. It occurs to me that if the sentiment behind this massive mourning for Dr. King could be quietly converted into community and national resolve to launch a decisive attack on racism in this country in all of its aspects, and in particular in its ghetto manifestations, the back of the American racial problem could be broken. . . .[56]

In public he denounced King's killing as a "national disaster, a profound American tragedy," and he returned once again to the urgent need for a basic effort to eliminate the ghettos, which constituted "an even greater threat to our security than Vietnam."[57]

Throughout the summer of 1968 Bunche brooded on the last tragic years which had culminated in King's death. In August he began to write "Notes on the Black Revolution" in order to "try to put down some of my thoughts on the crisis of race in America." These notes are characterized by the "monumental sadness" which the Southern writer, editor, and civil-rights reformer Harry S. Ashmore perceived in Bunche in the 1960s.[58] Bunche admitted that the process frightened him, as regards the future both of Black Americans and of the United States.

Although it never became a single organized study, many of the ideas Bunche scrawled in his by now nearly illegible handwriting found their place in his last public speeches. He was increasingly obsessed with the growing separation of two sharply conflicting societies in the United

States, and with the necessity of a vast effort "to move black Americans from the periphery of American economic and political and social life into its mainstream." He saw little sign of such an effort.

It is today tougher to be black in American society than at any period since abolition. . . . The Negro has reached the critical crossroad in the society, and he is forced to make the most fateful decision ever. He has to decide now whether there is still any real prospect, indeed any possibility, that, within the foreseeable future, the black minority which constitutes more than one-tenth of the nation's total population, can be accepted in full as an equal partner in all phases of the life of the society, can find a place in the society's mainstream. That is to say, is integration in the full sense a realizable goal, or is it only a dream that will always remain illusory, except in the realm of tokenism? Even the true believers of integration like myself, all of the firm advocates of it in the black segment, are assailed by unavoidable doubts these days. . . .
       Is it sound to speak of a black revolution? I have no doubt about it.

There was little comprehension among white Americans that a revolution was under way in their own country. A new pride in black ethnic identity was one symptom of this revolution. "To-day," Bunche wrote, "I am a partisan of black revolution as every black American must be, unless he is blind or craven, and unworthy of his birthright." Bunche's privileged position spared him "the discriminations, humiliations and the degradations which are so intolerably a part of the daily life of most black people." He did not live in a ghetto and had free contacts with all segments of society. But although it no longer applied to him personally, he felt the color bar acutely, because as long as it applied to other members of his group he would find no escape from the stigma of race.

When any black men are rejected by the dominant white society, all are rejected. . . . There is a decisive difference between being accepted genuinely, as an equal, and being tolerated for some reason, such as recognition of ability and need for it, a minimal bow to a pricking conscience or a missionary spirit of compassion. . . . I am not bitter, nor am I angry. I rely only on reason, candor and truth. They stand firmly enough without support from emotion. I am convinced that on the problem of race most Americans hide the truth or, more accurately, hide from it.[59]

Bunche had spent his formative years in California in a world of liberal optimism. Except for a very brief period during the Myrdal study, he had never experienced firsthand the total separation, and the stultifying mutual fear and basic hostility, of blacks and whites in the South. Until a late stage in his life, he seems to have underestimated the enormous and deep-rooted obstacles blocking the road to a real integration of the races in the United States. In the late 1960s, however, the rising tide of black rage and hostility and the festering problems of the ghettos finally undermined Bunche's lifelong optimism and gave rise to the agonizing doubts which pervade his "Notes on the Black Revolution."

Nearly blind, racked with a series of debilitating illnesses and living through a period of both national and international turmoil and disillusionment, Bunche did not completely lose his old sardonic brand of practical optimism, but he was more than ever skeptical of mere good intentions and well-meaning generalizations. When an interviewer mentioned "brotherhood," he responded:

May I speak a word or two against brotherhood? . . . We can save the world with a lot less. . . . Brotherhood is a misused, misleading term. What we need in this world is not brotherhood but coexistence. We need acceptance of the right of every person to his own dignity. We need mutual respect. Mankind will be much better off when there is less reliance on lip service to "brotherhood" and "brotherly love," and much more practice of the sounder and more realistic principle of mutual respect governing the relations among all people.[60]

In one of his last major speeches, in Honolulu in July 1969, Bunche addressed the problem of "Race and Alienation" as a worldwide phenomenon. He put side by side the situation of Black Americans and the pervasive issue of race on the international scene. "There is," he said, "a steady tendency toward polarization of the white and non-white peoples of the world which can lead to ultimate catastrophe for all."[61] The affluent people of the world were mostly white but constituted only 31 percent of the population. (The percentage is now dramatically smaller.) Bunche did not exclude the possibility of a worldwide conflict between white and nonwhite peoples, fueled by the population explosion and the development, in fifteen or twenty years, of severe famine in some areas.

There is no bigger obstacle to the building of solid foundations for a secure peace than the great and dangerously widening gap between the haves and have-nots in the world, especially in its racial overtones.[62]

Bunche ascribed to colonialism the major historical role in the estrangement between white and nonwhite peoples and quoted a 1947 speech by John Foster Dulles demanding the end of the colonial system. "It has borne some very evil fruit," Dulles had said, "primarily in that it has put people of one race to rule over peoples of another race and that has been very bad for both races. . . ."[63]

Bunche denounced the Vietnam War as having deep racial implications, and cited the dilemma of the many Black American soldiers who were in Vietnam to fight for the rights and freedom of seventeen million South Vietnamese but could not resort to force in their own country to secure the constitutional rights of twenty-two million Black Americans. Quoting President Nixon's remark that the American people were "fed up . . . with violence and lawlessness," Bunche added that Black Americans were also "fed up" with their inferior status. He urged white men everywhere to

find a way, if such there is, to purge themselves completely of racism or face an ultimate fateful confrontation of the races which will shake the very foundations of civilization and, indeed, threaten its continued existence. . . .[64]

This somber estimate, and his searing doubts about the possibility of full integration in the United States, clouded Bunche's last years. He had fought all his life for racial equality at home, and independence and equal opportunity abroad. In both spheres much progress had been made— some of it directly due to his own efforts. And yet immense obstacles remained, and new problems had arisen. Only Bunche's innate optimism and belief in basic human decency saved him from a descent into despair. Asked why he believed in human survival, he answered:

Because I've seen so many instances of man's ability to do the right thing. I see them every day. If man can do these things, he can do better things.[65]

33

Ending

"The prospect of death," Bunche wrote during a prolonged General Assembly debate,

comes more often to my mind these days, possibly because my various ailments are more aggravated and aggravating and my pains more acute. I believe that I have no fear of death and that I approach the subject calmly and philosophically. I hope so, but the decisive test comes when one's end is imminent. As I think of it I have only one real wish. I would not like to have an agonizing death, so as to be able to pass on with my characteristic smile on my lips. That would be entirely appropriate for me as I have always looked on life—and myself—with considerable amusement. Is a smiling corpse possible? Can the undertaker preserve it without it appearing macabre?[1]

Dark thoughts came more frequently as Bunche's ailments multiplied and the treatment of them intruded more and more on his working schedule. To the previous list had now been added pinched nerves in his neck, for which he wore a neck brace, and fits of hiccups which lasted for days at a time. In August 1970 he fell and broke a rib, an accident made the more agonizing by the hiccups. The day-and-night routine of conflict management and his chosen social program became increasingly hard to sustain.

The overall situation on the thirty-eighth floor of the UN Secretariat was in itself debilitating. U Thant, exhausted and a martyr to various stress ailments, was now frequently hospitalized. Bunche's fellow undersecretary for special political affairs, José Rolz-Bennett, had a brain tumor and was clearly dying. The burden of the office had to be carried mainly by the staff, but it never seems to have been seriously considered that Bunche, or indeed U Thant, should be allowed to bow out. We spent much of our time in hospital rooms getting signatures or going through urgent papers.

Bunche struggled on. He could no longer tell who was in the room until the person spoke, and everything had to be read to him, but his acute mind, his extraordinary memory, and his analytical powers remained. His talks and briefings, now unhampered by notes or scripts, were remarkable for their coherence, accuracy, and forcefulness. Being unable to see, his pleasure in music increased, and he continued to attend the opera with enthusiasm.

Bunche's health had become a matter of great interest to the UN press corps, a body not reticent about speculating on his departure. Their curiosity was only increased by his refusal to make any statements about the nature of his illness or his now frequent absences from his office. Speculation about his retirement led to further speculations about his successor, and lists of eminent American figures were circulated. There were sensational stories about "power vacuums" in Bunche's office, and even of Soviet intentions to execute a "power grab." Such stories were particularly irritating to Bunche's small staff,* which was now coping with both his and Rolz-Bennett's workload and the support of an often ailing secretary general.

As Bunche got sicker, he became more and more convinced that in some miraculous way he would regain his health. He was in no mood to hand in his resignation, and U Thant, who had insisted that Bunche stay on, did not want to ask him for it. Bunche's position in the UN was unique. His international stature and his ability were vital factors in the organization's, and particularly the secretary general's, work. U Thant himself was due to leave at the end of 1971 and felt that, in any case, such an important replacement must be made by his successor.

By the early months of 1971 Bunche's absences from the office had become more frequent as the progressive failure of his kidneys triggered other ailments. His attendance at high-level meetings had become an agony, although his advice and comments still commanded respect. His last important meeting was about the Middle East and took place on May 17, 1971, in U Thant's office. It was attended by U.S. Secretary of State William Rogers, Assistant Secretary of State Joseph Sisco, and George Bush, the United States representative at the UN, as well as Gunnar Jarring, the UN special representative in the Middle East, and myself. Rogers described his recent visit to the Middle East and his efforts to persuade Israel to be more responsive to Jarring. There was talk about an agreement on the Suez Canal. The new Egyptian president, Anwar Sadat,

*Bunche's principal staff at this time were: F. T. Liu; George Sherry; Colonel Lauri Koho; his secretaries, Ingrid Nagorski, May Davidson, and Lydia Fahon; and myself.

was being surprisingly reasonable. Rogers said that King Hussein of Jordan felt left out of the negotiating process and urged Jarring to take up negotiations between Israel and Jordan. In a two-hour meeting, Bunche, who had to struggle to stay awake, only intervened once. For those who knew him it was a very sad occasion.

From this time on Bunche was more and more frequently at home and in and out of New York Hospital. We kept him in touch and consulted him on all important decisions, but it was a losing struggle. Even so, no one was prepared to give up the hope that he would recover. In June he fractured his right arm in a fall at home and went back into hospital, where he fell into a coma for several days. Because he might well die without regaining consciousness, U Thant agreed formally to relieve him of his post in the Secretariat in order to protect his right, on the termination of his UN service, to withdraw a third of his pension as a lump sum, about the only capital Bunche was likely to leave to his family. He struggled on through the late summer and autumn with extraordinary grace and humor. Ruth was heroic, always at his side, supported by Joan and Ralph Jr.* He went on dialysis in July under the devoted care of Dr. Albert Rubin, and his condition notably improved. He was often his old sardonic self and was still passionately interested in people and events.

Outside the walls of New York Hospital, the world where Bunche had for so long played a leading role went on without him. In September U Thant announced that he would definitely be leaving at the end of the year. The People's Republic of China at last took its seat in the General Assembly on October 25. The people of East Pakistan, already stricken by flood and famine, rose against the Pakistani military government and began the struggle which ended with the creation of the state of Bangladesh.

Ralph Bunche died peacefully in New York Hospital at 12:40 A.M. on December 9, 1971, the same date on which his beloved uncle Tom had died nine years earlier. His death evoked eulogies from all over the world, recalling his many achievements and the nobility and integrity of his life and character. The General Assembly stood for a minute of silence in his memory. At his funeral, at noon on Saturday, December 11, in the Riverside Church in New York, a packed congregation heard eulogies from U Thant, Roy Wilkins, and myself. Leontyne Price sang, a cappella, a passionate and poignant spiritual, "I Want Jesus to Walk with Me." He was buried at the Woodlawn Cemetery, in the Bronx, in the Bunche family

---

*Joan worked throughout her career in the UN Secretariat on the economic and development side. After her retirement in 1992, she served as a UN observer in South Africa. Ralph Jr. has had a successful career as an investment banker based in London.

The Legacy of Ralph Bunche

In the *Los Angeles Times* after Bunche's death. December 12, 1971. DRAWING BY
PAUL CONRAD, COPYRIGHT 1971, *Los Angeles Times*, REPRINTED WITH PERMISSION

plot, which he had chosen himself after Jane's death.*

The world paid a heartfelt tribute to someone who had proved himself to be an outstanding servant of humanity. In the General Assembly U Thant hailed his faithful friend as "an international institution in his own right, transcending both nationality and race in a way that is achieved by very few. . . ."[2] At his funeral U Thant described the personality which had given Bunche his unique position in the world.

Ralph's character and temperament were uniquely suited for this most difficult of all tasks, and he succeeded in a number of cases where almost everyone else had failed. He was modest but tough, brilliant but unassuming, tireless but compassionate, strong but understanding, and he gained a position and a reputation in the world at large which any man might well envy. Even those who disagreed with him held him in the highest respect. Even those who opposed him never lost faith in his absolute fairness and integrity. And no one could doubt that beneath his extraordinary ability and performance was a driving passion for peace, for justice and for human decency and dignity. Ralph was both an idealist and a realist. He believed resolutely in the necessity of making the United Nations work, but he never underestimated the difficulties and frustrations of the peacemaker. He was never carried away by false enthusiasm or the desire for public acclaim and believed that work well done would speak for itself, whoever got the credit. He was a practical optimist who believed that whatever might go wrong in matters of peace or justice it was never too late to try again. His love of humanity and his belief in mankind's ultimate goodness carried him through many a crisis which would have broken a lesser man.[3]

In his journey from Detroit, Albuquerque, and Los Angeles through the universities and the capitals, the continents and the conflicts, of the world, Bunche left a legacy of principle, fairness, creative innovation,† and solid achievement which deeply impressed his contemporaries and inspired his successors. His memory lives on, especially in the long struggle for human dignity and against racial discrimination and bigotry, and in the growing effectiveness of the United Nations in resolving conflicts and keeping the peace. As Ralph Johnson Bunche would have wished, that is his living memorial.

*In 1980, a great steel monolith, *Peace Form One,* created by a young black sculptor, Daniel Johnson, whose father Bunche had known in his youth in Los Angeles, was dedicated in the small park on First Avenue opposite the main entrance to the UN. The park was rechristened "Ralph Bunche Park."

†In Los Angeles in early 1992, a former street-gang member, Anthony Perry, visited the library of the University of Southern California to research the Rhodes armistice talks of 1949. On the basis of the armistice agreements that Bunche had drafted, he negotiated a truce between the Bloods and the Crips, the two largest Los Angeles street gangs. At the time of writing, the truce is still in effect.[4]

Notes

The main depositories for Ralph Bunche's papers are the Library of the University of California, Los Angeles (UCLA) and, for his United Nations papers, the UN Archives in New York City. After Ruth Bunche's death some personal papers were also deposited at the Schomburg Center for Research in Black Culture in New York City.

Preface (p. 12)

1. Virginia Wicks, quoted by Whitney Balliett in *The New Yorker*, January 25, 1993.

1 Beginnings (pp. 23–35)

1. Handwritten note, July 15, 1967.
2. This, and many subsequent details, are from the history of the family compiled by Ralph Bunche's cousin Jane Taylor (née Johnson).
3. Letter to the Reverend Albert Bunch, September 30, 1969.
4. This and subsequent details are from Aunt Nelle Johnson's account of the early years of the family, which was written at Ralph Bunche's request.
5. Letter to Ralph Bunche, September 10, 1962.
6. Random Recollections and Comments, 1965–66.
7. Letter to William T. Noble of *Detroit News*, November 24, 1959.
8. Nelle Johnson's account.
9. Ibid.
10. Remarks at Golden Key Award, Atlanta, Ga., 1962.
11. Quoted in *The New Yorker*, January 1, 1972. Bunche had given the text to Lilian Ross early in the previous year.
12. Note on a Mr. Kennedy's interview with Bunche, May 7, 1968.
13. *Reader's Digest*, September 1969. The following quotations are from Bunche's second draft of the article, which, to his distress, was heavily edited and abridged in its published form.
14. Letter to Elizabeth M. Riley, January 25, 1956.
15. Interview with Pauline Frederick, *Today Show*, NBC-TV, February 20, 1969.
16. Letter to Rachel Gallagher, September 18, 1968.
17. Correspondence with Ralph M. Lloyd, March–April 1955.

2 UCLA, Harvard, and Howard (pp. 37–46)

1. Ralph Bunche, remarks at the dedication of Ralph Bunche Hall, UCLA, May 23, 1969.
2. Letter to Ronald W. Hosie, editor of *Cub*, UCLA, April 21, 1966.
3. UCLA *Daily Bruin*, September 29, 1950, quoted in Souad Halila, "The Intellectual Development and Diplomatic Career of Ralph J. Bunche," Ph.D. dissertation, UCLA, May 1988.
4. Ralph Bunche, "The Summer Job I Had as a Boy," *Esquire*, 1957.
5. Ralph Bunche, address to Fountain Club Youth Conference, Grand Rapids, Mich., April 24, 1954.
6. John and Laree Caughey, *Los Angeles: Biography of a City* (Berkeley, University of California Press, 1976), pp. 282–87.
7. Letter to Ronald Taylor, August 27, 1969.

8. Quoted in Benjamin Rivlin, *Ralph Bunche: The Man and His Times* (New York, 1990), p. 217.
9. Letter to Dean C. H. Rieber, October 26, 1927.
10. Robert C. Weaver quoted in Rivlin, op. cit., p. 6.
11. Bunche, address to Fountain Club Youth Conference.
12. Letter to Francis Phillips, September 11, 1956.
13. Sterling Brown, "Ralph Bunche at Howard,"

The Crisis, January 1972, quoted in Halila, op. cit., p. 30.
14. Kenneth B. Clark, in Rivlin, op. cit., pp. 212–13.
15. Charles P. Henry in ibid., p. 53.
16. Interviews with Robert Weaver and John Hope Franklin, 1992.
17. *The New Yorker,* January 1, 1972.
18. Peggy Mann, *Ralph Bunche: UN Peace Maker* (New York, 1975), p. 87.
19. From notes dictated by Ruth Bunche to her granddaughter Nina Bunche Pierce.

3 Howard and Beyond (pp. 51–63)

1. An admirable account of these years and of Bunche's part in them is to be found in John B. Kirby, *Black Americans in the Roosevelt Era: Liberalism and Race* (Knoxville: University of Tennessee Press, 1980).
2. Letter to Ruth, June 18, 1932.
3. Ralph Bunche, *Modern Policies of Imperialistic Administration of Subject Peoples,* p. 2. Address to Howard University Conference on Problems, Programs and Philosophies of Minority Groups. April 5, 1935.
4. *The Afro-American,* February 21, 1959.
5. Ralph Bunche, *A World View of Race:* (*The Associates in Negro Folk Education;* Washington, D.C., 1936).
6. Letter to Bobby Brunson, April 14, 1965.
7. Ickes quoted by John Kirby in Benjamin Rivlin, *Ralph Bunche: The Man and his Times* (New York, 1990), p. 33. Kirby's chapter of this book, "Race, Class and Politics," and his *Black Americans in the Roosevelt Era* are reflected in the following paragraphs.
8. Ralph Bunche, "Extended Memorandum on the Programs, Ideologies, Tactics and Achievements of Negro Betterment and Interracial Organization," prepared for the

Myrdal study, quoted by Kirby, "Race, Class and Politics," in *Ralph Bunche,* op. cit.
9. I am again indebted to John Kirby's analysis of this conference in *Ralph Bunche,* op. cit. The text quoted is entitled "Critique of New Deal Social Planning."
10. Ralph Bunche, "Triumph? or Fiasco?," *Race,* Summer 1936, vol. 1, no. 2.
11. Ibid.
12. "Official Proceedings of the National Negro Congress 1936," 1937.
13. Bunche, "Triumph? or Fiasco?," op. cit.
14. Ralph Bunche, address to 27th Annual Conference of the NAACP, Baltimore, Md., July 2, 1936.
15. *An African-American in South Africa,* edited by Robert R. Edgar (Ohio, 1992), pp. 4–12, gives a full account of the SSRC grant and Bunche's relationship with Melville Herskovits, Bronislaw Malinowski, and Isaac Schapera.
16. Herskovits to Henry Allen Moe, January 6, 1937, quoted in Edgar, op. cit., p. 12.
17. Herskovits to Schapera, August 9, 1937, quoted in ibid., p. 12

4 England 1937 (pp. 64–71)

1. Ralph Bunche, diary, April 1937.
2. Ibid., May 1937.
3. Ibid., February 1937.
4. Letter to Herskovits, May 20, 1937, quoted in *An African-American in South Africa,* edited by Robert R. Edgar (Ohio, 1992), p. 13.
5. Bunche, diary, February 1937.
6. Ibid., April 1937.
7. Ibid.
8. Ibid., March 1937.
9. Ibid., April 1937.
10. 4th US Civil Service Region, Investigations Division, report of special hearing, March

25, 1943 (a routine wartime security investigation).
11. Bunche, diary, April 1937.
12. Ibid.
13. Ibid., June 1937.
14. Ibid., July 1937.
15. Ibid., May 1937.
16. Ibid.
17. Ibid., September 11, 1937.
18. Ibid., March 1937.
19. United Kingdom Public Records Office, Colonial Office papers (CO 323/1517/7046/3).
20. Bunche, diary, August 1937.

5 Africa and Asia (pp. 72–80)

1. Ralph Bunche, diary, September 1937.
2. Ibid., October 1937.
3. Ibid.
4. Ibid.
5. Ibid., November 1937.
6. Ibid., November 9, 1937.
7. Letter to Essie and Paul Robeson, January 11, 1938, quoted in *An African-American in South Africa*, edited by Robert R. Edgar (Ohio, 1992), p. 23.
8. Bunche, diary, November 12, 1937, quoted in ibid., p. 137.
9. Ibid. p. 116.
10. Quarterly Progress Report to SSRC, December 1, 1937, quoted in ibid., p. 313.
11. Index-card notes, January 4, 1938, quoted in Souad Halila, "The Intellectual Development and Diplomatic Career of Ralph J. Bunche," Ph.D. dissertation, UCLA, May 1988, p. 59.
12. Bunche, diary, January 1938.
13. Ibid.
14. Ibid., February 1938.
15. Letter to Melville Herskovits, October 5, 1938.
16. Ralph Bunche, "The Irua Ceremony Among the Kikuyu of Kiambu District, Kenya," *Journal of Negro History,* January 1941.
17. Bunche, diary, April 1938.
18. Ibid.
19. Ibid.
20. Letter to Dean Louis K. Downing, November 22, 1938, quoted in Halila, op. cit., p. 64.
21. Bunche, diary, April 1938.
22. Ibid.
23. Ibid.
24. Ibid., May 1938.
25. Ibid.
26. Ibid.
27. Letter to Ruth, June 11, 1938.
28. Bunche, diary, June 12, 1938.
29. Ibid., July 1938.

6 An American Dilemma (pp. 81–91)

1. Letter to Prof. Melville Herskovits, October 5, 1938.
2. Ibid.
3. Charles P. Henry, "Ralph Bunche and the Howard School of Thought" (Institute of Governmental Studies, Public Affairs Report, May 1992).
4. Gunnar Myrdal, quoted in Dewey W. Grantham, introduction to Ralph Bunche, *Political Status of the Negro in the Age of FDR* (Chicago, 1973), p. xi.
5. Letter to Herskovits, May 23, 1939.
6. For the details of Myrdal's organization I am indebted to Grantham's introduction to Bunche, *Political Status*, op. cit.
7. Letter to Ira W. Williams, December 11, 1939, quoted in Walter A. Jackson, *Gunnar Myrdal and America's Conscience: Social Engineering and Radical Liberalism, 1938–1987* (Chapel Hill: University of North Carolina Press, 1990), p. 122.
8. Kenneth B. Clark in Benjamin Rivlin, *Ralph Bunche: The Man and His Times* (New York, 1990), p. 213.
9. Ralph Bunche, diary, October 1939.
10. Ibid.
11. Ibid.
12. Ibid.
13. Letter to Prof. Willard Z. Park, December 19, 1939.
14. Sissela Bok, *Alva Myrdal: A Daughter's Memoir,* Radcliffe Biography Series, (Cambridge, Mass., 1991), p. 84.
15. Bunche, diary, November 1939.
16. Ibid.
17. Ibid.
18. Ibid.
19. Ibid.
20. Ibid.
21. Ibid.
22. Grantham, introduction to Bunche, *Political Status*, op. cit., p. viii.
23. Ibid., p. vii.
24. Ibid., p. xx.
25. Ralph Bunche, "Political Status of the Negro," pp. 1455–59, quoted in John B. Kirby, *Black Americans in the Roosevelt Era: Liberalism and Race* (Knoxville: University of Tennessee Press, 1980) p. 208.
26. Ralph Bunche, "The Negro in Political Life," quoted in ibid., p. 208.
27. Two outstanding examples are: David W. Southern, *Gunnar Myrdal and Black-White Relations: The Use and Abuse of An American Dilemma, 1945–69* (Baton Rouge: Louisiana State University Press, 1987); and Jackson, op. cit.
28. Jackson, op. cit., pp. 319–20.

7 Prelude to War (pp. 92–100)

1. Ralph Bunche, "The Programs of Organizations Devoted to the Improvement of the Status of the American Negro," *Journal of Negro Education,* July 1939.
2. Ralph Bunche, "The Programs, Ideologies, Tactics and Achievements of Negro Betterment and Inter-Racial Organizations," monograph for the Myrdal study, p. 369. Quoted by John B. Kirby in Benjamin Rivlin, *Ralph Bunche, The Man and His Times* (New York, 1990), p. 38.
3. Ralph Bunche, "Notes on the Third National Negro Congress," Department of Labor Auditorium, April 26–28, 1940.
4. Ibid.
5. Ibid.
6. Ibid.
7. 4th US Civil Service Region, Investigations Division, report of special hearing, March 25, 1943.
8. Bunche, "Notes on Third National Negro Congress."
9. Letter to Charles Dollard, June 19, 1940.
10. Letter to the Committee to Defend America by Aiding the Allies, June 12, 1940.
11. Notes on meeting with Mrs. Roosevelt, May 13, 1940.
12. Ralph Bunche, "Talk on Position of Negro in Current International Crisis." No date or location given.
13. Letter to Julius Lewin, October 17, 1940.
14. Letter to Harold Laski, January 24, 1941.
15. Letter to Willard Z. Park, November 7, 1940.
16. Ralph Bunche, "Africa and the Current World Conflict," *Negro History Bulletin,* October 1940.
17. Ralph Bunche, foreword to "Anti-Semitism in the Negro Press," an article by a Miss Wedlock, December 11, 1941, publication unspecified.
18. Ralph Bunche, "The Negro in the Political Life of the United States," *Journal of Negro Education,* vol. 10, no. 3 (July 1941).
19. Personal note, 1941.
20. Interview with Pauline Frederick, NBC-TV, *Today Show,* February 20, 1969.
21. Letter to author from James Green, Memorial Day, 1988.
22. Ralph Bunche, interview in *Collier's,* June 1949.

8 World War II Washington and the OSS (pp. 101–10)

1. *Washington Star,* October 5, 1941.
2. Unsigned note from Harvard History Department, June 17, 1941.
3. Kenneth B. Clark quoted in Benjamin Rivlin, *Ralph Bunche: The Man and His Times* (New York, 1990), p. 214.
4. Memo to Conyers Read, October 4, 1941.
5. Ibid.
6. Memo to Conyers Read, February 6, 1942.
7. Ibid.
8. Letter from Edward R. Stettinius, March 27, 1943, quoted in Souad Halila, "The Intellectual Development and Diplomatic Career of Ralph J. Bunche," Ph.D. dissertation, UCLA, May 1988, p. 112.
9. Memo to Conyers Read, November 23, 1942.
10. Ibid.
11. Letter to the Capitol Transit Company, November 2, 1942.
12. Memo to Dr. Edgar Dale, OWI, September 23, 1942.
13. Memo to Malcolm Ross, OWI, December 2, 1942.
14. Conyers Read to John A. Wilson, November 12, 1942, in a memo urging Bunche's promotion.
15. Personal note, March 12, 1953.
16. Institute of Pacific Relations, 8th Conference, Mont Tremblant. Secretariat Document 15, December 12, 1942.
17. Letter to Ruth, December 11, 1942.
18. Personal note, January 1943.
19. Memo to John A. Wilson, March 21, 1943.
20. Conyers Read, memo to John A. Wilson, November 12, 1942.
21. Conyers Read to Dr. William Langer, October 29, 1942.
22. Memo to Sherman Kent, September 21, 1943.
23. Ibid.
24. Ibid.
25. Memo to Sherman Kent, September 23, 1943.
26. Ibid.
27. Ibid.
28. Personal note, September 1943.
29. Personal note, January 1943.
30. Letter to the author from Dean Rusk, December 17, 1981.
31. Ibid., and Dean Rusk, *As I Saw It: Dean Rusk as Told to Richard Rusk* (New York, 1990), p. 580.
32. Rusk, op. cit., p. 580.
33. Letter to Bunche, February 15, 1944.

9 The Road to San Francisco (pp. 112–23)

1. Cordell Hull, *The Memoirs of Cordell Hull* (New York, 1948), p. 1677.
2. Interview with James F. Green.
3. Lawrence Finkelstein in Benjamin Rivlin, *Ralph Bunche: The Man and His Times* (New York, 1990), p. 110.
4. Hull, op. cit., p. 1679.
5. "Post-War Foreign Policy Preparation 1939–1945," Department of State, 1949, p. 304.
6. Ralph Bunche, "The International Implications of Far Eastern Colonial Problems," Council on World Affairs, Cleveland, Ohio, February 3, 1945.
7. Bunche quoted in William Roger Louis, *Imperialism at Bay* (Oxford, 1987), p. 45.
8. Record of Meeting of the United States Delegation, Fifth Floor Conference Room, Fairmont Hotel, Thursday April 26, 1945, 8:40 P.M.
9. Letter to Ruth Bunche, April 29, 1945.
10. A full account of the work on non-self-governing territories and trusteeship is to be found in Ruth B. Russell, *A History of the United Nations Charter* (Washington, D.C.: The Brookings Institution, 1958), pp. 808–42.
11. Telephone interview with Harold Stassen, July 15, 1992.
12. Letter to Ruth, May 8, 1945.
13. Interview with Stassen.
14. Letter to Ruth, May 13, 1945.
15. Letter to Ruth, May 21, 1945.
16. Letter to Ruth, May 15, 1945.
17. Letter to Ruth, May 21, 1945.
18. Finkelstein in Rivlin, op. cit., pp. 124–25.
19. Letter to the author from Shabtai Rosenne, September 26, 1989.
20. Verbatim minutes of third meeting of Commission II, June 21, 1945, UNCIO Doc. 1144. II/16.
21. Interview with Stassen.
22. UNCIO Doc. 1144.
23. Ibid.
24. Letter to Ruth, June 17, 1945.
25. Finkelstein in Rivlin, op. cit., pp. 123–24.
26. Ralph Bunche, "Trusteeship and Non-Self-Governing Territories in the Charter of the United Nations," *Department of State Bulletin*, December 3, 1945.
27. Interview with All-American NewsReel, March 1, 1945.
28. Letter to Ruth, June 17, 1945.
29. Letter to Ruth, May 13, 1945.
30. Letter to Jane Bunche, May 28, 1945.
31. Letter to Ruth, n.d.

10 Building the United Nations (pp. 126–37)

1. Letters, October 4 and 6, 1945.
2. Personal note.
3. Letter to Ruth, September 25, 1945.
4. Letter to Ruth, October 3, 1945.
5. Letter to Ruth, October 9, 1945.
6. Letter to Ruth, October 15, 1945.
7. Lawrence Finkelstein in Benjamin Rivlin, *Ralph Bunche: The Man and His Times* (New York, 1990), p. 125.
8. Letter to Ruth, October 11, 1945.
9. Frances Perkins, "Working It Out," *Federation News* (Chicago Federation of Labor), February 2, 1946.
10. Personal note.
11. Letter to Ruth, October 21, 1945.
12. Personal note.
13. Letter from Ruth, September 18, 1945.
14. Letter from Ruth, September 21, 1945.
15. Letter from Ruth, September 20, 1945.
16. Letter from Ruth, September 22, 1945.
17. Letter to Ruth, September 29, 1945.
18. Personal note, November 9, 1945.
19. The description of Bunche at home is based on, among other things, talks with Joan Bunche and Ralph Bunche, Jr.
20. Personal note.
21. Letter to Ruth, January 14, 1946.
22. Letters to Ruth, January 11 and 26, 1946.
23. Letter to Ruth, January 26, 1946.
24. Letter to Ruth, January 14, 1946.
25. Personal note.
26. Personal note.
27. Personal note.
28. Personal note.
29. Finkelstein in Rivlin, op. cit., p. 126.
30. Ralph Bunche, address to 15th Annual Conference of the Canadian Institute on Public Affairs, August 21, 1946.
31. General Assembly Resolution 9(I), February 9, 1946.
32. Personal note.
33. John Foster Dulles, statement to the 27th plenary of the General Assembly, February 9, 1946, U.S. Delegation Press Release No. 23.
34. Letter to Wilfred Benson, February 6, 1946.
35. Benjamin Gerig, memo to Alger Hiss, April 8, 1946.
36. Ralph Bunche, speech to the Biennial Assembly of Methodist Women, Columbus, Ohio, May 1, 1946.
37. Letter from Benjamin Gerig, February 7, 1947.
38. Letter to Benjamin Gerig, February 10, 1947.
39. Letter to William Hastie, February 24, 1947.

40. Ralph Bunche, "Other People's Freedoms," Western Reserve University, Cleveland, Ohio, February 15, 1950.
41. Bunche, speech to Assembly of Methodist Women, May 1, 1946.
42. Finkelstein in Rivlin, op. cit., pp. 126–27.
43. Letter from Andrew W. Cordier, December 19, 1946.
44. "United Nations Weekly Bulletin," April 11, 1947, p. 309.
45. Personal note.
46. Letter from Vice-Principal William Eves III, June 26, 1946.

11   Palestine (pp. 140–51)

1. *Keesing's Contemporary Archives*, February 1–8, 1947, p. 8408.
2. Letter to Ruth, June 29, 1947.
3. Letter to Ruth, July 15, 1947.
4. Personal note.
5. Personal note.
6. Personal note.
7. Personal note.
8. Personal note.
9. Personal note.
10. Personal note.
11. Personal note.
12. Personal note.
13. Letter to Ruth, June 20, 1947.
14. Personal note.
15. Personal note.
16. There is a highly dramatic account of this episode in Samuel Katz, *Days of Fire* (London, 1968), pp. 159–63. Katz was a member of the Irgun and was present at the meeting.
17. Bunche's notes on the meeting.
18. Ibid.
19. Personal note.
20. Personal note.
21. Personal note, July 4, 1947.
22. Letter to Ben Gerig, July 23, 1947.
23. Letter to James Green, July 23, 1947.
24. Letter to Ruth, July 19, 1947.
25. Letter to Ruth, August 5, 1947.
26. Personal note.
27. Personal note.
28. Personal note.
29. Personal note.
30. Personal note.
31. Personal note.
32. Letters to Ruth, August 25 and 18, 1947.
33. Statement by delegation of Arab Higher Committee, Lake Success, N.Y., September 13, 1947.
34. William Roger Louis, *The British Empire in the Middle East 1945–1951* (Oxford, 1984), p. 484. This book contains a fascinating description of the inner workings of UNSCOP.
35. Evan Wilson, *Decision on Palestine* (Stanford, 1979), p. 115.
36. Letter to Ruth, July 6, 1947.
37. Letter from Ruth, July 6, 1947.
38. Letter to Ruth, July 7, 1947.

12   With the Mediator in Palestine (pp. 154–85)

1. General Assembly Resolution 181(II), November 29, 1947.
2. Trygve Lie, *In the Cause of Peace* (New York, 1954), p. 160.
3. Pablo de Azcarate, *Mission in Palestine, 1948–52* (Washington, D.C., 1966), p. 4.
4. Ibid., p. 9.
5. Ibid., p. 6.
6. Warren Austin to Secretary of State, January 19, 1948, *Foreign Relations of the United States* (hereafter *FRUS*), vol. 5 (1948), U.S. Department of State, p. 545.
7. Personal note.
8. Letter to Benjamin Gerig, March 25, 1948.
9. Security Council Resolution 48, April 23, 1948.
10. Security Council Resolution 46, April 17, 1948.
11. UN Document S/743, May 15, 1948.
12. General Assembly Resolution 186 (S-2), May 14, 1948.
13. Personal note.
14. Personal note.
15. Personal note.
16. Letter to Ruth, May 25, 1948.
17. Personal note.
18. Personal note.
19. Personal note.
20. Letter to Ruth, June 1948.
21. Azcarate, op. cit., p. 95 et seq.
22. Letter to Ruth, June 14, 1948.
23. Folke Bernadotte, *To Jerusalem* (London, 1951), p. 152.
24. Interview with John Reedman, June 20, 1988.
25. Security Council Document S/863, July 1948.
26. Letter to Ruth, June 23, 1948.
27. Personal note.
28. Personal note.
29. Letter to Ruth, June 30, 1948.
30. Letter to Bernadotte from secretary general of the League of Arab States, July 3, 1948, quoted in Sune O. Persson, *Mediation and Assassination: Count Bernadotte's Mission to Palestine in 1948* (London, 1979), p. 149.
31. Personal note.
32. John Bagot Glubb, *A Soldier with the Arabs* (London, 1957), pp. 148–51.
33. *FRUS*, vol. 5 (1948), pp. 1202, 1203.

34. Security Council Resolution 54, July 15, 1948.
35. Letter from Ruth, June 8, 1948.
36. Letter from Ruth, June 17, 1948.
37. Letter to Ruth, June 16, 1948.
38. Personal note.
39. Personal note.
40. Personal note.
41. Mediator's cable of July 29, 1948.
42. Personal note.
43. Cable from Bunche to secretary general, July 27, 1948.
44. Conversation with U.S. Chargé d'Affaires Patterson in Cairo on August 7, *FRUS*, vol. 5 (1948), pp. 1295–96.
45. Ibid., p. 1288.
46. Ibid.
47. Ibid., pp. 1295–96.
48. Letter to Ruth, July 29, 1948.
49. Account of talks with Marshall is from the record made by A. W. Cordier, who attended the meeting.
50. *FRUS*, vol. 5 (1948), p. 1308.
51. Ibid., p. 1340.
52. Documents on the Foreign Policy of Israel, vol. II, No. 487, p. 18.
53. Personal note.
54. Personal note.
55. Personal note.
56. Personal note.
57. Personal note.
58. Sidney Bailey, *How Wars End* (Oxford, 1982), p. 216.
59. For a detailed exposition of this thesis, see, for example, J. C. Hurewitz, "Bunche as UN Acting Mediator," in Benjamin Rivlin, *Ralph Bunche: The Man and His Times* (New York, 1990), pp. 157–75. See also William Roger Louis, *The British Empire in the Middle East, 1945–1951* (Oxford, 1984), pp. 547–50. Amitzar Ilan's *Bernadotte in Palestine, 1948* (New York, 1989) pp. 188–89, describes Bunche's alleged efforts to ensure "that the encounter [with Troutbeck and McClintock] must remain top secret 'forever.' " If there is any truth in this, Bunche's

efforts seem to have been remarkably unsuccessful. Ilan, however, is non-committal on how much influence the emissaries may have had on the text of the Bernadotte report.
60. *FRUS*, vol. 5 (1948), pp. 1399–1400.
61. General Assembly Document A/648, September 16, 1948.
62. Ibid.
63. General Assembly Resolution 181(II), November 29, 1947.
64. General Assembly Document A/648, para. 35.
65. Frank Begley, who was in Bernadotte's car, gave this account to Bunche.
66. I am indebted for much of the information on Bernadotte's assassination to Persson, *Mediation and Assassination*.
67. Buccarelli 1971 interview with Baruch Nadel, who had apparently intended to publish a book in Denmark in 1970 accusing Bernadotte of being anti-Semitic and pro-Arab.
68. Cable from British Middle East Office, Cairo, to the Foreign Office, September 18, 1946, U.K. Public Record Office, FO 371/68587-9581.
69. Letter to Ruth, September 19, 1948.
70. Personal note.
71. Personal note.
72. Personal note.
73. Personal note.
74. Keesing's Contemporary Archives, July 15–22, 1950, p. 10844.
75. Personal note.
76. Personal note.
77. Documents on the Foreign Policy of Israel, vol. II. No. 532, p. 623.
78. Security Council Document S/108, September 28, 1948.
79. Letter to Ruth, September 19, 1948.
80. Letter from Ruth, September 17, 1948.
81. Letter to Ruth, September 19, 1948.
82. Letter to Ruth, September 27, 1948.
83. Security Council Document S/1022, September 30, 1948.
84. Letter to Ruth, September 27, 1948.

13 The Acting Mediator in Paris (pp. 187–98)

1. Documents on the Foreign Policy of Israel, vol. II.
2. Verbatim record of 365th meeting, Security Council Official Records, third year, no. 116, pp. 17–18.
3. Dan Kurzman, *Ben-Gurion: Prophet of Fire* (New York, 1983), p. 306.
4. Personal note.
5. Security Council Resolution 59, October 19, 1948.
6. Documents on the Foreign Policy of Israel, vol. II, p. 117.
7. Statement to the Security Council, October 28, 1948.
8. Security Council Resolution 61, November 4, 1948.
9. Personal note.
10. Documents on the Foreign Policy of Israel, vol. II, p. 134.
11. Security Council Records, 378th meeting (private), November 9, 1948.
12. Security Council Resolution 62 (S/1080), November 16, 1948.
13. Documents on the Foreign Policy of Israel, vol. III (CV), p. 40.
14. Letter from acting mediator (Bunche) to president of the Security Council, December 10, 1948.

15. Cable to president of Security Council from acting mediator, Security Council Document S/1152, December 27, 1948.
16. Security Council Resolution 66 (S/1169), December 29, 1948.
17. *FRUS*, vol. 5, pt. 2 (1948), p. 1704.
18. Statement to the First Committee of the General Assembly, October 15, 1948.
19. Ibid.
20. Report of the mediator, General Assembly Document A/648, September 16, 1948, para. 10.
21. Statement to First Committee, October 15.
22. *FRUS*, vol. 5 (1948), p. 1494.
23. Documents on the Foreign Policy of Israel, vol. II, p. 75.
24. Personal note.
25. Elath to Sharett, October 25/26, Documents on the Foreign Policy of Israel, vol. II, p. 97.
26. General Assembly Resolution 194 (III), December 11, 1948.
27. Lillie Schultz, "Who Wrote the 'Bernadotte Plan'?," *Nation*, October 25, 1948. Bunche asked Lillie Schultz to come and talk to him. She refused.
28. Personal note.
29. James Barros, *Trygve Lie and the Cold War* (DeKalb, Ill., 1989), pp. 207–8.
30. Documents on the Foreign Policy of Israel, vol. II, p. 295.
31. Letter to Karel Lisicky, November 24, 1948.
32. Letter from Walter White, October 22, 1948.
33. Letter to Walter White, October 27, 1948.
34. Letter to Dr. E. Franklin Frazier, January 29, 1951.
35. Letter to Alain Locke, November 27, 1948.

14 Armistice Talks in Rhodes—Egypt and Israel (pp. 200–212)

1. Personal note.
2. Personal note.
3. Walter Eytan, *The First Ten Years: A Diplomatic History of Israel* (New York, 1958), pp. 29–30.
4. Bunche's text of his opening statement.
5. Cable to Trygve Lie, January 15, 1949.
6. Cable to Ruth, January 18, 1949.
7. Personal note, January 23, 1949.
8. Ibid.
9. Eytan to Sharett, Documents on the Foreign Policy of Israel, vol. III, p. 65.
10. Ibid., p. 72.
11. Letter to Ruth, January 25, 1949.
12. Cable to Trygve Lie, January 17, 1949.
13. Personal note.
14. Personal note, January 27, 1949.
15. Cable from the secretary general to Bunche, January 30, 1939.
16. *FRUS*, vol. 6 (1949), p. 702.
17. Personal note, January 31, 1949.
18. Ibid.
19. Ibid.
20. Yadin to Ben-Gurion, Documents on the Foreign Policy of Israel, vol. III, cv, p. 22.
21. Dean Acheson, *Present at the Creation* (New York, 1969), p. 258.
22. Handwritten note by Ernest Bevin on a Foreign Office memorandum, January 29, 1949, UK Public Record Office FO 371/75337-9581.
23. Letter to Ruth, February 2, 1949.
24. Personal note, February 3, 1949.
25. Personal note, February 3, 1949.
26. Personal note, February 4, 1949.
27. Ibid.
28. Eytan to Sharett, January 27, 1949, Documents on the Foreign Policy of Israel, vol. III, p. 77.
29. Personal note, February 6, 1949.
30. *FRUS*, vol. 6 (1949), p. 730.
31. Ibid., p. 731.
32. Interview with Yitzhak Rabin, August 23, 1991.
33. Letter to Ruth, February 8, 1949.
34. Letter to Ruth, February 14, 1949.
35. Cable to Trygve Lie, February 10, 1949.
36. Cable to Trygve Lie, February 11, 1949.
37. Cable to Trygve Lie, February 13, 1949.
38. Eytan to Sharett, Documents on the Foreign Policy of Israel, vol. III, p. 245.
39. Cable to Trygve Lie, February 14, 1949.
40. Cable to Trygve Lie, February 16, 1949.
41. Eytan to Sharett, February 17, 1949, Documents on the Foreign Policy of Israel, vol. III, p. 255.
42. Personal note, February 18, 1949.
43. Cable to Trygve Lie, February 20, 1949.
44. Ibid.
45. Personal note, February 24, 1949.
46. Ibid.
47. Eytan, op. cit., pp. 32–33.
48. Personal note, February 24, 1949.
49. Personal note, February 25, 1949.
50. Cable from Ruth, February 23, 1949.
51. Letter to Ruth, February 27, 1949.
52. *Time*, March 7, 1949.
53. *FRUS*, vol. 6 (1949), p. 766.
54. U.S. chargé in Egypt (Patterson) to secretary of state, *FRUS*, vol. 6 (1949), p. 766.
55. Interview with Yitzhak Rabin, August 23, 1991.
56. Abba Eban, *My Country* (New York, 1972), pp. 70–73, 89–90. See also Eytan, op. cit.

15   Armistice Talks—Jordan and Israel (pp. 213–19)

1. See Avi Shlaim, *Collusion Across the Jordan: King Abdullah, the Zionist Movement and the Partition of Palestine* (New York: Columbia University Press, 1988), for a full account of the Shuneh talks. A vivid personal account by Walter Eytan, "Three Nights at Shuneh," appears in *Midstream*, November 1981.
2. Personal note, February 28, 1949.
3. Cable to Lie, March 3, 1949.
4. David Ben-Gurion, *Israel: A Personal History* (New York, 1972), p. 319.
5. Personal note, March 10, 1949.
6. Personal note, March 11, 1949.
7. Ibid.
8. Dayan to Yadin, Documents on the Foreign Policy of Israel, vol. III, cv, p. 74.
9. Personal note, March 12, 1949.
10. John Bagot Glubb, *A Soldier with the Arabs* (London, 1957), pp. 227–37.
11. Personal note, March 16, 1949.
12. Documents on the Foreign Policy of Israel, vol. III, cv, p. 82.
13. Letter to Ruth, March 21, 1949.
14. Personal note, March 30, 1949. This is Percival L. Prattis' one and only appearance in Bunche's papers. I do not know who he was.
15. Personal note, April 1, 1949.
16. *FRUS*, vol. 6 (1949), pp. 900–901.
17. Statement at Israeli-Transjordan signing, April 3, 1949.
18. Personal note, April 3, 1949.
19. Personal note, April 4, 1949.
20. Letter to Ruth, March 3, 1949.
21. Cable to Trygve Lie, April 7, 1949.

16   The End of the Mediation and the Nobel Prize (pp. 221–32)

1. Brigadier General F. P. Henderson, U.S. Marine Corps retd., "How to Write an Armistice," *Marine Corps Gazette*, April 1984.
2. Press statement, February 29, 1968.
3. Letter to Gunnar Jarring, November 21, 1969.
4. Letter to Theodore Draper, September 27, 1967.
5. UN press briefing, July 1, 1970.
6. Walter Eytan, *The First Ten Years: A Diplomatic History of Israel* (New York, 1958), p. 32.
7. David Ben-Gurion, *Israel: A Personal History* (New York, 1972), pp. 318–19.
8. Interview with Yitzhak Rabin, August 23, 1991.
9. Moshe Dayan, *The Story of My Life* (New York, 1976), pp. 145–46.
10. Shabtai Rosenne, "At Rhodes: A Diplomatic Negotiator," in Benjamin Rivlin, *Ralph Bunche: The Man and His Times*, (New York, 1990), pp. 177–85.
11. Pablo de Azcarate, *Mission in Palestine, 1948–1952* (Washington, D.C., 1966), p. 114.
12. Security Council Resolution No. 73 (1949), August 11, 1949.
13. Letter to Ruth, March 30, 1949.
14. Dean Acheson, *Present at the Creation* (New York, 1969), p. 259.
15. Personal note, May 25, 1949.
16. Ralph Bunche, speech at American Association for the United Nations dinner in his honor, May 9, 1949.
17. "Ralph Bunche Speaks," remarks at the NAACP 40th Annual Convention, July 17, 1949, published in *The Crisis*, January 1972.
18. *FRUS*, vol. 6 (1949), pp. 931–32.
19. Documents on Foreign Policy of Israel, vol. III, p. 536.
20. Cable to Henri Vigier, May 14, 1949.
21. Sharett to Shiloah, Documents on Foreign Policy of Israel, vol. III, p. 564.
22. Aubrey Eban, letter to Trygve Lie, May 23, 1949.
23. Documents on the Foreign Policy of Israel, vol. III, p. 594.
24. Security Council Document S/1357, July 21, 1949.
25. Letter to Sam Souki, October 5, 1949.
26. UN Press Release PM/1264, April 18, 1949.
27. Ralph Bunche interview, *Psychology Today*, vol. 2, no. 11 (April 1969).
28. Ralph Bunche, statement of acceptance, Nobel Peace Prize, December 10, 1950.
29. Ralph Bunche, Nobel Peace Prize lecture, December 11, 1950, printed in *The Crisis*, January 1972.

17   Anticlimax (pp. 234–42)

1. Personal note, June 27, 1950.
2. Ralph Bunche, Nobel Prize Lecture, December 11, 1950.
3. Keesing's Contemporary Archives, Feb. 7–14, 1953, p. 12747.
4. Personal note, July 21, 1951.
5. Memorandum to Trygve Lie, November 29, 1951.
6. Ibid.
7. Letter to Ruth, November 25, 1951.

8. Personal note, December 19, 1951.
9. Letter from Ruth, November 7, 1951.
10. Personal note, December 20, 1951.
11. Personal note.
12. Recounted to Jane Taylor by Aunt Nelle Johnson.
13. Alvin J. Kugelmass, *Ralph Bunche: Fighter for Peace* (New York, 1962).
14. Interview with Pauline Frederick on NBC-TV *Today Show*, February 20, 1969.
15. Letter from William T. Thom 3rd, January 6, 1952.
16. Ralph Bunche, speech at Fountain Club Conference, Grand Rapids, Mich., April 24, 1954.
17. Ralph Bunche, address to 45th Annual Convention of the NAACP, Dallas, Texas, July 4, 1954.
18. Ibid.
19. Ibid.
20. Ibid.
21. Ibid.
22. Ibid.
23. Personal note, April 2, 1952.

18   The "Loyalty" Question (pp. 244–56)

1. Ralph Bunche interview, *Psychology Today*, vol. 2, no. 11 (April 1969).
2. Ralph Bunche, speech to Pigskin Club Banquet, January 2, 1953.
3. Personal note, June 18, 1953.
4. Personal note, November 20, 1953.
5. Personal note, November 22, 1953.
6. Ibid.
7. Interview with Constantin Stavropoulos, June 1981.
8. Keesing's Contemporary Archives. February 7–14, 1953, p. 12745.
9. "Machinations of American Warmongers in the UN," *Pravda*, January 30, 1953.
10. Letter to Senator William Jenner, March 12, 1953.
11. New York *Daily Mirror*, October 19, 1953.
12. Ambrose quoted in Porter McKeever, *Adlai Stevenson* (New York, 1989), p. 319.
13. Personal note, February 12, 1954.
14. Personal note, February 1954.
15. Personal note, February 12, 1954.
16. Letter to Alger Hiss, quoted by Charles P. Henry, "Civil Rights and National Security: The Case of Ralph Bunche," in Benjamin Rivlin, *Ralph Bunche: The Man and His Times* (New York, 1990), p. 56.
17. All the above quotations are from Bunche's answers conveyed to Pierce J. Gerety, chairman of the International Organizations Employees Loyalty Board, February 12, 1954.
18. Interview with Arthur Rovine, April 1966.
19. Penciled note to Hammarskjöld.
20. Joseph and Stewart Alsop, "Matter of Fact" column, *Washington Post*, July 2, 1954.
21. Letter to Professor V. O. Key of Harvard University, June 10, 1954.
22. *New York Times*, May 27, 1954.
23. *Dagons Nyheter*, March 28, 1953.
24. London *Times*, May 29, 1954.
25. Letter from Ruth, March 12, 1957.
26. Letter to Anson Phelps Stokes, January 1955.

19   Peaceful Uses of Atomic Energy (pp. 259–63)

1. Personal note, March 1955.
2. Personal note, August 1955.
3. Letter to Hammarskjöld, October 3, 1957.
4. Personal note, October 1957.
5. Letter to Hammarskjöld, October 9, 1957.
6. Letter to Joan Bunche, August 1958.

20   Suez and the First Peacekeeping Force (pp. 264–90)

1. Personal note, April 1956.
2. Keith Kyle, in *Suez* (New York, 1991), gives a magisterial account of the origins and unfolding of the Suez crisis.
3. Official Records of the General Assembly, ES-I, 561st meeting, November 2, 1956, para. 299.
4. Ibid., para. 307.
5. Cable to General E. L. M. Burns, November 4, 1956.
6. Dag Hammarskjöld, "Notes on my personal participation in the events of 29 October–20 November 1956," Dag Hammarskjöld Papers, Stockholm.
7. Press briefing at UN Headquarters, November 16, 1956.
8. Record of UNEF Advisory Committee, November 14, 1956.
9. Ibid.
10. Ibid.
11. Press briefing on UNEF, No. 1463, November 16, 1956.
12. Record of UNEF Advisory Committee, November 19, 1956.

13. Cable to Burns, December 23, 1956.
14. UN Press Release SG/540/EMF/28, November 28, 1956.
15. Record of UNEF Advisory Committee, December 4, 1956.
16. Record of UNEF Advisory Committee, December 8, 1956.
17. UN Press Release SG/549, December 10, 1956.
18. Cable to General E. L. M. Burns, December 9, 1956.
19. Record of meeting with Eban, December 12, 1956.
20. Ibid.
21. Letter to Arthur Hays Sulzberger, January 14, 1957.
22. Note from Bunche to Hammarskjöld, February 4, 1957.
23. Keesing's Contemporary Archives, March 23–30, 1957, p. 15441.
24. Dwight D. Eisenhower, *Waging Peace: The White House Years, 1956–61* (New York, 1965), pp. 187–88.
25. Statement to 659th plenary meeting of General Assembly, February 22, 1957, Press Release SG/563.
26. Hammarskjöld, cable to Burns, March 2, 1957.
27. Dag Hammarskjöld, "Diary Notes of the Gaza Take-over," Hammarskjöld Papers.
28. Personal note, March 8, 1957.
29. Ibid.
30. Ibid.
31. Cable to Bunche, March 8, 1957.
32. E. L. M. Burns, *Between Arab and Israeli* (Toronto, 1962), p. 263.
33. Personal note, March 13, 1957.
34. Personal note, March 17, 1957.
35. Letter to Ruth, March 18, 1957.
36. Robert S. Allen, *New York Post,* March 20, 1957.
37. Cable to Hammarskjöld, March 19, 1957.
38. Personal note, March 21, 1957.
39. Personal note, March 24, 1957.
40. Bunche's notes on the meeting.
41. Record of UNEF Advisory Committee, March 24, 1957.
42. Personal note, April 3, 1957.
43. Personal note, April 6, 1957.
44. Note to Correspondents No. 1580, April 12, 1957.
45. Record of UNEF Advisory Committee, April 15, 1957.
46. Hammarskjöld's notes for May, 1957. Hammarskjöld Papers.
47. Personal notes, May 9, 1957.
48. Penciled note to Hammarskjöld, May 9, 1957.
49. Personal note, May 10, 1957.
50. Personal note, May 9, 1957.
51. Hammarskjöld and Bunche, penciled notes, May 9, 1957.
52. Personal note, May 10, 1957.
53. Ibid.
54. Ibid.
55. Personal note, May 11, 1957.
56. Letter to Bunche, September 19, 1957.
57. UN Document SG/742, November 5, 1958.
58. Record of UNEF Advisory Committee, June 2, 1959.
59. Personal note, November 1, 1958.

21   Lebanon 1958 and the Middle East (pp. 291–98)

1. Personal note, October 1947.
2. Dwight D. Eisenhower, *The White House Years* (New York, 1965), p. 266.
3. Cable to Bunche from Hammarskjöld in Cairo, June 23, 1958.
4. Bunche's notes on talk with Jamali, June 27, 1958.
5. Handwritten note found in Bunche's calendar for July 16, 1958.
6. Penciled notes, December 4, 1958.
7. Note in Hammarskjöld's handwriting on cable dated April 17, 1959, from UNTSO Headquarters in Jerusalem.
8. Personal note, April 17, 1959.
9. Personal note, April 23, 1959.
10. Ibid.
11. Ibid.
12. Personal note, April 30, 1959.
13. Personal note, May 1959.

22   The Congo (pp. 299–355)

1. Personal note, January 4, 1960.
2. Personal note, January 8, 1960.
3. Personal note, January 11, 1960.
4. Personal note, January 12, 1960.
5. Personal note, January 13, 1960.
6. Personal note, January 13, 1960.
7. Personal note, June 20, 1960.
8. Handwritten letter to Hammarskjöld from Leopoldville, June 27, 1960.
9. Personal note, June 25, 1960.
10. Letter to Hammarskjöld, June 27, 1960.
11. Ibid.
12. Personal note, June 30, 1960.
13. Ibid.
14. Letter to Hammarskjöld, July 4, 1960.
15. Ibid.
16. Ibid.
17. Personal note, July 8, 1960.
18. Ibid.
19. Letter to Ralph Bunche, Jr., July 8, 1960.

20. Letter to Ruth, July 9, 1960 (mailed in Brazzaville by Bunche's secretary, Pauline Lacerte, who had been sent there for safety reasons).
21. Ralph Bunche in *The Quest for Peace: the Dag Hammarskjöld Memorial Lectures* (New York, 1965), p. 129.
22. Cable to Hammarskjöld, July 9, 1960.
23. Cable to Hammarskjöld, July 13, 1960.
24. Ibid.
25. Thomas Kanza, *The Rise and Fall of Patrice Lumumba: Conflict in the Congo*, (Cambridge, Mass., 1979), pp. 141–44.
26. Broadcast on Leopoldville radio, July 16, 1960.
27. Cable to Hammarskjöld, July 18, 1960.
28. Cable to Hammarskjöld, July 17, 1960.
29. Brian Urquhart's notes on meeting with Belgians, July 19, 1960, and cable to Hammarskjöld, July 21, 1960.
30. Cable to Hammarskjöld, July 18, 1960.
31. Cable to Hammarskjöld, July 17, 1960.
32. Security Council Records, S/PV.901, September 14, 1960.
33. Madeleine G. Kalb, *The Congo Cables* (New York, 1982), pp. 27–29. This book gives an invaluable account of the Congo crisis as seen from the American side.
34. Letter to Ruth, July 21, 1960.
35. Cable to Hammarskjöld, July 20, 1960.
36. Ibid.
37. Ibid.
38. Ibid.
39. Ibid.
40. *New York Post*, July 25, 1960.
41. Walter Lippmann, "Today and Tomorrow—the Congo and the UN," New York *Herald-Tribune*, August 1960.
42. Cable to Hammarskjöld, July 25, 1960.
43. Letter to Ruth, August 4, 1960.
44. Penciled note to Hammarskjöld, August 4, 1960.
45. Handwritten note in Heinz Wieschhoff's writing, initialed and addressed by Hammarskjöld, August 5, 1960.

46. Personal note, "Close Calls and Tight Spots," written later.
47. Letter from de Rothschild to Hammarskjöld, August 13, 1960; memorandum from Bunche to Hammarskjöld, August 15, 1960; memorandum from Sture Linner to Bunche, August 15, 1960.
48. UN press release, Note No. 2211, August 7, 1960.
49. Security Council Resolution 146, August 9, 1960.
50. Records of the Security Council, 85th meeting; and Press Release SG/941, August 18, 1960.
51. Cable to Hammarskjöld, August 7, 1960.
52. The account of Bunche's meeting with Lumumba is taken from Brian Urquhart's notes on the meeting.
53. Letter to Lumumba, August 18, 1960.
54. Cable to Hammarskjöld, August 16, 1960.
55. Letter to Ruth, August 15, 1960.
56. ONUC Leopoldville, Order of the Day, August 19, 1960.
57. Cable to Hammarskjöld, August 18, 1960.
58. Cable to Hammarskjöld, August 20, 1960.
59. Cable to Hammarskjöld, August 24, 1960.
60. Cable to Hammarskjöld, August 25, 1960.
61. Cable to Hammarskjöld, August 25, 1960.
62. Letter to Ruth, August 20, 1960.
63. Cable to Hammarskjöld, August 28, 1960.
64. Ibid.
65. Hammarskjöld, cable to Bunche, August 28, 1960.
66. UN Press Release CO/67, August 30, 1960.
67. UN press release, Note No. 2230, September 1, 1960.
68. Rajeshwar Dayal, *A Mission for Hammarskjold* (London, 1976), p. 13.
69. Letter to a Miss Ezell, May 8, 1961, quoted in Souad Halila, "The Intellectual Development and Diplomatic Career of Ralph J. Bunche," Ph.D. dissertation, UCLA, May 1988, p. 129.

23 The Loss of Hammarskjöld (pp. 337–46)

1. Handwritten notes passed in General Assembly on September 22, 1960.
2. *Note verbale* from secretary general to the permanent representative of Belgium, November 6, 1960.
3. Ralph Bunche, quoted in *New York Times*, September 28, 1960.
4. Official Records of the General Assembly 871st meeting, September 26, 1960, para. 143.
5. ORGA 883rd meeting, October 3, 1960, para. 12.
6. Handwritten note, Dag Hammarskjöld Papers, Stockholm.
7. See, for example, the memoirs of the British

ambassador in Leopoldville: Ian Scott, *Tumbled House: The Congo at Independence* (London, 1969).
8. Personal note, December 2, 1960.
9. Press statement, May 2, 1961.
10. Letter to Hammarskjöld, June 27, 1961.
11. Personal note, June 27, 1961.
12. This and subsequent quotations are all from Bunche's cable to Hammarskjöld, September 14, 1961.
13. This and subsequent quotations are from Hammarskjöld's cable to Bunche, September 14, 1961.
14. For a detailed account of Hammarskjöld's last mission to the Congo, see Brian Ur-

quhart, *Hammarskjöld* (New York, 1972), pp. 565–89.
15. This and subsequent quotations come from Bunche's cable to Hammarskjöld, September 16, 1961.
16. Cable to Bunche, September 17, 1961.
17. Madeleine G. Kalb, *The Congo Cables* (New York, 1982), pp. 303–4.
18. For O'Brien's personal story, see Conor

Cruise O'Brien, "My Case," London *Observer*, December 17, 1961, and a later account, *To Katanga and Back* (London, 1962).
19. Cable to Linner, September 22, 1961.
20. Personal notes, March 1955.
21. Letter to Gunnar Jahn, September 22, 1961.
22. Press statement, October 23, 1961.

24 U Thant and the End of the Katanga Secession (pp. 349–60)

1. U Thant, *A View from the UN* (New York, 1977), p. 113.
2. Security Council Document S/5002, November 24, 1961.
3. Madeleine G. Kalb, *The Congo Cables* (New York, 1982), p. 313.
4. Ibid., p. 316.
5. George W. Ball, *The Past Has Another Pattern* (New York, 1982), p. 256.
6. Kalb, op. cit., p. 317.
7. Ball, op. cit., p. 257.
8. For a full account of this process, see Kalb, op. cit., pp. 317–21.
9. Security Council Document S/5038, December 21, 1961, pp. 3–4.
10. The following quotations are from Bunche's press conference at UN Headquarters, December 22, 1961, UN Press Services, Note No. 2456, December 22, 1961.
11. Personal note, October 18, 1962.
12. Personal note, November 11, 1962.
13. *Congressional Record*, 87th Congress, vol. 108, part 5, April 3–24, 1962, p. 6538.

14. Speech to UAW Convention, Atlantic City, May 7, 1962.
15. *Congressional Record*, 87th Congress, vol. 108, part 6 p. 8044–45.
16. Letter to Adlai Stevenson, May 7, 1962.
17. U Thant, op. cit., p. 141.
18. Ibid., p. 381.
19. Kalb, op. cit., p. 368.
20. UN Press Release SS/1407, January 3, 1963.
21. U Thant, "Annual Report on the Work of the Organisation," June 16, 1962–June 15, 1963, p. 19.
22. Cable to U Thant, January 4, 1963.
23. Interview with Prem Chand, August 19, 1982.
24. Bunche's report to U Thant, written during his return flight to New York.
25. Ibid.
26. Cable to U Thant, January 8, 1963.
27. Cable to U Thant, January 9, 1963.
28. Ibid.
29. Ibid.
30. Personal note, January 21, 1963.

25 Yemen (pp. 361–67)

1. Ralph Bunche, press statement, "Why I went to Jackson," July 8, 1963, quoted by Charles P. Henry in Benjamin Rivlin, *Ralph Bunche: The Man and His Times* (New York, 1990), pp. 62–63.
2. Speech at Rebild, Denmark, July 4, 1963.
3. *New York Times*, February 27, 1963.
4. From the account of Tony O'Connell, the UN military observer accompanying Bunche,

and Bunche's later note, "Tight Spots and Close Calls."
5. The descriptions of Bunche's visit are from his special report to the secretary general, March 8, 1963.
6. Personal note, October 5, 1966.
7. Personal note on his vacation, summer 1963.
8. Personal note, September 20, 1963.
9. Personal note, December 6, 1963.

26 Cyprus and Kashmir (pp. 369–79)

1. George W. Ball, *The Past Has Another Pattern* (New York, 1982), pp. 340–48.
2. Security Council Resolution 186, March 4, 1964.
3. Interview with William Barton, May 1987.
4. Memorandum to U Thant on briefing General Gyani, March 21, 1964.
5. Ibid.
6. Ibid.
7. Personal note, April 9, 1964.
8. Cable to U Thant, April 15, 1964.

9. Thimayya, cable to U Thant, August 11, 1964.
10. V. P. Suslov, memorandum to Bunche, December 14, 1964.
11. Cable to Bunche, March 10, 1965.
12. Personal note, July 11, 1966.
13. Transcript of remarks at Nicosia International Airport, July 11, 1966.
14. Personal note, April 18, 1966.
15. Cable to Brian Urquhart, July 9, 1966.
16. Penciled note, December 1, 1967.

17. This and details above from handwritten note made on National Airlines flight 73, December 3, 1967.
18. Report to U Thant, April 18, 1964.
19. Messages to governments of India and Pakistan, September 15, 1965.
20. Security Council Resolution 211, September 20, 1965.
21. Personal note, October 1965.

22. Personal note, November 1965.
23. Personal note, October 7, 1965.
24. Letter to Valerie Betts, June 1965. Valerie Betts was an Englishwoman who had written to Bunche. Bunche liked her letter and the phrase "As I take up my pen . . . ," with which many of her letters opened, and replied to it. They established a regular correspondence, but they never met.

27 Vietnam (pp. 381–92)

1. U Thant, *A View from the UN* (New York, 1977), p. 58.
2. Ibid., p. 63.
3. Ibid., p. 67.
4. Dean Rusk, *As I Saw It: Dean Rusk as Told to Richard Rusk* (New York, 1990), p. 463.
5. Letter to Valerie Betts, January 8, 1965.
6. See Rusk, op. cit., p. 463: "Adlai was impatient with me and didn't think we were being responsible. Our conflict was rather sharp."
7. Personal note, June 26, 1965.
8. Ibid.
9. Letter to Hobart Taylor, February 2, 1965.
10. Personal note, July 19, 1965.
11. Ibid.
12. Ibid.
13. Personal note, March 29, 1966.
14. Personal note, July 20, 1965.
15. Personal note, July 28, 1965.
16. Ibid.

17. Letter from President Johnson, delivered to U Thant by Arthur Goldberg on July 28, 1965.
18. Personal note, January 6, 1966.
19. Personal note, March 12, 1966.
20. Ibid.
21. Bunche's note on a talk with Goldberg, June 4, 1966.
22. Personal note, March 1967.
23. Personal note, April 1, 1967.
24. Ibid.
25. Personal note, April 11, 1967.
26. Personal note, April 13, 1967.
27. Personal note, April 17, 1967.
28. Personal note, April 3, 1968.
29. Personal note, April 25, 1968.
30. Personal note, September 26, 1968.
31. Letter to Ralph Jr., January 8, 1969.
32. Personal note, November 3, 1969.

28 A Darkening Glass (pp. 393–99)

1. Handwritten note dated June 16, 1968, the day on which Ralph Jr. left to join the army.
2. Ibid.
3. Personal note, February 1966.
4. Personal note, September 26, 1967.
5. Personal note, October 6, 1966.
6. Personal note, July 1, 1967.
7. Personal note, July 9, 1967. Bunche was actually about to turn sixty-four.
8. Personal note, January 18, 1966.
9. Personal note, October 1965.
10. Personal note, March 1966.
11. Personal note, June 4, 1966.

12. Letter to U Thant, August 29, 1966.
13. Ibid.
14. "Yearbook of the United Nations," 1966, p. 201.
15. Personal note, September 14, 1966.
16. Personal note, December 1, 1966.
17. Ibid.
18. Personal note, December 3, 1966.
19. Personal note, February 18, 1967.
20. Letter to U Thant, February 20, 1967.
21. Letter to Dr. George Harrar, March 30, 1967.
22. Letter to Valerie Betts, February 1967.

29 The Six-Day War (pp. 400–416)

1. Personal note, November 29, 1966.
2. A revealing account of this process, based particularly on Egyptian and Soviet sources, is contained in Richard B. Parker, "Mysteries Explored," *Middle East Journal*, Spring 1992.
3. Parker, op. cit., p. 180.
4. Commander UNEF, cable to U Thant, May 16, 1967.

5. Parker, op. cit., p. 185.
6. Ibid., p. 188.
7. Indar Jit Rikhye, *The Sinai Blunder* (New Delhi, 1978), p. 19.
8. U Thant, *A View from the UN* (New York, 1977), p. 231.
9. Verbatim record of UNEF Advisory Committee meeting, 5:00 P.M., May 18, 1967.

10. U Thant, cable to General Rikhye, the commander of UNEF, May 18, 1967.
11. Security Council Document S/7896, May 19, 1967.
12. Bunche's notes on meeting with U Thant and Gideon Rafael, May 19, 1967.
13. Personal note, May 18, 1967.
14. All quoted in Andrew Boyd, *Fifteen Men on a Powder Keg* (New York, 1971), p. 196.
15. Transcript of background briefing by Ralph J. Bunche to correspondents on May 20, 1967.
16. Parker, op. cit., p. 191.
17. U Thant, op. cit., p. 233.
18. U Thant's talks in Cairo are described by Rikhye in *The Sinai Blunder* (New Delhi, 1978) and by Ramses Nassif in *U Thant in New York* (London, 1988). Both authors were in Cairo with U Thant.
19. Personal note, May 29, 1967.
20. Personal note, June 7, 1967.
21. UN Press Release EMF/449, June 3, 1967.
22. General Assembly Document A/6730, June 26, 1967.
23. James Reston, "Cairo: Quiet Flows the Nile," *New York Times*, June 4, 1967.
24. Ibid.
25. Ralph Bunche, letter to *New York Times*, June 11, 1967.
26. Interview with Eric Rouleau in *Le Monde*, February 18, 1970, quoted in U Thant, op. cit., p. 232.
27. Handwritten note to U Thant.
28. Note to the United States Mission to the UN, June 14, 1967.
29. Dean Rusk, *As I Saw It: Dean Rusk as Told to Richard Rusk* (New York, 1990), p. 384.
30. James Wechsler, "An Untold Story," *New York Post*, June 7, 1967.
31. Quoted in *Keesing's Contemporary Archives*, July 1967, p. 22153.
32. All quotes are from U Thant, statement to the General Assembly, June 20, 1967, UN Press Release SG/SM/753, June 20, 1967.
33. Personal note, July 11, 1967.
34. Personal note, July 15, 1967.
35. Ibid.
36. Ralph Bunche, "Note for the File," July 11, 1968.
37. Letter to Eugene Rostow, undersecretary for political affairs in the U.S. State Department, February 7, 1968.

30 Winding Down (pp. 417–25)

1. Letter to Valerie Betts, July 23, 1970.
2. Letter to Barbara Hepworth, October 30, 1970.
3. Personal note, January 26, 1968.
4. Personal note, November 22, 1968.
5. UN press briefing, December 29, 1969.
6. Personal note, September 9, 1969.
7. Personal note, April 4, 1966.
8. Personal note, August 8, 1968.
9. Personal note, December 18, 1968.
10. Personal note, October 1969.
11. Ralph Bunche, remarks at the dedication of Ralph Bunche Hall, UCLA, May 23, 1969.
12. Personal note, April 26, 1970.
13. Letter to London Sunday *Times*, October 1970.
14. Telegram to John V. Lindsay, February 12, 1969. The text bears a note: "Personal message for which Mr. Bunche is to be billed. He is sending it through UN channels because of difficulty in dictating to the commercial channels."
15. Second telegram to Mayor Lindsay, February 12, 1969.
16. U Thant, *A View from the UN* (New York, 1977), p. 334.
17. Notes exchanged in the Security Council, September 10, 1969.
18. Personal note, November 21, 1969.

31 Bahrain (pp. 426–29)

1. Sir Denis Wright, on a BBC program, "Peaceful Solutions," March 9, 1986.
2. Anthony Parsons, *They Say the Lion: Britain's Legacy to the Arabs* (London, 1986), p. 139.
3. Interview with Sir Anthony Parsons, November 1991.
4. Letter to the secretary general from the permanent representative of Iran to the UN, quoted in *Keesing's Contemporary Archives*, May 23–30, 1970, p. 23998.
5. Letter, drafted by Bunche, from U Thant to Vittorio Winspeare Guicciardi, March 20, 1970.
6. Report of the personal representative of the secretary general in charge of the good-offices mission, Bahrain, Security Council Document S/9772, April 30, 1970, p. 13, para. 57.
7. Letter from U Thant to Soviet Ambassador Jakob Malik, April 6, 1970, UN Security Council Document S/9738, April 6, 1970.
8. A good account of the process is to be found in an article by Husein al Baharna in *International and Comparative Law Quarterly*, vol. 22 (1973).
9. U Thant, *A View from the UN* (New York, 1977), p. 50.

10. U Thant, speech to the Royal Commonwealth Society, London, June 15, 1970.
11. Bunche, quoted in a confidential report by the British Mission to the UN, Ref. 3/2/438, May 25, 1970.
12. Ibid.

32 Civil Rights and Race in the United States (pp. 430–53)

1. W. E. B. Du Bois, *Souls of Black Folk* (Chicago, 1903), pp. 3–4 (republished, New York, 1990, pp. 8–9).
2. Ralph Bunche, interview in Chicago *Daily Tribune*, May 12, 1960.
3. Letter to Mr. Daniel Livingfree of the Anti-Racial Christian Association, September 19, 1959.
4. *Journal-American*, July 15, 1957.
5. Ralph Bunche, talk at the Polo Grounds, New York, Sunday, July 19, 1959.
6. Letter from Grace, July 7, 1961.
7. Letter from Ruth, May 29, 1959.
8. Interview with Pauline Frederick, NBC-TV, *Today Show*, February 20, 1969.
9. John Hope Franklin, *From Slavery to Freedom: A History of Negro Americans*, (New York, 1980) p. 447.
10. A. Philip Randolph, quoted in Peggy Mann, *Ralph Bunche: UN Peacemaker* (New York, 1975), pp. 332–33.
11. Charles P. Henry in Benjamin Rivlin, *Ralph Bunche: The Man and His Times* (New York, 1990), p. 51.
12. Ralph Bunche, talk to 53rd Annual NAACP Convention "Youth Night," Atlanta, Georgia, July 6, 1962.
13. Ibid.
14. Ralph Bunche, "Two Critical American Dilemmas: Vietnam and the Ghetto," speech delivered at UCLA, February 21, 1968.
15. Ralph Bunche, "Race in World Perspective," Texas Christian University, Fort Worth, May 6, 1963.
16. Ralph Bunche, interview in *Long Island Press*, June 9, 1963.
17. Bunche, "Two Critical American Dilemmas."
18. Letter to Mrs. John Berry of Greensboro, N.C., February 25, 1959.
19. Bunche, talk to NAACP "Youth Night," op. cit.
20. Jim Haskins, *Ralph Bunche: A Most Reluctant Hero*, (New York, 1974) p. 118.
21. Quoted by Marshall Frady, "The Children of Malcolm," *The New Yorker*, October 12, 1992.
22. Thomas J. Ladenburg and William S. McFeely, *The Black Man in the Land of Equality* (New York, 1969), p. 168, quoted by Souad Halila, "The Intellectual Development and Diplomatic Career of Ralph J. Bunche," Ph.D. dissertation, UCLA, May 1988, p. 93.
23. Ralph Bunche, *A World View of Race: The Associates in Negro Folk Education* (Washington, D.C., 1936), pp. 83–84.
24. Bunche, interview in *Long Island Press*.
25. Ralph Bunche, letter to Jackie Robinson, New York *Amsterdam News*, November 20, 1963.
26. Letter from Jackie Robinson, May 28, 1964.
27. Telegram to Martin Luther King, Jr., February 22, 1956.
28. Personal note, October 14, 1964.
29. *New York Post*, June 17, 1963.
30. Ralph Bunche, interview in *Washington Daily News*, January 1, 1960.
31. Ralph Bunche, speech to NAACP Convention, Atlanta, July 6, 1962.
32. Ralph Bunche, *Amsterdam News*, April 16, 1960.
33. Letter to Valerie Betts, September 13, 1963.
34. Telegram to Martin Luther King, Jr., March 19, 1965.
35. Personal note, March 24, 1965.
36. Charles P. Henry in Rivlin, op. cit., p. 62.
37. *St. Louis Post-Dispatch*, March 24, 1965.
38. Ralph Bunche, speech in Montgomery, Ala., March 25, 1965.
39. Letter to Michael Hirsch, March 16, 1966.
40. Ralph Bunche, "The Negro's Stake in the World Crisis," speech at Negro History Week meeting, Shaw University, Raleigh, N.C., February 9, 1941.
41. Ralph Bunche, "The Horizon Widens," address to Association for the Study of Negro Life and History, February 9, 1947.
42. Ralph Bunche, "Equality Without Qualifications," address to NAACP 42nd Annual Convention, Atlanta, July 1, 1951.
43. Ralph Bunche, address to 45th Annual Convention of the NAACP, Dallas, Texas, July 4, 1954.
44. Letter from Nelle Johnson, December 29, 1969.
45. Statement on the rioting in Los Angeles, August 17, 1965.
46. *New York Times*, October 2, 1966.
47. Untitled and undated note from the summer of 1967.
48. Interview in the *Purdue Exponent*, October 13, 1967.
49. Ibid.
50. Subsequent quotes are from "Upheaval in the Ghettos," undated paper written in summer of 1967.
51. Report of the National Advisory Commission on Civil Disorders, March 1, 1968, p. 1.
52. Letter to Thomas J. Watson, Jr., March 27, 1968.

53. Personal note, May 15, 1968.
54. Ibid.
55. Statement on the assassination of Martin Luther King, Jr., April 4, 1968.
56. Personal note, April 9, 1968.
57. Ralph Bunche, interview with William N. Oatis in *Long Island Press*, April 16, 1968.
58. Harry S. Ashmore, *Hearts and Minds: The Anatomy of Racism from Roosevelt to Reagan* (New York, 1982), quoted in Souad Halila, "The Intellectual Development and Diplomatic Career of Ralph J. Bunche," Ph.D. dissertation, UCLA, May 1988, p. 96.

59. All quotations from Ralph Bunche, "Notes on the Black Revolution," begun on August 20, 1968.
60. Ralph Bunche, interview with Mary Harrington Hall in *Psychology Today*, April 1969.
61. Ralph Bunche, "Race and Alienation," address to 5th East-West Philosophers' Conference, Honolulu, Hawaii, July 10, 1969.
62. Ibid.
63. Ibid.
64. Ibid.
65. Bunche, interview in *Psychology Today*.

33 Ending (pp. 454–58)

1. Personal note, December 4, 1969.
2. General Assembly, 2008th meeting, A/PV 2008, December 9, 1971.
3. Tribute by U Thant at the funeral of Ralph Bunche, December 11, 1971, UN Press Release SG/SM/1610.
4. *Los Angeles Times*, June 17, 1992.

Index